Political Repression in Bahrain

Exploring Bahrain's modern history through the lens of repression, this concise and accessible work spans the twentieth and twenty-first centuries, looking at all forms of political repression from legal, statecraft, police brutality and informational controls. Considering several episodes of contention in Bahrain, from tribal resistance to the British reforms of the 1920s, the rise of the Higher Executive Committee in the 1950s, the leftist agitation of the 1970s, the 1990s Intifada and the 2011 Uprising, Marc Owen Jones offers never before seen insights into the British role in Bahrain, as well as the activities of the Al Khalifa ruling family. From the plundering of Bahrain's resources, to new information about the torture and murder of Bahrain civilians, this study reveals new facts about Bahrain's troubled political history. Using freedom of information requests, historical documents, interviews and data from social media, this is a rich and original interdisciplinary history of Bahrain over 100 years.

MARC OWEN JONES is Assistant Professor in Middle East Studies and Digital Humanities at Hamad Bin Khalifa University, where his research focuses on issues of social justice and the Gulf. He is the co-editor of *Gulfization of the Arab World* (2018) and *Bahrain's Uprising: Resistance and Repression in the Gulf* (2015). In addition to his academic work, he contributes to the *Washington Post*, *New Statesman*, CNN, the *Independent*, PEN International, and appears frequently on the BBC, *Channel 4 News* and Al Jazeera.

Cambridge Middle East Studies

Cambridge Middle East Studies has been established to publish books on the nineteenth- to twenty-first-century Middle East and North Africa. The series offers new and original interpretations of aspects of Middle Eastern societies and their histories. To achieve disciplinary diversity, books are solicited from authors writing in a wide range of fields including history, sociology, anthropology, political science, and political economy. The emphasis is on producing books affording an original approach along theoretical and empirical lines. The series is intended for students and academics, but the more accessible and wide-ranging studies will also appeal to the interested general reader.

A list of books in the series can be found after the index.

Political Repression in Bahrain

Marc Owen Jones

Hamad Bin Khalifa University

CAMBRIDGE
UNIVERSITY PRESS

University Printing House, Cambridge CB2 8BS, United Kingdom

One Liberty Plaza, 20th Floor, New York, NY 10006, USA

477 Williamstown Road, Port Melbourne, VIC 3207, Australia

314–321, 3rd Floor, Plot 3, Splendor Forum, Jasola District Centre,
New Delhi – 110025, India

79 Anson Road, #06–04/06, Singapore 079906

Cambridge University Press is part of the University of Cambridge.

It furthers the University's mission by disseminating knowledge in the pursuit of education, learning, and research at the highest international levels of excellence.

www.cambridge.org
Information on this title: www.cambridge.org/9781108471435
DOI: 10.1017/9781108558822

First published 2020

Printed in the United Kingdom by TJ International Ltd. Padstow Cornwall

A catalogue record for this publication is available from the British Library.

Library of Congress Cataloging-in-Publication Data
Names: Jones, Marc Owen, author.
Title: Political Repression in Bahrain / Marc Owen Jones, Hamad Bin Khalifa University.
Description: Cambridge, United Kingdom ; New York : Cambridge University Press, 2020. | Series: Cambridge Middle East studies | Includes bibliographical references and index.
Identifiers: LCCN 2019060032 (print) | LCCN 2019060033 (ebook) | ISBN 9781108471435 (hardback) | ISBN 9781108458009 (paperback) | ISBN 9781108558822 (ebook)
Subjects: LCSH: Political persecution–Bahrain–History–20th century. | Political persecution–Bahrain–History–21st century.
Classification: LCC JC599.B26 J66 2020 (print) | LCC JC599.B26 (ebook) | DDC 323/.044095365–dc23
LC record available at https://lccn.loc.gov/2019060032
LC ebook record available at https://lccn.loc.gov/2019060033

ISBN 978-1-108-47143-5 Hardback
ISBN 978-1-108-45800-9 Paperback

Dedicated to my mum, dad and brothers

Contents

Figures

Tables

Acknowledgements

My acknowledgements section cannot possibly do justice to all those to whom I am indebted, both throughout my life but also across my academic studies at Durham, Tuebingen, Exeter and now Doha.

First, however, thanks to my Mum and Dad for tolerating me from a young age and giving me so much. I am also grateful to my wonderful siblings Owen and Gareth for allowing me to be the middle child, and Kate for being such an inspiration. As for my late grandparents Rhoda, Cyril, Charlie and Elsie, I am in awe of your wisdom and kindness. Cyril, aka, 'Little Grandad', your polemics on equal pay had such a formative influence. Zainah, you proofread this book in its nascent state and made me tea; enough said. I couldn't' have done it without you. Sooty, I miss you. Potem, you are acceptable as a cat.

My gratitude extends to the academics, activists, journalists and other human beings who prefer not to be labelled. As most of you are protagonists in this book, there is no need to mention you here – such is your incredible impact on the world.

As for the guys at Bahrain Watch – Ala'a Shehabi, John Horne, Luke Bhatia, Bill Marczak, Fahad Desmukh, Ahmed Ali, Maryam Al Khawaja, Reda al-Farhan, Ali Abdulemam, Travis Brimhall – there are few opportunities to work with such incredibly good and talented people. It has been a privilege.

The process of this research has made me lose a lot of friends but introduced me to some of my now closest, who have been unrivalled in their encouragement, understanding and tolerance. Thanks in particular to Ryaan, Alexei, Hussain, Mariam, Hasan, Nada, Mo, Esra, Huda, Kirstyn, Pep, and Siobhan. Michael B.; our burgers and BBQs, bunny patrols and road trips were restorative in the extreme. Special thanks to Dima – without your support, I do not even know if I would have finished.

I would also like to thank, for your various chats and inspiration, Abdulhadi Khalaf, Farida Vis, Kristian Ulrichsen, Marwan Kraidy, John Jewell, Marie Duboc, Ollie Schulmberger, Mirjam Edel, Christopher

Davidson, Reem Abou al-Fadl, Claire Wardle, Una McGahern, Mokhtar, Sophie Richter Devroe, James Thomas, Clive Jones, Philip Robins, Steven Wright, David Kaufer and Lucy Abbott.

Since the conception of this manuscript at Durham to finalizing it in Qatar, I have spilled countless cups of coffee with countless wonderful people who have endured me. Noha, thanks for helping me settle so well into Qatar. Exeter crew, you are among the best people I know in terms of integrity and research but also as human beings. Marc Valeri, Ross Porter, Claire Beaugrand – you guys are a source of inspiration: kind, patient, intelligent and thoughtful. Katie Natanel, I miss you as my office neighbour. Isabel, thank you for helping me through a rough summer with Fortnite and *Love Island*. Thank you Eliza for making me a little braver. Ollie and Rhian, drinking tea and writing songs are some of my best memories. Sophie, Wajdi, George, Julie, Amal, Steven, Hassan, Dilek, Hendrik Abdulrahman, Fatema, Clayton, Richard, Doha Footballers, thanks for help making Qatar a home from where I can write!

Thanks to Ustinov College. Your collegiate environment and atmosphere has been a source of strength and inspiration, especially during difficult times. In particular, it has been a great place to study and unwind. Thanks especially to Siobhan and Michael; the cafe working group has been a source of levity, irreverence and procrastination. Carole and Leanne, your tea, muffins and breakfasts sustained me! Thank you to all the staff whom I bothered incessantly and who made Ustinov such a home: Jonathan, Gary, Alan, Faye, Sam, Robin, Margaret, Ian, Sarah C., Sarah P., Lynsey, Glenn, Maggie and Sheila. Trevor, you're a legend; I shall miss induction week! Brian, keep on snapping (photos that is). Ray, your patience and calm temperament are incredible. Paddy, don't let any bastards grind you down.

Last, but certainly not least, thank you Bahrain for your inspiration, tragedy, hope and hopelessness. No one could ask for a better home, nor better people but certainly a better government. Viva the revolution.

Abbreviations

AI	Amnesty International
BCHR	Bahrain Centre for Human Rights
BDF	Bahrain Defence Force
BICI	Bahrain Independent Commission of Inquiry
BNA	Bahrain News Agency
BNC	Bahrain National Congress
CID	Criminal Investigation Department
CNU	Committee of National Union
GCCPS	Gulf Cooperation Council Peninsula Shield
HEC	Higher Executive Committee
IAA	Information Affairs Authority
IFLB	Islamic Front for the Liberation of Bahrain
HRW	Human Rights Watch
NLF	National Liberation Front
SIS	Security and Intelligence Services
SIU	Special Investigation Unit
MOI	Ministry of the Interior
NSA	National Security Agency
PSF	Public Security Forces

Introduction

Political Repression in Bahrain in the Twentieth and Twenty-First Century

> Shaikh Abdulla [Al Khalifa]'s servants abducted a girl, a native of Fars. Her parents after searching for her for some time returned home and left behind one Muhammad Abdulla to continue the search. He discovered that she was being kept by Shaik Abdulla. The latter then passed her on to an Arab of Zallaq, receiving Rs. 400. Muhammad Abdulla on behalf of the parents made efforts to recover the girl. He did so on payment of Rs. 500 and on condition that he himself married her. She was pregnant and subsequently died in childbirth.[1] —C. K. Daly, 1921

The abduction, trafficking and subsequent tragic death of a young Bahraini girl by a member of the Al Khalifa ruling family in the 1920s is a potent example of the historical continuity of repression and social injustice in Bahrain. Far from being an isolated incident, or simply a criminal act, the kidnap was a facet of what Bahraini sociologist Abdulhadi Khalaf calls the Al Khalifa's 'legacy of conquest'. The Al Khalifa ruling family conquered the small Persian Gulf island of Bahrain in 1783, establishing a form of settler colonialism that subjugated the indigenous *baḥārna*[2] population. This settler colonial rule included a conquering mindset, whereby the ruling Al Khalifa family treated Bahrain's resources, subjects and lands as their rightful property and inheritance.

From the correspondence of British East India Company officials to contemporary reports published by NGOs such as the Bahrain Centre for Human Rights and the testimonies of Bahrainis, the extent of the injustice stemming from this legacy of conquest has been documented, in its varying forms, for almost 200 years. In 1829, the British naval officer

[1] 'File 9/4 Bahrain Reforms. Introduction of Reforms in Bahrain' [5v] (27/224), British Library: India Office Records and Private Papers, IOR/R/15/2/131, in Qatar Digital Library, www.qdl.qa/en/archive/81055/vdc_100023403812.0x00001c

[2] The *bahārna* (adj. *baḥrānī*) are an ethno religious group that inhabit Bahrain, an area historically existing in modern-day Bahrain as well as parts of the present-day Eastern province of Saudi Arabia.

Major Wilson noted that 'the enormities practised by the Uttoobees[3] towards the original inhabitants of Bahrain far exceed what I have ever heard of tyranny in any part of the world'.[4]

Similarly, the British naval officer Captain Taylor said of the *baḥārna* under the Al Khalifa that: 'The aboriginal inhabitants of Bahrein, now subjected to a foreign power, suffer from the tyranny of their masters more keenly than language can express'.[5] Later, in 1878, Captain Edward Law Duran described a group of Shiʿa *baḥārna* from the village of A'Ali as a 'broken-spirited helpless lot', and noted that one of the most salient aspects of his survey of Bahrain was the 'innumerable complaints of the tyranny of the Sheikhs and their tribe'.[6] In 1921, the British Political Agent in Bahrain, Major Clive Kirkpatrick Daly, submitted a scathing condemnation of the Al Khalifa to his superiors. He simply titled it, 'Oppression of Bahrain Subjects by Members of the Ruling Family'. Daly focused in particular on ʿAbd Allah bin 'Isa Al Khalifa's[7] treatment of the *baḥrānī* community, writing, 'Instances of this oppression are far too numerous to quote, but details are on record of a large number of cases of recent date, which include illegal seizure of property, wrongful imprisonment with cruelty, and political murders, for which no one has been brought to trial, and no effort made to enforce justice'.[8] Daly added that 'oppression in the past two years has amounted to terrorism',[9] and that political murders were becoming common, as were 'outrages against respectable women'.[10] Things had

[3] The Uttoobees, is the British pluralization for the Arabic *al*-Utbī. *Banī ʿUtbah* is the name for the federation of Arab clans believed to originate in Najd.

[4] Major Wilson, 'Selections from the Records of the Bombay Government' [107] (149/733), British Library: India Office Records and Private Papers, IOR/R/15/1/732, in *Qatar Digital Library*, www.qdl.qa/en/archive/81055/vdc_100022870191.0x000096

[5] Anon, 'Selections from the Records of the Bombay Government' [23] (60/733), British Library: India Office Records and Private Papers, IOR/R/15/1/732, in *Qatar Digital Library*, www.qdl.qa/en/archive/81055/vdc_100022870191.0x00003d

[6] E. L. Durand, 'Notes on the islands of Bahrain and antiquities, by Captain E. L. Durand, 1st Assistant Resident, Persian Gulf', 1878–1879, in P. Tuson and E. Quick (eds), *Records of Bahrain 1820–1960*, vol. 2, Slough, Archive Editions, 1993, p. 545.

[7] Abd Allah was the son of the then ruler, ʿIsa Al Khalifa. His brother Hamad was heir apparent at the time and the eldest son of ʿIsa. ʿIsa, who was elderly and senile, was frequently referred to by the British as being dominated and under the influence of his wife. See 'Administration Reports 1920–1924' [119v] (243/412), British Library: India Office Records and Private Papers, IOR/R/15/1/713, in *Qatar Digital Library*, www.qdl.qa/en/archive/81055/vdc_100023385511.0x00002c

[8] C. K. Daly, November 21, in P. Tuson and E. Quick (eds), *Records of Bahrain 1820–1960*, vol. 3, Slough, Archive Editions, 1993, p. 668.

[9] Ibid.

[10] 'Administration Reports 1920–1924' [84v] (173/412), British Library: India Office Records and Private Papers, IOR/R/15/1/713, in *Qatar Digital Library*, www.qdl.qa/en/archive/81055/vdc_100023385510.0x0000ae

reached such a pitch that Daly wrote that there was no longer any 'security for persons or property'.[11]

A few decades after Daly wrote about the oppression of Bahraini residents at the hands of the Al Khalifa, the British were writing about how they themselves were engaging in violence against those living in Bahrain. Charles Belgrave, a political and financial advisor to the Ruler of Bahrain between 1926 and 1957 kept a diary almost every day for his thirty years of service. On 27 May 1932 Belgrave wrote about his interrogation of a suspect in a case of rioting: 'at first they would not speak but I beat a few of them till they did speak, it was all very barbarous and illegal but on some occasions, one has to behave illegally'.[12] In the latter half of the twentieth century, Bahraini citizens accused British police working in Bahrain's security of exacting even more egregious violations of personal integrity, including torture leading to death.

Throughout the twentieth and twenty-first centuries, modernization and state building have not fundamentally changed the nature of this Al Khalifa-dominated political system, despite the growth of internal opposition. The decline of the British Empire has resulted in the ascendency of United States' hegemony in the Gulf. This has not caused a reprieve from repression for the average Bahraini. As this book will argue, repression has changed form, becoming more violent, brutal and sectarian. US policy in the region, very much determined by its maintenance of close relationships with the conservative Kingdom of Saudi Arabia, has allowed repression to flourish. Indeed, since Bahrain's Independence, repression has fundamentally changed, highlighting again how the nature of repression in Bahrain is always a dialectic between the Al Khalifa family and whoever so happens to be its suzerain at a given era.

Contemporary accounts of human rights violations published by international NGOs such as Amnesty International and Human Rights Watch, or those now documented on mobile phones, highlight the similar repression of, not the *baḥārna* per se but the Bahraini Shiʿa – abandoning the ethnic identifier. From the 1980s onwards, we see Amnesty International stating that the 'majority of protesters, Shiʿa Muslims, have complained of being politically marginalized by the ruling Sunni Al Khalifa family who dominate all aspects of political and economic life in Bahrain'.[13] In 2011, the continued discrimination and

[11] Ibid.

[12] C. Belgrave, *Papers of Charles Dalrymple-Belgrave: Transcripts of Diaries, 1926–1957*, Library of the University of Exeter, 27 May 1932.

[13] Amnesty International, *Bahrain: Reform Shelved, Repression Unleashed*, London, Amnesty International Publications, 2012, p. 3.

ongoing lack of political participation, all of which has its roots in the legacy of conquest, resulted in what has variously been called the Bahrain Uprising, the 14th February Revolution or the Lulu Uprising.

The historical continuity of this repression demands an understanding of the methods and motivations used in maintaining a system of political domination. Repression is an apt conceptual lens and a suitable means of exploring Bahrain's unequal political contract between the rulers and ruled. Specifically, this book attempts to answer the following question: how has the dominant political and social order in Bahrain prevented, controlled or constrained potential radical change to their authority since the end of the First World War? Here, the dominant political and social order refers generally to the Al Khalifa ruling family and its external allies – mostly notably Britain, Saudi Arabia and the United States but also the increasingly ambiguous assemblage of repressive actors that benefit from such activities.

Using multiple sources in English and Arabic, including British Foreign Office archives, freedom of information requests, ethnographic data, social media data and newspaper clippings, this book seeks to examine the historical evolution of repression in Bahrain, exploring its causes, forms and, occasionally, its effects. It is foremost a book about the history of political repression in Bahrain between 1920 and 2011. According to Theda Skocpol, in interpretive histories, a historical concept is used as a heuristic device to 'facilitate the selection, organisation, and interpretation of empirical material'.[14] In the case of this book, the relevant concept is 'repression', a phenomenon that continues to impact the lives of thousands of Bahrainis negatively. Indeed, many Bahrainis have suffered and still suffer from the excesses of state and non-state repression, much of it deployed under the auspices of quasi-colonial rule and neo-imperialism. In line with the emphasis on social justice, interpretive historical sociology attempts to be meaningful in the sense that it is significant to the present and relevant to audiences beyond academia. With regards to Bahrain, the study of control and repression is highly relevant and meaningful. This is a modern history of Bahrain, mediated by the concept of repression. It is hoped that it will contribute to revisionism on a region dominated by the scholarly trappings of Occidentalism and Orientalism, often manifest in multiple studies on oil, nationalism, imperialism, tribe and shaykhs. Instead, by emphasizing the importance of repression, we can examine the plight of the subaltern and how their continued subjugation is carried out.

[14] V. E. Bonnell, 'The Uses of Theory, Concepts and Comparison, in Historical Sociology', *Comparative Studies in Society and History,* vol. 22, no. 2, 1980, p. 166.

Bahrain: A Short Modern History

Bahrain is a small archipelago of thirty-three islands in the Persian Gulf. While consisting of only around 765 square kilometres, Bahrain has occupied an important place in the history of the world, from Dilmun civilization to Alexander the Great, to the Persian and British Empire. The modern city of Hamad Town, for example, was built on thousands of burial mounds, and some say it is still occupied by Jinn or the spirits of its former residents. Bahrain was, for some time, the location of the headquarters of the British Empire in the Gulf. It was also the first place on the Arabian side of the Gulf where Europeans discovered oil. Despite the pitfalls of periodization, that is to say determining clear-cut eras within history, one could say that Bahrain's modern history broadly begins in 1785, when members of the Al Khalifa family, a tribe of the *al-*Utbī clan, left Zubara in present-day Qatar and invaded Bahrain. The Al Khalifa were, and remain to many, a colonial force. They occupied Bahrain, expropriated lands and created a series of fiefdoms, extracting tithes from indigenous farmers. The Al Khalifa still rule Bahrain today, despite numerous challenges to their authority. Their longevity has been sustained primarily because of formal and informal protection arrangements with outside powers, namely Britain, the United States and Saudi Arabia.

Recently, Ala'a Shehabi and the author argue that what has emerged in Bahrain is essentially a kleptocratic ethnocracy, where one ethnic group, the Al Khalifa tribe,[15] have captured the instruments of state in order to protect their position of material and political privilege.[16] At the heart of this regime is a 'ruling core' of mostly Al Khalifa family members, who have a high degree of personalist influence in internal policy. As a result, a system of domination has been created, and is reproduced through social, political, coercive and legal institutions that reflect the 'norms, values and interests of the dominant ethnic group'.[17] The ruling family's attempts to maintain a monopoly of wealth and resources lead to inherently repressive institutions that create differences in life chances that in turn fuel social conflict. The despotic rule that has emerged has, in part, been shaped by the 'settler-ruler' mentality of the Al Khalifa. Unlike in the neighbouring shaykhdoms, such as Qatar and Kuwait, where the

[15] The Al Khalifa, originally from Kuwait, migrated to Qatar. From there, they invaded the island of Bahrain in 1781/2, ejecting the Persians who had previously ruled.

[16] A. Shehabi and M. O. Jones, *Bahrain's Uprising: Resistance and Repression in the Gulf*, London, Zed Books Ltd, 2015.

[17] T. Sellin, *Culture Conflict and Crime*, New York, NY, Social Science Research Council, 1938.

ruling families assimilated into the local population, forming a more cohesive political entity, the Al Khalifa continue to 'jealously guard their identity/image as "settler-rulers"'.[18] Fuad Khuri expands on this and notes the 'exclusiveness and non-assimilative character'[19] of the Al Khalifa, whose legitimacy was based on historically claimed rights of conquest devoid of any substantial public delegation.[20] This settler-ruler mentality became within the Al Khalifa a 'legacy of conquest', which relates to how, even to this day, 'the ruling family in Bahrain ... refer to their conquest as the basis for establishing legitimacy of their dynastic rule'.[21] In short, Bahrain, its wealth and its people are seen as possessions or subjects of the conquering Al Khalifa.

While what might be described as a kleptocratic ethnocracy led by the Al Khalifa family might be a suitable shorthand for Bahrain, it is also imperative to acknowledge one of the country's most notable features: the role of external actors, especially Britain, Saudi Arabia and the United States. Indeed, if a state's most salient features define a regime, this must be reflected in the nomenclature. Toby Craig Jones argues that the Al Khalifa have only managed to perpetrate such continued repression against the indigenous people due to the protection afforded to them by outside powers.[22] On the recent uprisings, Curtis Ryan notes that 'the outcome of almost every case within the Arab uprisings has turned at least in part on the action and decisions of external powers'.[23] Initially, this was Britain, who in order to secure their domination of trade routes to India, conducted a series of treaties with tribal leaders along the Persian Coast in the 1800s. The first of these agreements was the General Maritime Treaty of 1820 that recognized the Al Khalifa as the legitimate rulers of Bahrain. A subsequent agreement in 1861 turned Bahrain into an informal British protectorate.

[18] A. Khalaf, *Contentious Politics in Bahrain: From Ethnic to National and Vice Versa*, The Fourth Nordic Conference on Middle Eastern Studies: The Middle East in a Globalising World, Oslo, 13–16 August 1998, www.smi.uib.no/pao/khalaf.html

[19] F. Khuri, *Tribe and State in Bahrain: The Transition of Social and Political Authority in an Arab State*, Chicago, IL, University of Chicago Press, 1981, p. 236.

[20] Ibid.

[21] A. Khalaf, 'Opening remarks, Bahrain: 30 years of unconstitutional rule', Parliamentary Human Rights Group, House of Lords, 25 August 2005, http://jaddwilliam2.blogspot.co.uk/2005/08/royal-dream.html

[22] T. C. Jones, 'Time to Disband the Bahrain-based U.S. Fifth Fleet', *The Atlantic*, 10 June 2011, www.theatlantic.com/international/archive/2011/06/time-to-disband-the-bahrain-based-us-fifth-fleet/240243/

[23] C. Ryan, 'New Opportunities for Political Science: IR Theory', in *Arab Uprisings: New Opportunities for Political Science*, Project on Middle East Political Science (POMEPS Briefings), 2012, p. 56.

As a consequence, Britain was bound to provide 'security' for its 'possessions against similar aggressions directed against them by the Chiefs and tribes of this Gulf'.[24] In 1880, the British completed an agreement with the Chief of Bahrain in which they forbade the Al Khalifa from engaging in negotiations or treaties without the consent of the British.[25] This treaty was updated again in 1892.[26] In exchange for control over Bahrain's foreign policy, Britain was now obliged to protect the Bahraini government from external aggression. As such, British Imperial influence in internal affairs increased. Most importantly, it enabled Britain to assert further imperial control over the Gulf by excluding or controlling the presence of other global powers.

Since the 1800s, 'special relations' with Britain provided the regime with a vital source of legitimacy. Britain, as an external source of power warded off external threats and helped the regime suppress its internal opposition. For more than a century, but especially since the discovery of oil, British might, including military force, was ready at hand to rescue the Al Khalifa from attacks by its opponents, whether tribal, confessional or nationalist.[27] In 2013, at a reception ceremony in London hosted by the current ruler, King Hamad, highlighted the historical Al Khalifa reliance on the British, noting his father's sadness at their departure, stating: 'Why, no one asked you to go?'[28] There was no altruism here on an Imperial level. Britain's motives of what seemed to be 'wholehearted support' of the Al Khalifa was due to her 'apprehension of the geopolitical consequences of Saudi ambitions, Iranian claims and, later, as part of its region-wide actions to restrain the growth of the Arab national liberation movement'.[29] However, the Al Khalifa's reliance on external protectors has meant that they never depended wholly on the 'support, material, political or otherwise, of their subjects'.[30] Instead, 'alliances with outsiders were meant to strengthen the family's grip over internal

[24] 1861 Agreement between Shaykh Mohamed bin Khalifa, independent ruler of Bahrain, on the part of himself and successors, and captain Felix Jones, Her Majesty's Indian Navy, political resident of her Britannic majesty in the Gulf of Persia, on the part of the British Government, 1861, in P. Tuson and E. Quick (eds), *Records of Bahrain 1820–1960*, vol. 1, Slough, Archive Editions, 1993, p. 725.

[25] Translation of agreement signed by the Chief of Bahrain, dated 22 December 1880, in P. Tuson and E. Quick (eds), *Records of Bahrain 1820–1960*, vol. 1, Slough, Archive Editions, 1993, p. 409.

[26] Exclusive Agreement of the Shaykh of Bahrain with the British Government, dated 13 March 1892, in P. Tuson and E. Quick (eds), *Records of Bahrain 1820–1960*, vol. 2, Slough, Archive Editions, 1993, p. 456.

[27] Khalaf, *Contentious Politics in Bahrain.*

[28] Bahrain News Agency, 'HM King Hosts Reception Ceremony in London', 12 May 2013, www.bna.bh/portal/en/news/560364

[29] Khalaf, *Contentious Politics in Bahrain.*

[30] Khuri, *Tribe and State in Bahrain*, p. 238.

affairs while retaining its local exclusiveness'.[31] The exclusivism facilitated by this externally bolstered protection means that the Al Khalifa suffer from limited legitimacy among ethnic groups excluded from political power. This dependency on Britain, which carved out a geopolitical niche for the Al Khalifa family, has nonetheless created a state that is, without international backing, small and weak. Indeed, as Nakhleh states, places like Bahrain 'cannot be an independent actor in the international arena. Whether Bahrain wills it or not, by its very location it will be caught in the squeeze of international politics'.[32]

Bahrain's cycles of instability over the past century have rendered it an interesting political case study. Despite intermittent growth of political democracy in the early 1970s and later in the early 2000s, and the ratification of a number of international treaties such as the International Code of Civil and Political Rights (ICCPR), the recent government crackdown that began in 2011 has been more brutal than any other in history, certainly in terms of total number of deaths. Vincent Boudreau states that one 'way of thinking about state reactions to social challenges is to argue that different kinds of regimes have different repressive potentials…',[33] or repressive capacity. Davenport argues in his uses of Giddes' typology of different types of regimes that 'autocratic governments repress in different ways',[34] and that a concerted effort must be made to understand the nature of this repression and reasons for its occurrence; 'for research, the implications are clear: in the future, there must be an effort extended to disaggregate regime type so that we can understand the circumstances under which civil liberties are restricted and human rights are violated'.[35] It is therefore incorrect to treat all autocratic governments in the same manner.[36] As such 'we would not expect repression to be comparably applied across all types of autocracy'.[37] The logical implications of the above arguments are clear, and suggest that the most comprehensive understanding of repression on a state level is naturally an examination on a case-by-case basis.

Crises in Bahrain have therefore impinged upon the interests of outside powers, and thus invited significant external involvement in

[31] Ibid.

[32] E. Nakhleh, *Bahrain: Political Development in a Modernizing Society*, New York, NY, Lexington Books, 2011, p. 111.

[33] V. Boudreau, 'Precarious Regimes and Matchup Problems in the Explanation of Repressive Policy', in C. Davenport, H. Johnston and C. Mueller (eds), *Repression and Mobilization*, Minneapolis, MI, University of Minnesota Press, 2005, p. 36.

[34] C. Davenport, 'State Repression and the Tyrannical Peace', *Journal of Peace Research*, vol. 44, no. 4, 2007, p. 486.

[35] Ibid., p. 486. [36] Ibid., p. 500. [37] Ibid., p. 489.

repression. While these shifts in 'international political re-alignments'[38] have impacted upon the political status quo and opportunities available to social movements, they have also affected repressive capacity and repressive choices. After all, Bahrain's crisis of sovereignty implies an inability by the regime to have full autonomy over its actions. In this regard, regime type becomes somewhat problematic, as it applies responsibility to an entity that is very much contingent on the actions of other regime types (i.e. Britain and Saudi). In 1996, a writer in *The Economist* eloquently summed up this interference.

For a tiny country, without even much oil to recommend it, Bahrain has an unusual number of big friends ready to rally enthusiastically to the ruling family's sides as it cracks down, yet again, on dissent. Several have their own reasons for doing so: dislike of the democracy (Saudi Arabia); eagerness to ingratiate itself with the Gulf states (Jordan); the desire to protect a useful military base (America and Britain). And most are happy to form a phalanx against Iranian meddling – if that is, indeed, what is happening.[39]

This multiple state-centric focus should also give way to factor in other actors, from private companies and entrepreneurs to new technological forms themselves. Indeed, rather than regime, the term 'assemblage' is perhaps more appropriate. Nonetheless, the question of how Britain and Saudi Arabia have demonstrated extensive interference in quashing political opposition designed to challenge the Al Khalifa has not been studied extensively.

Inevitably, the international realignments that followed Independence are important to Bahrain, whose ruling regime has sought to placate and be amenable to international players with varying ideologies and foreign policies. A regime that has summarily relied on outside forces to maintain its power does not necessarily fall neatly into any predefined category, and will never be a leading player, or ultimately determiner of its own destiny. That is not to dismiss the agency of the Bahraini government but merely to acknowledge that other forces are at work that shape, influence and often define the limits of the enactments of specific processes. While it is a truism now that international linkages have been influential in bolstering the resilience of Arab states,[40] the existence of the literature on how repression changes temporally over

[38] D. McAdam, 'Political Process and the Development of Black Insurgency 1930–1970', in V. Ruggiero and N. Montagna (eds), *Social Movement: A Reader*, London and New York, NY, Routledge, 2008, p. 179.

[39] *The Economist*, 'Spot the Villain', 3 February 1996, issue, 7951, p. 44.

[40] See, for example, Bellin and Heydemann.

time is small and non-existent for countries such as Bahrain.[41] If such changes do exist, they may be more discernible in a country like Bahrain that has been subject to two different spheres of influence: British and then Al Khalifa/Saudi Arabian imperial overrule, the latter coinciding with a rise of US influence in the region. Indeed, the argument is that repressive action is defined in part by the differing dual authority structures that have emerged in Bahrain, from a British Al Khalifa coalition to a Saudi Al Khalifa coalition. In this regard, exploring the 'legitimaters' of repression is essential. 'Legitimaters', according to Lopez and Stohl are 'a core group of technocrats, industrialists and, virtually always, military personnel and institutions',[42] who 'lend support to acts of state terror because they directly benefit from them or because such brutal use of state force permits the realization of goals that are highly salient to them'.[43]

Why Repression?

Bahrain presents a compelling case in itself regarding the study of repression for many reasons. It has been afflicted by internal political instability and conflict throughout its modern history. What began as the feudal oppression of the native *baḥārna* by the conquering Al Khalifa tribe and their allies has evolved into the neofeudal repression by the Al Khalifa-dominated regime (and their allies) of several uprisings spearheaded by different movements. These uprisings have had several different characteristics, from the more nationalist movements of the 1950s and 1960s and the labour and leftist movements of the 1970s to the exogenously branded 'Islamic' movements of the 1980s and 1990s. The most recent of these uprisings began in 2011, when Bahrainis, galvanized by the protests in Tunisia and Egypt in 2010, took to the streets on 14 February 2011 to demand greater political rights. In all cases, despite political reforms, or constitutional reformulations, the ruling Al Khalifa family have succeeded in preserving their monopoly on the country's material, political and military resources, highlighting what Eva Bellin

[41] For work that has sought to track methods of repression over long periods of time, see: R. J. Goldstein, *Political Repression in Modern America: From 1870 to 1976.* 1st Illinois ed. Urbana, IL, University of Illinois Press, 1978; R. J. Goldstein, *Political Repression in 19th Century Europe*, Oxford, Routledge, 2010 (first published 1983); J. Boykoff, *Beyond Bullets: The Suppression of Dissent in the United States*, Edinburgh, AK Press, 2007, p. 14.

[42] G. A. Lopez and M. Stohl, 'State Terrorism: From the Reign of Terror to Ninety-Eighty Four Terrorism', *Chitty's Law Journal*, vol. 32, no. 5, 1984–7, p. 25.

[43] Ibid.

describes as authoritarian 'robustness'.[44] All movements in Bahrain's history, whether organized political societies or indigenous groups who are subordinate to the superordinate Al Khalifa, have faced severe and repeated political repression, a fact that has not been tempered by nominal democratic reform.

However, when it comes to repression, counter-revolution and how social movements or dissidents are ended/inhibited, we have only just begun to 'scratch the surface of the topic'.[45] Even the definition of political repression itself is the subject of much debate. Given its contemporary and historical importance in Bahrain, and especially in light of the Arab Uprisings, political repression is perhaps one of the most useful and compelling conceptual lenses to 'mediate between meaningful happenings in the past and the concerns of present-day audiences'.[46] Charles Tilly once stated that collective action was often treated as a 'subsidiary form of political, social or economic history' but was something that required a history 'in its own terms'.[47] The same should be said of repression, given its importance in preserving extant political realities. It is also self-evident, from an ethical and social justice standpoint, that studying repression is vital simply by virtue that many often suffer as a result of it.[48] Perhaps surprisingly, repression has only received incidental references in historical accounts of Bahrain. Critical texts on Bahrain have retold its history using different lenses. Khuri's *Tribe and State in Bahrain*, for example, approaches the development of the state from the perspective of 'political authority' and the impact of imperial and tribal rule on political structures in Bahrain. Fred Lawson's history opts for a lens of modernization theory, tracking the development of Bahrain over the twentieth century. Abdulhadi Khalaf explores control strategies in his analysis of contentious politics on Bahrain, examining how tribal rule exerts a system of patronage related to Rentierism. Justin Gengler focuses on ethnic mobilization in Bahrain and its relation to the Rentier

[44] E. Bellin, 'Reconsidering the Robustness of Authoritarianism in the Middle East: Lessons from the Arab Spring', *Comparative Politics*, vol. 44, no. 2, pp. 127–49.
[45] C. Davenport, *How Social Movements Die: Repression and Demobilization of the Republic of New Africa,* Cambridge: Cambridge University Press, 2015, p. 21 [Kindle Edition].
[46] T. Skocpol, 'Emerging Agendas and Recurrent Strategies in Historical Sociology', in T. Skocpol (ed.), *Vision and Method in Historical Sociology,* Cambridge, Cambridge University Press, 1985, p. 362.
[47] C. Tilly, *From Mobilization to Revolution*, Ann Arbor, MI, University of Michigan, 1977, ch. 8, p. 14.
[48] C. Davenport, 'Repression and Mobilization: Insights from Political Science and Sociology', in C. Davenport, H. Johnston and C. Mueller (eds), *Repression and Mobilization,* Minneapolis, MI, University of Minnesota Press, 2005, p. xii.

State.[49] Stacy Strobl examines the importance of sectarianism in defining policing outcomes and attitudes towards the police in Bahrain, while Toby Matthiesen emphasizes the importance of sectarianism as a regime survival strategy. Yet, as Shehabi and Jones note, 'repression and dissent in Bahrain have generally remained outside of research focus and dominant approaches adopted by NGOs, think-tanks, and international relations experts have tended to focus through paradigms of sectarianism, modernisation, rentierism, or even democratisation, where "reform" and "dialogue" have become tired idioms'.[50]

The need for critical approaches to the Gulf is also necessary in a field dominated disproportionately by transatlantic security concerns, and perhaps a focus on the paradigm of oil economics, rentierism, Islamic finance, and tribal politics. As such, the research paradigm here is transformative. Integral to the transformative paradigm is its axiology. That is, it is a paradigm shaped as much by ethical concerns as it is anything else, and its intellectual justification is itself the need to focus on social justice. It is this axiology which forms an important part of defining other considerations of ontology, epistemology and methodology. Axiological considerations include respecting cultural norms of interaction, while beneficence is 'defined in terms of the promotion of human rights and increase in social justice'.[51] Axiomatic within this are the tenets of the transformative ontology, which reject 'cultural relativism and recognise the influence of privilege' in shaping what is real.[52] Furthermore, 'multiple realities are shaped by social, political, cultural, economic, gender, disability and other values'.[53] Like much critical research, shedding light on the extent of government repression will help empower people with new knowledge, expose the inequities of the status quo and underpin social changes that help 'equalise the distribution of resources'.[54]

The transformative paradigm can be applied to a study in any discipline so long as it is related to relevant social issues of the day. Empowerment, injustice, inequality, oppression, domination and alienation are

[49] Invariably, when control strategies are mentioned, they tend to reflect on a useful, yet a delineated, postcolonial emphasis on strategies of divide and conquer, as is the case with Kylie Moore's article on Bahrain.

[50] A. Shehabi and M. O. Jones, 'Bahrain's Uprising: The Struggle for Democracy in the Gulf', in A. Shehabi and M.O. Jones (eds), *Bahrain's Uprising: Resistance and Repression in the Gulf*, London, Zed Books Ltd, 2015, p. 33.

[51] D. M. Mertens, 'Philosophy in Mixed Methods Teaching: The Transformative Paradigm as Illustration', *International Journal of Multiple Research Approaches*, vol. 4, 2010, p. 11.

[52] Ibid. [53] Ibid.

[54] F. M. Cancian, 'Conflicts between Activist Research and Academic Success: Participatory Research and Alternative Strategies', *The American Sociologist*, vol. 24, no. 1, 1993, p. 92.

important objects of study, whether framed historically or in a contemporary context.[55] Such an approach is especially important in history, as more traditional historical enquiries have 'silenced members of oppressed and marginalised groups'.[56] This paradigm is not to denounce the importance of historical context. Indeed, a vital part of the transformative paradigm's methodological stance is to acknowledge 'contextual and historic' factors, 'especially as they relate to discrimination and oppression'.[57]

Why Bahrain?

The use of Bahrain as a case study seeks to add to our understanding of repression, expanding on the nuance of autocratic control, while also addressing the issue of the lack of conceptual clarity among the many manifested forms of repression.[58] In particular, it addresses the deficiency in literature outlying the 'specific contours' of the repressive methods and choices made in Bahrain over the past one hundred years, and fulfils the need to analyse Arab countries independently. This is especially true of Bahrain, which Schwedler argues is an 'outlier' in many respects in the studies of the region.[59] Justin Gengler, too, argues that Bahrain has always challenged the 'prevailing interpretation of politics in the Arab Gulf – the so-called rentier state paradigm – which holds that regimes can buy the political acquiescence of the citizenry through judicious distribution of oil revenues'.[60] Abdulhadi Khalaf argues that rentierism only partly explains a regime's resilience and that the movement of 2011 marked the end of rentierism politics in Bahrain.[61] Eva Bellin herself frequently refers to Bahrain as an exception to her more generalizable explanations of Arab State authoritarianism, and thus it becomes clear that a more in-depth investigation may reveal more idiosyncrasies about repression in what is a small, but important, Gulf Kingdom.

[55] J. W. Creswell, *Research Design: Qualitative, Quantitative, and Mixed Methods Approaches*, London, Sage, 2003.

[56] Ibid. [57] Mertens, 'Philosophy in Mixed Methods Teaching', p. 11.

[58] M. Khawaja, 'Repression and Popular Collective Action: Evidence from the West Bank', *Sociological Forum*, vol. 8, no. 1, 1993, p. 50.

[59] J. Schwedler, 'What Should Political Scientists Be Doing?', in *Arab Uprisings: New Opportunities for Political Science*, Project on Middle East Political Science (POMEPS Briefings), p. 57.

[60] J. Gengler, 'Bahrain's Sunni Awakening', *Middle East Research and Information Project (MERIP)*, 17 January 2012, www.merip.org/mero/mero011712

[61] A. Khalaf, 'Foreword', in A. Shehabi and M. O. Jones (eds), *Bahrain's Uprising: Resistance and Repression in the Gulf*, London, Zed Books Ltd, 2015.

However, while authoritarian resistance has been examined by numerous scholars, notable among them Eva Bellin, who focuses on the extensive will and capacity of the coercive apparatus in Arab states as making them exceptional, new approaches are necessary.[62] Repression is one such approach and there is little work done on how long-term changes of repression occur in countries that have experienced a shift in protectors. For a country like Bahrain, which suffers from a position of sovereign insecurity (an inherent dependence on the protection of larger states or entities), repression is crucial in understanding how international factors influence internal repression. Thus, repression and Bahrain are both relatively undernourished in the literature, and thus form a marriage of convenience regarding academic study on the region.

By adopting a fine-grained approach to repression, this study explores numerous deficiencies addressed by social movement scholars in the study of repression that tend to focus on creating general causal models based on narrow definitions of repression. By broadening yet conceptually refining different types of repression, and examining strategic decision-making processes by legitimaters, this research reveals that while repressive choices and methods are often dependent on specific contextual and temporal factors, there are also long-term trends in the repressive structure of Bahrain's political system. Furthermore, as repression is, like social movements, a phenomenon that is not concerned about disciplinary boundaries, the nature of the research expands into fields of legal research, politics and communications.

While it can be hard to summarize an argument in an interpretive history, this book makes several claims. These are that the nature of repression and control shifted according not only to the threat to the ruling Al Khalifa regime but also due to several other factors, such as those tools available to the government, the personality of those responsible for control policy and the nature of institutions themselves. Contextual factors, attitudes of elites, levels of accountability are all crucial in determining repressive choices. In addition to these micro-level transactions that influence repressive choices, this research also reveals how the shift from British Imperial overrule to Saudi overrule marked a fundamental shift in general trends of repression. Increasing Al Khalifa and Saudi autonomy following Independence in 1971 led to a reassertion of the Al Khalifa's 'legacy of conquest'.[63] Under this form of rule, public

[62] M. M. Howard and M. R. Walters, 'Response to Eva Bellin, Ellen Lust, and March Lynch', *Perspectives on Politics*, vol. 12, no. 2, June 2014, pp. 417–19.

[63] A. Khalaf, 'The Outcome of a Ten-Year Process of Political Reform in Bahrain', Arab Reform Initiative, 2008, www.arab-reform

delegation of issues of collective importance has been relegated and more coercive forms of control favoured. While the British protected the Al Khalifa, institutionalizing their rule and abetting their tribal authoritarianism, they also altered the 'modalities' of repression; whereas increasing Saudi influence prompted a reversion to traditional Al Khalifa methods of settler-colonial rule. In other words, repression became notably more severe in specific categories after Independence in 1971, especially for the country's Shiʿa population.

Aspects of statecraft have failed to temper ongoing government brutality. The relatively recent democratization, for example, lacked 'binding consultation between the agents of the government and the people, inhibiting a crucial aspect of democracy: the protection of citizens from an arbitrary state'.[64] Again, this has also raised questions about to what extent certain types of democratization can function as a tool of hegemonic control. Like any new history, revisionist or otherwise, this book also makes known new facts: from acts of British torture to the extent of the Foreign and Commonwealth Office's complicity in hiding knowledge of torture from Parliament. Contemporary investigations also reveal the depth of not only fake news in the recent uprising but fake journalists and sectarian robotic accounts. Through addressing the history of informational control, this book also problematizes the liberating potential of technology and critically examines how social media in the recent uprising was used as a tool of social control, propaganda and surveillance. The increased role of online vigilantism also highlights the need to examine further the role of non-state actors as agents of repression.

This study, therefore, seeks to revise current historical work on Bahrain, placing state repression and control as the focal point. By doing so, it hopes to raise awareness of methods of control that Bahrainis have been, and continue to be, subjected to. It is emancipatory in the sense that it contributes towards narratives of resistance, further positioning current claims of oppression within an expansive historical account of subordination and domination. Last, and perhaps it is this researcher's own naivety or waning optimism, it is hoped that revealing the structures of control may force some to question and revise certain assumptions that cause them to resist change and support oppression.[65]

[64] L. Kalmanowiecki, 'Origins and Applications of Political Policing in Argentina', *Latin American Perspectives*, vol. 27, no. 2, Violence, Coercion and Rights in the Americas, 2000, p. 37.

[65] It is important to note that in the context of this study, repression is predominantly the result of dominant groups attempting to maintain their monopoly of power, wealth and resources. Studying repression does not necessarily imply support for any of the

The Book: Structuring Repressive History

Following the outline of the theoretical framework in the introduction, the 'common-sense device of narrative storytelling' is frequently employed, accounting for the impetus for those repressive choices. As for the use of narrative, Lichbach notes that 'there are many ways in which a narrative "seeks to use history to construct the theory and to flesh out its implications" (Rosenthal 1998, 2)'.[66] Out of the narrative stream of happenings that begins in the 1920s, Bahrain's cycles of unrest represent a 'set of chronologically linked strategic situations'.[67] From this historical trajectory, we can 'derive many observable implications about the recurring pattern of politics (i.e., strategizing) manifested in the case's particular events, individuals, issues, groups, conflicts, regions or periods'.[68] This 'overall thesis, or meta-narrative, illuminates the general pattern or overall stylised facts of the case'.[69] The instances of contestation selected across the twentieth and twenty-first century represent the 'short-run equilibria' that 'compound to produce a long-run equilibrium as the series of within-case studies compounds to produce the overall case study'.[70] Given that the emphasis is on the methods of repression, this book is primarily organized around themes. Within each theme of repression, episodes and events are more or less analysed chronologically.

The episodes under scrutiny are *baḥrānī* resistance to tribal repression in the 1920s, the Higher Education Committee movement of the 1950s, the leftist movements of the 1960s and 1970s,[71] the religious unrest of the 1980s, the 1990s' Intifada and the Uprising of 2011. By focusing on these particular episodes of unrest, it is possible to offer a more analytical

individuals, social movements or groups attempting to create political change. Indeed, in some instances the wishes expressed by some social movements may not be conducive to the betterment of certain marginalized or oppressed groups. However, when social movements are fighting a system that deprives them of rights enjoyed by others, there is an immediate issue of social justice that must be addressed. It is unreasonable to refrain from such critique on the basis of fears that a new social order may be more repressive than the preceding one. To adopt such a mentality would negate any form of change, as people would accept inequality and marginalization on the premise that no one can anticipate future outcomes. Furthermore, in many cases, extreme manifestations of certain groups may derive themselves from government policy; thus the creation of radical groups can be contingent on acts of state and non-state repression. One must therefore oppose repression *on principle*, for it is often state repression that creates groups whose end goals may seem counter-productive to the promotion of social justice.

[66] M. Lichbach, 'How to Organize Your Mechanisms: Research Programs, Stylized Facts, and Historical Narratives', in C. Davenport et al. (eds), *Repression and Mobilization*, Minneapolis,MI, University of Minnesota Press, 2005, p. 241.

[67] Ibid., pp. 241–2. [68] Ibid. [69] Ibid., p. 240. [70] Ibid.

[71] These include the National Liberation Front, the Popular Front for the Liberation of Oman and the Arabian Gulf and various trade union movements.

focus, rather than examining every conceivable aspect of social control. As these episodes of unrest have acted as an opportunity for the regime to repress dissent, they are a logical unit of analysis for studying repression, and represent what Mark Lichbach calls 'episodic crises, recurring problems, periodic challenges, or key turning points in the case's history'[72] that form 'linked strategic situations'.[73] Although these situations remain separate, the recurring patterns of politics highlight both nuance for each occurrence and also a more generalizable trend. These, combined with other contextual factors – elite attitudes, resource availability, institutional capabilities, organizational structure – have had a significant implication for strategic choices and the repression of dissent. Fundamentally, this approach seeks to address the deficiency in historical work on contentious politics, which tends to be very restrictive in focusing on temporally limited events, such as a singular strike or episode of contention.[74]

Similar to Goldstein's work on America, this is a 'history and analysis of political repression, so naturally, it stresses events relevant to this subject'.[75] Emphasis is also placed on the shift to Independence in 1971, as it was at this time that regional hegemony transfered from British hands to Saudi and American influence. While there has never been a historical study on repression in Bahrain, other qualitative studies on the topic are worthy of note. Jules Boykoff pulls data from many sources across a fifty-year history in order to create his taxonomy of repression in the USA. Boykoff categorizes different types of repression, 'systematising an array of cases ranging from the early twentieth to the early twenty-first century'.[76] Austin Turk's research on political policing pulls data from a wide range of sources (including Amnesty International reports for example) in order to create a taxonomy of different methods of control. Turk, however, does not merely focus on the USA, and his taxonomy of methods of repression is more frugal than Boykoff's.[77] Robert Goldstein's history of repression in America between 1870 and 1978 covers a similar broad expanse of time, yet it is organized chronologically, as does his 1983 study on *Political Repression in 19th Century Europe.*[78]

[72] Lichbach, 'How to Organize Your Mechanisms', p. 239. [73] Ibid.
[74] B. Dill and R. Aminzade, 'Historians and the Study of Protest', in B. Klandermans and C. Roggeband (eds), *Handbook of Social Movements across Disciplines*, New York, NY, Springer, 2007, p. 269.
[75] Goldstein, *Political Repression in Modern America*, p. xxii.
[76] Boykoff, *Beyond Bullets*, p. 9.
[77] A. Turk, *Political Criminality: The Defiance and Defence of Authority*, Beverley Hills, CA, Sage Publications, 1982.
[78] See Goldstein, *Political Repression in Modern America*; Goldstein, *Political Repression in 19th Century Europe*.

Gary Marx, too, does the same, although his time frame is admittedly shorter.[79] While there is an emerging academic body of work looking at long-term studies of repression, their approaches differ somewhat. Goldstein's work was organised according to specific movements, this book, for example, is organized according to repressive categories, to see how they evolved in all spheres.

In Chapters 1 and 2, the justifications, concepts and theories for the study are laid out. There are four key issues. First, regime type analysis of repression yields unsatisfying results. Second, Bahrain exhibits many characteristics that make it an interesting case study, such as the Al Khalifa regime and its reliance on foreign powers. Third, studies of repression are often quantitative, and attempts to build generalizable causal models have reached often divergent conclusions, emphasizing the need for fine-grained approaches such as historical ones. Fourth, there is a lack of nuanced conceptualizations of repression, and this book proposes a new one, ideally positioned to create a rich net for studying repression. In other words, what types of repression are there, and how can we apply them to study Bahrain?

With the template of repression laid out, methods of statecraft are detailed and examined in Chapter 3. In particular, the chapter notes several compelling trends. First, the British desire to sail a Middle Course in Bahrain led to reforms designed to ameliorate dissent through indirect and pacific means, yet it also ultimately led to the crystallization of the Al Khalifa regime. These methods included the civil list, municipal reform and even the acknowledgement of primogeniture. It also notes that in the 1950s, growing Arab nationalism and a desire to follow this middle course of non-interference meant that Britain innovated and improvised techniques of statecraft in order to repress the Higher Executive Committee. Post-Independence diminishing British influence and increasing Saudi ascendency meant that the government eschewed tactics like public-delegation through parliament in favour of methods centred around patronage. This Saudi largesse had the simultaneous effect of binding Bahrain closer to Saudi, resulting in long-term dedemocratization and rentierism. Diminishing British influence following Independence also seemed to cause a manifestation of both Saudi and Al Khalifa animosity towards political opposition and the Shiʿa. In particular, this chapter contributes to knowledge by offering

[79] G. Marx, 'External Efforts to Damage or Facilitate Social Movements: Some Patterns, Explanations, Outcomes, and Complications', in M. Zald and J. McCarthy (eds), *The Dynamics of Social Movements*, Cambridge, MA, Winthrop Publishers, 1979, pp. 94–125.

new facts on Bahrain's transition to Independence, as very little primary document research has been done on this period.

Chapter 4 details the evolution of, and the repressive capacity and methods of Bahrain's security services. In particular it focuses on the police, for which most historical and current data is available. Ranging from the personalist explanations of repression, such as why Charles Belgrave himself engaged in beating detainees, to the institutionalization of deviance, Chapter 4 looks at how personal integrity violations in Bahrain are intrinsically tied up with the country's institutional and political structures. It also explores how Al Khalifa conservatism underlined by Saudi fear of Iranian expansionism has informed a militant and coercive policy of repression. In particular, the chapter notes that while the British established the police and continued to play an important role in training and technical assistance, a shift in power occurred leading up to and following 1971. Following Independence, the increasing Al Khalifa and Saudi control, coupled with diminishing British influence on policy, led to a more systemically repressive coercive apparatus, one in which the British influence became hidden behind the legal distancing of 'Independence'. As well as detailing the emergence of the police force, this chapter argues how tactics such as mass arrests and torture have emerged, not simply because of the criminalization of the Shiʿa threat but due to the embedded discrimination and sectarianism that pervades the security forces and the ruling regime.

By examining laws, legislation, and legal processes, it is argued in Chapter 5 that the legal system in Bahrain is becoming an increasingly comprehensive tool of repression. Despite the increasing standardization of law, the arbitrary nature of its execution during political unrest highlights the continuity of particularistic features of tribal law embedded within a standardized system. Also, legal repression has been facilitated by the emergence of specific legal structures and processes. As a consequence, laws have often been enacted as reactionary measures to control dissent, long outliving their initial utility while simultaneously generating future grievances. The extent of impunity as an enabling factor for repression is also investigated and highlighted. In particular, a re-examination of historical sources sheds new light on the trial of the al-Madani killers in 1977 and the trial of the Khawalid shaykhs[80] in the

[80] Khawalid is a pluralization of Khalids. The term is used to refer to a branch of the Al Khalifa family descended from Khalid bin Ali Al Khalifa (1853–1925). Khalid bin Ali was the half-brother of Isa bin Ali Al Khalifa, who ruled Bahrain between 1869 and 1923. From 2011, the term was used to refer to the two brothers Khalid bin Ahmed Al Khalifa, the Royal Court Minister and Khalifa bin Ahmed Al Khalifa, the Commander-in-Chief of the Bahrain Defence Force.

1920s. While the emergence of 'rule by law' instead of 'rule of law' is implicit, this chapter sheds light on the nuances within even those repressive authoritarian legal processes.

Chapter 6 explores how the control of information has become increasingly important throughout the twentieth and twenty-first centuries. In particular, modern communication technologies have been foundational in creating new forms of resistance and repression. Despite British involvement in the censorship of anti-regime material, their general encouragement to liberalize the media was again met with Al Khalifa hostility. This continued post-Independence, yet despite recent liberalization, the process of Al Khalifa control has persevered. In addition to exploring the historical development of repressive information practice, this chapter includes elements of a framing analysis and virtual ethnography. News coverage and social media content are examined to reveal that protesters and opposition are framed as violent, Iran-sponsored agents working to install a theocracy. This chapter also problematizes the liberating potential of technology by arguing how it was continually adapted as a tool of surveillance and control in the recent uprising. It also analyses the growth in importance of surveillance strategies, emphasizing the continued importance of transnational linkages in maintaining these repressive processes. Specifically, it assesses how private British and American companies are capitalizing on whitewashing human rights abuses.

1 Defining Political Repression

Breadth or Depth?

All states repress, yet the meaning of repression is subject to much scholarly debate. The following definition is rooted in conflict theory: 'conflict cannot be excluded from social life ... "Peace" is nothing more than a change in the form of the conflict or in the antagonists or in the objects of the conflict, or finally in the chances of selection.'[1] In order to gain and maintain access to material resources, both the state and private actors frequently use repression and control to prevent potential challenges to their position of privilege, often resulting in conflict. Such forms of control may be broad, as in the Durkheimian preservation of cultural, social or ethnic stratification, or much narrower, such as the use of torture to deter political dissidents or opponents of the regime. Whereas the former phenomenon may be more broadly termed a form of social control, the latter might more readily be considered a form of repression.

Nonetheless, drawing a distinction between broader forms of control and repression is not straightforward. Scholars of repression often disagree about what constitutes political repression. Robert Justin Goldstein provides a useful starting point, arguing that repression 'consists of government action which grossly discriminates against persons or organisations viewed as presenting a fundamental challenge to existing power relations or key government policies, because of their perceived political beliefs'.[2] More recently, and despite other definitions of repression, Goldstein has reiterated his commitment to his original definition, noting that it can 'defy even the most expert lexicographer'.[3] Scholars such as

[1] M. Weber, *On the Methodology of the Social Sciences*; *The Meaning of 'Ethical Neutrality'*, Glencoe, IL, The Free Press of Glengoe, 1949, p. 27. Cited in A. Turk, *Political Criminality: The Defiance and Defence of Authority*, Beverley Hills, CA, Sage Publications, 1982, p. 11.

[2] Goldstein, *Political Repression in Modern America*, p. XVI.

[3] Goldstein, *Political Repression in 19th Century Europe*, p. xiii.

Christian Davenport have embellished upon Goldstein's work,[4] defining repression as:

> the actual or threatened use of physical sanctions against an individual or organisation, within the territorial jurisdiction of the state, for the purpose of imposing a cost on the target as well as deterring specific activities and/or beliefs perceived to be challenging to government personnel, practices or institutions.[5]

Such measures may include 'harassment, surveillance/spying, bans, arrests, torture, and mass killing by government agents and/or affiliates within their territorial jurisdiction'.[6] Brett Stockdill provides a similar definition, classifying repression as 'any actions taken by [government] authorities to impede mobilisation, harass, and intimidate activists, divide organisations, and physically assault, arrest, imprison and/or kill movement participants'.[7]

Although social movement scholars have widely used these definitions of repression, Jennifer Earl notes that they place too much emphasis on the role of the state. For this reason, Earl defines repression as any 'state or private action meant to prevent, control, or constrain non-institutional, collective action (e.g., protest), including its initiation'.[8] Similarly, Charles Tilly defines repression as 'any action by another group which raises the contender's cost of collective action'.[9] Jules Boykoff's study on repression emphasizes that non-state actors such as the media play an integral role in vilification and turning public opinion against social movements. As a result, Boykoff argues that the role of non-state actors necessitates a broadening of the concept of repression.[10] As Davenport argues, there is a need to include 'alternative mechanisms' of control when analysing repression, including those that might usually be understood as aspects of normative or material power.[11] Luis Fernandez also agrees with the need to broaden our definitions of repression, arguing that it 'opens up the theoretical possibilities for broader studies of protest control'.[12] For example, private security firms, software firms, the arms trade and vigilantes may also play an important role in

[4] Ibid. [5] Davenport, 'State Repression and Political Order', p. 2. [6] Ibid., p. 1.

[7] B. C. Stockdill, Multiple Oppressions and Their Influence on Collective Action: The Case of the AIDS Movement, PhD Dissertation, 1996, Evanston, IL, Northwestern University, p. 146.

[8] J. Earl, 'Political Repression: Iron Fists, Velvet Gloves, and Diffuse Control', *The Annual Review of Sociology,* vol. 37, 2011, pp. 261–84, p. 263.

[9] C. Tilly, *From Mobilization to Revolution,* Ann Arbor, MI, University of Michigan Press, 1977, p. 100.

[10] Boykoff, *Beyond Bullets.* [11] Davenport, 'State Repression and Political Order', p. 19.

[12] L. A. Fernandez, *Policing Dissent: Social Control and the Anti-globalization Movement,* New Brunswick, NJ, Rutgers University Press, 2008, p. 9.

repression. As Earl notes, there is 'very little' study of non-state actors and private repression.[13]

Hendrix too argues that a state's administrative, bureaucratic capacity may be more important in determining a state's repressive capacity than the ability to put boots on the ground.[14] While the line between state and private actors is not always clear, studies of repression tend to be state-centric. The role of private actors tends to focus on national institutions such as the media. Over-broad definitions of repression run the risk of making it a 'theoretical umbrella' as opposed to a useful analytical tool.[15] On the other hand, focusing on one aspect of repression such as the policing of protest runs the risk of ignoring other aspects of repression that are important in understanding the broader web of control and, in the case of Bahrain, the reason for the regime's resilience.

As well as noting that repression is a contested concept, there is also the problem of the general limitations on academic studies of repression. Social movement scholars have tended to focus more on the study of the 'emergence, growth and effectiveness of social movements', as opposed to the role the state or private actors play in preventing or repressing their activity.[16] Furthermore, as states move towards more democratic forms of representation, more attention must be given to those institutions that do not necessarily form part of the traditional coercive apparatus. As Davenport notes, alternative mechanisms of control, separate from coercion, 'have not been examined extensively'.[17] Furthermore, 'The failure to incorporate coercive behaviour with other forms of state influence has hindered not only the study of repression but also the study of the alternatives.'[18] On a similar note, Goldstein notes that repression may be legal and peaceful, or illegal and violent.[19] Despite acknowledging that repression is a contested concept, defining repression is essential for conceptual clarity. For the purpose of this study, the definition of repression leans towards a more inclusive, open-ended definition, defined as *the process by which the dominant hegemonic order attempt to maintain power by destroying, rendering harmless or appeasing those organizations, people, groups or ideologies that potentially threaten their position of power or privilege*. The dominant hegemonic power is the Al Khalifa

[13] Earl, 'Political Repression', p. 265.
[14] C. S. Hendrix, 'Measuring State Capacity: Theoretical and Empirical Implications for the Study of Civil Conflict', *Journal of Peace Research*, vol. 47, no. 3, pp. 273–85.
[15] Earl, 'Political Repression', p. 272. [16] Boykoff, *Beyond Bullets*, p. 14.
[17] Davenport, 'State Repression and Political Order', p. 9. [18] Ibid.
[19] Goldstein, *Political Repression in 19th Century Europe*, p. xiii.

regime, a regime which Abdulhadi Khalaf describes as a 'despotic form of rule that has gradually evolved in the British-designed political and economic reforms of the first decades' of the twenty-first century.[20] In this instance, arguing repression as being the action of a dominant hegemonic power asserts that there is a group with a monopoly on governance, rulership and resources. In many respects, the use of repression is, axiomatically, an actualization of their ascendency.

The Case for Historical, Fine-Grained Studies of Repression

With a definition of repression outlined, and Bahrain and its protectors outlined as an interesting unit of analysis, it is useful to address *how* one can approach studying repression when simple measures of regime type may be determined as too encompassing, as repressive capacities are dependent on a myriad of interacting factors. While there may be similarities in how different states control dissent, it is useful to examine them on a case-by-case basis to best understand how regime response to control is dependent on specific temporal, geographical and political factors. Aurel Braun acknowledges this, stating, 'it is vital not to divorce intellectual history from its national, historical, and social bases' when examining dissent and repression.[21] Indeed, the systemic features of political organization and the historical context are necessary for having a sociologically informed understanding of repression.[22]

Furthermore, as repression changes according to time, space and context,[23] focusing on one country will allow a more 'fine-grained' approach in which similarities and differences can be identified to explain why the state or other actors chose specific courses of repressive action at specific times. As Charles Tilly, a pioneer in the area of contentious politics, argues, 'the repressiveness of a government is never a simple matter of more or less. It is always selective, and always consists of some combination of repression, tolerance and facilitation.'[24] This focus on nuance will address shortcomings that arise from creating generalizable

[20] A. Khalaf, 'Contentious Politics in Bahrain: From Ethnic to National and Vice Versa', Paper presented at The Fourth Nordic Conference on Middle Eastern Studies: The Middle East in Globalizing World, Oslo, 13–16 August 1998, www.smi.uib.no/pao/khalaf.html

[21] A. Braun, 'Dissent and the State in Eastern Europe', in C. E. S. Franks (ed.), *Dissent and the State*, Toronto, Oxford University Press, 1989, p. 113.

[22] A. Turk, *Political Criminality: The Defiance and Defence of Authority*, Beverley Hills, CA, Sage Publications, 1982, p. 202.

[23] Davenport, 'State Repression and Political Order'.

[24] Tilly, *From Mobilization to Revolution*, p. 14.

explanations about, for example, the robustness of authoritarianism in the Middle East, and be more akin to historical studies of repression undertaken by the likes of Goldstein and Boykoff who examine multiple incidents of contention across national or regional histories.[25]

The need for a historical understanding of repression also stems from the divergent findings and limitations of those studies that attempt to create overly broad explanatory models or grand causal theories. Indeed, quantitative studies of repression or studies that focus on numerical covariance between indexed forms of repression and other variables tend to produce very different results. For example, Douglas Hibbs argues that repression increases dissent, whereas scholars such as Mark Lichbach and Ted Gurr believe that repression decreases dissent.[26] Although there tends to be a general consensus that liberal political democracy decreases state repression, there is also the argument that 'mixed and transitional regimes, which combine elements of autocracy and democracy are the most coercive'.[27] Also, Daniel Hill finds the link between 'democracy and torture to be quite tenuous, particularly during periods of violent dissent'.[28] Studying Guatemala, Christopher Sullivan argues that repression will decrease dissent in cases where government challenges are directed at clandestine organizations, whereas repression can increase dissent if the government focuses on overt actions against it.[29] In actuality, one of the few relationships to have stood the test of time is that states are more likely to resort to repression when faced with a domestic threat.[30] However, this is hardly revelatory.

Similarly, quantitative measures, like the Political Terror Scale,[31] seem to have misleading results on Bahrain, offering little nuance or historical utility. The Cingranelli–Richards (CIRI) human rights project, while providing rich data used by scholars of repression for covariate analysis,[32] also offers little nuance with regard to specific countries. Quantitative

[25] See Boykoff, *Beyond Bullets*; Goldstein, Political Repression in Modern America.

[26] Davenport, 'State Repression and Political Order', p. 8. [27] Ibid., p. 11.

[28] D. W. Hill, The Concept of Personal Integrity Rights in Empirical Research, PhD Thesis, University of Georgia, 2013, http://myweb.fsu.edu/dwh06c/pages/documents/pi_concept13Aug13.pdf

[29] C. M. Sullivan, 'Project MUSE – Political Repression and the Destruction of Dissident Organizations: Evidence from the Archives of the Guatemalan National Police", *World Politics*, vol. 68, no. 4, October 2016, pp. 645–76.

[30] C. Davenport, *Paths to State Repression: Human Rights Violations and Contentious Politics*, New York, Rowman & Littlefield, 2000, p. 1.

[31] The Political Terror Scale, www.politicalterrorscale.org/countries.php?region=Eurasia&country=Syria&year=2010

[32] See, for example, D. Hill and Z. Jones, 'An Empirical Evaluation of Explanations for State Repression', *American Political Science Review*, vol. 108, no. 3, pp. 661–87, doi:10.1017/S0003055414000306.

studies can also lead to a simplification of definitions of repression and civil liberty restrictions, compressing complex types of state action into extremely broad categories.[33] The limitations of quantitative studies are also apparent in their failure to explain *why* repression and control might occur. For example, Lawson's[34] quantitative work on the contentious politics in the 1990s' Bahrain *Intifada*[35] is ambiguous in its attitudes to the motivations for state repression. When addressed in statistical studies, the results can be somewhat monolithic. Emily Ritter, for example, notes that the 'onset and severity of repression are a function of leaders' expectations of how the choice will influence dissent and thus their probability of remaining in power'.[36] Although interestingly, a study by DeMerrit and Young says that states that rely on oil, or other rents, are more likely to repress than others, or repress more severely in relation to personal integrity violations. Indeed, this is an odd supposition considering the tenets of the rentier paradigm that notes the exceptional stability of the oil monarchies versus Middle East republics. Indeed, the search for various independent variables has led to a swathe of broad generalizations.[37]

These generalizations have left many potentially interesting questions underexplored. For example, do elite attitudes impact upon type/frequency/consistency of repression?[38] This is an interesting assertion if we argue, as Gibson does, that elite attitudes and ideologies are more influential in defining the nature of repression.[39] Recent qualitative political science scholarship on Bahrain, for example, has argued that power in the palace in Bahrain shifted to the hardliners during 2011, leading to a far more violent and coercive crackdown by the authorities. Frederic Wehrey, for example, states that 'Conservative figures within the Bahraini royal family are redoubling their efforts to subdue the

[33] A. Escribà-Folch, 'Repression, Political Threats, and Survival under Autocracy', *International Political Science Review*, vol. 34, no. 5, 2013, pp. 543–60, doi:10.1177/0192512113488259.

[34] F. H. Lawson, 'Repertoires of Contention in Contemporary Bahrain', in Q. Wiktorowicz (ed.), *Islamic Activism: A Social Movement Theory Approach*, Bloomington, IN, Indiana University Press, 2004, pp. 89–111.

[35] *Intifada* [Arabic]; uprising [English].

[36] E. H. Ritter, 'Policy Disputes, Political Survival, and the Onset and Severity of State Repression', *Journal of Conflict Resolution*, vol. 58, no. 1, pp. 143–68, doi: 10.1177/0022002712468724.

[37] J. H. R. DeMeritt and J. K. Young, 'A Political Economy of Human Rights: Oil, Natural Gas, and State Incentives to Repress',*Conflict Management and Peace Science,* vol. 30, no. 2, 2013, pp. 99–120, doi: 10.1177/0738894212473915.

[38] Earl, 'Political Repression', p. 263.

[39] James L. Gibson, 'Political Intolerance and Political Repression during the McCarthy Red Scare', *American Political Science Review*, vol. 82, no. 2, 1988, pp. 511–29.

opposition. This conservatism is visible in new arrests, media censorship, warnings to Shiʿa clerics, and more aggressive counter-demonstration tactics.'[40] Jane Kinninmont, too, notes that the unrest shifted the country 'towards a more hardline, security-oriented',[41] form of governance. However, does this view hold up? How are decisions to use certain types of repression limited by available resources? Are authorities, as Gamson argues, opportunists who repress groups when they are weak or do they only repress when they perceive themselves to be more threatened?[42] Is it correct to make this generalization? Tilly argues that states will not repress groups if they fall below a certain threshold of weakness[43] and that the power of challengers and the size of demonstrations will influence the use of repression.[44] In Tilly's analysis, strong threats will more likely be co-opted. Conversely, Paul Gregory and Phillip Shroder argue that Stalin exacted more repression when enemies were perceived to increase above a threshold where they represented a challenge.[45] While this does not contradict Tilly, it also implies an upper threshold above which coercion becomes facilitation. As Pion-Berlin notes, 'it may be more important to study government perceptions about oppositional violence than to study the opposition itself.'[46] But how objective is a perceived threat, and to what extent does that perception rest on the attitudes of those in power? Will regimes repress even when not threatened with an existential threat? Can internal political battles impact upon the nature of repression? Can international actors play a role in influencing repression?

These questions can be rarely addressed by quantitative studies or facile causal models. Even Charles Tilly notes that scholars of social movements and sociologists should focus on 'sources rather than theories in their effort to overcome their "unawareness of the historical limits to their observations"'.[47] Indeed, 'because *history* is not often readily

[40] F. Wehrey, 'The March of Bahrain's Hardliners', Carnegie Endowment for International Peace, http://carnegieendowment.org/2012/05/31/march-of-bahrain-s-hardliners

[41] J. Kinninmont, *Bahrain: Beyond the Impasse,* Chatham House, London, 2012, p. 1, www.chathamhouse.org/sites/files/chathamhouse/public/Research/Middle%20East/pr0612kinninmont.pdf

[42] W. A. Gamson, *The Strategy of Social Protest,* Homewood, IL, Dorsey, 1968.

[43] Tilly, *From Mobilization to Revolution,* p. 22. [44] Ibid.

[45] P. R. Gregory, P. J. H. Shroder and K. Sonin, 'Dictators, Repression and the Median Citizen: An "Eliminations Model" of Stalin's Terror', Working Paper No. 91, CEFIR/NES Working Paper Series, 2006.

[46] D. Pion-Berlin, 'Theories of Political Repression in Latin America: Conventional Wisdom and an Alternative', *American Political Society Association,* vol. 19, no. 1, 1986, p. 51.

[47] Cited in B. Dill and R. Aminzade, 'Historians and the Study of Protest', in B. Klandermans and C. Roggeband (eds), *Handbook of Social Movements across Disciplines,* New York, NY, Springer, 2007, p. 305.

available for quantitative comparative analyses, cross-country analyses that treat countries as "like units," conditional on a few contemporary observables such as per capita income, are likely to suffer from bias due to the omission of historical factors'.[48] The study of repression in dictatorships or autocracies is difficult, in part due to the secrecy and retention of important internal documents. In her work on state repression in Iraq, Lisa Blaydes notes that the internal workings of such regimes are often described as 'black boxes'.[49] Like Blaydes' study of Iraq, re-examining existing sources and attempting to uncover new ones has yielded fascinating insights. At times, these insights may only be fleeting, temporally limited and confined to very specific situations, yet they are insights nonetheless. As Skocpol notes, 'the whole story can never be told in any work of history or historical sociology. However, interpretive works can convey the impression of fullness much more readily than works of historical sociology that aim to apply models or establish causal connections of relevance to more than one case.'[50] Indeed, the study is as much an exploration into repression as it is an acknowledgement of the importance of historiographical research in the social sciences. What the literature highlights, however, as Davenport notes, is that 'amid varying contexts, methodological approaches, and model specifications, different findings abound'.[51]

For this reason, hypothesis testing is eschewed in favour of more interpretive approaches. To simply focus on whether states are democratic or not, for example, is to miss the nuances that may define why or how repression occurs. As Turk argues, 'the perception of threat and the specifics of the control response will be determined by the knowledge and instruments available to them'.[52] Thus, in addressing questions like this, one must be prepared to qualitatively address historical studies of repression in order to see what repression existed, how it has changed and why it might have changed? Indeed, 'if neither the systemic features of political organisation nor the historical context'[53] of repression is specified, 'inquiry is very likely to flounder'.[54] Ultimately, one 'cannot assume but must establish the applicability to

[48] J. G. Hariri, 'A Contribution to the Understanding of Middle Eastern and Muslim Exceptionalism', *The Journal of Politics*, vol. 77, no. 2, 2015, p. 489.

[49] L. Blaydes, *State of Repression: Iraq under Saddam Hussein*, Princeton, NJ, Princeton University Press, p. 2.

[50] T. Skocpol, 'Emerging Agendas and Recurrent Strategies in Historical Sociology', in T. Skocpol (ed.), *Vision and Method in Historical Sociology*, Cambridge, Cambridge University Press, 1985, p. 371.

[51] Davenport, *How Social Movements Die*, p. 346.

[52] Turk, *Political Criminality*, p. 117.

[53] Ibid., p. 202.

[54] Ibid.

particular cases of any general conclusions about trends and prospects in political policing'.[55]

The temporal range of this study then is important for many reasons. First, to track change, and examine how and why repression has shifted, it is necessary to consider a period spanning a significant number of years. A temporally expansive study can help prise open the authoritarian playbook. Second, repression in an autocracy does not necessarily remain stable over time. While it has been argued that the demise of the Soviet Union made autocracies less repressive in view of their desire to appease the democracy-espousing principles of the singular global hegemon (USA), it is equally reasonable to assume that regimes had to repress more after the Cold War in order to stymie greater demands for liberty and democratization.[56] A temporally broad study will offer a more likely chance of finding these occasional sparks of insight into processes that are generally secretive and opaque. The aim, similar to works of interpretive historical sociology, is to present an account that is 'vivid and full'.[57] As an interpretive work, the aforementioned questions asked throughout these introductory chapters can be subsumed into the following. What methods have been utilized in order to resist these changes, and how have these methods evolved over time? When possible to identify, why did the authorities choose specific methods of repression in certain contexts, and what influenced those choices? To what extent have Bahrain's protecting powers had an impact on the nature, and type of repression, repressive choices and repressive capacity made?

[55] Ibid. [56] Davenport, 'State Repression and the Tyrannical Peace', p. 500.
[57] Skocpol, 'Emerging Agendas', p. 371.

2 The Repression Playbook

In order to address these questions, we first need to outline the specific contours, modalities or methods of repression in order to select relevant moments in history. After all, as Austin Turk stated, 'how political resistance is neutralised is as important to authorities as neutralizing it.[1] Many studies of what can be considered repression focus on limited facets such as protest policing and fail to consider "the variety of subtler ways the state attempts to exert social control"'.[2] Similarly, Marwan Khawaja notes that few studies of repression 'provide clear criteria for conceptually distinguishing among the many manifested forms of repression'.[3] More recently, Jennifer Earl notes that there is a lack of 'refined and powerful conceptualisation[s] of repression'.[4] The first was Gary Marx[5] in 1979, yet others have followed, such as Jennifer Earl and Jules Boykoff, who have enumerated different methods for studying repression. Jennifer Earl's 2011 work on political repression sets out a typology based on the following core distinctions: '(a) whether the repressive actor is a state, private or hybrid actor; (b) whether the repressive action is coercive or uses more carrot-based "channelling" ... and (c) whether the repressive

[1] Turk, *Political Criminality*, p. 137.

[2] J. Boykoff, 'Limiting Dissent: The Mechanisms of State Repression in the USA', *Social Movement Studies: Journal of Social, Cultural and Political Protest*, vol. 6, no. 3, 2007, p. 284.

[3] Cited in Boykoff, *Beyond Bullets*, p. 15.

[4] J. Earl, 'Tanks, Tear Gas, and Taxes: Towards a Theory of Movement Repression', *Sociological Theory*, vol. 21, no. 1, 2003, p. 44.

[5] Marx highlights the main purpose of repression as to: 'inhibit capacity for corporate action, direct energies of movement of defensive maintenance needs and away from pursuit of broader social goals, create unfavourable public image and counter-ideology, gather information on movement, inhibit supply of money and facilities, inhibit freedom of movement, expression, and action; create myth and fact of surveillance and repression; apply legal sanctions, damage morale, derecruitment' in G. Marx, 'External Efforts to Damage or Facilitate Social Movements: Some Patterns, Explanations, Outcomes, and Complications', in M. Zald and J. McCarthy (eds), *The Dynamics of Social Movements*, Cambridge, MA, Winthrop Publishers, 1979, pp. 94–125, http://web.mit.edu/gtmarx/www/movement.html

action is observable/overt or unobserved/covert'.[6] Boykoff outlines ten 'action modes', each referring to a specific method of repression: direct violence, public prosecutions and hearings, employment deprivation, surveillance and break-ins (including 'black bag jobs'), infiltration, 'badjacketing' and the use of agent provocateurs, 'Black propaganda', harassment and harassment arrests, extraordinary rules and laws, Mass media manipulation and Mass media deprecation.[7] Boykoff's categories are useful in that they break away from the somewhat normative idea that equates repression with physical violence undertaken by agents of the state against social movement organizations.

However, even a cursory glance at such typologies highlights that they are not always pertinent or comprehensive in Bahrain. Preliminary inductive research on Bahrain has highlighted methods of repression that were absent or underexplored in these typologies, such as exile, the removal of citizenship or demographic engineering designed to create a cordon sanitaire around the regime. With regard to Bahrain, Omar Al Shehabi outlines a summary of processes of state responses to dissent, noting that the rulers dealt with existential threats by sowing divisions, stalling for reform, co-opting and then using force.[8] Abdulhadi Khalaf too in the foreword to *Bahrain's Uprising* outlines three key elements of repression: '1) the security services' use of brutal force to disperse protesters, followed by sweeping police raids to arrest known activists and leaders of protest; 2) use of the media and traditional notables to discredit protest leaders and their lack of "patriotism"; 3) dispensing promises of political reforms in combination with offering lavish *makramāt* to protest leaders perceived as "moderate"'.[9] When taken together, these methods complement one another to form a richer net for conceptualizing repression, but it can be improved further. Repression, whether by that name or something else, (e.g. political policing, control), directly or implicitly, has been addressed by scholars from various disciplines, from criminology to history and political science. As Davenport notes:

> At present, an unwritten division of labour appears to exist: Scholars concerned with civil liberties, protest policing, human rights violations, and genocide/politicide focus on repression, while scholars interested in rhetoric, communication, and propaganda focus on persuasion, and scholars concerned with selective incentives, wages, bribes, oil profits, and welfare systems focus on material benefits. Clearly, however, there is some overlap.[10]

[6] Earl, 'Political Repression', p. 264. [7] Boykoff, 'Limiting Dissent'.

[8] A. Shehabi, 'Divide and Rule in Bahrain and the Elusive Pursuit for a United Front: The Experience of the Constitutive Committee and the 1972 Uprising', *Historical Materialism*, vol. 21, no. 1, 2013, pp. 94–127.

[9] Khalaf, 'Foreword', p. xv. [10] Davenport, 'State Repression and Political Order', p. 9.

Since studies of repression focusing on just one aspect of repression, such as protest policing, risk sacrificing 'breadth on the altar of depth',[11] it is useful to aggregate theories and concepts, and in particular typological approaches to repression across different case studies to create a more thorough *template* for analysing repression. As this is a historical work which seeks to 'use concepts and theories to develop a meaningful historical interpretation',[12] this section, in line with many interpretive works, presents the 'relevant concepts and theories at various levels of abstraction ... from various fields'[13] to create the lens through which to interpret Bahrain's history. We have defined repression generally, but by parsing different concepts of repression across disciplines, the nature of their change across different categories can better be assessed, as can the evolution of the repressive capacity. Davenport highlights the utility of delineating categories of repression, stating that 'disaggregation is specifically useful if we expect governments to respond to different challenges with distinct repressive strategies'.[14] There is the temptation in such a review of methods of repression to review every facet on the literature on any subcategory of control. While these have been looked at where possible in order to add more insight into particular aspects of repression, scholars who have approached categorizations of repressive methods have been emphasized in order to create a clearer focus.[15]

Templates versus Typologies

With this in mind, it is important to review theories of repression, and in particular typologies, to create a comprehensive template that can

[11] Boykoff, 'Limiting Dissent', p. 284.

[12] T. Tsou, *The Cultural Revolution and Post-Mao Reforms: A Historical Perspective*, Chicago, IL, University of Chicago Press, 1986, p. xxi.

[13] Ibid. [14] Davenport, 'State Repression and Political Order', p. 18.

[15] For this reason, useful reading, such as the literature on the National Security State, has been important rather than integral to the construction of the template. Indeed, the useful outline provided by Jack Nelsen-Pallmeyer in his 1992 book, a *Brave New World Order*, provides characteristics of the National Security State, which describe the nature of a specific state, as opposed to focusing on methods of repression. While these seven characteristics do include the ways such states behave, and include methods, they focus more on regime-type rather than regime methods. Pallmeyer's description of the state emphasizes the role of the Church in mobilizing ideology, making it an unusual point of reference for the Persian Gulf. In addition, such literature can be too state centric, focusing on the role of the state and not necessarily the bottom-up notions of control increasingly recognized by scholars of repression. Furthermore, other important texts, such as Michael Hogan's work on the National Security State, is very specific to the political development of America vis-a-vis its constitutional demands, and not necessarily any more pertinent to Bahrain than literature on the authoritarian states.

then be used to select empirical data. The term 'template' is preferable to typology or taxonomy because taxonomies rely solely on empirical observation, while typologies are ideal-typical. Given this rather rigid a posteriori and a priori binary, a template analysis, which combines elements of both empirical and theoretical influence for its definitions, bridges both.[16] In light of this overlap, this study codes different theories of repression to identify common aspects of repression in order to create a template for selecting data that can be deemed repressive.[17] As well as approaching repression through 'multiple lenses',[18] the purpose of what could be considered disciplinary triangulation is to create a more transparent, more complete lens with which to view Bahrain's history.[19] While some may level accusations of 'theoretical eclecticism',[20] this, as Tang Tsou argues, is 'a matter of necessity in an endeavour to achieve an informed understanding'[21] of repression in Bahrain. Studies of repression that focus, or are at least clear, on delineating methods have been the focus of the literature review as these provide a richer and more comprehensive means of parsing repression. However, many studies of repression, political policing or political power have been referred to when they offer useful definitions or insights.

A template analysis yields four broad categories of repression and control. These are *political statecraft, personal integrity violations, legal repression*, and *information control.* Figure 2.1 highlights how these categories are a useful heuristic but acknowledges that there are overlaps in categories. For example, creating visa restrictions to prevent political dissidents from entering or leaving a country may be considered an aspect of statecraft, yet if it were legislated, it would fall into legal repression too. The diagram was inspired by Luis Fernandez in his work on policing protests in Seattle.[22]

[16] J. McGarry and B. O'Leary (eds), 'Introduction: The Macro-Political Regulation of Ethnic Conflict', in *The Politics of Ethnic Conflict Regulation*, Oxford, Routledge, 1993.

[17] It also, inductively, harvests categories from empirical observations but this will be discussed later.

[18] Z. Hoque, M. A. Covaleski and T. N. Gooneratne, 'Theoretical Triangulation and Pluralism in Research Methods in Organizational and Accounting Research', *Accounting, Auditing & Accountability Journal*, vol. 26, no. 7, 2013, pp. 1170–98.

[19] To further the analogy, the process of this theoretical triangulation resembles white light going into a prism; the object is to disperse it into its myriad colours, each of which represents a facet of repression.

[20] Tsou, *The Cultural Revolution*, p. xxi. [21] Ibid.

[22] Fernandez, *Policing Dissent*, p. 32.

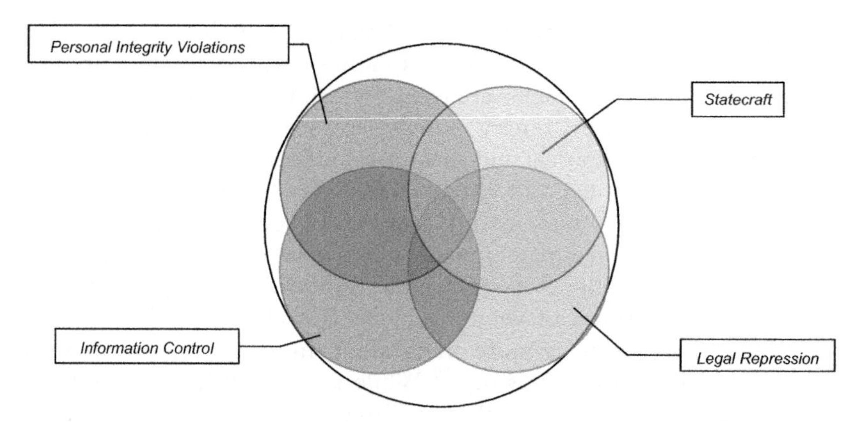

Figure 2.1 Heuristic illustrating interconnected categories of repression

Political Statecraft

Criminologists such as Austin Turk use the term 'statecraft' to describe the broader way in which political policing occurs. While policing can be normatively understood as the institutional development of methods of control and repression to prevent radical changes in political power, statecraft is defined as the art and science of social control as developed and used in the political organization of social life.[23] Building on sociologist William Gamson's 1968 work, Turk summarizes three of the four major strategic operations of statecraft as insulation, sanctioning, co-optation and persuasion (this will be discussed in more detail in the section on 'Informational Control'). Insulation is essentially the blocking of access to those perceived as a threat to positions or institutions that control resources 'that can be brought to bear on authorities'.[24] Methods include restricting visas, modifying immigration policies, exile, deportation, screening employees from potentially sensitive positions, gerrymandering, or restricting the movements of dangerous groups.[25] In this sense, dangerous groups may include political dissidents, or groups perceived in many spheres to be subordinate or subaltern, such as women (within the patriarchy) or the Shiʿa community in Bahrain. In his analysis of the former USSR, Robert Sharlet calls a similar process 'bureaucratic deprivation', which ranges from 'petty harassment, such as the suspension of telephone service, to more consequential deprivations such as job dismissal, eviction, and preventing a dissident's child from

[23] Turk, *Political Criminality*. [24] Gamson, *The Strategy*, 1968, p. 117.
[25] Turk, *Political Criminality*, p. 160.

entering university'.[26] Sanctioning is the general system of punishment or rewards. For the deserving, rewards may include job offers, promotions and increased salaries. For the troublesome, this may involve the loss of jobs or the withdrawal of status (perhaps even nationality).[27] As McCarthy and Zald note: 'the more than subsistence income, fringe resources, leisure, and flexibility offered by many jobs can indirectly be important in facilitating social movement participation. Conversely, the denial of such employment to activists can be a means of indirectly damaging a movement'.[28] Gary Marx adds that the removal of employment 'can damage morale, shrink resources, and make sustained actions difficult or impossible. For some activists, the cost of continued participation may become too great, and they may quit. However, more direct efforts toward this end may also be undertaken in the form of explicit de recruitment activities'.[29]

Co-optation, perhaps potentially the most dangerous, involves including former dissidents or oppositional forces in the internal apparatus so that they have a say and responsibility in decision-making. This can diminish social movement strength by removing structural support from former followers. Alternatively, newly co-opted agents can influence former followers into supporting the status quo.[30] Austin Turk notes that sanctioning is preferable to more traditional forms of bodily 'violence', as the latter can more readily incur legitimacy costs. Turk also notes that Western democracies, in particular, prefer to adopt strategies of 'field controls', whereby authorities control dissent through broader, more diffuse reforms that include, for example: import controls to defuse labour unrest, welfare reforms that can punish the defiant or cuts in educational funding to limit potential student militancy.[31]

Political scientists too, have examined strategies of repression and control in authoritarian states. Aurel Braun's work on the control of dissent in Eastern Europe offers a framework for studying how the dominant social order responds to dissent and overlaps with the work of Gamson and Turk. Braun includes the concepts of co-optation, containment, coexistence in his outline of political control.[32] Lustick too, according to Reudy, in the area of political science, offers a shorthand for talking about Israel's control strategies of the Arab minority, describing the 'three components of Israel's control system as

[26] R. Sharlet, 'Party and Public Ideals in Conflict: Constitutionalism and Civil Rights in the USSR', *Cornell International Law Journal*, vol. 23, no. 2, 1990, p. 345.
[27] Turk, *Political Criminality*, p. 161. [28] Marx, 'External Efforts'. [29] Ibid.
[30] Turk, *Political Criminality*, p. 162. [31] Ibid., p. 199.
[32] Braun, 'Dissent and the State in Eastern Europe'.

segmentation, dependence and co-optation. Segmentation refers to the isolation of the Arabs from the Jewish population and to the internal fragmentation of the Arab community; dependence means the forced reliance of the Arab population upon the Jewish sector for economic and political resources; and co-optation refers to material, social and political enticements to elites to elicit their cooperation'.[33] Here, co-optation is similar to that defined by Gamson, whereby elites or the state attempt to pacify dissidents by offering them positions in the public administration or government.

Similarly, inclusion and co-optation overlap considerably with Tilly's concept of 'facilitation', which is the process of legitimatizing a group by giving it publicity, paying it off or doing anything to increase the group's cost of collective action.[34] These strategies of co-optation ultimately aim to achieve pacification through partial inclusion,[35] and form part of a general political strategy pursued by many Middle Eastern states that appropriate and contain civil society, and manage political contestation[36] by limiting its ability to flourish independently. As Wiktorowicz notes in his work on Jordan, the Middle Eastern 'state attempts to limit the possibility of collective action in the niches of society by requiring that all group work is performed in the open through civil society organisations that are within reach of administrative practices'.[37]

Although labelled types of 'power', Dallin and Breslauer's concepts of normative and material power outline similar strategies used by authoritarian governments in repressing dissent. They are: Normative power (also referred to as positive or symbolic power), commonly called persuasion and including socialization, education, and the offer of prestige, recognition, or love; material power (also referred to as technical or utilitarian power), commonly called incentives and including such forms as wages, rewards, bonuses, bribes, and promotions.[38] Sociologist Abdulhadi Khalaf, whose research has explored the repression of labour

[33] J. Reudy, 'Review of Arabs in the Jewish State: Israel's Control of a National Minority', *Washington Report on Middle East Affairs*, 6 September 1982, p. 7, www.wrmea.org/1982-september-6/book-review-arabs-in-the-jewish-state-israel-s-control-of-a-national-minority.html

[34] Tilly, *From Mobilization*, ch. 4, p. 3.

[35] J. I. Ross, *The Dynamics of Political Crime*, London, Sage, 2003, p. 159.

[36] S. Heydemann, 'Upgrading Authoritarianism in the Arab world', Analysis Paper 13, The Saban Center for Middle East Policy at The Brookings Institution, October 2007.

[37] Q. Wiktorowicz, 'Civil Society as Social Control: State Power in Jordan', *Comparative Politics*, vol. 33, no. 1, 2012, p. 49.

[38] A. Dallin and G. W. Breslauer, *Political Terror in Communist Systems*, Stanford, CA, Stanford University Press, 1970, p. 2.

movements[39] and contentious politics[40] in Bahrain, draws on the work of Mann to examine various political strategies adopted by the 'Al-Khalifa regime' to contain challenges to its authority. Khalaf's work focuses more on statecraft, or what Mann calls 'infrastructural power', that is to say, the 'capacity of the state actually to penetrate civil society and to implement logistically political decisions throughout the realm'.[41] Khalaf focuses less on the state's coercive apparatus, or what Mann terms 'despotic power' arguing that the Al Khalifa regime is a 'ruling-core' who use a system of patronage and *makramāt* (gifts or rewards or sanctioning) to both give and remove privileges from different social groups, taking advantage of Bahrain's oil revenues to facilitate this process. This system of granting and withdrawing privilege is supported by the Al Khalifa's monopoly ownership of the country's resources, both materially and militarily. Khalaf also notes the importance of inclusion strategies in Bahrain that include the giving of 'gratuities and favours in the form of employment, cash, and plots of land' via regime-sponsored patrons.[42] This strategy might otherwise be termed 'coup-proofing', which includes the establishment of loyalties between officers and the regime through ethnic, religious or personal bonds. Precariousness and dependence on the regime can be established too through the recruitment of mercenary soldiers or those from certain minorities.[43] However, by providing incentives or rewards to some members of the group but not others, these methods may foster schism and disunity, leading to the fragmentation and weakening of certain groups, and the general stratification of society where the have and have-nots divide falls along religious, gender, ethnic, or identity-based cleavages. This study adds to Khalaf's work by giving a more theoretically broad emphasis on repression while also using updated data.

Statecraft, in particular, contributes to repression through 'problem depletion', which works by 'removing (1) the perceived need for the movement and/or (2) the perceived relevance of claims-making effort within the relevant population'.[44] Modern governments may, for example, create 'front' [social movement organisations (SMOs)]; that 'actually represent the status quo's interest but that maintain the veneer

[39] A. Khalaf, 'Labor Movements in Bahrain', *Middle East Research and Information Projects Report*, no. 132, 1985, pp. 24–9.

[40] Khalaf, 'Contentious Politics in Bahrain'. [41] Mann, Cited in Ibid. [42] Ibid.

[43] H. Albrecht, 'The Myth of Coup-Proofing: Risk and Instances of Military Coups d'Etat in the Middle East and North Africa, 1950–2013'. *Armed Forces & Society*, vol. 41, no. 4, 2015, pp. 659–87, doi: 10.1177/0095327X14544518.

[44] C. Davenport, *How Social Movements Die: Repression and Demobilization of the Republic of New Africa*, Cambridge, CambridgeUniversity Press, 2015, p. 23 [Kindle Edition].

of a challenger'[45] in order to compete with the threatening organization, and convince others the issue is being dealt with on official terms. Similarly, the creation of committees, investigatory panels on terms defined by the regime may undermine the perceived need to join other political forces to affect change. Demonstrable commitment to issues addressing key grievances such as corruption, land reform, injustice (as examples), is argued to be the most effective way of splitting support away from insurgent groups in particular. In this sense, reform can be considered repression. Limited democratization, for example, falls into repression according to the definition, as it serves to defuse general discontent by providing a forum for grievances but not to the extent it significantly alters the status quo.

While such an assertion that democratization can be seen as a form of repression may seem counter-intuitive or controversial to some, democratization can be argued to be a continuum. At one end of this continuum, where one believes a certain level of political democracy to have been achieved, scholars such as Davenport and Armstrong[46] argue that there is often a decrease in violent repression. However, this is based on the normative assumption that repression is necessarily an act of physical violence, a definition that this book rejects. Indeed, without labouring the point, 'physical violence' is somewhat probelamtic as it implies there is less physicality to other forms of behaviour designed to control behaviour through intimidation, socialization et cetera. For example, fear or anxiety, whether induced by surveillance or attacks by the police, are fundamental physical and physiological processes driven by neurotransmitters. To deny their physicality is, in many ways, to reject well-established biologial science.

Furthermore, given the importance of repression as a tool of hegemonic power maintenance, acts of 'democratic' reform that can be shown to be a deliberate tool designed to weaken social movements or opposition while disproportionately preserving the status quo can be considered repression. Until the level of democracy is achieved where the people are theoretically, and in practice, the source of power, such as in what Gerardo Munck calls 'high-quality democracies',[47] then one

[45] Ibid., p. 27.

[46] C. Davenport and D. A. Armstrong, 'Democracy and the Violation of Human Rights: A Statistical Analysis from 1976 to 1996', *American Journal of Political Science,* vol. 48, no. 3, 2004, pp. 538–54.

[47] Gerardo Munck argues that 'democracy is diminished by counter majoritarian institutions, such as (i) presidents with strong legislative powers, (ii) upper chambers with strong powers, (iii) rigid constitutions, and (iv) courts with the power of judicial review regarding matters of normal politics'. See G. L. Munck, 'What Is Democracy? A Reconceptualization of the Quality of Democracy', *Democratization,* vol. 23, no. 1, p. 13, 2014, doi: 10.1080/13510347.2014.918104.

Table 2.1 *Summary of methods of statecraft*

Statecraft	Insulation	Exile, restricting immigration policies, screening employees from sensitive jobs, removal of citizenship, social stratification
	Deprivation and sanctions	Cutting off access to essential resources, mass layoffs, removing scholarships, fines, targeted taxes, import controls, labour reform
	Rewards and makramāt	Jobs, increased salaries, promotions, co-optation
	Selective Reform	Grievance removal, reform stalling/temporary tolerance, superficial reform that fails to threaten distribution of resources, limited democratisation

must always be critical of whether those institutions are tools of power maintenance by a power elite or otherwise. Indeed, just as there is a difference 'between violence practised by the oppressed and by the oppressors',[48] there is a difference between democracy from and for the people and democracy designed to ensure the continuation of the dominant hegemonic order.

Of course, this is not a book about democracy in Bahrain, nor is it about to what extent democracies repress; it simply argues that certain institutions or procedures associated with democracy can be part of a repressive strategy. While some may argue that this type of liberalization (if not democratization) can 'relax' political repression, it depends on the definition of repression.[49] Furthermore, as we will see in Bahrain, incomplete reforms as responses to popular demands delay larger protests that are then repressed in the future with the more normative notions of police violence and torture. In such cases, the analytical power of arguing that reforms defray the need for political repression is constrained by short-term and limited temporal analyses.

Personal Integrity Violations

Pamela Oliver defines two of the three main goals of repression as deterrence and incapacitation.[50] Perhaps most obviously, such

[48] H. Marcuse, 'Repressive Tolerance', in R. P. Wolff, B. Moore, Jr. and H. Marcuse, *A Critique of Pure Tolerance*, Boston, MA, Beacon Press, 1965, pp. 95–137.

[49] R. Brynen, B. Korany and P. Noble, *Political Liberalization and Democratization in the Arab World*, vol. 1, Boulder, CO, Lynne Rienner Publishers, 1995, p. 4.

[50] P. Oliver, 'Repression and Crime Control: Why Social Movement Scholars Should Pay More Attention to Mass Incarceration as a Form of Repression', *Mobilization*, vol. 13, no. 1, 2008, pp. 1–24.

measures can be understood as torture, police violence, sexual violence, intimidation or incarceration. Dallin and Breslauer call this 'coercive power' or 'physical power', noting that it 'includes such forms as fines, penalties, terror, and regulatory and police power'[51] (although fines in this study would fall under statecraft). The extensive literature on Latin America notes the importance of disappearances,[52] while more extreme examples might include mass executions or assassinations.[53] Since disappearances are often a preliminary euphemism for execution or state terrorism, Howard Kleinman notes that the bureaucratic authoritarian regimes of Latin America used disappearances for highly idiosyncratic reasons. As the disappeared often do not reappear, it is difficult 'to classify a disappearance as a specific violation of international human rights law'.[54] Indeed, this modality of repression stemmed in part from a relationship with the US Under the Alliance for Progress, the pressure for moderate reforms from the Kennedy Administration as disappearances allowed the state to use 'terror against certain sectors of civil or political society while retaining a facade of formal democracy'.[55] It is a potent example of a modality of repression defined partly by external factors.

Austin Turk notes the importance of 'violence' in political policing, arguing that 'neutralisation of resistance by violence and/or other means, as well as intimidation tactics aimed at general deterrence' are the ultimate goals of political policing.[56] Personal Integrity Violations generally include repressive acts such as 'acts of harassment, intimidation, physical assault, arrests'.[57] Among these varied definitions of police power or coercive power, lie numerous similarities. Daniel Hill summarizes them succinctly in his definition of personal integrity violations as; '1) state-imposed deprivations of life, 2) physical harm at the hands of state agents, and 3) state-imposed detention'.[58] In addition to these three concepts, there are the more nebulous aspects of personal integrity

[51] Dallin and Breslauer, *Political Terror*, p. 2.
[52] J. Nieto, 'U.S. Security Policy and United States – Colombia Relations', *Latin American Perspectives*, vol. 34, no. 1, pp. 112–19.
[53] G. A. Lopez and M. Stohl, 'State Terrorism: From the Reign of Terror to Ninety-Eighty Four Terrorism', *Chitty's Law Journal*, vol. 32, no. 5, 1984–87, pp. 14–33.
[54] H. Kleinman, 'Disappearances in Latin America: A Human Rights Perspective', *N. Y. U. Journal of International Law and Politics*, 1986–87, pp. 1033–1060.
[55] Ibid., p. 1038.
[56] A. T. Turk, 'Social Control and Social Conflict', in J. P. Gibbs (ed.), *Social Control: Views from the Social Sciences*, London, Sage Publications, 1982, p. 253.
[57] L. A. Fernandez, *Policing Dissent: Social Control and the Anti Globalization Movement*, New Brunswick, NJ, Rutgers University Press, 2008, p. 8.
[58] D. W. Hill, *The Concept of Personal Integrity*, p. 16.

violations that may not constitute apparent harm but may include harassment or intimidation designed to deter activists from engaging in group action. These are not deprivations of liberty per se but might include curfews or other restrictions on movement that serve to limit or contain the movement of opposition in meatspace.

While governments may be seen to enforce certain forms of personal integrity violations in situations that may be seen as legitimate, this policy is based on laws and criminal codes as defined by a particular government. Hill notes: 'The fact that there are many instances of government violence that conform to domestic legal procedure has led some (e.g., Stohl et al., 1986) to suggest that "illegal" (i.e., not conforming to domestic legal code) is a useless category for the purpose of identifying and measuring violations of personal integrity'.[59] Thus personal integrity violations here refer to those actions, legal or illegal, that fall into the definition used by Hill, and that is deployed by the Bahrain government or its supporters to deal with political dissent.

Arrests too are a primary method for decreasing the efficacy of social movements. They reduce the number of opposition bodies in meatspace and disrupt the organizational capacity of political movements. Arrests 'divert activists from their social-change goals, undermine the morale of social-movement participants, and discourage support from potential recruits or bystander publics'.[60] The targeting of leaders can be particularly significant: 'Because social movement leaders are symbolically and instrumentally important, movement-damaging activities often focus on weakening them as the most visible and presumed central part of a movement'.[61] Arresting leaders may be preferable for the authorities, for if the repressive effect succeeds, this may negate the need for more problematic widespread mass arrests of activists. Furthermore, arrests also exacerbate paranoia among activists, while tying them up in lengthy and costly legal proceedings that drain valuable resources.[62] Earl notes such arrests can be challenging and painful experiences that increase costs by entangling the victim within the criminal justice system, thereby raising the costs of dissent.[63] Thus, in order to avoid such actions like police violence, activists, citizens or protesters will withdraw from organizations, institutions or actions deemed to be dissident. Personal integrity violations are essential for

[59] Ibid., p. 16. [60] Boykoff, *Beyond Bullets*, p. 140. [61] Marx, 'External Efforts'.
[62] Churchill and Vander Wall, in Boykoff, *Beyond Bullets*, p. 140.
[63] J. Earl, 'You Can Beat the Rap, but You Can't Beat the Ride: Bringing Arrests Back into Research on Repression', *Research in Social Movements, Conflicts, and Change*, vol. 26, 2005, pp. 101–39. Cited in Boykoff, 'Limiting Dissent', p. 291.

Table 2.2 *Summary of methods of personal integrity violations*

Personal Integrity Violations	Containment	Targeted or mass arrest of leaders, organizers or activists, roadblocks, curfews, kettling, kidnap.
	Physical Harm	Mass arrests, torture, disappearances, use of mass harm weapons, e.g. tear gas, collective punishment, extrajudicial killings, police violence, genocide, rape
	Threats	Threats of violence, other threats, general intimidation.

deterrence; 'general deterrence is the ultimate goal of political policing; it is the anticipated product of intimidation'.[64]

While some personal integrity violations, such as arrests, may more easily be the domain of state institutions such as the police, violence and intimidation can be undertaken by multiple agencies, whether official, quasi-official or unofficial. Indeed, vigilantism can emerge in an environment where the state refuses to, or is unable to, deploy means of coercion to prevent it. In this regard, the state may deliberately facilitate or turn a blind eye to vigilantism if it serves useful social control purposes, regardless of whether the state has full coercive control over its territorial jurisdiction. As Lopez and Stohl argue, the government may participate in repression through the '(covert) employment of the security forces and the condoning of unofficial vigilante groups or death squads against groups or individuals for the purposes of intimidation and compliance with state or majority interests'.[65] Indeed, personal integrity violations tend to reflect normative definitions of repression and violence, although it is preferable to parse this violence off as a subset of repression.

Legal Repression

Law is used as an instrument to extend control over society, subjecting persons to rules laid down through particular institutions. The establishment of specific laws[66] and the use of legal repression or unaccountability

[64] Turk, *Political Criminality*, p. 150. [65] Lopez and Stohl, 'State Terrorism', p. 21.

[66] Given the social context, an argument could be made about how the role of Sharia law and Islamic jurisprudence play out in the use of legal repression. Unfortunately, the nature of Islamic jurisprudence and the extent of the research required to delve adequately into this sphere is beyond the scope of this book. Having said that, Bahrain's Sharia courts mostly have jurisdiction over matters of personal status relating to Muslims of all nationalities. Furthermore, while Bahrain's legal system is influenced to a large extent by British common law, the predominant influence is

in authoritarian regimes can result in 'rule by law' instead of 'rule of law'. In 'rule by law', or repressive law, 'there is little or no separation between law and politics, and the dictates and policies of the rulers trump laws'.[67] Philippe Nonet and Philip Selznick conceptualize repressive law as those laws and systems in which law is designed to uphold the social order. It is often ad hoc, designed to punish disobedience and demands conformity.[68] Repressive laws and legal systems are characterized by the subordination of law to power politics.[69] As Tilly notes, legislation and law can be a useful index of a state's repressiveness. Indeed, 'legality matters because laws state the costs and benefits which governments are prepared (or at least empowered) to apply to one form of action or another'.[70] In this context, the law is an increasingly important category in repressing dissent. Laws accompanied by administrative actions and breaches of due process[71] should also be considered repression.

Michael Hardt and Antonio Negri state that emergency laws, in particular, allow the state to define the demands of interventions, as well as the 'capacity to set in motion the forces and instruments that in various ways can be applied to the diversity and the plurality of the arrangements in crisis'.[72] Given that Bahrain has been subject to emergency laws for about half a decade, political activity in Bahrain has been subject to what Georgio Agamben describes as a 'state of exception that has now become the rule'.[73] In other words, political activity has been criminalized, or has had the potential to be easily criminalized in a manner where 'increasingly numerous sections of residents [are] deprived of political rights'.[74] As James L. Gibson argues, such laws can reflect a 'repressive public policy', which is defined as 'statutory restrictions on political activities through which citizens, individually or in groups, compete for political power'.[75]

Non-emergency laws must be considered too. Dictating when people can and cannot meet, whom they can meet and for what purpose is

theoretically Islamic law. Thus analysis of legal repression inevitably takes into account aspects of Islamic legal rulings.

[67] R. Peerenboom, *China's Long March to Rule of Law*, Cambridge, Cambridge University Press, 2002, p. 64.

[68] P. Nonet and P. Selznick, *Law and Society in Transition towards Responsive Law*, Abingdon, Routledge, 2009, eBook, p. 18.

[69] Ibid. [70] Tilly, *From Mobilization*, ch. 4, p. 6. [71] Goldstein, *Political Repression.*

[72] M. Hardt and A. Negri, *Empire*, Cambridge, MA, Harvard University Press, 2000, pp. 1–17. Cited in Boykoff, *Beyond Bullets*, p. 157.

[73] G. Agamben, *Means without End: Notes on Politics*, Minneapolis, MI, University of Minnesota Press, 2000, p. 138.

[74] Ibid., p. 133.

[75] J. L. Gibson, 'The Policy Consequences of Political Intolerance: Political Repression during the Vietnam War Era', *The Journal of Politics*, vol. 51, no. 1, 1989, p. 15.

critical in controlling the outcomes of those meetings. Although such laws may seek to mitigate the use of coercive force by creating a more palatable framework for organizing dissent, the replacement of force with law serves to make repression less visible. By defining when, where and what social movements discuss, the state is better able to control and repress potential challenges to its authority before the need to use violent coercion. Drawing on Foucault, Quintan Wiktorowicz states that 'discipline orders individuals in spatial settings to maximise the ability of the state or those in power to maintain constant observation. By dictating when and where individuals are present and even their relations with one another, the state enhances its social control'.[76] Isaac Balbus argues that 'legal repression' is a means of repressing dissent by the 'formal rationality' of legal methods that 'depoliticise the consciousness of the participants, deligitimate their claims and grievances, and militate against alliances between participants and other non-elites or elite moderates'.[77]

Similarly, withdrawing a legal framework can hinder activists by delegitimating their rights when initially protected by law. The removal of legal outlets for opposition movements was frequent in Latin America. Patricia Weiss Fagen notes how the Brazilian government, for example, 'enacted a series of Institutional Acts and decrees that banished individuals from political participation; curtailed political activities; outlawed political parties, student organisations, and trade unions; ended direct elections; and reduced Congressional powers'.[78] Although their focus is on states of exception, Lopez and Stohl also note the importance of legal methods of repression in their typology of state terror, including 'the use of legislative and extra-constitutional or extra-systematic acts and policies; the adoption of martial law; a state of siege; a state of emergency, or other decrees which provide for a suspension of the normal protection of constitutional rule'.[79] Many of these laws, or forms of 'channelling', as described by Jennifer Earl, have been used in Bahrain in an attempt to limit, control or constrain the activities of social movements or political activists. The absence of overt coercive force also, as a corollary, imbues those whom the law benefits with the credibility that results from their resort to repression without the stain of violence.

[76] Wiktorowicz, 'Civil Society as Social Control', p. 48.

[77] I. D. Balbus, *The Dialectics of Legal Repression: Black Rebels before the American Criminal Courts*, New York, NY, Russell Sage Foundation, 1973 cited in Boykoff, 'Limiting Dissent', p. 291.

[78] P. W. Fagen, 'Repression and State Security', in J. E. Corradi and P. W. Fagen (eds), *State Terror and Resistance in Latin America*, Berkeley, CA, University of California Press, 1992, p. 47.

[79] Lopez and Stohl, 'State Terrorism', pp. 14–33.

Legal *processes* in an arbitrary state can be independent of the laws that set them in motion, but laws are still important in defining expectations of both the government and social movements. Otto Kirchheimer argued that the objective of the classical political trial is to 'incriminate its foe's public behaviour with a view to evicting [them] from the political scene'.[80] He adds that in the derivative political trial, perjury, defamation and contempt are 'manipulated in an effort to bring disrepute upon a political foe'.[81] Ultimately, the objective of the political trial is not the execution of impartial justice but a means to undermine or destroy power relations, or a way to discredit political leaders or social movements. In this sense, truth, evidence or standards of due process are subverted in favour of achieving political goals. These goals may be to assert the supremacy of the dominant order by giving them the authority to punish or sanction, or to remove potential threats to their authority. Legal processes are not necessarily consistent and represent 'differentiated political justice',[82] in which justice is meted out according to the nature of the threat, its intent, the government's objectives, and their scope for non-accountability.

In describing his modes of repression, Jules Boykoff includes legal processes as 'public prosecutions, hearings and extraordinary rules and laws'.[83] Like Kirchheimer, Boykoff notes that such trials, in addition to being part of legal processes that embroil activists in timely and costly legal labyrinths, are primarily a form of dissuasion in which negative associations are 'attached to the character, nature, or reputation of an individual or group based on perceptions of that individual or group'.[84] Although legal threats will not deter some, others may be discouraged from engaging in dissent if the consequences are publicized; while those who are further radicalized by such actions may play into the government's strategy by endorsing a more brutal government response. This high-profile stigmatization allows international actors or government supporters to potentially rationalize and justify their support for status quo policies. Such an issue is pertinent in Bahrain, where the regime-controlled press often portrays the Shiʿa population as an Iranian fifth column.

Facilitating this repression is the impunity of state officials guilty of egregious or illegal acts. As Turk states: 'Court and administrative decisions exonerating legal control agents are to be expected in any

[80] O. Kirchheimer, *Political Justice*, Princeton, NJ, Princeton University Press, 1961, p. 46.
[81] Ibid.
[82] R. Sharlet, 'Party and Public Ideals in Conflict: Constitutionalism and Civil Rights in the USSR', *Cornell International Law Journal*, vol. 23, no. 2, 1990, pp. 341–62.
[83] Boykoff, 'Limiting Dissent', p. 288. [84] Ibid., p. 296.

Table 2.3 *Summary of methods of legal repression*

Legal Repression	Specific Laws	Laws: that render collective action difficult, e.g. public gathering laws; that give security apparatus broad powers of arrest and incarceration, such as emergency laws; that criminalize freedom of expression and civil liberties; that suspend constitutional protections; laws that are so vague as to be applied arbitrarily to numerous cases
	Legal Processes	Summary trials, leniency for state control agents, show trials, unaccountability for elite officials, secret trials, refusal of access to lawyers, failure to adhere to a standard of due process, police witnesses. Limited inquiries or inquiries launched after control objective realized

polity. For official repression even to be subjected to legal review is an accomplishment, and for a regime to punish its own agents for using harsh tactics against its political enemies is unthinkable in most countries.'[85] Impunity can be intimidating for it demonstrates that the state can repress egregiously without fear of consequence. Impunity is also a fundamental function in the persistence of repression, for in the absence of meaningful oversight, crimes of power are likely to persist.[86] It also immunizes state actors while obstructing victims from seeking justice and/or compensation.[87]

Informational Control

Turk emphasizes the importance of information control techniques in repressing dissent, highlighting the role of 'intelligence gathering and information control (censorship propaganda)', in responding to dissent. Turk equates informational control with indoctrination, adding that 'free thinking and criticism are to be suppressed; celebrations and apologies are to be broadcast'.[88] As with strategies that seek to minimize coercive control, Turk argues that 'educational, research, religious and media institutions' should accomplish social control objectives with minimal recourse to police intervention.[89] Gamson notes that such strategies, if they achieve their utmost efficiency, aim to 'control the desire and not the ability'[90] to challenge authority. Gary Marx also emphasizes the

[85] Turk, *Political Criminality*, p. 147.
[86] M. Welch, *Crimes of Power and States of Impunity: The U.S. Response to Terror*, New Brunswick, NJ, Rutgers University Press, 2009, p. 160.
[87] Ibid., p. 161. [88] Turk, *Political Criminality*, p. 129. [89] Ibid.
[90] W. A. Gamson, *The Strategy of Social Protest*, Homewood, IL, Dorsey, 1990, p. 125.

importance of informational strategies to repress dissent and stresses how critical methods include the creation of an 'unfavourable public image' of the perceived dissidents.[91] Marx also argues that it is vital to mobilize a strong 'counter-ideology' to 'gather information on movements' and to 'inhibit freedom of movement, expression, and action'.[92]

Jules Boykoff emphasizes the role of informational control strategies in suppressing dissent, arguing that surveillance, infiltration, the use of agent provocateurs, black propaganda, mass media manipulation and mass media deprecation work to complement each other to crush movements. Ruud Koopmans stresses that in modern democracies, in particular, the interaction between violent agencies and protesters is less important than the act of repression as a form of 'strategic communication in the public sphere'.[93] Cottle, too, notes the changing imperatives of protest in the public sphere; 'Unlike in earlier times, the co-present public at demonstrations no longer count the most (Tilly, 2005); rather, it is the mass audience watching and reading the media coverage at home, and sometimes elites and authorities watching and coordinating responses, from afar (Koopmans, 2004: 368)'. Here, it is 'public discourse and the mass media [that] play a crucial role', and that it is futile to consider the impact of repression without examining the media and its relationship to the public sphere.[94] The media, in particular, plays a role in issue depletion which works by 'removing (1) the perceived need for the movement and/or (2) the perceived relevance of claims-making effort within the relevant population'.[95] There are numerous paths to this. States may use propaganda or ideological methods to convince people there are no problems. Boykoff argues that such tactics contribute to 'stigmatisation', a 'relational mechanism whereby discrediting attributes are attached to the character, nature, or reputation of an individual or group based on perceptions of that individual or group'.[96] The 'use of certain phrases and specific imagery tends to strip dissidents of credibility and make them appear irresponsible, fringe-like, and sometimes even violent'.[97] He adds that stigmatization creates a bifurcated world view among publics that seeks to establish groups of both insiders and outsiders, separating deviant actors from conformists. The proliferation and embedding of those terms may prevent those movements from gaining additional followers, adherents or

[91] Marx, 'External Efforts'. [92] Ibid.

[93] R. Koopmans, 'Repression and the Public Sphere: Discursive Opportunities for Repression against the Extreme Right in Germany in the 1990s', in C. Davenport et al. (eds), *Repression and Mobilization*, Minneapolis, MI, University of Minnesota Press, 2005, p. 239.

[94] Ibid., p. 161. [95] Davenport, *How Social Movements Die*, p. 23.

[96] Boykoff, 'Limiting Dissent', p. 296. [97] Boykoff, *Beyond Bullets*, p. 32.

supporters.[98] Pallmeyer notes that this stigmatization reflects an obsession with enemies that is a defining characteristic of the National Security State.[99]

The mass media has traditionally played an important role in stigmatizing movements, and Gamson argues that the rise of mass media contributed to the largest single most shift in the nature of repression in the United States. This form of persuasion is an aspect of information control, in that it attempts to induce a state of compliance, acceptance or indifference via all available ideological resources, whether educational, religious or otherwise. It is an imperative aspect of control as perceived by Middle Eastern governments, where traditional values of respect and deference to patrimonial authority are encouraged. As Steve Heydemann notes, controlling new communications technologies is one of the critical factors that allow authoritarian regimes to keep power.[100]

Boykoff also argues that information control strategies, such as encouraging the emergence of suspicion and discord through the use of infiltrators or saboteurs, can divide, split and weaken movements. Such division may be intra- or inter-group and can break up individual movements or prevent co-operation and solidarity between movements. However, while Davenport suggests that such issues are internally related to social movements, internal schism is often intricately connected to the outside.

Pamela Oliver describes one of the three main goals of repression as surveillance.[101] Surveillance, as with other methods, can contribute to burnout, where those engaged in struggle are worn down physically, emotionally and psychologically from their struggle.[102] Surveillance, which seeks to not only provide authorities with information conducive to undermining social movements, is also meant to modify the behaviour of those being monitored. Setting the foundations for modern surveillance studies, Michel Foucault used the notion of Bentham's Panopticon to explain the mechanism of surveillance, arguing that '[the] major effect of the Panopticon is to induce in the inmate a state of conscious and permanent visibility that assures the automatic functioning of power'.[103]

98 Ibid., p. 296.
99 J. N. Pallmeyer, *Brave New World Order*, Maryknoll, NY, Orbis Books, 1992, www.thirdworldtraveler.com/National_Security_State/Seven_Characteristics_NSS.html
100 Heydemann, 'Upgrading Authoritarianism'.
101 P. Oliver, 'Repression and Crime Control: Why Social Movement Scholars Should Pay More Attention to Mass Incarceration as a Form of Repression', *Mobilization*, vol. 13, no. 1, 2008, pp. 1–24.
102 Boykoff, 'Limiting Dissent'.
103 M. Foucault, *Discipline and Punish: The Birth of the Prison*, trans. A. Sheridan, New York, NY, Pantheon, 1997, p. 201.

Table 2.4 *Summary of methods of information control*

Informational Control	Media Control	Censorship, stigmatization of movements or leaders, selective release of information, selective release of state secrets
	Intelligence Gathering	Surveillance, agent provocateurs, infiltration of political/activist groups
	Ideological	Indoctrination, education, general mobilization of ideological resources through media, religion, culture, et cetera.

In this regard, surveillance should be 'permanent in its effects, even if it is discontinuous in its action'.[104] Thus it is the possibility of being watched rather than the act of watching itself that induces the most efficient forms of control.[105] Ben and Marthalee Barton stress the importance of surveillance as a form of repression, arguing that the 'asymmetry of seeing-without-being seen is, in fact, the very essence of power', and the 'power to dominate rests on the differential possession of knowledge'.[106] Even where surveillance does not occur, Marx notes that it is important to 'create myth and fact of surveillance and repression',[107] which can be done by publicizing incidences of surveillance. Indeed, the same is true of publicizing any egregious acts of repression. Earl too, notes the importance of surveillance, and argues that 'with more and more protest-related activity happening online, it will be increasingly important for scholars to consider how repression may work online'.[108] Mann, Nolan and Welman also state that 'surveillance techniques have increasingly become embedded in technology'.[109] With this in mind, social media as a tool of repression is a particular focus in Chapter six, as it represents the zeitgeist of the Arab Uprisings. Ultimately, information control is not only about gathering intelligence about potential dissidents but is also designed to convince potential challengers that dissent is an undesirable and costly choice.

[104] Ibid.
[105] M. O. Jones, 'Social Media, Surveillance, and Social Control in the Bahrain Uprising', *Westminster Papers in Communication and Culture: The Role of Social Media in the Arab Uprisings, Past and Present*, vol. 9, no. 2, 2013, p. 75.
[106] B. F. Barton and M. Barton, 'Modes of Power in Technical and Professional Visuals', *Journal of Business and Technical Communication*, vol. 7, no. 1, 1993, pp. 138–62.
[107] Marx, 'External Efforts'. [108] Earl, 'Political Repression', p. 278.
[109] S. Mann, J. Nolan and B. Wellman, 'Sousveillance: Inventing and using Wearable Computing Devices for Data Collection in Surveillance Environments', *Surveillance & Society*, vol. 1, no. 3, 2003, pp. 331–55.

Stylized Relations between Repressive Methods and Their Effects

Although it is important to delineate types of repression, it is also necessary to theorize how these elements might impact upon dissent. After all, repression can, according to its definition, only be considered repression if it foreseeably plays a role in allowing the dominant hegemonic order to fend off challengers. Although some of these aspects have been referred to above, a further discussion will enrich our concept of repression and also provide more insight into those methods of repression suitable to insert into the template. Many processes inherent within statecraft – personal integrity violations, legal repression and information control – are designed to be repressive and contribute to resource deprivation,[110] that is, the 'hindering of SMO efforts to generate the human and financial resources necessary to continue engaging in channelling behaviour'.[111] As discussed, this may be through deportation, exile, arrest, murder, depriving members of their livelihood or preventing them from accessing institutions that could give them political leverage to impact change. It may also involve cutting funding to movements, limiting personal advancement by preventing access to employment, scholarships, positions of office et cetera. Such acts may eventually demoralize or weaken movements, leaving them unable to function efficiently or effectively. Indeed, without resources, movements cannot 'pay rent; travel; offer decent salaries; training, seminars, and workshops; obtain equipment, food, and medicine; and engage in a wide range of dissident activities, such as strikes, demonstrations, petitions, sit-ins, teach-outs, terrorism, guerrilla warfare, and insurgency'.[112]

While methods describe what legitimaters do, scholars like Boykoff have argued that so-called mechanisms of repression theorize *how and why* these state actions have their effect.[113] Boykoff's description of mechanisms is appealing. Social mechanisms are explanatory accounts of a series of events that bring about a change between two variables. As Hedstrom and Swedberg state: 'Assume that we have observed a systematic relation between two entities, say I and O. In order to explain the relationship between them we must search for a mechanism, M, which is such that occurrence of the case or input, I, it generates the effect or outcome, O'. In the case of this study, I is repression, and O is demobilization.[114]

[110] Davenport, *How Social Movements Die*, 2015. [111] Ibid., p. 23. [112] Ibid., p. 24.
[113] Boykoff, 'Limiting Dissent', p. 288.
[114] P. Hedstrom and R. Swedberg, *Social Mechanisms: An Analytical Approach to Social Theory*, Cambridge, Cambridge University Press, 1998.

Accordingly, focusing on mechanisms allows one to 'move beyond covariation' (i.e. the positive or negative relationship between two variables)[115] and identify the 'cogs and wheels'[116] that explain why cause and effect relationships might come about between variables. The study of mechanisms moves away from the study of grand theory and towards a more middle-level approach that seeks to identify similar processes that can occur within different historical and political contexts. For this reason, social mechanisms 'inhabit the intermediate space between laws and descriptions, between grand theory and historiography'.[117] Given that the explanatory power of social mechanisms lies in the fact that they ought to achieve a certain level of generality, they serve as an important underlying theoretical assumption of how the state represseds dissent.

> When working with mechanisms, one is not necessarily in search of a one-to-one, mechanism-to-outcome causal relationship ... Mechanisms are dependently connected: they intersect with, play off of, and in some cases, amplify each other in interlocking configurations, or 'concatenations of mechanisms' ... Such concatenations constitute the 'workhorses of explanation'.[118]

However, Mechanisms are inherently problematic by their very nature, because they invite one to criticize them because there may be sub-mechanisms that operate within the mechanisms themselves. This could lead to a zero-sum game in which the search for mechanisms is subordinated by a never-ending quest to expose the 'nuts and bolts'. As Lichbach states, it is difficult to identify in any one situation what mechanisms are fundamentally at play.[119] As such, it is useful to add the caveat that while mechanisms may offer some explanatory power, it is perhaps better, albeit more modest, to adopt stylized explanations of causal relations. In this sense, we can *theorize* how methods of repression contribute to several outcomes: for example, short- and long-term demobilization, nascent mobilization, escalation and radicalization. This is perhaps more appropriate when attempting a long-term analysis of Bahrain's history.

Not all methods lead to the single outcome of demobilization. Some, for example, may lead to short- or long-term escalation. Violent or not, repression can simply breathe life into social movements or causes by imbuing in people a sense of anger or indignation. The benefit of talking

[115] Boykoff, 'Limiting Dissent'.

[116] J. Elster, *Nuts and Bolts for the Social Sciences*, New York, NY, Cambridge University Press, 1989, p. 3.

[117] Boykoff, 'Limiting Dissent', p. 286. [118] Ibid.

[119] M. Lichbach, 'How to Organize Your Mechanisms: Research Programs, Stylized Facts, and Historical Narratives', in C. Davenport et al. (eds), *Repression and Mobilization*, Minneapolis, MI, University of Minnesota Press, 2005, pp. 239–40.

Table 2.5 *Summary of stylized categories of repression*[120]

Intimidation	Frightens people into stopping
Incapacitation and Containment	Physically restrains or prohibits people from protesting, physically removes people from space, including arrests of leaders, roadblocks et cetera, killing.
Embroilment and Regulation	Puts people into complex processes or situations that prevent or hinder them from protesting. Can drain resources, reduce morale, divert time away from activism, can create negotiation with the state that tempers impact of activism.
Co-optation and Placation	Make those more amenable to a certain course of action through incentivizing actions and disincentivizing others.
Persuasion/Dissuasion	Dissuades people from getting involved in such activity, whether educationally or ideologically, through demoralization or surveillance.
Fragmentation	Reduces cohesive solidarity of movement as a whole, and even whole social groups, facilitating control through disunity.
Strengthening	Augments forces designed to protect the status quo.
Escalation	Creates resentment, anger and fuels protest

about how these methods lead to repression is simply to offer a more thorough justification for the selection of these repressive methods. The term 'mechanisms' might be better described by the term 'stylized categories of repression' – in other words, simplified notions of processes that *theorize* how repression works to squash protest movements. Like mechanisms, stylized categories are perhaps more modest, providing 'a how-possible explanation; [they tell] us how the effect could in principle be produced'.[121] The reasons for preferring stylized categories is that they acknowledge their lack of generality, and by doing so, do not run the risk of creating an 'endless … inventory of mechanisms'.[122] Stylized categories then show how the methods within the categories of Statecraft, Personal Integrity Violations, Legal Statecraft and Informational Control may accomplish a number of objectives. Table 2.5 represents a table of

[120] It is important to note the distinction between categories. Not all methods will intimidate people into stopping, nor may those who are intimidated actually want to stop, for example. In these cases, incapacitation, embroilment, co-optation or persuasion may provide alternative strategies. Fragmentation may occur when groups are targeted through legal procedures, or if a number of their members are incapacitated or intimidated into withdrawing their support. The potential interactions or concatenations are large, but it is important to note them. In other instances we may have an overlap of nomenclature. For example, should co-optation be a method of repression, or does it explain why repression works?

[121] P. Hedstrom and P. Ylikoski, 'Causal Mechanisms in the Social Sciences', *The Annual Review of Sociology*, vol. 36, 2010, p. 52.

[122] Lichbach, 'How to Organize', p. 233.

Repression in Bahrain: Methods and Stylized Mechanisms

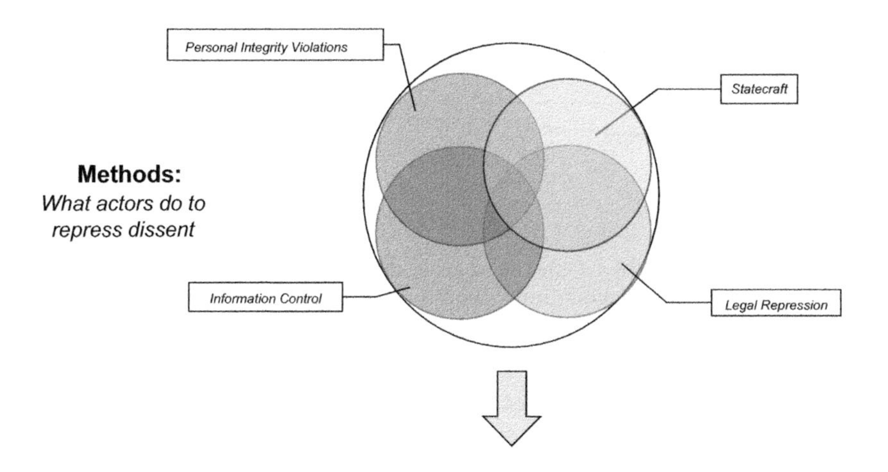

Stylized Categories:
How the methods may lead to the following outcomes

Intimidation
Incapacitation
Embroilment and Regulation
Containment
Fragmentation
Co-optation and Placation
Persuasion/Dissuasion
Strengthening

Outcomes *Demobilization (long and short term); Radicalization; Nascent Mobilization; Negative Stability*

Figure 2.2 Summary of types of repressive action and how they impact upon dissent

'stylized categories', which are essentially regularities distilled from a range of theoretical explanations of how repression impacts upon dissent. They illustrate how repressive processes may impact psychologically or physically on group or individual processes.

3 Political Statecraft

Between Democratization, Discord and Division

> Unfortunately, some members of the ruling family still think in the old way – that Bahrain is the spoils of war 'gained by the sword', where the land, wealth and positions of authority are to be distributed amongst the sons of the victorious tribe and its supporters.[1] —Ibrahim Sharif, 2011

The process of political statecraft, including the allocation of resources, the management of communal issues and the calculations of institutional figures all form a part of explaining why certain repressive choices were made. In Bahrain, repressive choices related to statecraft – from exile and the removal of citizenship to certain types of labour reform and democratization – have been contingent on specific contextual factors: from the inclinations of hawkish groups to the apparent whim of certain individuals; from regional politics to the availability of resources. Much has been determined by the political objectives of Bahrain's protectors. The change in suzerain from the United Kingdom to Saudi Arabia in 1971 resulted in changes to strategic decision-making within the Al Khalifa regime, prompting changes in the nature, intensity and type of repression. This shift, compounded by resource availability and ideological inclination, has resulted most notably in political strategies designed to exclude Bahrain's Shiʿa from political life. However, as this chapter highlights, it is difficult to distinguish any specific variable as being the driver of certain types of repression. We can, of course, argue for certain truisms. For example, the shrinking of the British Empire and the growth of information technology limited the efficacy of exile as a means of repression. Bahrain's natural wealth has been used to moderate internal conflict within the ruling family, which has also prompted unrest, unequal land distribution and further repression. Despite this factor, we do see other patterns over time: from the recurring importance of co-optation and *makramāt* to the process of administrative reform

[1] E. Sharif, 'A Trial of Thoughts and Ideas', in A. Shehabi and M. O. Jones (eds), *Bahrain's Uprising: Resistance and Repression in the Gulf*, London, Zed Books Ltd, 2015, p. 55.

designed to act as an ameliorating remedy to dissent. Modernity and its accompanying industrialization also brought with it new roles involving labour, resistance and repression. The rise of the oil and aluminium industry, and their various accoutrements, whether factories or shipyards, created organized and salaried labour that had to be tackled with new methods, such as mass layoffs, union manipulation and the import of cheap labour. Political dissent has coloured almost every decision, or piece of policy advice. Even the import of labour has been conceived of as a means of potentially controlling dissent, while the planning of land and the nature of urban topography have been designed in part to militate against unrest. Underneath all, the desire of the ruling family and its protectors to maintain the primacy of the ruling dominance of the Al Khalifa has underpinned all aspects of statecraft.

Pacification of Internal Factionalism through Co-optation and the Civil List

> With the exception of Shaikh Khalid, all the old oppressors are still alive and willing to resume their former ways if not repressed.[2]

The above quote, written by C. C. J. Barrett in 1929, the British political agent based in Bahrain, highlights the recent memory of Al Khalifa 'intrigues' and oppression of the *baḥārna* population. Here Barrett uses the term 'former ways' to describe the behaviour of members of the ruling family, many of whom were competing for power, engaging in internecine strife and challenging British interference in their perceived right of rule. By using the word 'repressed', Barrett is conscious of the imperial power dynamic regarding British hegemony over the Al Khalifa.

By the end of the 1800s, Britain found themselves increasingly drawn into Bahrain's internal affairs for numerous reasons, including internal strife, and the ruling family's oppression of the indigenous population, as well as their own desire to exclude other regional and European powers from gaining advantages in the Gulf. This process contravened what the British had long stressed, particularly in the first half of the twentieth century, which was that their influence in Bahrain should be brought about by 'indirect and pacific means, and through the increase of influence with the Shaykh by gaining his confidence and trust'.[3] Instead, British attempts

[2] C. C. J. Barrett, Letter to the Foreign Sec. to the Gov. of India, 28 August 1929, No. 385-S, in P. Tuson and E. Quick (eds), *Records of Bahrain 1820–1960*, vol. 4, Slough, Archive Editions, 1993, p. 570.

[3] C. K. Daly, Note on the Political Situation in Bahrain, November 1924, in P. Tuson, A. Burdett and E. Quick (eds), *Records of Bahrain 1820–1960*, vol. 3, Slough, Archive Editions, 1993, p. 669.

at methods of indirect and pacific means that might readily be considered statecraft were increasingly about interceding directly in matters of internal rule. While ship captains of the British Navy passing through the Gulf had long documented the mistreatment of the *baḥārna*, increasing oppression of the local population and the potential international outcry it would generate spurred them to act. In the early 1920s, Persia was threatening to go to the newly established League of Nations to hold Britain accountable for the misrule of Bahrain's Shiʿi subjects. This Persian disquiet over the treatment of their fellow co-religionists undermined Britain's commitment to emerging international norms of accountability. However, Britain's treaty obligation to protect the Al Khalifa from external aggression was paramount in securing their continued, oppressive rule. Major Clive Daly, the British Political Agent in Bahrain, succinctly documented this problem in 1921: 'Why do you not remove British protection then we would at least have the redress usually resorted to by Arabs. We should appeal to another Arab ruler to take over our country and treat us better.'[4]

While Britain's impetus to intervene increased on account of internal instability, self-interest and changing international structures, its continued encroachment in Bahrain's affairs was, in many ways, an inevitability. One of the most salient examples was their involvement in the royal succession of the Al Khalifa rulers. Here, British intervention was executed according to the notion that dynastic struggles and resistance over the succession process could result from the death of Shaykh ʿIsa bin Ali, Bahrain's ruler between 1869 and 1923.[5] It would also secure Britain's influence over the ruling line. As a result, in 1898, and as a response to a request by Shaykh ʿIsa bin Ali Al Khalifa, the British had already acknowledged that they would recognize a system of primogeniture, and Hamad bin ʿIsa Al Khalifa, Shaykh ʿIsa's eldest and, in the eyes of the British administrators, more malleable son, would become successor. Hamad's ascent to the throne was expedited to ameliorate growing unrest. When the ruler, Shaykh ʿIsa, proved unable and unwilling to control belligerent elements of his family who were reacting against British reforms, the British deposed him, putting his son Shaykh Hamad in his place in 1923. This, the British argued, would 'bring the affairs of Bahrain more under our [British] control and aid towards securing the inhabitants against a despotic rule'.[6] Following this, British officials were

[4] Daly, 21 November, p. 674.

[5] The date of Isa's forced abdication is 1923. If one does not accept the legitimacy of this, Isa ruled until 1932.

[6] J. C. Gaskin, A Reply to First Assistant Resident's Request Conveyed in His Memorandum of the 1st April 1898, 30 April 1898, in P. Tuson and E. Quick (eds), *Records of Bahrain 1820–1960*, vol. 3, Slough, Archive Editions, 1993, p. 25.

quick to remind Hamad of the debt he owed them for acknowledging his right to the throne.

The justification for putting Hamad on the throne was in small part due to the activities of a faction of the ruling family headed by Hamad's brother, ʿAbd Allah bin ʿIsa Al Khalifa. This faction was attempting to resist British encroachment upon what some members of the ruling family perceived as their legitimate rights as conquerors of Bahrain. This resistance was coloured, at least from the British perspective, by ʿAbd Allah's desire to secure the rule of Bahrain from his older brother and fits within the broader picture of internecine conflict within the Al Khalifa family, as opposed to broader anti-imperialist ambitions. Together with their tribal allies, the Dawasir, located in both Bahrain and on the Arabian Peninsula, this Al Khalifa faction was engaged in the oppression of the indigenous *baḥrānī* population throughout the 1920s. The British desire to mitigate complaints by various parties about internal misrule to Bahrain required a strong response to what they saw as belligerent and uncooperative members of the Al Khalifa family, whose control was necessary for preserving the ill-named 'Pax Britannica' in the Gulf. The problem was clear: although the British were treaty-bound to protect the Al Khalifa from external aggression, it was members of that family, mainly led by the ruler's son, ʿAbd Allah bin ʿIsa Al Khalifa, that were the prime fomenters of intrigues and resistance to British reforms through their support of Hamad.

The British were now in an even more invidious position, acting as a deterrent to those potentially able to end the Al Khalifa' oppressive rule. Indeed, it was only British protection of the ruling family that made the *baḥārna* fearful of resisting the Al Khalifa and potentially ending their subjugation. The British political agent between 1921 and 1926, Clive Daly, was fully aware of this. Writing in 1921, Daly noted 'Bahrain subjects are afraid to take the law into their own hands as the Sheikh is under our protection, and they urge, with some reason, that we ought, in consequence, to take steps to prevent the Sheikh from abusing his authority.'[7] Daly went as far as to say that the pitch of misrule was Britain's failure as a protecting power.[8] Despite sympathy from the likes of Daly and other British political agents, the *baḥrānī* pleas for extensive reform were generally rebuffed by the Government of India, who, unlike

[7] C. K. Daly, Tyranny of the Sheikh of Bahrain and His Family over Bahrain Subjects, 30 December 1921, in P. Tuson and E. Quick (eds), *Records of Bahrain 1820–1960*, vol. 3, Slough, Archive Editions, p. 663.

[8] 'Administration Reports 1920–1924' [158r] (320/412), British Library: India Office Records and Private Papers, IOR/R/15/1/713, in *Qatar Digital Library* www.qdl.qa/en/archive/81055/vdc_100023385511.0x000079

agents on the ground in Bahrain, believed that they should continue to sail a 'middle course' between treating Bahrain as a full 'British protectorate' and 'an independent principality'.[9]

However, Britain's position was ambiguous regarding this middle course. It was clear that political agents in Bahrain were advised to avoid invasive (but vaguely stipulated) reforms. Instead, the Government of India were morally indifferent and instructed local agents to focus on customs reform and courting influence with the Shaykh. This emphasis on customs reform reflected the trade-orientated priorities of the British colonial project, and perhaps the Government of India's own view that the Gulf was an irrelevant and often irritating peripheral appendage to the Empire. However, despite egregious acts undertaken by members of the ruling family, British policy towards repressing dissenting members of the Al Khalifa was primarily co-optation and monetary incentivization. This dovetailed with the Government of India's advice to bring about placation through 'indirect and pacific', as opposed to violent, means. However, following repeated pressure by Major Daly for the Government of India to do something about the ruling family tyranny, it was generally agreed in 1922 that only in 'glaring cases of oppression' could the political agent intervene, yet this brought with it a great deal of subjectivity in what was termed oppression.[10]

While the British had on many occasions threatened to shell the Al Khalifa and their allies from their gunboats, a standing military force was considered costly. However, gunboats were not always speedily available in the Gulf. Instead, less militant methods were encouraged. Britain's viceroy stated in 1923; 'All we want is to put ourselves right with the world and the Bahrainis by the introduction of some measure of justice and equitable taxation.'[11]

Consequently, one of the most significant and enduring acts of statecraft that the British used to repress the Al Khalifa was the reforming of the privy purse. The privy purse effectively was the creation of a mechanism of distributing Bahrain's wealth through the British-appointed Hamad. The attempt to bring the Al Khalifa under control

[9] Draft Letter (Unapproved) from The Secretary to the Government of India to Major P. Z. Cox, 1905–1906, in P. Tuson and E. Quick (eds), *Records of Bahrain 1820–1960*, vol. 3, Slough, Archive Editions, p. 281.

[10] A. P. Trevor, Tyranny of the Sheikh of Bahrain and His Family over Bahrain Subjects, 6 January 1922, in P. Tuson and E. Quick (eds), *Records of Bahrain 1820–1960*, vol. 3, Slough, Archive Editions, 1993, p. 677.

[11] Viceroy, Foreign and Political Department, to Secretary of State for India, 14 May 1923, in P. Tuson, A. Burdett and E. Quick (eds), *Records of Bahrain 1820–1960*, vol. 3, Slough, Archive Editions, 1993, p. 761.

was a prime example of how context influenced the methods of repression. The root of what Major Daly had called Al Khalifa's 'tyranny' of the *baḥārna* lay in extortive practices. This system of appropriation reflected, in part, the feudal system that existed in Bahrain. The *baḥārna* were often farming tenants on lands owned by members of the Al Khalifa family that were administered by various *wazirs* (Wazir were generally Shiʿa trusted by the shaykh). In addition to the regular tithes that the *baḥārna* would pay to the Al Khalifa via the Wazir, members of the ruling family who found themselves hard up for cash would either draw money from the customs revenue or extort money from *baḥārna*. As the Al Khalifa had, *before* the reforms, drawn money without check from customs revenues;[12] customs reforms were seen by the British as imperative, as they would limit the shaykhs' unfettered borrowing, and thus help to prevent them arbitrarily extorting *baḥārna* to pay back ever-increasing debts. Various changes were made. The Director of Muharraq Customs, Jasim al-Shirawi, a good friend of ʿAbd Allah bin ʿIsa and pecuniary beneficiary of the status quo, was illegally deported by Major Daly for an 'alleged conspiracy against the Bahrain Order in Council'.[13] Now, on the orders of the British, money earned through customs would be distributed solely through the Privy Purse of the British-appointed Hamad. Members of the ruling family who did not step in line would receive no income, a repressive policy that reflected both a desire to secure control indirectly and pacifically yet tailored to undermine the exploitative aspects of Al Khalifa feudalism.

This policy was far from subtle. In his speech to a Majlis convened to announce Shaikh Hamad's accession as the Ruler of Bahrain, the Political Resident Stuart George Knox warned that those [Khalifas] who did not work in supporting Hamad would live on a 'bare pittance for subsistence', and that those who committed mischief would be 'cut off absolutely and punished accordingly'.[14] This policy deliberately curtailed interactions between the *baḥārna* and the Al Khalifa. Under the reforms, the baḥārna would be paying their 'tribute' directly to the 'head office' in Manama, thereby obviating the obvious mechanisms of extortion: namely the *al-fidawiyya*, the notorious, and frequently violent, enforcers-cum-debt-collectors of Al Khalifa rule.

[12] Their ability to do this was facilitated by the fact customs were farmed out to a Hindu firm not approved by the Government of India. The Hindu firm even kept their accounts in Sindhi so as to make auditing and accountability more difficult.

[13] M. G. Rumaihi, *Bahrain: Social and Political Change since the First World War*, London and New York, Bowker, 1976, p. 173.

[14] S. G. Knox, Speech to Majlis in Bahrain, 26 May 1923, in P. Tuson and E. Quick (eds), *Records of Bahrain 1820–1960*, vol. 4, Slough, Archive Editions, 1993, p. 11.

The civil list reform had a notable legacy. In 1929, for example, the Amir did not want to reduce Shaykh ʿAbd Allah's payment from the civil list for fear he would cause trouble again.[15] The effectiveness of the Civil List in co-opting the Al Khalifa was also evidenced anecdotally in 1959 when, in a private meeting with an honorary consul general, Khalifa bin Muhammad Al Khalifa said that none of the Al Khalifa dared put a foot wrong because the ruler 'held the purse strings and could cut off an allowance when he pleased'.[16]

Thus, by introducing the Civil List, and by deposing ʿIsa and instating Hamad as Amir, the British mitigated the Al Khalifa's ability to extract wealth arbitrarily and violently as they had done in the past. Ultimately, the Civil List was a form of 'socialism for the rich', for it sought to repress the elite classes by giving them access to funds on the explicit condition that they: (a) ceased to oppose the British reforms; (b) fall in line with Hamad's rule and stop oppressing the *baḥārna*. The Civil List was also a form of material repression, whose purpose was to ameliorate dissent by giving the tribal shaykhs other sources of income beyond extortion and customary privileges, and by limiting the perceived improvidence of Al Khalifa shaykhs by defining a fixed income. While the British believed that ensuring the unity of the ruling family was imperative in creating a functioning government and ending anti-British agitation and the oppressive practices of the tribal shaykhs, it also created a vested interest group with access to massive power and wealth. In the future, revenues accruing to the ruling family, and their protectiveness of this right given under Britain's imperial oversight would be a key grievance among Bahrain's increasingly politically aware population, highlighting the short-sightedness of British policy in Bahrain. In fact, the Civil List and payment to the Privy Purse accounted for about 25 per cent of mean annual state revenue between 1922 and 1971.[17] Upon the discovery of oil, the percentage reduced, but the overall gross sums of money going to the ruling family increased dramatically. This lucrative stipend was due to an arrangement whereby the ruling family got one-third of all oil revenues, regardless of the amount produced. Such an

[15] C. Belgrave, Letter to Prior, 12 July 1929, in P. Tuson and E. Quick (eds), *Records of Bahrain 1820–1960*, vol. 4, Slough, Archive Editions, 1993, p. 488.

[16] H. C. G. Lian, Secret letter from British Residency in Bahrain, 23 July 1959, in A. Burdett (ed.), *Records of Bahrain 1820–1960*, vol. 7, Slough, Archive Editions, 1993, p. 375.

[17] This figure was derived from analysing the annual reports between the specified dates. They are summarized here: M. O. Jones, 'How the Al Khalifas Took a Quarter of Bahrain's Wealth'. *Your Middle East*, 29 April 2013, www.yourmiddleeast.com/opinion/marc-owen-jones-how-the-al-khalifas-took-a-quarter-of-bahrains-wealth_doi:11643

arrangement was common throughout the Gulf, and while in Bahrain it had initially sought to repress the *baḥārna* from agitating for reforms from the British, and keep the Al Khalifa house in order, it later became a bone of contention that spurred on unrest, provoking other means of repression.

The payments to the ruler and the ruling family were frequently a source of political discord, especially in the 1950s, when the ruler asked that his personal income be removed from annual financial reports to avoid embarrassment.[18] Even in 1942, the Privy Purse was explicitly mentioned as a source of tension. Social problems as a result of economic stagnation were perceived as particularly outrageous given the ruling family's share of the state's revenues. As a form of repression, the cost of this particular method was exorbitant. Numerous British officials believed in limiting the Civil List but accepted that tolerating the costs associated with it were better than generating dissent within the ruling family. Indeed, most seasoned imperial officials believed that the primary source of trouble in the Gulf at the time came from within ruling families themselves and that overall political stability resulted from securing the unity of the ruling elite. It was in this mutually beneficial, patron–client relationship with Gulf ruling families that the British secured their geopolitical interests, while the Al Khalifa secured enormous wealth and power.

For the British, preserving the material power of the ruling family facilitated a social structure in Bahrain conducive to British needs. Although this enforced fiscal structure came at a significant cost to Bahrainis, Charles Belgrave, the British financial advisor the Ruler, felt that aggressive attempts to limit the Civil List would risk ceding his influence over Hamad, noting in particular that the high cost lowered the amount of discontent within the ruling family. Despite this, Belgrave once stated with disdain; 'The Khalifa family is the Royal Family of Bahrain, & very much so. They are paid allowances by the Govt & do nothing apparently considering it infra dig to do any work, they are lazy conceited oppressive people, for the most part, living on being royalty.' Certainly, for a social group who had sought power and extracted wealth through means of piracy and feudalism, fiscal forms of repression were an effective means of ensuring the unity of the Al Khalifa family and ensuring continued British influence until Independence. However, the consequences were the creation of a political structure that preserved Bahrain's feudal inequality.

[18] E. P. Wiltshire, Annual Review of Bahrain Affairs for 1960, in A. Burdett (ed.), *Records of Bahrain 1820–1960,* vol. 7, Slough, Archive Editions, 1993, p. 387.

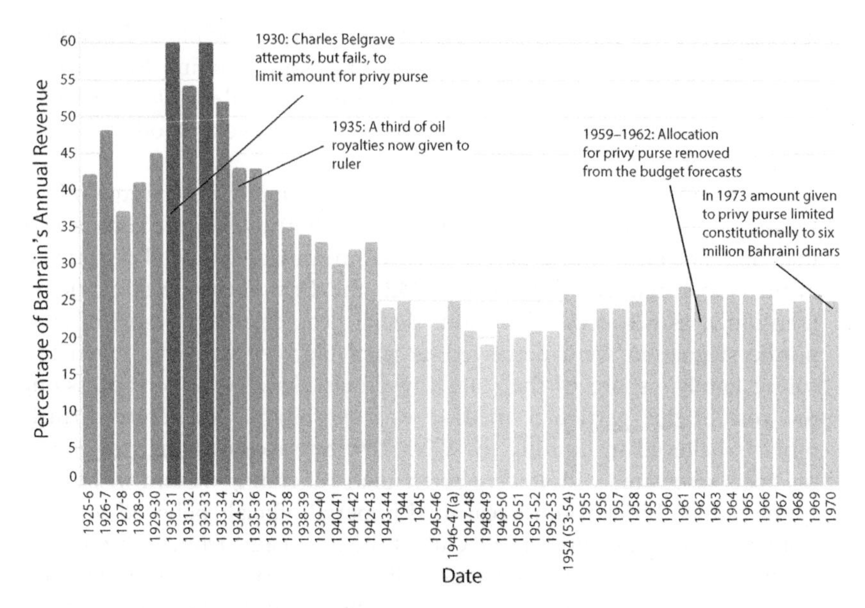

Figure 3.1 Graph showing percentage of Bahrain's national revenue going to the Privy Purse and Civil List between 1927 and 1970

The Legacy of the Civil List and Other Forms of Restraining the Al Khalifa

The British took other indirect and pacific measures to repress the ruling family. The Al Khalifas were prohibited by the British in the 1930s from selling their land to anyone else but other Al Khalifas.[19] This was done to stop Al Khalifa shaykhs selling off their ancestral land at low prices for short-term funds, an issue which led to them becoming destitute and either pestering Shaykh Hamad for more money from the Civil List or extorting members of the public. Gifts of land given by the ruler to his relatives were also an issue, as they included large villages and districts, and the same plots were often regifted, leading to confusion as to who actually owned what. This confusion often turned to anger, fuelling instability and conflict within the ruling family. It was eventually decided that gift holders could only keep the property in their lifetime and that after death, the property should revert to the ruler. This Belgrave noted, would help Hamad 'establish his authority over his family', and

[19] C. Belgrave, 'Annual report for the year 1351 (1932–33)', in *Bahrain Government Annual Reports 1924–1970*, vol. 1, Gerrards Cross, Archive Editions, 1986, p. 284.

strengthen his ability to continually reaffirm his patronage networks.[20] This reform would, the British believed, 'do more than anything else to stop oppression of Shiʿahs [sic] ', owing to the fact their land would not be constantly usurped and regifted to the Al Khalifa's tribal allies.[21]

While originally designed to prevent what one colonial officer described as 'the worst features of Arab misrule',[22] the reform 'overran its original limited objective'.[23] It soon became clear to the Agency that all they could do was mitigate future land disputes, rather than rectify old wrongs. 'Nearly all the property of the Shaikss [sic] has been looted from Bahrainis in the lifetime of Shaikh Easa [sic]. It would be impossible and undesirable to try to right these old cases now but sufficient we could put a stop to further exploitation of the[Shiʿi] subjects'.[24] Indeed, Daly noted that most gardens confiscated from the 'original owners' [*baḥārna*] occurred under ʿIsa's rule and that they now owned about two-thirds of the gardens, very few of which had been obtained legally.[25] While it is unclear what Daly meant by 'legally', the land policies designed to benefit the *baḥārna* and police the Al Khalifa resulted in the ruling family's monopoly of land ownership. The pattern of land ownership settled their conquest, underscoring modern-day grievances by excessively privileging a limited social group for the sake of British short-term repressive policy. This ownership was solidified in the Tabu (land registry) reforms of 1934, the final article of which stipulated that any lands not claimed within ten years of the law's passing would automatically go to the government of Bahrain.[26]

The legal validation and protections of land ownership, itself fetishized by the logic of British imperialism, bolstered the Al Khalifa's power over Bahrain's resources. This move in effect accelerated the process of primitive accumulation, rapidly fossilizing existing feudal structures in such a way as to simultaneously dispossess the native population.

[20] C. Belgrave, 'Annual report for the year 1352 (1933–34)', in *Bahrain Government Annual Reports 1924–1970*, vol. 1, Gerrards Cross, Archive Editions, 1986, p. 371.

[21] The Agency Bahrain, 11 February 1923, in P. Tuson and E. Quick (eds), *Records of Bahrain 1820–1960*, vol. 3, Slough, Archive Editions, 1993, p. 743.

[22] J. G. Acheson, the Deputy Secretary to the Government of India in the Foreign and Political Department, 'British Administration in the Bahrain State', 28 May 1929, in P. Tuson and E. Quick (eds), *Records of Bahrain 1820–1960*, vol. 4, Slough, Archive Editions, 1993, p. 540.

[23] Ibid. [24] The Agency Bahrain, p. 743.

[25] 'Administration Reports 1920–1924' [158r] (320/412), British Library: India Office Records and Private Papers, IOR/R/15/1/713, in *Qatar Digital Library*, www.qdl.qa/en/archive/81055/vdc_100023385511.0x000079.

[26] [Translated from Arabic] Abode and residency from registration papers for the Tabu department, www.legalaffairs.gov.bh/AdvancedSearchDetails.aspx?id=4406#.Wte_o4jwZyw

This 'dispossession by accumulation' as David Harvey might call it, has underpinned existing tribal, ethnic and religious divisions in Bahrain.[27] The accumulation of state wealth and endogamy between members of the same tribe have consolidated this accumulative structure, leading to a power elite with numerous cultural and legal mechanisms designed to preserve their monopoly on the means of production. Ultimately, the British emphasis on repressing discord from the ruling family was shortsighted and led to a legacy of problems that formed the backbone of many of today's grievances. The land reforms under the British, designed initially to prevent internecine and communal strife, would sow the seeds for a future of contention, for it was the British-led formalization of private land ownership that formed the basis of modern-day accusations of displacement and appropriation.

Regarding repression, this was not done without a lack of foresight. In a poignant act of prescience, a British officer acknowledged that much of the land to be formally and legally (under British-led legal reforms) owned by the ruling family and 'well-to-do-Sunnis' were 'filched' from the 'original' Bahrainis.[28] However, their concerns were trumped by their desire for short-term solutions. Like the Civil List and the Privy Purse, the land reforms represented the vestiges of political control rooted in Britain's ambiguous position towards Bahrain. They were a product and repressive choice born from a poorly named 'middle course' between stronger intervention and allowing the Al Khalifa to continue a form of rule that was provoking the *baḥārna* and generating civil unrest.

Kleptocratic Ethnocracy: Rewards, Makramāt and Sanctions

Rentierism and Patronage

Despite the curtailing of the Civil List in 1971, the Al Khalifa family was growing, a problem once foreseen by British official Charles Geoffrey Prior, who noted with the kind of contempt frequently demonstrated by British officials that they were 'breeding like rabbits'.[29] While this disdain from the British reflected familiar tropes of Orientalism, it also highlighted that the British relationship with the Al Khalifa was more strategic than it was a 'friendship'. Nonetheless, maintaining the unity of an expanding power elite necessitated the bestowing of privilege to other family members, and

[27] D. Harvey, *The New Imperialism*, New York, NY, Oxford University Press, 2003, p. 148.

[28] 'File 9/1 Institution of Reforms & Sunni opposition intrigues' [97r] (208/504), British Library: India Office Records and Private Papers, IOR/R/15/2/127, in Qatar Digital Library www.qdl.qa/archive/81055/vdc_100023321443.0x000009

[29] C. G. Prior, Letter to the Political Resident, 28 July 1929, in P. Tuson and E. Quick (eds), *Records of Bahrain 1820–1960*, vol. 4, Slough, Archive Editions, 1993, p. 483.

increasingly by other means, such as through institutions of the state, ministerial roles, land or other favours. The need to ensure the unity of a power elite with ever-dwindling resources has led to a form of Al Khalifa cronyism that has itself become a source of tension with the public but also a means of ensuring their continued position of power. This form of repression has resulted in an underlying structure of kleptocratic ethnocracy. That is, the ruling family continue to maintain unity through the disbursement of inherited privilege (oil revenues) to mostly tribal allies. Even by 1988, oil also made it possible for the Al Khalifa to allocate a monthly stipend to the '2500–3000 members of the ruling family according to an elaborate classification'.[30] This classification was often laid out in rich detail by the British administration, who kept lists of payments going to each member of the ruling family. Also, these resources allowed the ruling family to disburse rewards in the 'form of employment, cash, and plots of land'.[31] However, by doing so, their continued monopoly of the surplus product antagonized an increasingly large number of the population.

As argued by Abdulhadi Khalaf, the ruling core, for its part, had discretion over the distribution of *makramāt*, enabling them to enhance or weaken the influence enjoyed by intermediary patrons.[32] From a Marxist perspective, the ruling family's monopoly of the surplus product was solidified by British protection, allowing them to be the ultimate arbiters in a system of selective patronage and surplus distribution. Khalaf writes: 'Loyalty to the regime of divergent, and among themselves conflicting forces, have been maintained through an elaborate segmented system of intermediary patrons. On the top of the segmented pyramid of patrons stands the Amir himself, as a supreme patron.'[33] Upon the consolidation of the Al Khalifa regime under the British, the process of state-building necessitated the creation of social services, specialized offices and institutions. With this came the provision of opportunities, jobs and increased life chances to members of the public. While the provision of such 'rewards' to ward off discontent can be framed within broader aspects of ameliorating dissent through fulfilling or meeting growing expectations, the Bahrain example often highlights how such benefits are a common form of repression designed to divide or maintain loyalties, fragment opposition or remove the brunt of popular discontent. The acquisition of oil was particularly significant, as it enabled the government to ward off discontent by investing in social-welfare programmes that positively 'privileged' certain citizens on the basis that their loyalty did not waver. This administrative reform was regularly pushed forward

[30] Khalaf, *Contentious Politics in Bahrain.* [31] Ibid. [32] Ibid. [33] Ibid.

under the British, who were particularly mindful that although they had set in motion the mechanisms for this kleptocratic clientelism, peace could not be maintained if benefits accruing to the ruling family continued without some form of wealth sharing with the wider population. When it appeared that the Al Khalifa would renege, or lapse in this duty to disperse this wealth to the population, the British would periodically threaten the Al Khalifa that they [the British] were not obligated to help them should they face internal dissent.[34] The issue was not necessarily that this wealth would not be shared but rather the manner in which disbursement took place. In the early 1900s for example, money was often dispersed to Arab tribesmen from the Arabian Peninsula. In the 1940s, it was noted that a large chunk of the ruler's wealth went to the Na'im tribe. Such expenditure irked the British, who believed that within the context of the normative modern state such payments and favours should be limited to those within the new territorial jurisdiction of Bahrain. As such, their threats to remove their protection of the Al Khalifa functioned as a means of mitigating Al Khalifa dissent against the British.

Operation Fig Leaf: Declining British Influence and Growing Saudi Hegemony

It is perhaps unsurprising then that the departure of the British and their coercive clout altered the extent of their political influence. The build-up to Bahrain's Independence in 1971, and the resultant withdrawal of British military forces prompted much concern about Bahrain's security, especially given that British protection of the ruling family, and periodic threats to withdraw that protection, had hitherto restrained aspects of Al Khalifa oppression, checked their spending and deterred or contained their opposition to British rule. While the Al Khalifa had relied on British protection to ensure their continued dominance in Bahrain, they used Independence to promote the idea that now, unfettered from the strictures of British imperialism, they were better able to meet the needs of their people through the announcement and introduction of a constitution. This rebuke to imperialism was entirely superficial, a cynical attempt to accrue legitimacy through appealing to widespread anti-colonial sentiment in the Middle East. Indeed, its lack of sincerity was highlighted by business-as-usual. The use of *makramāt* to placate potentially restive citizens was not abandoned. Indeed, the British methods of attempting to steer the policies of the ruling family to include limited redistribution of wealth continued.

[34] C. K. Daly, From the Agency in Bahrain, 11 April 1922, in P. Tuson and E. Quick (eds), *Records of Bahrain 1820–1960*, vol. 3, Slough, Archive Editions, 1993, p. 771.

This legacy of the 1920s' reforms was in many ways both habitual and ingrained into the governance of Bahrain. Upon Independence, however, the lack of a protecting military deterrent meant that British influence was best achieved through diplomatic pressure and British citizens in the police. For post-Independence diplomats like Andrew Sterling, the British ambassador to Bahrain in 1970, British policy relied on encouraging rent-distribution as a solution to political crises, suggesting that rentierism itself was as much a method of repression as it is an analytical concept. Indeed, it was certainly *perceived* by some officials as being an effective antidote to the visible activity of social movements. Sterling noted in 1970: 'Bahrain's attainment of full Independence, a twelve-and-a-half per cent pay rise of Government employees, the redemption of the Amir's debts and the waiving of instalments due on the purchase of Government houses took the edge off discontent.'[35] Officials like Sterling clearly felt that these moves to stave off revolution had to be pushed 'hard...if anything is actually to be done'.[36] However, Sterling's regard for such a policy was not without equivocation. He also noted, 'these domestic reforms cannot be a sure guard against revolution, but they can make the revolutionaries' task longer and harder'.[37] These comments came at a time where Britain acknowledged that its already limited internal influence was further giving way in light of Bahrain's new but contested sovereignty. Instead, British attempts at retaining stability in Bahrain and dousing revolutionary urges centred around the encouragement of certain domestic factors. In addition to encouraging positive economic conditions, they argued that the Bahraini Government needed to identify itself more closely with the people. If these conditions could be maintained, 'the present regime's chances of survival appreciably beyond are none too bad'.[38] For Sterling, domestic policy was about securitizing democratic institutions. Sterling reflected on such methods as an alternative to the presence of armed forces, noting: 'non-military means of influence were disrespectfully christened Operation Fig leaf ... a fig leaf is not to be despised when it covers the awkward evidence of castration'.[39]

Despite this metaphorical fig leaf, and British protestations that they now occupied a diminished military role, British officials still stressed the importance of British personnel in the police, noting, for example, that if the British head of Special Branch, Colonel Ian Henderson, were to

[35] A. J. D. Sterling, 'Bahrain: Annual Review for 1971', FCO8/1823, The National Archives.
[36] A. J. D. Sterling, 'Bahrain: Annual Review for 1970', FCO8/1638, The National Archives.
[37] Ibid. [38] Ibid. [39] Ibid.

leave, then subversion would be 'more difficult to contain'.[40] Ian Henderson, who came to Bahrain in 1965, was kicked out of Kenya following its Independence in 1963. However, he had gained a reputation among British government officials as a counter-insurgency expert after the often brutal repression of the Mau Mau. Like Belgrave before him, Henderson stayed in Bahrain for several decades, working in some form of security capacity until the 1990s. Robert Tesh, Britain's ambassador to Bahrain between 1975 and 1979, indicated that Ian Henderson influenced Sterling's recommendations for staving off revolution – so much so, that there was even a name for it: 'Ian's recipe'.[41] Tesh described Ian's recipe as a 'Saudi–Bahrain Treaty of Friendship specifying the right of each to help the other maintain law and order, followed by a big programme of social welfare spending'.[42] Indeed, this policy of rent-spending underpinned by the threat of Saudi coercion was similar to the system that had taken place under the British. However, now, with Saudi wealth factored largely into this recipe, it meant an increasing lack of autonomy for Bahrain. Whereas the personal financial difficulties of the shaykhs had previously impacted upon the *baḥārna*, there is evidence to suggest that post-Independence, the Saudis picked up the financial slack to help continue the consolidation of the unity of the ruling family. As Francis Trew noted in 1985: 'Apart from the official economic support, the Saudis helped the Amir and other members of his family out of some of their personal financial difficulties.'[43] The skyrocketing of oil prices assisted methods of repression through patronage after the oil crisis of 1973. The subsequent revenue accruing to oil-producing states allowed the Al Khalifa regime, now increasingly under the patronage of Saudi Arabia, to fall back on policies of rentierism and patronage, obviating the need to extract wealth from citizens. Indeed, with this Saudi patronage, came Saudi influence. By 1974, Bahrain had, according to one British diplomat, become 'economically, and therefore politically, very dependent on Saudi Arabia'.[44]

In 1974, British officials noted that the 'increase in revenue [had] enabled the Government to embark on a whole range of additional social and infrastructure projects as well as schemes for development

[40] Ibid.

[41] R. M. Tesh, Bahrain Elections, 11 December 1973, FCO8/1975, The National Archives.

[42] Ibid.

[43] F. S. E. Trew, Bahrain: Annual Review 1985, 23 January 1986, FOIA Request from the FCO, The National Archives.

[44] R. M. Tesh, Form at a Glance (FAAG), 24 June 1974, FCO8/2180, The National Archives.

aimed at the "formation of a modern industrial state"'.[45] The national minimum wage and food subsidies were increased, and the cost of living controlled.[46] While the Bahraini government's policy was still to 'deal firmly with the political labour agitators' until further modernization had taken place,[47] they responded to some short stoppages with conciliation, as opposed to force. Tesh noted that in 1974, twenty-six of the twenty-seven labour disputes 'had been settled, or were in the process of being settled, by the processes of mediation, statutory conciliation, and statutory arbitration provided by the Labour Ordinance of 1957'.[48] In 1975, the salaries of civil servants and parastatal employees (Aluminium Bahrain, Bahrain Petroleum Company) were purposely increased by 15 per cent to defuse 'the main source of labour discontent'.[49] The increase in oil revenues also allowed electricity bills to be halved in the hope that such measures would 'convince the Bahraini man in the street that he is better off with this regime than with any conceivable alternative'[50] – in other words, a genuine democracy. Where ideological confrontations were necessary, Shiʿa Islamists were often appeased with token gestures that were, according to British official P. F. M. Wogan, 'patently paternalistic and designed to secure their quiescence'.[51] Such examples included the tightening of alcohol provision during Ramadan.[52] The government also allowed them to 'blow off steam' through protests even if they had no intention of meeting their demands.[53] It is important to note that this limited tolerance of protest was less an indicator of openness but itself a means of repression through the diffusion of tension.

These superficial concessions marked a reassertion of Saudi-facilitated *makramāt* as opposed to a continued commitment to identification with the Bahraini people through democracy or political reform. Although the British had encouraged some sort of democratic system since 1963, they were also pursuing a policy that attempted to obviate its necessity. For

[45] R. M. Tesh, Bahrain National Assembly, 12 November 1974, FCO8/2180, The National Archives.
[46] R. M. Tesh, Bahrain: Internal, 9 April 1974, FCO8/2180, The National Archives.
[47] R. M. Tesh, Bahrain's First Parliament, 8 July 1974, FCO8/2180, The National Archives.
[48] R. M. Tesh, Bahrain: Internal, 23 June 1974, FCO8/2180, The National Archives.
[49] R. M. Tesh, Letter to Ivor Lucas, 6 May 1975, FCO8/2415, The National Archives.
[50] R. Kinchen, Dissolution of the Bahrain National Assembly, 29 August 1975, FCO8/2415, The National Archives.
[51] P. F. M. Wogan, Iran and the Gulf, 23 August 1982, FCO8/4332, The National Archives.
[52] US Embassy Manama, 'Bahraini Political Developments: Foreign Minister's Comments', 11 September 1975, Wikileaks, https://file.wikileaks.org/oc/2476/163374.pdf
[53] H. B. Walker, Bahrain: Annual Review for 1979, FCO8/3490, The National Archives.

the relatively oil-poor Bahrain, moving closer into Saudi's orbit meant the ability to sustain rentierism-as-policy. Without Saudi largesse, and the money from the economically shared but Saudi-controlled oilfield Abu Safah, it would have been challenging to implement these costly policies that deferred or depleted some demands for further political pluralisation. Unsurprisingly, many of the projects fuelled by oil rents were criticized for offering only a superficial and temporary fix to growing political problems. This theme of short-sightedness that had so far characterized imperial and Al Khalifa governance of Bahrain was reflected upon by Given, who stated: 'Circuses to supplement bread are a very old-fashioned remedy for discontent, but notoriously ineffective in the long run.'[54]

It is difficult to determine how effective these *makramāt* were, but at they reflected the political intentions of the regime. There was undoubtedly a clear link between the bestowing of this monetary largesse and Bahrain's abandonment of democracy. According to US cables, when Saudi Arabia 'voiced displeasure at Bahrain's parliamentary experiment',[55] the latter agreed 'to help finance certain economic reforms and development schemes'.[56] Instead, the government pursued these methods precisely to mitigate demands for democracy. By 1976 the British noted the 'sycophantic attitude of the local press towards the country [Saudi]',[57] and the 'stream of official visits'.[58] It was the 'proliferation of projects built with Saudi aid' that prompted one British official to say that Bahrain was becoming a 'Saudi pensioner'.[59]

Growing Saudi dominance over Bahrain was also evident in the arms trade. The oil boon allowed Saudi Arabia, described by 'GOB [Government of Bahrain] leaders' as 'the "backbone" to stability on the Arab side of the Gulf',[60] to finance or underwrite arms sales for Bahrain, including the procurement of rockets, or the retransfer of military equipment. While the procurement of arms for military purposes may be seen as a means of buttressing newfound sovereignty without British protection, the Saudis made it clear that they wished to buy the arms themselves, as they could then gain political influence by being the party to hand over the weapons to Bahrain. In a discussion on Bahrain's desire to purchase 2.75-inch rockets, one US cable reported in 1978 that, 'Mansouri [Foreign Ministry Undersecretary] said SAG [Saudi Arabian Government]

[54] E. F. Given, Bahrain 1976, 15 March 1977, FCO8/2873, The National Archives.
[55] US Embassy Manama, 'Bahraini Political Developments: Foreign'. [56] Ibid.
[57] Given, Bahrain 1976, 15 March 1977. [58] Ibid. [59] Ibid.
[60] US Embassy Manama, 'Bahrain's Foreign Policy', 9 February 1975, Wikileaks, https://search.wikileaks.org/plusd/cables/1975MANAMA00163_b.html

would prefer to purchase the rockets themselves since SAG is footing the bill. This was so SAG could have the benefit of some political leverage over GOB'.[61] Indeed, even Bahrain's defence purchases were kept on a tight Saudi leash. As Roger Tomkys noted about the BDF's decision to buy British-made military Hawk jets: 'The contracts may still come as the Amir wishes, but Saudi Arabia holds the purse strings tight and will continue to have the real say.'[62] In the end, the Hawk deal fell through due to Saudi influence. Instead, the Saudis handed down their 'superseded F5s', no doubt because they did not want Bahrain to have superior equipment. Unsurprisingly, this lack of Independence, along with the inevitable consequences of a lack of strategic military depth, meant that Bahrain 'looked to Saudi Arabia, and particularly the Saudi Air Force, to protect it against any overspill from the [Iran/Iraq] war'.[63] Indeed, not only was Bahrain dependent on Saudi for superior protection, the Saudis could now justify their need to protect Bahrain on account of their purposefully inferior arsenal of weaponry.

For their part, the British believed post-Independence that positive economic performance led to less political agitation. While Saudi funding cannot be ignored regarding its effect on potentially placating the population, given the existence of ongoing economically rooted grievances, the main issue was that the distribution of these resources was uneven, discriminatory and plagued by corruption. In many cases, redistribution just increased the Al Khalifa monopolization of land and commerce, a problem that was growing more acute through the 1970s and 1980s.[64] As a result, underlying grievances, such as discrimination or political representation, were not addressed. The oil price dip in the 1990s exposed this, forcing spending cuts and reducing the government's ability to fight unrest and the formation of opposition with a carrot-only policy.[65] Even during times of economic difficulty, the growth of the Gulf Co-operation Council (GCC) and its shared security policy entrenched the habit of *makramāt* and blatant paternalism as a substitute for inclusive politics. As a seemingly instinctive reaction to the 1990s Intifada in Bahrain, Saudi Arabia raised Bahrain's allocated income from the Abu Safah oilfield from 70,000 barrels a day to

[61] US Embassy Riyadh, 'Bahrain's Arms Requests', 1 March 1978, Wikileaks, https://search.wikileaks.org/plusd/cables/1978JIDDA01545_d.html
[62] W. R. Tomkys, Farewell to Bahrain, 1984, FOIA Request from FCO.
[63] F. S. E. Trew, Bahrain: Annual Review 1984, FOIA Request from FCO.
[64] E. F. Given, Prospects for Bahrain, 29 October 1976, FCO8/2643, The National Archives.
[65] *The Economist*, 'Morning and Questioning, in Bahrain', 13 March 1999, issue 8110, p. 86.

100,000. As the unrest showed no sign of abating, Saudi reportedly gave Bahrain the full allocation of 140,000 barrels.[66] In addition to this, 'Saudi Arabia, Kuwait and the United Arab Emirates reportedly resumed annual subsidies of $50 million each to Bahrain's rulers[67] following the onset of the political unrest at the end of 1994'.[68]

This policy of 'ignoring the protests while trying to improve standards of living'[69] had a questionable impact upon unrest, and reflected the Gulf monarchies' fear of democratic empowerment. Following the outbreak of the unrest in 2011, the ruling family offered 1,000 dinars to every family in March the same year, shortly after the outbreak of protests.[70] Concerned that Bahrain's instability might be a bellwether for their own autocratic regimes, the Gulf Cooperation Council (GCC) offered a $21 billion aid package ('Marshall Plan') to Bahrain.[71] Given the salience of housing grievances, $5.56 billion of this was earmarked for the building of 47,000–57,000 houses.[72] Although this general policy of patronage has continued to the present day, it has not been enough, especially when the ideological inclinations of protesters have constantly moved beyond simple demands for improved living standards. Not only does the reliance of the Al Khalifa on traditional *makramāt* and patronage highlight the deficit of democracy in Bahrain but also the unwillingness to rectify it. Indeed, as Al Naqeeb noted: 'the effective monopoly of the sources of power and wealth which the ruling elites practise, creates "mobility closures" in society which will lead, with the passage of time, to increasing friction between social classes and ranks'.[73] One could argue that this point was reached some time ago and, as a consequence, the Al Khalifa have very little political capital remaining with which to affect change using welfare-based incentives. While rentierism-based theories are

[66] Human Rights Watch, *Routine Abuse, Routine Denial, Civil Rights and the Political Crisis in Bahrain*, 1997.

[67] It is interesting that unrest in Bahrain often results in the GCC pouring money into Bahrain, via the rulers. It would be interesting, yet difficult given the ruling family's secretive accounts, to see how such money was distributed, or found its way into the pockets of elites. Rampant corruption could make unrest in Bahrain a lucrative business.

[68] Cited in Human Rights Watch, *Routine Abuse*.

[69] *The Economist*, 'Mourning and Questioning'.

[70] T. Fuller, 'Bahrain's Promised Spending Fails to Quell Dissident', *New York Times*, 6 March 2011, www.nytimes.com/2011/03/07/world/middleeast/07bahrain.html?_r=0

[71] U. Laessing, 'Gulf States Launch $20 Billion Fund for Oman and Bahrain', Reuters, 10 March 2011, www.reuters.com/article/2011/03/10/us-gulf-fund-idUSTRE7294B120110310

[72] Trade Arabia, 'Bahrain to Build $5.59bn Housing Units', 19 September 2012, www.tradearabia.com/news/CONS_222196.html

[73] K. H. Al Naqeeb, *Society and State in the Gulf and Arab Peninsula*, London, Routledge, 1990, p. 125.

simply capturing a facet of strategies designed to stave off unrest, it is important to note that the distribution of wealth initially favoured maintaining peace within the ruling family. The redistribution of rents in Bahrain has, at times, mitigated aspects of political unrest but also been a prime source of instability and discontent. One must also consider that unrest has, in some ways, been a boon for members of the ruling class. Increased moneys from Saudi and the GCC, ostensibly to alleviate social unrest through the funding of social welfare programmes, inevitably benefits members of the ruling elite. Perversely, they seek to benefit from these cash injections necessitated by domestic unrest. Whether such benefits can lead to the purposeful exacerbation of such tensions is not clear, although not unlikely.

Sanctioning and the Withdrawing of 'Privilege'

> My third piece of advice is in regard to rewards and punishments, the two principal functions of a ruler.[74]

Just as state benefits have been framed as a benevolent form of gratuity in exchange for loyalty, the growth of a reward and punish culture among Bahrain's institutions has meant that failure to be loyal has prompted a withdrawal of these 'privileges'. The importance of loyalty as a particularistic form of repression is evident in the statements of the government and in particular the Al Khalifa, who continuously emphasize the importance of 'loyal citizens'.[75] During the 2011 Uprising, the Sayegh family set up a campaign and encouraged people to come and pledge their loyalty to the king by signing an allegiance oath. Bahrainis were invited to the National Stadium to sign the pledge. Many feared that if they did not, there would be recriminations. These fears were underlined by the fact that many of the signatures would be engraved on a 'sword of allegiance', which would then be presented to the king.[76]

Tactics of demonstrating loyalty were evident as early as the 1920s. During an outbreak of Al Khalifa oppression of Bahrain subjects, Manama residents were 'coerced' by various loyal parties into signing a

[74] Col. S.G. Knox, Appendix IV to Report on Bahrain Reforms, 26 May 1923, in P. Tuson and E. Quick (eds), *Records of Bahrain 1820–1960*, vol. 3, Slough, Archive Editions, 1993, p.791.

[75] J. Gengler, 'Bahrain's Sunni Awakening', *Middle East Research and Information Project (MERIP)*, 17 January 2012, www.merip.org/mero/mero0117122012.

[76] Bahrain News Agency, 'Shaikh Nasser to launch the Youth Sword and Patronise the Allegiance Pledge Signing', 12 April 2011, www.bna.bh/portal/en/news/452594?date=2011-04-15

pledge showing their approval of Shaykh ʿIsa Al Khalifa to the British.[77] From the British perspective, Shaykh ʿIsa was attempting to gain legitimacy for his reforms and opposition to British rule, yet this was largely against the interests of the *baḥārna*, who were generally complaining of oppression. Similarly, in the 1920s, members of the *baḥārna* co-opted into various positions of low-level power by their feudal chiefs tried to force Bahrainis to sign these documents, at least to give the impression that they were content.[78] At other times, such as in 1939, when members of the *baḥrānī* community in Bahrain were pushing for political representation, Charles Belgrave used petitions signed by non-Manama *baḥārna* communities to underscore that the *baḥārna* were content with the status quo.[79]

While such petitions were eventually forbidden under government proclamations in the first half of the twentieth century, their re-emergence in the 1990s has highlighted a reassertion of tribal politics, where the ruling family, and not the British, became the go-to mediator for political demands. In one instance, Rashid bin ʿIsa Al Khalifa, the head of the General Organization for Youth and Sports, reportedly forced Shiʿa clubs based in Sanabis and Diraz to sign loyalty pledges to the Amir, in a move designed to humiliate them.[80] Reflecting an ingrained sense of hostility by the ruling class towards the Shiʿa underclass, Shaykh Rashid bin ʿIsa Al Khalifa was reported to have said about the eventual Shiʿa acquiescence to the petitions: 'You see, they came like dogs'.[81] Thus petitions have served different purposes when deployed by the regime. Historically they were often used by the ruling family to attempt to convince the British that the *baḥārna* supported the status quo. They can also be designed to humiliate, functioning as a reassertion of ruling hegemony designed to remind the Shiʿa of extant power relations. In the 2011 Uprising they were used as a tool of intimidation: with those not signing them leaving themselves open to accusations of disloyalty and privilege removal.

Over the years, and due to the changing nature of the modern state, withdrawal of privilege has taken the form of employment deprivation and other means of lowering life chances of those perceived as oppositional forces. This has resulted in at times explicit but other times inadvertent sectarianization of repression. During the 1990s Intifada,

[77] A. P. Trevor, Letter to Mr. Denys de S. Bray, Tyranny of Shaikh of Bahrein and His Family over Bahrein Subjects, 13 January 1922, in P. Tuson and E. Quick (eds), *Records of Bahrain 1820–1960*, vol. 3, Slough, Archive Editions, 1993, p. 685.

[78] Knox, 'Report on Bahrain Reforms', p. 779.

[79] Belgrave, 18 January 1939, p. 165.

[80] Human Rights Watch, *Routine Abuse.*

[81] Ibid.

collective punishment in the form of withdrawing state utilities was a form of repression enabled by Bahrain's inherently sectarian topography. This topography was the result of Sunni urban in Manama and Muharraq being prioritized in development over the more historically rural *baḥrānī* areas. As part of this embedded logic of settler–tribal privilege, mostly *baḥārna* villages like Jidd Hafs and Bilad al-Qadim became poor satellites of Manama, lacking both modern housing and adequate public services. Indeed, this urban manipulation decreased the ability of the Shiʿa underclass to integrate into the socio-economic fabric of modern Bahrain, which in turn has led to a culture of marginality, underdevelopment and political/religious militancy whose capacity for mobilization draws on the historical memory of old rural and agricultural communities.[82] Unsurprisingly, this government neglect has resulted in the ghettoization of some Shiʿi villages, a feature which facilitated certain forms of communal/collective punishment. For example:

> By the fall of 1997, the security services started punishing communities that provided material and moral support to the protesters. Supplies of electricity and water were periodically shut off to predominantly Shi'i residential districts. Mysterious fires destroyed the homes and businesses of suspected dissidents. The military commander in charge of the National University abruptly cancelled mid-year examinations, disrupting students' progress toward their degrees.[83]

Sectarian Quadrillage

Foucault described quadrillage as the policing of a virtual or physical space that had been portioned meticulously in order to facilitate control.[84] The parsing of the population into disparate, and thus containable units, is a system of discrimination implemented both implicitly and explicitly. This quadrillage facilitates repression, and has been embedded in Bahrain's town planning. For example, in a somewhat contradictory but telling communique called the 'Shiʿa of Bahrain', Simon Collis, the Second Secretary in Bahrain from 1981 to 1984, noted that 'There is no discrimination against the Shiʿa in the allocation of government housing, loans or land sales by the Ministry of Housing'.[85] However, in the same paragraph Collis wrote that the knock-on effect of this was

[82] N. Fuccaro, *Histories of City and State in the Persian Gulf: Manama since 1800*, Cambridge, Cambridge University Press, 2009, p. 224.

[83] F. H. Lawson, 'Repertoires of Contention in Contemporary Bahrain', in Q. Wiktorowicz (ed.) *Islamic Activism: A Social Movement Theory Approach*, Bloomington, Indiana University Press, 2004, p. 104.

[84] M. Foucault 1975, cited in L. Lambert (ed.), *The Funambulist Pamphlets Volume 02: Foucault*, Brooklyn, NY, Punctum Books, 2013, p. 50.

[85] S. Collis, 'The Shiʿa in Bahrain', Bahrain Internal Political, 1984, FCO8/5442, The National Archives.

institutional discrimination in other sectors: 'Given the population structure the Shiʿa, therefore, occupy the majority of new Government housing, except in Isa Town where a semi-official system of land and housing grants to BDF officers and senior government officials favours the Sunni, who are over-represented in these positions.'[86] Collis alludes to conscious government efforts to implement the social engineering of religious demographics, especially in Manama. He noted that government housing schemes had attempted to mix the religious communities, especially in Manama,[87] in order to purposefully dilute Shiʿa political influence. Collis's allusion to displacing Shiʿa communities in Manama was also due in part to the value of land. 'The inner-city Shiʿa quarters of Manama are prime targets for redevelopment for political reasons as well as economic and social in the neutral sense.'[88] Indeed, the Shia were seen as both a threat to redevelopment in the sense that they might not so easily subscribe to the government's visions of neoliberal redevelopment but also as undeserving of owning potentially valuable tracts of real estate. In addition Collis stated that the layout of each new town was done according to an over-arching sectarian logic. Each new town project built by the government was equipped with an exactly equal number of Sunni and Shiʿa mosques sited in pairs. Of each pair, the Sunni mosques were reputed to be the further from Mecca 'to prevent the Shiʿa from praying over [the Sunnis], as one prays over the dead' according to a popular Sunni belief.[89] While housing is a crucial *makramāt* distributed by the ruling elite, it is done according to the quadrillagial logic of limiting subversive, and especially Shiʿa, influence. Although one may applaud this attempt to establish parity among religious communities through the building of an equal number of mosques, clearly the motivation in Bahrain was to enforce Sunni hegemony over the majority Shia population.

From Jobs to Scholarships: Employment and Education Deprivation

As Bahrain industrialized, those who were formerly involved in more subsistence forms of income-generation such as farming or fishing became reliant on salaried labour. Tilly argued that these significant changes in an industrializing nation affect 'the interests and the organisation of various contenders for power, and thereby affected their mobilisation and collective action'.[90] In Bahrain, these changes created a greater dependency of the new industrial classes on the benevolence of

[86] Ibid. [87] Ibid. [88] Ibid. [89] Ibid. [90] Tilly, *From Mobilization*, p. 11.

the tribal overlords, who maintained extensive influence on the offices and industries of state. In addition, the formalization of the tribal ownership of the means of production under the British meant a blurring of boundaries between the role of Bahraini citizen and Bahraini wage labourer. As a consequence of this assimilation of existing powerholders into the government and commercial apparatus, mass employment deprivation has become a more noticeable tactic during times of political unrest, especially when Shiʿi employees dominate certain professions.

The tactic of employment deprivation was evident as early as the 1950s, during the emergence of salaried labour working in expanding industries. In 1956, the government threatened to cut the salaries of employees who did not go to work during strikes organized by the Higher Education Committee, a political group consisting of Bahrainis from all walks of life demanding political change.[91] In June 1974, 113 employees of Aluminium Bahrain (ALBA) were dismissed after the Ministry of Interior declared the strikes that they were undertaking were illegal.[92] While one may believe such a tactic simply reflects the impact of autocratic governance monopolizing its influence within the public sector, such dismissals also occurred in the private sector. In some cases, core members of the ruling family have used their prerogative to ensure that such dismissals have occurred. In one instance, the American construction firm, Brown and Root, and its 'local civilian labour contractor... were allowed to by-pass the Labour Ministry, involve the Prime Minister, and lay off, with doubtful legality a number of labourers' who were considered unruly.[93] In this case, we see corruption and cronyism influencing potentially extra-legal repressive choices.

This interference by the prime minister came at a time when the Amir's Privy income was theoretically limited to six million dinars per year, with two million being invested for the Amir's family. With the ostensible diminution of Privy Purse payments, it is perhaps unsurprising that members of the ruling family were attempting to secure wealth through their encroachment in the business world. A frequent complaint was that some members of the ruling family, through their business practices, were acquiring larger stakes in Bahrain's commercial ventures, industry, and trade. This ability was enabled both by their hegemonic position but also the fact that oil had allowed them to accrue significant purchasing power. As Rob Franklin notes: 'The ruling family and its allies [were] now well integrated into the administrative machinery, and [were] in a particularly good position to exploit the growth of the real

[91] Office Notice, 29 October 1956, FO371/120548, The National Archives.
[92] Tesh, Bahrain's First Parliament. [93] Tesh, Bahrain: Internal, 23 June 1974.

estate market'.[94] This was by no means ubiquitous, but Given noted in 1977 an 'increasing tendency' among some shaykhs and merchants to 'steer lucrative contracts in the direction of companies in which they have shares'.[95] As a consequence, this personal stake in Bahrain's commercial activities has led to a sort of ethno-tribal fascism, in which a conservative attitude towards dissent is a natural tendency when one's interests are so firmly embedded to the commercial success of state and non-state enterprises.

The tactic of removing people from their jobs became more acute in the 1990s when people were dismissed simply for making political demands – as opposed to engaging in strikes. Rather than indicate a reassertion of the arbitrary state, this practice highlighted a reassertion of *makramāt* in exchange for loyalty in the provision of jobs and services. In 1995, several of the sponsors of a popular petition demanding the reinstating of the 1973 National Assembly were arrested, including Shaykh 'Abd al-Amir al-Jamri and 'Abd al-Wahab Husayn 'Ali. Others faced non-custodial punishments. For example, Sa'id 'Abd Allah 'Asbul was dismissed from his job at the Ministry of Works and Electricity after resisting pressure by the authorities to take his name off the petition.[96] At the end of March 1995, twenty professional women and two hundred others signed a petition and handed it to the Amir. Although its requests were reasonable, calling for the Amir to initiate a national dialogue, and 'to restore democratic rights and to ensure that the rights of those held in custody are respected ... a number of them were threatened with dismissal from their jobs if they failed to withdraw their names from the petition and to "apologise" for their action'.[97] At least two of them, 'Aziza al-Bassam and Hasa al-Khumayri, were dismissed[98] On April 1995 seven teachers[99] and several of their pupils were arrested at Madinat 'Isa Secondary School for Girls, and then dismissed from their jobs, reportedly when the authorities discovered that a demonstration was to be held at a school.[100] Others, such as Sa'id al-Asbul, were dismissed from their work for being involved in the petition campaign, and also blacklisted from obtaining other work following government intervention.[101]

[94] R. Franklin, 'Migrant Labour and the Politics of Development in Bahrain', *Middle East Report 132*, www.merip.org/mer/mer132/migrant-labor-politics-development- bahrain?ip_login_no_cache=a7ae599f50b951b5145fca37baa546b4#_12_

[95] E. F. Given, *Annual Review 1997*, FCO8/3091, The National Archives.

[96] Amnesty International, *Bahrain: A Human Rights Crisis*, 1 September 1995, www.refworld.org/docid/3ae6a9984.html

[97] Ibid. [98] Ibid.

[99] Fatima 'Abd Allah Abu Idris, Khatun Ahmad Khalaf, Samira 'Abd 'Ali Saif, Sawsan Ahmad Mansur al-Halwachi, Fathiyya al-Saffar, Wadad Shubbar and Muna Hussain.

[100] Amnesty International, *Bahrain: A Human Rights Crisis*, p. 15. [101] Ibid., p. 10.

As a matter of policy, the unrest in the 1990s prompted measures to securitize the Shiʿa problem, enforcing discrimination through institutional changes. Most notably, the progressive technocrat ʻAli Fakhro was replaced as Minister of Education by General ʿAbd al-Aziz al-Fadhil, who had been previously in charge of training in the Bahrain Defence Force (BDF). Soon, al-Fadhil, along with another former BDF Officer, Colonel Muhammad Jasim al-Ghattam, replaced Dr Ibrahim al-Hashmi as president of Bahrain University. After this change, increased discrimination against Shiʿa applications, as well as the purging of Shiʿa from senior positions was documented by Human Rights Watch.[102] Unconfined to the educational sector, Human Rights Watch noted numerous unconfirmed reports of new hiring and firing policies designed to reduce the number of Shiʿa in ministries and state companies formerly considered to be Shiʿa employment redoubts, such as the Ministry of Electricity and Public Works and BATELCO, the state telecommunications company'.[103]

While the documentation of such layoffs has improved since the 1990s, the Uprising in 2011 saw, on an unprecedented scale, the use of mass layoffs to punish those who had engaged in strikes that were actually 'within the permissible bounds of the law'.[104] The Bahrain Independent Commission of Inquiry (BICI) report noted that 'during the events of February/March 2011, 2,075 public sector employees and 2,464 private sector employees were dismissed'.[105] According to the International Trade Union Confederation (ITUC), many of those dismissed were prominent trade union leaders, whose firing diminished the organizational capacity of the labour movement.[106] While the government claimed a year after the dismissals to have reinstated the majority of those who had lost jobs, in 2013, two years after the firings, the General Federation of Bahrain Trade Unions (GFBTU) claimed that 657 workers still had not been reinstated.[107] There is little doubt that the purpose of the lay-offs was to intimidate those engaging in strikes and to reassert the premise that the life chances and livelihoods of civilians were dependent

[102] Human Rights Watch, *Routine Abuse.* [103] Ibid.
[104] M. C. Bassiouni, N. Rodley, B. Al-Awadhi, P. Kirsch, and M. H. Arsanjani, *Report of the Bahrain Independent Commission of Inquiry [BICI Report]*, 23 November 2011, BICI, Manama, p. 353, www.bici.org.bh/BICIreportEN.pdf
[105] Ibid., p. 420.
[106] International Trade Union Confederation [ITUC], *Countries at Risk: Violations of Trade Union Rights*, 2013, p. 35.
[107] Ibid.

on loyalty to the Al Khalifa-dominated government. A former employee from BAPCO described his experience during the mass layoffs:

> On 13th March we were asked to ring all our employees who had been absent from work that day to urge them to come into work the following day. I vividly remember calling one of our employees who lived in one of the Shiʿa villages off Budayia Road and hearing him say, 'how can I leave my family, there are armed police and army people kicking in doors and ransacking houses in the village, they are taking people from their homes, I can't leave my family alone!' The following day, GCC Forces swept over the causeway to assist the Bahrain Government to suppress the protests. A month or so later, I received a request to accompany one of our Bahraini employees to an interview with our Human Resources Dept. I was surprised and shocked when he was shown photographs of himself at one of the peaceful protests. When he was asked what he was shouting at the protest, he replied, 'No Sunni, no Shiʿa, just Bahraini.' He was sacked about three weeks later after over 30 years of loyal service to the company; He had just six months to go before retirement. Over the coming days over 30 more of our divisional employees were sacked or suspended for attendance at the protests or for 'unauthorised absence'. Company-wide, over 290 employees were sacked for similar 'offences'. They were almost exclusively Shiʿa employees and included many well respected and experienced people.

Although the strikes were legal, a recourse to extra-legal means of punishment is not new in Bahrain. The policy of repress first and ask questions later has characterized authority responses to political unrest and has been a function of Bahraini political repression since at least the 1950s. As demonstrated, legal protections are relatively meaningless in curbing the nature of this form of repression as the state subverts them when it deems it necessary to protect its interests.

Targeting Students

In addition to firing those in state-run companies and requiring private companies to fire those accused of 'absenteeism', the government has also targeted the country's youth. Students, an integral part of Bahrain's protest movements across the decades, have consistently been the object of sanctions. This tactic emerged with the advent of public education in Bahrain. In the 1920s and 1930s, some children of the ruling family and wealthier merchants were sent for education in places ranging from Beirut to Brighton. This policy eventually extended to a broader government strategy of providing scholarships to promising students to study abroad. It was anticipated that these students would be grateful to the state for their opportunity, and return in order to help modernize Bahrain. However, these scholarships were contingent on the continued political acquiescence of those students. As early as 1956, the Bahrain

Government were reported to have cancelled the tuition fees of a critical Bahraini student studying law in London.[108] Such decisions were not without high-level interference. In the 1960s and 1970s, the conservative nature of the prime minister became more apparent, especially where it concerned Bahraini students. Khalifa bin Salman was riled by Kuwait's 'softness' towards radicals living there, the majority of whom were Bahraini nationals studying at Kuwait University[109] – so much so, that in 1974 the Bahraini Government pressured Kuwait to expel a Bahraini leftist from university in Kuwait.

The year 2011 marked a deepening of this tactic of targeting students. In order to intimidate and raise the costs for students taking part or planning to take part in the protests, the government ordered the expulsion of hundreds of students from higher-education institutions across the country, taking the repression of students to an unprecedented level. Between March and June of 2011, 427 students were expelled from the University of Bahrain, while another 54 were expelled from Bahrain Polytechnic.[110] Many of those expelled found it hard to obtain work or study in universities in the region as a result of being expelled. In line with the idea of loyalty in exchange for *makramāt*, the University of Bahrain later required that all students sign a loyalty pledge to the king and the Kingdom of Bahrain. The terms of the pledge stated that those 'who do not sign give up their right to university study, and those who break the pledge can be expelled'.[111] While many students were reinstated, those facing criminal charges were not. The BICI report found too that most students had been expelled as a result of investigations that relied on 'hearsay and circumstantial evidence'.[112] In many cases, the only evidence was photographs of the students attending peaceful demonstrations.[113] Also, many students had their scholarships withdrawn as a sanction for engaging in pro-democracy protests. By 31 March 2011, 97 students had had their scholarships revoked.[114] Although the government eventually reinstated these scholarships with retroactive pay, the message was clear – continue to engage in protest and face consequences.

The unrest also prompted a re-evaluation of how the government and companies distributed scholarships. Employees at the Bahrain Petroleum

[108] Higher Executive Committee, 29 March 1955, Higher Executive Committee, 29 March 1955, in A. Burdett (ed.), *Records of Bahrain 1820–1960,* vol. 7, Slough, Archive Editions, 1993, p. 150.

[109] R. A. Stein, Security on Gulf and Bahrain, US Embassy Manama, 30 April 1973, www.wikileaks.org/plusd/cables/1973MANAMA00248_b.html

[110] *BICI Report*, p. 356. [111] Ibid. [112] Ibid., p. 364. [113] Ibid.

[114] Ibid., p. 406.

Company (BAPCO) stated that, previously, technical experts had administered the scholarship exams, conducted interviews and selected those students deemed the most academically gifted. However, following 2011, the delegation of the often non-Bahrain technical experts to select scholarship applicants was escalated to management. Since then, one employee reported that many of those receiving scholarships were now from the 'Sunni side of the street'. Scholarships in technical jobs, which were traditionally a means for the Shiʿa community to gain skilled employment, were now being reduced based on the need to appease the ruler's support base. More so than before, the 2011 Uprising prompted a sectarianization of scholarship awards.

Education staff seen as giving any form of succour to the opposition were also not immune from state repression. Dr Mike Diboll, a former instructor at Bahrain Polytechnic, was sacked due to his online commentary on the Uprising. He personally attributed this repression to the sidelining of a so-called reformist cadre under the Crown Prince, Shaikh Salman bin Hamad Al Khalifa. Specifically, Diboll argued that these hardline policies were due to the 'influence of a cabal of hardliners, including the Prime Minister, and the brothers Khalid bin Ahmed Al Khalifa, the Royal Court Minister and Khalifa bin Ahmed Al Khalifa the Commander-in-Chief of the Bahrain Defence Force (also referred to as the Khawalid).[115] However, this is only part of the reason. During times of political dissent, the ascendency, or at least the influence, of hardliners in Bahrain should be assumed as a matter of course. Issues of security, especially since Independence, have tended to fall under the influence of the prime minister, or the general anti-reform cadre that currently includes the Khawalid. The problem with attributing repressive shifts to changing influence within the ruling family seems to be descriptive rather than explanatory, as draconian responses to unrest have always been the rule, rather than the exception, in Bahrain's history. Hardliners tend to take control when political expedience demands it.

The politics of loyalty in exchange for privilege as a method to punish or retaliate against those perceived as attempting to tarnish Bahrain's reputation was evident ahead of the 2014 general election. Unconfirmed governmental sources announced that only those who could prove that they had voted would be entitled to certain provisions and jobs.[116] As a

[115] M. Diboll, 'Written Evidence from Dr. Mike Diboll', Parliamentary Foreign Affairs Committee on the UK's Relationship with Saudi Arabia and Bahrain, 12 November 2012', www.publications.parliament.uk/pa/cm201314/cmselect/cmfaff/88/88vw25.htm

[116] E. Dickinson, 'Bahrain's Elections and the Opposition', Middle East Institute, 23 December 2014, www.mei.edu/content/article/bahrains-elections-and-opposition

result, some people felt intimidated into voting,[117] an act which, at the time, was considered one of support for the government, who were attempting to affirm their democratic legitimacy to the outside world by flaunting high voter turnout numbers. Indeed, the scale of the tactic in the recent Uprising marks a new era of state reach into both public and private affairs, highlighting further the ability of the government to withdraw what they perceive as citizen 'privileges' (e.g. jobs), as opposed to rights. The fact that democratic engagement directly relates to one's life chances certainly reflects the punitive nature of the reform process in Bahrain, one that punishes even the choice not to participate. The expansion of the role of the state, whether through the provision of education, or voting, has opened up new 'field controls' and possibilities for repression, yet

Insulation

Selective Recruitment and 'Docile Labour'

While firing those deemed disloyal is a reactive strategy, it is generally preferable to avoid such measures. Indeed, the government has sought to obviate the need for mass layoffs through the judicious selection of what one official once described as 'docile labour' in the first place. Docile Labour is defined as those employees less likely to be politically active or involved in unionization. Bahrain's rapid industrialization outstripped the ability of the country to provide appropriate local labour. As such, migrant workers from abroad have been in demand since the 1960s. While migrant labourers may be considered more docile simply because their existence in a given polity is contingent on their employment, the Bahrain government have sought to ensure that incoming labour is more likely to be politically acquiescent. For example, as Robert Tesh wrote in 1972: 'Palestinians, Iraqis, Syrians and Egyptians have not been politically welcome'.[118] The conception here was that Arabs from those countries were more hostile to the Gulf monarchies' relationship with imperial powers. Teachers, in particular, tasked with moulding the minds of impressionable children, were subject to screening.

Tactics of insulating the labour force from threatening ideologies have been dynamic, temporally dependent on emergent threats, as well as the

[117] The National Democratic Institute for International Affairs, 'Bahrain's October 24 and 31, 2002 Legislative Elections', 2002, www.ndi.org/files/2392_bh_electionsreport_engpdf_09252008.pdf

[118] R. M. Tesh, Bahrain: Annual Review for 1972, FCO8/1974, The National Archives.

relatively short-term outlook of Bahrain's protectors. Arab nationalism and its perceived roots in revolutionary Arab states such as Egypt and Syria turned Bahrain, a traditional monarchy, closer to Saudi Arabia. In the 1960s, one British official explained the reasons for this. 'It is not surprising at a time when the Gulf states are increasingly feeling the draught of Arab nationalism that Bahrain should be turning to Saudi Arabia in whose friendship she has, in any case, such a stake.'[119] However, this was also due to British Cold-War paranoia. They had previously dedicated significant effort to rooting out left-wing sympathizers and nationalists. When workers were accepted from perceived problem countries (i.e. Egypt, Syria, Palestine), consideration was also measured. For example, while Egyptians were generally eschewed, they were 'cautiously' accepted into some 'higher' level positions.[120] The Iranian Revolution and the Iran–Iraq war, which heightened political sensitivities in Bahrain at a time of less overt Arab nationalism, meant employment policy in the security forces focused more on perceived loyalty of sect and tribe, as opposed to Arab allegiance. As such, the relative moratorium on the recruitment of Syrians, Iraqis and Yemenis into the security services ended from the 1980s.

While the employment of other Arabs has long been sensitive for reasons ranging from orientalist conceptions of Arab capabilities to reasons of political sensitivity, the employment of perceived docile labour from abroad, in particular South Asia, has been encouraged. The Indian subcontinent was, and still is, seen as a key source of 'docile' labour and management. However, this was certainly the case during the 1970s. In 1974, it was suggested that the labour force would have to be increased by 50 per cent with workers from 'India, Pakistan and elsewhere'[121] – amounting to around 30,000 people.[122]

As well as supplying the workforce in a small but rapidly modernizing state, the process of altering the makeup of the foreign labour force has been a deliberate strategy in attempting to ensure labour docility. As Abdulhadi Khalaf notes, the government has sought to fragment the 'working class along ethnic, lingual and religious divides',[123] weakening their collective bargaining power. At times, certain officials have referred

[119] M. Joyce, 'Ruling Shaikhs and Her Majesty's Government 1960–1969', London and Portland, OR, Frank Crass, 2003, p. 63.
[120] Ibid.
[121] R. M. Tesh, Annual Review for the Year 1974, FCO8/2414, The National Archives.
[122] R. M. Tesh, Internal Political 1974, 17 December 1974, FCO8/2180, The National Archives.
[123] A. Khalaf, 'Labor Movements in Bahrain', Middle East Research and Information Projects Report, no. 132, 1985, pp. 24–9.

to foreign labour as a 'buffer' that can be disposed of during times of political instability. In 1984, British Ambassador Roger Tomkys wrote that rising unemployment would disproportionately impact the Shiʿa, but 'before that stage is reached, there is a comfortable cushion of expatriate labour that could be dispensed with'.[124]

Such labour policies have prompted tensions during times of high unemployment of Bahrainis. Despite apparent attempts to Bahrainiize the workforce, the use of foreign, docile labour continued to increase in many sectors. In 2001, the number of non-Bahrainis in the workforce was 181,220,[125] while in 2015 the figure jumped to 551,859.[126] However, as Franklin noted, development policies, especially throughout the 1970s and 1980s, 'served the interests of the ruling elite'.[127] However, 'at the same time, this sort of dependent development has substantially added to the list of problems the society must deal with'.[128] The calculated assumption is that the risk of creating unrest through unpopular hiring policies is preferable to further hindering the use of foreign labour in Bahrain, which both strengthens and furthers the political and material interests of the regime.

Shiʿa Containment through Labour Restrictions

For some time, the British development of the security services seemed inherently focused on eliminating any potential leftist or socialist tendencies, but the ruling family's concerns were somewhat different. Independence brought with it the refocusing of threat perceptions, and an employee's sect became an important consideration. British officials in the 1980s started to document the number of Shiʿa employees in specific industries. In addition to acknowledging the general discrimination of Shiʿa in Bahrain, especially in sensitive ministries such as the Ministries of Defence, Justice, Foreign Affairs and the Land Registry, they were mindful of the employment of *baḥārna* in 'strategically important sectors', a fact which had prompted 'officially inspired' efforts to

[124] R. Tomkys, Internal Political Situation Bahrain 1984, FCO8/5442, The National Archives.

[125] Bahrain Central Informatics Organization, Labour Force by Nationality and Sex in Census Years – (1959, 1965, 1971, 1981, 1991, 2001), www.cio.gov.bh/cio_ara/English/Publications/Statistical%20Abstract/ABS2009/CH11/1.pdf

[126] Bahrain Labour Market Indicators, Labour Market Regulatory Authority, Q2, 2015, http://blmi.lmra.bh/2015/06/mi_dashboard.xml

[127] R. Franklin, 'Migrant Labour and the Politics of Development in Bahrain', *Middle East Report 132*, www.merip.org/mer/mer132/migrant-labor-politics- development-bahrain?ip_login_no_cache=a7ae599f50b951b5145fca37baa546b4#_12_

[128] Ibid.

Table 3.1 *Shiʿa employment in the technical sector*

	Company Name	Total Workforce	Percent Shiʿa
BATELCO	Bahrain Telecommunications	1,800	87
BANOCO	Bahrain National Oil Company	4,500	80
ALBA	Aluminium Bahrain	2,000	79
BSED	Bahrain Electricity	1,900	78

'control their numbers'.[129] Simon Collis documented several statistics about Shiʿa employment in Bahrain that revealed their preponderance in the technical sector.

In 1997, Bahry noted that although some ministries had a Shiʿi labourer workforce of up to 80 per cent, these were all areas deemed 'non-sensitive', and certainly did not include the military.[130] The failure to secure funding for modernization projects in sectors such as heavy industry also shrank opportunities for employment, generating protest.[131] Meanwhile, the Shiʿa continued to face alienation. As one merchant told the Washington Post, 'We are totally kept out of all the major ministries... If you switch on the TV, there is not a single program that refers to us, our history, our folklore, our geography. We are nothing.'[132] The ITUC has documented that Bahraini Shiʿa face further discrimination in the workplace, a problem compounded following the 2011 Uprising.

> With growing regularity, jobs are now being denied to Shiʿa. Some companies, such as Gulf Air, have actually fired Bahraini workers, targeting Shiʿa specifically, under the pretext of restructuring. This was done unilaterally and without prior consultation with the GFBTU. At the same time, the companies are hiring non-Bahrainis and Sunnis with lesser qualifications and announcing new job vacancies. Furthermore, the Government has allegedly pressured many contractors to fire qualified Shiʿa workers by denying them tenders. These violations are continuous and recurrent, and the labour legislation fails to protect workers[133]

Again, the criminalization of the country's Shiʿa, and the fact they form most of Bahrain's disgruntled opposition, has led to a form of policy that

[129] S. Collis, Internal Political 1984, FCO8/5442, The National Archives.
[130] L. Bahry, 'The Opposition in Bahrain: A Bellwether for the Gulf', *Middle East Policy*, vol. 5, no. 2, 1997 p. 51.
[131] F. H. Lawson, 'Repertoires of Contention in Contemporary Bahrain', in Q. Wiktorowicz (ed.), *Islamic Activism: A Social Movement Theory Approach*, Bloomington, IN, Indiana University Press, 2004, p. 92.
[132] Ibid, p. 91.
[133] International Trade Union Confederation, *Countries at Risk: Violations of Trade Union Rights*, 2013, p. 36.

works to undermine the ability of workers to 'withhold their labour power through strikes and work stoppages',[134] often a key component in exercising their collective power. While hiring policy has reflected the perceived nature of the threat to the Al Khalifa regime, the government's exclusion and suspicion of Shiʿa has led to a process by which policy motivates discontent and simultaneously seeks to disarm it. It is, however, important to add that while this exclusion of Shia worsened following Independence and the Iranian Revolution, it was occurring well before the 1950s – especially in the police (see Chapter 4).

Exile and Deportation

As Austin Turk once wrote, 'manipulating entry or exit in reference to polity or sub polity boundaries' is important in maintaining control of power within a certain geographical jurisdiction.[135] Exclusion through exile has been a standard method of repression in Bahrain's history, particularly for the leaders of political movements and members of the ruling family. It perfectly exemplifies a regime's desire to maintain a geographical jurisdiction devoid of threats, political or otherwise. In the early part of the twentieth century, the British in particular favoured exile as a form of repressive action. At a time of relatively poor communication and slow travel, it was seen as an effective way of preventing 'troublemakers' from spreading their influence. The main target of exile in the early days of British reforms were fledgeling nationalists and members of the Al Khalifa family who were resisting British influence and reforms. During the 1920s there were frequent clashes between Najdis and Persian residents in Manama (events which have been coloured by partisan dispute). Following the Najdi–Persian riots in 1923, in which the British official Knox stated 'it is unthinkable that Persians are the aggressors'[136] the alleged agent of Ibn Saud, Qusaybi, was arrested and kicked out of Bahrain. While Britain's intercession on the decision to deport Qusaybi was made because they believed the Al Khalifa were afraid to punish an agent of Ibn Saud, the British too were mindful not to anger him. To ameliorate potential discontent from Ibn Saud about this repression of Qusaybi, Knox noted that despite the Persians being the victims in the affair, he would have to get rid of a Persian or two.[137] Here repression

[134] A. Austin Holmes, 'Working on the Revolution in Bahrain: From the Mass Strike to Everyday Forms of Medical Provision', *Social Movement Studies: Journal of Social, Cultural and Political Protest*, 2015, doi: 10.1080/14742837.2015.1037265.
[135] Turk, *Political Criminality*, p. 160.
[136] Knox, 'Report on Bahrain Reforms', p. 757.
[137] Ibid.

was highly politicized, coloured by Britain's geostrategic considerations. As such, several of those who were deported were acknowledged to be innocent.

Exiling the Anti-British

Despite British treaty obligations to the Al Khalifa, members of the ruling family were not spared exile in the early twentieth century. However, the nature of repression on the part of the British oscillated wildly depending on what was seen as politically expedient at the time. The British were harsher when repressing activities that could be construed as anti-British political crimes. In reality, this meant any action that sought to undermine British power. In 1929, a man was deported for anti-British propaganda,[138] while two men accused of trying to kill Shaykh Hamad were deported to the Andaman Islands.[139] Generally, the British attempts to repress the ruling family were fiercely resisted, even by British allies among the Al Khalifa. For example, after two members of the ruling family – ʿAli bin Khalid Al Khalifa and his brother Ibrahim who were both deported for organising attacks on *baḥārna* villages – returned to Bahrain without British permission, officials did little to enforce such rulings. Charles Belgrave highlighted his frustration at the return of these two shaykhs in 1927, writing: 'Rather annoyed at Ali b Khaled being present, he later served six months for being mixed up in a murder case, banished, & came back without permission.'[140] Belgrave's inability to enforce the rulings highlights not so much the limitations of British influence but the desire of the British to avoid making political decisions that could provoke discord among the ruling families of the Gulf.

Perhaps the most notable example of British involvement in wholesale exile was their mass expulsion of the Dawasir, a powerful tribe loyal to the Al Khalifa, and once described by Charles Belgrave as a 'saucy crowd'.[141] The tribe, which had harassed Jewish merchants and assisted in the Al Khalifa's attacks on the *baḥrānī* population, did not accept the legitimacy of Hamad's succession. They were implicated in numerous acts of oppression, including an attack on the village of ʿAli on 19 June 1923[142] that killed three, and seriously injured four of its *baḥrānī*

[138] C. Belgrave, 5 January 1929, *Papers of Charles Dalrymple-Belgrave: Transcripts of Diaries, 1926–1957,* Library of the University of Exeter.

[139] C. Belgrave, Annual Report for the Year 1956, *in Bahrain Government Annual Reports 1924–1970,* vol. 5, Gerrards Cross, Archive Editions, 1986, p. 47.

[140] Belgrave, Papers, 11 February 1927. [141] Belgrave, Papers, 19 February 1930.

[142] S. G. Knox, Attack on 'Ali by Dawasir Tribesmen, in P. Tuson and E. Quick (eds), *Records of Bahrain 1820–1960,* vol. 4, Slough, Archive Editions, 1993, p. 118.

residents. They also took 5,000 rupees as loot.[143] Their attacks were reportedly encouraged by 'Nejd',[144] where the *Ikhwan* were also repressing Shiʿa and *baḥrānī* residents on the Arabia peninsula. The final straw for the British administration came after some Shiʿa notables who gave evidence in the case against the Dawasir were murdered, most likely in revenge for their testimony. The Dawasir tribe were given an ultimatum by the British; fall in line with Hamad's rule or leave Bahrain. Although some Dawasir chose to stay in Bahrain and submit to Hamad's rule, many left to the Eastern province of Saudi Arabia.

The decision to exile the Dawasir was based on the premise that they were not falling in line with British-backed Hamad's rule. The British legally justified their removal from Bahrain as being in accord with their treaty with Bahrain's rulers. Resources and the limits of intervention also meant that the British could not afford and did not wish to keep deploying gunboats as a deterrent. Nor did they wish to use violent action as there was suspicion that the Dawasir were encouraged by Ibn Saud, and any attacks would increase tensions with him. The exile of the Dawasir removed the backbone of resistance to Hamad's, and therefore resistance to British influence. One official noted that 'their [the Dawsir's] departure from Bahrain has assisted Hamad to assert his authority more than would ever have been possible had they remained'.[145]

However, like many measures undertaken by the British, short term acts of repression often caused long-term problems, both anticipated and unanticipated. The Dawasir were a case in point. Many of them returned to Bahrain, reportedly with approval from Ibn Saud. Their return then became a source of financial tension. Although their expulsion by the British had included forfeiture of all their lands and property in Bahrain, upon their return they successfully pressured the government to get their back rents. Charles Belgrave did not want to return their property, lest the British and the ruler's authority be undermined. The problem was escalated to the Political Residency in Bushire who agreed to return much of what had been confiscated. It is likely that the British were sensitive about not upsetting Ibn Saud – who Shaykh ʿIsa warned would be upset by a British refusal on this issue.[146] Indeed, British

143 Ibid.

144 C. K. Daly, Relations of Shiʿa and Sunnis in Bahrain, in P. Tuson, A. Burdett and E. Quick (eds), *Records of Bahrain 1820–1960,* vol. 4, Archive Editions, Slough, 1993, p. 126.

145 'Administration Reports 1920–1924' [159r] (322/412), British Library: India Office Records and Private Papers, IOR/R/15/1/713, in *Qatar Digital Library*, www.qdl.qa/en/archive/81055/vdc_100023385511.0x00007b

146 Belgrave, Papers, 20 April 1927.

unwillingness to upset tribal allies of Ibn Saud tempered their repressive policies. The British also thought that bearing the cost of appeasing the Dawasir might be better than potentially reigniting hostilities. So while their exile may have resulted in a short-term reprieve in their resistance to British reform, their return simply enflamed existing communal tensions in Bahrain.

Exiling Nascent Nationalism

While the expulsion of the majority of the Dawasir stymied Al Khalifa factionalism by reducing the ruling tribe's coercive capabilities over the *baḥārna*, the emergence of political opposition with reformist and nationalistic agendas posed a new challenge for the emerging regime. This opposition included the Bahrain National Congress (BNC), who came to prominence in the 1920s. Nelida Fuccaro argues that the BNC was inspired by the ideas of constitutional and representative governance championed by the Khilafaat Movement and the Indian National Congress.[147] Muhammad Rumaihi, on the other hand, is more critical, noting that all of the elected representatives were Sunni. Nonetheless, the demands of the Bahrain National Congress were perceived as radical at the time, and the British were inclined to see anything vaguely democratic as 'bolshie'. They perceived the Bahrain National Congress as a radical challenge to British hegemony and deported its two ringleaders, Ahmad bin Lahij and ʿAbd al-Wahab Zayani, to Bombay on 7 November 1923. It was here that Zayani sadly died in exile.[148] Similarly, when ʿAbd Allah Al Khalifa was working to undermine his brother Shaykh Hamad, Daly exiled two of his advisers, Jasim al-Shirawi and Hafiz Wahba. This, according to Rumaihi, was to isolate ʿIsa and ʿAbd Allah from their 'evil advisers'.[149]

Although it is fair to say the British were rarely tolerant of democratic movements, their repression of the BNC should be understood as being in line with their desire to consolidate power over those opposing their reforms. There is some debate as to whether the objectives of the BNC genuinely included broad-based representation of all Bahrain's communal groups. While it has been suggested that the BNC attempted to reach out to Shiʿi ʿAbd ʿAli bin Mansur Rajab, the historian Mahdi Abdalla Al-Tajir argues that few meetings took place.[150] Omar Al Shehabi critiques an analysis of the composition of

[147] N. Fuccaro, *Histories of City and State in the Persian Gulf: Manama since 1800*, Cambridge, Cambridge University Press, 2009, p. 158.
[148] Khalid Bassam, 'Bahrain Personalities' [Arabic], Jadawel, 201, p. 56.
[149] Rumaihi, *Bahrain: Social*, p. 173.
[150] M. A. Al-Tajir, *Bahrain 1920–1945, Britain, the Shaikh and the Administration*, London, Croom Helm, 1987, p. 62.

the sects of the Bahrain National Congress as the use of an 'ethnosectarian gaze', which privileges sectarianism as an analytical category. However, to ignore categories that have been demonstrably used as a means of dividing society would be remiss. Rumaihi argued that the failure of the attempt to reach out highlighted an 'unbridgeable' mistrust between the two communities.[151] That most of their demands concerned the protection of traditional mercantile privileges suggests that they were adopting a new language to resist the British reforms at the expense of the indigenous *baḥārna*.

Furthermore, criticism of the BNC was not solely on sectarian terms. It is curious, too, that the BNC supported Shaykh ʿIsa, who had been deposed by the British in favour of his son Hamad. Al Shehabi argues that the Congress's alignment with the ex-ruler ʿIsa was important for it signified that he 'was no longer the ruler but one of the opposition, a symbol to them of a usurped power and an anti-colonialist drive'.[152] However, this neglects to mention that those lobbying accepted that Hamad could be ruler so long as Shaykh ʿIsa decided it to be so: "Should Shaikh Isa decide to appoint his son Shaikh Hamed as ruler we would expect from him as we would expect from his father."[153] Their motives for supporting ʿIsa should not be assumed to be that he was a symbol of resistance at the time. If so, it would show a lack of regard for the *baḥrānī* community. Ultimately, the Bahrain National Congress's support for Shaykh ʿIsa, who was opposing British-led reforms, did little to assuage concerns that the BNC desired to preserve a status quo amenable to the interests of an existing elite.

The process of exile or incarceration of political figures continued throughout the 1920s. It was indicative of growing British interference in Bahrain's internal affairs and the strengthening of their influence by eradicating Hamad's enemies. However, the tactic of exile frequently backfired. For example, ʿAbd al Aziz Shamlan, a key leader of the opposition movement in the 1950s, was deported in the 1920s to India. Despite this, he later returned to Bahrain but only after being exposed to many of the ideas and methods of peaceful resistance popularized by Gandhi.[154] Such ideas, which have become a mainstay of Bahraini opposition tactics, would further influence British policies of adaptation to repression. Indeed, it was such cases that most likely

[151] Rumaihi, *Bahrain: Social*, p. 312.

[152] O. H. Al Shehabi, 'Contested Modernity: Divided Rule and the Birth of Sectarianism, Nationalism, and Absolutism in Bahrain', *British Journal of Middle Eastern Studies*, vol. 44, no. 3, 2017, pp. 333–55, doi: 10.1080/13530194.2016.1185937.

[153] Rumaihi, *Bahrain: Social*, p. 311.

[154] Bassam, 'Bahrain Personalities'.

prompted Britain to exile political prisoners to remote prison islands, such as St Helena.

In 1938, growing national consciousness among an emergent middle class led to the creation of a new group with several demands. These were: (a) a legislative council, (b) reforms to the police department, (c) the codification of Bahraini laws, (d) the dismissal of the education inspector and the dismissal of two Shiʿa Qadis, (e) that Bahrainis should get preference of employment in BAPCO and (f) that the council should be formed of Sunna and Shiʿa. Despite these demands, the British suspected that some aspects of the agitation were being exploited once again by ʿAbd Allah bin ʿIsa Al Khalifa, who was to be the head of the proposed council of five Arabs (Sunna) and five *baḥārna*. Given ʿAbd Allah's previous record, the British feared that he was using the council to wrestle control from his brother.[155] Another member of the ruling family with an axe to grind, Hamud bin Sabah Al Khalifa, was also alleged to be mixed up in the agitation. He had issues with the government since his conviction for attacks on *baḥrānī* villages.[156] Regardless of the motives of ʿAbd Allah, demands for reform were very real. However, the British viewed any such agitation as subversive and were insecure about creating an elected forum that they felt would be under the influence of their internal enemies. ʿAli bin Khalifa al-Fadil, the suspected ringleader, was exiled for two and a half years, a comparatively light sentence for a movement that was considered 'directly against the Government'.[157]

Exiling the St Helena Three

The 1950s in Bahrain was characterized by the rise of the Higher Executive Committee (the HEC), originally called the Committee of National Union (CNU). The ruler objected to the word "Higher" as he felt it usurped his authority. The HEC was a political group demanding greater political representation in Bahrain. They opposed Belgrave's autocratic influence and, like many other political groupings before them, demanded a penal code and democratic representation. Although the British employed numerous tactics in trying to dismantle the influence of the HEC, some of which will be discussed later in this chapter, they eventually conspired to have three of the original eight leaders of the

[155] H. Weightman, Report, 27 October 1938, in A. Burdett (ed.), *Records of Bahrain 1820–1960,* vol. 5, Slough, Archive Editions, 1993, p. 174.

[156] Ibid., p. 185.

[157] C. Belgrave, Annual Report for Year 1357 (1938–39), *in Bahrain Government Annual Reports 1924 –1970,* vol. 2, Gerrards Cross, Archive Editions, 1986, p. 29.

movement deported to the Crown Colony of St Helena. The original eight were ʿAbd al-Rahman Bakir – Secretary c, Ibrahim Fakhro, Ibrahim al-Musa, Ibrahim bin Mousa, ʿAbd ʿAli al-ʿAlaiwat, Sayyid ʿAli Kamal ad-Din, Shaykh ʿAbd Allah Abu Dib and Shaykh Muhsin al-Tajir. Those exiled were ʿAbd al-Rahman Bakir, ʿAbd al- ʿAziz al-Shamlan and ʿAbd ʿAli al-ʿAlaiwat. The British worried that any elected body would not guarantee British military infrastructure in the Gulf; they could not risk losing a crucial geostrategic base in the context of the Cold War.

Although the British decided not to support the HEC, it was the ruling family who decided to exile the prisoners to a British territory outside Bahrain. This was unsurprising given that the charges made against the leaders of the HEC included an assassination attempt of the ruler.[158] For fear of further criticism, the British were keen to emphasize that the decision to exile was one requested by the ruler. They were aware that decisions seen as heavy-handed would provoke further anger towards them, especially with the rise of Arab nationalism in the region. In this regard, what they did in Bahrain mattered further afield, especially in Egypt. The British were also worried that keeping such popular leaders in Bahrain would be a 'constant irritant and keep local agitation alive'.[159] This was especially true as inadequate prison facilities and a lack of security meant that the accused could pass messages to their supporters.[160] Indeed, incarcerated political opposition were still seen as a potent threat, underscoring the perceived importance of exile-as-repression.

In an attempt to balance their security concerns with the concerns of the ruling family, the British administration entertained numerous repressive measures before they eventually decided to exile the prisoners to St Helena. This process of internal deliberation aptly reflects strategic decision-making regarding repressive choices. At first, the British attempted to use financial incentives. It had, after all, worked with the ruling family. According to Charles Belgrave, the British Residency secretly bribed Abd al-Rahman al-Bakir, the leader of the HEC, with 5,000 rupees to leave on one occasion. Belgrave noted: 'It has now got out that the Residency paid Bin Bakr Rs5000 when he left – in fact, to get him to leave, as I knew, but it won't be believed that this was the case.'[161] On another occasion, when al-Bakir was out of the country, the British instructed their consulates not to renew his passport without a reference

[158] Foreign Office, Communique to Bahrain, Intel 223, 24 December 1956, in A. Burdett (ed.), *Records of Bahrain 1820–1960*, vol. 7, Slough, Archive Editions, 1993, p. 287.
[159] Ibid.
[160] B. A. B. Burrows, 15 November 1956, FO371/120548, The National Archives.
[161] Belgrave, Papers, 17 December 1956.

from Bernard Burrows, the Political Resident.[162] Of course, Bernard Burrows would not give this permission. This did not succeed, and the British realized that the deportation, or exile, of the HEC leaders to Beirut, Syria or Cairo would only result in agitation or the setting up of a 'Free Bahrain Government'.[163] The British then considered sending two of the leaders to England, and two to Beirut on a one-way ticket. They even considered the Seychelles. In the end, it was decided to deport ʿAbd al-Rahman Bakir, ʿAbd al- ʿAziz al-Shamlan and ʿAbd ʿAli al ʿAlaiwat to St Helena. This strategic decision-making provides an interesting and rare insight into the often unseen processes of deliberating repressive methods. It also indicates how certain methods may be attempted and discarded in favour of other approaches.

For some, the exile was a success. Edward Parr Wiltshire, the Political Agent between 1959 and 1962, concluded that the deportation had been effective, resulting 'in a peaceful four years'.[164] He added, 'out of sight and so almost "out of mind"'.[165] In the months following the deportation of the St Helena three, others deemed to be threats to security were deported, such as schoolteacher Hassan Geshi and Bedreech Khalfan, a 'young woman' who had become a 'political leader'.[166] It is interesting to note that Bedreech Khalfan may have been the first woman to have been deported from Bahrain for political reasons. In some cases, Belgrave had attempted to discourage the deportation of certain individuals. However, decisions to deport were often contentious. In the case of Hassan Geshi, who had worked in Bahrain for twenty years, members of the Al Khalifa deported him without legal justification (according to Belgrave).[167] Although there were frequent moments where Belgrave lacked influence regarding internal security, the British saw deportation as a legitimate strategy as late as the 1950s and 1960s. Indeed, Bernard Burrows noted that 'banishment [was] a traditional method in the Gulf States',[168] and that there was a general 'belief' that deportation was 'beneficial to security'.[169] The idea that such a practice could perhaps be self-reinforcing, based on a perception that it was a 'traditional method', highlights how some repressive tactics reflect institutional learning.

Exile as a repressive method had numerous drawbacks. The political scandal created by the St Helena affair made the British more sensitive in

[162] B. A. B. Burrows, 22 September 1956, FO371/120548, The National Archives.
[163] Foreign Office, Communique to Bahrain, 14 November 1956, FO371/120548, The National Archives.
[164] E. P. Wiltshire, 30 December 1960, FO1016/691, The National Archives. [165] Ibid.
[166] Belgrave, Papers, 6 January 1957. [167] Belgrave, Papers, 8 January 1957.
[168] B. A. B. Burrows, 12 November 1956, FO371/120548, The National Archives.
[169] B. A. B. Burrows, 15 November 1956, FO371/120548, The National Archives.

their dealing with Bahraini internal political affairs. The ailing British Empire and Bahrain's Independence in 1971 also meant that political prisoners could not be whisked away to remote places where they would be less likely to cause trouble for Britain's protectorates. Although exile as a method of repression fell out of favour with the British administration, the ruling family still advocated this method throughout the 1960s. British Political Agent Peter John Tripp noted in 1963 that the 'ruling family' preferred the 'clandestine deportation of known trouble-makers',[170] rather than a public spectacle that might be generated by a drawn-out court case. A victim of this was 'Abd Allah Rashid, a member of the National Liberation Front, who was deported in 1960 for distributing leaflets and writing slogans on walls. He was also forcibly exiled in 1970, and again in 1974.[171] So, while this tradition was often adopted by the British, it was becoming clearer throughout the 1960s that security decisions not necessarily approved by the British administration were being advocated by the government of Bahrain.

Mass Deportations of the Shiʿa

Post-Independence, there was a marked increase in exile as repression, sometimes en-masse, by the Al Khalifa regime. However, the scale of these deportations, and that most of those deported were Shiʿa, reflected both a differing sense of challenges and threat perceptions in Bahrain, as well as a resurgence of ethnosectarian and tribal rule by the ruling family. Ostensibly, the increasing deportations were prompted by the desires of the ruling core. The decision to expel the Shiʿa was often in conflict with the advice of the British-officered Bahrain security services. On one occasion in 1982, Ian Henderson complained that he was 'very concerned over the increasing number of deportations being carried out by the Bahraini authorities acting for Shaikh Hamad or the Prime Minister'.[172] Many of those were deported on the pretext that they supported Khomeini's Islamic Revolution and would thus support political agitation against the ruling Al Khalifa family. However, Ian Henderson added that the deportations had 'no legal basis', and by the beginning of 1982, he stated that '300 people had by now been deported, many of them Bahraini passport holders'.[173] He further argued that there was also no political threat posed by these Shiʿa, and they were just rounded up

[170] J. P. Tripp, The Internal Situation in Bahrain, 1 June 1963, FO371/168670, The National Archives.
[171] Human Rights Watch, *Routine Abuse.*
[172] W. R. Tomkys, Internal Political Situation Bahrain 1982, 10 April 1982, FCO8/4332, The National Archives.
[173] Ibid.

and put on board 'willy nilly'.[174] It is probable that the Bahrainis who were deported were Iranian migrants (ajami) and their children who had migrated to Bahrain generations before, as opposed to the *baḥārna*. In 1985 Peter Ivey, the Third Secretary at the British Embassy in Bahrain, noted that the authorities often deported the 'implacable' opposition who were Shiʿa or of Iranian heritage.[175]

While Ian Henderson maintained some degree of influence in Bahrain, he was opposed to what he saw as a unilateral move on the part of the ruling core to collectively punish the Shiʿa population in Bahrain. The deportations highlighted a worrying aspect of what Tomkys described as the 'multiplicity of pseudo-security organisations',[176] operating on behalf of members of the Al Khalifa family. In July 1982 Tomkys noted that:

> The total number of Bahrainis deported in recent years to Iran is put at 182. In some cases, whole families have been deported at short notice on the basis of a single unsubstantiated allegation against one of their members. The legality of their deportation, particularly for those who are arguably Bahraini rather than Iranian by nationality is doubtful semicolon nor is there much political wisdom in the practice which is bitterly resented in the Shiʿa community here which may simply serve to provide recruits for subversive training schools in Iran.[177]

The deportation of some members of the Shiʿa community is in some ways similar to the British expulsion of the Dawasir tribe. Both were done on the premise of attempting to maintain some degree of internal stability. However, while the Dawasir were assisting the ruling family in the oppression of the *baḥrānī* population, the Shiʿa community was not really in a position of power. Nor does it seem apparent that any of those deported were particularly threatening. Given their previous egregious treatment by the ruling family, it would be specious to argue that the deportation was solely a reaction to the success of the Iranian Revolution.

While the tactic of exile was common in the twentieth century, this shift to Al Khalifa control of Bahrain's various security organs, coupled with the Islamic revolution and increasing Saudi influence, undoubtedly contributed to a vindictive policy of collective punishment against the country's Shiʿa. Although this could suggest individual Al Khalifa prejudice may have manifested itself in state repression, it also illustrates how regional tension between Saudi Arabia, Iraq and Iran played out in Bahrain. However, the deportation of Shiʿa cannot be assumed to be an obvious reaction to deep-rooted paranoia about Iranian expansionism. On the contrary, its impact on Bahrain's security was challenged.

[174] Ibid. [175] P. R. Ivey, FCO8/5817, The National Archives. [176] Ibid.
[177] W. R. Tomkys, Return of Bahraini Deportees from Iran, 5 July 1982, FCO8/4332, The National Archives.

Henderson strongly argued that the deportations would probably have a negative effect in terms of security. As such, the decision to deport does not necessarily follow the realist implication that it was done for internal security reasons. A generous interpretation would be that the disagreement highlighted a divergence in threat perceptions between the ruling family and the British-officered security forces. However, it was more likely that Saudi-pressure and the ruling family's historical animosity towards the Shiʿa community played out in this decision.

The increasing criminalization of the Shiʿa meant that these deportations reached into the hundreds. Within the rather unnuanced paradigm of the New Middle East Cold War between Iran and Saudi Arabia,[178] government action against the Shiʿa may simply be written off as part of Bahrain's alliance with Saudi Arabia. Instead it reflects an embedded and historically rooted process of discrimination reasserted after 1971. Indeed, the seeming ease with which hundreds of people were deported itself reflects a discriminatory, hostile and prejudiced attitude to those communities.

Regional political crises would continue to have an impact on the nature of exile in Bahrain. Following the Iraqi occupation of Kuwait in 1990 and the subsequent Gulf War in 1991, Amnesty International noted that hundreds of political dissidents had been exiled. Amnesty also documented that hundreds of Bahraini nationals who had previously been expelled from the country were attempting to return, including whole families.[179] They added that 'scores of people were permitted to return although usually after more than one unsuccessful attempt. Many others, however, were denied entry'.[180] It is not clear how many of these people were those same families and individuals deported in the early 1980s.

Throughout the 1990s Intifada, the government deported influential members of the Shiʿa community. In January 1995, the Bahrain authorities exiled at least eleven Bahrainis upon their return to the country.[181] In 1995, the arrest of ʿAli Salman, a prominent Shiʿa religious figure and critic of the government, prompted a chain of events that resulted in the forcible exile of Salman and two other religious scholars, Hamza al-Dayri, and Sayyid Haydar al-Sitri.[182] Salman had irked the authorities through his influential role in encouraging people to sign petitions and

[178] F. G. Gause, *Beyond Sectarianism: The New Middle East Cold War*, Foreign Policy at Brookings, no. 11, 2014, www.brookings.edu/research/beyond-sectarianism-the-new-middle-east-cold-war/

[179] Amnesty International, *Bahrain: A Human Rights Crisis*, 1996, London, Amnesty International Publications, www.refworld.org/docid/3ae6a9984.html, p. 42.

[180] Ibid. [181] Ibid., p. 44. [182] Ibid.

was probably targeted because of this.[183] The somewhat archaic tactic of exile was actually quite an anomaly in the global context. Human Rights Watch (HRW) noted that Bahrain was one of the few countries in the world to carry out such forcible deportations of citizens. Indeed, HRW stated that roughly 500, mostly Shiʿa, Bahrainis had been exiled by 1995, with 128 being deported in 1993 alone.[184]

Distrust directed towards the country's Shiʿa population perhaps explains why many of them were exiled. However, the need to accentuate sectarian divisions as a means of legitimizing harsh government repression is also important. Episodes of contentious politics in Bahrain serve as periodic reinforcers of the status quo, redividing society and maintaining the strategic fragmentation of religious and non-religious opposition. As such, the government are keen to publicise certain acts of sectarian repression in order to provoke fear of an Islamic-style revolution. In 2011, the Bahraini government announced that they were deporting sixteen Lebanese nationals who they claimed had links to Hezbollah.[185] Although the government did not deport them in the end, other countries in the region such as the United Arab Emirates went ahead with the expulsion of dozens of mostly Lebanese Shiʿa, pointing to a region-wide surge in sectarian-fuelled securitisation.[186]

Things have changed somewhat in the twenty-first century. It is harder to deport or exile people legally, and it is now assumed that ideologues, activists or dissidents can foment unrest from distant lands.[187] It is also important to note, however, that the intimidation of political dissidents has prompted many to flee Bahrain, resulting in an involuntary exile. Indeed, while exile may have seemed like a solution sixty years ago, in the 2011 Uprising, the chickens have come home to roost. As predicted by government officials in the 1950s, generations of activists who were deported or fled abroad have consolidated an effective international opposition network. This is especially true in the former protecting power. Since 2011, Bahrain has put pressure on Britain to hand over those convicted of political crimes in absentia. During the time of Empire, Britain had some latitude with where they could deport convicts,

[183] Bahry, 'The Opposition in Bahrain'. [184] Human Rights Watch, *Routine Abuse.*

[185] *Now Lebanon*, 'Mikati Thanks Bahrain for Halting Deportation of Lebanese Nationals', 19 April 2011, https://now.mmedia.me/lb/en/archive/mikati_thanks_bahrain_for_halting_deportation_of_lebanese_nationals

[186] *The New Arab*, 'Lebanese Families Given 48 Hours to Leave the UAE', 18 March 2015, www.alaraby.co.uk/english/news/2015/3/18/lebanese-families-given-48-hours-to-leave-the-uae

[187] It is important to note, however, that the intimidation of political dissidents has prompted many to flee Bahrain, resulting in an involuntary exile.

and slow communications meant it was more difficult for exiles to spread political ideas. However, this became increasingly ineffective, and frequently exiled convicts would continue political activities abroad or return to Bahrain. It is perhaps ironic to note that while globalization of communication has perhaps facilitated the generation of opposition networks, it is for that the reason the state seeks to attempt to secure its physical jurisdiction over the dissident's body.

In the 2011 Uprising, other means of political exclusion, not confined to Bahraini nationals, were used on those deemed sympathetic to opposition demands. Several US officials were asked to leave by the Bahrain government for their perceived support of the opposition. Thomas Malinowski, the then US Assistant Secretary of State for Democracy, Human Rights and Labor, was expelled from Bahrain after he met with representatives of the opposition group Al Wefaq.[188] Ludovic Hood, an American diplomat, was withdrawn after the US government feared for his life. These incidents followed a loyalist backlash that resulted from video footage of Hood innocently giving Krispy Kreme doughnuts to members of the opposition. Like Hood, US envoy Thomas Krajeski was the subject of a petition endorsed by nine Sunni Islamist societies, who claimed he was 'interfering in political matters' and giving support to the opposition.[189] The focus of attacks on US diplomats reflected the United States' slightly less sycophantic position towards Bahrain under the Obama administration (as opposed to the UK's more obsequious foreign policy). The deterritorialization of protest and advocacy has warranted the need for adaptive responses by the Al Khalifa regime.

Nonetheless, the deportation, harassment and subsequent replacement of a foreign diplomat marked a new form of repression, one that came about because of the perceived ability of opposition groups to lobby diplomats. It is also possibly indicative of a more American style of diplomacy (if we can say such a thing); giving doughnuts to protesters is almost certainly something the British would never do. Nonetheless, the expulsion of Hood assists government repression by removing sympathetic, or at least receptive, ears with whom the opposition can share their grievances. In this regard, it is an attempt to isolate opposition groups from channels of international lobbying that could culminate in political pressure on the Bahrain government for reform.

[188] BBC News, 'US Diplomat Tom Malinowski Expelled from Bahrain', www.bbc.co.uk/news/world-us-canada-28204511

[189] *Gulf Daily News*, 'Societies Seek to Expel Envoy', 12 June 2013, http://archives.gdnonline.com/NewsDetails.aspx?date=04/07/2015&storyid=355162

Shaping Civil Society

Removal of Citizenship, Tajnīs and Denial of Entry

The Al Khalifa regime has worked to reduce the number of persons with ideologically opposing views from infiltrating Bahrain, whether as citizens or migrant workers. While exile was relatively ad hoc before the existence of laws governing citizenship status, the citizenship law of 1937 laid out some clear government prerogatives of inclusion and exclusion. Since the creation of the law, the authorities have frequently resorted to tactics such as removing or changing citizenship status to control access to polity boundaries. In 1956, the Bahrain government removed the citizenship of ʿAbd al-Rahman Bakir, who in addition to being a leading member of the HEC, was also the editor of a newspaper critical of the Bahraini government. Shiʿi figure ʿAbd al-Hadi Al - Mudarrasi was stripped of citizenship and deported in 1981.[190] The scale of this citizenship removal seemed to increase throughout the 1980s. The Committee for the Defence of Political Prisoners in Bahrain, an NGO-in-exile, published a pamphlet in March 1990 with the names of sixty-five people who were stripped of their Bahraini nationality and deported during the 1980s.[191] According to Bahraini human rights activist Sayed Al Wadei, between 2011 and 2018 the Bahraini government removed the citizenship of at least 608 citizens.[192] Sometimes this was done en masse. In March 2018 Amnesty International reported that 115 citizens were stripped of citizenship in a single trial. Lynn Maalouf, Amnesty International's Middle East Research Director, stated: 'The Bahraini government is using revocation of nationality – rendering many of its citizens stateless in the process – and expulsion, as tools to crush all forms of opposition, dissent and activism.'[193] The ruler's legal ability to decide over citizenship has put him in the position of the ultimate arbiter of what it means to be a Bahraini, at least legally. In this regard, Bahraini citizenship is a gift bestowed by the ruler, as opposed to an inalienable right enjoyed by citizens.

By their very nature, attempts to change such prerogatives of the ruling elite automatically invite accusations of treachery and treason.

[190] *BICI Report*, p. 29.

[191] Committee for the Defence of Political Prisoners in Bahrain, Violations of Human Rights in Bahrain, March 1990.

[192] S. Al Wadei, 18 April 2018, https://twitter.com/salwadaei/status/986709424403308544?s=12

[193] Amnesty International, Bahrain: Citizenship of 115 people Revoked in 'Ludicrous' Mass Trial, www.amnesty.org/en/latest/news/2018/05/bahrain-citizenship

To challenge the ruler's ability to determine who is Bahraini is also to challenge the essence of being Bahraini.[194] 'Ali Shucair notes that stripping citizenship represents a shift from merely punitive, to tyrannical, 'since the Bahraini judiciary is not only issuing prison sentences against opposition members for 5 to 15 years but also depriving them of their citizenship'.[195]Abdulhadi Khalaf argues that in 'Qatar, the UAE, Saudi Arabia and Bahrain, threatening to revoke – or not renew – one's citizenship has become one of the tools used by security forces to control citizens, as well as a form of punishment for those whom the authorities wish to deny their generosity'.[196] Some of those who have had their citizenship removed have not even been involved in a specific court case, pointing to a punitive sectarian policy targeting mostly Shiʿa journalists, human rights activists and lawyers.[197] On a technical level, the removal of citizenship makes various other procedures difficult, such as the ability to give power of attorney to lawyers in order to lobby for their appeal.[198] It also prevents the stateless from leaving the country or accessing important public services for which citizenship is required. They effectively become prisoners in their own country.

Statelessness may yield further problems for those affected and their children, such as securing employment, healthcare and education. Bank accounts are frozen and identity documents are removed. Those who live in Bahrain at the time of the removal of their citizenship must find a sponsor or risk deportation.[199] Those who have had their citizenship removed have complained that they have lost their jobs, their businesses and their overall sense of wellbeing. Hussein Kurailla Mohammed stated that his life became 'like a hell' following the removal of his citizenship after the 2011 Uprising.[200] On other occasions, the Bahraini government have also denied re-entry to numerous Bahrainis who left the country for various reasons and attempted to return. Bahrain Human Rights Organization documented 211 cases between 1990 and 1994 in which

[194] Ibid.

[195] A. Shucair, 'Bahrain Begins to Revoke Dissidents' Citizenship', *Al Monitor*, 4 September 2014, www.al-monitor.com/pulse/politics/2014/09/bahrain-citizens-deprived-revolution

[196] A. Khalaf, 'GCC Rulers and the Politics of Citizenship', *Al-Monitor*, 26 December 2012, www.al-monitor.com/pulse/politics/2012/12/gcc-rulers-use- citizenship

[197] Bahrain's Policy of Revoking Shiʿa Protesters Citizenship [Documentary].

[198] Human Rights Watch, Bahrain: Citizenship Rights Stripped Away, August 2014, www.hrw.org/news/2014/08/21/bahrain-citizenship

[199] Interview with Bahraini activist, 2018.

[200] Bahrain's Policy of Revoking Shiʿa Protesters Citizenship [Documentary].

Bahrainis had been denied entry to Bahrain and sent back to different countries.[201] Many of those were children.

Throughout the century, the process of exile has widened from targeting specific political leaders and dissidents to targeting hundreds of mostly Shiʿi families. While some may wish to attribute this shift to a changing threat perception following the Iranian Revolution, this is too reductionist. Overstating the importance of the Islamic Revolution in Bahrain's history underpins government strategies that seek to disproportionally criminalize or securitize Shiʿi members of society.[202] This overemphasis can result in the attribution of 'inferiority and/or radical alienness' of the Shiʿa as the other, perpetuating cycles of discrimination. It also attributes Bahrain's problems as being primarily exogenous, reinforcing the status quo by making government repression seem like a necessary condition in preserving stability, plurality and sovereignty from the spectre of a looming Iranian theocratic threat. It also shifts attention from important issues that drive discontent, such as corruption and socio-economic marginalization.

Tajnīs and Citizenship

Controlling subpolity boundaries and make-up also involves the deliberate exacerbation of communal differences and demographics. This is especially true with regard to the manipulation of sectarian loyalties. While the Arab/Persian divide may have been more acute during the 1920s, the Shiʿa–Sunni demographic balance is now a significant point of contention. An indication of the sensitivities of demographics is evidenced by the fact that the only official census to include data on sects was undertaken in 1941. It noted that Bahrain had 46,354 Shiʿa residents and 41,944 Sunni residents.[203] Segregation generally followed an urban–rural divide, with the Shiʿa population concentrated in the countryside and villages. Manama was roughly half and half, while Muharraq and Hidd were mostly Sunni. The government at the time feared feelings of majoritarianism among the Shiʿa. As a result, they believed that counting

[201] 'Denied the Right to Enter Bahrain', Bahrain Human Rights Organization, Centre for Arab Gulf Studies, January 1996.

[202] M. Jones, 'Contesting the Iranian Revolution as a Turning-Point Discourse in Bahraini Contentious Politics', in M. Valeri, R. Porter and M. O. Jones (eds), *Gulfization of the Arab World*: Exeter Critical Gulf Series, Berlin, Gerlach Press [eBook], 2018. Read more at https://socialsciences.exeter.ac.uk/iais/staff/marcjones/#auGLaHy0SzHv3XyH.99

[203] 'File 6/70 Census of Bahrain population' [45r] (91/228), British Library: India Office Records and Private Papers, IOR/R/15/2/1289, in Qatar Digital Library, www.qdl.qa/archive/81055/vdc_100035874045.0x00005c

sects in the census would legitimize this majority demographic status and could lead to further demands for political power. Belgrave also noted in 1950 that recording a citizen's sect would risk causing 'ill-feeling' between Sunni and Shiʿa, especially because the ruling family belonged to the less numerous sect.[204]

This belief, underpinned by a general distrust of the Shiʿa, has formed the basis of attempts to exclude them from specific institutions. Throughout the twentieth and twenty-first centuries, the government has sought to strengthen its position and weaken opposition by boosting its own popularity vis-a-vis the issuing of citizenship to foreign, predominantly Sunni nationals. More recently, this has reflected a growing sectarian issue in the region, exacerbated undoubtedly by a number of factors, including Saudi conservativism, ingrained prejudice and the fear of Shiʿi expansionism following the Iran/Iraq conflict. The government has reportedly naturaliszed thousands of foreign nationals in a 'decade-long program of naturalising foreign Sunna in return for police and military service'.[205] (This naturalization is often referred to locally as *tajnīs*. Those considered to have been naturalized are also called, often pejoratively, *mujanisīn*). One *Financial Times* journalist described the ruling family's naturalization programme as an attempt to build a 'cordon sanitaire' around the regime. Justin Gengler argues that the regime naturalized between 8,000 and 10,000 Sunna from Pakistan, Jordan, Syria and Yemen during the perceived Shiʿa uprising in 1998.[206]

Both naturalization and the use of migrant labour ensures that oppositional movements will always have to contend with either docile labour or a cadre of naturalized and therefore de facto government loyalists. This method of repression naturally reduces the likelihood of broad-based popular resistance to the regime while maintaining the loyalty of the coercive arm of the state. Of course, this is not to crudely deny agency of those individuals and assume loyalty based on sect. However, because citizenship is contingent on continued loyalty, potential dissidents among these ranks can be disposed of through denaturalization and deportation. Indeed, there have been cases where police officers from elsewhere in the world have been deported, despite having been naturalized. In 2013, it was reported that the government deported five hundred

[204] 'File 6/70 Census of Bahrain population' [89r] (179/228), British Library. India Office Records and Private Papers, IOR/R/15/2/1289, in Qatar Digital Library, www.qdl.qa/archive/81055/vdc_100035874045.0x0000b4

[205] J. Gengler, 'Bahrain's Sunni Awakening', Middle East Research and Information Project (MERIP), 17 January 2012, www.merip.org/mero/mero011712

[206] J. Gengler, 'Ethnic Conflict and Political Mobilization in Bahrain and the Arabian Gulf', PhD Thesis, University of Michigan, 2011.

Pakistani workers serving as special forces in Bahrain due to their alleged participation in strikes.[207]

Granting citizenship has also been used as a political tool to secure support for Bahrain's top-down democratization policies in 2001. The descendants of the aforementioned Sunni Dawasir tribe have mostly been repatriated by the Bahraini government, with up to 20,000 reported to be holding dual Bahraini–Saudi Arabian citizenship, a move permitted under a Decree Law of 2002. A documentary by the Bahrain Center for Human Rights revealed that the Dawasir living in Damman (Saudi Arabia) were voting in the Bahrain elections in polling booths located on the Bahrain–Saudi causeway while also obtaining housing and state benefits from the Bahraini government.[208] When asked for whom they voted in the elections, a number of them said that the chief of the Dosari (Dawasir) tribe, ʿAli bin ʿIsa, instructed them in their choice.[209] Thus the regime ensured that the Dawasir voted for a pro-government candidate through their influence over ʿAli bin ʿIsa,. The documentary caused a stir in Bahrain, prompting a parliamentary enquiry. However, this was deliberately scuppered by the government's insistence that naturalization cases prior to a Decree of 2002, or those 'special cases' determined by the 1963 Naturalization Law, be exempted. Given that virtually all cases fell under one of these laws, the investigation yielded little fruit.[210] The policy also seems to demonstrate a contemporary reversal of the British policies of the first half of the twentieth century that sought to exclude the Dawasir from Bahrain precisely because they refused to co-operate with the British-led Hamad's rule. However, it is interesting to note how a century-old tactic of exile strengthened the presence of the present-day Dawasir community in the Eastern Province of Saudi Arabia, something that has led to their instrumentalization in government gerrymandering. So while the Dawasir had previously assisted the government in coercing members of the *baḥārna* community, they now assist the continuation of Al Khalifa hegemony and legitimacy through the ballot box.

In 2006, the problem of naturalization and anti-Shiʿa discrimination became more acute after the election of Nouri-al-Maliki in Iraq. It spawned a fear of Shiʿa expansionism among some Middle Eastern governments. In Bahrain, a clandestine group was set up to insulate the country from any potential Shiʿa 'takeover'. Salah al-Bandar, an adviser

[207] *Daily Pakistan*, 9 May 2014, https://dailypakistan.com.pk/09-May-2014/100742 [Urdu].

[208] Political Naturalisation in Bahrain II [online video], 2011, www.youtube.com/watch?v=QBzFRVY79jA

[209] Ibid. [210] Gengler, 'Bahrain's Sunni Awakening'.

to the Minister of Cabinet Affairs in Bahrain, was deported after he blew the whistle on the actions of a cabal closely linked to the Al Khalifa family. Al-Bandar alleged that this group were engaged in a conspiracy to rig the elections and manipulate the country's sectarian balance in order to ensure Sunni domination over the country's majority Shiites.[211] Al-Bandar's report singled out Ahmed Attiyatallah Al Khalifa, the then head of the Central Informatics Organization (CIO), the body responsible for the organization of the elections. In 2006, the *Al-Wasat* newspaper published an investigation that documented how 17,000 names on the voter roll could not be accounted for. They also suggested that 5,000 South Asian expatriate workers had been naturalized before the elections, presumably as an act of pro-status quo gerrymandering.[212]

Al-Bandar's report documented a five-year plan to 'put political control of the country firmly into the hands of militantly anti-Shiite Sunnis'.[213] According to Justin Gengler, the network arose in response to a report written by an Iraqi academic in 2005, titled 'A Proposal to Promote the General Situation of the Sunni Sect in Bahrain'.[214] The paper was itself a by-product of the fall of Saddam Hussein's regime that was perceived to empower the Shiʿa in both Iraq and Iran. Before the release of the Al-Bandar report, American officials had noted that the emboldening of Shiʿa in Iraq had prompted a response in Bahrain that sought to focus on containing Shiʿi influence. This response according to the US Embassy had been led by the two Al Khalifa brothers, Shaykh Ahmed bin Attiyatallah and Muhammad bin Attiyatallah.[215] The US ambassador to Bahrain at the time, William Monroe, noted the importance of regional politics in developing these tactics of political repression:

> there can be no doubt that regional developments – Shiʿa empowerment in Iraq, belligerent rhetoric and actions out of Iran, unhappy election experiences in Egypt and the Palestinian Authority, concerns about Shiʿa advancements enunciated publicly or privately by key allies like Jordan and Saudi Arabia – have frightened or emboldened those in Bahrain who want to protect traditional Sunni power and privileges[216]

[211] H. M. Fattah, 'Report Cites Bid by Sunnis in Bahrain to Rig Elections', *New York Times*, 2 October 2006, www.nytimes.com/2006/10/02/world/middleeast/02bahrain.html?pagewanted=all&_r=0

[212] W. T. Monroe, 'Elections Highlights No. 1: Dates Announced, E-Voting Out', US Embassy Manama, 8 October 2006, https://wikileaks.org/plusd/cables/06MANAMA1756_a.html

[213] Fattah, 'Report Cites'. [214] Gengler, *Ethnic Conflict and Political Mobilization.*

[215] W. T. Monroe, 'Bahraini Political Scene Part II: Royal Family Conservatives Tighten Reins on Politics', US Embassy Manama, 24 May 2006, https://wikileaks.org/plusd/cables/06MANAMA907_a.html

[216] Ibid.

The scandal demonstrated the ability and desire of high-level members of the ruling family to mobilize identity politics in order to counter the perceived Shiʿi threat. This mobilization was again evident in the recent uprising, where Sunni groups, backed by societies like Manbar al-Islamic and other tribal outfits, staged a popular counter-revolution[217] that helped quell the anti-government uprising in March 2011.[218] In many respects, the events of 2006 reflected the same distrust of Shiʿa that had been evident throughout the 1980s. Undoubtedly, the government's manipulation of identity politics, whether through the withdrawal or issuing of citizenship, drove mobilization among the country's Shiʿa, promoting grievances along ethnic lines while also ensuring a cadre of supporters for the regime. Along with recent complaints that *makramāt* are predominantly being given to the Sunni community, the selective distribution of wealth undermines the broad brush, economically deterministic approach that positions rentierism as a phenomenon with little nuance.[219] Through the removal of citizenship from dissidents and the naturalization of those seen as likely to be pro-government; the government have undertaken social engineering designed to create citizens more amenable to the ideological inclinations of the ruling elite. If not amenable, then the government has reduced institutional or organizational mechanisms available to opposition groups to challenge the status-quo.

Co-optation

Political Amnesties, Taming Revolutionaries and Benevolent Change

While tactics such as exile and the removal of privileges such as citizenship or jobs highlight the power of the ruling regime, the ability to restore them underlies the regime's perception of themselves as the ultimate authority – both vindictive and merciful. Often this restoration of privileges is a form of conciliation that seeks to reduce both animosity and potential subversion among political dissidents. Such gratuities and

[217] Interestingly, this supposed hardline cabal led by the Khawalid descend from the same family exiled by the British in the 1920s for orchestrating attacks on *baḥārna* villagers.

[218] J. Gengler, 'Bahrain Drain; Why the King's Sunni Supporters Are Moving Abroad', *Foreign Affairs,* 5 September 2014, www.foreignaffairs.com/articles/middle-east/2014-09-05/bahrain-drain

[219] G. Okruhlik, 'Re-thinking the Politics of Distribution: Lessons from the Arab Uprisings and the Lack Thereof', in *Arab Uprisings: New Opportunities for Political Science,* Project on Middle East Political Science (POMEPS Briefings), pp. 42–3, www.ssrc.org/publications/docs/POMEPS_Conf12_Book_Web.pdf

Amiri prerogatives also include the return of exiles, or what Khalaf describes as the 'symbolic release of political detainees'.[220] Belgrave proposed these amnesties as early as 1956, although the Al Khalifa always had the final say. As Belgrave noted: 'Went out to see His Highness, Shaykh Abdulla was there, took a list of 10 of the prisoners recommending their release, but he crossed out 2; however, it's a good political gesture.'[221] Similarly, before the authorities deported the leaders of the HEC to St Helena, they attempted to co-opt them. ʿAbd al-Rahman Bakir was invited to be on an administrative committee, a move the regime hoped would draw Al-Bakir away from the movement and thus weaken the demands of the HEC.[222] However, this did not succeed.

Individual attitudes among the ruling family impacted on the deployment of this tactic, often to the chagrin of others in government. In 1965, the ruler Shaykh ʿIsa bin Salman Al Khalifa upset the head of police Shaykh Mohammed by ordering the release of prisoners. According to Tripp, Mohammed was allegedly disheartened that the ruler had not allowed him to exercise 'arbitrary and independent control over arrests'.[223] Tripp noted that Isa's 'reputation for softness' meant he was often easily pressured by influential families to release their relatives. The fact ʿIsa had such a reputation implies too that it was often his personal characteristics that impacted upon the nature of methods of political control. Despite this, his natural inclination towards lenience was generally tempered by the wishes of his more conservative relatives. Again, this situation reveals how the personal characteristics of members of the ruling family have led to the vascilating exercise of particular methods of repression.

The three Bahrainis deported to St Helena in 1956 for their alleged role in subversion were eventually invited back to Bahrain. Some of them became part of the short-lived National Assembly in 1973. Whether this was a tactic favoured by either the British or the ruling core is not clear. The British Ambassador Robert Tesh alluded in 1973 to some inertia on the part of the Al Khalifa regarding such a policy. Tesh stated: 'I pointed out that the political prisoners of today could easily become the chosen leaders of tomorrow'.[224] Fuad Khuri noted that this policy of co-optation was 'led by the Prime Minister', and that he 'deliberately employed many of the "freedom fighters" of the past', in order to '[weaken] the opposition ideologically and organizationally'.[225]

[220] Khalaf, *Contentious Politics in Bahrain.* [221] Belgrave, Papers, 24 December 1956.
[222] *Al Nida Al Arabi,* Issue 1, September 1956, FO371/120548, The National Archives.
[223] J. P. Tripp, 14 February 1965, FO371/179790, The National Archives.
[224] Anon, 18 July 1960, FO1016/684, The National Archives.
[225] Khuri, *Tribe and State in Bahrain,* p. 224.

An example of this co-optation is the case of Hassan al-Jishi, who was exiled from Bahrain for his *Ba'athi-influenced* agitation in 1957. He returned in 1971 and was elected President of the National Assembly in 1973.[226] Similarly, Abdul Aziz Shamlan, described by one British official as a 'tamed exile', was actually the Amir's candidate for Speaker of the Assembly in 1973.[227] The pardon and return of Shamlan was organized in close coordination with the police. Although the government believed Shamlan's return would reflect government confidence in tackling dissent, the pardon was not publicized to avoid a demonstration at the airport.[228]

In 1977, as a consequence of a period of relative stability, the government 'were able to release a number of political detainees for National Day'.[229] Occasions such as National Day have often been used to release political prisoners, affirming the benevolence of the regime while imprinting the ultimate authority of the elite under the banner of nationalism. However, this behaviour has been moderated by the spectre of Saudi displeasure. The fear of an adverse Saudi reaction had previously discouraged the government from releasing prisoners;[230] a fact noted by Robert Tesh in 1973. In this regard, the use of amnesties as a tool to dampen the desire of social movements can be understood as a measure permitted in times of relative government confidence. However, in recent years, it appears that such amnesties are less concerned with the appearance of benevolence or goodwill but more so that political societies can police their own political constituencies. During the outbreak of contentious activity in the 1990s, the release of political prisoners was often on condition that those released would calm down their followers.[231,232] The Bahraini government's concern for agitation even meant the release was contingent on them controlling agitators living abroad, a bizarre turn of events considering state policy had created this exiled opposition overseas. In one instance, Shaykh Khalil and Hasan Mushayma' were released on the understanding that they would travel to Damascus and London to persuade exiled regime opponents to end their activities'.[233]

The tactics of releasing prisoners did not always have the desired effect. The government blamed an outbreak of labour unrest in

[226] R. M. Tesh, From Bahrain Embassy, 18 December 1973, FCO8/1975, The National Archives.
[227] Ibid. [228] Records of Bahrain, Volume 6, 1971, p. 177.
[229] E. F. Given, Bahrain: Annual Review for 1977, FCO8/3091, The National Arcbive.
[230] Tesh, 'Bahrain Elections', p. 11. [231] *The Economist*, 'Spot the villain', p. 44.
[232] Bahry, 'The Opposition in Bahrain', p. 49.
[233] Human Rights Watch, *Routine Abuse*.

1974 on the release of 'two dozen or so political detainees'.[234] Similarly, in 2007, the king sought to defuse tension by ordering the public prosecution to drop its legal case against Hassan Mushayma', Abdulhadi Al Khawaja and Shaker 'Abd al-Husayn, who had been charged, among other things, with promoting change to the political system using illegitimate means. The hope was to have the newly released oppositional figureheads police and calm their supporters. Instead, clashes broke out between security forces and civilians in areas where these figures were popular.[235] Here, the attempted co-optation had been a failure. The regime had underestimated the strength of the oppositional sentiment, and their gamble did not pay off.

As well as releasing prisoners, the government has issued amnesties in order to ameliorate dissent by forging the illusion of a new era. Conciliatory gestures aimed at promoting new beginnings were most controversial following the death of Shaykh 'Isa's in 1999.[236] 'Isa's successor, his son Hamad, made himself king and promised a new era of democratic reforms, earning much international praise in the process.[237] However, his accession was only a fig leaf for the continuation of business as usual. Initially, Hamad initiated a number of steps designed to diffuse social tensions. In May 1999, 'Hamad ordered large quantities of lamb and rice to be distributed at government expense to *matams* throughout the country for use in the upcoming 'Ashurah ceremonies, and in early June he ordered the release of 360 leading detainees.'[238] In addition, Hamad pardoned Shaykh 'Abd al-Amir al-Jamri in July, but only after al-Jamri submitted a statement expressing his regret over various events that had occurred during the 1990s' Intifada.[239] Under Hamad's reforms new forms of collectivization were allowed. Political societies such as Wa'ad formed, with their membership consisting mostly of returned exiles.[240] This included Rahman Al Nuaimi, a Sunni liberal exiled in 1970.[241]

[234] R. M. Tesh, Bahrain: Annual Review for 1974, 2 January 1975, FCO8/2414.

[235] W. T. Monroe, 'Court Case against Activists Dropped, But Clashes Flare Up Anyway', US Embassy Manama, 24 May 2007, https://wikileaks.org/plusd/cables/07MANAMA476_a.html

[236] G. P. Parolin, 'Reweaving the Myth of Bahrain's Parliamentary Experience', in M. A. Tetreault, G. O. Okruhlik and A. Kapiszewski (eds), *Political Change in the Arab Gulf States; Stuck in Transition*, London, Lynne Rienner, 2011, p. 21.

[237] Ibid.

[238] F. H. Lawson, 'Repertoires of Contention in Contemporary Bahrain', in Q. Wiktorowicz (ed.) *Islamic Activism: A Social Movement Theory Approach*, Bloomington, IN, Indiana University Press, 2004, p. 105.

[239] Ibid.

[240] A. Ereli, 'A Field Guide to Bahraini Political Parties', US Embassy Manama, 4 September 2008, www.wikileaks.org/plusd/cables/08MANAMA592_a.html

[241] Ibid.

Other religious figures exiled in the 1990s, including Shaykh Ali Salman Shaikh Hamza al-Dayri and Sayyid Haydar al-Sitri, were also invited to return. While some continued their political activity, the government attempted to co-opt others into the institutions of state. Murtadha Badr, a former IFLB activist, was elected head of the Manama Municipal Council.[242] Hamad's gestures throughout 2001 should be seen more critically as a means of assuaging popular discontent through the grandiose issuing of amnesties. Fundamentally, the traditional processes of *makramāt* were still in place, and the new reforms were a strategic calculation as opposed to deep-rooted constitutional change. The perception of this personal benevolence was highlighted in the testimony of one member, Al Wefaq, who said: 'Then the king sat with the opposition and opened a dialogue, a new page. He took steps we highly appreciated: he released all political prisoners, allowed exiles to return, cancelled the emergency law and staged a referendum on the National Charter.'[243] However, the amnesties ultimately served to allow the continued impunity for the state security forces, who had been accused of torture during the 1990s Intifada (See Chapter 4).

Between GONGOization and Authoritarian Upgrading

The government have also tried to limit the flourishing of critical opposition and meaningful change by placing stringent controls on civil society organizations and institutions, a key driver for political change. As Steven Heydemann notes: 'the hallmark of authoritarian upgrading is the ability of Arab regimes to exploit rather than resist broad social, political, and economic trends, both to blunt the challenges they might contain and to generate political resources that bolster regimes' hold on power'.[244]

This has been particularly relevant following King Hamad's reforms of 2001 that permitted the creation of new civil society institutions. In particular, the government has attempted to limit the effectiveness of NGOs and civil society organizations that, if left unfettered, could provide extra momentum to social movements, institutions or individuals

[242] C. Beaugrand, 'The Return of the Bahraini Exiles', Mapping Middle Eastern and North African Diasporas, BRISMES Annual Conference, July 2008, Leeds, United Kingdom, https://halshs.archives-ouvertes.fr/halshs-00511588/document

[243] International Crisis Group, *Popular Protest in North Africa and the Middle East (VIII): Bahrain's Rocky Road to Reform, MENA Report, No. 111*, 28 July 2011, www.crisisgroup.org/~/media/Files/Middle%20East%20North%20Africa/Iran%20Gulf/Bahrain/111-%20Popular%20Protest%20in%20North%20Africa%20and%20the%20Middle%20East%20VII%20-%20%20Bahrains%20Rocky%20Road%20to%20Reform.pdf

[244] Heydemann, 'Upgrading Authoritarianism'.

desiring change. Human Rights Watch noted that the body responsible for overseeing non-government organizations, the Ministry of Social Development, far exceeded international standards in the restrictions it placed on such groups. They noted that the ministry 'routinely exploited its oversight role to stymie the activities of NGOs and other civil society organisations'.[245] They achieved this through the process of 'arbitrary rejection of registration applications and intrusive governmental supervision of NGOs'[246] and the 'takeover and in some cases dissolution of organisations whose leaders have criticised government officials or their policies'.[247] One Bahraini activist stated that the objective of this was 'to interfere, restrict, and attempt to control the activities of civic organisations'.[248] The government have also put considerable limits on the ability of groups to raise local or foreign funding,[249] fearing funding could be given by nefarious organizations who desired to create instability in Bahrain. However, NGOs in Bahrain also rely on donations from legitimate international funding sources to sustain their activities.

Crucial to the strategy of controlling civil society organizations is the use of co-opted agents or loyal opposition figures, who, to varying extents, consent to the limitations imposed upon them by the government. While this tactic has become more salient in the recent uprising, it can, according to an interview between the US ambassador and Shaykh ʿAbd al-Aziz bin Mubarak Al Khalifa, be attributed also to anti-opposition and anti-Shiʿa hardliners in the ruling family, especially the Khawalid. Through their personal relationships with the king and their officials' positions, the Khawalid have worked since at least 2006 to '"throttle" civil society' by advocating for the clamping down of such groups.[250]

The shift to the manipulation of civil society was a critical development in the arsenal of repression, reflecting to some extent the development from more personalistic approaches to institutionalized paternalism. As protesters in Bahrain adopted a modern human rights agenda and discourse throughout the 1990s and the 2000s, the 'framing of demands on a popular level according to international legal conventions [illustrated] a new articulation and platform for legitimacy'.[251] This shift has seen human rights activists emerge as leaders of the movement. Subsequently, the role of NGOs in lobbying international and regional bodies for

[245] Human Rights Watch, *Interfere, Restrict and Control,* p. 1. [246] Ibid. [247] Ibid.
[248] Ibid., p. 1. [249] Ibid., p. 2. [250] Monroe, 'Bahraini Political Scene Part II'.
[251] L. Bhatia, and A. Shehabi, 'Shifting Contours of Activisms and Policies for Justice in Bahrain', in A. Shehabi and M. O. Jones, M. (eds), *Bahrain's Uprising: Resistance and Repression in the Gulf,* London, Zed Books Ltd, 2015, p. 95.

change has increased. The government now have to fight an uphill battle against the discourse of human rights, the appeal of which lies in 'its capacity to imagine and assert universal rights possessed by every human rather than the specific political rights of citizens or members of a particular political community'.[252] In response, the regime have attempted to appropriate the discourse of human rights themselves. Given that the language of human rights has provided Bahrain's opposition with moral resources and agency, the ruling family have learned to play the 'human rights game', engaging with the United Nations Human Rights Council (UNHRC) while celebrating its 'track record' on human rights.[253] By doing so, the illiberal regime has given itself a liberal facade that has enabled itself to reinforce and rejuvenate its position in the international community.[254]

The government have also tried to wrestle the human rights mantle back from activists and protesters through the creation of Government Owned Non Governmental Organizations (GONGOS). These co-opted organizations attempt to legitimize government repression through the lens of human rights. Following the execution of three men accused of planting a bomb that killed three police officers, the National Institute for Human Rights (NIHR) released a report condoning capital punishment. To endorse capital punishment is generally unheard of among human rights lobbyists, highlighting the extent to which such organizations have been created to whitewash state repression. The regime has also tried to reinvent the rhetoric of human rights. They have been especially keen to emphasize how the protests have impacted upon on the human rights of an undefined and apolitical 'silent majority'. This mysterious silent majority allegedly desires a peaceful and undisrupted existence. The language used by the government here reflects neoliberal sensibilities of peace, security and stability. For example, people should be able to have the 'right' to drive to work without fear of legitimate civil disobedience.

The government's desire to position itself as an authority on human rights was embodied most strongly by the commissioning of the Bahrain Independent Commission of Inquiry (BICI), a team of international experts tasked to investigate the unrest of 2011. Bahrain's European and transatlantic allies lauded the move, for it also gave them a fig leaf with which to continue their relationship with a regime widely known to have committed gross human rights violations. While the move reflected the government's desire to construct its human rights mantle, it was also designed to defuse tensions and build confidence with

[252] Ibid. [253] Ibid., p. 130. [254] Ibid.

citizens. However, as the government have learned in previous decades, such investigations, amnesties or reforms can be used to buy time while they consolidate their strength. As Bernard Burrows once noted in the 1950s, a commission set up to look into communal violence would give authorities 'breathing space', to strengthen the armed forces. Similarly, in 2011, following the setting up of the BICI, John Yates, a former assistant commissioner of the Metropolitan Police, and John Timoney, a former head of Miami Police, were brought in to 'reform' the police. In reality, they were in Bahrain to ensure the ability of the police to continue to resist dissent.

The government used the BICI Report as a platform to launch a cadre of GONGOS funded by the Bahrain government.[255] In addition to setting up a Ministry of Human Rights and the NIHR, the government have legalized a number of superficially independent Human Rights organizations, including the Bahrain Human Rights Watch Society, Bahraini Monitor, the Manama Centre for Human Rights and others. Recently one of these three GONGOS[256] contributed to a witch hunt by publishing the photos of well-known and internationally respected human rights activists, saying that they were responsible for terrorism. This human rights turn was also evident in the ruling regime's desire to position Bahrain as a bastion of regional human rights. King Hamad stated that he wanted Bahrain to become home of the Arab Court for Human Rights, an idea that Cherif Bassiouni dismissed as a 'Potemkin tribunal' – an empty vessel giving a facade of justice.[257] Thus, prompted by pressure for reform, the government have dealt with demands for pluralization by creating a heavily regulated and co-opted civil society that extends the means the regime has to control the population.

Charles Wright Mills once argued that the unity of a power elite, when combined with a fragmented polity, facilitates control.[258] It was noted as early as 1923 that the ruling family had been attempting to weaken opposition to their rule by encouraging enmity between Sunni and Shiʿa. British officials described the consequents of this sectarian divide-and-rule: 'Owing to the extremely bitter relations in Bahrain between Sunnis

[255] Ibid., p. 126.

[256] Bahrain Human Rights Watch Society, Karama Human Rights Society and Gulf European Center for Human Rights.

[257] R. Lowe, 'Bassiouni: New Arab Court for Human Rights Is Fake "Potemkin Tribunal"', International Bar Association, 1 October 2014, www.ibanet.org/Article/Detail.aspx?ArticleUid=c64f9646-15a5-4624-8c07-bae9d9ac42df

[258] C. W. Mills, *The Power Elite*, New York, NY, Oxford University Press, 1967.

Figure 3.2 Cartoon by the author showing how the BICI report was used to appease the international community while shielding the regime's continued human rights violations

and Shaihs [sic], which attitude has, for their own ends, been deliberately encouraged by the rulers for years'.[259]

Despite the seemingly indignant attitude of some European officials, the British also used such tactics when it suited them. Various British policies sought to facilitate the unity of the Al Khalifa regime under Hamad, a tactic that was complemented by dividing potential opposition to the government. In the 1930s and 1940s, when the 'Arabs' (a term often used by the British to refer to Sunna in Bahrain) attempted to get the *baḥārna* to join strikes, Belgrave reminded them that the British had always looked after their interests and thus sought to compound *baḥārna* reluctance to get involved.[260] Similarly, in the 1950s, Persian merchants who opposed the goals of the HEC were granted permission to set up a group that directly opposed the actions of the HEC, a calculated strategy designed to create some opposition to the HEC. The HEC argued that 'the policy of the Persian Committee will be to oppose the Committee of National Union – the people's committee'.[261] Inevitably, such a move also contributed to creating broader divisions between the Bahraini and

[259] The Agency Bahrain, p. 739.

[260] T. Fowle, Agitation in Bahrain, 12 November 1938, *RoB*, in P. Tuson and E. Quick (eds), *Records of Bahrain 1820–1960*, vol. 5, Slough, Archive Editions, 1993, p. 132.

[261] *Al Nida Al Arabi*, Issue 1, September 1956, FO371/120548, The National Archives.

'Persian' community as a whole, setting the stage not only for future sectarian tensions but further tensions between Arabs and Persians. At that time, the message of sectarian unity touted by the HEC was perhaps not as significant as it has been made out to be.[262] In 1953, many Shiʿa went to the Political Agency for protection following the outbreak of sectarian skirmishes in Muharraq,[263] highlighting a lack of depth to the cross-sect unity espoused by the HEC. The existence of interest groups along ethnic lines also facilitated this divide-and-rule strategy.

Despite the creation of a temporary loyal opposition in the form of a Persian Committee, it was still hard for the British to find a pretext to justify cracking down on the HEC. Indeed, the British were forced to admit that the HEC was not particularly anti-British and that even Gamal Abdul Nasser and the Syrians had told the HEC to co-operate with the Bahraini government.[264] However, Britain still feared that a democratic government would prohibit a British military presence. As such, their decision to support the Al Khalifa was also one that meant dismantling the HEC.

Given the popularity of the HEC, Bernard Burrows thought it might be best to resort to political techniques to destroy the movement. It was believed interceding coercively at the moment of the movement's highest popularity might be dangerous. While the creation of divisions was often encouraged deliberately, sometimes they were driven by a lack of material resources or other political imperatives. In his reluctance to see British intervention, Bernard Burrows eschewed using British troops in favour of other methods. They could not move too quickly or violently against al-Bakir lest they risk making him a martyr among his followers.[265] Instead, efforts were made to divide the opposition and turn public opinion against the HEC. Interestingly, there is evidence to suggest that members of the National Front at the time, led by 'prominent younger members of the Ruling Family',[266] deliberately provoked unrest at an HEC Rally in March 1956 in order to prove that the HEC was 'entirely unreliable'.[267] This theory was based on the notion that the ruling family wished to expedite British involvement and highlight that a 'foreign police force

[262] O. Shehabi, 'Political Movements in Bahrain, Past, Present, and Future', *Jadaliyya*, 14 February 2012, www.jadaliyya.com/pages/index/4363/political-movements-in-bahrain_past-present-and-fu
[263] Belgrave, Papers, 20 September 1953.
[264] Minutes from Meeting, 1956, FO371/120548, The National Archives.
[265] Burrows, 1 October 1956, FO371/120548, The National Archives.
[266] B. A. B. Burrows, 4 March 1956, in A. Burdett (ed.), *Records of Bahrain 1820–1960*, vol. 7, Slough, Archive Editions, 1993, pp. 209–12.
[267] Ibid.

[was necessary] to maintain order'.[268] Before this outbreak of violence, the HEC had 'remained almost entirely within the bounds of the law' according to Burrows.[269]

The British did not provide any further evidence in their correspondence about whether the Al Khalifa's involvement in provoking agitation actually occurred. However, they noted that it fit with the ruler's request for British support in a conversation he had had with British Foreign Secretary Selwyn Lloyd.[270] It is plausible that members of the Al Khalifa acted as provocateurs in order to put pressure on the British to intervene. After all, the first half of the century was characterized by the ruling family's selective mobilization of sections of society in order to defend their interests. Despite the ensuing crackdown of the HEC, Burrows believed statecraft had lessened the popularity of the HEC. Musing on the sudden demise of the HEC, Burrows suggested that by persuading the ruler to 'make reasonable reforms and to give time for the more extreme demands of the Committee to disgust moderate opinion', they had 'ensured that there was, in fact, a very wide measure of support in November for the action eventually taken by the ruler against the CNU'.[271] In other words, they had successfully fragmented the movement by undermining its popularity.

Even during Bahrain's brief democratic experiment from 1973 to 75, tactics of divide and rule were used to try and split the fledgling National Assembly, which was threatening to stymie the introduction of the government's draconian security law. An Islamic bloc and a leftist bloc were bucking expectations and joining forces to oppose government policy. The government responded in kind. Robert Tesh noted that the 'rulers [were] deliberately encouraging the Right (particularly the Religious group) to react against the Left'.[272] One minister stated that, as a result, the Left was being successfully smeared as communists and were becoming generally unpopular. Tesh offered a stark warning about such repressive methods, stating that a '"divide and rule" policy does, however, have its dangers and creates the possibility of violence'.[273] This prophetic comment was realized in 1976 when leftist activists of the Popular Front for the Liberation of Oman and the Arabian Gulf (PFLOAG) were accused of killing the notable Shiʿi editor of *al-Mawaqif*, ʿAbd Allah al-Madani. Following his murder, the government feared violence breaking

[268] Ibid. [269] Burrows, 4 March 1956, p. 211. [270] Ibid., pp. 209–10.

[271] D. M. H. Riches, 11 April 1957, in A. Burdett (ed.), *Records of Bahrain 1820–1960*, vol. 7, Slough, Archive Editions, 1993, p. 345.

[272] R. M. Tesh, Bahrain Internal, 6 May 1974, FCO8/2180, The National Archives.

[273] Ibid.

out between leftists and more conservative villagers.[274] However, the circumstances of al Madani's death are disputed, and discussed in further detail in Chapter 5.

As Tesh had warned, the consequences of this divide and rule policy were manifest in growing fringe religious radicalism in Bahrain. As early as 1978, the police were keeping tabs on any possible Shiʿa support for Iran. The risk of radicalism was compounded by government discrimination against the Shiʿa following the Iranian Revolution in 1979. However, despite the work of more extreme groups like the Islamic Front for the Liberation of Bahrain (IFLB), the Shiʿa in Bahrain remained relatively quiet following the revolution.

Growing divisions between the leftists and Shiʿa, especially after the murder of al-Madani, meant that a united leftist Shiʿi front was an impossibility at the time of the Iranian Revolution. As such, it was not an appropriate opportunity for pressing for regime change. Following the Iranian Revolution, the government eschewed what P. F. M. Wogan described as a 'low key' approach to the Shiʿi problem, and instead drove 'young Shiʿa into the extremist camp'.[275] The abandonment of a more relaxed approach to Shiʿi opposition was manifest in the 1990s when Shiʿa marginalization combined with economic woes created an acute political crisis. As expected, the government curtailed political cooperation between moderate Sunna and Shiʿa to divide the movement, driving the Shiʿi movement further underground, making it both more radical and religious.[276] In 1991, Amnesty noted the government's move against the Shiʿa was a 'deliberate policy' designed to target and 'harass and intimidate entire communities – particularly Shiʿa communities' living in villages near the capital city.[277] Amnesty International's accusation appears to correctly reflect the sectarian policies that emerged following Independence.

With the rise of a large Shiʿi bloc following the reforms of 2001, the government feared an overwhelmingly strong Shiʿi mobilization. The rise of this large bloc, initially consisting of Al Wefaq, had in no small part been down to the exclusionary policies fostered by the Bahraini government. The creation of the Shiʿa bloc, according to some Bahrainis, required further division in order to weaken it within the new democratic context. When Al-Wefaq split over a decision to participate

[274] A. J. D. Sterling, Bahrain: Annual Review for 1971, FCO8/1823, The National Archives.
[275] P. F. M. Wogan, 23 April 1982, FCO8/4332, The National Archives.
[276] Bahry, 'The Opposition in Bahrain', pp. 42–57.
[277] Amnesty International, *Bahrain: Violations of Human Rights*, May 1991, pp. 5–6.

in 2006 elections, prominent Shiʿi cleric Shaykh Hussein Najati speculated that the government's arrest of Hassan Mushaymaʿ, 'Ali Salman's rival, was designed to make him a hero among the Shiʿi community, driving a wedge between Al-Wefaq and Haq in order to divide the Shiʿi street.[278] Naturally, the danger of pushing elements of the population to more radical fringes creates the potential for more instability. Despite this split, and subsequent splits of Al Wefaq into groups like Haq and Wafa', opposition groups generally maintained unity during the 2011 Uprising.

Attitudes to the Shiʿa after 2011

In the build-up to the uprising of 2011, repressive government policy towards the Shiʿa can be understood as a product of hawkish ascendency following 2001. As US Ambassador Monroe stated in 2007:

> The royal family is, in fact, divided on how to deal with the Shiʿa...royal family hard-liners, exemplified by the Prime Minister, are wary of reform for many reasons: the demographic threat posed by the majority Shiʿa, whose loyalty to Bahrain (i.e., connections with Iran) has long been questioned; concern that democracy, and by extension noisy street demonstrations, will scare investors away; and – most importantly – the potential threat to the Al-Khalifa regime that reform may ultimately pose. Although one of the key hard-liners is Royal Court Minister and close King confidant Shaikh Khalid bin Ahmed, the views of the King are less clear. It was the King, after all, who launched the reform movement, talks of a day when the King will serve as a constitutional monarch paternalistically protecting the interests of all Bahrainis and infuriates hard-liners by regularly ordering the release or pardon of Shiʿa extremists and demonstrators. And yet, he does little to reign in Shaikh Khalid bin Ahmed and his hard-line allies.[279]

The alleged split in the ruling family mentioned by Monroe, along with Hamad's reform-orientated approach, have arguably long been subservient to the interests of hardliners. The limited nature of the reforms of 2001 had all but ensured the containment of Shiʿi activism, implying that it was always a conservative and sectarian group within the Al Khalifa that had dictated policies facilitating anti-Shiʿa discrimination. Given this high-level distrust of the Shiʿa, it is unsurprising that the government

[278] W. T. Monroe, 'Prominent Shiʿa Paint Gloomy Picture of Shiʿa Outlook in Bahrain', US Embassy Manama, 9 April 2007, http://webcache.googleusercontent.com/search?q=cache:eZh_8zJoqAoJ:https://wikileaks.org/plusd/cables/07MANAMA328_a.html+&cd=1&hl=en&ct=clnk&gl=uk

[279] W. T. Monroe, 'Future of Bahrain: Ambassador's Parting Thoughts', US Embassy Manama, 19 July 2007, https://wikileaks.org/plusd/cables/07MANAMA669_a.html

instrumentalized sectarianism in order to divide the opposition. This instrumentalization was most notable in 2011 when the government enflamed religious tensions by deliberately destroying Shi'i religious structures, a move that Amnesty International considered to be 'collective punishment'.[280] They also targeted Sunni members of the opposition who bridged the sectarian gap. Ibrahim Sharif, the General Secretary of Wa'ad, was arrested, as was Muhammad al-Buflasa, a former member of the Bahrain military. Justin Gengler posited that Ibrahim Sharif and al-Buflasa were the most dangerous men in Bahrain, not because they were violent, but because both Sharif and al-Buflasa's stances placed them 'against the royal family and government', which, 'as Khuri observed three decades ago, is especially intolerant of social and political groupings that cut across Sunni–Shi'i lines'.[281] In reality, it was not just these high-profile figures that were the 'most dangerous'. In the age of social media, new inadvertent figures emerged. Manaf al-Muhandis, for example, was arrested for starting a successful online campaign called #UniteBH (Unite Bahrain). The purpose was to unite Bahrainis, irrespective of sect, via Twitter.[282] Others espousing principles of unity were ridiculed. For example, guards at a checkpoint abused a driver for wearing a t-shirt saying, 'No Sunni, No Shi'a, Just Bahraini'.[283] While the government no doubt were extremely wary of any form of perceived dissent during 2011, acts of cross-sect unity were especially dangerous.

However, as Justin Gengler notes, the problem with this balancing act is that the 'more the state succeeds in convincing "loyal citizens" of the need to defend Bahrain against Shi'i and Iranian designs, the more it opens itself to the charge of not acting firmly enough'.[284] This dangerous game has led to a state of affairs where loyalist-dominated democratic institutions support draconian and repressive legislation in the name of national security, giving a veneer of popular legitimacy to discriminatory practices. King Hamad's empowerment of Sunni Islamists has compounded this problem. In 1997 'Ali Salman stated that the current state of sectarian tensions was unprecedented in Bahrain's history.[285] As of

[280] Amnesty International, 'Human Rights in Bahrain – Media Briefing', 31 April 2012, www.amnesty.ca/news/news-item/amnesty-international-human-rights-briefing-on-bahrain

[281] J. Gengler, 'The Most Dangerous Men in Bahrain', Religion and Politics in Bahrain [web blog], 5 June 2011, http://bahrainipolitics.blogspot.co.uk/2011/06/most-dangerous-men-in-bahrain.html

[282] @Redbelt, 'Today is the anniversary of my detainment. Just because someone posted my picture on Facebook. Also because I started #UniteBH', [Tweet by @Redbelt], 29 March 2012, https://twitter.com/Redbelt/status/185324439934738432

[283] M. Yusif, 'Just Bahrain' not welcome at checkpoints', Mahmood's Den [web blog], http://mahmood.tv/2011/03/19/just-bahraini-not-welcome-at-checkpoints//

[284] Gengler, 'Bahrain's Sunni Awakening'. [285] Monroe, 'Future of Bahrain'.

2017, they were certainly no better, especially now that the government were repressing both out of perceived necessity but also to appease their own loyal constituency.

There Is Power in a (Dis)Union

As well as driving a wedge between different sects to prevent the rise of large-scale formal political organizations, the Bahraini government has opposed the foundation of political parties, societies, labour unions or clubs that cut across regional, ethnic or religious groupings. This resistance to formal political organization has been particularly acute in the labour sphere. Trade unions or worker activity has been highly fragmented by the regime, especially after the 1965 Uprising, which resulted from the state-controlled oil company BAPCO laying off expatriate workers. Following the unrest, committees at BAPCO were subsequently and deliberately created to be a 'safety valve should any disturbances take place in the future'.[286] The committees were purposefully organized in a way that would prevent social and political items getting on the agenda.[287] The resultant committees could only bargain on mundane[288] issues, and the ballot system was arranged so that a company-wide lobby was avoided. Thus, bylaws ensured that no 'Bahraini personalities could emerge as the few representatives of a mass of workers'.[289]

Eschewing labour legislation, the government sought to engage in industrial arbitration that would prevent the emergence of a strong labour power base.[290] Occasionally this involved selective incentives and divide and rule. In 1973, the British noted how the 'government and management contrived to drive a wedge between the striking employees of two BAPCO contractors and their ringleaders, making some concessions to the former and dispersing the latter'.[291] In 1980 the Bahrain government were firmly committed to keeping labour groups 'small, not centralised'.[292] Although they were distrusted by the majority of underground worker movements, the government introduced co-opted 'Workers' Committees'[293] to prevent a manageable outlet for worker grievances. In 1981 these committees contributed, albeit

[286] Anon, 1965, in A. Burdett (ed.) Records of Bahrain, vol. 5, Cambridge Archive Editions, 1961–1965, 1997, p. 422.
[287] Ibid., p. 423. [288] Ibid., p. 412. [289] Ibid., p. 422.
[290] G. Foggon, 28 October 1974, FCO8/2180, The National Archives.
[291] R. M. Tesh, 23 July 1973, FCO8/1975, The National Archives.
[292] H. B. Walker, Bahrain Internal, 18 May 1980, FCO8/3489, The National Archives.
[293] This was via the 'joint commission of workers and employers to attend to matters related to industrial relations'. Order 9, the ordinance issued by the ministry.

marginally, to the process of labour pacification.[294] Like the reforms of 1965, the activities of these groups were deliberately and heavily curtailed to prevent strikes.

The promulgation of the 1981 Labour Law paved the way for the introduction of an eleven-member elected General Committee to oversee labour disputes. These eleven members were elected from the forty-eight elected worker representatives, who were joined with an equal number of management-appointed members from the Joint Committees (JC). The Joint Committees had their roots in the nominated Joint Consultative Committees (JCCs) created in 1971. Interestingly, the companies that were permitted to have JCCs were mostly ones that had Westerners in management. This prejudice in allocating JCCs in Westerner-managed companies was primarily due to the experience held by such staff in dealing with labour issues. It was assumed that those who had worked in Europe or the United States would be familiar with how to deal with workers' committees and strikes. The focus on having an appointed body to balance the will of elected members reflected the government's fear of providing political space to those deemed subversive. Even those who ran for the elected positions were vetted by the Secret Intelligence Services.[295] Furthermore, the prime minister was reported to have personally intervened to prevent specific candidates from being elected. As Simon Paul Collis noted: 'The Prime Minister has involved himself closely in the process and allegedly turned down several quite presentable candidates on his own account.'[296] Also, while the Joint Committees and the General Committee could write their own constitutions in accordance with the Labour Law, the JC's committee had to be ratified by the Ministry of Labour. Reflecting the relative improvement of the labour situation, but one that nonetheless guaranteed government control over labour matters both at the international and national level, Simon Collis wrote in 1983 that 'the General Committee will present Bahrain with a rather more decent fig leaf to sport in international labour circles'.[297] In other words, the creation of a convoluted system of checks and balances ensured government dominance over union activity.

King Hamad's reforms saw the emergence of labour law reform, and the umbrella union, the General Federation of Bahrain Trade Unions (GFBTU) was created. However, strikes organized by the GFBTU in the 2011 Uprising prompted the government to dismantle the newly

[294] Khalaf, 'Labor Movements in Bahrain'.
[295] S. P. Collis, Bahrain Labour, 12 March 1983, FCO8/4920, The National Archives.
[296] Ibid. [297] Collis, 12 March 1983.

empowered unions. While the strikes had been entirely legal according to the BICI report, their effectiveness demonstrated to the government the potential impact of industrial action, which had never occurred on such a large scale in Bahrain's history. In response, the government issued legislation that paved the way for the creation of a new umbrella trade union that the union official Cathy Feingold[298] described as an 'absolutely blatant attempt to split the union movement'.[299] Initially, and perhaps fittingly, the acronym of the new union spelt BLUFF (Bahrain Labour Union Free Federation), and critics such as Khalil Boazza, a Bahraini labour activist, believed that the new movement would weaken Bahrain's previously 'opposition-dominated' unions.[300] Some union activists even argued that unions representing workers at some major corporations went over to BLUFF without the consent of their members.[301] BLUFF was called out, and rearranged its name to FFBTU. However, the new trade union amendments highlighted the government's attempts to limit effective collective action, contributing to the process by which the 'state erodes the capacity of social movements, thereby diminishing the ability to engage in contentious politics'.[302] By dividing and disempowering the GFBTU, the government reduced the union's ability to call effective strikes and lobby on behalf of Bahraini workers both nationally and internationally.[303] Given the importance of Bahrain's labour force, the absence of strikes meant that the opposition lost crucial political leverage. Furthermore, by maintaining the existence of the unions, the government were making their repression superficially acceptable, as they could defend their action by pointing out that they had not banned or dissolved the unions.

The nature of political repression is not just about preventing people from engaging in collective action but is also about shaping the nature of that collective action in order that it can be best controlled. Fragmentation and reshaping are a dynamic process whereby the government assesses potential oppositional coalitions, dividing them accordingly. Whether through trade unions, or religion, the regime in Bahrain has maintained a degree of organizational fragmentation. This method is not

[298] Cathy Feingold is the director of the international department for the AF-CIO, the American Trade Union federation.
[299] B. Law, 'New Bahrain Trade Federation Splits Union Movement', BBC News, 17 November 2012, www.bbc.co.uk/news/world-middle-east-20324436.
[300] H. T. al-Hasan, 'Bahrain's New Labour Scheme: One Step Forward, Two Steps Back?', *Open Democracy*, 5 August 2012, www.opendemocracy.net/hasan-tariq-al-hasan/bahrain%E2%80%99s-new-labour-scheme-one-stepam-forward-two-steps-back
[301] Law, 'New Bahrain Trade Federation'. [302] Boykoff, 'Limiting Dissent', p. 294.
[303] Austin Holmes, 'Working on the Revolution in Bahrain'.

always consistent. For example, following the murder of the newspaper editor ʿAbd Allah al Madani in 1976 (see Chapter 3), the police reportedly made rapid arrests to reduce the possibility of leftist versus religious bloc violence, whereas in the recent uprising, the government sought the deliberate exacerbation of communal tension. The possible explanations are numerous. It could be that the unrest following 1976 was not widespread or substantial enough to warrant wholescale divide and conquer tactics on a societal level. If this were the case, it could be hypothesized that once unrest in Bahrain crosses a particular threshold of threat, the sectarian card is deployed actively (or perhaps just resonates more significantly). Alternatively, the police policy of arrest could be separate from the government's desire to enact a divide and rule strategy, perhaps itself reflecting some degree of command and control conflict within the police. It also reflects, as Charles Tilly stated earlier, how repression can be selective, often defined contextually and in view of temporally based factors. In such a case, it cannot simply be argued that the sectarian card is always deployed but rather is deployed strategically and/or ambiguously.

From Municipal Councils to Democracy: Reform as Repression

> Bahrain is rapidly industrialising in a period of rampant inflation; in which there is great maldistribution of wealth together with universal education; in which semi-feudalism has already largely given way to broad-based cabinet government; in which the mushrooming towns contrast with the neglected villages and the Islamic traditionalists with the modernists: such a country needs a representative organ to balance and adjust the strains.[304]

Demands for democracy, or at least democratic ideals, have been a critical driver of reform since the early 1900s. The British realized as early as 1922 that the spread of 'democratic ideas'[305] had made what they called 'the tyrannical rule of the Al Khalifa' difficult. State concessions to political liberalization in Bahrain have generally been made to provide a 'safety valve' for popular politics, thus mitigating the chances of direct violent action. Several democratic forums have been expressly created to repress potential dissent. For example, the Manama Municipality established by Major Daly in 1919 was tasked with 'forging' a new political and sanitary regime in the town as the antidote to Bahrain's social and political malaise'.[306] The municipal councils established in urban areas

[304] Tesh, 'Bahrain's First Parliament'. [305] Daly, 11 April 1922.
[306] N. Fuccaro, *Histories of City and State in the Persian Gulf: Manama since 1800*, Cambridge, Cambridge University Press, 2009, p. 118.

across Bahrain were efforts to extend the influence of the Government of India and allay social turmoil through a functional administrative apparatus. Indeed, administrative reform as an antidote to unrest is well rooted in Bahrain's modern history.

However, the limitations of the municipal councils in Manama, Muharraq and Hidd were made apparent when certain groups pushed to have more democratic institutions established. Until the 1940s, both the Al Khalifa and the British were reluctant to institute such reforms for fear of ceding too much control. However, in 1935, the Political Resident of the Persian Gulf, Trenchard Craven Fowle, sought to impress upon the ruler that 'times [had] changed and governments must now depend, to a large extent, on the public opinion of the majority of their subjects'.[307] Despite this view, demands for a democratic council in the 1930s, mostly by the community of Persian Holis, and not the *baḥārna* or Arabs, were rebuffed by the Al Khalifa who thought that councils would be the 'swan song of the Al Khalifah as Rulers of Bahrain;'[308] However, the British noted that if the agitation spread beyond the Holis, it would be foolish not to implement at least an advisory body for the Shaykh.

While the British, and specifically the Government of India, had put the breaks on suggesting democratic institutions, they had pressed for reforms both during and after the agitation of the Manama *baḥārna* in 1934/1935. However, this mostly related to having more representation on the commercial council and the municipalities, as well as improvement to education and the creation of a criminal code.[309] As a middle course, the British began pushing more for administrative reform to curb dissent. During the strikes and rise of the HEC in the 1950s, timely administrative reform was framed by officials as a means of defusing social tension. Referring to the ongoing strikes, Burrows noted in 1954 that 'the removal of some justifiable grievances will leave the subversive virus with less to feed on'.[310]

Generally speaking, the British believed that a solid legal system would actually increase the power of the administration and, as a consequence, bolster Al Khalifa authority. Burrows stated that 'It [was] the object of the reforms which the Bahrain Government have announced on our

[307] T. C. Fowle, Communique to Government of India, in P. Tuson and E. Quick (eds), *Records of Bahrain 1820–1960*, Slough, Archive Editions, vol. 5, 1993, p. 109.

[308] Political Agent, Express Letter, in A. Burdett (ed.), *Records of Bahrain 1820–1960*, Slough, Archive Editions, 1993, pp. 200–4.

[309] G. Loch, Communique to the Political Resident, 18 February 1935, in A. Burdett (ed.), *Records of Bahrain 1820–1960*, vol. 5, Slough, Archive Editions, 1993, p. 94.

[310] B. A .B. Burrows, 20 July 1954, in A. Burdett (ed.), *Records of Bahrain 1820–1960*, vol. 7, Slough, Archive Editions, 1993, p. 59.

advice to increase both the impartiality and the power of the administration'.[311] If these reforms failed to ameliorate dissent, the British knew that it would at least allow time to strengthen the coercive apparatus. Burrows also sought reforms as a means of buying time, implying that there remained an ulterior motive to political change. He argued that timely reform would 'give a breathing space in which [the government] might strengthen the Public Security Department, and at the same time satisfy the more intelligent section of the people now discontented'.[312] Despite Burrows' suggestion, the ruler was reluctant to pursue administrative reforms that could empower the Shiʿa. J. W. Wall and Charles Belgrave had to convince the Emir to carry out administrative changes.[313] The resulting agreement between the Emir and the British was conditional. Eventually, the government published an ordinance that stated reforms would only be announced if those on strike returned to work.[314] Certainly, in order to encourage the ruling family to enact such reforms, the British phrased it in a way that suggested it would ultimately increase Al Khalifa's strength and power. Thus reform sought not only to defuse oppositional tension but to improve the long-term survivability of the regime. Reform can actually be, in some cases, a most insidious form of repression.

The National Assembly as Counter-Revolutionary Insurance

In the 1970s, the British were still emphasizing the need for reform as a form of counter-revolutionary insurance. This time, however, they were pushing for popular representation.[315] British Ambassador Andrew Sterling noted that the British wanted 'the government to affect its promised constitutional reforms' and 'improve the system of administration' in order to help 'guard against revolution'.[316] Sterling also noted in his 1971 Annual Report to the Foreign and Commonwealth Office that such constitutional advance was the 'best defence against subversion',[317] as if democratic representation was a means of ameliorating dissent rather than empowering Bahrainis. However, upon Independence, the British had already reported that the hawkish prime minister had halted moves towards popular representation', demonstrating what Stirling disparagingly called a 'native talent for procrastination'.[318] Democracy was also reportedly opposed by Bahrain's neighbours, including

[311] Ibid., p. 57. [312] Burrows, 20 July 1954, p. 54. [313] Ibid. [314] Ibid.
[315] R. M. Tesh, Bahrain: Internal, 17 December 1973, FCO8/1975, The National Archives.
[316] A. J. D. Sterling, Annual Review 1970, FCO8/1638, The National Archives.
[317] Ibid. [318] Ibid.

Saudi Arabia, the UAE, Qatar and even Kuwait.[319] Tesh wrote in 1972, that 'there is some irritation that Saudi Arabian conservatism puts the breaks on popular representation in Bahrain'.[320] Despite this opposition, and in order to smooth over the transition to Independence and build confidence, Shaykh ʿIsa announced that a constitution would be introduced in 1971.[321] Two years later, Robert Tesh reflected on the effect of the reforms on unrest. 'Judging by the absence of violence and the paucity of strikes since the outbreak of March 1972, the steps taken towards popular representation are having the desired effect.'[322]

The reforms themselves reflected a lack of political will among many ministers. The parliament was criticised for only being 'representative enough to be credible'.[323] That the 'Shiʿi villages' were 'underrepresented'[324] demonstrated a Saudi-Al Khalifa animosity towards the Shiʿa and a general fear of majoritarianism. The veneer of credibility was evident in the amended constitution, which superficially 'appeared to curtail the Amir's powers but in fact was calculated to give the government and the Prime Minister an assured position for the first four-year parliament at least – after which they would take their chance'.[325] In effect, the National Assembly would still guarantee continued Al Khalifa rule. As Tesh noted: 'The aim of the Al-Khalifah inner circle was to delegate sufficient power to the People to satisfy them that its intentions were genuine, but not to concede so much that the administration would be hamstrung, or rash measures forced on it, or powerful neighbours antagonised, or the position of the Al Khalifa irredeemably undermined.'[326]

The perceived perils of the 1973–5 National Assembly were also obviated by carefully crafted procedural obstacles. In addition to a distribution of power that favoured the Al Khalifa regime and its allies, the government also engaged in tactics designed to limit the power of elected members. For example, the government angered elected members by 'insisting on priority for its own bills' and using 'parliamentary devices – closed sessions, the committee system, the rules of reply, etc. – to curb the elected members' powers'.[327] They also chose to pass controversial legislation, like the security decree, in the summer recess by Amiri

[319] R. M. Tesh, Bahrain's Elections, 11 December 1973, FCO8/1975, TNA.
[320] Tesh, Bahrain: Annual Review for 1972, 31 December 1972. [321] Ibid.
[322] R. M. Tesh, Bahrain: Constitutional Development, 12 June 1973, FCO8/1975, The National Archives.
[323] R. M. Tesh, Bahrain: Annual Review for 1973, FCO8/2181, The National Archives.
[324] Ibid. [325] Ibid. [326] Tesh, Bahrain: Constitutional Development.
[327] R. M. Tesh, Bahrain: Internal, 4 March 1975, FCO8/2415, The National Archives.

decree; as they knew that parliament would not accept it.[328] The decree, which had been opposed by the assembly, was legal until the Assembly declared it null.[329] When the Assembly did not ratify the bill, it was dissolved in order to 'contain the growing influence of opposition and alter the power balance to the advantage of the ruling family'.[330] Even the timing of the dissolution was calculated for maximum repressive effect, and done in the summer where it was assumed that the heat would 'provoke the least reaction'.[331]

The tactics of democratization and constitutional reform as a means of guarding against revolution had been profoundly influenced by Saudi encroachment in Bahrain's internal affairs. The British believed that 'Saudi Arabia, though an immensely powerful friend, [was] too rich, too Islamic, and too close for comfort'.[332] It was under this growing Saudi influence that the Bahraini government reportedly 'became less inclined towards political change, no doubt under Saudi influence'.[333] Saudi influence undoubtedly emboldened the anti-reform nature of hardliners, such as the prime minister. Even the British Ambassador Edward Given was inclined to attribute this shift away from support of political reform to the pressure from Saudi Arabia: 'this may be due to the influence of the Saudis, whom I believe greatly disapproved of the Bahrain experiment in democracy'.[334] As the British had done in the 1920s, the Saudis used their own *makramāt* to secure influence among the ruling family, who could then be leaned on to pressure the Bahraini Amir into supporting Saudi foreign policy.

Bahrain was not alone in the region. The British diplomat Ivor Lucas wrote in 1978 that 'all the traditional regimes in the Gulf are becoming increasingly dependent on Saudi support and that they must to a greater or lesser extent accept what goes with it'.[335] Given elaborated on how Saudi Arabia was keen to secure favour, stating that 'grotesquely expensive sports facilities' were given 'to please some of the younger shaykhs'. He believed that such gifts were 'conditional on the abandonment of [democratic] experiments which might prove dangerous to the Al Sa'ud as well as to the Al Khalifa'.[336] In other words, Saudis sought to co-opt

[328] Tesh, Bahrain: Annual Review for 1974.
[329] R. M. Tesh, Bahrain Internal, 1 March 1975, FCO8/2415, The National Archives.
[330] Khuri, *Tribe and State in Bahrain*, p. 234.
[331] H. B. Walker, Bahrain Internal, 28 June 1980, FCO8/3489, The National Archives.
[332] R. Tomkys, First Impressions, 4 February 1982, FCO8/4332, The National Archives.
[333] E. F. Given, Bahrain: Annual Report for 1976, 5 January 1977, FCO8/2873, The National Archives.
[334] Ibid.
[335] I. T. M. Lucas, Bahrain 1977, 9 February 1978, FCO8/3091, The National Archives.
[336] E. F. Given, Prospects for Bahrain, 5 July 1976, FCO8/2643, The National Archives.

influential Bahrainis with monetary incentives – a form of rentierism-as-foreign policy.

While successive British political agents had initially rejected but eventually encouraged the idea of democracy, it was now chiefly Saudi conservatism, and fear of Shiʿi subversion, that prompted the question of democracy to be firmly ignored. In 1980, the Bahraini leadership insisted that there would be no return to parliamentary life.[337] Al Khalifa antipathy towards Bahrain's Shiʿa community was also a factor. In the Assembly's early days, Robert Tesh reported that the Amir had 'growled about "All these Shiʿa"' in the parliament.[338] The prime minister too was reportedly insistent that democracy in Bahrain would mean a parliament populated by men in Turbans who take their orders from Khomeini.[339] The feeling that the government gave too much in the way of representation in 1973 may explain the reneges on promises made by the king in 2001. Whether or not the British pressure for reform after 1963 was sincere or even significant, the Al Khalifa could indulge their habitual disdain for democratic institutions by 'clinging' not to Britain but to Saudi Arabia instead.

Thus, democratization as a means of grievance removal and a safety valve to mitigate potential unrest was a temporary tactic, not sustained enough to affect Al Khalifa hegemony. Attempts to resurrect the democracy were prevented by Bahrain's new patron, Saudi Arabia. The Al Khalifa Ruling Family Council were also disillusioned with democracy and reportedly blamed Shaykh ʿIsa for ever having agreed to it.[340] Indeed, it is interesting to note once again that Shaykh ʿIsa was far more inclined towards administrative reform that could be seen to fall within the spectrum of power-sharing. This 'softness', as the British once called it, was not shared by his brother Khalifa. Indeed, the prime minister, who was already, according to Stirling, firmly 'in the saddle' by the late 1970s, was apparently 'reluctant to defy King Faisal'.[341] Thus, the reassertion of Al Khalifa authoritarianism and Saudi pressure can offer further insight into the repressive measures taken by the Al Khalifa regime following Independence. However, this was not just general Al Khalifa authoritarianism. Clearly ʿIsa was seen as a soft touch, and more willing to consider measures of change that did not fit with the desires of his brother Khalifa or other hardliners.

[337] H. B. Walker, 26 October 1980, FCO8/3489, The National Archives.
[338] Tesh, Bahrain: Constitutional Development.
[339] H. B. Walker, Bahrain Internal – Representative Assembly, 19 February 1981, FCO8/3893, The National Archives.
[340] R. M. Tesh, 10 June 1974, FCO8/2180, The National Archives.
[341] A. J. D. Stirling, 'Bahrain: Annual Review for 1971', The National Archives.

The creation and subsequent dissolution of parliament in 1975 were enough to raise and then dash expectations of many Bahrainis. As Robert Franklin noted: 'The dissolution of Parliament in 1975 abruptly terminated this political development without ending the sentiments in favour of reform, creating and reinforcing a profound sense of deprivation and frustration.'[342] If a significant part of this failure was due to Saudi pressure, then Saudi influence continued being important in stymying any democratic advance in the 1990s. Instead, co-opted councils with limited advisory powers were the administrative repressive method of choice. In a time-honoured tradition, the 1990s Intifada resulted in the construction of an appointed council to form a safety valve for popular grievances. In 1993 a thirty-member council with fifteen Sunna and fifteen Shiʿa was appointed by the Amir, but they had no legislative function. One Bahraini businessman interviewed by Human Rights Watch perceived the strategy as being exogenous to Bahrain, noting that the 'Shura proposal was ninety-five percent made-in-Saudi Arabia';[343] pointing again to the perception that repressive reform was dictated by Saudi interests.

While the new Shura council was criticized as pointless, several Bahrainis, including a former cabinet minister, alluded to how policymaking was increasingly the role of a small cabal headed by the conservative, Saudi-influenced prime minister. He noted that 'even the cabinet itself was no longer the site of useful policy discussion, and in recent years assembled only to rubber-stamp the decisions of Prime Minister Khalifa bin Salman Al Khalifa, and to hear from a small number of other influential officials, most notably Minister of Interior Muhammad bin Khalifa Al Khalifa, a first cousin of the Amir'.[344] Unsurprisingly, the regime's attempt at defusing tension through a facade of popular representation was a failure, and unrest continued through the 1990s. While the council was updated in 1996 to forty members,[345] it was dissolved in 2002 upon the creation of the country's bicameral parliament. Like the National Assembly, committees and municipal councils before it, the latest Shura council had been a tentative experiment designed to defuse unrest while the regime consolidated power. It would certainly make sense to assume that the idea for such a council was agreed upon by Saudi Arabia. It reflected Saudi's own attitude to domestic trouble. In Saudi, the government were actively rejecting any political *infitah* (opening).[346] As such, they were pushing hard against democratic tendencies in the region. For

[342] R. Franklin, 'Migrant Labour and the Politics'.
[343] Cited in Human Rights Watch, *Routine Abuse*. [344] Ibid.
[345] T. Lansford, 'Bahrain', *Political Handbook of the World 2014*, London, Sage, p. 109.
[346] P. Menoret, *The Saudi Enigma*, London, Zed Books Ltd, p. 125.

example, in 1997 the Saudi interior minister, Prince Nayef 'urged his Yemeni counterpart to cancel the parliamentary elections' on the basis that they were a 'threat to stability in the region'.[347]

A Faulty Safety Valve: Towards King Hamad's Facade Democracy

The death of Shaykh ʿIsa in 1999 and the succession of his son Hamad to Amir marked a new era of politics in Bahrain. Hamad drove forward several reforms that included the eventual establishment of a bicameral parliament and the liberalization of laws governing civil society. Ostensibly a step-change towards more representative politics, when viewed through a critical lens, the reforms of 2001 can best be described as a constitutional coup. On the surface, the reforms were a response to US foreign policy promotion goals of democratization. On the ground, the actual reforms were tempered by a fear of giving the Shiʿa too much power. A member of the ruling family told Ambassador William Monroe that: 'The Saudi leadership opposes open elections in Bahrain for fear that the Shiʿa would gain too much power.'[348]

Indeed, Bahrain's close alliance with Saudi Arabia facilitated the execution of Saudi foreign policy objectives, which revolved around countering internal democratic development in Bahrain. The Saudis believed that democracy would result in Iranian expansion in the Gulf region.[349] As they did in the early 1970s, the government sought to restrict the threats posed by social movements and opposition by defusing tensions through democratic reforms, while also ensuring mechanisms for the executive's continued political dominance. As the International Crisis Group (ICG) noted, the structures of democracy chosen 'virtually guaranteed that ultimate decision-making power remained in the palace'.[350] This assessment supported British assertions in 1982, when they noted that the 'Al Khalifa [intended] to continue to control Bahrain themselves'.[351] In addition to curbing Iranian expansionism, the simple fact that the ruling family did not want to have their

[347] Human Rights Watch, *Routine Abuse.*

[348] Monroe, 'Bahraini Political Scene Part II'.

[349] O. Hassan, 'Undermining the Transatlantic Democracy Agenda? The Arab Spring and Saudi Arabia's Counteracting Democracy Strategy', *Democratization*, vol. 22, no. 3, pp. 479–95, doi: 10.1080/13510347.2014.981161.

[350] International Crisis Group, 'Popular Protests in North Africa and the Middle East (III): The Bahrain Revolt', MENA Report No. 105, 6 April 2011, www.crisisgroup.org/~/media/Files/Middle%20East%20North%20Africa/Iran%20Gulf/Bahrain/105-%20Popular%20Protests%20in%20North%20Africa%20and%20the%20Middle%20East%20-III-The%20Bahrain%20Revolt.pdf

[351] W. R. Tomkys, 8 May 1982, FCO8/4332, The National Archives.

spending curtailed by an elected body also influenced Al Khalifa reticence to reform. As the British Ambassador Roger Tomkys stated in 1982, 'the way in which the Amir and his family spend their funds will certainly be off limits'.[352] As such, under Hamad's reforms, constitutional amendments required a two-thirds majority of both elected and appointed chambers, rendering change highly improbable. Furthermore, 'while power to pass laws rested with both chambers, the cabinet alone [had] the right to initiate and draft them'.[353] Meanwhile, the 'appointed Shura chamber has in effect veto power over initiatives and decisions by the elected chamber'.[354] Perhaps most importantly, the King of Bahrain retains the 'power to rule by decree (*marsūm bi-qanūn*), provided such decrees do not violate the constitution'.[355] However, as we will see in Chapter 5, the constitution's National Safety caveat essentially suspends constitutionally guaranteed protections of civil liberties and rights.

In addition to this, a few political prestidigitations were undertaken during the initial reforms in 2001. The government issued several statutory decrees before the creation of the new parliament. As with any statutory decrees issued before the first meeting of Bahrain's new 'democratic' National Assembly, none could be amended unless both houses voted to rescind them.[356] These included the draconian press law, which although suspended after protests, was enforced at the government's discretion.[357] The reality of this move was that it became virtually impossible to rescind any laws decreed before the creation of the National Assembly in 2002, no matter how draconian.

Electorally, the reforms also put in systems of redundancy to ensure the disempowerment of the country's Shiʿa. Before 2014, Bahrain's electoral boundaries were drawn in order to to minimize the impact of the Shiʿi vote. The boundaries meant that Sunni constituencies numbering only a few hundred were given the same voting power as a Shiʿa-dominated block consisting of thousands of citizens. In some cases, one Sunni vote equalled twenty-one Shiʿi votes.[358] Influential in this strategy were members of the ruling family, namely two influential Al Khalifa brothers – the Minister of State for Cabinet Affairs Shaykh Ahmed bin Attiyatallah and President of the Royal Court

[352] Ibid. [353] International Crisis Group, 'Popular Protests in North Africa'.
[354] Ibid. [355] Ibid. [356] Ibid.
[357] Carnegie Endowment for International Peace, 'Arab Political Systems: Baseline Information and Reforms – Bahrain', 2008.
[358] F. Desmukh, 'Gerrymandering in Bahrain. Twenty-One Persons, One Vote', 2013, Bahrain Watch, https://bahrainwatch.org/blog/2013/02/11/gerrymandering-in- bahrain-twenty-one-persons-one-vote/

Shaykh Mohammed bin Attiyatallah – who led 'the effort to contain the electoral process'.[359]

As the ruling family feared, the nature of the democratization yielded new power formations and groups that, if left unmanaged, would gain further influence. Before the 2014 elections, the democratization prompted by the King had given more clout to Sunni Islamists to balance the increasingly empowered Shiʿi bloc in parliament, a move that the American ambassador noted made Bahrain more conservative. King Hamad's empowerment of this Sunna bloc reflected a conflict in his 'desire to be a regional leader on reform' and the desire of 'neighbours – especially Saudi Arabia – who [worried] about the influence his reforms might have elsewhere in the region'[360] Yet although the King '[counselled] patience and understanding with the Shiʿa', he still '[permitted] hard-line royal family members to crack down hard against Shiʿi interests'.[361] The influence of these hardliners was noted by *Al-Wasat* editor (and former Shiʿi exile) Mansur al-Jamri, who said that the Minister of the Royal Court Shaykh Khalid bin Ahmed had become the de facto prime minister and that the actual prime minister was currently more focused on protecting his business interests and his family's future.[362]

Whether or not this faction exerted more power than the prime minister is debatable, and perhaps irrelevant, as their interests seem generally aligned on matters of internal security. The limited nature of democratization as a repressive safety valve, evident in the constitutional coup, reflects again a middle course between appeasing US and European interests while also bending to the Saudi and Al Khalifa desire not to empower the Shiʿa too much. Since 1979, any transatlantic democracy promotion has itself become muted by a strategic 'interest in containing Iran'.[363]

Following the advent of the War on Terror, combating Sunni Islamism has also been a strategic concern of the United States that has manifested itself in Bahrain's democratic processes. In 2014, for example, the Bahrain government eventually redrew electoral districts to tackle issues of blatant gerrymandering that weakened the Shiʿi vote. However, the popular Shiʿi Islamist Al Wefaq opposition complained that it was done in a way that disempowered both them and the other Islamists. Such an accusation makes sense, for, in Bahrain, democratic reform is usually a response to an emerging security threat, whether the rising popularity of Al-Wefaq, or the emergence of Sunni Islamism. Very much like his

[359] Monroe, 'Bahraini Political Scene Part II'.
[360] Monroe, 'Future of Bahrain: Ambassador's Parting Thoughts'. [361] Ibid.
[362] Ibid. [363] Hassan, 'Undermining the Transatlantic Democracy Agenda?', p. 480.

British colleagues, William Monroe noted the view that Bahrain's international protectors took on the nature of democracy, stating that Bahrain's allies will 'prioritise immediate security interests over promoting democracy'.[364] As for democratization in its current guise, the limits, as defined by Saudi Arabia and the Al Khalifa, have already been reached.

Conclusion

> We should not dismiss as unimportant a simple interest in freedom from arbitrary arrest, in equality before the law and the right to help elect the country's leaders.[365] —Sir (William) Roger Tomkys, British Ambassador to Bahrain 1981–4

By parsing the different methods of political statecraft, this chapter has highlighted several important considerations regarding the development of repression in Bahrain. Most generally, the deployment of a number of tactics have been contingent on particular foreign policy objectives of Bahrain's suzerains. In particular, British intervention in the 1920s and the 1950s was tempered by a desire not to be seen to be too involved in Bahrain's internal affairs. Nonetheless, the prospect of instability in Bahrain always prompted intervention by Bahrain's protecting powers, whether the United States or Saudi Arabia. Indeed, almost every facet of change, whether through the creation of municipalities or parliaments, was always discussed in the context of combating unrest or revolution.

What we have also seen is that the reasons for using specific tactics in specific instances are difficult to generalize. For example, in the 1950s reform was born out of a desire to divide the HEC through grievance removal, and partially necessitated by the UK's unwillingness to commit its own troops – even though this is what the ruling family desired. In the 1970s, democratic changes were perceived differently by Bahrain's key foreign allies, the UK and Saudi Arabia. The British viewed them as a means of mitigating unrest, while the Saudis feared they could embolden opposition particularly among the Shiʿa. The nature of rewards and co-optation also followed different contexts. While the British created the Civil List to combat Al Khalifa/Dawasir aggression against the *baḥārna*, Saudi funding was largely responsible for the cutting short of democratic experimentation or administrative reforms in favour of more blatantly paternalistic and patrimonial distribution of makramāt. The fear of democracy itself stemmed from the Saudi fear of emboldening Bahrain's Shiʿa, and subsequently the Shiʿa in Saudi's Eastern province. This

[364] Ibid. [365] Tomkys, Internal Political Situation 1984.

fine-grained study has demonstrated the importance of temporal, geographical and political context. International shifts in protectors matter to domestic repression, affecting both the methods used, the severity of their application and their future consequences.

It is important, however, to remember that the impact and outcome of such tactics has always been somewhat difficult to assess, a fact thrown into sharp relief in the 2011 Uprising, which Khalaf calls the mark of the death of rentier economics.[366] Underlying all this, one cannot underestimate the agency of the ruling family itself, who, in conjunction with their allies, have sought to define the methods of statecraft as their relative autonomy under the umbrella of protection grew. Even here, we can see how individual members of the ruling family initiated and encouraged certain courses of repressive action. From Shaykh Isa's apparent 'softness', to the hard-line nature of the prime minister, personality matters when it comes to repression. Some figures stand out for other reasons. Bernard Burrows, the British Political Resident in the 1950s, and who we heard from first hand, played an instrumental and calculating role in dividing and ensuring the fragmentation of the HEC. However, the relative power of individuals to execute their wishes depends on the tactic itself, and the moderating influences of internal and external actors. Individual agency is influenced by the shifting nature of the system.

Over the progression of the twentieth century, a certain distinct modality of statecraft has sought to embed sectarianism in complex ways. While the Shiʿa and *baḥārna* have always been the primary object of repression, it is crucial to bear in mind that the ruling family, nationalists, communist and Islamists of all stripes have been targeted at times. Nonetheless, specific methods of exclusion and quadrillage disproportionately affect the Shiʿa, whether through gerrymandering, denationalization or the refusal to hire. While the persecution of the Shiʿa was particularly notable in the 1990s Intifada and the 2011 Uprising, it is also a permanent feature of social life. Indeed, as this chapter has shown, even the urban topography of Bahrain has been influenced by decisions to disempower the Shiʿa community or limit inter-communal cooperation. Although the Iran–Iraq war and the Iranian Revolution were catalysts for further repression of the Shiʿa, the tendency towards a more draconian policy was resurrected following Independence in 1971 as a result of Saudi ascendency and the reassertion of the Al Khalifa's legacy of conquest.

[366] A. Khalaf, 'Foreword', in A. Shehabi and M. O. Jones (eds), *Bahrain's Uprising: Resistance and Repression in the Gulf*, London, Zed Books Ltd, 2015, pp. xiii–xvii.

4 Torture, Arrests and Other Personal Integrity Violations

> The officers responsible for interrogation are Arabs and the more brutal among them, according to Ian Henderson, are invariably Bahraini. The encouragement they get from some members of the Al Khalifa is to be more rather than less tough in their methods.[1]
>
> —Sir (William) Roger Tomkys, 1982

Violations of personal integrity such as torture, police violence, sexual violence, intimidation or incarceration have been a crucial method of containing dissent in Bahrain over the past hundred years. As the key actor responsible for the processes of *intimidation, incapacitation* and *containment,* this chapter focuses mostly on the repressive potential of Bahrain's security services, charting its development over this period. It highlights several factors that have come together to create a historical persistence of security service militancy, from the personal influence of specific people and inadequate training to social conditions leading to high levels of antagonism against the government itself. In addition to the foreign and sectarian make-up of the police, Independence prompted a decline in British control over police and a subsequent reassertion of Al Khalifa and Saudi influence in matters of internal security. While this coincided with the rise of the Islamic Republic of Iran, it is important to note that changes in repressive policy were set in motion before this and that growing repression seems to be more a reassertion of brutal policy prior to the reforms of the 1920s. Furthermore, a culture of permissibility has arisen in Bahrain's security services, in which extreme forms of coercion seem to be perceived as valid means of social control, a phenomenon buttressed by the increasing use of sectarianism to legitimize oppression and the Al Khalifa's legacy of conquest. The inability of the government to secure legitimacy has necessitated the need for a 'strong arm' of government to deal with frequent political agitation. Indeed, personal integrity violations have been used frequently to repress dissent,

[1] W. R. Tomkys, 16 February 1982, FCO8/4332, The National Archives.

and despite the creation of a constitution and parliament, they appear to have become worse over the last hundred years.

Policing: The Struggle between Force and Consent

A Brief History

Before discussing personal integrity violations, and how and why they have changed, it is useful to look at the political milieu that has shaped Bahrain's security apparatus in order to explore why it has emerged as it has. The term 'security apparatus' is preferable to police since the Criminal Investigation Department (CID), the National Security Agency, the Bahrain Defence Force, the National Guard, Bedouin, auxiliaries and Levy Corps have all been used at various points in the past to repress dissent. Policing in Bahrain evolved as did many colonial forces in the region, as a 'complex mixture of paramilitary, civil and tribal organisations; of civil and tribal courts administering different law'.[2] At times of political crisis, the differing roles between such agencies or groups become increasingly nebulous, and cooperation between institutions makes the encompassing term 'security services' more meaningful.[3] While this compression of different institutions in times of crisis is true of many types of regime, it is in itself a distinctive feature of repression in Bahrain.

As the primary institutions responsible for violating personal integrity, the security apparatus has historically been a contentious force in Bahrain, suffering from both a legitimacy deficit and an authoritarian disposition. While the security apparatus has modernized and become more professional over the past 100 years, this should not be considered synonymous with an evolution towards 'consensual' policing. The term 'modernize' belies the fact that many of the problematic characteristics planted in the early 1920s have remained, except now in a more extensive apparatus with more sophisticated tools of coercion at its disposal.

Indeed, while the apparatus of control has been modernized in a technical sense, there has been little public input on this change, resulting in a force with a disputed mandate. The inability of the police to maintain public approval and respect, and thereby minimize the need for repressive force, stems from the fact that their primary function in

[2] D. H. Johnson, 'From Military to Tribal Police: Policing the Upper Nile Province of the Sudan', in D. M. Anderson and D. Killingray (eds), *Policing the Empire: Government, Authority and Control, 1830–1940*, Manchester University Press, Manchester, 1991, p. 151.

[3] A. Turk, 'Organizational Deviance, and Political Policing', *Criminology*, vol. 19, no. 2, 1981, p. 248.

Bahrain has been to defend British, other foreign and ruling family interests while insulating the elites from anti-constitutional agitation. While Bahrain was a British protectorate, tactics of policing, especially since Independence, resembled that of other colonies, having 'little to do with serving the community and everything to do with upholding the authority of the colonial', and in Bahrain's case, the recolonized state.[4] Indeed, the security services were, and continue to be, little more than the 'agents of arbitrary "traditional" rule' and, in this case, Al Khalifa domination.[5] In some literature on policing, they might be considered a private police force, largely unbeholden to civilian oversight.

This proximity of the security services to the regime was embodied by the British adviser Charles Belgrave, who was both financial adviser to the ruler, as well as commandant of the Police.[6] His joint responsibility as an officer of public service and as an employee protecting the wealth of the ruling family inevitably led to some role confusion. This blurring of roles between public servant and enforcer of Al Khalifa hegemony continued well into the 1960s. Benn, the British superintendent of the police, was given a supplementary monetary sum 'paid for privily'[7] out of the personal pocket of the present prime minister, Khalifa bin Salman Al Khalifa. This personal payment '[became] embarrassingly widely known', contributing to the legitimate 'perception that the British were mercenary enforcers of Al Khalifa hegemony'.[8] As a result, it is unsurprising that the security apparatus have long reflected the political intentions and prejudices of the dominant power.

Before the formation of the police, the ruler and other members of the ruling family had reportedly relied on 'wild Bedouin' as a source of strength.[9] They also used armed retainers called *al-fidawiyya* (warriors).[10]

4 D. Killingray, 'Guarding the Extending Frontier: Policing the Gold Coast, 1865–1913', in D. M. Anderson and D. Killingray (eds), *Policing the Empire: Government, Authority and Control, 1830–1940*, Manchester University Press, Manchester, 1991, p. 123.

5 D. M. Anderson and D. Killingray (eds), 'An Orderly Retreat? Policing the End of empire', in *Policing and Decolonisation: Politics, Nationalism, and the Police, 1917–65*, Manchester University Press, Manchester, 1992, p. 4.

6 Belgrave, Annual Report for the Year 1956, p. 47.

7 J. P. Tripp, Communique to A. D. Parsons, 14 February 1965, FO371/179788, The National Archives.

8 M. O. Jones, 'Rotten Apples or Rotten Orchards: Police Deviance, Brutality, and Unaccountability in Bahrain', in A. Shehabi and M. O. Jones (eds), *Bahrain's Uprising: Resistance and Repression in the Gulf*, London, Zed Books Ltd, 2015, p. 212.

9 F. B. Prideaux, Communique from the Agency in Bahrain, 24 June 1904, in P. Tuson and E. Quick (eds), *Records of Bahrain 1820–1960*, vol. 3, Slough, Archive Editions, 1993, p. 274.

10 The *al-fidawiyya* were the armed retainers of the feudal shaykhs who were responsible for coercion and enforcement.

There was little central co-ordination of these *al-fidawiyya*, most of whom were acting on the orders of their individual tribal chiefs. Their role as enforcers of often arbitrary rulings by their employers was a prime source of irritation for the British authorities. The *baḥārna*, in particular, complained about the behaviour of the *al-fidawiyya*. The violence perpetrated against the Shiʿa inhabitants of Bahrain by the *al-fidawiyya* prompted anger from Persia. The British therefore sought to control the errant *al-fidawiyya* by centralizing the coercive apparatus under their protégé Hamad. The police and security apparatus would bolster Hamad's authority. Although the British were concerned that such reforms would anger Ibn Saud, they were also keen to appease Persia. As such, they forced the Al Khalifas and (Ibn Saud) to put their house in order, frightening them with the bogeyman of potential Persian aggression.[11]

As with many such reforms undertaken by the British Empire, the urban centres of trade took precedent. As a means of addressing these multiple grievances, the creation of the Manama Municipality was significant, as it prompted the creation of an embryonic police force (a collection of *Nāturs*, i.e. watchmen), designed to prevent disorder, oppression and what the British called 'rowdyism' in the capital. Crucially, however, the move was about trade, for it would also allow European merchants to go about their business without fear of extortion or violence.

Poor Quality of Recruits: Mercenaries, Baltajiyya and Foreigners

As well as the Municipality police, Hamad, Britain's protégé, was given a personal body of Levy Corps. This was not done primarily to protect him but 'to remove the excuse that he had no force to maintain order and could not restrain his relatives, *al-fidawiyya* and other Sunna from armed attacks on his Shiʿa subjects'.[12] The establishment of the Baluchi Levies, most of whom were originally from Muscat, followed what was termed 'the second Sitra Outrage'. The first Sitra Outrage involved shaykhs of the Khawalid line, who killed *baḥrānī* tenants in Sitra for failing to pay their rents. The killers fled to the Arabian Peninsula and were banished by Hamad. They then returned and shot nine *baḥrānī* inhabitants of Sitra. Hamad, for his part, insisted that he did not have the authority to control them.[13] This paved the way for a British-backed military

[11] Viceroy, Foreign and Political Department, to Secretary of State for India, 14 May 1923, p. 761.

[12] Horner, Express Message, 1923–1932, in P. Tuson and E. Quick (eds), *Records of Bahrain 1820-1960*, vol. 4, Slough, Archive Editions, 1993, p. 222.

[13] C. G. Prior, Communique from Political Agency Bahrain, in P. Tuson and E. Quick (eds), *Records of Bahrain 1820–1960*, vol. 4, Slough, Archive Editions, 1993, p. 550.

intervention on the mainland. The setting up of the Levies also accompanied the creation of a small police force totalling eighty-nine people. However, it was soon decided that there was no need for a separate police and Levy force in 1926.[14] The Levies were short-lived, and were disbanded following an incident in which one of them shot and killed their commanding officer and wounded Major Daly, the political agent. The sudden disbanding of the Levies required the prompt arrival of an Indian regiment and Indian Police.[15] However, the Indians did not speak much Arabic, which meant that they were replaced by a force of local men, a move which was completed in 1932.

Aside from a somewhat chaotic inception, the police force was initially popular, especially among the oppressed *baḥārna* and residents of Manama. On one occasion, civilians lent their weapons and support to the police following an attack on a police outpost by unknown persons. According to Charles Belgrave, the Shiʿi *baḥārna* at this time supported Hamad. This is unsurprising given his alignment with the British, who were intervening, largely out of self-interest, to protect the *baḥārna*.

The establishment of a standing force of armed enforcers of Hamad's authority did not come without resistance. The faction of the Al Khalifa who opposed the British-led reforms directed attacks against the police in the early days, as they saw it as an extension of British imperial control and an encroachment on their tribal privilege. Contrary to British colonies, where the police were a source of widespread hostility,[16] the police force in Bahrain was popular with an indigenous population attempting to protect themselves from oppression – in the beginning at least.

Despite the initial popularity with the country's Shiʿi population, the early security apparatus in Bahrain was the result of a balancing act, an attempt to control the Al Khalifa while also not overly antagonizing Ibn Saud or the Persians. As British support for the Al Khalifa continued and strengthened, several Al Khalifa were co-opted into joining the police. Their suitability for the roles was questionable. The British Political Agent in 1929, Captain Charles Prior, held the Al Khalifa in low regard, describing them as 'nonentities, incapable, or vicious, or all three'.[17] Having such members of the ruling family in the police meant that the security apparatus, even in its nascent form, was populated by characters perceived by the British as villainous, cruel and unpopular. In addition to

[14] Notes on formation of New Police Force, in P. Tuson and E. Quick (eds), *Records of Bahrain 1820–1960*, vol. 4, Slough, Archive Editions, 1993, p. 223.
[15] Belgrave, Annual Report for the Year 1956, p. 48.
[16] Anderson and Killingray, 'An Orderly Retreat?', p. 9.
[17] 'File 9/1 Institution of Reforms & Sunni opposition intrigues'.

this, 'many of the recruits were also drawn from the country's *al-fidawiyya*, the notorious henchman and enforcers used by the Al Khalifa to extract tax, intimidate the populace, and uphold their feudal rule'.[18] Unsurprisingly, they were disliked by many of the population. The fact that equally unpopular characters led them meant that there was also an issue in maintaining discipline, authority and control.

An example is the Amir of Manama, whose role was 'Governor and Chief of Police combined'.[19] He was described by one British official as 'one of the worst characters in Bahrain'[20] and could be 'trusted by the Sheikhs to support them in every form of extortion'.[21] He had also reportedly 'arbitrarily collected taxes, practically the whole of which were devoted to his personal expenditure'.[22] When Hamad removed him in 1923, this angered those who benefited from his corruption. Representatives of the Al Khalifa demanded the reinstatement of the Amir of Manama.[23] The Amir of Muharraq, who had also served as the Amir of Manama, was also not spared from Belgrave's fastidious attention to criticism. In 1929 Belgrave described him as a 'fat useless one-eyed rascal who never [did] any work'.[24] Belgrave's disdain of the Municipal Amirs did not abate. In 1930, he described the Amir of Manama, who was appointed in 1927, as a 'fat lazy scoundrel'[25] who did nothing but 'strut(s) about with a belt full of pistols and daggers', and whose watchmen '[treated] people very badly'.[26] Whether Belgrave's words are entirely accurate is difficult to verify, although they do tally with the general British administration's disdain towards members of the Al Khalifa. References to this dislike of the ruling family frequently included references to their oppressive character. In 1923, for example, Political Resident Lieutenant Colonel A. P. Trevor wrote about Salman bin Hamad – Bahrain's ruler between 1942 and 1961: 'Selman bin Hamad has all the worst qualities of the Al Khalifa family. He is totally uneducated, vain, lazy, and inclined to oppress and

[18] Jones, 'Rotten Apples or Rotten Orchards', p. 220.

[19] C. Belgrave, The Bahrain Municipality, in P. Tuson, A. Burdett and E. Quick (eds), *Records of Bahrain 1820–1960*, vol. 3, Slough, Archive Editions, 1993, p. 651.

[20] The Amir of Manama was later in charge of watchmen (not police): Belgrave, Papers, 8 February 1927.

[21] Ibid.

[22] C. K. Daly, Note on the Political Situation in Bahrain November 1921, 6 January 1922, in P. Tuson, A. Burdett and E. Quick (eds), *Records of Bahrain 1820–1960*, vol. 3, Slough, Archive Editions, 1993, p. 669.

[23] C. K. Daly, 'Memorandum', 4 October 1923, in P. Tuson, A. Burdett and E. Quick (eds), *Records of Bahrain 1820–1960*, vol. 4, Slough, Archive Editions, 1993, p. 141.

[24] Belgrave, Papers, 9 October 1929.

[25] Belgrave, Papers 11 February 1928.

[26] Belgrave, Papers, 19 February 1930.

tyrannise over anyone who is powerless to resist. Selman is absolutely unfit to succeed his father as ruler.'[27]

The British creation of the police and municipalities had irked the Al Khalifa, usurping their ability to forcibly extract wealth. By creating the police, the British had modified the Al Khalifa's broad monopoly on arbitrary violence, creating a system whereby the British were the main bulwark against Al Khalifa oppression of the *baḥārna*. Although this position would eventually be eroded in the subsequent decades, the change set in place a dynamic that served to moderate but not fundamentally alter, an antagonistic relationship between the Al Khalifa and the residents of Bahrain. Subsequent members of the Al Khalifa family holding important positions in the police have been criticized for either their hostility towards the Shiʿa, or tendency towards criminality. In 1956, Major William Oscar Little, a British officer in the Bahraini police described Shaykh Khalifa bin Muhammad, the Director of Police and Public Security, 'as a debauchee and a drunkard', and 'a leading crook, with a finger in every nefarious and profitable racket, from drug smuggling to the slave transit traffic and procurement of girls'.[28] Shaykh Khalifa's replacement Muhammad bin Salman Al Khalifa, and son of the ruler – who was head of the police between 1961 and 1965 – also had a reputation for anti-*baḥārna* violence.[29] When he was young, Muhammad bin Salman Al Khalifa and a group of Bedouin broke into the house of a *baḥārna* and beat up the resident. Charles Belgrave personally persuaded the victim not to make a complaint.[30] In this instance, the ruler had, according to Belgrave, ordered his sons to attack the *baḥārna*, indicating further antipathy towards the indigenous community.[31] That the ruler could be encouraging these direct forms of repression again indicates a personalist element to the nature of discrimination. The fact that Belgrave forced the victims to turn a blind eye highlights both a complicity and an unwillingness to hold elites accountable. What remains clear is that for much of the 1900s, the employment in the security forces of characters 'who were inclined to oppress and discriminate has contributed to the systemic institutionalisation of deviance, embedding it within the policing culture in Bahrain'.[32]

[27] A. P. Trevor, Bahrain Reforms, in P. Tuson and E. Quick (eds), *Records of Bahrain 1820–1960*, vol. 4, Slough, Archive Editions, 1993, p. 189.
[28] W. O. Little, 'Report by Major Little', in Pamphlet on Bahrain, Part IV, p. 4, 1957, FO371/126918, The National Archives.
[29] See Chapter 5 on legal control for more on Muhammad bin Salman's attitude towards the *baḥārna*.
[30] Belgrave, Papers, 5 December 1954. [31] Ibid.
[32] Jones, 'Rotten Apples or Rotten Orchards'.

Nāturs, Bedouin and Vigilantes

As well as the questionable nature of recruits, the complex mix of paramilitary, tribal and official security organizations made issues of coordination, discipline and role delineation complicated. These complexities and blurred boundaries have inclined the Bahrain Security Services towards deviance. The Bahraini police grew out of a force of *Nāturs*. These ill-trained, often illiterate guards, initially commanded by the maligned Amirs of specific municipalities, would eventually supplement the work of the police. Described in 1929 as 'rather a wild body' but suitable to local requirements, they were, according to C. G. Prior, the only force that Arabs would join as they could 'resign easily', go diving and were 'not obliged to wear uniforms'.[33] Belgrave in 1927 described *Nāturs* as a 'sort of civil police',[34] and they were frequently called upon to help police unrest, even though their training and discipline was questionable. For example, in the pearl diver riots of 1932, many of the *Nāturs* started firing guns 'wildly' in an effort to control the situation.[35] In 1965, five hundred *nawātir* were used to help quash the March uprising, assisting the already stretched police.[36] However, according to Belgrave, the Naturs 'were greatly feared, especially by the Shiʿa villagers'.[37]

The incorporation of the *al-fidawiyya* into the *Nāturs* partly explains the continuation of this aggressive and informal type of policing. This problem was augmented by the fact that several shaykhs kept their Bedouin retainers, who would also help enforce elements of their rule. These Bedouin retainers were reportedly violent in their approach. In 1938, the *Shabab al-Watani (The Youth of the Nation)*, a group of young, politically minded Bahrainis, claimed that they were beaten by a 'number of Bedouins' when they protested outside the British Agency.[38] The ruler's retainers also had some powers of detention, arresting a picket of boys in 1938.[39]

In 1954, during Sunni and Shiʿa communal disturbances, the police and the 'Ruler's Bedouin'[40] patrolled Bahrain. Charles Belgrave argued that such ancillaries were necessary, even though the Higher Executive

[33] C. G. Prior, 29 June 1929, in P. Tuson, A. Burdett and E. Quick (eds), *Records of Bahrain 1820–1960,* vol. 4, Slough, Archive Editions, 1993, p. 556.

[34] Belgrave, Papers, 8 April 1927. [35] Belgrave, Papers, 26 May 1932.

[36] P. E. Turnbull, A review of the structure and organization of the Bahraini State Police Force, 1965, FO371/179788, The National Archives.

[37] Belgrave, Annual Report for the Year 1956, p. 47.

[38] Al-Shabab al-Watani, 1938, in A. Burdett (ed.), *Records of Bahrain 1820–1960,* vol. 5, Slough, Archive Editions, 1993, p. 130.

[39] Belgrave, Annual Report for the Year 1956, p. 29.

[40] J. W. Wall, Communique to FO, 4 December 1954, in A. Burdett (ed.), *Records of Bahrain 1820–1960,* vol. 7, Slough, Archive Editions, 1993, p. 86.

Committee had protested against the 'provocative attitude of the Bedouin police auxiliaries'.[41] At the time, Al Khalifa oppression of the 1920s was still well within living memory. Unsurprisingly, in 1954, when the Shaykh's Bedouin set up roadblocks and intimidated people, Belgrave noted that citizens were 'very scared of them'.[42]

The problem of incorporating ancillary forces was exacerbated by an ill-disciplined, nervous and jumpy police force. Belgrave wrote in 1954 that police refused to go out without their rifles but also that they were 'utterly useless'.[43] He attributed this disposition to Khalifah, the Head of the Police, describing him as 'lazy, cowardly & incompetent'.[44] He also noted that Khalifah kept himself 'out of the way if there [was] any possibility of trouble'.[45] However it would seem that the *baḥārna* were singled out for particularly brutal behaviour. On several occasions, the British authorities had to intervene to prevent young Al Khalifa shaykhs leading attacks of hundreds of Bedouin against the *baḥārna*. The ruler even joined the Bedouin in war dances after they gathered in Rifa'a to show support and intimidate the *baḥārna*.[46] This level of perceived incompetence reflects to some extent why violence eventually broke out. It also explains why Bernard Burrows wished to try and bring about an end to the unrest with minimal use of the police.

However, the presence of multiple agencies of coercion under Al Khalifa control remained acute following Independence. The British Ambassador Roger Tomkys complained that a multiplicity of pseudo-security organs were illegally deporting Shi'a in the early 1980s.

In the 2011 Uprising, para-state security organizations continued to provide law enforcement functions. Numerous reports, videos and accounts have shown how thugs in civilian clothes have attacked activists or protesters. In 2012, Ahmad Ismail, a citizen journalist, was shot and killed by unknown assailants in an unmarked car as he filmed a protest. Mike Diboll, a teacher at Bahrain Polytechnic, described how '"loyalist" vigilantes equipped with pickaxe handles, iron bars, swords, spears and machetes...supported by Ministry of the Interior Police', came to campus to confront protesters in March 2011.[47] Since 2011, numerous videos have emerged of vigilantes, or *baltajiyya* [thugs], attacking civilians. The term *baltajiyya* has become engrained in the Bahrain lexicon since 2011. This vigilantism reflects the creation, perhaps deliberate, of a

[41] Ibid., p. 87. [42] Belgrave, Papers, 4 December 1954.
[43] Belgrave, Papers, 6 September 1954. [44] Ibid. [45] Ibid.
[46] Belgrave, Papers, 6 July 1954.
[47] M. Diboll, 'Written evidence from Dr Mike Diboll', Parliamentary Foreign Affairs Committee on the UK's Relationship with Saudi Arabia and Bahrain, 12 November 2012, www.publications.parliament.uk/pa/cm201314/cmselect/cmfaff/88/88vw25.htm

certain type of lawlessness, which itself can lead to pro-democracy activists silencing their calls for change in exchange for the security afforded by authoritarian policing methods. Indeed, the psychological implications of unfettered and unrestrained vigilantism can be telling; its lateral nature symbolizes a breakdown of traditional non-state mechanisms of protection, such as community and neighbourliness. In combination with state violence, vigilantism is therefore among the most insidious forms of political violence. That the authorities do little to restrain vigilantes indicates the important social control function it has played during political unrest in Bahrain.

Foreign Mercenaries

The Bahraini government's recruitment policy in the officially state-sanctioned security services has often motivated political unrest. Indeed recruitment policy is both a source of discontent and a driver of repressive action, especially due to the high number of foreign employees in the Public Security Forces (PSF) and the National Guard. Ala'a Shehabi and Nazgol Kafai reflect on this diversity: 'The running joke in Bahrain is that you can expect to be arrested by a Pakistani, interrogated by a Jordanian, tortured by a Yemeni, and judged by an Egyptian, but at least you can expect your fellow prisoners to be Bahraini.'[48]

The historical recruitment of foreigners termed pejoratively, *al-murtazaqa* (mercenaries) has bred resentment, and resulted in a security apparatus that is, as David Killingray described many colonial police forces, 'for the most part alien and thus mercenary in nature'.[49] In the first half of the twentieth century, police recruitment policy was shaped to a large extent by British foreign-policy considerations, with the historic tensions between Persia and Saudi Arabia informing how candidates were selected. In the 1920s, having to appease the Saudis, *baḥārna* and the Al Khalifa, the British adopted an ambivalent strategy to recruitment. When the British were seeking to restrain Al Khalifa piracy and banditry, it was expedient, yet expensive, to have Punjabi Indian Muslims as policemen. However, locals saw them as 'expensive foreign mercenaries',[50] and they were phased out and replaced by a force of 'Bahrain Arabs, Shiʿa baḥārna, manumitted slaves, local Persians', and a mixture

[48] N. Kafai and A. Shehabi, 'The Struggle for Information: Revelations on Mercenaries, Sectarian Agitation, and Demographic Engineering in Bahrain', *Jadaliyya*, 29 May 2014, www.jadaliyya.com/pages/index/17912/ the-struggle-for-information_revelations-on-mercen.

[49] Killingray, 'Guarding the Extending Frontier', p. 106.

[50] C. Belgrave, Annual Report for the Year 1937, *in Bahrain Government Annual Reports 1924–1970,* vol. 2, Gerrards Cross, Archive Editions, 1986, p. 10.

of 'Kurds, Iraqis, Swahili and Sudanese'.[51] This delicate balance was short-lived. Discontent at the presence of Persian policemen, many of whom were recruited initially by the head of the Manama Municipality – Khan Sahib Mohammed Sharif Kutbaddin[52] – excited further historical animosity between the Al Khalifa, Al Saud and Persia, culminating in the Najdi Persian riots in 1923, in which a number of Persians were killed. As most of the Naturs at the time were *al-fidawiyya* and Persians,[53] and Ibn Saud's anger more acute than Persia's, Knox dismissed several Persians in order to appease Ibn Saud.[54]

On the periphery of colony and Empire, Bahrain was always vulnerable to global geopolitics. Further shifting political imperatives changed the nature of recruitment policy, and they always brought with them questions of police legitimacy. Following India's Independence in 1947, and the growth of Arab nationalism and communism in parts of the Middle East, the British were careful when seeking out new police recruits. This did not necessarily mean recruiting non-Arabs. In the 1950s, soldiers from Iraq and tribal militias from *al-Hasa* were brought in to help keep order.[55] These militias, for example, were seen not as nationalists but as those whose tribal ties could be manipulated by the Bahrain regime.

While both the Al Khalifa and the British favoured the use of foreigners, Bahrainis protested over the presence of what they saw as mercenaries in the police. Despite their protestations, the tradition of recruiting strangers to police 'strangers' continued into the 1960s when the British commandant of the police, Winder, went to Pakistan to recruit ex-servicemen.[56] Indeed, Pakistan became a useful recruiting ground for officers who were neither Arab nationalists nor Communists. In 1965, of the 921 strong police force in Bahrain, only one quarter was actually Bahraini. In 1970, this had increased slightly to 32 per cent.[57]

There were numerous, often questionable, reasons why local police officers were eschewed in favour of foreigners. In 1965, Commandant Winder maintained that 'Bahrainis [did] not make good policeman being

[51] Belgrave, Annual Report for the Year 1351 (1932–33), p. 358.
[52] Rumaihi, *Bahrain: Social and Political Change*, p. 295.
[53] A. P. Trevor, From the British Residency – Bushire, 10 November 1923, in P. Tuson, A. Burdett and E. Quick (eds), *Records of Bahrain 1820–1960*, vol. 4, Slough, Archive Editions, 1993, p. 196.
[54] S. G. Knox, From Bushire to Secretary of State for Colonies, in P. Tuson, A. Burdett and E. Quick (eds), *Records of Bahrain 1820–1960*, vol. 3, Slough, Archive Editions, 1993, p. 757.
[55] Khuri, *Tribe and State in Bahrain*, p. 207.
[56] Jones, 'Rotten Apples or Rotten Orchards', p. 212.
[57] J. S. Bell, Annual Report for 1970, *in Bahrain Government Annual Reports 1924–1970*, vol. 8, Gerrards Cross, Archive Editions, 1987, p. 95.

Table 4.1 *Percentage of foreigners in the Bahrain police*

	1934–5	1957	1960	1965	1970	2015
Percent Bahraini	6[58]	24	21	25	32	50[59]

lazy and not amenable to discipline'.[60] In addition to this, very few Bahrainis applied, especially in the early days of the police, when the pay was bad, and the British physical requirements of policemen favoured the ethnic Arab-African, and not the *baḥārna*. In 1961, of the 360 recruits who applied, only four were Bahraini.[61] Following the disturbances of March 1965, British police expert Peter Edward Turnbull was commissioned to write a report on the Bahrain police. He argued that more Bahraini policeman should be recruited, ostensibly to create a less acrimonious disposition between the police and the policed. Despite this, the trend of employing foreigners continued unabated post-Independence. The unwritten policy was also adopted by the newly formed military.[62] In 1974, three hundred 'kindred tribesmen' from Saudi Arabia were reportedly brought in to join the growing Bahrain Defence Force (BDF).[63] The imperative of recruiting loyal foreigners, specifically Sunna, was especially apparent after the Iranian Revolution. As of 2011, it was believed that around 50 per cent of Bahrain's security apparatus are foreign Sunna.

Although it would be easy to say that recruitment has tended to favour non-Bahraini Sunna, the truth is more complicated. Being Sunni is not a sufficient condition. The fact the police have gained a reputation as the coercive arm of Al Khalifa rule has not endeared it to multiple segments of the local population. In the 1980s, it was no longer the case that Bahrainis were not willing to apply to the police. Instead, it was seen as a domain for younger members of the ruling family.[64] An interesting

[58] This number is derived from a total force of 172, and 10 Shiʿa baḥārna. No 'Bahrainis' were mentioned, only Arabs, Persians, Manumitted Slaves, Swahilis, Sudanese, Iraqis, Yemenis, Kurds, Malabaris and Baluchis. Annual Records/Belgrave, vol. 1, p. 523. On p. 445 he mentions all enlisted locally – not all local.

[59] S. E. Nepstad, *Nonviolent Struggle: Theories, Strategies, and Dynamics*, Oxford, Oxford University Press, 2015, p. 140. (This figure includes all armed forces.)

[60] J. P. Tripp, 14 Feb 1965, FO371/179790, The National Archives.

[61] M. b. S. Al Khalifah, Annual Report for Year 1961, *in Bahrain Government Annual Reports 1924–1970,* vol. 6, Gerrards Cross, Archive Editions, 1987, p. 46.

[62] K. Oldfield, 30 August 1965, FO371/179790, The National Archives.

[63] R. M. Tesh, Bahrain: Annual Review for 1974, FCO8/2414, The National Archives, 2 January 1975.

[64] W. R. Tomkys, Tel 75: Internal Security, FCO8/4332, 27 April 1982, The National Archives.

example of the relative complexities of hiring policies was illustrated with the creation of the BDF. When in discussions about replacing the British heads of police Henderson and Bell, the British noted that the prime minister would be reluctant to hire Pakistanis as superiors. The deputy was reluctant to have Englishmen, while the prime minister eschewed Jordanians because there were so many in senior positions in the BDF, and the prime minister feared that they might be more loyal to Hamad, who ran the BDF, than to him. This, he feared, would undermine the public security's role as a potential defence against the BDF.[65]

Although there is still much reliance on non-Gulf personnel in the security apparatus, in the 2011 Uprising the government actually relied on fellow Gulf countries for security assistance. At least five hundred policemen from the United Arab Emirates entered Bahrain in 2011 to augment the Bahraini forces.[66] These Emirate policemen remained in Bahrain until at least March 2014.[67] In April 2014, the *Bahrain Mirror* published leaked documents revealing that there were at least 499 Jordanian citizens working in the Bahraini security sector.[68] Furthermore, according to Pakistan's foreign minister Naila Chohan, 10,000 Pakistanis were serving in Bahrain's 'defence services' in 2014.[69] Many of Bahrain's PSF are still recruited from Yemen, Syria, Jordan and other countries in the Arab world, although the military tends to be predominantly Bahraini.

The use of such *al-murtazaqa* has been provocative on a number of levels. Not only does it raise issues of employment by depriving Bahrainis of many state sector jobs, thus promoting antagonism along political and economic lines, but it also means that a non-native police force are tasked with policing a foreign citizenry – an issue that erodes the legitimacy of the police. It has also prevented the emergence of what Douglas Johnson calls a positive 'link between government and the people'.[70] Fuad Khuri concurs, arguing that the use of foreign police in Bahrain '[hardens] their hearts',[71] imbuing the police with less empathy to the local population

[65] Tomkys, Internal Political 1984, FCO8/5442, The National Archives.
[66] J. Lessware, 'State of Emergency Declared in Bahrain', *The National*, 16 March 2011, www.thenational.ae/news/world/middle-east/state-of-emergency-declared-in-bahrain
[67] *The National*, 'Emirati Officer Dies in Bahrain Bomb Explosion', 3 March 2014, www.thenational.ae/world/emirati-officer-dies-in-bahrain-bomb-explosion
[68] *Bahrain Mirror*, 'Bahrain Mirror Publishes Important Document Regarding Jordanian Police: 499 Policemen Are Costing Bahrain 1.8 Million Dollars Per Month', 3 April 2014, http://bmirror14feb2011.no-ip. org/news/14724.html
[69] P. Muhammad, 'Foreign Relations: Tit-for-Tat Proposed over Visa Rejections', *The Express Tribune*, 1 April 2014. http://tribune.com.pk/story/689833/ foreign-relations-tit-for-tat-proposed-over-visa-rejections
[70] Johnson, 'From Military to Tribal Police', p. 153.
[71] Khuri, *Tribe and State in Bahrain*, p. 123.

Table 4.2 *Outline of the multiple modern security organs in Bahrain*

	Bahrain Defence Force (BDF)	**National Guard**	**Public Security Forces (PSF)/Police**	**National Security Agency**	**Criminal Investigation Department (CID)**
Established	1968	1997[a]	1920s	2002[b]	1966
Responsible to	The king, who is the Supreme Commander of the BDF	The King of Bahrain	Ministry of the Interior. Formerly the Bahrain Police Directorate, the Ministry of the Interior was created in 1971.	Separate entity reports through a director (who has the rank of cabinet minister) to the prime minister	Ministry of the Interior
Formerly known as	This was established ahead of Bahrain's Independence from Britain.	Established in 1997, the National Guard was intended to add strategic depth to Bahrain's Army and Police.	The police, established in the 1920s, has evolved considerably over the past century. The PSF is the main law enforcement arm of the police and is responsible for most riot control operations.	General Directorate of State Security (est. 1996), formerly known as the Security Intelligence Services (est. the 1970s), formerly known as Special Branch (amended as special branch in Arabic meant penis)	This has always been known as the CID.

[a] The National Guard was established in 1997 pursuant to Emiri Order No. 1 of 1997 and is governed by Emiri Decree Law No. 20 of 2000. According to Emiri Decree Law No. 20 (*BICI Report*).

[b] Decree No. 14 of 2002 established the National Security Agency (NSA) to replace the General Directorate of State Security that was formerly under the authority of the Ministry of Interior (*BICI Report*).

and increasing the likelihood of more egregious behaviours including violence and torture. While policing may be understood 'as a continuum of activities ranging from a pole of service, protection, and concern for individualizing justice to a pole of domination, exploitation, and concern for maintaining order',[72] the security services in Bahrain have long inhabited the latter end of the continuum, an aspect potentially facilitated by many being mercenaries. Even the Bahraini Minister of Interior acknowledged that using Bahrainis to police Bahrain's problems would be problematic. In an interview on Bahrain Television in 2012, Shaykh Rashid bin Abd Allah Al Khalifa indicated that it in a small country such as Bahrain, where people know and are known to each other, it would be hard to expect them to police others.[73] Therefore in a real way, this lack of empathy between the police and the policed is understood as politically useful by the authorities. It also helps explain a disposition towards violence or aggressiveness, one justified, at least if the authorities are to be believed, by Bahrain's small physical size.

Anti-Shiʿa Discrimination

> The Shiʿa would not rise against the Al Khalifa unless police oppression became much more brutal than hitherto. If they did, they would expect, rightly, to be crushed eventually (and no doubt inefficiently) by Saudi forces[74]

In addition to the recruitment of aliens to police locals, there has always been deep-rooted discrimination of Shiʿa, and specifically the *baḥārna*, in the security services. This discrimination has led to a contentious disposition towards the police and resulted in the increased occurrence of personal integrity violations. During the communal disturbances of the 1950s, Belgrave wrote that the 'police were obviously in sympathy with the Sunna and the Muharraqis'.[75] When a fracas broke out in 1953, the police sided with the Sunna after the unrest devolved into a sectarian affair.[76] Following another disturbance in 1953, Charles Belgrave noted that, 'one of the policemen referred to the Shiʿa as "the enemy" & that is the way they regard it'.[77] He also wrote that all the police 'showed a strong anti-Shiʿa basis' and that this 'feeling sticks to them all'.[78]

[72] Turk, *Political Criminality,* p. 116.
[73] Minister of Interior Bahrain, Mercenaries Are Our Brothers [online video], 13 February 2012, www.youtube.com/watch?v=rOQon8MjDLI
[74] R. Tomkys, First Impressions. 4 February 1982, FCO8/4332, The National Archives.
[75] Belgrave, Papers, 20 September 1953. [76] Ibid.
[77] Belgrave, Papers, 6 October, 1953. [78] Belgrave, Papers, 1 October 1953.

On a personal level, Belgrave criticised the impact of this sectarianism within the police. So much so that he even sided with the Shiʿa when they wished to hold a general strike to protest police violence: 'the Shiʿa propose to have a general strike tomorrow & I entirely sympathise with them'.[79] Belgrave was not the only British official to see this sectarian bias as a reason for police partisanship. John W. Wall, the British political agent, noted in 1953 that the police were mostly Sunna, who 'naturally enough, felt the best way to restore order was to hit a Shiite [sic]'.[80] Unsurprisingly, this problem was accentuated during the holy month of Ashura. In 1953, Belgrave noted there were 'police beating up people, sometimes indiscriminately during Muharram[81] altercations'.[82]

Both discrimination and subsequent repression against the recruitment of Shiʿa were exacerbated after Independence. This worsened after the Iranian Revolution, which created even more contempt for the country's Shiʿi population, effectively placing the majority of Bahrainis under suspicion. However, the sectarian explanation is not wholly sufficient. Nor is the Iranian Revolution. The Shiʿa had been excluded from the police force in Bahrain long before the Revolution. Charles Belgrave, for example, often rejected *baḥrānī* recruits on account of their 'their physique and eyesight…not being as good as that of the Arabs and men of African origin'.[83] Belgrave's personal prejudices also influenced recruitment. On one occasion he argued: 'in my opinion, the best type of men are those of mixed Arab and African extraction, they have more intelligence than the pure African and are tougher than the local Arab or Bahrani'.[84] While Belgrave's opinion reflects the salience of imperial prejudices about race and culture in defining British policy,[85] it also indicates how police recruitment was rooted in social, political and economic discrimination. Despite the health issues presented by the *baḥārna*, undoubtedly enforced by their general poverty and their poorer life chances, recruitment was also defined by whom was being policed. Indeed, the purpose of the security forces at their inception was to reduce Al Khalifa oppression, which necessitated a force not entirely subservient to them. For example, recruiting locally was problematic, as the likely candidates would be Najdis, 'over whom there would be no control, and

[79] Belgrave, Papers, 20 September 1953.
[80] J. W. Wall Communique to B. A. B. Burrows, 5 October 1953, in A. Burdett (ed.), *Records of Bahrain 1820–1960,* vol. 7, Slough, Archive Editions, 1993, p. 22.
[81] Muharram is a holy month celebrated by Muslims, and in particular, by Shiʿa.
[82] Belgrave, Papers, 20 September 1953.
[83] Belgrave, Annual Report for Year 1357 (1938–39), p. 14.
[84] Belgrave, Annual Report for the Year 1351 (1932–33), p. 358.
[85] Anderson and Killingray, 'An Orderly Retreat?', p. 7.

all security would then cease in Bahrain'.[86] To this effect, it was actually a Shi'i *baḥārna* (Hajji Salman) who became the first superintendent of police. He worked in the Bahrain police from its creation in the Manama Municipality until his death in the summer of 1934/35.[87] Hajji Salman also survived an assassination attempt in 1926[88] that the British believed was a plot to wipe out the police, possibly by 'Abd Allah bin 'Isa Al Khalifa, who still resented the usurpation of Al Khalifa privilege, especially by *baḥārna*.

Hajji Salman represented an important symbol of protection against tribal oppression. His eventual death prompted members of the Manama Shi'a community to attempt to 'secure the appointment of Hajji Salman's son as Superintendent of Police'.[89] Belgrave was displeased by this lobbying, and was indignant at the fact such positions were often perceived by locals as hereditary. He refused the request on the grounds that Salman's son was not qualified. However, Belgrave's cynicism is perhaps misplaced. In fact, what the mobilization of the Shi'a community highlighted was the belief that a member of the *baḥrānī* community in the police would probably secure them against arbitrary Al Khalifa oppression. After all, the police, as Charles Prior noted in 1929, were part of the reason that the *baḥārna* 'had security and justice for the first time for 150 years'.[90] Even in 1929, uniformed constables were 'mostly Persians'.[91]

However, the presence of Persians or *baḥārna* in influential positions in the police would be short-lived. Britain's treaties with the Al Khalifa meant that they still recognized them as the true rulers of Bahrain. As a result, it was inevitable that members of the family would, over time, occupy senior positions in the police. Certainly for those members of the ruling family who had resisted the creation of the police, it soon became clear that it would be more productive to occupy rather than oppose the coercive arm of the state. For their part, the British were happy that an increasingly compliant ruling family were taking responsibility for issues related to governance. However, the continued co-optation of members of the ruling class into positions of authority caused a further reassertion of Al Khalifa influence in recruitment matters. In 1939, shortly after Hajji

[86] Secretary, Communique to Resident, 12 August 1926, in P. Tuson, A. Burdett and E. Quick (eds), *Records of Bahrain 1820–1960*, vol. 4, Slough, Archive Editions, 1993, p. 217.

[87] C. Belgrave, Annual Report for the Year 1353 (193–35), *in Bahrain Government Annual Reports 1924–1970*, vol. 1, Gerrards Cross, Archive Editions, 1986, p. 523.

[88] Belgrave, Papers, 3 August 1926.

[89] Belgrave, Annual Report for the Year 1353 (1934–35), p. 523.

[90] Prior, 29 June 1929, p. 551. [91] Ibid.

Salman's death, Shaykh Khalifa bin Muhammad bin ʿIsa Al Khalifa, was appointed superintendent of police.[92] The reassertion of Persian claims to Bahrain in 1948 catalysed anti-Shiʿa sentiment in the ruling family, contributing to less Shiʿa in the Bahrain police.[93] This became so noticeable that Belgrave even commented on the ruler's increasingly sectarian disposition: 'HH [was] beginning to be very unreasonable, against the Shiʿa, naturally all the Sunni have been talking to him'.[94]

In 1955, when it became increasingly clear that the policing apparatus was key to control, more and more members of the Al Khalifa were recruited into officer positions.[95] By 1965, the British argued that the police should no longer be controlled directly by the ruling family, partly to prevent members of the Al Khalifa from the political exposure of being head of the police.[96] The British were less concerned about Al Khalifa heavy-handedness but that members of the ruling family could be directly implicated in potential violent coercion. To solve this, ministerial cover was seen as a means of devolving direct ruling family accountability in matters of internal repression. This problem served as an acknowledgement that the Al Khalifa were increasingly filling positions in the police. This nepotistic approach arguably got worse leading up to Independence. In 1970, expatriates were replaced in police headquarters by Inspector Khalifa Muhammad Al Khalifa and Assistant Superintendent Ahmed Sultan Al Khalifa.[97] Shaykh Mohammed bin Khalifa Al Khalifa was also promoted to deputy commandant, under the British Commandant Jim. S. Bell,[98] while Shaykh ʿIsa bin 'Ali Al Khalifa was appointed director of immigration.[99]

After Independence, and in particular after the Iranian Revolution, Bahrain's Shiʿi population were excluded from the higher echelons of the security forces. They required 'a certificate of good behaviour before getting a job'.[100] The same was true in the military. Ten years after the establishment of the Bahrain Defence Force (BDF) in 1968, a British official noted that the BDF contained no Shiʿa.[101] This reluctance persisted, although abated somewhat. In 1984, a British official stated that

[92] C. Belgrave, Annual Report for Year 1358 (1939–40), *in Bahrain Government Annual Reports 1924–1970,* vol. 2, *Gerrards Cross, Archive Editions,* 1986, p. 21.
[93] Belgrave, Papers, 29 May 1951. [94] Ibid.
[95] Belgrave, Annual Reports for Year 1955, p. 47.
[96] M. S. Weir, 7 October 1965, FO371/179788, The National Archives.
[97] J. S. Bell, Annual Report for 1970, p. 89. [98] Ibid., p. 89. [99] Ibid., p. 91.
[100] S. Strobl, 'From Colonial Policing to Community Policing in Bahrain: The Historical Persistence of Sectarianism', *International Journal of Comparative and Applied Criminal Justice*, vol. 35, no. 1, 2011, p. 30.
[101] Miers, Attempted Coup in Bahrain, 26 February 1982, FCO8/4332, The National Archives.

the Shiʿa were underrepresented in the security forces, and deliberately so. There were only six Shiʿa officers in both the BDF and the Public Security Forces combined. In the BDF, there were 300 Shiʿa out of a total strength of 2,500. However, none of them were in combat roles, while in the public security forces, there were only 750 out of a total of 8,000 employees who were Shiʿa.[102] According to political activist Ibrahim Sharif, the situation as of 2011 was largely unchanged. Indeed, when the Shiʿa were actually included in the security forces, they were still being recruited in non-critical roles

The British were quick to argue that Saudi influence was crucial to maintaining this sectarian imbalance. As the UK Ambassador at the time, Francis Trew, noted, 'Saudi Arabia is funding the development of the Bahrain Defence Force and calls the tune.'[103] But it was not simply the Al Khalifa and the Saudis that were suspicious of the Bahrain Shiʿa. The hysteria following the Iranian Revolution was keenly felt throughout the security services. After 1979, Ian Henderson showed suspicion of those Shiʿi policeman taking part in the ʿAshura processions. Henderson worried they could not be called upon when duty required.[104]

As with Charles Belgrave, the attitude and influence of influential individuals had an impact on the nature of the police. For example, Yemenis were seen as treacherous, while Najdis unreliable (in the 1920s and 1930s) due to their allegiance to Al Saud. Just as Belgrave's impressions of race, ethnicity and perceived loyalty/independence defined recruitment policy, so too did the Al Khalifa's distrust of the Shiʿa. Anti-Shiʿa prejudice, and increasingly anti-Shiʿa sentiment, in the upper echelons of the security services post-Independence has not abated. There have even been recordings of the Shiʿa's precarious employment in the security forces being used as a bargaining chip. As recently as 2007, the king's brother and head of Bahrain's National Guard, Shaykh Muhammad bin ʿIsa Al Khalifa reportedly said to Shiʿa notable Shaykh Hussain al-Najati that the Shiʿa 'should appreciate that he did not dismiss Sunnis married to Shiʿa from the security services, even though it was in his power'.[105] This indicates that there is still considerable opinion against having Shiʿa in the security services among the ruling core, and that such a 'privilege' could easily be revoked should certain key individuals decide to do so.

[102] S. Collis, Internal Political 1984, FCO8/5442, The National Archives.
[103] F. S. E. Trew, Bahrain: Annual Review 1984, FOIA Request from the FCO.
[104] S. P. Collis, Bahrain Internal: Ashoora, 15 November 1981, FCO8/3893, The National Archives.
[105] Monroe, 'Prominent Shiʿa Paint a Gloomy Picture'.

The endurance of a political structure dominated by one family suggests that social control methods have been preserved generationally. During 2011, after the rise to prominence of certain hardliners, the notoriously anti-Shiʿa Khalid bin Ahmed stated that only the older members of the Al Khalifa family knew the mentality of these protesters and 'how to deal with them'.[106] Khalid bin Ahmed's statement is indicative of an authoritarian memory, one in which successful tactics of control are perceived to be preserved generationally. Indeed, given the dominance and long tenure of members of Al Khalifa in the security apparatus, it makes sense that tactics of repression would be seen as a skill acquired through experience and lineage.

The discriminatory recruitment policy highlights that the police in Bahrain have never been a force created for the benefit of the public as a whole. It is more accurate to characterize them as a private force protecting the interests of a hegemonic elite. As such, they are not generally shackled by regards for the restraint that might be expected of a force that serves to protect and uphold the general rights of the community. Of course, such a force is more likely to exist in a country where civilians cannot fully elect their Minister of the Interior.

Failure of Policing 'by Consent' and the Resurgence of Collective Punishment

The general exclusion of the indigenous *baḥrānī* Shiʿa from the police has corroded the legitimacy of the institution, as well as the ability to win public consent for policing tasks. This has set up a contentious disposition to policing operations, especially when involving political protest. As one British official said in 1982: 'So long as the Al Khalifa continue to discriminate against the Shiʿa majority, there will be a supply of restless young men trying to subvert the Bahraini government.'[107] In this regard, a discriminatory recruitment policy creates a self-fulfilling cycle, wherein the policy creates societal tensions and thus legitimizes the securitization of a manufactured Shiʿa threat. Indeed, the exclusion of the Shia and the *baḥārna* from the security services become the raison d'être of its bloated size. The inherent discrimination in the policing institution, coupled with

[106] J. Gengler, 'The Khawalid, Al Khalifa Politics Lurch into the Open', 22 February 2013, Bahraini Politics [web blog], http://bahrainipolitics.blogspot.co.uk/2013/02/the-khawalid-al-khalifa-politics-lurch.html

[107] Miers, 'Attempted Coup in Bahrain', 26 February 1982, FCO8/4332, The National Archives.

the general discrimination faced by the Shiʿa, has led to some accusing the state of engaging in collective violence against civilians, particularly those living in Shiʿi areas.

Tear Gas

Bahrain's urban geography has contributed to accusations of collective sectarian repression, especially with regard to the use of tear gas. In 2011, videos and reports of security forces indiscriminately firing tear gas into enclosed places and Shiʿi neighbourhoods raised concerns about the use of chemical agents on civilians. Tear gas was first introduced into Bahrain in 1956 by the British, and its capacity as a less than lethal method has facilitated collective punishment, as it inhabits the nebulous area between deadly force and a 'less-lethal' method of crowd control.[108] Initially introduced to disperse crowds with minimum casualties, its use is now routinized in Bahrain, partly due to the rituals of contestation that have emerged in Bahrain's Shiʿa villages, but also because of the general tendency of Bahrain police to resort to more coercive methods early on in any confrontation. Yet the 'less-lethal' branding of tear gas belies its deadly nature. During the 1990s Intifada, there were at least two reported deaths from tear gas, sixty-year-old Sakina al-Ghanimi, and eighteen-month-old 'Aqil Salman ʿAli al-Saffar, who both died in 1995.[109] This figure jumped during the 2011 Uprising, with Physicians for Human Rights (PHR) reporting that up to twenty-four people had died from tear gas-related injuries between February 2011 and March 2012.[110]Many more deaths as a result of tear gas have been reported since then. PHR have even argued that the Bahraini authorities were 'weaponizing toxic chemical agents', and using tear gas to intentionally impair people's health, and in particular those of the Shiʿi sect.[111] This level of intimidation has extended to the security forces preventing ambulances[112] reaching the wounded, the

[108] B. A. B. Burrows, Letter from Bahrain to Foreign Office, 12 March 1956, in A. Burdett (ed.), *Records of Bahrain 1820–1960,* vol. 7, Slough, Archive Editions, 1993, p. 227.
[109] Amnesty International, *Bahrain: A Human Rights Crisis*, p. 40.
[110] Physicians for Human Rights, 'Weaponizing Tear Gas: Bahrain's Unprecedented Use of Toxic Chemical Agents Against Civilians', August 2012, https://s3.amazonaws.com/PHR_Reports/Bahrain-TearGas-Aug2012-small.pdf
[111] Ibid.
[112] It is interesting to note that Daly reports how after an attack on the Shiʿa village of A'ali in 1923, Khan Sahib Yusuf Kanoo was told not to rent cars to Shiʿa trying to take their wounded women and others to hospital. 'Administration Reports 1920–1924' [159r] (322/412), in *Qatar Digital Library.*

occurrence of which has been reported in both the 1990s Intifada[113] and the 2011 Pearl Uprising.[114]

This weaponization of tear gas is also symptomatic of sectarian state policy, which is itself compounded by the relative ease of the procurement of tear gas on the international market. Tear gas inhabits an unusual position in the Chemical Weapons Convention (CWC). Indeed, while Bahrain has signed the CWC, which prohibits signatories from using tear gas in a war with another state, it does not prohibit the police using it on civilians in a domestic context. How tear gas is used as a form of collective repression in Bahrain is also particularistic to the country's sectarian topography. Continued government discrimination in areas of town planning, such as the alleged banning or controlling of sales of land to Shiʿa in 2007 in the Sunni-dominated governate of Muharraq, has led to the emergence of Shiʿa ghettos.[115] Other social engineering projects, as revealed in the Al Bandar report, also highlight this policy. As Staci Strobl notes:

> There is visible segregation of poor Shīʿ communities from surrounding wealthier areas. Entire Shīʿ villages are tucked away, off the main roads, with only one or two points of access to them. The containment of these pockets of squalor, notably the outskirts of Manama, Sitra, and Sanabis, has come in handy during demonstrations against the detainment of Shīʿ activists and leaders. According to reporting by al-Wasat newspaper, riot police use the villages to dead-end protest marches and contain demonstrators.[116]

The ghettoization of Shiʿa communities, along with the aforementioned quadrillage of Bahrain's topography, explains how riot police can launch dozens of tear gas canisters into whole villages without generally having to be concerned about angering non-Shiʿa, Sunni or expatriate residents.

Violent Coercion, Paramilitary Policing and the Authoritarian Reflex

From Britain's gunboat diplomacy to the arrival of over two thousand GCC troops, the policing of Bahrain's internal affairs has always blurred the lines between military intervention and regular policing. While gunboat diplomacy existed at a time when 'British prestige rested on fear and not on respect', the decision to achieve change by more pacific means

[113] Amnesty International, *Bahrain: A Human Rights Crisis.*
[114] See, for example, M. C. Bassiouni, N. Rodley, B. Al-Awadhi, P. Kirsch, and M. H. Arsanjani, 'Report of the Bahrain Independent Commission of Inquiry' [*BICI Report*], 23 November 2011, BICI, Manama, www.bici.org.bh/BICIreportEN.pdf
[115] Monroe, 'Prominent Shiʿa Paint a Gloomy Picture'.
[116] Strobl, 'From Colonial Policing to Community Policing in Bahrain'.

meant more emphasis on how domestic institutions, and thus administrative measures, could facilitate control.[117]

However, like the security apparatuses in other parts of the British Empire, 'continuity of personnel between the army and the police, the military style of police training and organisation, meant that the police presence…retained something of the aura of an army of occupation'.[118] Consequently, 'popular hostility to the police and political realities dictated that policing remained predominantly a paramilitary activity'[119] throughout both the British Administration and after Independence. In the latter half of the twentieth century, protest policing in Bahrain tended to be paramilitary in style. Paramilitary policing involves the 'military style deployment of large police and army formations, numerous detentions and arrests as well as use of water cannons, mounted police and dogs, tear gas, and rubber bullets'.[120] This style of policing protest is indicative of an 'authoritarian reflex'[121] – that is, the tendency of states with authoritarian histories to revert to draconian techniques when changing political opportunity structures threaten the status quo. However, Bahrain's fragile sovereignty has prompted a near permanent sense of anxiety and perceived threat. This, coupled with the distrust of the Shiʿa population, meant that the authoritarian reflex was engaged frequently, This reflex has been aggravated by a lack of any real accountability or procedural oversight, resulting in frequent accusations that the police fail to adhere to standards of due process, such as issuing warrants for searches and arrests (see Chapter 5 for more on legal repression).

The lack of respect for due process by the police has been a perennial issue in Bahrain's history. A group of Bahrainis complained about this problem as early as the 1940s, stating that while Bahraini houses could be raided without warrants, police required a warrant from the political agent to raid the house of a foreigner. As cooperation and compliance with the police is fundamentally structured by public consent to being policed,[122] the bifurcation in treatment based on race, nationality and ethnicity posed serious problems for police legitimacy. Indeed, the lack of parity in procedural justice has aggravated police–society relations. While such treatment erodes the legitimacy of the police in the eyes of

[117] Khuri, *Tribe and State in Bahrain*, p. 88.
[118] Johnson, 'From Military to Tribal Police', p. 151.
[119] Killingray, 'Guarding the Extending Frontier', p. 106.
[120] A. Juska and C. Woolfson, 'Policing Political Protest in Lithuania', *Crime, Law and Social Change*, vol. 57, no. 4, 2012, p. 405.
[121] Ibid.
[122] J. Sunshine and T. R. Tyler, 'The Role of Procedural Justice and Legitimacy in Shaping Public Support for Policing', *Law and Society Review*, vol. 37, no. 3, 2003, pp. 513–48.

Bahrain's marginalized and dissident communities, the lack of legitimacy can also encourage a lack of compliance with the law, resulting in the creation of two groups with conflicting goals. It can also create a sense of hierarchy, one in which those afforded fewer rights might be perceived as worthier of incurring personal integrity violations.[123]

There is also continued evidence over the twentieth and twenty-first centuries that influential members of the ruling family encouraged the police to use more coercive repressive techniques. This has been particularly acute during times of political unrest. In 1954, Belgrave wrote that the ruler's 'idea is more Police & more force to enforce law & order & no sign of any concessions to public opinion'.[124] The results of this encouragement, along with poor training and inexperience became evident on 1 June 1954, when a group of Shiʿi civilians, angry at the sentencing of a co-religionist who had been involved in an altercation in Sitra, gathered at the police force to protest. The police opened fire and killed three of them.[125] Two years later, in 1956, the police opened fire in a market, killing five civilians and injuring seventeen. Despite this, the emphasis remained on quantity and not quality of police. Even after the suggested expansion of the police before 1956, the ruler, ignoring the advice of Charles Belgrave, increased spending on the security apparatus, even though this resulted in a massive budget deficit.[126]

The police would be put to the test again ten years later. In 1965, during unrest provoked by the state oil company's laying off of workers, the police killed between six and eight civilians using Greener guns. This occurred when they were breaking up strikes led by the National Liberation Front (NLF) – a leftist group with Nasserist leanings and who were advocating more workers rights.[127] The military mindset of the authorities was evidenced by the fact that the political resident was given standing authority to commit British troops if necessary. The need for this measure arose from both the residency's lack of faith in the Bahrain police and also because the British were concerned that the strikes were a pretext for leftist agitation. This situation was not entirely unusual in the British Empire. With Cold War paranoia and fear of Arab sympathies lying with the Soviet Union, policing in the colonies often 'took on an

[123] Ibid. [124] Belgrave, Papers, 28 December 1954.

[125] Many of those present then ran to the Political Agency where they demanded the protection of British soldiers and the disarming of the Bahrain police. In a poignant moment, a member of the crowd grabbed a British flag and wrapped it around one of the deceased as a 'makeshift symbol of al-kafan', the white linen symbolizing the ordeal of the family of Imam Hussein.

[126] Belgrave, Papers, 19 January 1957.

[127] J. P. Tripp, April 1965, FO371/179788, The National Archives.

increased security function in dealing with unrest and insurrection prompted by anti-colonial politics'.[128] Although British troops were not committed in Bahrain, Royal Navy helicopters were used to drop tear gas on protesters. The British were extremely reluctant to commit their armed forces to defend Bahrain, which meant the police had to be increasingly capable of performing a duty that might be expected of the military during a period of martial law. In this regard, Britain's desire to maintain control but appear to be taking a backseat directly resulted in the emergence of paramilitary-style police forces.

However, the deaths of the six to eight civilians served as useful ammunition for Britain's enemies, both in Bahrain and abroad. There was no institutional accountability for the civilian deaths. Instead, the ruler was rewarding, arguably incentivizing, the use of violence as a legitimate response to any unrest. The ruler and Shaykh Mohammed personally bought new armoured vehicles for the police in 'recognition of their good work during the disturbances'.[129] As with the 1950s, justice was replaced with an official report, this time one that focused on reforming the police. Peter Edward Turnbull, was commissioned to do the work. However Turnbull's report, which recommended significant police reform, including a severe reduction in numbers but increases in pay and efficiency, was duly ignored by the Al Khalifa. Instead, the ruling family bolstered the police.[130,131] As a result, the police force almost doubled in size between 1965 and 1970, increasing from 1,012 personnel to 2,012.[132]

The ill-advised expansion of the police was a product of the security-minded, fragile position of the Al Khalifa, whose fear of popular insurrection was validated by the British, who were clear that if there were to be an armed uprising, the police would be quickly overcome. As Tripp noted, 'the British commandant of police considers that an actively hostile crowd would very quickly get beyond the control of his police and believes that only the intervention of British troops could restore the situation'.[133] This fear, and diminishing British influence leading up to and following Independence, coupled with Saudi fear of Iranian expansionism, meant that ruling family tendencies towards securitization could continue relatively unhampered. The British had little motivation to

[128] Anderson and Killingray (eds), 'An Orderly Retreat?', p. 5.
[129] M. S. Weir, 22 April 1965, FO371/179788, The National Archives.
[130] J. P. Tripp to M. S. Weir, 5 April 1965, FO371/179788, The National Archives.
[131] M. S. Weir, 7 October 1965, FO371/179788, The National Archives.
[132] These figures are taken from the statistics provided in the annual reports of Bahrain between 1924 and 1970.
[133] J. P. Tripp, The Internal Situation in Bahrain, 1 June 1963, The National Archives.

pressure for the implementation of the Turnbull report. Indeed, it was the tension in this duality in how to develop the police that contributed towards the institutional foundations that formed the basis of an aggressive disposition. Paradoxically, while the British had initially attempted to pressure the regime into accepting the Turnbull Report, they also fully backed the expansion and strengthening of police numbers following Independence. The British believed that the fledgeling Bahrain military needed to be contained, and that a powerful police force was the only way to do this. As such, British Officer Jim Bell was brought in to oversee this expansion.

Ruling Family Rivalries and Coercive Strengthening

According to one US official, the 1970s witnessed a 'Gulf Arms Race'.[134] The growth of new armed forces to make way for the retreat of the British after Independence was perhaps obvious. However, in Bahrain, the arms race was catalysed by intra-family rivalry and tensions between the then Crown Prince, Hamad Al Khalifa, and Prime Minister Shaykh Khalifa bin Salman Al Khalifa. Hamad controlled the newly established BDF, while Khalifa controlled the Ministry of the Interior. The rivalry resulted in the growth of a police force that was purposefully designed to deal with any potential BDF insurrection or rebellion. This rivalry resulted in security inflation, in which the government diverted more and more resources to strengthening and equipping a police force designed to contain a military threat. As Andrew Sterling noted:

> The greatest danger is still the Bahrain Defence Force, against which the Special Branch efficiency offers almost the only protection. The Cabinet claim to recognise the danger and they have allowed no increase in the Defence Force while ensuring a considerable expansion of the police, but the menace remains[135]

A few years after Sterling talked of the expanding BDF, the British Ambassador Edward Given wrote that the police: 'ordered large quantities of anti-riot equipment, including some which would enable the police to take on the Defence Force'.[136] The growth of the BDF was not the only security concern for the police. The presence of internal subversion in the form of the Popular Front for the Liberation of Oman and the Arabian Gulf (PFLOAG) prompted the prime minister to boost

[134] US Embassy, 18 July 1978, 'Bahrain's Financial Plight', Wikileaks, https://search.wikileaks.org/plusd/cables/1976MANAMA00964_b.html

[135] A. J. D. Sterling, Bahrain: Annual Review for 1971, FCO8/1823, The National Archives.

[136] E. F. Given, Bahrain: Annual Report for 1976, 5 January 1977, FCO8/2873, The National Archives.

the strength of the police. In some ways the leftist threat was simply cover for the expansion of the police designed to 'coup proof' the regime from the new military. Indeed, Robert Tesh noted in 1974 that a 'by-product of the "security situation"' was 'the increasing strength of the police'.[137] The police budget was also doubled again in the mid-1970s.[138] While the increase in the size of the security service may have had an impact on its efficacy, it perhaps also reflects the siege mindset of the Al Khalifa. This attitude, coupled with the large and well-equipped security force, suggests a greater willingness to deploy force against political dissent.

Union Busting

The strengthening of the National Liberation Front and the various trade union movements in the 1970s was accompanied by a resurgence of political activity. Other factors also helped create a febrile environment for unrest, including increased urbanization, rises in the cost of living, changes in political opportunities and further industrialization. However, despite the arms race between the BDF and the police, both institutions generally united to fight threats against the regime. Police often using armoured cars and tear gas, dealt with protesters with little restraint. In many cases, they were backed up by the newly formed army, as if they were dealing with an insurgency and not a protest. In March 1972, labour activists took to the streets after negotiations with the government on labour unionization broke down. As with their predecessors, their 'major demands concerned the improvement of labour laws, freedom of association (including the right to unionise) and the release of political prisoners and detainees'.[139] The full force of the security apparatus was called upon, perhaps due to the regime's fundamental disdain for unionization. Anti-riot squads combined with the BDF to crush the demonstrations led by the Constitutive Committee (CCWBWPU), an alliance between the NLF, the Bahraini section of the PFLOAG and independent opposition figures. Afterwards, 'most known leaders of the CCBWPU were detained for a year but never brought to trial'.[140] At the time, units of the Saudi National Guard were also frequent visitors to Bahrain, including during the 1972 'uprising'.[141] Whether or not they were deployed is unclear. Nonetheless, the heavy-handed tactics used during the March 1972 uprising reflected the government's desire to show a firm hand before the creation of the National Assembly in 1973. This show of strength was also a result of government fear that the creation of a parliament showed weakness to the opposition.

[137] R. M. Tesh, Bahrain Internal, 8 October 1974, FCO8/2180, The National Archives.
[138] Ibid. [139] Khalaf, 'Labor Movements in Bahrain'. [140] Ibid. [141] Ibid.

However, after the promulgation of the constitution in 1973, initial oppositional success in the newly formed parliament increased opposition morale and led to a spate of actions designed to secure more rights.[142] Thirty-six strikes took place 'during the first six months of 1974, affecting all major employers on the island'.[143] The government's initial confusion emboldened the activists into thinking that the former were weak. Further strikes helped gain certain concessions, including a rise in the minimum wage. However, the government were not willing to concede to any further demands, and, during one incident, failed negotiations prompted the whole of the ALBA workforce to go on strike. This strike, which reportedly cost the government twenty million dinars, prompted the regime to respond with militaristic and non-militaristic actions. As Khalaf noted, 'the security forces took charge. Anti-riot squads and units from the Bahraini Defence Force were sent in around the smelter's area. Troops were also positioned at every "strategic point" in main towns and crossroads.'[144] In this case the government exhausted their willingness to give concessions and resorted to force in order to highlight their line in the sand. This was in part due to the fact that they wanted to reassert their strength but also that they did not want to concede too much to unions during the early days of parliament. The authorities knew that political liberalization could bring with it increased enthusiasm for further reform, an enthusiasm they wished to dampen.

The acts of cooperation between the BDF and the police reinforced a general sense of combined purpose among the hitherto rival institutions, and also added extra deterrence power to what has often been perceived as a relatively weak police force. Before Independence, the intervention of British and Saudi troops had always been deemed essential only in cases of serious insurrection. Now, the BDF and the National Guard had proved themselves as a useful deterrent against internal threats.

However, the deployment of the BDF in 1972 also showed that increases to the size and budget of the Ministry of the Interior were not, in themselves, an adequate solution to Bahrain's security problems. If anything, they compounded them. The perceived interchangeability between a military body and the police marked a continuation of a tendency to react with military means to any domestic threat. The leadership and quality of training were also called into question. Ian Henderson lamented what he saw as a 'total failure' of 'the Al Khalifa to face up to the

[142] Ibid. [143] Ibid. [144] Ibid.

need to train their own officers to take over responsibility for the security services'.[145] While this could reflect Henderson's personal prejudice, or desire to appear indispensable, it also reflects a perception of how changes in leadership affected the ability, competency and repressive capacity of the police force. Indeed, it seemed that no matter how well equipped the police were, they were not sufficient to contain unrest. In many cases, they simply served to enflame tensions. For Henderson, much of this was down to the leadership of the ruling family.

The continued ascendency of the prime minister buttressed the militancy within the security forces. It also brought with it a general anti-Shiʿa and anti-*baḥrānī* ideological position that contributed to severe repression in the 1980s and the 1990s Intifada. Writing in 1984, Roger Tomkys noted: 'All the Shiʿa may be subject to the unwelcome attention of the Public Security forces (not just the Special Branch).'[146] The perceptions of this sectarian disposition, according to numerous Bahrainis interviewed by Human Rights Watch, was not because of the cabinet but reportedly the work of a small cabal including the prime minister and the Minister of Interior, Muhammad bin Khalifa Al Khalifa.[147] For their part, the cabinet existed to rubber stamp the policies of this conservative grouping.[148] Such speculations, while valuable in themselves in terms of perceptions, appear to be accurate given the prime minister's reported behaviours in the 1970s and 1980s.

Security apparatus antipathy towards the Shiʿa manifested itself in confrontations between opposition members and the police. In 1994, government forces, without provocation, fired multiple tear gas canisters into the open area outside a Shiʿa mosque. They then arrested about two dozen people and shut down the mosque.[149] The lack of provocation seemed to reflect the government's willingness to manufacture a pretext on which to clamp down on growing unrest. In 1995 a paramilitary approach galvanized by hawkish influence resulted in an atmosphere of permissive police violence. Throughout the 1990s security forces and riot police routinely beat 'unarmed civilians, including women and minors'.[150] Extrajudicial killing outside of prison was common, with most protesters dying during altercations with the police. A number of these cases occurred during peaceful protests, and early on during the Intifada. The facts that these deaths occurred before any opposition

[145] W. R. Tomkys, Tel 75: Internal Security, 27 April 1982, FCO8/4332, The National Archives.
[146] W. R. Tomkys, Internal Political Situation 1984, FCO8/5442, The National Archives.
[147] Human Rights Watch *Routine Abuse.* [148] Ibid. [149] Ibid.
[150] Amnesty International, *Bahrain: A Human Rights Crisis,* p. 40.

violence became established suggested a policy of deliberate escalation by the police. Indeed Amnesty argues that of the ten initial civilian deaths occurring between December 1994 and May 1995, most occurred during marches 'described as peaceful, with the participants calling on the government to restore democratic rights'.[151]

Increased police brutality marked the realization of Henderson's fear of how Al Khalifa control of the police could lead to more unrest. While a sectarian force with a repressive and sectarian disposition had emerged under British stewardship, after Independence an aggressive attitude to dissent, furnished by an institutional conservatism underscored by anti-Shiʿa sentiment, became notably more acute. As was noted by one observer: 'A defensive regime – the Al Khalifa family – which has an even more defensive Saudi Arabia breathing down its neck, responded aggressively, cracking down on all dissent.'[152]

The 2011 Uprising and Evidence of Police Rioting

Despite cyclical instances of police violence over decades, the 2001 reforms symbolized hope for many, even after it became clear that King Hamad had led a constitutional coup to prolong monarchical rule. As if to illustrate this hope, the *baḥārna* of Sitra carried King Hamad in the air. Indeed, immediately after the reforms, there were ten years of relative quiet on the streets. However, the mass protests that erupted on 14 February 2011 showed that the Bahraini authorities were still quick to engage their authoritarian reflex when confronted with bodies in meatspace.

Even though popular protests in 2011 had remained peaceful, the response by the security services was not. Police tactics reflected the increasing self-reliance of the Saudi-backed Al Khalifa regime in tackling internal dissent. The killing of civilians in February led to more significant protests that resulted in further deaths. The BICI report specifically attributed the deaths of innocent civilians to the 'forceful confrontation of demonstrators involving the use of lethal force'. According to the BICI report, the paramilitary style of policing was key: the 'heavy deployment of Public Security Forces led to the death of civilians. This caused a marked increase in the number of persons participating in protests and led to a palpable escalation in their demands.'[153] Thirteen people were killed by the security forces, while eight deaths 'could not be attributed to

[151] Ibid., p. 34.
[152] *The Economist*, 'Gazing Backward', 25 March 1995, issue 7907, p. 74.
[153] Ibid., p. 223.

a particular person or agency'.[154] Despite the BICI's lack of clarity on the eight deaths mentioned above, the security services were implicated in most of them.

Social Media and Police Brutality

The rise of social media has led to an increase in documentation of police tactics that hitherto would have remained unknown or unverified. This new evidence of police violence serves to legitimize previous accusations of police behaviours in Bahrain. The evidence on social media, coupled with the narratives in the BICI report and those compiled by various international NGOs indicates a culture of 'police rioting'. This term was initially used in the United States in 1968 to describe 'unrestrained and indiscriminate police violence' against protesters or property.[155] Videos depicting gross acts of police rioting are now commonplace in Bahrain. There are countless hours of footage showing police officers attacking subdued and unarmed civilians,[156] deliberately damaging property and shooting at civilians. In 2011, Tony Mitchell, an expat working in Bahrain at the time, witnessed police smashing up cars parked near the Pearl Roundabout: 'Several cars belonging to the protesters were still parked on the sides of the footpath, the owners having abandoned them in their haste to leave. Every single one of them had had their windows smashed.' Mitchell, whose apartment overlooked the Pearl Roundabout, also described the clearing of the site that occurred on 17 February 2011. His testimony highlighted the extremely aggressive police tactics seemingly unrelated to protest militancy: 'My wife and I watched the last of the protesters flee the vacant lot on foot; the security forces were pursuing them too aggressively for them to have time to get into cars and drive away. It was obvious that the police were not content on merely clearing the area; they seemed hell-bent on injuring as many of the protesters as possible.'[157]

[154] Ibid., p. 226.

[155] Summary of report submitted by Daniel Walker, Director of the Chicago Study Team, to the National Commission on the Causes and Prevention of Violence, introduction by Max Frankel, E. P. Dutton, New York, 1968, www.fjc.gov/history/home.nsf/page/tu_chicago7_doc_13.html

[156] As part of the online virtual ethnographic, I collated a database of videos I could find demonstrating police deviance. This list can be viewed here: https://docs.google.com/spreadsheets/d/12489YCwvB-boyzQgYzPfU2q_nBJiS85WjTPEc7HGRuM/pub?output=html

[157] T. Mitchell, 'Witness to an Uprising: What I Saw in Bahrain', *The Atlantic*, 14 December 2011, www.theatlantic.com/international/archive/2011/12/witness-to-an-uprising-what-i-saw-in-bahrain/249977/

These police behaviours are not modern anomalies. Interviews with Bahrainis in 1996 by the Associated Press reveal how towns were 'systematically ransacked' by the security services.[158] News clips even show images of cars with smashed windshields. Between 2011 and 2012, police were often filmed in large groups, throwing Molotov cocktails, stones, metal construction rebars and other non-standard weapons.[159] The methodical and widespread nature of much of this deviance imply that it was either encouraged, tacitly accepted or completely ignored. Indeed, the historic lack of accountability in punishing those engaged in such actions also points to a tacit approval within the security services of such behaviours.

Accusations of this type of behaviour are frequently levelled at the Bahrain police. However, the term 'police rioting' implies an anomaly. The frequently aggressive tactics used by the Bahrain police point to an entrenched institutionalization of such methods. Reliance on military-style methods has further delegitimized the police and reduced cooperation with the general public. Indeed, the Bahrain authorities frequently responded to demonstrations with 'violence and minimal concessions',[160] the hallmark of paramilitary policing. In the recent uprising, the BICI report noted that the weapons and the way they were used violated principles of 'necessity and proportionality'.[161] Often, the police fired without due care as to whether the victim was injured or killed.[162]

Numerous attempts to reform the police have generally been prompted by the Al Khalifa's desire to increase its coercive capacity, as opposed to creating political solutions to increase consent to being policed. The term 'reform' is also somewhat euphemistic, implying a positive and progressive change, as opposed to an attempt to improve the repressive potential of the institution. Indeed, the attitude of the Al Khalifa towards policing highlighted by Belgrave in 1954 seems to have endured; 'more Police & more force to enforce law & order & no sign of

[158] Associated Press Archives, 'Bahrain – Crises' [video] 4 December 1996, www.aparchive.com/metadata/Bahrain-Crises/12dd0996a99586175645c5ab8800cf71?query=bahrain¤t=30&orderBy=Relevance&hits=330&referrer=search&search=%2fsearch%2ffilter%3fquery%3dbahrain%26from%3d21%26orderBy%3dRelevance%26allFilters%3d1990%253ADecade%26ptype%3dIncludedProducts%26_%3d1398682372621&allFilters=1990%3aDecade&productType=IncludedProducts&page=21&b=00cf71

[159] M. O. Jones, 'For the record: police in Bahrain throw Molotov cocktails', *Marc Owen Jones* [blog], 18 March 2012, http://marcowenjones.wordpress.com/2012/03/18/for-the-record-police-in-bahrain-throw-molotov-cocktails/,

[160] Physicians for Human Rights, *Weaponizing Tear Gas: Bahrain's Unprecedented Use of Toxic Chemical Agents against Civilians*, August 2012, https://s3.amazonaws.com/PHR_Reports/Bahrain-TearGas-Aug2012-small.pdf

[161] *BICI Report*, p. 418. [162] Ibid.

any concessions to public opinion'.[163] Indeed, the security apparatus in Bahrain has been more 'reactive than proactive',[164] and fears of militant policing have not been assuaged recently. Matthew Cassel[165] argued in 2011 that the so-called Miami model of policing was coming to Bahrain after the government invited former Miami police chief John Timoney to help reform the police. Jeremy Scahill notes that the Miami model is more akin to 'paramilitary soldering'.[166] The model is characterized by the deployment of military-style armoured personnel carriers and the use of helicopters, making many protests seem like war zones. Despite these fears, the Manama model existed before the Miami model. Violence has long been, and continues to be, an essential aspect of maintaining Al Khalifa hegemony. It has, however, become quantitatively worse over the past century, and shows no sign of abating.

Methods of a Mild Spanish Inquisition: Use of Torture and State Terror

Torture[167] is a form of repression aimed at harming the integrity of the flesh and has been used as early as the 1920s in Bahrain. Torture aims to deter individuals, extract confessions and warn others of the costs of engaging in dissent. Torture is also instrumental and has been used in Bahrain for a number of reasons, including: extracting confessions, gathering information about political movements, forcing detainees to relinquish their political beliefs, forcing detainees to report on the activities of their friends and forcing detainees to promise to cease engaging in political activity.[168] In this respect, torture seeks to damage and debilitate social movements through intimidation, intelligence gathering and

[163] Belgrave, Papers, 28 December 1954.

[164] Anderson and Killingray, 'An Orderly Retreat?', p. 10.

[165] M. Cassel, 'Even Bahrain's Use of "Miami Model" Policing Will Not Stop the Uprising', *The Guardian*, 3 December 2011, www.Theguardian.Com/commentisfree/2011/dec/03/bahrain-miami-model-policing

[166] J. Scahill, 'The Miami model', Democracy Now! on *Information Clearing House*, 24 November, www.informationclearinghouse.info/article5286.htm

[167] Torture is defined by the United Nations as 'any act by which severe pain or suffering, whether physical or mental, is intentionally inflicted on a person for such purposes as obtaining from him or a third person information or a confession, punishing him for an act he or a third person has committed or is suspected of having committed, or intimidating or coercing him or a third person, or for any reason based on discrimination of any kind, when such pain or suffering is inflicted by or at the instigation of or with the consent or acquiescence of a public official or other person acting in an official capacity. It does not include pain or suffering arising only from, inherent in or incidental to lawful sanctions'. UN Convention Against Torture, www.ohchr.org/en/professionalinterest/pages/cat.aspx

[168] Amnesty International, *Bahrain: A Human Rights Crisis.*

persuasion. Although it has existed for decades, its severity and occurrence in Bahrain appears to have increased markedly since Independence, and even more so since the 1990s Intifada.

Amnesty International reports document torture occurring as early as 1972,[169] although a more thorough consultation of British records shows that detainees were exposed to physical harm to extract information from as early as 1926. Indeed, British officials were directly involved in torturing political prisoners themselves, a fact that has not been addressed in much of the literature on Bahrain. This was particularly true during the 1920s when the British administration was beset by numerous challenges to its authority, whether it was perceived Bolshevik agitation or the actions of groups working on behalf of a faction of the ruling family to undermine British authority.

On one occasion, ʿAbd Allah bin ʿIsa's and his mother sought to undermine the reforms of the 1920s by disrupting the newly established security services.[170] Dissent was sown in the ranks of the armed forces, allegedly via a Persian Bolshevik Mullah, culminating in a Baluchi Sepoy killing two other Levies. This was the same attack that resulted in the injury of Major Daly, who was stabbed, shot and wounded. Given that the attack attempted to undermine British authority, extreme methods were used to extract information. Belgrave admitted to using 'methods of a mild Spanish Inquisition' to get information from one of the conspirators.[171] Interestingly, he also wrote how he 'felt sorry for the boy' being tortured.[172]

Following a raid on the village of Sanābis in 1926, again thought to be orchestrated by the rebellious faction of the Al Khalifa, the British Police Captain Parke used sleep deprivation over a few nights to get suspects to talk.[173] Belgrave noted that such methods were, 'not exactly torture'.[174] In another case, a small cabal, likely headed by Shaykh ʿAbd Allah bin ʿIsa Al Khalifa but attributed to Shaykh Khalid, organized an assassination attempt on the ruler. The suspected perpetrators were rounded up, and Captain Parke ordered the police to use 'rather oriental methods'[175] in order to extract information. Despite Belgrave's initial use of euphemism, he goes on to detail that one of the methods used involved the placing of pieces of lighted papers between the toes of the prisoners.

[169] Amnesty International, *Annual Report 1972–1973*, London, Amnesty International Publications, p. 70.
[170] A paramilitary force of troops.
[171] Belgrave, Papers, 15 August 1926. Interestingly, Belgrave here expresses remorse for these deeds.
[172] Ibid. [173] Belgrave, Papers, 12 November 1928. [174] Ibid.
[175] Belgrave, Papers, 16 April 1929.

Belgrave's diary reveals how the torture from his subordinates occurred at their own volition, highlighting a significant amount of police autonomy in such matters. When the political agent was informed about the torture, he expressed his anger at Parke, but no action was taken to discipline him. Whatever Parke had done, he had managed to successfully extract a confession as to who organized the crime.[176] Belgrave was more concerned with the negative publicity but felt no 'compunction' for the men on account of their actions. Indeed he noted that it was a 'pity' that the news came out, and a 'pity that Parke took part in it himself'.[177] Despite the obvious acknowledgement by both Belgrave and Barrett that such methods were somehow undesirable, the combination of police autonomy and a lack of accountability clearly created an enabling environment for such methods to be used. In addition, contextual factors, such as the perceived severity of the crime, undoubtedly contributed to the severity of repression used.

In 1932, following the outbreak of riots related to reforms of the Pearling Industry, Belgrave 'beat' a few detainees in order to get them to reveal who had incited them to protest.

> I spent the whole morning till two o'clock interrogating the prisoners, at first they wouldn't speak, but I beat a few of them till they did speak, it was all very barbarous and illegal, but on some occasions, one has to behave illegally. They gave me the information that I needed, and on that, I was able to make a list of the names of the men who were the ringleaders and who actually broke into the Police Office and took the man out.[178]

While some may say that the 1920s were 'different times', and attitudes to violent methods of coercion were less pronounced, there are several issues with that argument. First, such methods were clearly perceived as an effective way of achieving certain objectives, whether information gathering or punishment. In the aforementioned example, Belgrave attributes and justifies his 'barbarous' methods by emphasizing the successful results. Indeed, he believed by beating the prisoners, he got the names of the ringleaders. Second, Belgrave himself acknowledged the deplorable nature of his actions. Similarly, the Political Resident Barrett had expressed his anger about Captain Parke's use of torture. Belgrave even noted with remorse that he had acted 'illegally' after beating inmates (although no penal code existed at the time).

Evidence of torture in the 1940s, 1950s and 1960s is harder to come by, and the Foreign and Commonwealth Office's refusal to comply with Freedom of Information requests confounds further research into the

[176] Ibid. [177] Ibid. [178] Belgrave, Papers, 27 May 1932.

issue. It is also important to bear in mind that information about Belgrave's torture came from Belgrave's diary, and after 1957 he was no longer recording his daily activities. Belgrave's own admittances tend to confound any illusions of a civilizing British colonial presence. However, and euphemisms notwithstanding, the extent and frankness of Belgrave's diary suggest that torture was the exception as opposed to the rule, and reserved mainly for high-level political crime. Indeed, Belgrave personally engaged in acts of torture when the crime being investigated related to challenges to his own, or indeed, British authority. In this regard, torture did not appear to be haphazard, but directly related to the perceived severity of challenges to the British/Al Khalifa nexus of authority.

The increasing professionalization of the police in the 1960s and the shift to more intelligence-led policing under Ian Henderson did not appear to create an initial documented increase in torture. Despite reports of police brutality in 1965, a surprise visit by the Red Cross in the same year revealed nothing suspicious.[179] Under Henderson's methods, the police were, at some point, forbidden from arresting suspected dissidents, let alone torturing them. This implies a general, although perhaps temporary, shift in policing behaviours. For their part, British diplomatic officials believed that Henderson and Bell's methods were less draconian than their predecessors, and were initially 'regarded with favour' by Bahrainis.[180] However, the activities of bodies like Amnesty International and the Red Cross, coupled with the increasing press scrutiny of the British role in its former protectorates, meant that the authorities were aware that such actions could no longer be done with total impunity.

Torture Post-Independence

Reports of torture after Independence in 1971 became more frequent and consistent.[181] Deaths as a result of torture began to occur and be documented by both British officials and human rights organizations. Even though Amnesty International and Human Rights Watch improved their reporting of human rights violations in the Gulf during the 1970s and 1980s, the increase in torture likely reflects a spike in occurrences rather than better documentation.

[179] Visit to Bahrain by International Red Cross Official, 1965, FO371/179809, The National Archives.

[180] K. Oldfield, 15 August 1965, Amnesty International and Political Prisoners, FO371/185355, The National Archives.

[181] Amnesty International Annual Reports from 1973–74, 1977, 1980 and 1982 all report torture.

Eight political detainees were killed in custody between 1976 and 1986.[182] Amnesty International as well as the British Parliamentary Human Rights Group reported that at least six of those were believed to have been killed as a result of torture.[183] This means that deaths known to be caused by torture began following Independence. The British, who had excellent contacts in the police through Ian Henderson, discussed some of these killings. The first so-called 'Shiʿa martyr' was considered to be Jamal ʿAli, who was killed in police custody in 1980. The local English newspaper, the *Gulf Daily News*, reported that Jamal ʿAli had died of kidney failure as a result of bad health.[184] (Similarly, in 2011, the Bahrain News Agency noted that Karim Fakhrawi, who was found to have been tortured, also died of kidney failure.) British officials were not convinced by the GDN's reporting. In fact, they acknowledged that ʿAli was likely an 'innocent party', was 'electrocuted'[185] and was 'beaten up in custody' where he later 'died of his injuries'.[186] Civil society groups were also not convinced by the government's official line. The Bahrain Workers Union (BWU) claimed that Jamal ʿAli was arrested and tortured for his trade union activities. Despite British knowledge of his torture, the BWU's complaint about Ali's death to the International Labour Organisation (ILO) in 1981 was dismissed in part due to the government's story that ʿAli was being treated in Salmaniya hospital for a 'diseased and defective kidney condition'.[187] Inevitably, the BWU could not substantiate their claims without evidence.

In most cases of deaths by torture, there was no investigation, internal or otherwise. In three of the cases between 1976 and 1986, investigations found that the deceased had died of suicide or medical illness – a common excuse used to absolve the security services of accountability. For the most part, the government sought to conceal their actions. In 1981, twenty-three-year-old Muhammad Hassan

[182] Amnesty International, *Bahrain: A Human Rights Crisis*, p. 2.

[183] R. Wilkingson, 'Speak Together of Freedom. The Present Struggle for Democracy and Human Rights in Bahrain', *The Parliamentary Human Rights Group*, March 1996, http://bahrain.wikia.com/wiki/Speak_Together_of_Freedom:_The_Present_Struggle_for_Democracy_and_Human_Rights_in_Bahrain,_Robert_Wilkinson,_The_Parliamentary_Human_Rights_Group,_March_1996

[184] *Gulf Daily News*, 'Ministry Denies Death Rumours', April 1980, FCO8/3489, The National Archives.

[185] K. J. Passmore, Letter from Roland Moyle, MP: Bahrain, 16 September 1981, FCO8/3893, The National Archives.

[186] H. B. Walker, Bahrain: Annual Review for 1980, 10 February 1981, FCO8/3894, The National Archives.

[187] Definitive Report – Report No 230, November 1983, Case No 1043 (Bahrain) – Complaint date: 01-JUN-81 – Closed, www.ilo.org/dyn/normlex/en/f?p=1000:50002:0::NO:50002:P50002_COMPLAINT_TEXT_ID:2900571

Madan was beaten to death by three policemen in Muharraq police station.[188] The circumstances of his death prompted a public outcry. In the ensuing protests, police ran over and killed nine-year-old ʿAdel Hasan Khoki.[189] It is said that the bodies of both Madan and Khoki were buried in secret graves,[190] and that the Khoki incident was deliberately not reported for fear of stirring up more anger.[191] Indeed, there is perhaps no clearer example here of how torture breeds anger, which breeds further repression.

A number of factors can best explain the rise of torture. In addition to an increased sense of vulnerability brought about by Bahrain's Independence in 1971, there was a notable shift in power at the Ministry of Interior that empowered hard-liners within the ruling family. Harold Walker, the British ambassador at the time, singled out these hardliners as the prime minister and a merchant elite that included the al-Muyyad and al-Zayani families. The coercive disposition of this elite towards opposition actions was highlighted in 1974, when 'the government and the merchant class thought it was time to take a firm hand'[192] against any unrest.

The prime minister himself exhibited a personal antipathy towards the Shiʿa, feelings that were no doubt significant in increasing repression especially against the country's *baḥārna* population. The shift in power to these hardliners was accompanied by a corollary diminishing of British influence in the security apparatus. By 1973, it was reported that the prime minister had the last word on matters of internal security and basic foreign policy'[193] and kept police and Special Branch 'closely under his own control'.[194] The British were still well represented in the Bahraini police, yet this seemed to have little impact on moderating torture. Foreign Office correspondence, corroborated by US State Department cables from the 1970s, both acknowledge the declining influence of the British heads of police, Jim Bell and Ian Henderson.[195] The British embassy reported that:

[188] Copson, Telegram No 165, 16 September, 1981, FCO8/3893, The National Archives.
[189] Ibid.
[190] Bahrain Martyrs [Instagram Account], 16 February 2014, https://instagram.com/p/ke8XaLxEnT/
[191] Copson, Telegram No 165, 16 September, 1981.
[192] R. M. Tesh, Bahrain Internal, 1 July 1974, FCO8/2180, The National Archives.
[193] R. M. Tesh, Bahrain: Annual Review for 1973, FCO8/2181, The National Archives.
[194] Tesh, 17 December 1974, The National Archives.
[195] 'Advisory Roles of the UK and Certain Other Countries in the Persian Gulf States', US Embassy Manama, 20 February 1975, www.wikileaks.org/plusd/cables/1975MANAMA00217_b.html

> Two years ago the Chief of the Police and the Head of the Special Branch, both British, came directly under the Prime Minister and were regularly and visibly in close and constant touch with him. Now they hardly ever see him but work to a Bahraini Minister of the Interior who is fortunately conscientious and hard-working. The Chief of Police is now 'Director-General of Public Security', advising and administering from the background rather than exercising direct executive control. He has lost much of his power, and rather sadly accepts this. The Head of Special Branch – which is now, at the top, wholly expatriate – is no longer allowed to detain or interrogate; his intelligence network must, therefore, function by other means, and the power of deterrence has dwindled.[196]

As a result, Henderson and Bell were 'excluded from various private lines of command influence'.[197] However, they were still seen as an 'inestimable advantage in practical terms', as they did, according to one British official, offer some assurances about the maintenance of law and order despite the renewed force of Al Khalifa conservatism.[198]

This shift to hardliners was solidified further in 1976. The murder of newspaper editor Shaykh ʿAbd Allah al-Madani in the same year signified the real overturning of Henderson's influence and the rejection of a surveillance-led policy that had hitherto restricted interrogation and torture. The Bahraini authorities used al-Madani's murder to justify a crackdown on leftist political groups in Bahrain. They also used it to overturn a policy that had previously prevented targets of subversion from being arrested and therefore tortured. As Edward Given noted, 'the "murder" removed the restriction on the interrogation of Popular Front suspects and enabled the police to acquire a clearer picture than before of its ramifications and activities'.[199] Prior to this, 'the absence of interrogation of suspects meant that the police received only the amount of intelligence which their sources in the NLF cared to give them'.[200]

The impact of this change in policy was immediate. Two Bahrainis, Muhammad Ghulum Busheri and Saʿid al-ʿUwaynati, were killed as a result of torture following their arrest. Although the trial of the remaining living suspects in the murder case was entirely unsafe, it was used as a pretext for clamping down on political opposition. The trial also came at a time where the ruling family were reportedly 'closing ranks'[201] and concentrating in their hands both politically sensitive posts such as

[196] R. M. Tesh, 1 March 1975, FCO8/2415, The National Archives.
[197] Tomkys, Bahrain Internal Security, 10 April 1982.
[198] P. F. M. Wogan, Letter to W. R. Tomkys, 23 April 1982, FCO8/4332, The National Archives.
[199] E. F. Given, Political Murder in Bahrain, 29 January 1977, FCO8/2874, The National Archives.
[200] Ibid. [201] E. F. Given, 5 July 1976, FCO8/2643, The National Archives.

security as well as posts relating to social affairs.[202] Again, this had gone on in opposition to the recommendations of the Turnbull Report, which had advocated 'removing direct control from members of the Ruling Family'.[203] In short, the 1970s represented a tightening of grip by hard-liners over the security apparatus, a factor that correlated with, and more likely caused, the increase in torture.

The legislative provisions of the State Security Decree introduced several years previously also facilitated and incentivized the torture of prisoners in Bahrain.[204] Detainees could be held incommunicado for months, or even years, isolated from the outside world, with no access to legal counsel until the time of their trial and only infrequent visits from their family. Provisions governing trial before the Supreme Civil Court of Appeal also allowed the court to base its judgment solely on confessions given to the police, or even on police testimony alone (even in the absence of witnesses). In the 1980s, confessions were allowed as the sole basis for a conviction, even if uncorroborated. In this regard, the incentive of using torture was increased for the police. It was an efficient means of getting convictions in a timely manner. There were few safeguards ensuring that such evidence would or could be discarded in the courts.[205] Combined with the new State Security Law, the al-Madani affair consolidated a shift from an intelligence-gathering approach to one that encouraged the interrogation and torture of suspects. While this shift reflected a difference of opinion in tactics between Henderson and the Al Khalifa, it eventually became routine, thus ending what had been described by Given as a 'lack of a coherent policy' on dealing with political opposition.[206] What had previously vacillated, according to Given, 'between inactivity and excessive zeal',[207] now erred more on the side of excessive zeal.

Following the increase in torture, the British Embassy in Bahrain wished to impress upon the Bahrainis that such a method was not only 'morally undesirable'[208] but also self-defeating. They used the example of SAVAK (the secret intelligence-gathering organization of Iran known for their brutal treatment of dissidents) to get their point across. However, the British were also reluctant to upset the Al Khalifa by criticizing their methods of policing.[209] This reluctance reflected a lack of influence, and led to a bifurcation of labour between the British and Arab police,

[202] Ibid. [203] M. S. Weir, 7 October 1965, The National Archives.
[204] Amnesty International, *Bahrain: Violations of Human Rights*, p. 10.
[205] Amnesty International, *Bahrain: A Human Rights Crisis.*
[206] E. F. Given, 5 July 1976, FCO8/2643, The National Archives. [207] Ibid.
[208] 'Bahraini Police Methods', FCO8/4332, The National Archives. [209] Ibid.

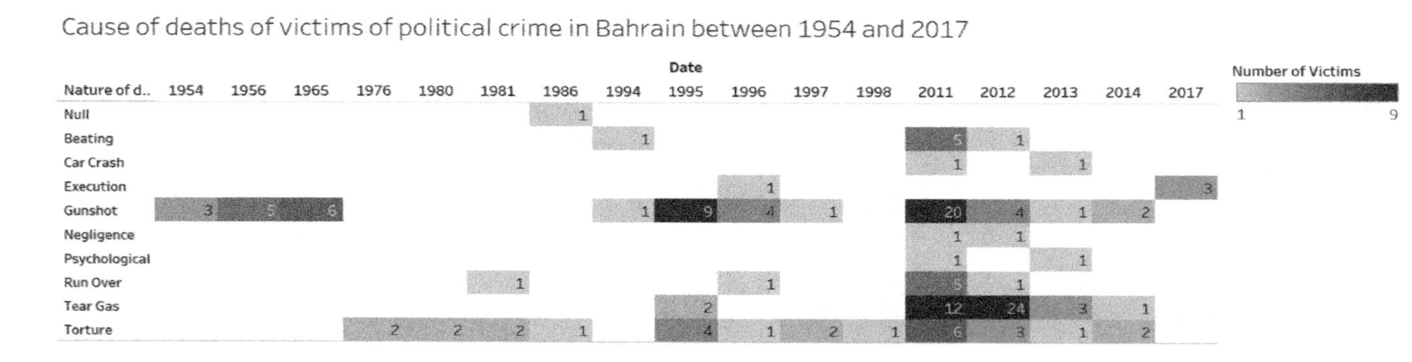

Figure 4.1 Graph showing the cause of deaths of victims of political crime in Bahrain between 1954 and 2017

whereby local recruits, as opposed to British officers, would be the ones engaging in torture. The use of torture was directly attributed by British officials to pressure from the ruling family. Roger Tomkys reported that the most brutal among the torturers were Bahrainis and that the 'encouragement they get from some members of the Al Khalifas is to be more rather than less tough in their methods'.[210] Tomkys' perception, based on meetings with the likes of Ian Henderson, again suggests that the reassertion of Al Khalifa control had a direct impact on the methods and severity of repression used.

Torture also became functional and important in creating intelligence networks that had previously been raised through other, more ambiguous, methods. In 1991, Amnesty International reported that 'detainees are tortured and ill-treated to obtain information, or confessions which may then be used as a basis for their conviction and sentence... or threatened and warned against taking part in any form of political opposition activity in the future'.[211] Amnesty International also reported that many prisoners were 'subjected to torture or threats in order to force them to cooperate with the authorities, reporting back on the activities and friends of particular individuals'.[212] Between 1994 and 1998, Human Rights Watch received reports of at least seven deaths in custody due to torture.[213] The need for information and the continued relevance of confessions without sufficient safeguards to ensure confessions are coerced have allowed the method of torture to flourish. Although it is not clear how Henderson's original intelligence networks were coerced or co-opted into providing information to the authorities, certainly any willing cooperation would have been destroyed by the increasing use of torture. In this regard, as police brutality and the willingness to use torture has increased in general, so too has the forced cooperation through torture.

Modern Methods of Torture, Patterns and Explanations

With more accurate documentation of torture comes more insight into the methods used. Torture in the 1980s frequently involved the following: beatings with lengths of hosepipe/electric cable, enforced standing upright for hours or days, sleep deprivation, prevention from going to the toilet, the extinguishing of cigarettes on the body and suspension in contorted and painful positions.[214] In addition to this,

[210] Tomkys, 16 February 1982, The National Archives.
[211] Amnesty International, *Bahrain: Violations of Human Rights*, pp. 8–9. [212] Ibid.
[213] Human Rights Watch, *Torture Redux*.
[214] Amnesty International, *Bahrain: Violations of Human Rights*, pp. 8–9.

some prisoners were threatened with sexual abuse or execution, or had their skin pierced by a drill. Others were sometimes forced to eat faeces or lizards.[215] The multitude of techniques highlight the importance of humiliation and the destruction of the victim's self-esteem. Psychological methods such as threats to the family of the detainee have also been used. It is also worth noting that the consistency of techniques since the 1980s has remained relatively stable.

Some of the methods of torture that have been employed are particular to Bahrainis and the Shiʿa. For example, the prevalence of sickle-cell anaemia (a condition of the blood) in Bahrain is exploited to facilitate torture, as is the derision of the Shiʿi faith by officials. This technique has been more salient since the Bahrain Intifada. Sickle-cell anaemia patients in the 1990s and the 2011 Uprising have often been kept in cold, air-conditioned rooms during winter for extended periods of time exposing them to the risk of organ damage, especially of the kidneys or eyes.[216] Sufferers also risk 'leg ulcers, gall stones and bacterial infection, and suffer generalised body pain'.[217] Shiʿa detainees are also frequently prevented from 'saying their prayers or performing ablution', highlighting how the profile of the target specifically influences methods.[218] Often when those with sickle-cell anaemia (called *siklar*) have died in custody, the authorities have blamed the disease by attributing it to kidney failure,[219] reflecting a tendency to use cause of death without referring to the underlying proximate cause of death. Of course such distinctions are important in determining why the person died. At least three deaths, two in custody and one from tear gas, were blamed by the government on sickle-cell anaemia. In the case of the custodial deaths of Hasan Jasim Muhammad Maki[220] and Zakariya Rashid Hasan al-Asheri[221] in 2011, the BICI report found the deaths had been as a result of torture. In the third case, they concluded that Sayid Jawad Ahmed Hashim Marhun did not even suffer from sickle-cell anaemia.[222] The BICI Report noted that the level of mistreatment was dependent on the 'categories of detainees', again, emphasizing the relationship between threat, potential religiosity or method of torture.[223]

The continuance of torture throughout the 1990s seemed to be indicative of a casual and permissive attitude towards state violence. This was emphasized when Shaykh Muhammad bin Mubarak Al Khalifa, a member of the ruling family and the then foreign minister, dismissed claims of torture and mistreatment by saying, 'I think there is a lot of

[215] Ibid., p. 7. [216] Amnesty International, *Bahrain: A Human Rights Crisis*, p. 28.
[217] Ibid. [218] Ibid. [219] *BICI Report*, p. 244. [220] Ibid., p. 242.
[221] Ibid., p. 244. [222] Ibid., p. 254. [223] Ibid., p. 417.

exaggeration, I am not say [sic] we are perfect, I am not saying that, I am not saying there aren't some mistakes'.[224]

In addition to this lack of accountability, there appears to be a widely held attitude among security officials that those detained on suspicion of criminal activity are automatically guilty. Human Rights Watch acknowledged that there is 'a sense that anyone in custody for whatever reason must deserve punishment, which ordinary police and security officials feel entitled to administer'.[225] This attitude appears to have been aggravated by the sectarian divide between perceived Shiʿa dissidents and the mostly Sunni police. In addition, the historic marginalization and more recent criminalization of the Shiʿa at large may have a knock-on effect. Their perception as an underclass, with a lack of *wasta* (political influence), makes them more liable to mistreatment in custody.[226]

Torture was reported to have decreased following the advent of the National Action Charter in 2000. This is unsurprising, as the reforms prompted a period of relative calm. However, in 2007, there was, according to Human Rights Watch, a 'reversion to past practices' in the security services.[227] Security officials 'utilised a specific repertoire of techniques' that mimicked precisely those from the 1990s, implying an institutional memory to methods of torture.[228] This resurgence coincided with a regional fear of Shiʿa empowerment prompted by the fallout of the coalition invasion of Iraq in 2003. The King of Jordan, for example, noted that Shiʿi victories in Iraq were leading to a rising Shiʿi Crescent. While it might be reasonable to assume that this engaged a 'Gulf-wide obsession with Iran's potential influence',[229] there is an argument to say that it was Shiʿa empowerment in Iraq, and not Iran, that resulted in stronger action towards Shiʿa dissent in Bahrain.

Certainly there is evidence to suggest that some officials were more fearful of Shiʿi empowerment in Iraq, as opposed to Iran. In 1983, paraphrasing Sir Geoffrey Arthur, one British official stated that 'the Bahraini ruling family were far less worried by the direct influence which Khomeini and the Iranian revolution might have on the Shiʿi majority in Bahrain than by the risk of the installation of a Shiʿi

[224] Associated Press Archives, 'Bahrain Crises' [video], 4 December 1996.
[225] Human Rights Watch, *Routine Abuse.* [226] Ibid.
[227] Human Rights Watch, *Torture Redux.* [228] Ibid.
[229] G. Abdo, 'The New Sectarianism: The Arab Uprisings and the Rebirth of the Shi'a Sunni Divide', The Saban Center for Middle East Policy at Brookings, Analysis Papers, no. 29, April 2013, www.brookings.edu/~/media/research/files/papers/2013/04/sunni%20shia%20abdo/sunni%20shia%20abdo

government in Baghdad'.[230] The growing strength of the Shia in Iraq following the toppling of Saddam Hussein coincided with the creation of an almost entirely Bahraini-run security services. This was a development that the British heads of police had anticipated with gloom in the 1970s, when they explicitly noted that a Bahrain-run Special Branch could lead to civil unrest.[231] Ian Henderson reportedly mentioned to David Tatham of the Middle East Department in 1977 that if he (Henderson) were to retire, 'the effect on the efficiency of the security apparatus generally would be severe'.[232] Henderson maintained that he and Jim Bell 'were trying hard to keep up standards, but a general sloppiness was creeping in'.[233] Indeed, Henderson and Bell feared that a decline in standards would simply result in the increasing repression of both criminals and political prisoners.

The increasing localization of the police may have also contributed to the increase in torture. In 2009, Shaykh Khalifa bin ʿAbd Allah Al Khalifa was tasked by the king to Bahrainiize the Bahrain National Security Agency (NSA) in order to remove 'the last vestiges of British influence'.[234] This, coupled with a legislative amendment of 2008, gave the NSA powers of arrest and interrogation[235] and paved the way for the NSA involvement in violence during 2011. These powers given to the NSA were singled out in the *BICI Report* as a contributor to the torture of inmates. Although the BICI recommended powers of arrest be withdrawn from the NSA (a recommendation the government briefly implemented) in 2016, the king decreed that the NSA once again be given powers of arrest in 'terror' cases. This reneging no doubt reflects the dying down of international pressure in Bahrain a few years following the beginning of the Arab uprisings.[236] It also implies a habitual tendency to 'regress' to particular strategies when the temporally limited focus of

[230] Cited in M. O. Jones, 'Saudi Intervention, Sectarianism…, and De-democratization in Bahrain's Uprising', in T. Davies, H. Ryan and A. Pena (eds), *Protest, Social Movements, and Global Democracy since 2011* (Special Issue), *Research in Social Movements, Conflict and Change*, vol. 39, 2016, pp. 251–79.

[231] P. F. M. Wogan, Iran and the Gulf, 23 August 1982, FCO8/4332, The National Archives.

[232] D. E. Tatham, 'Internal Security in Bahrain', 1977, FCO document, www.whatdotheyknow.com/request/164213/response/531538/attach/3/FOI%200544%2013%2

[233] Ibid.

[234] C. Henzel, 'Scenesetter for Manama Dialogue, December 11–13', US Embassy Manama, 2 December 2009, https://wikileaks.org/plusd/cables/09MANAMA681_a.html

[235] *BICI Report*, p. 45.

[236] J. Gambrell, 'Bahrain, Reversing Reform, Restores Arrest Powers to Spies', Associated Press, 2017, https://apnews.com/d1d7dc18390a485cb9461b7b496ef279/Bahrain,-reversing-reform

certain international bodies expires. Thus international pressure can impact upon the nature of these repressive techniques but only in a limited capacity. Whether or not reduced external (foreign power) oversight impacted upon the methods of repression and violence used by the security services is open to debate, although certainly this was the fear that Henderson expressed in the 1970s.

In 2011, the Bahrain Independent Commission of Inquiry documented that a 'systematic practice of physical and psychological abuse' had taken place during 2011.[237] As with before, the forms of torture[238] and abuse were similar to those in the 1990s and 1980s.[239] The historic similarity points again to an institutional memory of repression, where the transmission of memories, tactics, behaviours occur between members of the ruling class, their associates and the institutions that they control. As the *BICI Report* noted, 'the very fact that a systematic pattern of behaviour existed indicates that this is how these security forces were trained and how they were expected to act'. Indeed, it is highly improbable that without some institutional memory, or training, that similar techniques would have spontaneously manifested themselves.[240]

While the brutality in the recent uprising has been attributed to a shift to hardliners, it has been prevalent since Independence, growing steadily more endemic since. This implies a number of more high-level explanatory reasons, such as the increasing involvement of Saudi in Bahrain's affairs, the Al Khalifa's mentality of conquest, the criminalization of Shiʿa, the sectarian imbalance of the police, the Bahrainiization of the police, higher popular mobilization and the demise of sufficient external moderating influences.

Torture and Technological Change

Technology and the dissemination of images of torture were also a defining aspect of the 2011 Uprising. Whereas images of tortured bodies have existed since the 1970s in Bahrain, the proliferation of digital media has meant that gruesome images of violence have been disseminated far more widely, from more angles and in greater detail. One of the most iconic images, not of torture, but police brutality, was of Ahmed Farhan, who had half his head blown away by the riot police. Videos taken on

[237] *BICI Report*, p. 298.

[238] E.g. excessive handcuffing and blindfolding, forced standing, severe beatings, electric shocks, cigarette burns, beating the soles of feet (falaqa), sleep deprivation, threats of rape, sexual abuse, religious insults (usually anti-Shiʿa), electric shocks, hanging or suspension, solitary confinement, expose to extreme temperatures and other forms of humiliation.

[239] *BICI Report*, pp. 288–90. [240] Ibid., p. 281.

handheld devices showed him at the hospital, surrounded by people videoing his dead body, some even putting their phones into the vacated cavity of his skull to get a close-up shot. The process of vicarious trauma, that is, the psychological and harmful impact of exposure to such images, cannot be underestimated in its ability to induce fear and fragment oppositional morale. Police brutality, and torture, in particular, are often perceived as an act that regimes wish to keep secret. However, regimes are less concerned about keeping the fact that it happens a secret. Instead, they seek to minimize publicity about the extent to which it happens. As Austin Turk has noted, torture is vital in 'making the consequences of political resistance so gruesome that no one who has experienced it is psychologically and/or physically capable of further resistance – if he or she survives'.[241] Torture therefore, must be publicized at some point. The advent of mobile phones and social media allows the consequences of political resistance to be disseminated instantaneously. Just as the purpose of public punishment in town squares was intended to have a deterrence effect, so too is the strategic dissemination of state brutality.

Impunity and Cover-Ups Legitimizing Torture

Amnesty International wrote in 1996 that 'the impunity with which such practices are carried out, and the absence of any official accountability has resulted in torture being regarded as a legitimate method of interrogation'.[242] This lack of accountability has been an ongoing problem, yet its historical persistence can also be explained by a culture of impunity buttressed by reactionary attitudes to dissent. Underpinning much of the persistence of torture in Bahrain has been a lack of accountability, coupled with a shift to policymakers and officials who perceive its value as both a right as well as a tool of social control. Although it is purposefully difficult to prove that torture is ordered by those in key political positions, their influence, or failure to influence, implies some level of complicity that points to a systemic combination of negligence, willful blindness, active encouragement or tacit approval of the practice. Certainly, conversations between British officials and British police in the 1980s were explicit in stating that such methods were actively encouraged by the Al Khalifa family. This would not be surprising as there is no specific reason to suggest that the brutality reported in the 1920s was ever remedied through socialization strategies. Indeed, the discovery of oil merely created more distance between the ruling family and the native population.

[241] Turk, *Political Criminality,* p. 137.
[242] Amnesty International, *Bahrain: A Human Rights Crisis.*

The British and Torture: From a Direct Role to Insidious Indifference

Influential officials, including British diplomats and political agents in Bahrain, have had varying attitudes towards torture over the past century. While at least one political agent expressed strong disapproval when he heard about Captain Park's use of torture in the 1930s, British officials after Independence adopted a more 'c'est la vie' attitude. Indeed, Roger Tomkys noted in 1982 that brutality from the security apparatus 'is normal and expected'.[243]

At times, this attitude could not be attributed to indifference or ambivalence. On the contrary, there is evidence to suggest British diplomats helped to cover up the use of torture. In the 1970s, the British Embassy was fully aware of torture going on within Bahrain's Ministry of the Interior. However, they appeared to do little to stop it, even though they had the chance. On some occasions, British diplomats actively misled the British public about their knowledge of the occurrence of torture in Bahrain. When Bahraini army officer Saʿid al-ʿUwaynati was tortured and killed by the Bahrain Defence Force for his alleged role in the murder of the newspaper editor ʿAbd Allah al-Madani in 1976, the British Embassy in Bahrain forcefully denied the extent of their knowledge to Stan Newens, a British Labour Party MP making enquiries about human rights abuses in Bahrain. They also misled Newens on the explanation of the death of Muhammad Ghulum Bucheeri, who was killed in police custody during the same round of arrests as al-ʿUwaynati. The British knew that al-ʿUwaynati had been tortured and killed by the Bahrain Defence Force. However, because the information about his murder was regarded as a secret by the Bahrain government, and told to the British ambassador in confidence, the British said nothing. When Stan Newens, who was also a member of the Gulf Committee, wrote to ask about the death of Ghuloom and al-ʿUwaynati, the British simply said they could not confirm the report about the latter's death. Of course, this was untrue, and during a careful series of edits, the British officials in Bahrain were careful not to let on how much they knew about al-ʿUwaynati's death to Newens. They thought it would compromise the source that had given them useful information on Bahrain's internal situation.[244]

Although the British did not divulge much information to Newens and the Gulf Committee, they sent a report of the incident along with the full details of al-ʿUwaynati's death to Anthony Crosland, the British secretary of state at the time. What Crosland did with the information is unclear

[243] Tomkys, 16 February 1982, The National Archives.
[244] The name of the source is omitted, but presumably it is Ian Henderson.

(assuming he received it), although what is clear is that British officials actively hid details of the incident from the British public. It is likely the British Parliament was not a party to the information about Ghulum's death. Indeed, no parliamentary records show a discussion of torture until at least 1992. It seems unlikely that the source (probably Ian Henderson) who knew about al-ʿUwaynati torture did not also reveal more about Ghulum's torture and the torture of the others. Regardless, hiding knowledge of torture from the British public was crucial in preventing pressure being brought on the Bahraini government to potentially adapt their repressive methods and refrain from such practices.

Some British officials justified torture by saying that Bahrain was moderate compared to other regimes, repeatedly using euphemisms to trivialize what they acknowledged to be brutal behaviour. For example, during the interrogation of members of the Islamic Front for the Liberation of Bahrain (IFLB) who were arrested for the alleged coup attempt in 1982, Ian Henderson reported that the security forces 'got the job done without any of the prisoners being severely or lastingly' injured.[245] Henderson added that this was a 'creditable achievement' in 'local terms'.[246]

While the British were defensive about accusations of abuse in Bahrain on account of the number of British officers in the police (especially at a time when British mercenaries were receiving unwanted attention from the press in Angola), other factors played a role in their reticence. Due to increased global competition for trade contracts in Bahrain, the British were sensitive about losing out on trade opportunities by upsetting the Al Khalifa-led government. As a case in point, J. C. Moberly was explicitly unwilling to press the Bahraini authorities on issues regarding torture as it might prejudice their relationship with Bahrain.[247] What British leverage and influence there may have been on issues of police tactics or otherwise diminished as they sought now to curry favour with Bahrain in order to gain business contracts and investments that would benefit the United Kingdom. As Ambassador Sterling noted in 1971:

> Bahrain is one of our best Arab markets. So it is worth continuing to give the Bahrainis the things that they want from us: help for the police, who are the best guarantee of local stability; training for the Defence Force officers, both to keep them happy and to stop them going to Iraq; favourable consideration for ECGD cover and, in particular, a continuingly effective technical assistance program.

245 W. R. Tomkys, 16 February 1982, The National Archives. 246 Ibid.
247 J. C. Moberly, Bahrain: Use of Torture by the Special Branch, 19 February 1982, FCO8/4332, The National Archives.

Our position here is strong. We can best maintain it by giving help and advice at least as readily in the future as hitherto, but always remembering that the Bahrainis are now fully independent and expect to be treated accordingly.[248]

In reality, the United Kingdom benefited from an Al Khalifa-led status quo that facilitated torture. Most British officials working in Bahrain avoided raising the issue of torture because of materialistic concerns about trade. Thus through a policy of wilful negligence and demonstrative obfuscation, British officials were directly complicit in a brutal policy facilitated by British police officers. They attempted to ease their conscience through constant reiterations that Bahrain was independent and that such egregious behaviour was commonplace in the Middle East. The most compelling evidence of this is that Britain conveniently distanced itself when it came to complaints about British citizens serving in the Bahrain police but took a very active role in facilitating and influencing decisions that involved strengthening the Bahrain police.

Who Was the Real Butcher of Bahrain?

Colonel Ian Henderson, frequently referred to by many Bahrainis as the 'Butcher of Bahrain' for his role as head of CID, has been singled out for his role in torture. Many Bahrainis allege that Colonel Ian Henderson engaged personally in torture.[249] One victim stated in a documentary made by Carlton ITV in the UK that he had been digitally raped by Ian Henderson while in custody. Attempts to shed light on Henderson's role have been scuppered. A Metropolitan Police investigation into Ian Henderson collapsed at the early stages. The Metropolitan Police have also resisted my own attempts to gain documents obtained by the Crown Prosecution Service (CPS) for an investigation.

Despite these reports, Ian Henderson may have had a more ambiguous and perhaps less salient role in promoting specific forms of torture. According to Foreign Office documents, Henderson was reportedly trying to reign in the direct influence of the Al Khalifa hardliners on police behaviour, frequently trying to dissuade the prime minister from taking more draconian forms of action. For their part, the British Embassy comforted themselves with the argument that the presence of Henderson and other British officials was a positive influence on police behaviour. Writing on Bahrain, Emile Nakhleh suggested that torture was tacitly accepted by the authorities in Bahrain and that a division of

[248] A. J. D. Sterling, Bahrain: Annual Review for 1971, The National Archives.
[249] R. Fisk, 'Britain at the Heart of Bahrain's Brutality Rule', *The Independent*, 18 February 1996, www.independent.co.uk/news/world/briton-at-the-heart-of-bahrains-brutality-rule-1319571.html

labour had emerged whereby Arabs did the torturing and the British concerned themselves with intelligence.[250]

Ultimately, Henderson's influence on police brutality is hard to determine. However, the British, disavowed from their treaty obligations to rule with a moderating influence (less they provoke a backlash), gave tacit support to coercive security measures. While knowledge of Henderson's role is still shrouded in mystery, he may have been, quite controversially, a man who restrained the more brutal intentions of hardliners in the government. Throughout the 1970s, there are numerous examples of Henderson complaining about the harsh treatment of the Shi'a by the Al Khalifa. He frequently opposed Al Khalifa policy, pressuring them not to carry out executions or deport citizens. These exhortations were never framed out of compassion per se but merely on the pragmatic basis that they would be bad for future stability in Bahrain. In some ways, Henderson has become a lightning rod for general accusations against the brutality of the police. This is understandable, given Britain's historic overrule both in Bahrain and across the rest of its Empire. Indeed, revelations about British brutality in putting down the Mau Mau uprising in Kenya highlight a likelihood of continuity of such practices in Bahrain. After Independence, the British may have objected to these brutal methods, but when they did, they did so exceptionally quietly.

Unfortunately, details of the inner workings of the security apparatus, including the conduct of its British officers, will be hindered by both the British and Bahrain governments' attempts to repress such information coming to light. During the reforms of 2001, an amnesty was granted to anyone in the state security apparatus who committed crimes before 2001. Although the government framed this as an attempt to start Hamad's reign with a blank slate, it was actually a means of ensuring a lack of accountability and scrutiny on past practices of torture. Indeed, until the publication of the *BICI Report* in 2011, government officials often claimed that reports about ill-treatment were exaggerated in order to generate sympathy for the opposition. In 1996, for example, the then foreign minister, Shaykh Mohammed bin Mubarak Al Khalifa,[251] when

[250] E. Nakhleh,'Op-Ed: Ian Henderson and Repression in Bahrain: A Forty-Year Legacy', *Inter Press Service*, 18 April 2013, www.ipsnews.net/2013/04/op-ed-ian-henderson-and-repression

[251] Associated Press Archives, Shaikh Mohammed bin Mubarak Al Khalifa, 'Bahrain Crises' [video], www.aparchive.com/metadata/Bahrain-Crises/12dd0996a99586175645c5ab8800cf71?query=bahrain¤t=30&orderBy=Relevance&hits=330&referrer=search&search=%2fsearch%2ffilter%3fquery%3dbahrain%26from%3d21%26orderBy%3dRelevance%26allFilters%3d1990%253ADecade%26ptype%3dIncludedProducts%26_%3d1398696824995&allFilters=1990%3aDecade&productType=IncludedProducts&page=21&b=00cf71

challenged about reports of police abuse and torture, responded, 'believe me, this exaggeration is part of the campaign'.[252] More recently in 2011, officials claimed that doctors or protesters had inflicted wounds to generate international sympathy.[253]

After receiving the *BICI Report*, the government accepted that systematic torture had taken place in Bahrain during 2011 – despite their claims to the contrary. However, efforts at redress have been a fig leaf to hide business-as-usual. The promise of reforms designed to mitigate the occurrence of future torture has been executed in a manner designed to prevent actual accountability (see the Chapter 5 on legal control).[254] The fact that torture follows similar patterns and has been occurring throughout Bahrain's history with little to no accountability suggests that it has moved beyond a systematic problem to a systemic one. Now, torture is accepted as a legitimate method of coercion, as well as an important instrument of state control, surveillance and deterrence. Indeed, the problem has deepened following Independence and remains ongoing. Part of the problem, of course, is that torture continues due to a British-Bahraini mutual unwillingness to confront past practices in a meaningful way.

Cutting off the Head of the Snake: *Arresting Leaders*

As leaders of movements are symbolically and organizationally important, detaching them from a movement through arrest can weaken the ability of the social group to mobilize. The Bahraini authorities have engaged in the process of arresting leading members of the political opposition since the very inception of organized political activity. In late 1934/early 1935, when a group of Manama *baḥārna* inspired by Gandhi's demonstrations against the British campaigned for more rights for labourers, the British threatened the eight people they perceived to be the ringleaders. The British claimed that any disruption would result in the eight being held accountable, essentially forcing the ringleaders to police their own followers lest they get arrested.

While such threats may have worked while combating Bahrain's nascent political opposition, it was not always so straightforward. The complexity of targeting political leaders came into sharp relief in 1956.

[252] Ibid.

[253] P. Cockburn, 'Bahrain Regime Jails Doctors Who Dared to Treat Protesters', *The Independent*, 30 September 2011, www.independent.co.uk/news/world/middle-east/bahrain-regime-jails-doctors-who-dared-to-treat-protesters-2363331.html

[254] *BICI Report*, p. 298.

The British realized that the popularity of the Higher Executive Committee[255] meant that unrest would probably break out if they arrested the leaders. This was partly due to the widespread popularity of the movement itself but also as the methods of the HEC had remained 'within the bounds of the law'.[256] This gave the British no pretext on which to introduce more aggressive measures of repression.

However, the ruling family, who were worried by the fact the British were entertaining the HEC as potential partners, were pressuring Charles Belgrave to take 'immediate and drastic action' by arresting its leaders. Belgrave thought such an action might not actually degrade the movement but lead to even more unrest.[257] Sometimes sectarian elements played into this calculation. British caution in making arrests was also evident in 1956 when they refused to arrest the Shiʿi leaders of the HEC on the basis they thought them harmless but also because an arrest would upset the villagers and lead to unrest.[258] The reticence in making arrests was also due to the perception that the police were too weak to contain any potential fallout. The Foreign Office, for their part, encouraged a policy of delaying arrests, stating that, '[we] hope that you will be able to prevent [the ruler] provoking a dangerous situation unnecessarily before his police are capable of dealing with [it]'.[259]

Reluctance to undertake arrests, itself based on the British perception of police weakness, prompted consideration of other repressive methods. At one point, it was argued that the 'better elements' should be detached from the reformists but in a timely fashion.[260] This process of 'divide and conquer' would be enacted through careful government political manoeuvring such as selected reforms. The fulfilling of such reforms would, according to the British, result in moderate elements who supported the HEC turning against their leaders. This type of grievance removal would serve to deplete those issues around which HEC supporters mobilized. They would, according to the British, soften public opposition to an eventual arrest. In addition to government manoeuvring, the HEC faced growing divisions based on the fact that they were appealing to a broad spectrum of Bahrainis. Indeed, they had to 'respond to the whims and

[255] This was the original name before they were forced to change the name to the Committee of National Union. The Amir reportedly did not like 'higher', which implied they were above his rule.
[256] Burrows, 4 March 1956, p. 211. [257] Ibid., p. 210.
[258] B. A. B. Burrows, Bahrain Internal Situation, 6 November 1956, FO371/120548, The National Archives.
[259] Foreign Office, 'Foreign Office to Bahrain', 6 March 1956, in A. Burdett (ed.), *Records of Bahrain 1820–1960,* vol. 7, Slough, Archive Editions, 1993, p. 216.
[260] Ibid.

moods of various incoherent factions within the broad spectrum of opposition'.[261] This growing fragmentation, itself a result of the combination of government policy and HEC tactics, paved the way for the arrest of the leaders. According to the British, after the arrests the HEC's supporters reportedly faded 'into thin air',[262] with others going underground.

During the March Uprising of 1965, the authorities arrested school students and strike leaders. Schools, in particular, were a source of contention for the Bahrain government, and the British blamed non-Bahraini Arab teachers for riling up students with anti-imperialist ideas. The British claimed that the settling of the strike, along with the 'arrest of the ringleaders' in 1965 returned everything 'back to normal by mid-April' of the same year.[263] Thus they deemed the removal of organization leadership as an effective strategy.

In the 1970s, attention was paid to the leaders of leftist movements and workers rights' groups, as opposed to those perceived as Arab nationalists. In 1973, the British claimed that pro-communist PFLOAG cells in Bahrain were broken after most of their leaders were arrested.[264] Following an outbreak of strikes in the 1970s, the authorities arrested numerous trade union leaders. Between 'June 15 to 25, the SIS rounded up the leaders of the strike and a number of other labour activists and political figures'.[265] As a strategy of repression, the British believed that arresting the leaders 'was effective' in that it encouraged them to police their own followers. In the early 1970s, Robert Tesh stated that 'left-wing leaders themselves hastily restrained those workers outside ALBA who wanted to strike in sympathy [with other workers]'.[266] The British also noted that such arrests encouraged the leftists in the Assembly to step more in line with what the government wanted. Despite British officials' positive view of such arrests, they still did not result in opposition factions agreeing to the draconian state security legislation. Further arrests did little to get people on board. Twenty-nine trade unionists were arrested in June 1974,[267] while more were arrested in 1975 before the eventual dissolution of the National Assembly. In 1975, the mass arrest of political

[261] Khuri, *Tribe and State in Bahrain*, p. 207.

[262] Belgrave, Annual Report for the Year 1956, p. 8.

[263] G. W. R. Smith, Annual Review for the year 1965, *in Bahrain Government Annual Reports 1924–1970*, vol. 7, Gerrards Cross, Archive Editions, 1987, p. 1.

[264] Tesh, Bahrain: Annual Review for 1973, The National Archives.

[265] Khalaf, 'Labor Movements in Bahrain'.

[266] R. M. Tesh, Bahrain's First Parliament, 8 July 1974, The National Archives.

[267] Amnesty International, Annual Report 1974/1975, London, Amnesty International Publications, p. 126.

leaders was no longer about getting them to be more malleable parliamentarians. Instead, these arrests were designed to destroy opposition leadership immediately prior to the unpopular political decision of dissolving the National Assembly. A well-led opposition would undoubtedly have protested the destruction of the assembly.

The destruction of the leftist threat led to a vacuum that was filled with the religious opposition. In 1981, after an alleged coup attempt by the Islamic Front for the Liberation of Bahrain, seventy-three people were given steep sentences (three of them life imprisonment, sixty of them fifteen years each, and twelve juveniles seven years each).[268] Despite acknowledging that they did not present a severe threat, the prime minister argued that a strong response was necessary to deter others. His attitude indicates that regimes do not always repress strongly simply because they feel threatened but that they wish to perpetuate a state of fear. As Shaykh Khalifa said: 'They didn't represent anything dangerous to us, but we are not used to this sort of thing, so we had to take strong action.'[269] It is possible that Shaykh Khalifa was bluffing, but it is interesting to note that he chose to take stronger action based more on the desire to appear tough, as opposed to necessarily feeling more threatened. Indeed, the personalistic element highlights just how a small group of people can have an impact on the specific methods of repression used.

On other occasions, arrests have been made in order to reduce the potential for societal tension – the opposite of what we saw in 1956. Following the murder of ʿAbd Allah al-Madani in 1976, the police were under pressure to make arrests lest the incident result in communal strife between the religious community and left wingers. After the arrest of three culprits, it was reported that tension 'subsided' between religious elements and leftists.[270] What is notable about this incident is that the regime had been deliberately raising tensions between the left-wingers and the religious elements. Nonetheless, the fast arrests highlight that while the government wanted to maintain strategic fragmentation among opposition elements, they did not necessarily want full-blown communal violence. As mentioned previously, the strategy of polarization through divide and conquer is a risky one that can provoke dangerous consequences.

In the 1990s Intifada, the targeting of political leaders continued under an almost identical Al Khalifa core. As in the 1980s, the prime minister,

[268] W. R. Tomkys, Trial of Detainees, 15 March 1982, 8/4332, The National Archives.
[269] *Gulf Daily News*, 'Interview with Shaykh Khalifa bin Salman Al Khalifa', 15 Saturday 1982, FCO8/4332, The National Archives.
[270] Given, Political Murder in Bahrain.

beholden to Saudi, was the main driver of policy. Unsurprisingly, the nature of repression deployed was generally highly coercive. Prominent religious leaders were accused of inciting hatred against the regime and arrested by the authorities. Those arrested included Shaykh ʻAbd al-Amir al-Jamri, ʻAbd al-Wahab Hussain, Shaykh Khalil Sultan, Shaikh Hassan Sultan and Hassan Mushaimaʼ.[271] Similarly, in the 2011 Uprising, twenty-one political and religious leaders were rounded up and put in prison.[272] While some were tried in absentia, the rest, who were imprisoned, became known as the Bahrain Thirteen.[273] Summary justice followed, and the fledgeling protest movement suddenly lost a lot of its important figureheads. Religious figures and human rights activists were also arrested, including Nabeel Rajab, Sayyed Yousef al-Mahafdha and Zainab al-Khawaja. This action reflected the importance of Bahrain's advocacy revolution as Bahrain activists were keen to stress the universal discourse of human rights instead of exclusionary religious or ideological tropes.

Although it is challenging to determine strategic decision-making in modern times due to the secrecy surrounding high-level communications, the empowerment of the Shiʿa in the region, the influence of Saudi and the power of hawkish Al Khalifa, all point to the reason for a reactionary arrest policy. Clearly, the arrest of leaders is still seen as an important tactic, regardless of the short-term problems and unrest it can create. For the regime, it can disrupt the organizational capacity of protest movements and make leaders so fearful of further sanction that they work to police their own constituency. The disruption of the organizational capacity of protest movements is clearly a strategic calculation, one that generally usurps the desire not to provoke potential violence. In theory, any resulting violence or action will be less organized, and thus easier for the state to repress.

The Shiʿi Threat and the Rise of Mass Arrests

While the leaders of various opposition groups have been targeted consistently throughout Bahrain's modern history, the process of mass

[271] Amnesty International, *Bahrain: A Human Rights Crisis.*

[272] Protest leaders currently in prison: Abd al-Hadi al-Khawaja (also a citizen of Denmark), Abd al-Wahab Hussein, Hassan ʻAli Mushaima, Muhammad al-Muqdad (also a citizen of Sweden), Abd al-Jalil al-Muqdad, Abduljalil al-Singace, Seed al-Nuri, Abd al-Hadi al-Mukhudar, Mirza al-Mahrus, Muhammad ʻAli Rida Ismail, Muhammad Jawwad Muhammad, Ibrahim Sharif, Salah al-Khawaja, Nabeel Rajab, Zainab al-Khawaja (also a citizen of Denmark). See Human Rights Watch, *Interfere, Restrict, Control.*

[273] S. Bery, 'Nabeel Rajab: Why Did the U.S. State Department Drag Its Feet?', *Amnesty International Blog,* 21 August 2012, http://blog.amnestyusa.org/middle-east/nabeel-rajab-why-did-the-u-s-state-department-drag-its-feet/

arrests has become more widespread over the past fifty years. This is partly due to changing opposition tactics and sensibilities. The devolution and horizontal stratification of opposition movements has made the arrest of leaders problematic. Often, leaders live abroad and foment unrest remotely without running the risk of being arrested. Improvements in communication and travel within the region means that it has become easier for those in exile to lead movements in Bahrain. The British acknowledged this in 1965 when they argued that exiled Bahrainis in Kuwait were sewing discord. With the growth in technology and travel, rising levels of education and growing awareness of ruling family corruption have resulted in more considerable popular discontent. The Turnbull Report of 1965, commissioned primarily to audit the Bahrain police, singled out education as a problem. It noted that the 'relative spending on education compared to security had meant that the "insurance rate" for security had, in five years, fallen considerably below the increased risk which a liberal education policy is liable to create'.[274] Turnbull, even attributed the 1965 March Uprising as a product of this discrepancy.[275] Thus, British security experts at the time believed that the rise in education spending relative to money spent on the police meant that increased education was increasingly linked to instability. A smarter population meant a population less reliant on charismatic leaders for information and inspiration. Broad-based arrests were necessitated in part due to the increasing organizational resilience of leadership removal. Indeed, the existence of a small cache of charismatic and educated leaders was no longer as crucial in mobilizing political unrest.

It is perhaps in this context that Arab nationalism resonated so profoundly, not simply because many of Bahrain's foreign teachers promoted it, but because people were more aware of the various inequities promoted by British imperialism. In the 1950s, numerous Bahrainis were drawn to the appeal of pan-Arabism. In this context, the Al Khalifa and the British were increasingly perceived as an imperialist anachronism and a remnant of Western colonialism. Consequently, this widespread appeal meant that larger-scale arrests began in earnest in the 1950s, as arresting political leaders alone did not address the broad-based allure of anti-imperial sentiment. After the British invasion of Suez in 1956, the authorities stepped up the process of mass arrests. They imprisoned dozens of people, even building a new camp in Rumaitha in order to hold them. In 1965, when workers mobilized to oppose BAPCO's plans

[274] P. E. Turnbull, 1965, A review of the structure and organisation of the Bahraini State Police Force, 1965, FO371/179788, The National Archives.
[275] Ibid.

for making redundancies, the arrest of leaders was buttressed by widespread arrests of strike participants.

Although growing labour agitation had resulted in the 1965 Intifada, it was in the 1970s that strikes became commonplace. In March 1972, police arrested over five hundred people after what Amnesty International described as a series of 'non-violent strikes and demonstrations'.[276] In all cases, the size of the initial arrests was designed to have a salutary effect on demonstrators while also removing bodies from meatspace. This reactionary and short-term approach was highlighted by the fact that about 400 of those arrested were released almost immediately after they were detained.[277] Sometimes agitators were targeted for no apparent reason other than intimidation. As Amnesty International noted in March 1978, '35 employees in the shipbuilding and aluminium smelting industries were arrested and imprisoned for several days, during which time they were beaten. These arrests do not seem to have been connected with any particular activities on the part of those detained.'[278] Undoubtedly the rise of mass arrests correlated with increasing resources being put into the Ministry of Interior. The increase in budget meant more prisons, more police officers and a growing need to keep a large security service occupied and trained in duties that history had demonstrated were an inevitability in Bahrain. In short, it meant more capacity to realise the hardline tendencies of the conservative ruling core. Furthermore, the differing reasons for initiating arrests points to the tactic of detention-as-crowd-control. Indeed, arrest was not always about perceived wrongdoing but about intimidation and protest management.

The Bahrain authorities also frequently retained a reserve of political prisoners in order to maintain a level of deterrence. In 1978, Amnesty International documented that 'the number of political prisoners held for more than short periods [had] remained constant at approximately thirty, releases being matched roughly by new arrests'.[279] They also reported that 'in many cases...the same people [were] arrested, released and re-arrested several times over a period of years, without ever having been charged with an offence'.[280] Amnesty International documented a bizarre feature, in which arrests followed a specific 'pattern', in which they were 'made from time to time simply in order to discourage dissent'.[281]

[276] Amnesty International, *Annual Report, 1971–1972*, London, Amnesty International Publications, p. 48.
[277] Ibid.
[278] Amnesty International, *Annual Report 1978*, London, Amnesty International Publications, p. 252.
[279] Ibid. [280] Ibid. [281] Ibid.

Although the al-Madani murders may have encouraged a policy of deterrent arrests, his killing was was used as a pretext to justify a more draconian policy advocated by the prime minister. Afterall, by 1973 it was reported that the prime minister had 'his own way on security matters which were his sole responsibility'.[282] The prime minister's ascendency since Independence resulted in a notably more hawkish approach to arrests. In 1973, a group of PFLOAG members, including two women, were arrested and put in prison on the Bahrain Island of Um al-Hassan. The prime minister, 'determined to act firmly', said that they would stay there.[283] In the same year, a PFLOAG member accused of storing weapons and explosives was also given a stiff sentence, reflecting the government's desire to deter other potential recruits.[284] Accordingly, the British believed that PFLOAG's structure was destroyed after the arrest of most of its prominent members.[285] The political murder of Al-Madani provided an excellent opportunity to move against PFLOAG, and an even better opportunity to ensure continued division between religious elements and leftists. The PFLOAG arrests in the al-Madani case happened quickly,[286] perhaps too quickly, in order to keep the peace. The hawkish response of the government was evident in the fact they did not appear willing to keep many PFLOAG members at large, a tactic usually advocated by Henderson. Instead, the arrests of suspected PFLOAG members and sympathizers only stopped because the authorities ran out of room in prison.[287]

The prime minister's attitude to dissent and arrests also reflected the growing autonomy and independence of Bahrain's police. This shift in policy was evident as early as 1974, when the British complained about being kept in the dark about certain police operations that they would have hitherto been privy to, such as the early morning arrests of ALBA labour agitators. Quoting Shaykh Muhammad bin Mubarak, Robert Tesh stated: 'For once we have taken the initiative.'[288] However, Tesh added, 'What they did not tell me is that the police were going to pounce.'[289] In addition to reflecting how British officials were

[282] R. M. Tesh, Bahrain Internal, 18 November 1973, FCO8/1975, The National Archives.
[283] US Embassy Manama, 'Security on Gulf and Bahrain', 30 April 1973, www.wikileaks.org/plusd/cables/1973MANAMA00248_b.html
[284] US Embassy Bahrain, 'Bahraini Subversive Given Stiff Sentence', 12 May 1973, www.wikileaks.org/plusd/cables/1973MANAMA00279_b.html
[285] Tesh, 'Form at a Glance (FAAG)'.
[286] Given, Bahrain: Annual Report for 1976, The National Archives. [287] Ibid.
[288] R. M. Tesh, Bahrain Internal, 1 July 1974, FCO8/2180, The National Archives.
[289] Ibid.

increasingly kept out of the loop with regard to police activity, Tesh's commentary on this series of arrests indicates that hardliners were taking more and more initiative. This group included members of the ruling family but was also reported to include members of the 'Government and the merchant class'.[290]

The Securitization of the Shiʿa

It was not simply the increasing 'initiative' taken by hardliners that led to more and more mass arrests. The rise of the so-called 'Shiʿi threat' and the subsequent criminalization of the Shiʿa has also impacted upon mass arrests. As Roger Tomkys warned in 1981, the 'increasing numbers of arrests among the Shiʿi community in the last few days, not confined to young hotheads, may alienate them more widely'.[291] Contrary to narratives that posit that the Iranian Revolution was the sole reason for Shiʿi insurrection in Bahrain, the Shiʿa were relatively quiet when that was happening. The police even acknowledged this and noted that there had been 'virtually no visible signs of support among the Bahraini Shiʿa for the Imam Khomeini' since the Iranian Revolution in 1979.[292] It was rather the Iran–Iraq war and growing Shiʿi anger at how Saddam Hussein's regime was treating Iraq's Shiʿa that generated discontent. Nonetheless, the Iranian Revolution was seen as a moment of Shiʿa ascendency, rather than a specific reason for promoting unrest in Bahrain. The prime minister, now ubiquitous in all aspects of Bahrain's affairs, decided to move against the country's Shiʿi population. In the early 1980s, at least 650 Shiʿa were arrested, reportedly for no reason. Indeed, many Shiʿa were arrested because they did not protest. Bizarrely, the fact that the Ashura holiday (usually a time when Shiʿa express political grievances) had been peaceful actually encouraged the prime minister to make the mass arrests, bringing the new total of those incarcerated to 850. Indeed, it was perceived opposition weakness in this regard that made him act in such a way. It is likely too, that such arrests would have conveyed to the Shiʿa community that no matter how they behaved, they would always be subject to the arbitrary actions of the security forces.

[290] Ibid.

[291] W. R. Tomkys, Meeting between Minister of State and Bahraini Prime Minister, 18 December 1981, FCO8/3893,The National Archives.

[292] H. B. Walker, The Shiʿa in Bahrain, 26 October 1980, FCO8/3489, The National Archives.

This punitive approach to mass arrests may have in part stemmed from the prime minister's own ethnocentric prejudice. In a conversation with Christopher Wilton, the British First Secretary in Bahrain, Ian Henderson said that the prime minister's reason for moving against the Shiʿa was reportedly to demonstrate to them that the 'Bahrain Government were true Arabs'.[293] Even Ian Henderson, the so-called 'Butcher of Bahrain' disagreed with the decision to order this crackdown, stating that it would 'probably have the opposite effect from that desired'.[294] Again, theoretically, this is interesting, as it points to an instance where a repressive action was not necessarily made to bring about short-term peace and/or stability. If the prime minister did believe it would, his difference in opinion with Henderson highlights how it is hard to generalize about the inevitability of individual repressive choices.

The British Embassy reported that over one thousand Shiʿa were arrested between 1979 and 1982, although it is not clear for what reason, if any. Amnesty International corroborated these numbers in their annual report on human rights abuses around the globe.[295] With the advent of Independence, the Iran–Iraq War, the Iranian Revolution, the empowerment of the Al Khalifa, the growing influence and enabling factor of Saudi Arabia and the diminishing of British Influence in the police, the Bahraini government had 'abandoned their tolerant and low key approach to Shiʿa unrest'.[296] The sectarian dimension to this repression continued and became entrenched. In 1991, Amnesty International argued that the government's repression against the Shiʿa was a 'deliberate policy' designed to target and 'harass and intimidate entire communities – particularly Shiʿa communities' living in villages near the capital city.[297] Amnesty International reported that the authorities arrested as many as 4,000 people between December 1994 and September 1995, with many being held for months without charge or trial.[298] Of course, the growing persecution of the Shiʿa in Bahrain meant that the community had even more legitimate grievances to mobilize around, as was anticipated in the early 1980s.

The legal framework for mass arrests of Shiʿa Bahrainis was initially facilitated by the State Security Law, which, since its inception in the 1970s, has given a legal pretext for the arrests of thousands of protesters.[299] The law essentially allowed for indefinite incommunicado

[293] Ibid. [294] Ibid.
[295] Amnesty International, *Annual Report 1982*, London, Amnesty International Publications.
[296] K. J. Passmore, 3 December 1980, FCO8/3489, The National Archives.
[297] Amnesty International, *Bahrain: Violations of Human Rights*, pp. 5–6.
[298] Amnesty International, *Bahrain: A Human Rights Crisis*. [299] Ibid.

detention. In the 1980s, detainees such as 'Shaykh Muhammad ʿAli al-ʿIkri, ʿAbd al-Karim Hassan al-ʿAradi and ʿAbd al-Nabi al-Khayami were held under the State Security Law's 'provisions, without charge or trial, for as long as three to seven years'.[300] Even after the abolition of the State Security Law, the introduction of the Anti-Terrorism Law has given the security services very expansive powers of detention and arrest. Those suspected of engaging in a variety of different acts stipulated in the anti-terror law can be detained for up to sixty days without being charged.[301] This preliminary incarceration can then be renewed by order from the High Court for a period of up to six months.[302] These laws have subsequently allowed the authorities to incarcerate citizens on the scantest suspicion of wrongdoing. Indeed, the Bahrain Centre for Human Rights reported that 'in 2013 alone, there were 38 terrorism cases where 318 defendants, including women and children, were sentenced to prison, or [were] awaiting verdicts'.[304]

The shift from arresting political leaders to mass arrests has marked a corollary shift from 'cutting off the head' of the snake to attempting to destroy or incapacitate the 'body'. The advent of the Iran–Iraq war, the Iranian revolution, as well as a reversal to more Saudi-backed Al Khalifa autonomy in matters of internal security, has led both to a more hawkish approach but also a more extensive coercive apparatus, one that was less fearful of a backlash should they deploy draconian measures of enforcement. Technological changes, oppositional adaptation facilitated by Soviet training, as well as the rise of education have also horizontalized oppositional movements to the extent that arresting leaders is no longer sufficient to destroy their effectiveness. This has helped necessitate mass arrests.

Similarly, the growing criminalization of the Shiʿa, in large part due to hard-line members of the Al Khalifa, has resulted in a phenomenon whereby Shiʿa are, by default, perceived as potential opposition. Legal changes and the rise in broad anti-terror laws has also facilitated the ease by which people can be arrested with little or no evidence of wrongdoing. There has thus been a general trend over the twentieth and twenty-first

[300] Ibid., p. 4.

[301] Bahrain Center for Human Rights, 'The Terrorism Law in Bahrain: A Tool to Silence Dissidents', 13 March 2014, www.bahrainrights.org/sites/default/files/Terrorism%20Laws%20in%20Bahrain%20-%20FINAL.pdf

[302] Article 29, Law no 58, Protecting Society from Terrorist Acts, July 2006, www.legalaffairs.gov.bh/AdvancedSearchDetails.aspx?id=2125#.U49LEfldXD1

The mention of 'six months' comes from Civil Procedures. Also reported in www.bahrainrights.org/sites/default/files/Terrorism%20Laws%20in%20Bahrain%20-%20FINAL.pdf

[304] Bahrain Center for Human Rights, 'The Terrorism Law in Bahrain'.

centuries towards mass arrests, facilitated by political will, a vast security apparatus and a permissive legal framework.

Conclusion

As in many former colonies, the security services in Bahrain have long been an ambiguous amalgamation of mercenary bodies, quasi-military bodies and other 'informal structures of authority'.[303] This habit of the police functioning like a 'military garrison'[304] is not only a legacy of Bahrain's imperial past but also indicative of Bahrain's status as a peripheral frontier. The police force, initially created to prevent uncooperative members of the Al Khalifa family from undermining British-led reforms, has since become an instrument of Al Khalifa-regime power maintenance. This militarized control function has been exacerbated by Bahrain falling under Saudi influence which prompted a shift in the violent intensity of policing .

From the evidence, it is clear that personal-integrity violations have become worse in a quantitative sense. Arrests have shifted from a leader-focused approach to mass arrests, indicating a change from criminalizing the individual to collective punishment. This is particularly true of the arrest and targeting of Bahrain's Shiʿi population. Torture too has become more prevalent, consistent and routinized since Bahrain's Independence, and superficial democratization has, unsurprisingly, failed to temper its severity. The paramilitarization of the police has continued unabated, and despite advances in training, the absence of consent means that policing will continue to involve military-style soldiering.

The worsening of personal integration violations have largely been facilitated by a lack of accountability, inadequate regulatory bodies, a lack of transparency, the sectarian make-up of policing institutions, the militant nature of police, a multiplicity of security forces, willful blindness by authorities and Bahrain's allies, poor training and loyalist demands for protection. While many of these traits are a hangover from the Bahrain police under the British, the transfer of power after Independence resulted in key changes to the repressive potential of the police. The police remained an alien body that served, and were

[303] D. M. Anderson and D. Killingray (eds), 'Consent, Coercion and Colonial Control: Policing the Empire 1830–1940', in D. M. Anderson and D. Killingray (eds), *Policing the Empire: Government, Authority and Control, 1830–1940*, Manchester University Press, Manchester, 1991, p. 5.

[304] Ibid., p. 4.

responsive to, the narrow political interests of the colonial and recolonized regime. However, the new regime was an increasingly emboldened and empowered Al Khalifa ruling core, one that still had not abandoned its ideological attachment to a deeply entrenched legacy of conquest. This, along with a profound new Saudi authoritarianism, has resulted in an increasingly autocratic and brutal form of policing.

5 Repressive Law and Legal Repression

> Even if the police stick to the book, Bahrain has a repressive enough legal system to squash most dissent.[1]
>
> —*The Economist*, 1999

Laws, legal processes and the legal system have been a persistent framework for repression in Bahrain. Over the decades, they have become an ever more substantial and more comprehensive part of the repressive capacity of the state. The establishment of certain legal traditions has defined the scope of legal interference by the Al Khalifa regime throughout the twenty-first century. While initially stemming from the British desire to retain order through indirect and pacific means, law is now integral to the repression of social movements through *embroilment, regulation and persuasion.* The hegemonic order so completely dominate the process of lawmaking and legal processes in Bahrain that 'rule by law' has replaced any sense of 'rule of law'. By examining legislation, legal structures, legal processes and, where possible, the strategic decision-making behind these, this chapter argues for the emergence of what Nonet and Selznick call 'repressive law' in Bahrain. While one must acknowledge that any given legal order or legal institution is likely to have a mixed character, Nonet and Selznick argue that within their typology of law – responsive, autonomous and repressive – elements of one category tend to be more salient in individual states.[2] This chapter argues that Bahrain most closely approximates the repressive law model, in which law tends to reflect the will of the politically powerful rather than any commitment to impartial justice. During political unrest in Bahrain, the law has become an arbitrary instrument that sets out the processes whereby intolerable political opposition may most effectively be limited in their actions.

[1] *The Economist*, 'Whitewash', 23 January 1999, issue, 8103, p. 60.
[2] Nonet and Selznick, *Law and Society in Transition*, p. 18.

A Repressive Legal Structure

A Brief Outline of Systemic Legal Bias from Tribal to Colonial

The legal system in Bahrain has always been populated by members of the ruling family or those whose interests are aligned with the ruling elite. This, of course, has been deliberate. Historically, Al Khalifa feudal lords had considerable autonomy when it came to dishing out justice in their individual 'fiefdoms', with justice often being at the discretion of local tribal shaykhs governing individual estates. The process of reforms pushed forward by the British from the 1920s increased Imperial encroachment, centralizing authority while maintaining much of the particularized tribal law that had defined the pre-reform period. While Fuad Khuri asserts that tribal societies like the Al Khalifa refuted a standardized penal code, as it 'opposes the principles that bind a tribal group together – namely, exclusiveness based on kinship and the ability to "particularize" or make law without legislative bodies',[3] this is not strictly true. A code has emerged in Bahrain but one that is subservient to the ruling elite's interests. Nonetheless, Khuri is correct in in his assertion about the Al Khalifa's reluctance to cede control over the legal system – which has been a persistent problem over the past century. Indeed, past rulers have struggled to relinquish tribal justice in favour of implementing standardized laws. In the 1920s for example, Shaykh Hamad bin ʿIsa was continually unwilling or unable to use his powers of punishment that had been agreed on with the British. Instead of bringing them to justice, he allowed members of the Al Khalifa family to rule over their 'individual spheres' by conducting 'ruthless oppression'.[4] While the introduction of laws did not stop their arbitrary implementation, the Al Khalifa still remained wary of legal reform. In 1954, the ruler Salman bin Hamad Al Khalifa thought judicial reform would mean ceding his absolute authority over Bahrain.[5] Naturally the best antidote to this fear was to maintain Al Khalifa domination of the judiciary. Failing that, coercion of the judiciary could be implemented. In 1976, the prime minister, and Shaykh Salman's son, Shaykh Khalifa bin Salman Al Khalifa said he would put the judges on trial if they did not agree to his sentence on a case of political murder.[6] His attitude seems to have

[3] Khuri, *Tribe and State in Bahrain*, p. 216.

[4] 'Administration Reports 1920–1924' [158r] (320/412), in *Qatar Digital Library*.

[5] J. W. Wall, 25 October 1954, in A. Burdett (ed.), *Records of Bahrain 1820–1960*, vol. 7, Slough, Archive Editions, 1993, p. 73.

[6] British Embassy Bahrain, Letter to Rt Hon Anthony Crossland MP, 29 January 1977, FCO8/2874, The National Archives.

remained the same. In 2013, he was filmed telling a man accused of torture that both he and the Al Khalifa were above the law.[7] Indeed, the lack of political dynamism and the continuation of tribal rule has led to a form of 'sticky authoritarianism', where the influence of conservative members of the Al Khalifa (within or without the judiciary) have impacted upon the legal apparatus, whether in specific legal decisions or general processes of legislative development.

While the British had sought to reform the legal system in the 1920s, partly in order to alleviate Persian disquiet over the oppression of *baḥrānī* subjects, it only ever became a hybrid entity – one that fused tribal and imperial interests at the expense of a judicial system that better served the interests of the entire population. The implementation of the Bahrain Order in Council in 1919 (although it was drafted in 1913) created numerous courts, most of which had some degree of British influence – namely through the presence of judges. For the most part, the judicial advisor, who was Charles Belgrave in 1925, would either act as a magistrate, or the appointer of various *Kazis* (judges or persons on the various legal organs). In practice, Belgrave himself had a substantial degree of autonomy in giving out punishments. Indeed, he even whipped criminals himself. Thus regardless of who determined law in Bahrain, its implementation was always the purview of a very limited section of the hegemonic elite.

The Order in Council, and its quasi usurpation of traditional authority, led to some degree of tension. While the British were often less reactionary than the Al Khalifa on some issues, legal reforms were usually secondary to British commercial interests. They were also reactive more than pre-emptive, and the impetus for their creation frequently derived from crises instead of forward-thinking policy, as it was crises that prompted Britain to deviate from the middle course between intervention and the light touch they were keen to steer. However, increasing British reforms to the legal system initiated in 1919 by the Political Agent Major Dickson reflected the problems of this dual authority system, in which the tribal and imperial authority systems came into conflict.[8] This conflict and tension between the British and the Al Khalifa would often centre around the need to change both laws and the legal system. The British hoped that the creation of a more transparent legal system would help ameliorate dissent and control political unrest by providing people with appropriate channels from which to conduct agitation. The Al Khalifa feared it was an encroachment on their authority, especially in

[7] Jones, 'Rotten Apples', p. 228. [8] Khuri, *Tribe and State in Bahrain*, p. 88.

terms of maintaining their hegemony through the religious courts. Indeed, the Sharia courts that had been used to adjudicate on civil and criminal matters were deemed unjust by the British, who were concerned in particular about cases of violence perpetrated by Sunna against the Shiʿa. The British administration noted that if such cases were referred to a Sunni *qadi* (judge) the perpetrator would escape 'scot free or with light punishment'.[9]

The British saw legal reform as a means of controlling opposition, and attempted to convince the Bahrain government of this useful purpose. As Trenchard Fowle said in 1938, protesters had 'no legal means of putting forward their grievances, whether real or imaginary, and are therefore reduced to illegal channels such as agitation'.[10] By arguing that people have a 'legal' means of expressing themselves, the government was in a stronger position to deal firmly with those who employed 'illegal' means. This was particularly true with regard to those protesting for the implementation of a penal code. Indeed, Fowle accused the Bahrain government in 1938 of being 'responsible for the agitation' due to being 'remiss about initiating reforms, e.g. the Bahrain [Penal] Code'.[11] This 'remiss' attitude, prompted by squabbling and apathy among the British and Al Khalifa, dogged the implementation of a legal channel for dissent. As late as 1963, Peter Tripp noted the intractable problem of how the Al Khalifa saw justice as a 'shaykhly' prerogative, where the 'idea of an independent judiciary is abhorrent'.[12] He added that he did not think the ruler nor his family believed in a system of 'impartial justice', and that British attempts to help reform them had failed or were doomed to fail.

Following Independence, the Al Khalifa and the merchant elites reasserted themselves, with Saudi Arabia gaining influence in Bahrain, primarily through the prime minister, who was amenable to Saudi pressure.[13] With the absence of any democratic safety valve following the 1975 dissolution of parliament, and with Bahrain slowly becoming a Saudi vassal state,[14] the legal framework continued to be shaped by an autocratic elite.

[9] 'File 19/165 IV (C 57) Bahrain Reforms' [106r] (242/476), British Library: India Office Records and Private Papers, IOR/R/15/1/340, in Qatar Digital Library www.qdl.qa/en/archive/81055/vdc_100023555763.0x00002b

[10] T. C. Fowle, 17 November 1938, in A. Burdett (ed.), *Records of Bahrain 1820–1960*, vol. 5, Slough, Archive Editions, 1993, p. 139.

[11] Ibid.

[12] J. P. Tripp, The Internal Situation in Bahrain, 1 June 1963, FO371/174521, The National Archives.

[13] Leading Personality Reports 1977, FCO8/3090, The National Archives.

[14] E. F. Given, 'Bahrain 1976', 15 March 1977, FCO8 2783, The National Archives.

In the twenty-first century, much remains the same. Despite the introduction of a constitution in 2002 that stipulates that the judicial system should be independent and that judges should not be subject to any outside influence, the International Commission of Jurists argues that the 'the Bahraini judiciary has typically been subject to inappropriate government influence'.[15] In 2012, a decade after King Hamad's 'reforms', many senior judges still belong to the ruling family, and the king appoints all judges.[16] Furthermore, those members of the judiciary who are members of the ruling family may still issue verdicts that are aligned with the will of the ruling family. The International Commission of Jurists further argued that many of the judges not affiliated with the ruling family were Egyptians on two-year contracts. The ICJ argued that such judges would be unwilling to issue rulings unfavourable to the government for fear of not having their contracts renewed.[17] In times of social upheaval, this pressure is even more acute, and social movements may find themselves at the receiving end of decisions made by judges whose concern for their jobs and livelihoods transcends their desire to mete out impartial justice.

Parliament has remained relatively powerless in having any impact on curtailing legal repression. Since 2011, the weak lower house has become a bastion of reactionary and loyalist sentiment. This situation resulted from a political (mis)calculation by the political society Al Wefaq. In a move of political principle, the almost exclusively Shi'i al-Wefaq withdrew from parliament to protest government repression, vacating eighteen out of forty seats. This move prompted bi-elections that resulted in the election of a largely pro-government coalition who ratified, among other things, laws that gave the state even deeper powers to deal with dissent.[18] Nonetheless, Al Wefaq's point of principle, an attempt to win supporters among those factions more tempted by the confrontational politics of the illegal opposition, such as al-Wafa', Haq, and the Bahrain Freedom Movement, backfired. The government capitalized on this, pushing draconian legislation through the lower house in order to give some semblance of popular legitimacy to measures that sought to legally enshrine the continued stifling of civil society. While Bahrain's parliament was already structurally biased in favour of the regime, the

[15] International Commission of Jurists, 'Bahrain Attacks on Justice 2002', 26 August 2002, www.refworld.org/docid/48a57efa0.html

[16] Freedom House, Bahrain 2012, https://freedomhouse.org/report/freedom-world/2012/bahrain-0

[17] Ibid.

[18] Freedom House, *Freedom in the World 2015,* https://freedomhouse.org/report/freedom-world/2015/bahrain#.VWius8_BzGc

withdrawal of al-Wifaq simply encouraged a more repressive public policy that would be difficult to undo.[19]

In short, Bahrain's legal system is constructed in such a way as to reflect the will of the ruling elite, especially during times of political agitation. While most conflict criminologists would argue that any legal system is one that ultimately favours the dominant social grouping, the degree to which this is evident in Bahrain is perhaps clearer than in many other countries. In Bahrain, the odds are, and always have been, stacked against political dissidents.

However, this legal repression represents a qualitative change in the evolution of control methods. The advent of legal reforms led by the British in the 1920s symbolized a shift from a place in which sheer coercive power and tribal justice as repression were replaced by channelling in the form of an entire 'body of laws, announcements, decisions, or decrees made and enacted by government'.[20] While these may be subservient to political interests, they still exist as a framework for governing state responses to political challenges. This combination of arbitrary rule and more standardized laws has resulted in a system which is not only reflective of ruling class interests, but also a legal system that can be subverted more readily when ruling class interests are threatened. Certainly, the tensions inherent in this dual authority system impacted the timely implementation and execution of laws and legal processes in the face of dissent. In some ways, this tension was perhaps unwarranted, as the existence of law has done little to circumvent its utility as a means of political control.

Laws

Emergency Laws and 'Legal Form'

Bahrain has been subject to emergency laws for the majority of the past fifty years, and, as with most repressive legal systems, a 'spirit of martial law prevails'.[21] These laws have been: the Emergency Law of 1956, the

[19] Existing laws already regulate people's right to freedom of association, expression and peaceful assembly. For example, the 'Public Gathering Law of 1973 and the Press Law of 2002 also unduly restrict the activities of political societies as they relate to freedom of assembly and expression'. See Human Rights Watch, 20 June 2013 'Interfere, Restrict, Control: Restraints on Freedom of Association in Bahrain', www.hrw.org/report/2013/06/20/interfere-restrict-control/restraints-freedom-association-bahrain. While existing legislation is restrictive enough, the new moves saw an entrenchment of authoritarianism and the emergence of even more repressive public policy.

[20] Khuri, *Tribe and State in Bahrain*, p. 216.

[21] Nonet and Selznick, *Law and Society in Transition*, pp. 34–5.

Public Security Law of 1965, the State Security Decree of 1974 and the State of National Safety of 2011. Over time, emergency laws in Bahrain have expanded their definitions of dissent and have facilitated the process of the incarceration, trial and incapacitation of political 'criminals'. The British, who had embarked on a process of influence designed to be spread by 'indirect and pacific' means, had been encouraging legal reform, yet they blamed the Al Khalifa for its slow implementation. However, the vagueness of the terms of Britain's suzerainty over Bahrain has made the implementation of law haphazard and unclear. Furthermore, while Britain preferred non-interference, laws were often introduced brashly as reactionary measures to what the British perceived as, initially, Al Khalifa misrule, and then later on as threats to the Al Khalifa. Because Britain decided to take the reins when emergencies necessitated it, the laws were often harsh and draconian.

A decades-long delay in implementing a penal code meant that a legal framework had failed to set the terms for legitimate dissent during the agitation of the 1950s, and the first formalized emergency 'notice' came in 1956. This was a reactionary measure that gave the authorities significant powers to deal with the HEC, a movement that threatened British and Al Khalifa hegemony. Crucially, the uprising of 1956 drew government attention to its own weaknesses and lack of security laws[22] and the issuing of the notice was not without equivocation. Indeed, the British knew the ruler would be reluctant to implement legal reforms, and so sought to persuade him that the laws would serve to boost his authority. First, the British thought emergency laws would 'make clear to the reformists that the 'Bahrain Government is determined to preserve order and that political activity must be kept within proper constitutional bounds'.[23] It would also 'enable the Ruler to act in proper legal form against the reformist leaders if their conduct merited it'.[24] Without legal resources, it would be necessary to use non-legal power to deal with any problems of social interaction.[25] This power would include coercion, which incurred more legitimacy costs. However, the British knew that the HEC would see the move as 'provocative',[26] and it might prompt disorder that would necessitate the intervention of British troops. Contrary to their advice, the British also considered the advantages of

[22] Khuri, *Tribe and State in Bahrain*, p. 216.
[23] D. M. H. Riches, 10 April 1956, in A. Burdett (ed.), *Records of Bahrain 1820–1960*, vol. 7, Slough, Archive Editions, 1993, p. 239.
[24] Ibid.
[25] A. Turk, Law as a Weapon in Social Conflict, Social Problems, vol. 23, no. 3, 1976, pp. 276–91, especially p. 284.
[26] Riches, 10 April 1956, p. 239.

the ruler being able to use his more discretionary tribal laws.[27] Afterall, not being constrained by laws also appealed to the more militant sensibilities of some imperial officers. Ultimately, the Emergency notice of 1956 was issued, and it gave the authorities 'legal form' to crack down on absolutely any dissent, whether from the HEC or otherwise. Specifically, it gave magistrates, including state officers, the authority to ask people gathered in public spaces to disperse on pain of death.

The 1956 emergency law was superseded by the equally broad Bahrain Public Security Law of 1965, which was also brought in hastily following strikes at the Bahrain national oil company (BAPCO). Again, the emergency law was seen as necessary due to the continued absence of a proper legal framework for managing dissent. Peter Tripp stated that the emergency laws, 'although repugnant to normal British notions of justice, are regrettably necessary in Bahrain'.[28] Despite this apparent repugnance, the British persuaded the ruler of Bahrain to issue the Public Security Ordinance,[29] saying that the recent disorder was an 'ideal peg with which to hang the enactment of a Public Order decree' on.[30] Article 3 (1) of the Public Security Law of 1965 gave the ruler of Bahrain ultimate power to 'lay down any regulations which he consider[ed] necessary or suitable in the interests of public security or for the preservation of public order or the safety of the country'. Furthermore, any regulation invoked by the ruler under the Public Security Law voided any other laws that might run contrary to it.[31] On 22 April 1965, and in accordance with Article 3 of the Public Security Law, the ruler issued Public Security Regulation No. 1. This gave him the power to lawfully detain anyone deemed to be a 'danger to public security or the safety of the country'.[32] These broad laws, which deepened the government's ability to legally repress anyone deemed a threat to the state (itself a broad and nebulous concept), reflected both the British fear of nationalistic forces and the Al Khalifa's fragile position. Indeed, while the British had to persuade the Al Khalifa to issue the Public Security Law, the ruler's reluctance may have stemmed from no real respect for justice, but more that Shaykh ʿIsa objected to having to legally justify his actions when it came to dealing with anyone wishing to 'harm Bahrain'.[33] While the law was a reactionary measure, it could also be seen as an authoritarian opportunity in which crisis was exploited to legitimize more draconian forms of rule.

[27] Ibid. [28] Tripp, Communique to M. S. Weir, 26 April 1965, p. 389. [29] Ibid.
[30] R. F. Brenchley, Communique to JP Tripp, 26 March 1965, in A. Burdett (ed.) Records *of Bahrain, 1961–1965,* vol. 5, Cambridge Archive Editions, 1997, p. 385.
[31] Public Security Law, in A. Burdett (ed.) *Records of Bahrain, 1961–1965,* vol. 5, Cambridge Archive Editions, 1997, p. 385.
[32] Ibid. [33] Ibid., p. 383.

It was somewhat more sophisticated than the 1956 notice, and did not simply threaten death for those failing to comply with an order to evacuate public space. On the contrary, it used the language of safety and order to position the law as an ostensibly neutral means of mediating political conflict.

Through these emergency laws, the government increased their ability to justify containment and trap protesters in embroilment and increased regulation. The introduction of such laws partly reflected the success of Britain's middle course but also its failure. Indeed, it was successful in that laws could theoretically mean committing fewer military resources to protect the Al Khalifa. On the other hand, the laws were a reaction to unrest that had partly resulted from an inability to push through timely 'legal form'.

The British were also under pressure to protect British subjects. As a result, they were often overzealous in their application of emergency laws that would have been unthinkable at home but seemingly fine on the periphery of an embattled empire in retreat. In addition to the creation of this vague law, the growing influence of the police was a problem. They were obstructing the introduction of a Code of Criminal Procedure as it would involve them having to disclose in open court the evidence and sources on which their cases against subversives might rest'.[34] This attitude, coupled with the Public Security Law, marked the growing asymmetry between the rights of the police and the public, fuelling a disparity that facilitated the incarceration of perceived agitators with no moderation of police or state power.

The State Security Decree

The 1965 Public Security Law was replaced by the State Security Decree of 1974, another draconian piece of legislation that sought to manage the inherent risk of a new legal system and Bahrain's venture into Independence. The new law, encouraged by Ian Henderson,[35] was an attempt by the government to maintain their ability to control dissent in the face of uncertainty, posed by the deliberative and partially legislative capacity of the National Assembly. Indeed, the new parliament established in 1973 had exposed the government to the risk of legitimate and legally sanctioned dissent, yet the unprecedented need to devolve issues of national security to an elected body was anathema to the tribal politics of the Al Khalifa regime. Indeed, it threatened the notion that justice was

[34] Ibid.
[35] Author Unknown, Letter to ITM Lucas, 22 June 1975, FCO8/2415, The National Archives.

their prerogative. However, this did not last long. When parliament failed to vote in accordance with how the government had expected due to a surprise coalition between leftists and the religious bloc, the prime minister, according to British documents, led the decision to dissolve the parliament. The dissolution of the National Assembly meant that the State Security Decree remained in force.[36] In order to legitimize the dissolution, the Bahraini government fabricated a coup as a pretext. A leaked document from the US State Department revealed that the coup was indeed a pretext: 'GOB seized on ineffectual intent of certain radical elements as a justification for taking, on "security grounds", moves it felt otherwise necessary'.[37] The State Department added that there was 'no clear security threat to the regime', highlighting that even threat perception is not necessary for implementing repressive laws.[38] Given this lack of threat, one could argue that the ruling family's belief of justice as a tribal prerogative was sufficient in enabling this particular avenue of legal repression.

Although Ian Henderson had encouraged the State Security Law, it is more likely that it was pushed for by a small group within the ruling family. The foreign minister of Bahrain told the US Embassy in 1975 that the decision to implement the law had 'come from the Prime Minister who, over the summer in consultation with the Amir, Foreign Minister and Interior Minister, had come to the conclusion [that the] continuation of [the] National Assembly as it had been constituted and operated for the last two years was harmful to Bahrain's national interest'.[39]

The broad nature of the law,[40] and its lack of clear definition of the acts it sought to criminalize, led to it being used to target the long-term detention of political criminals for the non-violent expression of their opinions.[41] In addition to offering a broad description of what might constitute a crime under the State Security Law, the scope for lodging an appeal was limited. Detainees could submit a complaint regarding their arrest to the Supreme Court of Appeal but only after spending three

[36] Leading Personality Reports 1977, The National Archives.
[37] US Embassy Manama, 'Bahraini Political Developments'. [38] Ibid. [39] Ibid.
[40] For example. Article One permits administrative detention for the following: if there is serious evidence that a person has made statements, committed acts, undertaken activities or made contacts which are damaging to the internal or external security of the country, or to the country's religious or national interests, or to its fundamental structure, or social or economic systems, or amount to discord, which affects, or could affect, relations between the people and the government, or between the various institutions of the state, between sectors of the people, those working in establishments and companies, or which aim to assist in the commission of acts of sabotage or harmful propaganda, or the dissemination of heretical principles. State Security Law, in Internal Political Situation in Bahrain, FCO8/2415, The National Archives.
[41] Amnesty International, *Bahrain: Violations of Human Rights,* p. 4.

months in detention.[42] This initial period of three months' detention not only deprived the defendant of the right to be brought promptly before a judge, but it also allowed the authorities to sweep potential dissidents off the street without fear of bureaucratic slowdown when they felt necessity demanded it. Indeed, this reflected a repress first, ask questions later approach. It also meant that Special Branch no longer had to persuade a judge every six days to keep those charged with sedition detained, freeing up their capacity to engage in operational policing. If a complaint did go to the Supreme Court of Appeal, hearings would be held 'in camera' and only attended by members of the 'prosecution, the complainant and his representative'.

Furthermore, as stipulated by Article 3 of the State Security Law, the Supreme Court of Appeal did not have to adhere to the Code of Criminal Procedure.[43] So while a successful appeal would still necessitate at least an obligatory three-month period of detention, the odds of securing an appeal were heavily weighted in favour of the state. Thus, the decree facilitated the state's legal repression by loosely determining what activities constituted as subversive, and laid a framework for criminalizing behaviour that could be defined at the whim of the state. In short, Independence saw the deepening and further codification of a legal apparatus that sought to legitimize the processes of containment, embroilment and incapacitation, while giving the intelligence apparatus greater scope for increasing its knowledge in Bahrain's affairs. It also freed up the administrative burden on other security agencies, theoretically making them more efficient as control organs.

The challenge posed by the 1990s Intifada forced the government to make changes to the State Security Law. Despite the broad nature of the State Security Law, the Amir issued a decree in March 1994 whereby suspected cases involving arson or violence were handed to the State Security Court.[44] This was after ʿIsa Qambar, a twenty-year-old Bahraini accused of killing a policeman, had his case shifted to the criminal court after his lawyers successfully argued that his case was not in the jurisdiction of the State Security Court. The government, concerned it would have 'to prosecute other destruction of property and bodily harm cases in the criminal court, with its higher standards of evidence and more substantial adversarial procedure... transferred jurisdiction over some fourteen additional articles of the penal code from the criminal courts

[42] Amnesty International, *Bahrain: A Human Rights Crisis*. [43] Ibid.

[44] Amnesty International, *Report: Bahrain, 1 January 1997*, www.refworld.org/cgi-bin/texis/vtx/rwmain?page=publisher&docid=3ae6a9fe0&skip=0&publisher=AMNESTY&coi=BHR&searchin=title&sort=date

to the State Security Court'.[45,46] Ten months after these changes, the state security courts tried 130 more people than they had the previous year, pointing to an increase in the efficacy of this repressive law.[47] This legal sleight of hand sought not only to criminalize sedition but to broaden the definitions of sedition so that more and more crimes could be dealt with in a manner that allowed the state to cope more punitively with dissident tactics. After the changes, notwithstanding this modification, the State Security Decree was, in principle and as practised, barely less draconian than the 1965 law. It amounted to an equally repressive yet more verbose and sophisticated legal ambiguity, augmented by the ability of the executive to modify it when political expediency necessitated.

The State Security Decree lasted over thirty years and was instrumental in repressing dissent in the 1980s and the 1990s. Although draconian, it was somehow more sophisticated than the 1965 emergency law. Instead of just stipulating the authorities' right to detain individuals, it detailed sentences and various crimes. However, this sophistication in practice merely allowed potential oppositional forces to better manage their expectations. The law was still deeply repressive. It allowed the state to detain – without trial for up to three years – anyone convicted of a range of ambiguous activities: from spreading 'atheistic principles' to the spreading of 'subversive propaganda'.[48] The risk created by the creation of the parliament encouraged the more formal legislation of Al Khalifa power, reflecting the growing assertiveness and legal sophistication of a ruling core worried both by Independence and the formative results of Bahrain's brief democratic liberalization.

2001, An Unofficial State of Emergency

While 2001 saw the official demise of the State Security Law, existing legal strictures still ensured the continuation of an unofficial state of

[45] 'The additional offenses that can now be prosecuted in the security court include arson and use of fires or explosives' (Articles 277–281), and assaults or threats "against a civil servant or officer entrusted with a public service" (Article 220), or "against another in any manner, even though without having the intent of killing the victim, if the assault leads to death of the victim" (Article 336). Also in early 1996 the government quietly expanded the security court from one chamber to three chambers in order to cope with the increased number of arrests. Over the following ten months, more than 180 persons were convicted under the state security process, compared with one estimate of fewer than fifty in 1995. This period also saw increased detention of women and children.'. Human Rights Watch, *Routine Abuse, Routine Denial: Civil Rights and the Political Crisis in Bahrain*, 1997.

[46] Human Rights Watch, *Routine Abuse, Routine Denial.* [47] Ibid.

[48] Amnesty International, *Bahrain: A Human Rights Crisis.*

emergency. The rapid proliferation of new legislation following Hamad's reforms led to legal ambiguities that have been interpreted in a manner favourable to the regime in times of political crisis. For one, the 1976 penal code voided civil liberties enshrined in the 1973 constitution.[49] Likewise, provisions of the 1976 penal code voided articles of the 2002 constitution, 'giving the government the right to suspend key human rights or encroach on them for "national security" reasons'.[50]

In 2006, and in light of the emboldening of the Shiʿa in Iraq, Bahrain passed a law on counter-terrorism that threatened to undermine the constitution and reform moves initiated in 2001. By defining terrorist acts so broadly, the law has, according to the ICJ, allowed the 'criminalisation of rights that are internationally recognised, such as freedom of assembly, freedom of expression or the right to strike'.[51] The Bahrain

[49] Bahrain's 1973 constitution guarantees freedom of speech (Article 23), the press (Article 24), communication (Article 26), association, including the right to form trade unions on a national basis (Article 27), and assembly (Article 28). In many cases, however, the 1976 Penal Code effectively nullifies those rights, particularly in the following articles: Article 134A calls for imprisonment and a fine for 'any citizen who has attended abroad in whatever capacity and without authorization from the Government, any conference, public meeting or seminar, or has participated in any manner whatsoever in the deliberations thereof with the intent of discussing political, social or economic conditions in the State of Bahrain or in any other state so as to weaken financial confidence in the State of Bahrain or undermine its prestige or standing or to worsen political relations between Bahrain and these countries.' Article 163 more broadly penalizes 'any person who establishes, sets up, organizes or runs in the State of Bahrain without a license issued by the Government, international societies, organizations or institutions of any kind whatsoever or branches thereof,' or 'any person who joins the aforesaid societies, organizations and institutions', including any citizen who 'join[s] or participate[s] in any manner without a Government license in any of the aforesaid organizations which are based outside the country'. Article 164 authorizes the closure and dissolution of 'aforesaid societies, organizations and institutions.' Article 165 authorizes an unspecified prison sentence for 'any person who expressly incites others to develop hatred or hostility toward the system of government'. Article 168 penalizes 'any person who deliberately disseminates false reports, statements or malicious rumours, or produces any publicity seeking to damage public security, terrorize the population or cause damage to the public interest', and penalizes possession of 'any publication or leaflet' containing such material or possession of any device intended for the reproduction or dissemination of such material. Article 169 penalizes publication of 'untrue reports' that 'undermine the public peace or cause damage to the country's supreme interest or to the State's creditworthiness'. Article 178 proscribes any assembly of five or more persons 'aimed at undermining public security, even though for the realization of a legitimate objective'. Article 222 penalizes 'any person who offends with the use of signs, saying, writing or by any other method a civil servant or officer entrusted with a public service'.

[50] Interview with Bahraini Lawyer, 20 November 2013.

[51] International Commission of Jurists (ICJ), 34th Session of the UN Committee Against Torture, 10 May 2005: Submission by the International Commission of Jurists (ICJ) on the impact of the draft law on counter-terrorism of the Kingdom of Bahrain on its obligations under the United Nations Convention against torture and Other Cruel,

Centre for Human Rights described the law as a 'tool to silence dissidents',[52] and despite Bahrain being a State Party to the International Covenant on Civil and Political Rights (ICCPR), the law allows for ill-treatment in detention, enforced disappearances and arbitrary detention.[53] The ICJ also argued that the terms in the law were too nebulous and unclear, and ran contrary to the cornerstone of criminal law *nullum crimen, nulla poena sine lege*[54] [no crime without law].

The principle of no crime without law is founded on the idea that no one can be tried for a crime that is not stipulated in law, nor its punishments defined. However, when it comes to repression, vagueness is an asset to authoritarian regimes. The ambiguity of the laws in Bahrain is such that the government have almost unlimited discretion in determining what is considered a crime under the anti-terror act.

According to the legislation, a demonstration that leads to clashes with the police could theoretically result in the protesters being branded terrorists and detained for ninety days upon the basis of secret and undisclosed evidence. Such a law does not simply criminalize civil disobedience, a key method used by social movements, but also renders it a terrorist act, further empowering the state in its legal ability to prevent legitimate freedom of expression. The law also limits the discretionary powers of judges, further empowering the state regarding sentencing outcomes.[55] The context of the law is important too, as it came during the global War on Terror initiated by the United States after the 11 September terror attacks in New York. As such, there was considerable US pressure on countries in the Gulf to clamp down on terrorism.[56] Other terror attacks in Saudi, Kuwait and Oman also prompted support among a number of influential Bahrainis for a crackdown.[57] In this regard, the global war on terror led to political pressure to change laws but also provided a convenient pretext on which to criminalize legitimate political dissent. For the regime, the war on terror was a useful opportunity in

Inhuman or Degrading Treatment or Punishment (UNCAT), 10 May 2005, www.refworld.org/docid/48a57eff2.html

[52] Bahrain Center for Human Rights, 'The Terrorism Law in Bahrain: A Tool to Silence Dissidents', 13 March 2014, www.bahrainrights.org/sites/default/files/Terrorism%20Laws%20in %20Bahrain%20-%20FINAL.pdf

[53] International Commission of Jurists (ICJ), 34th Session of the UN Committee Against Torture, 10 May 2005.

[54] Essentially means that a law has to exist prohibiting an action before it can be deemed as criminal.

[55] Law Number 58 for the year 2006, Law for the protection of society from terrorist acts, www.legalaffairs.gov.bh/Media/LegalPDF/K5806.pdf

[56] W. R. Tomkys, Mahdi Tajjir, 16 May 1982, FCO8/4332, The National Archives.

[57] W. T. Monroe, Bahrainis Publicly Acknowledge Regional Terrorist Threat, US Embassy Manama ,16 February 2005, https://wikileaks.org/plusd/cables/05MANAMA224_a.html

which to attack opposition through comprehensive anti-terror legislation. With its limited powers and distorted representative make-up,[58] parliament can do little to challenge the law, even though it carries many of the hallmarks of its state security predecessor.

From State Security to National Safety

Although the State Security Law lasted until the advent of the National Charter in 2001, the creation of a constitution and a bicameral parliament under the then Amir Hamad was no more than a gilded legal cage. Amir Hamad sought to build his legacy on a platform of democratization, as well as the abandonment of the legal structures that had been the source of much repression and discontent. However, Hamad's 'constitutional coup'[59] shattered the illusion of an authentic reform process, and illustrated the continuation of new forms of control – ones that reflected both a Saudi and Al Khalifa fear of emboldening political opposition or giving it more power, especially the power to make laws.

This was evident following the outbreak of protests in 2011, where the government introduced the Orwellian-named 'State of National Safety'. This law, which was passed by decree and not subject to ratification by parliament, allowed the authorities broader scope in dealing with dissent without democratic oversight. The prime minister and the Supreme Defence Council, a non-elected body created to monitor matters of national security made up exclusively of members of the ruling family, approved the law.[60] In other words, the decision to initiate the State of National Safety bypassed even the already disempowered parliament. This decision not only lacked any binding consultation between the state and society but also between the ruling family and society. Unsurprisingly, the law was passed the day after 2,000 Saudi soldiers from the Peninsula Shield entered Bahrain to 'defend Bahrain as a bulwark against perceived Iranian expansionism'.[61] However, while this draconian measure reflected a significant degree of fear by both the Al Khalifa and the Saudis of political unrest, it cannot simply be said to be the work of hardliners such as the Khawalid or the prime minister, as it was voted on by the Supreme Defence Council, whose makeup included people outside this group.

[58] See Chapter 3 on statecraft.

[59] A. Gresh, 'Bahrain: Divide, Repress and Rule', April 2011, http://mondediplo.com/blogs/bahrain-divide-repress-and-rule

[60] A. Shehabi. 'Bahrain's Sovereign Hypocrisy', The Middle East Channel, *Foreign Policy*, 14 August 2013, http://mideast.foreignpolicy.com/posts/2013/08/14/bahrains_sovereign_hypocrisy?wp_login_redirect=0

[61] Kinninmont, *Bahrain: Beyond the Impasse*, p. 20.

The State of National Safety removed the restraining barriers of role delineation between different coercive institutions of state, giving a legal pretext for multiple enforcement agencies to work together to impose curfews, search citizens, censor or confiscate publications and regulate or ban public gatherings.[62] This lack of 'separating functions' or role delineation within various security organs, is a move that Austin Turk associates with increased deviance and coercion.[63] The absence of a statute 'identifying the exact powers to be exercised by the Government during a State of National Safety',[64] contributed to an increase in violations of due process.

This outcome was not undesirable for the regime, for it benefited the Bahrain government to induce a temporary state of lawlessness in order to create a wide sense of disorder that would generate panic and thus a desire for 'law and order'. During March 2011, the government's withdrawal of the police from the streets created a chaotic atmosphere that was later used to justify a heavy-handed deployment of security forces.[65] Federico Ferrara describes the deliberate creation of social disorder as a form of repression. The breakdown of law and order creates a Hobbesian dilemma, where anarchy is pervasive, and where 'violence and indiscriminate pillage [is] not only tolerated but promoted by the armed forces'.[66] Ferrara adds that such manufactured dilemmas create a corollary demand for the status quo, usually brought about by intervention from the armed forces of the state.

The decree also created a two-tiered quasi-military court system. Those arrested under the National Safety Law's broad mandate were tried in courts in which one of the three judges were members of the military – a generally Sunni-dominated institution whose experience lay with military as opposed to civil justice. Human Rights Watch described the courts as 'as a vehicle to convict defendants of alleged crimes stemming from the exercise of fundamental rights of freedom of expression, association, and assembly, in violation of international and Bahraini law'.[67] No matter how nefarious, the State of National Safety was crucial in giving the authorities the correct, yet highly repressive, 'legal form' to arrest and put on trial important leaders of the political opposition. Twenty-one high-profile opposition activists were tried and given harsh sentences (ranging from five to twenty-five years), even though much of their testimony had been extracted under torture and that most of the

[62] *BICI Report.* [63] Turk, 'Organizational Deviance and Political Policing', p. 248.
[64] *BICI Report*, p. 418. [65] Kinninmont, *Bahrain: Beyond the Impasse,* p. 20.
[66] F. Ferrara, 'Why Regimes Create Disorder: Hobbes' Dilemna during a Rangoon Summer', *The Journal of Conflict Resolution,* vol. 47, no. 3, 2003, p. 310.
[67] Human Rights Watch, *No Justice in Bahrain: Unfair Trials in Civilian and Military Court,* 2012, p. 3, www.hrw.org/sites/default/files/reports/bahrain0212webwcover.pdf

evidence related 'almost entirely to peaceful political activities and raised serious due process issues as well'.[68]

Despite these issues, the judges argued that the provisions of the decree took precedence over those in the Bahrain constitution that protect a citizen's right to free speech and association.[69] The legal interpretation was certainly not lenient. According to the BICI Report, the military attorney general interpreted statutes in a way 'least favourable to the arrested persons and to the defendants appearing before the National Safety Courts'.[70] Far from being an illegal move, the right to declare a State of National Safety is enshrined in the Bahrain constitution, highlighting how the constitution itself ceases to provide a useful function in protecting political rights when the safety of the regional status quo is challenged.

Despite the name of the decree, the State of National Safety was simply a way of increasing the efficiency with which the Bahrain government could justify the detention and arrest of a large number of people. Indeed, over 3,000 people were arrested shortly following its implementation.[71] This depleted the strength and efficacy of much of the active political opposition. In particular, the incarceration of political leaders reduced the organizational capacity of the opposition in Bahrain. The use of law gives a veneer of legitimacy to a process that would otherwise be seen as an entirely arbitrary means of repressing social movement activism. Given that the prime minister has stated on a number of occasions that all citizens are 'equal before the law',[72] the process also allows the government to argue that procedures are undertaken in a way that does not selectively target certain parts of the population. Indeed, to state that all people are equal before the law is a superficially appealing but intellectually dishonest endeavour. On the contrary, laws are specifically purposed to target and criminalize political opposition.

Perhaps most crucially, the State of National Safety was a litmus test for the limits of the constitution. Rather than preventing repressive law, the constitution enshrined it by having a caveat that allows for a state of martial law. Most tellingly, while a memorandum attached to the constitution states that measures undertaken in a State of National Safety are meant to be less restrictive than the Martial Law Decree of 1981, they were interpreted in a manner that 'exceeded those stipulated in Amiri Decree No. 27 of 1981'[73] [Martial Law]. Thus, the state of national

[68] Ibid., p. 4. [69] Ibid. [70] *BICI Report*, p. 418. [71] Ibid.

[72] *Gulf Daily News*, 'No Place for Anarchy'', 13 March 2013, http://archives.gdnonline.com/NewsDetails.aspx?date=04/07/2015&storyid=349200

[73] *BICI Report*, p. 57.

safety set in motion an efficient judicial apparatus that was squarely within a militaristic, Al Khalifa-dominated sphere of influence. Indeed, the protection afforded to subjects by the constitution is ultimately subservient to the security of the Al Khalifa regime.

Bahrain's precarious position has always made it vulnerable to increased uncertainty, prompting the almost constant existence of a state of emergency, one in which the regime has justified the 'suspension of normal legal principles and procedures'.[74] The State of National Safety simply reflected the implementation of the legal redundancies put in place to deal with popular unrest. The fact that such emergency laws have always been accompanied by foreign intervention simply shows that legal cover is a useful means to legitimize the strengthening of the coercive apparatus. While Humphreys argues that a constitutional endorsement of a state of exception is a 'pragmatic recognition of limited constitutional dominion',[75] the power to institute National Safety in Bahrain is done solely by decree. There is no binding consultation between state and the king, demonstrating that legalizing lawlessness in the form of emergency law is a discretionary right initiated by the king in defence of private interests. The emergency laws in Bahrain highlight foremost the 'close integration of law and politics',[76] especially when enacted as a response to widespread popular discontent. In such cases, the 'direct subordination of legal institutions'[77] preserves local minority elite interests in the face of populist demands. The limits of constitutional dominion are defined by the ruling family and external interests. Unlike during various repressive moments in Latin American history, where the constitution was 'rendered inoperative by continuing states of emergency',[78] in Bahrain the constitution enshrines the power of the king to hold a state of national emergency. The swift arrival of Saudi troops also indicates that the decision to enact the National Safety Law was not solely a Bahraini one but one made by the de facto suzerain – Saudi Arabia.[79]

Ordinary law, Ordinances and Regulations: The Expansion of Repressive Law

While emergency laws in Bahrain can be conceived of as highly reactive, designed as a rapid response to agitation in a context where administrative

[74] Welch, *Crimes of Power and States of Impunity*, p. 18.
[75] S. Humphreys, 'Legalizing Lawlessness: On Giorgio Agamben's State of Exception', *The European Journal of International Law*, vol. 17, no. 3, 2006, p. 678.
[76] Nonet and Selznick, *Law and Society in Transition*, pp. 50–2. [77] Ibid.
[78] Fagen, 'Repression and State Security', p. 48.
[79] S. Mabon, 'The Battle for Bahrain: Iranian-Saudi Rivalry', *Middle East Policy Council*, vol. xix, no. 2, 2012.

and non-coercive controls are not sufficient to give the authority vague enough parameters to deal with dissent – non-emergency laws or ordinances are also important tools of legal repression. Many such laws concern the regulation of public meetings, labour organizations, the regulation of the press and the association of people in clubs and societies.

Attempts in the early 1900s to clamp down on what the British called Al Khalifa 'rowdyism' resulted in the creation of the Manama Municipality (see Chapter 3 on statecraft). The Municipality offered one of the first legal frameworks in Bahrain for regulating public space. A curfew was introduced, and systems of taxation and discipline were regulated and formalized. This set a precedent that urban centres would be subject to the law before the rural 'hinterland'. The Al Khalifa, for their part, sort to strangle the legal reforms from within, resisting British encroachment on what they saw as tribal law, which had previously allowed them to undertake arbitrary justice in their oppression of the *baḥārna.*

While unpopular with the ruling family, the relative transparency offered by Municipal rules was welcomed by others. In 1935 and 1938,[80] popular demands for reform highlighted the widespread desire to end forms of arbitrary rule. However, petitions for a penal code fell on deaf ears, despite British encouragement for them at the time.[81] It is perhaps telling that during the 1990s Intifada, and despite numerous 'legal reforms', protesters were still taking to the streets and using petitions due to there being no legal means of expressing their discontent.[82] Petitioning the government marked a resurgence of the tactics used by the *baḥārna* in the early 1900s. This was not simply an oppositional tactic but reflected the post-Independence resurrection of a relationship between the ruling family and the population that been somewhat subdued between the 1920s and the 1960s.

A Poisoned Chalice: The New Penal Code

It was only in 1954 that the British finally got around to drafting a penal code. They also brought in a labour code in 1955. Certainly, the lack of timely reforms impacted upon dissent with subsequent repressive choices reflecting a decades-long absence of legally defined protest parameters. While the attempted standardization of law originally stemmed from the British administration's idea that the ruler needed 'proper legal form'[83]

[80] Fowle, 12 November 1938, p. 132.
[81] T. C. Fowle, Communique to the Foreign Secretary, in A. Burdett (ed.), *Records of Bahrain 1820–1960,* vol. 5, Slough, Archive Editions, 1993, p. 4.
[82] *The Economist,* 'Bahrain's Spreading Flames', 19 July 1997, Issue 8026, p. 56.
[83] D. M. H. Riches, 10 April 1956, in A. Burdett (ed.), *Records of Bahrain 1820–1960,* vol. 7, Slough, Archive Editions, 1993, p. 238.

to repress dissent, the British were initially worried that laws at the time would antagonize the Higher Executive Committee.

For the British, tackling the HEC via administrative and legal measures in the face of Al Khalifa obstinance was preferable to British boots on the ground. As a result, Britain's so-called middle-course was once again abandoned in favour of greater pressure on internal reform. In 1954, Bernard Burrows reflected on this: 'We shall be involved in a greater degree of direct participation in the administration, through the Judicial Adviser and the British police officers, than would otherwise be necessary or perhaps desirable.'[84]

Burrows compared Bahrain to Kuwait, the latter of which, he argued, involved a stronger British presence in the administration. The reality was, however, different. In Bahrain, given the recent memories of Al Khalifa oppression, the British often portrayed their intervention in legal affairs as unavoidable if some form of peace was to be kept. Although these motives were rarely altruistic, there was some truth in them. As Burrows noted, there was 'no alternative method of reassuring the people of Bahrain that impartial justice will in future be done and that police will be in a better position to maintain order without the unwarranted use of firearms'.[85]

With this justification in place, the British sought to exploit the popular demand for a penal code as a foil to contain dissent. Being an amalgamation of Egyptian, Sharia and English Common Law, it is unsurprising that Bahrain's new penal code contained articles that sought to curtail the rights of assembly. It had been honed previously in other British chapters of colonial repression. The HEC opposed the introduction of the code on 'the grounds that it incriminated whoever took part in sedition or civil disturbances'.[86] However, the HEC had already been worn down by several unilateral government notices, and their opposition to the penal code caused the government to engage new strategies of control. These strategies can only be described as legal pedantry. The straw that broke the camel's back for the HEC came when the government claimed that a march planned by the committee had deviated from its intended route, and, as such, the HEC had failed to control people and was thus responsible for these 'grave disorders'.[87]

Perhaps paradoxically, while the desire for a penal code ultimately drove forward the standardization of law in resistance to tribal particularized law,

[84] B. A. B. Burrows, 20 July 1954, in A. Burdett (ed.), *Records of Bahrain 1820–1960*, vol. 7, Slough, Archive Editions, 1993, p. 58.
[85] Ibid. [86] Khuri, *Tribe and State in Bahrain*, p. 206.
[87] Bahrain State Radio Transcript, 6 and 7 November 1956, Bahrain Internal Political, 1956, The National Archives.

the penal code and emergency law, when implemented, were designed to facilitate repression and British-supported Al Khalifa domination. In this respect, the rise of the HEC marked the widespread beginning of the conflict between 'de facto rights from below', and 'de jure' rights from above'. The HEC had pushed for the creation of standardized law, but its execution had been undertaken by a government who then used it as an opportunity to manage dissent.

Limiting Organization, Maintaining Fragmentation

Public Spaces

Following the eventual dismantling of the HEC in 1956, the regime reflected upon how they would deal with such issues in the future. However, with the HEC out of the picture, the Bahrain government felt less need to hurry reform, legal or otherwise. A familiar apathy had set in. Nonetheless, the government endeavoured to engage, at their own slow pace, a swathe of legal changes without the political pressure from the HEC. However, tensions between the ruling family's and Britain's vision for Bahrain resulted in the piecemeal introduction of legal reforms that tended to reflect the more conservative tendencies of the Al Khalifa. The introduction of the Labour Ordinance in 1957 did little to permit unionization or organization. The updated Labour Ordinance that was considered in the late 1960s and encouraged by the British provided for registered union organization. However, it was scuppered by Al Khalifa and merchant class interests on the grounds that the law would 'conflict with those vested interests among the members of the Ruling Family and the more influential merchants which are still effective obstacles in the way of progress'.[88]

The British eventually stopped pressuring to introduce such a law as they feared that such measures might be seen as facilitating subversion.[89] The undermining of the Labour Law highlighted the Al Khalifa fear of legal changes giving groups the power to collectively organize, whether through unionization or within public spaces. This was partly due to an embedded sense of tribal conquest but also because the experience with the HEC had simply made them fear such forms of organization, whether legal or not. Thus, the ability to formulate laws of collective bargaining, and the nature of the laws themselves, was something that remained the prerogative of the ruling family and their merchant allies.

[88] G. Middleton from the British Residency, 18 July 1960, in A. Burdett (ed.), *Records of Bahrain 1820–1960,* vol. 7, Slough, Archive Editions, 1993, p. 820.
[89] Ibid.

Laws that did eventually emerge reflected a general disregard for civil liberties and freedom of association. The fact they were created shows some sense of shared purpose between British officials and the ruling family, perhaps as a result of the Cold War creating panic about communist subversion. The first proper law concerning the regulation of public meetings was the Amiri Decree Law No. 18 of 1973 on the Organization of Public Meetings, Rallies and Assemblies. The law was passed hastily in September 1973, two months before the establishment of the National Assembly, to prevent it being subject to public debate. The law gave legal form to the containment of public order deliberately before Bahrain's democratic reforms – an underhand move that emphasized how officials regarded elected bodies as a general risk to stability. The law, which was subsequently amended in 2006 and 2011, stipulated, among other things, that the head of public security be informed of the time, place and subject matter of all public meetings and demonstrations. Similarly, Law No. 32 of 2006 states that organizers are also responsible for 'forbidding any speech or discussion infringing on public order or morals', although it does not define 'public order or morals'.[90] It also permits the authorities to deem whether a police presence should be necessary, thus giving the authorities the legal scope for positioning legal control agents to pre-empt any serious attempts at dissent or even civil disobedience.

Human Rights Watch has argued that the Bahrain government have used the law to prosecute both organizers and participants in gatherings arbitrarily deemed as 'illegal'.[91] Combined with stiff sentences, charges of illegal gatherings have been a means for the authorities to scoop up activists expressing publicly their right to free expression. In one high-profile case in 2012, prominent human rights activist Nabeel Rajab was given a three-year sentence for charges related to illegal gathering.[92] The extent to which such charges of illegal gathering have been used to clamp down on perceived troublemakers is evident in that the authorities have 'arrested hundreds of mostly young men and imprisoned them on charges of '"illegal gathering", "rioting" or "arson" after trials that failed to comply with international fair trial standards'.[93]

[90] *BICI Report*, p. 209.

[91] Human Rights Watch, 'Human Rights Watch UPR Submission on Bahrain', 21 November 2011, www.hrw.org/news/2011/11/21/human-rights-watch-upr-submission-bahrain

[92] Index on Censorship, 'Bahrain Activist Nabeel Rajab Sentenced to Three Years in Prison', August 2012, www.indexoncensorship.org/2012/08/bahrain-activist-nabeel-rajab-sentenced-to-three-years-in-prison/

[93] Amnesty International, *Behind the Rhetoric: Human Rights Abuses Continue in Bahrain Unabated*, London, Amnesty International Publications April 2015, p. 11.

The Law on Public Gatherings and its subsequent amendments came into place ahead of the establishment of the National Assembly in order to manage the risks posed to the regime by the democratic body. The law, which again reflected the policies of an unelected government, treated the right to peaceful assembly 'as if it were a mere privilege, imposing arbitrary obstacles in the way of those who wish freely to exercise this right, including to demonstrate against the government'.[94] Two constitutions later, both of which enshrined freedom of expression, its draconian tenets are still being utilized to give legal form to preventing freedom of expression.

Clubs, Societies and NGOs

As well as dictating where and when people can meet, legal channels to constrain dissent have also been useful in defining the nature and size of the opposition. Since the rise of Arab nationalism and the proliferation of para-political institutions such as the Uruba club, laws of association have been important in attempting to create organizational fragmentation. This fragmentation is intended to weaken potential challengers to Al Khalifa hegemony.

In 1959, the government issued an ordinance that regulated the foundation and operation of clubs and societies in Bahrain, ensuring that they were 'ethnically divided between Shiʿa and Sunni, Arab and Persian, Indian and Pakistani'.[95] The principal of fragmentation extended to both foreign labour and expatriates. While the introduction of such a law sanctioned the creation of clubs, it also regulated them in an attempt to minimize their potential to act as institutions that encouraged widespread political mobilization. Indeed, clubs were forbidden to extend membership beyond a particular geographic location, especially if eligibility for joining was broad.[96] As Fuad Khuri notes: 'The proliferation and fragmentation of club organisation have not been haphazard; it is an expression of government policy and the factional divisions of communities and ethnic groups'.[97] This much was acknowledged by a British official in 1985, who stated that only allowing clubs to recruit locally was deliberately designed to militate against countrywide political formation.[98] Therefore while the authorities used the law to permit the establishment of clubs and societies, the law also helped ensure that the membership of those clubs was constrained and limited in order to maintain some degree of disorganization and disunity, further weakening potential opposition. Consequently, clubs believed to foster any form of political

[94] Ibid., p. 24. [95] Khuri, *Tribe and State in Bahrain*, p. 185. [96] Ibid., p. 185.
[97] Ibid. [98] P. R. Ivey, Internal Political 1985, FCO8/5817, The National Archives.

dissidence were targeted by the authorities. Following the killing of the newspaper editor ʿAbd Allah al-Madani in 1976, for example, clubs in the villages of al-Dayh and Abu Saybaʿ were shut down. In the 1990s Intifada, clubs had to seek permission from the authorities to hold public meetings. More recently, when the ʻUruba Club asked to have an event on the theme of 'freedom of the press and condemning violence',[99] they had to submit all the names of invitees to the Ministry of the Interior, who subsequently denied permission to hold the event. They clearly deemed it too seditious.

Although the legislation of clubs has served to stymie political organization or shape it in such a way that political debate is skewed in a manner that benefits the government (e.g. promoting affiliation according to religious sect, for example), it has never been a panacea and has required upgrading. For this reason, the Law of Associations, amended in 2002, was written to further constrain the operation of the burgeoning civil society organizations and NGOs.[100] As Human Rights Watch argue, the Law of Associations has been used to

> to suppress civil society and restrict freedom of association in three main ways: by arbitrarily rejecting registration applications and intrusively supervising NGOs; taking over and dissolving—more or less at will— organisations whose leaders have criticised government officials or their policies; and severely limiting the ability of groups to fundraise and receive foreign funding.[101]

With the advent of the Law No. 26 of 2005 concerning political societies, passed by a Sunni Islamist-dominated parliament, the government also sought to draw a legal distinction between legitimate political societies and illegitimate political societies. As the law required all groups to register with the Ministry of Justice, those that did not could be construed as rejecting the legitimacy of the constitution promulgated in 2002. According to Justin Gengler, the state's purpose here was clear: to delegitimize and criminalize those groups who did not, through their willingness to succumb to the state's legal-bureaucratic apparatus, register with the Ministry of Justice.[102] Furthermore, the law enables a judge to seek a court order to shut the political society down for up to three months if they violate either the constitution or the law. Although the courts are obliged to reach a decision within thirty days, the political society is suspended during this time, giving the government the ability to

[99] Human Rights Watch, *Routine Abuse: Routine Denial.*
[100] Human Rights Watch, *Interfere, Restrict and Control*, p. 2. [101] Ibid.
[102] J. Gengler, 'Bahrain's Legal "War on Terror"', Religion and Politics in Bahrain, 17 September 2013, http://bahrainipolitics.blogspot.co.uk/2013/09/bahrains-legal-war-on-terror.html

disrupt the activities of such groups even before the courts have ruled any wrongdoing.[103]

The law also prevents Bahrain's restive teenagers from forming legally sanctioned political allegiances, with the minimum joining age set at twenty-one. This age limit also reflects an interesting contextual element, as Bahrain has historically seen dissent originate in the country's high schools, a fact believed by the authorities to be a result of Arab school teachers from outside the Gulf instilling Arab nationalist ideas in the youth. Thus youths, who were seen as perhaps more politically impressionable and therefore restive, were deliberately prioritized in terms of exclusion from avenues of legitimate political organization.

Cross-group cooperation has also been discouraged, with it being illegal to be a member of more than one society. In June 2012, Law Number 26 was invoked to dissolve the Islamic Action Society (Amal) – a Shia Islamist party representing the Shirazi faction within Bahraini politics. The government accused Amal of the following: failing to submit their annual reports, failing to convene a general conference for more than four years and taking decisions from a religious authority that openly advocates and incites hatred.[104] Despite the official reasons, Amal had been a thorn in the regime's side for some time, and their dissolution was the culmination of the government's antipathy towards Amal as opposed to their failure to adhere strictly to laws and regulations. The emphasis on their procedural shortcomings was notably to detract from the fact that most of its board members and over 200 active members were arrested in 2011. Thus, Amal's failure to comply with specific laws enabled the government to prevent them from engaging in legally sanctioned protest, even though their inability to rally supporters had been curtailed by specific government repression.[105]

Despite King Hamad's political openings of 2001, various legal legerdemains undermined most of the advantages bestowed upon civil society organizations who sought to take advantage of the new liberalization. The Law of Associations (no. 21/1989) has also been used by the government to interfere in the work of NGOs. It gives the government the authority to replace board members and forbids the NGO from engaging in ill-defined 'political' activities.[106] The law has been used as a weapon by the regime in dealing with dissent. In 2011, the Ministry of Social

[103] Human Rights Watch, *Interfere, Restrict and Control*. p. 52. [104] Ibid. p. 63.

[105] Bahrain Center for Human Rights, 'Bahrain: Right to Association under Attack as Ministry of Justice Moves to Dissolve Islamic Action Society "Amal"', 20 June 2012, www.bahrainrights.org/en/node/5326

[106] *Human Rights Watch*, 'Human Rights Watch UPR Submission on Bahrain', 21 November 2011.

Development used the Law of Associations to dissolve the Bahrain Teachers Society and 'replace the board of the Bahrain Medical Society', after they had supported protesters demanding more political rights.[107] The Law of Associations has also curtailed sources of funding for NGOs. As a result, those groups who refuse to accept government funds for fear of appearing to be co-opted and complicit in government strategy have severe restrictions on how they can raise money. As Gary Marx noted, social movements require funding, and government actions work to restrict funding in order to weaken them.[108]

As always following widespread political unrest, the progression of legal repression gained pace after 2011. In September 2013, Ministerial Order No. 31 of 2013 stipulated that political societies must liaise with the Ministry of Foreign Affairs (MoFA) before meeting with representatives of foreign parties or political societies.[109] The MoFA authorized itself to send a representative to any meetings.[110] Such a move represents the increase of state surveillance over the activities of political groups and reflects a deliberate government strategy to prevent NGOs from alerting sympathetic foreign governments and audiences to relevant political grievances. This, in turn, creates further obstacles for social movements trying to draw attention to their cause by the international community. Such laws do not simply reflect government fears of, for example, groups like Al Wefaq meeting with Shiʿi figures in other countries but also their fears born out of Bahrain's advocacy revolution, which has seen a burgeoning number of groups seeking assistance from international organizations.

Legal Repression of Trade Unions

In additions to curtailing the work of NGOs that might hold the government to account, the Bahraini authorities have sought to weaken and control another conventional institution for political mobilisation – the trade unions. The authorities viewed this as necessary following Bahrain's increasing industrialization in the 1950s and 1960s. Changes to the labour market altered the social base of power and created a shift towards 'issue-orientated' politics that threatened to transcend traditional and more predictable (at least for the ruling family) forms of organization

[107] Ibid., p. 12. [108] Marx, 'External Efforts'.

[109] Bahrain Youth Society for Human Rights, *Report: The Recommendations of the Bahraini National Assembly Restrain Human Rights*, 8 September 2013, http://byshr.org/wp-content/en-reco.pdf

[110] *Gulf News*, 'New Rule for Bahrain Societies over Contacts', 4 September 2013, http://gulfnews.com/news/gulf/bahrain/new-rule-for-bahrain-societies-over-contacts-1.1227200

such as sect or ethnicity. While trade unions have been illegal throughout much of Bahrain's history, there have been calls for workers' rights from as early as the 1930s. The eventual introduction of a Labour Ordinance of 1957 did little to allow collective bargaining, while the updated Labour Law for the Private Sector created in 1976 deliberately excluded those who were civil servants or working in public corporate entities. In other words, those working in industries perceived strategic to Bahrain's economy were not covered by the private labour law of 1976. The Bahrain Workers Union, which was based in Damascus, raised several concerns with the ILO about how this law limited association. In 1981, they noted the autocratic nature of the inception of the law and its contents:

> it does not give workers the right to form trade unions of their own choosing; that the workers were not consulted during the drafting of the Code; that it does not recognise the right to strike; that part-time and agricultural workers are excluded from its terms; that it does not fully treat arbitrary dismissal but only mentions indemnities and in fact allows dismissal without indemnity or notice for reasons including non-recognition of employers' directives concerning workers' safety; that it enforces the use of an intermediary to settle labour disputes; that it allows the Minister to decide on the methods of designating workers' representatives on joint Committees and that it includes various unsatisfactory provisions concerning maternity leave, hours of work, etc.[111]

Any ostensible advances in labour law were undermined by mechanisms that deliberately limited the power of such organizations. The permitting of Joint Worker/Employer Committees in 1981 was done in a manner designed to circumvent the emergence of powerful unions (see Chapter 3 on statecraft) while appearing to look progressive. Specifically, resolution number 15 of 1981 allowed the Secret Service to vet candidates running for positions on a company's elected Joint Committee.[112] This, presumably, was done through article two, which required the composition of the committees to be approved by the Ministry of Labour and Social Affairs.[113] Later stipulations clarified who could and could not run to represent workers. Resolution 9 of 1981 explicitly laid out six conditions that would forbid certain candidates from running. People eligible for exclusion were those who had a previous criminal conviction in the past five years; had been dismissed from work for a breach of trust issue; and had engaged in activities that could be construed as being against the

[111] Interim Report – Report No 211, November 1981
Case No 1043 (Bahrain) – Complaint date: 01-JUN-81 – Closed, www.ilo.org/dyn/normlex/en/f?p=NORMLEXPUB:50002:0::NO::P50002_COMPLAINT_TEXT_ID:2900570

[112] Collis, Bahrain Labour, 12 March 1983, FCO8/4920.

[113] www.legalaffairs.gov.bh/AdvancedSearchDetails.aspx?id=8908#.WNQ6CCaLSUm

state or national unity.[114] Indeed, the caveats above deliberately excluded anyone who might have been involved in trade union activity before 1981, targeting established defenders of workers' rights. Inevitably, complaints from the BWU to the ILO revealed continued attempts by trade unionists to improve their freedom of association and right to organize:

> As regards the specific allegation that three named trade unionists, Mr Abdallah Addawi, Mr Majid Abd Ali Almadi and Mr Adnan Assaid Kazem were arrested, detained, interrogated or tortured, and in one case even forced to resign from office as Vice-President of the Bahrain Workers' Union because of their trade union activities, the Committee notes the Government's reply that the complaint is incorrect and misleading since the persons concerned were, as private citizens, and not as trade unionists, assisting the police in an investigation into other matters.[115]

When trade unions were actually permitted to form, strict laws were implemented, and breaking those laws resulted in severe penalties. What is more, even abiding by those laws and exercising the right to strike within legal parameters has resulted in state repression.

Although Bahrain has not ratified the Freedom of Association and Protection of the Right to Organise Convention and the Right to Organise and Collective Bargaining Convention, in 2002, as part of King Hamad's reforms, the 2002 Workers Trade Union Law was ratified, with a provision to allow strikes.[116] Naturally, this was widely lauded as a progressive move. In 2011 when the General Federation of Bahrain Trade Unions (GFBTU) organized a legal action to protest the advent of martial law, thousands of workers went on strike. Despite the legality of the strike, the government responded with a series of witch-hunts that resulted in the dismissal of thousands of workers. In addition, they hastily passed Decree Law 35 of 2011 that sought to divide, fragment and ultimately weaken the GFBTU. The amendments to the trade union law included only allowing unions chosen by the Ministry of Labour to represent Bahraini workers in national and international bargaining. The International Trade Union Confederation (ITUC) argued the change would prevent the GFBTU from voicing its concern that the new amendments were designed to prevent them from further denouncing

[114] www.legalaffairs.gov.bh/AdvancedSearchDetails.aspx?id=5730#.WNQ_LyaLSUm

[115] Interim Report – Report No 233, March 1984 Case No 1211 (Bahrain) –Complaint date: 27-MAY-83 – Closed, www.ilo.org/dyn/normlex/en/f?p=1000:50002:0::NO:50002:P50002_COMPLAINT_TEXT_ID:2901041

[116] Workers Trade Union Law General Provisions, International Labor Federation, www.ilo.org/dyn/natlex/docs/ELECTRONIC/65397/62838/F553283085/BHR.65397.pdf

government violations.[117] The amendment also included a clause that the ITUC argued would prevent trade union leaders convicted of actions leading to the dissolution of a trade union (e.g. leading strikes in 2011) from being elected for five years following the date of their conviction.[118] In other words, trade union leaders who organized the legal strike in 2011 would be targeted by the new law. These measures severely curtailed the ability of the opposition to lead effective protests.

Maintaining a Neoliberal Facade in the Capital

Laws have also sought to govern strategic locations in Bahrain. The need to keep Bahrain's image in the international community a pristine amalgam of skyscrapers and modern infrastructure, devoid of conflict, has resulted in specific laws designed to keep disorder out of the capital. In line with how challenges to authority have honed the Bahrain's government's use of repressive law, the Ministry of the Interior claimed that it was considering studying sites that would be specifically for protests and demonstrations.[119] Although the outcome of the study was unclear, the government banned all protests between 30 October 2012 and 13 December 2012, citing 'repeated abuse' of the right to protest.[120] In August 2013, a ban on protests in Manama was then formalized into law via an amendment to Article 11 of the Public Gatherings Law,[121] highlighting how the government were not satisfied with the existing laws' effect on the behaviour of protesters. The new amendment banned public meetings, marches, gatherings and demonstrations in the capital, 'excluding sit-ins outside international organisations', which can be held with the written authorization of the Public Security Chief.[122] However, in addition to this condition, the Public Security Chief may also define the time, place and number of people participating in any demonstration.

As with the introduction of the Manama Municipality in 1921, Manama's position as capital was prioritized in terms of law designed to prevent protest or dissent. The exclusion of protests from the country's

[117] International Trade Union Confederation, 'ITUC Statement on Recent Attacks on Rights of Bahraini Trade Unionists', 11 October 2011, www.ituc-csi.org/IMG/pdf/ITUC_Bahrain_Statement_Final_3_.pdf
[118] Ibid.
[119] Kingdom of Bahrain Ministry of Interior, Study to Identify Sites for Approved Rallies, 12 July 2012, www.policemc.gov.bh/en/news_details.aspx?type=1&articleId=13799
[120] Bureau of Human Rights, Democracy and Labor, US Department of State, Bahrain 2012 Human Rights Report, April 2013, www.state.gov/j/drl/rls/hrrpt/2012/nea/204355.htm
[121] Amnesty International, *Behind the Rhetoric.*
[122] Trade Arabia, 'Bahrain bans public meetings in Manama', 7 August 2013, www.tradearabia.com/touch/article/LAW/240713

capital represents an attempt to limit the visibility and occurrence of dissent as well as mitigate the effects of civil disobedience. Since part of the purpose of a protest is to garner public and media attention, relegating them to discreet locations, far from the eyes of the media or other citizens, is a way of reducing their effectiveness as a means of expressing discontent or gaining public support.[123] These laws function as a form of censorship and containment, attempting to persuade potential investors and tourists, via omission, that Bahrain is indeed, 'business friendly'. Thus, the legal system in Bahrain has explicitly been designed to restrain the visibility of organizations, activities and discourses that might be harmful to the reputation of Bahrain. While such laws offer useful tools for imposing and outlining order, they are 'far less competent at securing stability founded in consent'.[124]

Legislating the Private, Religious and the Face

Since the 1990s, the state has been introducing legislation that seeks to penetrate more private spheres. While family and personal status laws have been the jurisdiction of the religious courts, the unrest in the 1990s prompted the government to introduce legislation that increased the state's reach into what was traditionally the religious domain. Decree-law 19 of 1996 established a High Council for Islamic Affairs, a body of Sunni and Shiʿi scholars appointed by the prime minister. As a reaction to the perceived independence of Shiʿa clerics, the law designated that the council be responsible for the promotion of religious materials that espoused unity between all Muslims, and removed any 'impurities'. To this end, the second article mandates that the committee screen all appointees whose job might include speaking in mosques or matams. As *the New York Times* reported in 1996, this article was perceived by many members of the opposition as a means of 'muzzling' Shiʿa clerics[125] and regulating religious discourse in a manner conducive to the maintenance of the status quo. Isa Qasim, a Shiʿa cleric, established the Islamic Scholars Council in 2004 in order to provide a non-state-controlled outlet for religious discussion. The government dissolved it in 2014, soon after the 2011 Uprising, claiming that it was violating the constitution, and conducting political activities under cover of religious sectarianism.[126]

[123] In a more 'humorous' example of this idea, someone wrote into the *Gulf Daily News* to suggest that protesters should be confined to small islands or zones.

[124] Nonet and Selznick, *Law and Society in Transition*, pp. 52–3.

[125] 'Bahrain curbs clerics', 25 Apr 1996, *New York Times* (1923–Current File), https://0-search-proquest- com.lib.exeter.ac.uk/docview/109599851?accountid=10792

[126] 'Bahraini Court Dissolves Islamic Scholars Council, *Al Monitor*, 30 January 2014.

The protests in 2011 have also prompted a swathe of legislation designed to extend state repression further into the private sphere. The 1976 Juvenile Law was amended so that the parents of anyone under sixteen who took part in an unauthorized public gathering would be warned on the first offence and imprisoned or fined on the second.[127] Again, this attempt to raise the costs of protest through legislation that informally makes parents part of the policing apparatus, is designed to weaken opposition through a process of intimidation. Using families to police their offspring has increased the state's pervasive role in the private sphere.[128]

This also marks a further shift to collective responsibility and punishment. That is, those other than the people carrying out criminal activity are being held accountable for crimes. This asymmetry is matched by a similar yet opposite degree of state unaccountability. Essentially, families are explicitly expected to police what the state has failed to, and the burden of accountability has extended further from the state to the citizens. Thus, the political rights of parents or guardians now become contingent on the behaviour of those under their care, representing a deepening of the police state. This widening the net of accountability has also been directed at those providing first aid to people wounded by the security forces. The government announced that those offering medical care to protesters outside official clinics would be held 'legally responsible' for the victim's 'health and well being', forcing protesters to either suffer or turn themselves into a hospital, and by extension, the police.[129]

The use of law as an instrument of control has also verged on the petty. In 2013 the government made the importation of 'V for Vendetta' masks illegal.[130] The masks, which can symbolize anarchism have become a mainstay of protest movements the world over, somehow irked the Bahrain authorities. The move came a few months after authorities in the UAE did the same, and authorities there stated that the police could question anyone wearing the mask. So, although Bahrain's nebulous emergency laws were guilty of no crime without law, regular laws have

[127] Amnesty International, 'Bahrain: New Decrees Ban Dissent as Further Protests Organized', 7 August 2013,www.amnesty.org/en/latest/news/2013/08/bahrain-new-decrees

[128] M. Al A'Ali, 'Rioters' parents may face jail', *Gulf Daily News*, 4 December 2013, www.gulf-daily-news.com/NewsDetails.aspx?storyid=366155

[129] Bahrain News Agency, 'Northern Police Directorate/ Statement', 24 February 2013, www.bna.bh/portal/en/news/548078

[130] S. Mustin, 'Anti-Protest: Bahrain Bans Import of Plastic Guy Fawkes Masks', 25 February 2013, *The Independent*, www.independent.co.uk/news/world/middle-east/anti-protest-bahrain-bans-import-of-plastic-guy-fawkes-masks-8510615.html

resulted in a legal system often so specific that it has criminalized all facets of collective action, whether in theory or practice. From wearing a mask symbolizing dissent to engaging in protests, Bahrain's laws are both specific and vague. Interpreted according to the political will of the elite, they are not irrelevant but arbitrary when it comes to challenges to state authority.

Legal Processes

The Political Trial and Political Justice

While laws may set out the legal framework for managing dissent, the use of legal processes and the courts to repress dissent is also important. A political trial is one such method. It is, as Otto Kirchheimer argued, designed to 'incriminate its [the state's] foe's public behaviour with a view to evicting him/[her] from the political scene'.[131] The political trial, while somewhat vaguely defined by Kirchheimer, is a useful description for any judicial trial that is undertaken with the object of renegotiating the balance of power within a specific polity. When it is used to eliminate or weaken political opposition, it fits within the definition of repression.

Political trials have been used throughout Bahrain's many episodes of contentious activity. In the 1920s, when the British were attempting to end ruling family persecution of the indigenous *baḥrānī* community, a few members of the ruling family were put on trial for various crimes in order to convince the public that not even the Al Khalifa were above the law. The trials were meant to create trust in the British-led reforms of that era, asserting a new era of imperial hegemony. Even at what was arguably the peak of British influence, justice was, to borrow Sharlet's description of justice in the USSR, 'meted out differentially' based not just on the 'offender, the intent, and the offence' but also on the goals of the regime.[132]

In an attempt to put an end to the arbitrary trials being enacted against the *baḥārna*, the British further consolidated Shaykh Hamad bin Isa's rule by giving him exclusive power among the Al Khalifa to try certain cases or inflict punishment.[133] However, the reality of political trials is

[131] Kirchheimer, *Political Justice*, p. 46.
[132] Sharlet, 'Party and Public Ideals in Conflict'.
[133] 'Administration Reports 1920–1924' [119r] (242/412), British Library: India Office Records and Private Papers, IOR/R/15/1/713, in *Qatar Digital Library*, www.qdl.qa/en/archive/81055/vdc_100023385511.0x00002b

that they they are political. So while some members of the ruling family were put on trial, their sentences were barely enforced, highlighting the limits of imperial overrule. For example, on 18 September 1923, a group of *al-fidawiyya* killed a *bahrāni*[134] villager after a camel belonging to Shaykh Khalid Al Khalifa was found wounded near the village of Sitra. Shaykh Khalid was found guilty of having 'encouraged and approved of the attack',[135] and was made to forfeit his property in the town of Sitra and pay blood money of 2,000 rupees.[136] His son ʿAli bin Khalid Al Khalifa, who was found guilty of 'organising and accompanying the attack' was banished to India.[137] Salman Al Khalifa, another son of Khalid Al Khalifa, was banished from Bahrain for a year. According to Charles Belgrave, the punishment so 'annoyed' the Khalid shaykhs that they briefly returned to Sitra and shot nine people[138] in what became known as the second Sitra outage.[139] Following this, Shaykh Khalid's sons were sentenced to death, a move that was intended to establish the new regime under Hamad.[140] Although ʿAli bin Khalid was banished to India, he returned to Bahrain about six months later without British permission.[141] Much to Belgrave's chagrin, the political resident Barrett also allowed Shaykh Hamad to issue a retrial of the two Khalids involved in the Sitra outrage. Attempts to undermine the political trial of the Al Khalifa shaykhs were then undertaken by the new Emir. Shaykh Hamad proceeded to 'square' the thirty-four witnesses who had seen the Khalids shoot nine villagers.[142] Belgrave wrote a letter to Barret complaining about his decision to let the Khalids return, and also complained to the Shaykh about the 'persuasion' that the *baḥrānī* witnesses in the Sitra case were being subjected to.[143] In February 1928, the Shiʿa *Qādi* Sayyid ʿAdnan wrote a letter to Hamad saying he had managed to 'square' the witnesses in the case.[144]

While the Khalids were not imprisoned, the illusion that justice had been done was seen by the British as an important step in securing the authority of the courts and the legal system. Whether or not many

[134] *Baḥrānī* is the adjective of *baḥārna.*

[135] C. K. Daly, 25 September 1923, No. 123-C, in P. Tuson, A. Burdett and E. Quick (eds), *Records of Bahrain 1820–1960,* vol. 4, Slough, Archive Editions, 1993, p. 130.

[136] Ibid. [137] Ibid. [138] Belgrave, Papers, 30 January 1928.

[139] 'Administration Reports 1920–1924' [159r] (322/412), British Library: India Office Records and Private Papers, IOR/R/15/1/713, in *Qatar Digital Library,* www.qdl.qa/en/archive/81055/vdc_100023385511.0x00007b

[140] 'Administration Reports 1920-1924' [195r] (394/412), British Library: India Office Records and Private Papers, IOR/R/15/1/713, in *Qatar Digital Library,* www.qdl.qa/en/archive/81055/vdc_100023385511.0x0000c3

[141] Belgrave, Papers, 11 February 1927. [142] Ibid., 30 January 1928.

[143] Ibid., 22 February 1928. [144] Ibid., 25 February 1928.

perceived this as the case is, of course, difficult to determine. Nonetheless, the return of the Khalids highlighted the limits of Britain's ability to press for high-level accountability. Instead they had to concede that mitigating conflict within the ruling family was more of a priority than the execution of substantial justice. The facade of justice that hides elite impunity has been an enduring aspect of Bahrain's history, and this case has never been accurately documented.[145]

The Attempted Assassination of the Ruler of Bahrain in 1926

In addition to the retrials of 1929, one Ibrahim bin Khalid bin ʿAli Al Khalifa was convicted for instigating an assassination attempt on Shaykh Hamad in 1926. Ibrahim had allegedly coordinated this plan during his exile on the mainland (present-day Saudi Arabia) after his involvement in the Sitra Outrages. The attempt to shoot Hamad failed, and the underlings who had carried out the attack were given varying prison sentences, while Ibrahim was exonerated by Shaykh Hamad. As was permissable in customary law, the victim or intended target of the attack (Hamad) had the option to issue clemency.[146] (It is interesting to note that Ibrahim eventually worked in Hamad's house – presumably so Hamad could keep an eye on him.)

Other members of the Al Khalifa family and shaykhs were also convicted for crimes including rape and murder. This included Shaykh Hamad bin Sabah and Shaykh Hamad bin ʿAbd Allah al-Ghattam.[147] However, only fines were imposed, even though the relatives of the victims demanded the death penalty.[148] Here, customary law was clearly only the prerogative of the elite. Hamad's issuing of lenient sentences again to his extended family stemmed from his weakness and desire to maintain family unity, itself an important factor in preventing further challenges to his rule. It is interesting to note that initial investigations suggested that it was the ruler's brother Shaykh ʿAbd Allah who had been behind the assassination attempt.

Despite this, ʿAbd Allah was brought in to augment the judges on the Bahrain Court that convicted Ibrahim. When it was suggested that ʿAbd

[145] Khuri ends the discussion of the case by noting that the Khawalids were given the death sentence but then fled. Al-Tajir mentions a fine and prison sentences.

[146] C. Belgrave, Annual Report for the Year 1348 (1929–30), *in Bahrain Government Annual Reports 1924–1970*, vol. 1, Gerrards Cross, Archive Editions, 1986, p. 153.

[147] Shaykh Hamad bin Sabah was found guilty of instigating an attack on the house of one of his tenants in the village of Tubli in around 1981. The house owner was killed. Shaykh Hamad bin Abdulla Al Ghattam had been previously tried by Shaykh Hamad for instigating murder and rape in a tenant's house in Farsia. After being retried he was found guilty and a payment of blood money was ordered.

[148] Ibid.

Allah be added to the court, Belgrave wrote in his diary: 'As ʿAbd Allah is one of the people implicated he would be certain to condemn the men to shield himself, and if they accused him in court he is quite clever enough to suppress any such idea. I think it would be a good idea to put him on the Court.'[149] Unless Belgrave had made a grammatical error, he appeared to be supporting ʿAbd Allah's position as a judge in order to protect himself from accusations against his involvement in the assassination attempt on his brother. Given ʿAbd Allah's previous attempts to undermine Hamad's rule, his involvement would not be unlikely. Such evidence, in addition to ʿAbd Allah's continued attempts to work against Hamad, contradicts Khuri's assertion that ʿAbd Allah committed himself to maintaining unity within the ruling family following the abdication of Shaikh ʿIsa in 1923.[150] Indeed, Khuri's idea that ʿAbd Allah became a conciliator as opposed to a party to conflict seems too simplistic, and it was perhaps the fear of losing a generous stipend from the state that induced ʿAbd Allah to limit his intrigues against Hamad.

Furthermore, despite ʿAbd Allah's attempts to work against Hamad, he was perceived by the British as the most competent Al Khalifa and one who was important in securing Shaykh ʿIsa's supporters to cooperate more fully with the British reforms. While these attempts to repress dissident members of the Al Khalifa resulted in reprisals or amnesties, they highlighted the limits of British control over Al Khalifa agitation. Indeed, the British political trials did have an ameliorative impact, but they were never in full control, and the decision not to enforce the law fully against the ruling family also reflected the perception that the British would lose influence entirely among the Al Khalifa if they pressed too hard.

The Trial of the St Helena Three

Both the British and their increasingly strategically aligned Al Khalifa 'clients', came together in opposition to the agitation of the 1950s. While the HEC represented a threat to the imperial order in Bahrain, they always demonstrated willingness to cooperate with the authorities. However, the British feared that in the midst of the Cold War a democratically elected body aligned with the spirit of Arab nationalism would refuse a British military presence. The Al Khalifa feared they would lose their lucrative monopoly on Bahrain's land and material resources. The political trial of the HEC leaders was therefore a means of attacking the legitimacy and reputation of dissenters while consolidating the position of the Al Khalifa.

[149] Belgrave, Papers, 4 February 1929. [150] Khuri, *Tribe and State in Bahrain*, p. 98.

In 1956, after Bahrain had been subject to two years of political campaigning by the Higher Executive Committee, the government decided to move against the leaders of the HEC. Following a highly political summary trial, in which a British officer from the Criminal Investigation Department (CID), Benn, acted as government prosecutor, three leaders of the HEC were illegally deported to the British island of St Helena.[151] However, the trial was a textbook example of political justice. Major William Little, a former member of the Bahraini police, compiled a report of the shortcomings of the trial. This report was kept secret until around 2005. Little submitted this report to the British Parliament arguing that the trial was simply a means of publicly discrediting the movement.[152] Belgrave, who disliked Little, and had at one point called him 'absolutely useless' and a 'mischief-maker',[153] actually did not disagree with all the contents of the report. He conceded that much of the evidence used in the trial would be 'inadmissible' in a 'strict court of law'.[154] The notorious ʿAbd Allah Al Khalifa once again acted as a judge for the trial, thus making those responsible for administering justice against those challenging the status quo the same parties interested in maintaining Al Khalifa hegemony. It later transpired that Benn, the prosecutor, received private payments from the future Prime Minister Shaykh Khalifa PM, a fact that indeed calls into question his partiality in administering justice. In addition to questionable evidence being presented by a police prosecutor, one of the main issues of the trial was that those accused refused to defend themselves on the basis that the trial was held in secret. The British argued that they had shifted the location of the trial to avoid creating a public security issue. However, they conveniently shifted the trial to a place where it would be difficult for the public to scrutinize. It remains uncertain whether the evidence found with those accused of leading the HEC was planted or not, although it is probable that it was. The integrity of the trial was very much in doubt. As Belgrave noted, it was not 'a strict court of law', reflecting instead how justice on the periphery of Empire was subordinated to the desires of the political elite.

Unlike earlier trials, where Al Khalifa legitimacy was threatened due to them being in the docks, the new arrangement consolidated their power and legitimacy by allowing them to arbitrate on matters of sedition and treason. Indeed, it cemented their role as figureheads of a new imperial arrangement. British complicity in this political trial was highlighted by

[151] Belgrave, Papers, 22 December 1956.

[152] The report was kept secret for about fifty years, highlighting the British authorities desire not to generate criticism of their policy abroad.

[153] Belgrave, Papers, 14 February 1957.

[154] Belgrave, Papers, 23 December 1956.

the collusion of local officials in shipping the detainees off to the island of St Helena. Although the defendants applied for a successful habeas corpus action to the 'Supreme Court of St Helena and to the Judicial Committee of the British Privy Council',[155] the trial had already achieved its purpose: to dull the political momentum of the HEC.

The Killing of ʿAbd Allah al-Madani

Although the British played a crucial role in logistically and politically supporting the demise of the HEC, political trials became somewhat routine after Independence in 1971. Indeed, they have become a predictable feature of Bahrain's frequent contentious episodes. In 1976, five alleged members of PFLOAG were put on trial for the murder of ʿAbd Allah al-Madani, editor of the weekly paper *al-Mawaqif*. The names of the men were Muhammed Taher al-Mahari, Ibrahim Abdulla al-Marhun, Ali Ahmed Falah, Ahmed Makki and Abdul Amir Mansour. Despite a lack of evidence, which was mostly based on confessions allegedly extracted under torture, three of the five were given the death penalty.[156] The questionable nature of the evidence and the provisions of the State Security Decree meant that the men had little chance of defending themselves properly. Their fate was also sealed by the pressure of hardliners in the Bahraini and Saudi governments demanding death sentences.[157] Indeed, while divisions within Bahrain's political elite and other influential members of the 'inner circle' informed the outcome of the trial, the prime minister evidently favoured a more draconian approach. According to the British ambassador, the prime minister had threatened to put the judges on trial if they did not secure death sentences. Eventually, after a lengthy delay, which reportedly reflected 'dissension within the Ruling Family to the degree of severity to be shown, two were sentenced to death and one to life imprisonment, while the instigators were acquitted'.[158] This decision was then altered; it was decided that the person sentenced to life imprisonment was also to be executed. Even though several others implicated in the case were acquitted, they languished in jail for eight years simply to prevent them from becoming opposition heroes.[159] The executions of those found guilty happened quickly. According to Given, this was in order to avoid international pressure for a reprieve.[160] The speed of the trials, the use of

[155] M. Joyce, 'The Bahraini Three on St. Helena, 1956–1961', *Middle East Journal*, vol. 4, 2000, p. 618.
[156] Given, Political Murder in Bahrain. [157] Ibid. [158] Ibid.
[159] صحيفة الوطن.. الفرعنة عندما لا تجد من يردعها. WAAD, National Democratic Action Society [website], 22 October 2010, www.aldemokrati.org/details.php?artid=6765
[160] Given, 'Political Murder in Bahrain'.

torture and the imposition of the political elite in influencing the outcome of the trial all point to a classic example of a political trial designed to subordinate justice in the pursuit of eliminating political opposition. The executions indicated the ascendency of the politically conservative prime minister. Francis Trew reported that the prime minister had lamented Kuwait's approach of merely imprisoning terrorists, and favoured Saudi's more hardline approach. Trew indicated that the prime minister would 'have no hesitation in executing terrorists in Bahrain'.[161] The Al-Madani trial was significant as it shows one of the first clear examples (at least in the British archives) of Saudi influence in the repressive choices of Bahrain's government.

The death of Al-Madani is still shrouded in mystery. With question marks remaining about the integrity of the trial, it remains uncertain who actually killed him. While there had been tensions between the leftist and religious blocs during the time of the assembly, Al-Madani, according to US State Department documents, more often than not found himself opposing the ruling family and siding with the leftists – making him an unlikely target for PFLOAG. US documents also alluded to al Madani being a government shill or operative, raising the question about whether or not his death may have been the state-sponsored eradication of a government asset.

> [Al Madani was] a populist-style critic of the government and ruling family. In pursuit of his anti-government goals, he and his assembly group were often found in tactical alignment with the leftist people's bloc in the assembly. In his youth, Madani had leftist leanings which apparently were 'cured' by his arrest and interrogation in the early 1960s.[162]

The killing of al-Madani had a substantial repressive impact. Certainly, the framing of the killing as a leftist ploy frustrated growing cooperation between the religious bloc and the leftists, an outcome that benefited the regime in their maintenance of a fragmented opposition. Furthermore, Edward Given noted that the execution of those accused of killing al-Madani, combined with the 'soft-centred nature of the Bahrainis' had a salutary impact on the National Liberation Front. This led, according to Given, to the clandestine opposition becoming 'virtually dormant'.[163]

Partially due to the successful repression of the leftist threat and their subsequent demise in the 1970s, the oppositional vacuum was filled to

161 Trew, 17 December 1984, FCO8/5442, The National Archives.
162 US Embassy Manama Bahrain, 'Murder of Journalist/Politician', 21 November 1976, https://wikileaks.org/plusd/cables/1976MANAMA01942_b.html
163 Given, Annual Review 1977, The National Archives.

some extent by the Islamist threat, which had been gaining ground since the establishment of the National Assembly. Also, further punitive treatment of the Shiʿa, combined with no substantial political outlet fuelled further animosity towards the government. In 1981, the government arrested seventy-three people from the Islamic Front for the Liberation of Bahrain (IFLB). Again, the trial was held in camera, and the defendants' lawyers were not given sufficient access to their clients. There had been a virtual media 'blackout' of the trial which was closed to international observers and the press – no doubt to reduce the likelihood of international criticism. Indeed, the patterns of the political trials in the 1970s and 1980s mirrored those of the St Helena Three.

In the trial of the IFLB members, the British attempted to dissuade the Bahrain government from giving death sentences for fear of further isolating the Shiʿa community.[164] Different officials had different outlooks on how sentencing could be used to combat dissent. Ian Henderson advocated passing death sentences but not actually carrying them out, as he believed carrying them out would be disastrous for stability.[165] However, British officials were generally wary of expressing their views on the trial, for fear of damaging their relationship with the ruling family and on the basis that they were not fully informed on the issue. The British instead relied on their excellent relationships with influential Bahrainis such as Yusufi Shirawi. Yusuf bin Ahmed Shirawi had been exiled after 'riots' in 1935 but now served as a useful conduit of British opinion[166] The British line was that executions would strengthen opposition to the regime. Tomkys noted in 1982:

> I am far from clear that we know the facts sufficiently, at any rate from any source other than Mr Henderson himself, to back up anything that would come under the heading of remonstrating with the Bahrainis. So far as clemency for those found guilty is concerned, I do not believe it would be right to go any further than suggested by Mr. Tomkys in paragraph 4 of his teleletter of 16 February to Mr, Passmore. I believe we should be wary of seeming to arrogate to ourselves a role in all this which does not accord with the present relationship between the British Government and the fully independent Gulf States. From what we heard from Yusuf Shirawi we can leave it in the main to influential Bahrainis who think as he does to make the case for giving the opponents of the Al Khalifa the satisfaction of having any martyrs for the cause.[167]

[164] Wogan, 23 April 1982, The National Archives.
[165] W. R. Tomkys, The December Coup, 21 March 1982, FCO8/4332, The National Archives.
[166] Staff at UK Embassy Bahrain, Biography of Yusuf bin Ahmad al Shirawi, Leading Personalities, 1976, FCO8/2643, The National Archives.
[167] Moberly, 'Bahrain: Use of Torture'.

As well as this, Tomkys told the minister of the interior that executions might make martyrs for the cause but emphasized too that the Bahrainis 'know their business and their own society'.[168] The Saudi government were concerned that Bahrain was a petri dish for insurrection in the region. They believed that if dissent 'were not stamped on hard, Bahrain would bear the responsibility for subsequent similar attempts (coups) in the region'.[169] However, the decision ultimately lay with the Al Khalifa, whom it was reported, 'may not have decided what penalties would be appropriate', and thought it advantageous to take a 'slow course'.[170]

Interestingly, there seemed to be an overnight decision to change death sentences to imprisonment, a decision, British sources say, that reflected the Amir's unwillingness to push the Shiʿa too far. Evidently, the Amir himself had sought more liberal council in the trial of the IFLB. However, his interference clearly highlights the lack of separation between the judicial system and the ruling family. The verdicts were subsequently harsh, with sixty of those accused given sentences of fifteen years, three to life imprisonment and ten given seven years. The harsh sentencing was no doubt designed to have a salutary effect on other potential dissidents, while the lack of death sentences was sufficient to limit international pressure for a reprieve. Indeed, these harsh but non-capital sentences struck a balance between repressive effect and an international outcry. The decisions were, nonetheless, the result of disagreements and deliberation among the ruling elite.

While Ian Henderson was said to be relieved at the outcome of the trial,[171] the decision was unpopular with hardliners, to the extent that the minister of interior even considered resigning. Those close to the prime minister seemed surprised by the sentences, suggesting that the decision was perhaps made by an extremely small circle. Again, the Al Khalifa were caught between Saudi Arabia and hardliners advocating for harsh punishments and the British and more liberal Bahrainis advocating a slightly less stringent approach. However, the trial highlighted the extent of Saudi influence in Bahrain's repressive choices. As one British diplomat foresaw, 'the danger is that Bahrain will snuggle so closely under Saudi Arabia's protection that it will eventually lose its independence and liberal traditions'.[172] The alleged coup attempt also resulted in the

[168] W. R. Tomkys, Police Brutality in Bahrain, 16 February 1982, FCO8/4332, The National Archives.
[169] S. M. J. Lamport, Bahrain Security, 8 March 1982, FCO8/4332, The National Archives.
[170] Tomkys, Internal Political Situation Bahrain 1982, 10 April 1982, The National Archives.
[171] W. R. Tomkys, 23 May 1982, FCO8/4332, The National Archives. [172] Ibid.

lessening of evidential requirements necessary to incriminate perceived political opponents. Anyone implicated in a plot could stand trial 'without obliging the authorities to demonstrate that they were full parties to the conspiracy'.[173] Essentially, the authorities gave themselves a carte blanche to arrest anyone they deemed politically inconvenient. At this time, that mostly meant anyone Shi'a.

Whether or not the coup attempt was genuine, it served as an important pretext for crushing Shi'i dissent. Saudi fear of Iranian expansionism undoubtedly played a role in political pressure. Perhaps most interestingly, however, is that the current King of Bahrain, considered a reformist by many, was believed by the influential Shi'a Mahdi Tajir to have been pressing for a 'root branch extirpation of the Shi'a opposition following the alleged coup'.[174] This does cast some doubt on his more recent reformist credentials.[175] Certainly, the presence of the IFLB reflected how the revolution in Iran had emboldened certain groups and refocused Saudi and Bahrain security attention onto Iran. However, the attitude of hardliners, and the fact that Shaykh Khalifa noted that the 1982 coup attempt 'didn't represent anything very dangerous to us' suggests that it may have been mostly a pretext to clamp down on the Shi'a.[176]

The Execution of 'Isa Qambar

The next major political trial in Bahrain occurred in 1996, when 'Isa Qambar, a twenty-nine-year-old Bahraini from the village of Nuwaidrat was convicted of taking part in the killing of policeman Ibrahim al-Saidi in 1995. At the time, the prime minister was reported to still be responsible for the draconian judicial policy[177] Qambar's prosecution contained all the tenets of the political trials that had preceded. For example, 'Isa Qambar and his co-defendants were arrested without judicial warrants and denied access to their family and legal counsel until the day of their trial.[178] In addition, the evidence relied on confessions extracted in pre-trial detention, allegedly under torture.[179] Defendants also argued that there was no forensic evidence linking them to the murder weapon. Furthermore, defendants in a separate case gave evidence against 'Isa Qambar and his associates, even though this violated Article 137 of the

[173] S. P. Collis, Bahrain Internal, 20 February 1982, FCO8/4332, The National Archives.
[174] Tomkys, 16 May 1982, The National Archives.
[175] The British document in which this is mentioned is redacted immediately after the quote about extirpation.
[176] *Gulf Daily News*, 'Interview with Shaykh Khalifa bin Salman Al Khalifa', 15 Saturday 1982, The National Archives.
[177] *The Economist*, 'Sheikhly fall-out'.
[178] Amnesty International, *Bahrain: A Human Rights Crisis*, p. 26. [179] Ibid.

Code of Criminal Procedure.[180] The defendant who gave evidence reportedly did so in exchange for his release.[181] As with the al-Madani case, there was also reportedly pressure to reach a verdict before the judicial recess on 15 July.[182] The state media widely publicized the trial of those accused of killing the policemen, yet the government remained silent on the issue of civilians being killed by police.[183] This smear game, assisted by a convoluted programme of legal embroilment and legal deviance, threw Qambar and his defence team into a lengthy process of deliberation and distraction. Amnesty International said that the trial 'ignored internationally accepted human rights standards'.[184] Clearly, the authorities in Bahrain were seeking to raise the costs for those planning on engaging in dissent. Although the case was eventually tried by the High Court (and not the State Security Court) because the defendants' lawyer successfully argued that the case was a murder, the accused were denied fundamental rights in pre-trial detention.[185] Following the trial of Qambar, eight leading Shiʿi Muslim activists were also put on trial, a move that reportedly was made by the prime minister to undermine the comparatively conciliatory approach of the then Crown Prince Shaykh Hamad.[186]

Although it is plausible to assume that someone among the opposition might kill a police officer, it is equally plausible that the regime might seek to utilize the death of a policeman for political purposes. Indeed, the repressive purpose of a political trial confounds the very nature and veracity of the crime being scrutinized. In addition, history in Bahrain has taught us that the social control intent of such trials transcends the notion of justice. The priority has always been to use such trials as a means of deterring other dissidents.

'The Bahrain Thirteen'

High profile trials of important political figures occurred in the 2011 Uprising. Thirteen opposition activists and political leaders were arrested between 17 March and 19 April 2011. The number of those put on trial was actually twenty-one, although seven were tried in absentia – all by the National Safety Courts. According to Human Rights Watch, many of the charges against the accused related to 'the exercise of freedom of expression, assembly and association'.[187] The sentences given were harsh,

[180] Ibid. [181] Ibid. [182] Ibid. [183] Ibid., p. 34.
[184] Associated Press, 'Execution Stirs Protests In Bahrain', 27 March 1996, www.nytimes.com/1996/03/27/world/execution
[185] Amnesty International, *Bahrain: A Human Rights Crisis*, p. 25.
[186] *The Economist*, 'Sheikhly fall-out'.
[187] Human Rights Watch, 'Bahrain: Vital Reform Commitments Unmet', 28 March 2012, www.hrw.org/news/2012/03/28/bahrain-vital-reform

ranging from between two years and life (twenty-five years) in prison.[188] Despite a retrial under a civilian court as demanded by the recommendations of the BICI report, the original rulings were upheld, even though the evidence was based on confessions extracted under torture. The late Cherif Bassiouni, an international legal expert and the head of the BICI team expressed his outrage at this decision, declaring:' I cannot think of a more egregious and specious legal decision.'[189] Like all the other political trials, press access was limited. The defendants eventually refused to show up to the hearings, complaining that they were being held in 'secret' and thus not subject to the scrutiny of either the public or the local and international media. As with other high-profile trials, this was no doubt to avoid subjecting the legal process to scrutiny, a process that could have given opposition more ammunition with which to use against the regime.

Similar trials of other reputable figures were undertaken in the 2011 Uprising, frequently on the basis of questionable evidence. On 29 September 2011, the Lower National Safety Court convicted twenty medics of several offences, including 'instigating hatred against the ruling system', 'spreading false news' and 'incitement to overthrow the regime'.[190] The medics claimed that they were tortured, and Human Rights Watch stated that procedural flaws meant that the trials violated both international human rights law and Bahrain law.[191] Although most of the medics had their conviction quashed in March 2013, the interim period saw a process of vilification by the state media. The medics were smeared in the press by sensationalist stories, one of which claimed that Kalashnikov rifles were found in the hospital in which the medics worked.[192] Interestingly, in 2019 an interview with a member of the army present in Bahrain at the time confirmed that the rifles were planted by the state. Given the medics' role as front-line witnesses to atrocities carried out by the authorities and the inherent respect associated with the medical profession, it was likely that any testimony given by the medics would be viewed favourably by international NGOs, news organizations and the wider Bahraini society. Thus, they represented a threat to the regime. In their attempts to make trials look fair, authorities have also been accused by Amnesty International of trying, en masse, those

[188] Human Rights Watch, 'Bahrain: Promises Unkept, Rights Still Violated', 22 November 2012, www.hrw.org/news/2012/11/22/bahrain-promises-unkept-rights-still-violated
[189] Law, 'Bahrain Reconciliation Distant among Slow Pace of Reform', *BBC News*, 23 November 2012, www.bbc.co.uk/news/world-middle-east-20449587
[190] Human Rights Watch, 'Bahrain: Medics Describe Torture in Detention', 22 October 2011, www.hrw.org/news/2011/10/21/bahrain-medics-describe-torture
[191] Ibid.
[192] Zahra, 'Kalashnikovs drama in medics' trial…', *Gulf Daily News*, 29 November 2011.

convicted of crimes, and then releasing a few.[193] Sometimes others are exonerated on appeal. However, the process of appeal is lengthy. By the time the retrial or appeal comes around, the social control objectives have been completed.

Whenever the regime faces a severe challenge, the general processes of procedural unfairness and 'rampant official discretion'[194] are implemented. The discretion with which law is interpreted and the inability to subject that process to scrutiny due to in-camera trials or media blackouts make it difficult for opposition groups to verify their claims of justice when lobbying for support. The political trial has been used repeatedly in Bahrain's history to attack the credibility and liberty of oppositional forces. The continuity of the ruling core, and particularly the prominent role of the prime minister, point to a routinization of the political trial. In many ways, it has become somewhat formulaic: breaches of due process, confessions under torture, vilification in the local media, banning of international media, conviction with harsh sentences and potential reprieve after appeal. In the more extreme cases, executions take place. Although such occurrences are certainly not unique to Bahrain, a study of political decision-making has revealed the extent to which the legal system is subverted according to the political needs of the ruling core and its international allies.

Selective Accountability and Asymmetric Justice

The 1950s: Investigate, Ignore and then Exonerate

In addition to the use of legal processes such as the political trial, Bahrain's legal control agents, such as the police and employees of the intelligence services, have been given wide scope to carry out their duties with minimal disruption. This broad mandate has contributed to the emergence of repressive law. Accountability of legal control agents accused of committing crimes or violations is disruptive for the regime's repressive capacity for it reduces the ability of the authorities to quash dissent. Having legal control agents tried for crimes erodes the authority of the state and is often avoided – especially in times when the regime faces an existential threat. As such, impunity for state officials is essential in maintaining the efficacy of the security apparatus when repressing dissent. This impunity has been a reoccurring aspect of repression in Bahrain's history.

[193] Amnesty International, *Bahrain: A Human Rights Crisis*, p. 25.
[194] Nonet and Selznick, *Law and Society in Transition*, pp. 50–2.

Between 1953 and 1956 the nature of the coercive apparatuses' impunity was very much determined by the unwillingness of Britain to draw itself more overtly into Bahraini politics. The British were concerned with creating a local security force that could be autonomous in its dealing with dissent. This would allow the preservation of a status quo in Bahrain conducive to British interests but one that did not require the embarrassing possibility of British intervention during times of unrest. The British knew that such controversy would simply add weight to accusations of continued colonial overrule. This attempt at distancing themselves was put to the test in 1954 when three people were shot and killed by the British-led police. Citizens were angry and demanded accountability. The authorities, fearing an increasingly tense situation, sought to defuse matters by forming a Commission of Inquiry headed by a British judge named Haines. The British argued that a foreign judge was necessary, with one official describing the judiciary 'as inept and discredited members of the Ruling Family'.[195] Indeed, the British believed that the inquiry would hold no weight without the appointment of a British judge.[196] Shiʿi leaders also requested that the British police the town, highlighting the pitch of sectarian tension between the police and the Shiʿa. The tensions between the public and the police were further noted by the British Commandant Colonel Hammersley,[197] who stated that there had not been 'good feeling' between the police and the public for a long time.

As a consequence of this ill-feeling, the political agent also advised the inclusion of a prominent Shiʿa to sit on the board with the British judge Haines.[198] This was mostly because the victims had been Shiʿa. The Commission of Inquiry found that while two officers had acted commendably, 'severe disciplinary action' needed to be taken against those policemen who had fired without orders.[199] Despite this, the ruler later pardoned those policemen responsible, a decision that angered the British administration, not least because the Bahraini government were still showing reluctance in reforming the courts.

The Commission of Inquiry appointed to investigate the events of 1 July 1954 was the first documented investigation into civil unrest and

[195] Wall, Letter to Political Resident in Gulf.

[196] B. A. B. Burrows, 1 July 1954, in A. Burdett (ed.), *Records of Bahrain 1820–1960*, vol. 7, Slough, Archive Editions, 1993, p. 40.

[197] Colonel Hammersley was third in command of the Bahrain police at the time. Above him was Director of Police Shaykh Khalifa and Commandant Charles Belgrave.

[198] Burrows, 1 July 1954, p. 39.

[199] *Report into July Disturbances*, 1954 in A. Burdett (ed.), *Records of Bahrain 1820–1960*, vol. 7, Slough, Archive Editions, 1993, p. 63.

the role of the police. Yet, the poor implementation of disciplinary measures against state officials reflects both weaknesses in the ruling family and the limits of British influence. The decision of the ruler not to prosecute any of the policemen found responsible illustrates what might be termed the beginning of a culture of impunity within the Bahrain police. Indeed, the lack of accountability would suggest that the police, at this time, were given more autonomy to commit deviant acts. Similarly, the prosecution of low-ranking police officers would have done little to address the systemic problems in the police, such as growing sectarianism.

With few lessons learned from the investigation in 1954, it is unsurprising that history repeated itself. On 11 March 1956, an altercation between some vegetable sellers and the market inspector in Manama led to a serious incident that culminated in the police firing on a crowd of civilians. The shooting killed five people and injured seventeen, six of them seriously.[200] Given growing political unrest in Bahrain throughout 1955 and 1956, the government was concerned that the event would be exploited by the opposition, and sought to engage in damage limitation. In anticipation of a circular from the HEC that would be critical of the police, Political Resident Burrows said explicitly that statements from the British administration 'should not (repeat not) criticize police'.[201] However, another inquiry was launched into the incident. It was to be headed up by Geoffrey L. Peace, the Judicial Adviser, and William P. R., Mawdsley, the Assistant Judge for Her Majesty's Court for Bahrain. Judge Haines, who had led the previous inquiry into the 1954 police shootings, was asked to advise what action ought to be taken on the board's findings.[202] Haines argued that the police fire was 'grossly excessive' and unjustified. Despite this, he concluded that the culpability[203] of the police could not be sufficiently proven, and therefore no criminal procedures ought to be taken, calling instead for departmental disciplinary action.

Further investigations were not recommended. Bernard Burrows[204] and whistle-blower Major William Oscar Little argued that it was

[200] B. A. B. Burrows, 12 March 1956 in A. Burdett (ed.), *Records of Bahrain 1820–1960*, vol. 7, Slough, Archive Editions, 1993, p. 218.

[201] Ibid.

[202] Judge Haines, Comments on Disturbances, in A. Burdett (ed.), *Records of Bahrain 1820–1960*, vol. 7, Slough, Archive Editions, 1993, p. 269.

[203] (1) the policemen fired their rifles without orders with intent to do grievous bodily harm or to kill and that the death or wounding of any particular individual resulted from this action, or (2) that they attempted to commit such an act.

[204] D. M. H. Riches, Minutes, 26 June 1956, in A. Burdett (ed.), *Records of Bahrain 1820–1960*, vol. 7, Slough, Archive Editions, 1993, p. 267.

Colonel Hammersley and not Charles Belgrave[205] who was probably guilty of negligence. A report in the Times, documenting some witness testimonies of the shooting, offered a more damning insight. The author noted that a British police officer fired a revolver shot, while a Pakistani police officer shot a youth with a Sten gun as he ran into a market.[206] Whether true or not, the report found that the firing had been excessive, with 85 policemen firing 478 rounds, mostly into the air.[207] The government responded to the inquiry by saying that the public was 'mainly to blame for these disturbances', and stated that training of the police would focus on 'modern methods of crowd dispersal'.[208] No mention was made of the fact that during the inquiry into the shootings of 1954, Haines recommended that something much 'less lethal than rifles' be used for 'mob dispersal'.[209] This was not implemented, reflecting a dismissive attitude to the judicial investigation.

An explanation for the unsatisfactory and dismissive nature of Haines's recommendations can be understood in the context of Britain's political considerations at the time. Indeed, the Foreign Office had pledged to support the Bahraini government with British troops if order was to break down,[210] yet this was seen as a last resort, as the British believed direct involvement would invite harsh criticism of British 'colonial' interference at a time of rising anti-colonialism and Arab nationalism. For this reason, the British were keen for the Bahrain police force to be capable of acting autonomously and without British assistance. In order for this to happen, it was imperative that morale among the police remained high. Bernard Burrows argued that the criticism of the police in the 1954 inquiry resulted in a severe lowering of their morale over a long period and that the 'diminution of it [police morale] would bring nearer the possibility of intervention by British forces'.[211] In this respect, there were compelling political pressures that meant that the outcome of the inquiry should not

[205] It is often argued, perhaps unfairly, that Belgrave is responsible for much of what went on in Bahrain.

[206] 'Inquiry Into Bahrain Shootings', *The Times* [London, England] 5 April 1956, p. 6, The Times Digital Archive.

[207] 'Findings On Riot In Bahrain', *The Times* [London, England] 11 June 1956: p. 8, The Times Digital Archive.

[208] Government Comments on March Disturbances 1956, in A. Burdett (ed.), *Records of Bahrain 1820–1960,* vol. 7, Slough, Archive Editions, 1993, p. 273.

[209] *Report into July Disturbances,* in A. Burdett (ed.), *Records of Bahrain 1820–1960,* vol. 7, Slough, Archive Editions, 1993, p. 63.

[210] Foreign Office, Communique to Agency Bahrain, No. 202, 6 March 1956, in A. Burdett (ed.), *Records of Bahrain 1820–1960,* vol. 7, Slough, Archive Editions, 1993, p. 63.

[211] B. A. B. Burrows, Burrows to Foreign Office 12 March 1956, in A. Burdett (ed.), *Records of Bahrain 1820–1960,* vol. 7, Slough, Archive Editions, 1993, p. 226.

be too critical of the police. Indeed, it was police weakness that prompted reforms and further foreign interference while the security apparatus was strengthened. The second enquiry, with its foregone conclusion, was simply a means of embarking upon conciliatory measures in order to provide a 'breathing space in which they might strengthen the Public Security Department'.[212] Furthermore, the police had been tired and overstretched at the time of the shooting, and while Belgrave had asked the ruler to lend some of his personal armed retainers, the ruler refused.[213] As such, the actions taken by the police were the result of an unwillingness by the British and the Bahraini government to both adequately train the police and hold them accountable . This confluence of different factors was instrumental in informing continued police violence. In both cases, the inquiries were a fig leaf designed to project a veneer of accountability while ensuring the continued survival of the status quo.

The Era of Reform: Factors Encouraging Impunity[214]

Amnesty International believes that not one single member of the Secret Intelligence Service (SIS) or CID have been brought to justice for engaging in acts of torture prior to 1995.[215] The same seems to be largely true after the period of reform that began following King Hamad's accession to the throne in 2002. My own research would seem to corroborate this. In 2011, following the outbreak of unrest, the Bahrain Independent Commission of Inquiry Report revealed that dozens of people were tortured, tens killed and thousands imprisoned by the State Security Forces.[216] Following recommendations by the BICI report to create a mechanism to hold both junior and senior officials accountable, the government demonstrated a superficial commitment to reform by prosecuting several low-level officials. By November 2012, the highest-ranking official charged with 'abuse' was a lieutenant-colonel.[217] As of 2016, it is not clear how many have been held accountable. The tactic of selectively holding only low-level security officers accountable represents an attempt to paint police deviance as the work of a couple of 'rotten

[212] B. A. B. Burrows, 20 July 1954, in A. Burdett (ed.), *Records of Bahrain 1820–1960*, vol. 7, Slough, Archive Editions, 1993, p. 54.
[213] Belgrave, Papers, 14 March 1956.
[214] Much of the data gathered concerning the impunity of state officials was gathered from tracking local news reports, NGO sources and State Department reports.
[215] Amnesty International, *Bahrain: A Human Rights Crisis*, p. 9. [216] *BICI Report*.
[217] BICI Follow Up Team, *BICI Follow-Up Report*, November 2012, p. 10, http://iaa.bh/downloads/bici_nov2012_en.pdf

apples', i.e., 'rogue officers operating with individual motives but whose actions are not reflective of the police institution as a whole'.[218] A less critical analysis 'would suggest that police deviance in Bahrain was the result of what O'Connor describes as "rotten barrels", namely, groups of police acting together but whose misconduct is also not representative of the police institution in general. However, given the habitual nature of police deviance in Bahrain, the concept of a 'rotten orchard' seems more appropriate'.[219]

Considering the nature of the abuses carried out by the police in Bahrain, both historically and more recently, the concept of a 'rotten orchard' is more fitting. This metaphor, originally put forward by Maurice Punch in 2003, outlines how 'deviance is not merely the fault of individuals or groups, but the result of systemic problems that either encourage, reward or necessitate police deviance'.[220] In this definition, the systemic issue refers to the formal structures such as 'the police organization, the criminal justice system and the broader socio-political context'.[221] Indeed, as Turk notes, 'legal deviance is much more likely to be attributed to individuals than to organisations. Indeed, it is easier to punish individuals, and scapegoating will as far as possible be used to block the imputation of legal deviance to the organisation'.[222] Deviance and impunity become more necessary, the more widespread the abuses, and the more those organizations are intertwined with the regime. They are indeed a hallmark of repressive law.

Despite the findings of the BICI report, which documented systematic torture, the authorities were reluctant to charge any of their officers with torture. When prosecutions did occur, the sentences were extremely lenient, reflecting only a desire to appease international actors or local opposition. Indeed, a clear pattern of legal manipulation emerged, one that involved the use of a series of legal procedures that initially incriminated those officials but ultimately repealed or commuted their sentences.[223] The examples of such trials are extensive. Originally sentenced to ten years in prison, the two policemen who tortured and killed the Bahraini civilian ʿAli Saqr in custody had their sentence reduced to two years. The policemen who tortured and killed civilian and journalist Karim Fakhrawi were 'sentenced to seven years for manslaughter, but had their sentences reduced to three years after appeal'.[224]

[218] Jones, 'Rotten Apples', p. 210. [219] Ibid. [220] Ibid.

[221] M. Punch, 'Rotten Orchards: "Pestilence", Police Misconduct and System Failure', *Policing and Society*, vol. 13, no. 2, 2003, p. 172.

[222] Turk, Organizational Deviance, p. 240. [223] Jones, 'Rotten Apples', p. 229.

[224] Ibid., p. 230.

Similarly, the officer accused of shooting and killing civilian ʿAli ʿAbd al-Hadi Mushaymaʿ was first sentenced to seven years for manslaughter but only to three years on appeal.[225] In another controversial case, the officer who shot Hani ʿAbd al-ʿAziz Jumʿa was initially sentenced to seven years for manslaughter. This was then reduced to six months on appeal.[226] In addition, ʿAli al-Shayba, an officer accused of permanently disabling a man by shooting him in the leg, first had his five-year sentence reduced to three, and then to six months on account of his ill-health.[227]

Others have simply been acquitted, such as the two officers accused of shooting Fadhil al-Matruq on February 2011, and the five policemen accused of beating blogger Zakariyya al-ʿAshiri to death in custody.[228] Amnesty International reported that in at least one case where an officer was sentenced to seven years for abuses committed in 2011, he was 'free pending the outcome of his appeal'.[229] In other cases, police officers being prosecuted for abuses have been accused of remaining on duty through the trial,[230] although the government say they remain on administrative detail.[231] These prosecutions also reflect a minimal commitment to investigating the deaths of those killed by the security forces in 2011. Forty-five cases of death believed to have been caused by the security apparatus were thrown out by the government by 2012. On the other side of the coin, no case of violence against police officers has ever been left unpunished.[232] This bifurcation of justice is indicative of an absence of equality before the law, especially regarding actions taken during political unrest.

Members of the security forces are also charged under more favourable legislation. They are often accused of manslaughter and not murder, which holds a maximum sentence of only seven years.[233] Manslaughter also implies a lack of menace and thus has the effect of portraying state agents as unintentionally violent. Ultimately, even this wrangling does not obscure the fact that the state is using such cases to project a veneer of accountability mostly to the international community. Little is likely to change. The BICI recommendations to improve redress for victims of state violence have been implemented to the extent they do not

[225] Ibid. [226] Ibid. [227] Ibid. [228] Ibid., p. 229.

[229] Amnesty International, *Bahrain: Reform Shelved, Repression Unleashed,* London, Amnesty International Publications, 2012, p. 9.

[230] N. Zahra, 'Officer Jailed in Shooting Case', *Gulf Daily News,* 26 June 2012, www.thefreelibrary.com/Officer+jailed+in+shooting+case.-a0294433698

[231] Ministry of the Interior Media Center, 'MOI Response to US State Department's 2013 Country Report on Human Rights', 8 May 2014, www.policemc.gov.bh/en/print.aspx?articleId=22819&mode=print

[232] BICI Follow Up Team, *BICI Follow-Up Report,* p. 10.

[233] N. Zahra, 'Sentences Slashed for Officers', *Gulf Daily News,* 28 October 2013, www.gulf-daily-news.com/NewsDetails.aspx?storyid=363780

threaten government control. For example, five of the eight people on the newly created Special Investigations Unit (SIU), tasked with investigating torture, are former MOI prosecutors.[234] The idea is that those investigating human rights abuses have a vested interest in covering up evidence of human rights abuses. In 2015, Human Rights Watch argued that the SIU had not released information to determine how many police officers were being held accountable for causing deaths in detention, so it is impossible to know what is actually being done.

> The SIU has not conducted investigations or prosecutions that have led to the conviction of any individuals for acts of torture in cases relating to Bahrain's political unrest. The ombudsman, who accepts individual complaints and directs them to the appropriate investigatory authority, did not provide details concerning the 83 cases his office referred to the SIU, so it is unclear how many may have related to allegations of torture.[235]

Decree 56: Enshrining Impunity

The legal whitewash in 1956 of the killing of civilians highlighted how maintaining the morale of the police was a priority for the government. In 1965, not one mention was made of investigations into the police's killing of eight protesters in the March Uprising. The same was true following government repression in the 1990s, and no officials were held accountable. On the contrary, upon becoming king in 2001, Hamad Al Khalifa sought to exonerate those employees of the state who were guilty of committing crimes during the unrest, and issued Decree Law No. 10 of 2001 and Decree Law No. 56 of 2002. While the former allowed political prisoners accused of state security crimes to go free, the latter allowed those who had potentially engaged in torture or extrajudicial killing to go free. In other words, Decree 56 conferred immunity from prosecution and investigation upon security officials accused of human rights abuses before 2002.[236] As Khalaf notes, 'Decree 56 saved many senior al-Khalifas and SIS officers'[237] and was an important precondition in securing ruling family consent to any reforms. Unsurprisingly, any suggestion to the contrary was quashed. A US diplomatic cable from Manama revealed that when ʿAbd al-Aziz Al Khalifa suggested to

[234] Bureau of Human Rights, Democracy and Labor, US Department of State, Bahrain 2013 Human Rights Report, 27 February 2013, www.state.gov/j/drl/rls/hrrpt/2013/nea/220348.htm

[235] Bahrain: Events of 2015, www.hrw.org/world-report/2016/country-chapters/bahrain

[236] Human Rights Watch, *Torture Redux.*

[237] M. O. Jones, 'Bahrain's History of Political Injustice', *Your Middle East*, 29 April 2013, www.yourmiddleeast.com/opinion/marc-owen-jones-bahrains-history-of-political-injustice_14064

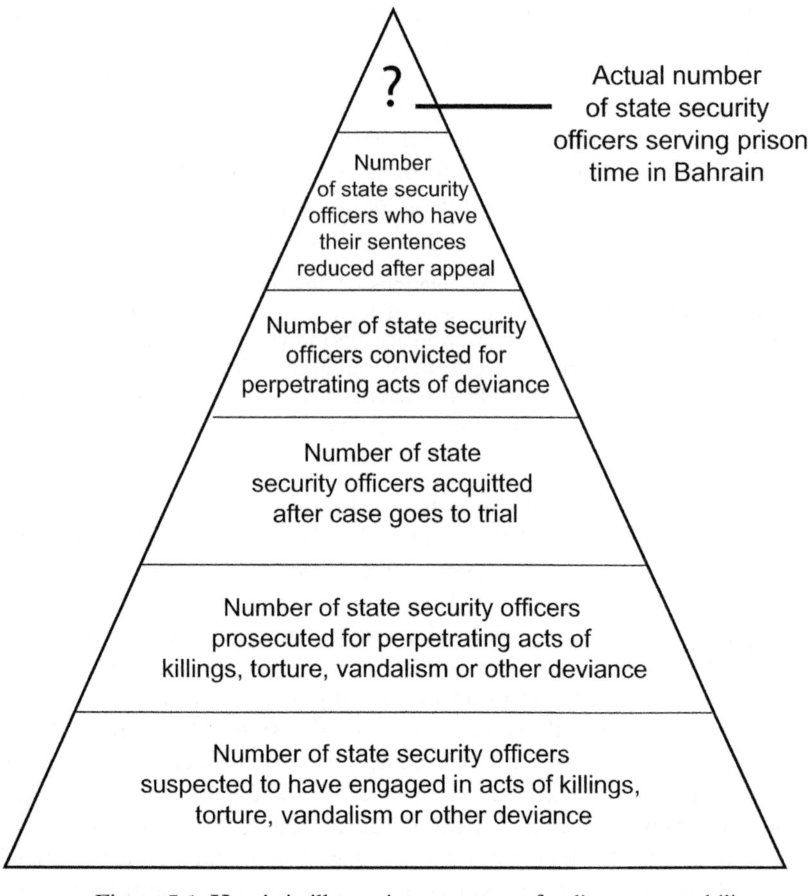

Figure 5.1 Heuristic illustrating structure of police accountability

the media that some form of transitional justice was necessary, he incurred so much Al Khalifa 'wrath' that he offered to resign.[238]

Impunity has been routinised in Bahrain's history, indicating the subservience of legal processes to power politics. While granting impunity may exacerbate conflict by promoting anger, it is secondary to ensuring that the morale and integrity of the security forces are maintained. In addition to the lack of accountability, those accused of political crimes have never properly acknowledged to have been innocent, meaning that the state maintains some degree of moral high ground by avoiding positioning itself as the guilty party in its perpetual conflict with society.

[238] Monroe, 'Bahraini Political Scene Part II'.

Al Khalifa Influence in Shielding Loyalists

It is interesting to note that the prime minister still plays a role in this impunity. Reflecting his commitment to his loyal constituency, a former US ambassador to Bahrain stated that 'the PM…is determined to demonstrate that the Al Khalifa remain loyal to those who faithfully serve the Al-Khalifas'.[239] Although these words by W. T. Monroe were uttered in 2007, they held true in the 2011 Uprising. A leaked video emerged in 2013 of the Bahraini prime minister meeting with Mubarak bin Huwayl, an exonerated security officer who had been accused of torture. In it, the prime minister demonstrated his continued commitment to protecting and rewarding those who most likely transgressed laws in order to protect the regime, saying;

> I am here to thank you, Mubarak, for your patience and good work. A human, as they say, is judged by his work, and your work as a family is the reason for your reputation, which is exemplary. A human is left with nothing but his reputation in life and death, and yours is a great one as a family. We are one family.[240]

The prime minister also mentioned to the gathered loyalists that they were above the law, saying 'These laws cannot be applied to you. No one can touch this bond. Whoever applies these laws against you is applying them against us. We are one body.'[241] Indeed, this pronouncement highlights both an absence of reformist influence in the legal apparatus but also the confidence of conservative members of the Al Khalifa in ensuring continued unaccountability.[242] It would not be an exaggeration to say that people such as the prime minister have played a pivotal role in ensuring the impunity of the security forces since the 1960s.

In addition to this high-level lenience for legal control agents, the government also sought to repress dissent and strengthen their position by raising the legal penalties for those engaging in attacks on the state's legal control agents. In 2012, Amendment 221 of Law no. 33 imposed stringent sentences on those who attacked or injured members of the security forces, even if it was done unintentionally.[243] Similarly, while Law 52 of 2012 also criminalized official use of violence such as torture, it excludes from accountability those who cause injury in the name of legal punishments or 'procedures'. This law could potentially be a get out

[239] Monroe, 'Future of Bahrain'.
[240] Khalifa bin Salman Al Khalifa, 'Prime Minister's Speech to Mubarak bin', www.youtube.com/watch?gl=GB&client=mv-google&hl=en&feature=plcp&v=YVundvyyNS8&nomobile=1, translated by the author.
[241] Ibid. [242] Jones, 'Rotten Apples'.
[243] Law Number 33 for the year 2012, Amendment to number 221 for the penal code decreed by the law 15 for the year 1976, www.legalaffairs.gov.bh/Media/LegalPDF/K3312.pdf

clause for those legal control agents accused of excessive force in the protection of the state.[244] As such, it gives the regime a stronger remit to engage in repression, for it does not clearly curtail the use of harsher methods of suppression, disincentivizing restraint by precluding legal control agents from sufficient accountability.

In addition to raising the penalties for those who attack the security services, laws have been introduced that criminalize those who incite hatred against the security forces, including the NSA, the police, the National Guard and the Bahrain Defence Force.[245] The government also increased the penalties for insulting the king, the country, the flag of Bahrain and the 'regime'.[246] By 2013, six people had been jailed for up to a year for allegedly insulting the king on the social-networking website Twitter.[247] In a worrying, yet unsurprising, event that highlighted Saudi's influence in Bahrain, the authorities arrested nine people on 23 January 2015 for making statements on social media that were deemed defamatory to the late King ʿAbd Allah of Saudi Arabia.[248] Thus the authorities have shut down the potential for legitimate criticism of the security apparatus, meaning that criticism of heavy-handedness is also grounds for arrest.

Societal Pressure and 'Legitimaters' of Repression

Repressive choices such as impunity are also necessary due to societal pressure, itself manufactured by the government's invocation of an exogenous threat. Just as the prime minister has been said to have been loyal to those who serve the Al Khalifa, a number of pro-government rallies held in support of the security forces were held between 2011 and 2013. In addition, groups have been established to pressure the government into protecting those policemen accused of abuses.[249] Following the outbreak of protests in 2011, groups from the mostly loyalist villages of al-Hidd and Busaiteen erected billboards around Bahrain depicting a noose with the slogan: 'We Demand from the Government the Maximum Punishment [No Pardon] for the heads of Fitna and the

[244] Law Number 52 of the year 2012, amendment to some of the penal code stipulated by Decree 15 from the year 1976. www.legalaffairs.gov.bh/Media/LegalPDF/K5212.pdf

[245] M. Al A'Ali, '20 years jailed backed for inciting hatred', *Gulf Daily News*, 30 April 2013, www.gulf-daily-news.com/NewsDetails.aspx?storyid=352350

[246] Amnesty International, *2014–15 Report Bahrain*, www.amnesty.org/en/countries/middle-east-and-north-africa/bahrain/report-bahrain/

[247] S. Yasin, 'The Cost of Tweeting in Bahrain', *Index on Censorship*, July 2013, www.indexoncensorship.org/2013/07/the-cost-of-tweeting-in-bahrain/

[248] Amnesty International, *Behind the Rhetoric: Human Rights Abuses Continue in Bahrain Unabated*, London, Amnesty International Publications, 2015.

[249] M. Al A'Ali, Group formed to help Policemen', *Gulf Daily News*, 1 January 2012, http://www.thefreelibrary.com/Group+formed+to+help+policemen.-a027611748

Misguided Elements'.[250] Such campaigns were validated by state media, who published sycophantic speeches by the likes of Dr ʿAbd al-Latif al-Mahmud, the head of the Gathering of National Unity, who demanded that those who carry out crimes against the state not be given amnesty.[251]

Thus, coercive violence by the state is endorsed by many who support the regime or internal state 'legitimaters'.[252] This is perhaps not surprising, as it is not uncommon 'for residents in places with endemic crime problems to adopt a "tough on crime" mentality. In such environments, there is more tolerance for what might ordinarily be termed police 'deviance'.[253] For this reason, 'police abuse does not stem simply from police authority alone, but also from a larger belief system shared by citizens in which brutality is acceptable as long as it is directed against "bad people".'[254] However, this argument attempts to legitimize deviant policing by invoking an element of consent, when, in actuality, the fear that allows people to exercise greater tolerance towards police deviance is constructed from the regime's exaggeration of the sectarian threat.[255] In Bahrain, tolerance of state violence has become increasingly high among loyalist elements in society, in part due to the state exaggeration of the danger posed by the opposition.

Demands for security from specific citizens can have an impact on police accountability, as holding accountable legal control agents runs the risk of angering those constituents on whom the regime rely for support. This is emphasized by the fact many of the local security forces are drawn from the country's Sunni communities, whose support for the ruling regime is often contingent on jobs provided in what is often colloquially referred to as *al-Amin (the security forces)*. The 2011 Uprising saw the emergence of conservative elements 'angry about even the government's limited steps to put the BICI report's suggestions into practice'.[256] In January 2012, the decision by the Court of Cassation to overturn the death sentences against two opposition activists who had been convicted by a military tribunal of killing two police officers sparked a furious protest from loyalists, prompting demonstrators to hang photographs of the spared men from a mock

[250] Gengler, 'Guilty by Billboard'.

[251] Bahrain News Agency, 'جلالة الملك يزور مجلسي ال محمود والمسلم بالحد ويحث على تعزيز اللحمة الوطنية التي تجمعنا كأسرة واحده متكاتفة ومترابطة' [His Majesty Visits the Majlises of al Mahmud and al Musallim in Hidd] 21 June 2011, http://bna.bh/portal/mobile/news/461875

[252] Lopez and Stohl, 'State Terrorism'. [253] Jones, 'Rotten Apples', p. 233.

[254] N. W. Pino and L. M. Johnson, 'Police Deviance and Community Relations in Trinidad and Tobago', *Policing: An International Journal of Police Strategies & Management*, vol. 34, no. 3, 2011, p. 459.

[255] Jones, 'Rotten Apples'.

[256] G. Carlstrom, 'In the Kingdom of Tear Gas', *MERIP Online*, 13 April 2012, www.merip.org/mero/mero041312?ip_login_no_cache=a560e0ddfd87c30e7b1e14c337e587ee

gallows.[257] It is, of course, difficult to determine how organic such protests are.

This bifurcation of justice was not confined simply to the country's political opposition demanding reform. In 2007, following the worldwide 'war on terror', the US Ambassador W. T. Monroe noted that the lack of prosecutions against loyalists in Bahrain was a 'reminder of the difficulty of actually prosecuting Sunni extremists in Bahrain'.[258] Monroe also noted that the rise of Iran and Al Qaeda, and the sharpening of the Middle East Cold War had highlighted the long-standing 'Bahraini reluctance to move against or alienate the Sunni Islamist community at a time of heightened concern about Iran and rising Shiʿa influence in the region'.[259] The policy of exacerbating ethnic tension and fragmenting opposition along sectarian and political lines has given the ruling regime more ability to exercise a policy of impunity and violent repression. Here the repressive legal capacity of the government is contingent on the extent to which it relies on ethnic polarization as a strategy of control. The more the regime adopts a policy of divide and conquer, the more the execution of justice is affected by politicization.

Conclusion

Austin Turk once wrote that 'the mandate to prevent radical changes in the distribution of power and privilege is incompatible with the idea of a legally or ethically limited effort to do so'.[260] While this may explain recourse to violence when legal controls fail to contain dissent, it does not account for the fact that 'legality' may, paradoxically, be both so parsimonious or so vague as to criminalize almost any activity, political or otherwise. Theoretically speaking, this work rejects the moral functionalist idea that law is simply a means of resolving problems, and adopts a critical perspective that emphasizes how law reflects the norms, values and interests of a ruling elite.[261] With significant interference from Britain and Saudi Arabia, the Bahraini government has frequently used laws, legal processes and legal deviance to repress dissent, facilitated by a repressive legal structure that primarily represents the interests of the Al Khalifa ruling core. Through a combination of emergency laws, political trials, regular laws, non-accountability and systemic legal bias, the Al Khalifa regime have sought to ameliorate dissent, both before and after its inception. While scholars on Latin America have noted military

[257] Ibid. [258] Monroe, 'Future of Bahrain'. [259] Ibid.
[260] Turk, 'Organizational Deviance and Political Policing', p. 241.
[261] Sellin, *Culture Conflict and Crime.*

dictators suspended 'judicial protection, due process and executive accountability'[262] during their period of rule; Bahrain has more or less existed in such a state for much of the twentieth and twenty-first centuries – only with varying levels of intensity.

Although Fuad Khuri argues that the British introduction of uniform laws curtailed the particularity of tribal law, particularism has re-emerged through the structures of the state. It is evidenced in the state's ability to produce laws that have the primary purpose of protecting the interests of the ruling elite. Whether this is achieved through decree, or through the ossification of punitive laws enacted through parliament, the legislative functions are suitably co-opted by the regime to ensure the protection of the status quo. Khuri too was perhaps too optimistic when he asserted how the trial of the Khalids in the 1920s represented the establishment of public over private law.[263] His argument assumes a clear binary between a pre-modern period and a period of modernity. No such distinction can be that clear-cut. The authorities have subverted the law in the interests of protecting their position of power. In times of political crisis, such laws have proliferated and remained pervasive, preserving in law palimpsests of Bahrain's past crises.

In its most modern guise, the Al Khalifa government and a loyalist parliament demonstrate the permeation of tribal structures through parliamentary institutions. The inability of opposition movements to truly formulate legislation means that the legal framework offers many segments of society no safeguard from an 'arbitrary state'.[264] Where legal controls fail to contain or constrain social movement activity before its inception, the system in Bahrain is manipulated in order that social control objectives take precedent. Indeed, the legal order is broken to save the social order.[265] As Austin Turk stated, law is a form of power, one that can be used as a weapon in social conflict, generating and exacerbating conflicts rather than resolving them.[266]

262 Fagen, 'Repression and State Security', p. 48.

263 The myth that the Khalids (or Khawalid) were deported has been propagated as recently as 2013. For example Charles Levinson of the *Wall Street Journal* wrote an article stating that the deportation of the Khawalid in 1923 had left a wound that festered for decades.

264 L. Kalmanowiecki, 'Origins and Applications of Political Policing in Argentina', *Latin American Perspectives*, vol. 27, no. 2, Violence, Coercion and Rights in the Americas, 2000, p. 37.

265 G. Agamben, *State of Exception*, Translated by Kevin Attell, Chicago, University of Chicago Press, 2005, p. 26.

266 A. Turk, 'Law as a Weapon in Social Conflict', *Social Problems*, vol. 23, no. 3, 1976, p. 276.

6 Information Controls

From Surveillance to Social Media and Fake News

All expressions of political thought are regarded as subversive[1]

From the humble political pamphlet, to social media, the control and regulation of information have formed an integral part of repression in Bahrain over the past hundred years. New technologies pose new challenges, and modernization has necessitated ever more extensive measures of allowing the state to interfere in the informational sphere. This has primarily taken the form of censorship, propaganda and surveillance. These broad terms cover a myriad of complex intersecting forms of information control, perpetrated largely by the security forces and various media and PR outlets.

Much of this chapter focuses on the evolution of the media in Bahrain, which has been a key instrument of repression, particularly since the 1950s. While globalization and the increasing liberalization of the press have resulted in difficulties in controlling the flow of information, elite strategies to throttle the media or shape the message have also bolstered narratives designed to stigmatize and demonize resistance. With the rise of Saudi Arabia, and its bolstering of tyranny in the region,[2] coupled with at times specious fears of Iranian expansionism, there has been a growing demonization and stigmatization of Bahrain's Shiʿa in the press. The traditional media have undertaken efforts to frame protesters as violent revolutionaries beholden to outside power or Shiʿa religious zealots. Whether on television, or in newspapers, traditional media usually attempts to hide certain narratives while promoting those desired by the state.

In general, over the course of the twentieth century, the ruling core, and the constituency on which they depend for some legitimacy, have

[1] J. P. Tripp, Communique 16 April 1963, FO1016/684, The National Archives.

[2] G. Greenwald, 'The US Alongside Saudi Arabia Fights for Freedom and Democracy in the Middle East', *The Guardian,* 12 January 2013, www.theguardian.com/commentisfree/2013/jan/12/us-saudi-arabia-libya-freedom

adapted to technological developments. Indeed, they have been adept at utilizing technologies to extend the state's surveillance and informational control abilities, making the process of repression more rhizomatic in the information realm.[3] While the advent of social media poses new challenges for authoritarian regimes, these challenges have been met with repressive solutions that problematize the democratizing and liberalizing potential of technology. Like all forms of repression documented in this book, it is important to acknowledge the increasingly collaborative effort between various external powers and the Bahrain regime in enacting information control. In particular, this chapter notes the increasing outsourcing of propaganda and surveillance strategies to opaque actors – from British public relations companies to Silicon Valley itself. It is perhaps more useful to see repression here as a good example not simply of state action but as the result of an assemblage between states, elites, and private corporations.

Censorship and Insulation

Insulation

Limiting the availability of information and knowledge likely to be critical of or that foster criticism of regimes is perhaps the most basic level of information control. If one can control access to what people know, one can, in theory, educate a polity to be acquiescent, docile and amenable to the desires of the status quo. In the early half of the twentieth century, the British, ever sensitive of their treaty obligations to Bahrain and 'stability' in the Gulf, were cautious about external ideas or criticism provoking disturbances in Bahrain. In the 1920s, they feared Bolshevik propaganda, while through the 1930s, 1940s and 1950s it was independence movements in India or Arab nationalist movements. Consequently, throughout the twentieth and twenty-first centuries, editors or publications thought to be critical of Bahrain's protecting powers Britain, Saudi or the Al Khalifa have often been censored, highlighting the importance of British and Saudi sensitivity with regard to the information sphere.

Censorship was used early on in the reforms of the 1920s to stymie the flow of ideas and information to those groups that may have exerted pressure or provided support to potential agitators in Bahrain. Although Bahrain did not have much in the way of a press at this time, efforts were made to curtail the availability of what the British saw as dangerous publications from neighbouring Arab countries. Press attacks on the

[3] 'Rhizomatic' here is in the Deleuzian sense and refers to increasingly horizontal, bottom-up forms of control in which citizens begin to take charge of surveillance.

British were often stirred up by certain members of the Al Khalifa, such as ʿAbd Allah bin ʿIsa, the ruler's brother, who was trying to undermine British interference in the 1920s. As early as 1922, ʿAbd Allah was reportedly paying the Persian and Arab press huge sums of money to stoke up what officials described as anti-British propaganda.[4,5] Charles Belgrave was particularly irked by any unfavourable coverage and resorted to bribery in at least one case to prevent criticism. Writing in 1927, Belgrave noted:

> Then [I] interviewed a Syrian journalist. They have a system which is very like blackmail, they come to places like this & demand subscriptions & if not heavily bribed they write abusive articles about people. Squared him with Rs 300/– he asked for more having first produced a most fulsome article all about Barrett & myself – the two people from whom he expected to get money[6]

For those not lucky enough to be bribed, a different approach was used. Aspiring journalists living in Bahrain who engaged in writing anti-British articles were subject to harsh treatment. At one point, the Political Agent Alban had deported one Khalid bin Faraj for writing 'violently' anti-British op-eds in Cairo Papers.[7] Alban was inclined to view everyone as anti-British, and at one point Belgrave worried that Alban would resort to 'wholesale deportations'. However, as was frequently the case during Britain's attempts to exert their hegemony, Alban's actions were frustrated by Shaykh ʿIsa, who sent Bin Faraj a letter saying that he could return. Much to Belgrave's chagrin, the Political Agent Barrett did not pressure for the Shaykh to undo this decision, and Belgrave stated that he [Barrett] was as weak as the Shaykh.[8] Such episodes highlighted not only a tension between factions of the Al Khalifa and the British about repressive choices but even within the ranks of the British officials, who had differing views on how to deal with dissent, especially when it came to challenging the authority of the ruling family.

Problems of enforcing censorship were compounded by a lack of transparency on what constituted the limits of acceptable speech. As was often the case in Bahrain, the advent of British intervention had disrupted existing norms of public behaviour. Consequently, the British administration decided it was better to issue formal boundaries

[4] 'Administration Reports 1920–1924' [119r] (242/412), British Library: India Office Records and Private Papers, IOR/R/15/1/713, in *Qatar Digital Library* www.qdl.qa/en/archive/81055/vdc_100023385511.0x00002b

[5] 'Administration Reports 1920–1924' [159r] (322/412), British Library: India Office Records and Private Papers, IOR/R/15/1/713, in *Qatar Digital Library* www.qdl.qa/en/archive/81055/vdc_100023385511.0x00007b

[6] Belgrave, Papers, 28 December 1927. [7] Ibid., 4 January 1929. [8] Ibid.

concerning regulating the flow of information, and particularly criticism. Charles Belgrave, in his far-reaching role as 'adviser', was concerned about any anti-British propaganda in Arab, Iraqi and Iranian newspapers. In order to counter it, insulation measures were taken in 1933, and foreign journalists were required to obtain visas[9] before entering Bahrain. Belgrave claimed that this measure helped decrease propaganda in Bahrain.[10] In 1936, Charles Belgrave signed off the correspondents and newspapers proclamation (law). This stipulated that anyone writing in a newspaper, whether they were Bahraini or not, had to register their names with the government. Failure to do so could result in a 2,000 rupee fine or a spell of six months in prison. Given the relatively sparse numbers of laws and ordinances at the time, it is quite striking that Belgrave sought to focus his attention on the media. Indeed, it highlights the importance with which he viewed potential propaganda.

Despite the existence of this law, it is not clear how successful many journalists were in actually entering Bahrain. According to Major Little, there had been a complete ban on the British press entering Bahrain before the 1956 riots, and Charles Belgrave (the ruler's adviser) had been the local correspondent for *The Times*. Whether there had been a complete ban on the British press is unclear, although Belgrave does mention in his diary that he entertained British journalists. One example includes a reporter called Hodgkin,[11] and James Morris, the *Times* correspondent for Cairo.[12] As well as contributing occasional pieces for the *Times*, Charles Belgrave was very keen to keep the press onside and fostered a relationship with various *Times* personnel. On holiday back to the UK, Belgrave invited a man he called Norman, who was the new foreign editor at the *Times*, for lunch.[13] This effective embedding of Charles Belgrave as the chief voice of progress in Bahrain undoubtedly shaped the world's perception of the country.

The British desire to keep press coverage favourable was particularly evident during the rise of the HEC in the 1950s. Political Resident Bernard Burrows was keen that any publicity of the trial of the St Helena three in 'the *Times* and the Associated Press should focus on the convictions, and that their removal from here and detention in a British possession should obtain as little publicity as possible'.[14] Subsequent reporting

[9] Belgrave, Annual Report for the Year 1352 (1933–4), p. 393. [10] Ibid., p. 489.
[11] Belgrave, Papers, 2 November 1954. [12] Belgrave, Papers, 12 December 1955.
[13] Belgrave, Papers, 6 September 1955.
[14] B. A. B. Burrows, Secret to Foreign Office, 15 December 1956, in A. Burdett (ed.), *Records of Bahrain 1820–1960*, vol. 7, Slough, Archive Editions, 1993, p. 303.

of the trial in January in the London *Times* was perfunctory, although it stated that it was the Bahraini rulers who asked the British for 'assistance'. This was no doubt to detract from the significant role the British had played in the deportation.

The lack of criticism of British policy in international media outlets during the 1950s can largely be explained by this ban on the press. Notwithstanding, the British administration in London was quick to intervene in any criticism of Bahrain. In 1957 Major William Little, a former employee of the Bahrain State Police circulated a pamphlet among British members of Parliament entitled 'Memorandum on Bahrain and Related Problems'.[15] The document offered a highly critical assessment of how the British and Bahrain authorities handled the 1954–56 crisis and included scathing accounts of British officers in the Bahrain Police. The Foreign Office described the pamphlet as 'scurrilous and tendentious',[16] and debated how to prevent the further circulation of the pamphlet. They certainly made no effort to investigate Little's serious claims. Instead, they considered getting those mentioned in the pamphlet to issue a writ for libel in the hope that it would discourage Little from further propagation. At the same time, however, the Foreign Office worried that if a libel case were pursued, it might give rise to 'undesirable publicity and might well encourage a further spate of Parliamentary Questions'.[17] In the end, Little was 'exposed' and dismissed from his job at the Joint Intelligence Bureau in the UK after he, and another former employee of the Bahrain State Police, Captain Hills, were caught taking and copying documents about Oman. It is not clear what the documents detailed. Despite Bahrain only being a British protectorate, the British were keen to mitigate any criticism of the government or the ruling family and the police, especially so after the unwelcome intervention by British forces in 1956.

In 1955, in order to further the government's monopoly on distributing information, the country's newly established press was targeted. In the context of the Cold War, anything left-leaning or sympathetic to Arab nationalism was viewed by the authorities with alarm. The two major local newspapers, *Sawt al-Bahrain* (Voice of Bahrain) and *Al-Qafilah* (The Caravan), were suspended because they made 'offensive remarks about neighbouring friendly states'.[18] Indeed, the editor of the former

[15] W. O. Little, 'Report by Major Little', in *Pamphlet on Bahrain*, 1957, FO371/126918, The National Archives.

[16] Foreign Office, 1957, FO371/126918, The National Archives. [17] Ibid.

[18] C. Belgrave, Annual Report for the Year 1955, in *Bahrain Government Annual Reports 1924–1970*, vol. 5, Gerrards Cross, Archive Editions, 1986, p. 3.

was 'Abd al-Rahman al-Bakir, one of the eight leaders of the HEC. Al-Bakir had his nationality temporarily revoked by the ruler in 1954.[19] Far from having a pacifying impact on the opposition, Khuri argues that this punishment gave many Sunna an 'immediate and personal grievance comparable to those enjoyed by the Shi'a. This had a mobilising effect, prompting more Sunna to be involved in HEC meetings'.[20] The Bahrain government obviously believed the merits of censorship and punishment of editors outweighed the costs. Consequently, in 1956, the Bahrain government banned the nationalistic newspaper *Al-Watan* [The Nation] for its anti-Saudi and anti-British editorial stance. *Al-Shu'lah* [The Flame], a rebranded version of *Al-Watan,*[21] was also banned a month afterwards for its criticism of Iraq and the information section of the British administration (and the British in general. The news editor of the Bahrain wireless news bulletins was also removed because his views reportedly tended to 'present the Egyptian view to the exclusion of others'.[22,23] In 1956, Charles Belgrave personally spoke to the 'Censor' of a local paper after some controversial headlines were published.[24] In short, newspapers in Bahrain were closed down almost as soon as they were started.

It is interesting to note that despite this rampant censorship during the 1950s, the British had encouraged the setting up of Bahrain's first newspaper (*Al Bahrain*) in 1939. However, its chief purpose was as a vehicle for Allied war propaganda.[25] Again, crisis necessitated a means of controlling the message. During the 1950s the British began again to see the value of the press as a means of spreading pro-government propaganda to counter the adept strategies of Arab nationalists in Egypt and Kuwait who were using wireless technologies to foment support. Such publications would be conducive to aligning local interests with the foreign policy objectives of the British. The British also thought that the press would be a means for Bahrainis to blow off steam through the outlet of moderate opinion.

Bernard Burrows suggested that an independent newspaper be set up, arguing that this would be complemented by an information office and the Bahrain Government Public Relations Office. Combined, these would make it easier to 'guide' without resorting 'to censorship and

[19] Wall, Letter to Political Resident in Gulf, p. 71. [20] Ibid.
[21] Anon., 6 September 1956, FO371/120548, The National Archives. [22] Ibid.
[23] For a complete history of Bahrain's Print and Broadcast Media, see E. M. H. Al-Rumaihi, 'The Development of Mass Media in the Kingdom of Bahrain', PhD Thesis, University Exeter, 2002.
[24] Belgrave, 18 April 1956. [25] Al-Rumaihi, p. 355.

suppression'.[26] This attitude reflected a growing realization that if information could not be stopped, it should at least be controlled. However, the Bahrain authorities erred too much on the side of caution. In 1956, the new criminal code contained an article designed to tackle the publication of inflammatory pamphlets and circulars that were issued by the HEC. While the HEC objected to the law, Belgrave thought that the laws, which prescribed what could be written, signified the abolition of censorship.[27] The 1950s were instrumental in the development of information control strategies in Bahrain, as the rise of mass media and wireless technologies posed new problems for the British, whose presence in the Middle East provoked the ire of anti-colonial Arab nationalists. Stymying the press was not always straightforward. The strength of the HEC in Bahrain highlighted the limited efficacy of simply trying to repress newspapers.

Indeed, the papers commanded a wide readership and advocated governmental reform, unionization and the improvement of living and labour conditions. As such, they were seen as inherently subversive by both the British and the Al Khalifa. In many ways, this continued censorship may have generated more discontent, especially among fringe groups. Major Little claimed in his pamphlet that the information control strategies failed to guide the beliefs of dissenters as Bernard Burrows had intended. Instead, Little argued, the repression of the local media prevented the 'emergence of moderate opinion' and that the Bahrain radio station was ineffective against Egyptian propaganda. In short, the Bahrain government had failed to create a credible alternative to foreign news outlets.

While the 1950s were characterized by a somewhat ambivalent and experimental attitude towards the press, the 1960s saw the further legislation of censorship. The British administration once again thought it necessary to create media to combat external propaganda. However, it was difficult to balance both the regime's security while maintaining the credibility of the media. Yet it appears that the more conservative elements won the debate. Certainly in the eyes of British officials, some members of the Al Khalifa family were particularly hostile to a relatively free press. In 1960, William Lyall noted how the ruler 'obstinately refused to allow the broadcast of any subject of a controversial nature'.[28] Similarly, in 1963, the British political agent noted that the ruling

[26] B. A. B. Burrows, 5 March 1955, in A. Burdett (ed.), *Records of Bahrain 1820–1960*, vol. 7, Slough, Archive Editions, 1993, p. 129.

[27] Belgrave, Papers, 20 May 1956.

[28] W. C. Lyall, 22 October 1960, FO1016/684, The National Archives.

family's attitude was entirely security-orientated, and for this reason allowed no newspapers.[29] Indeed, Peter Tripp stated in 1963 that all 'expressions of political thought were regarded as subversive'[30] by the ruler. Despite this, the British seemed oblivious to their own seemingly visceral fear of anti-communist propaganda. In 1960, when a British official saw a man reading the Indian left-leaning publication *the Blitz*, he wrote a missive suggesting that such material be banned.[31]

Regardless of divergent sensibilities, the triumph of conservative voices in the media debate was reflected in the further legislation of censorship. In 1960, the law regulating recitals, concerts and plays meant that anyone wishing to perform or host such a performance must first obtain written permission from the authorities. The law was specifically created to tackle the perceived politicization of the country's various clubs and societies, which provided important venues for discussing current affairs and politics. The law imposed a month-long prison sentence or 200 rupee fine (or both) for those who contravened it. Soon after, in 1965, Bahrain's formalized publication law came into effect.[32] The law offered formal legal control that limited who and what could be published. Among its stipulations was that no one writing in a newspaper could insult any ruling figure or anyone in the ruling family unless they had secured their permission. The law was also thorough and far-reaching, and 'newspaper' was deemed to be any magazine, paper, newsletter or circular issued in Bahrain. Indeed, it was so broad that any conceivable medium was subject to the laws. Also, to instigate regime change, whether through advocating violence or other means, became illegal, further limiting the opportunities for expressing discontent with the constitutional makeup of the country. Furthermore, the law stipulated that those who wished to own a newspaper or become its editor must have a 'good reputation'. Such subjective prerequisites naturally precluded those who may have been seen as a threat to the existing regime and allowed the judgement of good reputation to be determined by the British and Al Khalifa-dominated government institutions.

In practice, the publication law and the law on public performances and plays also limited access to material that could potentially encourage dissent. This was true not just of newspapers but all cultural production. Books or publications that were critical of, or embarrassing about, the

[29] J. P. Tripp, 18 April 1963, FO1016/684, The National Archives.
[30] Tripp, Communique, 16 April 1963, FO1016/684, The National Archives.
[31] Confidential, 11 July 1960, FO1016/684, The National Archives.
[32] Publication Law of 1965, www.legalaffairs.gov.bh/AdvancedSearchDetails.aspx?id=2184#.Us_OsvRdWwt

Al Khalifa were banned. This includes most histories, including Khuri's *Tribe and State in Bahrain*, and the papers of Charles Belgrave.[33] Many of these contain references to the Al Khalifa's oppression of the indigenous population, an aspect of history that has been replaced by a discourse that seeks to position the Al Khalifa as the liberators of Bahrain. This discourse is often problematic. For example, King Hamad mentioned in 2012 that both Shi'a and Sunna had come from Zubara together to drive the Persians out of Bahrain.[34] There is no evidence that this actually happened.

Despite Hamad's words, *baḥārna* and Shi'a culture are marginalized in Bahrain's historical and cultural output. TV shows produced by Bahrain's national television are mainly made in Sunni dialect, marginalizing the *baḥrānī* dialect almost completely.[35] The National Museum of Bahrain tends to promote the history of Bahrain's Sunni-dominated pearl industry and pre-Islamic civilization of the Dilmun to the almost complete exclusion of the 'Ajam and the *baḥārna*, the latter of whom mostly formed a settled agricultural class. As Amal Khalaf notes, the state-controlled image economy emphasizes the ruling family and therefore privileges Sunni Muslims or those loyal to the ruling tribe.[36] Thus political repression extends as far as attempting to remove potential deviant identities from the Al Khalifa's perception of the national fabric. The marginalization of particular Shi'a or *baḥrānī* voices, abetted implicitly by censorship laws, from Bahrain's media and cultural fabric has undermined the king's attempt to project the regime as tolerant and exclusive and perhaps served to strengthen this native identity.[37] With regard to repression, it has merely served to strengthen oppositional grievances and undermine the support of fellow citizens who are denied access to alternative and inclusive understandings of Bahrain's history.

Return to Hardline Influence on Censorship

If the sixties were characterized by a paranoia of the press induced by a turbulent period in the 1950s, Bahrain's brief democratic experiment in

[33] Cited in J. Gengler, *Ethnic Conflict*, p. 56.

[34] الملك: كنا معاً منذ تواجدنا في الزبارة سنة وشيعة وأتينا البحرين معاً [The King: We were together since Zubara, Sunni and Shia, and we came together to Bahrain] www.alwasatnews.com/news/636387.html?utm_source=Direct

[35] C. Holes, 'Dialect and National Identity: The Cultural Politics of Self-Representation in Bahrain Musalsalat', in P. Dresch and J. Piscatori (eds), *Monarchies and Nations: Globalization and Identity in the Arab States of the Gulf*, London, I. B. Tauris, 2005.

[36] A. Khalaf, 'The Many Afterlives of Lulue', Ibraaz, 28 February 2013, www.ibraaz.org/essays/56

[37] Cited in J. Gengler, *Ethnic Conflict*, p. 56.

the 1970s was accompanied by a more relaxed attitude to the media. Indeed, the ruling family's attempts to build legitimacy through political liberalization following the departure of their protectors necessitated this. British Ambassador Robert Tesh noted that 'criticism of the government in a reasonably polite way was pretty free'.[38] While it is not entirely clear what 'reasonably polite' meant, Tesh still described Bahrain's media establishment as a 'puppet press'.[39] Opposition groups such as the Marxists, who were democratically represented in parliament at the time, were still denied permission to open a newspaper.[40]

Post-Independence, as Bahrain tilted further into the political influence of its neighbour's orbit, criticism of Saudi Arabia, or indeed other friendly nations in the Gulf, was penalized heavily. For example, in 1975, a local paper was suspended for a month after it published comments critical of Saudi Arabia that were made by a visiting official from the People's Democratic Republic of Yemen.[41] The stringent censorship resumed after the demise of parliament. One Ibrahim Muhammad Bashmi was imprisoned by the regime in 1975 for being the editor of a paper that published an article that contravened the 1955 Penal Code and the 1965 Press Ordinance.[42] Indeed, without parliament, and with conservative Saudi Arabia filling the vacuum left by the British, Bahrain's press became an increasingly barren wasteland.

Censorship and scrutiny by the international press were particularly acute during times of political upheaval. The *Guardian* journalist David Hirst was prevented from entering Bahrain to cover the trial of those accused of plotting a coup on the pretext he had not given advanced notice. Similarly, Amnesty International observers were allowed into Bahrain, but they were not allowed to enter the courtroom.[43] The diverging sensibilities on censorship between the British and the Al Khalifa were still evident in 1982. British officials, who were now firmly of the opinion that the Al Khalifa's attitude to censorship was 'shortsighted',[44] said that the Bahraini authorities should be encouraging the press and Amnesty to cover it,[45] in order to remove plausible suspicion that the trial was a kangaroo court. Such transparency would prevent the Shiʿa from using what the British official Wogan once described as their

[38] R. M. Tesh, 'Bahrain Internal', 1 March 1975, FCO8/2415, The National Archives.
[39] Ibid. [40] Ibid. [41] Tesh, Bahrain Internal, 4 March 1975, The National Archives.
[42] Amnesty Report Clipping, FCO8/3893, The National Archives.
[43] P. F. M. Wogan, Bahrain Coup: Trial of Detainees, 16 March 1982, FCO8/4332, The National Archives.
[44] W. R. Tomkys, The December Coup, 21 March 1982, FCO8/4332, The National Archives.
[45] Wogan, Bahrain Coup: Trial of Detainees, The National Archives.

'predilection for martyrdom' to 'weave an effective political and religious mythology' out of any mishandling.[46] Indeed, the coverage of the IFLB trial was minimal, and David Hirst noted that the local newspapers were 'as insubstantial as their headlines [were] bold',[47] and that not even the head of Bahrain's state television could get access. Roger Tomkys noted that news of the trial was heavily filtered and that all the press got their information from a 'Ministry of Information handout'.[48]

The British believed that the reason for this stringent censorship policy was due to the direct influence of the prime minister. Indeed, Roger Tomkys was explicit; 'all concerned thought the Prime Minister was responsible for this policy'.[49] Such minimal press coverage was usual on issues related to political mobilization. The extent of the prime mnister's micromanagement of press affairs was also evident in his interest in union elections. After the formation of joint labour committees tasked with easing labour disputes, the government instructed the press to keep the coverage of committee elections as 'low-key' as possible.[50] No doubt this was to prevent any controversy that could lead to unrest. Indeed, by the onset of 1985, the Ministry of Information's control of the media actually exceeded that stipulated in the press laws.[51] By this time, editors and journalists had already learned what they could and could not get away with, indicating that a culture of 'self' censorship had emerged.

A draconian attitude to censorship continued into the 1990s. During the Intifada, Amnesty International complained that the government resorted to several tactics to prevent information[52] from being released that could have aided social movements in their attempts to lobby local and international actors to pressure the government. The rise of more

[46] Ibid.
[47] D. Hirst, 'Putting the Gulf's Resistance on Trial', *The Guardian*, 15 March 1982.
[48] Tomkys, Trial of Detainees, The National Archives.
[49] Tomkys, The December Coup, The National Archives.
[50] Collis, Bahrain Labour, The National Archives.
[51] P. R. Ivey, Political Expression in Bahrain, 7 July 1985, FCO8/5817, The National Archives.
[52] Article 5(4) of Amiri Decree No. 7 of 1976 stipulates that sessions of the State Security Court shall be public unless it is deemed necessary to hold them 'out of consideration for public order, public security or the higher interests of the state'. The same article stipulates that sentencing shall be pronounced in public session. In practice, sessions are always held, attended only by members of the courts' bench, the defendants, defence lawyers and representatives of the Public Prosecution. Relatives of the defendants as well as independent observers and the media are barred from attendance. Sentencing also takes place in closed session. Such in-camera proceedings are inconsistent with the right to a public trial guaranteed by Article 10 of the UDHR and Article 14(1) of the ICCPR. Amnesty International, 'Bahrain: A Human Rights Crisis'.

newsworthy and egregious incidents also meant more stringent control of information. The absence of any independent local news sources also meant an inability to corroborate government narratives.

Nonetheless, the Bahraini government remained committed to censoring local organizations. On 4 April 1995, one of the state-controlled daily newspapers, *al-Ayam*, published a statement issued by the then Minister of Information Tareq al-Mu'ayyed, highlighting the government's fear of negative press going outside Bahrain. The statement said that the 'ministry wishes to draw attention to the fact that no citizen is permitted to transmit news abroad without obtaining authorisation from the ministry'.[53] Those that did so would be liable for legal action, according to Human Rights Watch.[54] Although the threat of legal action had, according to Amnesty International, no basis in law since no decree had been issued, 'a number of people were summoned by government officials and reportedly told to refrain from giving interviews to the media and transmitting information abroad on the situation in Bahrain'.[55] A Saudi hand in determining press policy was evident when both the 'editor of the newspaper and the minister of information separately warned' a Bahraini journalist 'that Saudi officials had complained about the reporter's articles'.[56] As had become the norm since the 1980s, verbal warnings issued by the Ministry of Information with no basis in law, ones that often exceeded written laws, set the boundaries for press freedom.

Hiding Brutality

The government's fear of Bahrain obtaining a negative image was highlighted with their treatment of casualties or victims of police brutality. As police brutality can be a potent mobilizing element for most social movements, it was strategically necessary that victims had to be carefully hidden (sometimes it is also necessary to publicize police brutality). In the 1990s, these victims were frequently sequestered away so that the visibility of their injuries or testimonies remained hidden. Often, they were secretly transferred to Bahrain's Military Hospital, where their identity was better hidden as Bahrain's military lies closely under regime control. The sequestering of victims allowed the government to claim that people were 'fabricating' evidence or injuries, further adding to the stigmatization of social movements.

[53] Human Rights Watch, *Routine Abuse.* [54] Ibid.
[55] Amnesty International, *Bahrain: A Human Rights Crisis.*
[56] Human Rights Watch, *Routine Abuse.*

The government also sought to punish those facilitating outflows of information that could damage Bahrain's international reputation and thus lead to pressure for leniency against the opposition. The reaction of the government to people attempting to assist journalists also marked new heights for punitive dissuasion. In the 1990s, at least three residents of Bahrain, two of whom were Bahraini (one was Omani), were arrested and interrogated for acting as a fixer for BBC Middle East correspondent Martin Ingram and BBC Television Reporter Sue Lloyd Roberts.[57] Similarly, in the 2011 Uprising, medics were targeted, probably due to their credibility as witnesses combined with their proximity to the victims of state violence. Dr 'Ali al-Akri, one of many medics to be arrested, tortured and prosecuted by the government, claimed they did it because the medics were witnesses to the atrocities.[58] A number of them also gave interviews to international media, a perennial sticking point for the Bahrain authorities.

Censoring Civil Society Post-2001

Even after the reforms of 2001, which were meant to herald a new era of press freedom, six of Bahrain's seven daily newspapers remained 'either pro-government or owned by figures affiliated with the royal family'.[59] In 2011, these newspapers were *Al Ayam, Gulf Daily News, Bahrain Tribune, Akhbar Al Khaleej, Al Watan, Al Ayam* and *Al Wasat.* Attempts by opposition forces to provide balance, apart from through non-official means, such as social media, have been stymied by the government's refusal to issue newspaper and television licenses to opposition groups such as Al Wefaq.[60] In 2015 Bahrain pulled the plug on Saudi Prince Alwaleed bin Talal -al Saud's television channel *Alarab* within 24 hours of its first broadcast, reportedly because it aired an interview with a senior member of the opposition group Al Wefaq.[61] Again, the government did not wish to provide a platform for the opposition, and especially not for the Shiʿa.

This generally draconian attitude to censorship can, in part, be explained by conservativism within the ruling family. Both recently and historically, media and informational strategies have come further under

57 Ibid.

58 M. Chulov, 'Bahrain doctors await the call that will send them to prison', *The Guardian*, 30 September 2011, www.theguardian.com/world/2011/sep/30/bahrain-doctors-prison-uprising

59 POMED, 'One Year Later: Assessing Bahrain;s Implementations of the BICI Report', November 2012, http://pomed.org/wp-content/uploads/2013/12/One-Year-Later-Assessing-Bahrains-Implementation-of-the-BICI-Report.pdf

60 Ibid.

61 S. Kerr, 'Bahrain Pulls Plug on Saudi Media Tycoon's TV Station', *Financial Times*, 20 February 2015.

the control of hawkish members of the Al Khalifa, many with allegedly anti-Shiʿa viewpoints, such as the Khawalid. A former US Ambassador to Bahrain once expanded on the role of conservative shaykhs in the press, noting, for example, that 'royal court elements' had a 'direct hand in a scathing press campaign launched by Arabic daily *Al Watan* against NDI, the National Democratic Institute, other NGOs, and even the U.S. Embassy'.[62] The newspaper *Al Watan*, in particular, is noted for its close ties to the royal court.[63] Paradoxically, it was the reforms of 2001 and Hamad's rise to power that empowered anti-Shiʿa hardliners like the Khawalid, who have continued to maintain a tight grip on informational control strategies. After the 2011 Unrest, renewed efforts of censorship appeared to be driven forward by Saudi Arabia. A leaked cable from the then Saudi Foreign Minister Saud bin Faisal bin Abdulaziz Al Saud indicated that the 2011 Unrest prompted Saudi Arabia to ask Bahrain for co-operation between its media agencies to adopt strategies to counter what it claimed were efforts by foreign agencies to attack the reputation of Bahrain and Saudi Arabia.[64] Subsequent reports leaked from the latter indicate that such agencies inevitably meant Iranian press channels. As such, the 2011 Uprising prompted a mutual desire to counter opposition media strategies, a tactic that undoubtedly resulted in the proliferation of anti-Iranian and anti-Shiʿa media coverage/propaganda. Other leaked documents from the Saudi Foreign Ministry show the increasing overreach by Saudi Arabia in determining what should or should not be shown on TV in Bahrain and on regional satellite channels. Writing in the *New York Times*, Ben Hubbard and May El Sheikh noted:

> From 2010 to 2013, [Saudi Arabia] tried to force an Iranian Arabic-language satellite television station, Al Alam, off the air. These efforts included issuing royal decrees aimed at stopping the broadcast, pressuring the Riyadh-based satellite provider Arabsat to drop the channel, and using "technical means" to weaken the channel's signal, so it did not reach Bahrain and eastern Saudi Arabia, where Shiites complain of discrimination by their Sunni monarchs. A Beirut-based manager of Al Alam acknowledged that the channel had faced Saudi pressure since 2010, which had succeeded in getting two Arab satellite providers to drop the channel.[65]

[62] Monroe, 'Bahraini Political Scene Part II'.

[63] W. T. Monroe, 'Government Committees Warn Newspapers about Anti Regime Coverage, 21 June 2006, https://wikileaks.org/plusd/cables/06MANAMA1116_a.html

[64] F. Al Saud, 'Secret and Urgent', Kingdom of Saudi Arabia Ministry of Foreign Affairs, 2011–2012 (1433 Hijra), Wikileaks, https://wikileaks.org/saudi-cables/doc46685.html [Arabic]

[65] B. Hubbard and M. El Sheikh, 'Wikileaks Shows a Saudi Obsession with Iran', 16 July 2015, www.nytimes.com/2015/07/17/world/middleeast/wikileaks-saudi-arabia-iran.html

While the denial of access to journalists as a form of censorship started under Belgrave, the proliferation of news outlets has resulted in a vast increase of such access prohibitions. The NGO Bahrain Watch added that 'Methods of access denial include: denial of visa, refusal at a port of entry, changing regulations to prohibit planned visits, deportation, and blacklists'.[66] Between 14 February 2011 and the end of November of the same year, there were at least 221 instances 'where a foreign journalist, NGO member, politician, trade unionist, aid worker, or activist was denied access to Bahrain, alone or as part of a group. This total included representatives from at least 17 NGOs and 22 media organisations.…Access denials to Bahrain increased from 2011 to 2012: of the 221 cases of access denial, 74 were in 2011, and 147 were in 2012.'[67] In 2013, three journalists from the British broadcaster Channel 4 were deported after attempting to film protests while in Bahrain. Officially, they had been granted a visa only to cover the Formula One Grand Prix.[68] The denial of an organization whose access could facilitate and support the work of opposition social movements severely represses the abilities of those organizations to garner regional and international support. The larger the scale of abuses, the more profound the censorship. Numerous journalists have also reported that even the advent of Google has facilitated the ability of border control agents in Bahrain to deny entry. There have been a number of accounts whereby those suspected of being representatives of the media or a human rights organization have been taken aside at the airport while senior officials 'vet' them (Google them) from a computer.

Censorship through Intimidation: Targeting Liberal Media Outlets and Journalists

While the proliferation of new media and traditional newspapers has inevitably enabled information to get out, both within Bahrain and to the international community, the government's authoritarian reflex has meant that tactics apart from insulation are required. The recent uprising in Bahrain has seen the most egregious targeting of journalists, not simply because there have been more journalists, citizens and otherwise, covering the protests but also due to the increased influence of security minded, anti-reform elements of the regime. As Wehrey notes, 'the hardline faction, which controls the security forces as well as the

[66] Bahrain Watch, *Access Denied*, 2012, https://bahrainwatch.org/access/viewreport.php#findings
[67] Ibid.
[68] J. Halliday, 'Channel 4 Journalists Arrested and Deported from Bahrain', *The Guardian*, 23 April 2012, www.theguardian.com/media/2012/apr/23/channel-4-journalists-arrested-bahrain

instruments of censorship, is now very open about its intention to silence the opposition'.[69] The nature of this intimidation started long before the 2011 Uprising, and is not merely the result of a spontaneous or 2011-induced shift to hardliners, as is implied by some discourses on the uprising. In 2006, Shaykh Ahmed Attiyatallah Al Khalifa, a conservative and influential member of the ruling family, reportedly established two media watch committees under the auspices of his office to intimidate journalists and editors into not writing articles that were deemed anti-regime. While such directives could only, in theory, come from the Information Affairs Authority (the rebranded Ministry of Information), Shaykh Atayitallah's interference signified the influence of elements of the ruling core in controlling press freedom despite superficial institutional and constitutional safeguards.[70]

The general harassment and intimidation of local journalists escalated sharply during the 2011 Uprising. In early 2011, Bahrain's only opposition newspaper, *Al-Wasat*, was targeted by pro-government thugs, who attacked the company's printing press.[71] Other threats were issued, and a video appeared on social media of masked thugs burning the newspaper while calling it 'Al-Wasakh' (Arabic for dirty). Al-Wasat was suspended on 2 April 2011 after the government used a raft of legal arguments to quash it. They accused *Al-Wasat* of 'publishing fabricated news', 'harming public safety' and 'damaging national interests'. Mansur al-Jamri, the paper's award-winning editor, admitted to publishing six incorrect articles but also claimed he was the victim of a campaign to plant disinformation. Al- Jamri argued that this information that had been sent from accounts with IP addresses in Saudi Arabia, indicating a deliberate attempt to bait him into posting misleading information. The editorial staff were replaced by government-appointed personnel, and the newspaper's stance became less critical overnight.[72] *Al-Wasat* was then forcibly closed in June 2017, after fifteen years of operation.

In addition to the intimidation, and subsequent censorship of *Al-Wasat*, attacks and extrajudicial killings of other journalists also increased. The 2011 Uprising was the deadliest for journalists, citizen or

[69] F. Wehrey, 'The March of Bahrain's Hardliners', Carnegie Endowment for International Peace, 31 May 2012, http://carnegieendowment.org/2012/05/31/march-of-bahrain-s-hardliners

[70] W. T. Monroe, 'Government Committees Warn Newspapers'.

[71] M. Tran, 'Bahrain Accuses Human Rights Leader of Faking Pictures of Beating', *The Guardian*, 11 April 2011, www.theguardian.com/world/2011/apr/11/bahrain-human-rights-activist-accused

[72] Freedom House, *Freedom on the Net 2012:* Bahrain, 2012, www. freedomhouse.org/sites/default/files/Bahrain%202012_0.pdf

otherwise, in Bahrain's history. Reporters Sans Frontier (RSF), an NGO defending the human rights of journalists, noted that the citizen-journalist Ahmed Ismail Hussain was 'killed while covering a peaceful demonstration in Salmabad on 31 March 2012'.[73] Although it is not known who killed him, RSF stated that the Bahraini authorities were clearly to blame in several other cases. They blamed the Bahraini authorities for the torture and 'deaths of Karim Fakhrawi, a co-founder of the newspaper *Al-Wasat* and member of its board, and Zakariya Rashid Hassan'.[74]

The authorities have also harassed, tortured, arrested and tried other journalists in an attempt to prevent them evoking support for Bahrain's opposition by publishing potentially damning news stories. Photographers wearing bright-coloured clearly marked press vests, such as Hamad Muhammad and Amer Muhammad, were targeted by direct shots from tear gas canisters. No one has been held accountable. Bahraini photographer Mazen Mahdi joked that journalists were not targeted at protests but that the police are aiming for the cameras.[75] Others have been arrested or convicted on spurious charges, including Mustafa Rabea, Ammar ʿAbd al-Rasul, Ahmed al-Musawi, Sayid Baqir al-Kamal, Qassim Zayn al-Din, Ahmad Zayn al-Din, Ahmad al-Fardan, and Hussam Surur. Again, spurious legal charges have been used to set in motion the processes of legal embroilment. The alleged crimes range from 'participating in an illegal gathering' to 'attacking policemen'.[76] Between 2011 and 2012, sixty-eight journalists were charged with treason or 'publishing news that defamed the image of Bahrain abroad'.[77] Some, such as Naziha Sa'id and Mohammed al Oraibia, have accused the police of torturing them. Journalists like Mohammed al Najer claimed to have been arrested and beaten by police while covering protests.[78] New technologies allowed for more information to cross Bahrain's borders at a time when the government had not anticipated the pre-emptive measures required to prevent information from getting out. The unprecedented killing of journalists is not just an indication of increasing authoritarianism but an acknowledgement of the perceived dangers of new flows of information created by citizen journalists as well as by professional media personnel. A new information nexus of bloggers, journalists and netizens, all armed with highly connective audio-visual technology in the form of mobile phones, have challenged the state's monopoly on information. The result

[73] Reporters Without Borders, 'Bahrain', http://surveillance.

[74] Ibid.

[75] Interview with Mazen Mahdi, 26 March 2017.

[76] Reporters Without Borders, 'Media Freedom Still Under Attack in Bahrain', 11 March 2015, http://en.rsf.org/bahrain-media-freedom-still-under-attack-11-03-2015,47675.html

[77] POMED, 'One Year Later'.

[78] Reporters without Borders, 'Media Freedom Still Under Attack in Bahrain'.

from the state has been a backlash, repression designed to maintain the infrastructures of modernity such as the Internet but on terms that still allow the regime to regulate the nature of the information being distributed. Overall, there is a clear bifurcation in repressive strategies when dealing with journalists. While most foreign journalists are just deported, torture is reserved for nationals over whom the government believe they have more impunity to exact grisly punishments. However, the hardline influence and loyalist control of Bahraini mass media has facilitated an aggressive policy towards censorship, itself enabled by hardline control of security institutions.

While many Bahraini journalists have paid with their lives, foreign news agencies have also found themselves in different kinds of trouble. Bahrain Watch has noted that 'Some individuals who gain access to Bahrain are harassed by security forces, have their movements restricted, or are only granted access to attend Government events'.[79] Theoretically, this policy of restricting access to foreign observers reduces impartial coverage of the situation in Bahrain, while putting pressure on already stretched local NGOs and activists.[80] An absence of impartial coverage may result in international policymakers consulting erroneous, outdated or incorrect information, leading to suboptimal policy decisions with regard to Bahrain.[81]

Social Media and the Epoch of Trolling

Because traditional media can be subjected more easily to state forms of control, the Bahrain authorities have always been suspicious of new technologies. In the 1990s, government offices issued strict control of photocopier and fax machines. In 1996, international calls from public phones were banned as they could not be traced. The government suspected citizens might use public phones to contact subversive elements abroad or journalists/members of NGOs.[82] What set the 2011 Uprising apart from previous contentious episodes was the use of social media in conjunction with mobile technology. The advent of social media has led to a proliferation of media outlets and citizen journalists, creating an information deluge that provided numerous challenges to the repressive apparatus.

However, hegemonic forces have adapted, and new tactics have emerged to silence critical voices. In addition to the intimidation of official journalists and agencies, unaffiliated activists and netizens have been harassed and 'trolled' into silence. Trolling, cyberbullying and

[79] Bahrain Watch, *Access Denied.* [80] Ibid. [81] Ibid.
[82] Human Rights Watch, *Routine Abuse.*

cyber harassment can be defined as 'aggressive internet communication where people use anonymous or non-anonymous accounts to engage in abusive behaviour towards others'.[83] These behaviours vary in severity, from provocative comments and death threats to bullying and logically fallacious argumentation.[84] In Bahrain, intimidation has become prolific on social media since 2011. People reported that they often felt intimidated into not criticizing the government due to the prevalence of online harassment – mostly from Twitter trolls, or what was termed 'e-thugs' at the time. In a small country like Bahrain, with a lot of overlapping personal and familial networks, such threats were taken seriously. Some users admitted that online intimidation had stopped them tweeting or writing anything critical of the regime.[85] One informant noted that trolling stopped him tweeting: 'Don't know how long [I will be away for] Marc, my heart is heavy. Even my moderate views get attacked by trolls.'[86] Another was simply worried about being too vocal on account of the presence of perceived loyalists: 'I'd like to keep the news of me protesting on the DL (down low).. too many pro gov ppl on here..don't want to be attacked!'.[87] Others have 'protected' their Twitter accounts, meaning that what they write can only be read by those followers permitted by the author, thereby contributing to the censorship and silencing of oppositional voices on Twitter. Amid the mass arrests and killing of journalists in 2011, one informant stated, 'I feel people are scared now to talk publicly about the situation after the arrests. Some accounts here were made private'.[88]

The tactic of trolling was especially effective amid the political upheaval in 2011 when there was the very real possibility of arrest and torture. Often Twitter accounts would crop up simply to reveal the identity of previously anonymous accounts. One person told me: 'Just worried about [a friend]. That troll *name redacted* revealed his identity, so he stopped tweeting.'[89] There was much media convergence, with content criticizing critical voices posted both on social media and more traditional web platforms, such as blogs like Wordpress and Tumblr. One website appropriated the term 'troll' to refer to human rights activists and ranked prominent commentators on Bahrain according to their

[83] Jones, 'Social Media, Surveillance'. [84] Ibid., p. 77.
[85] The phrase 'self-censorship' is problematic, as it implies that there is no stimulus that causes the censorship, shifting the responsibility from the hegemonic order to the individual.
[86] Conversation with victim of trolling, 2011.
[87] Correspondence with informant, 19 March 2011.
[88] Correspondence with informant, 21 March 2011.
[89] Correspondence with informant, 9 June 2011.

'troll' level. The overall tropes painted human rights activists as disingenuous, attention-seeking, opportunistic and even fat. Journalist Erin Kilbride noted that troll accounts insulted opposition figures by making references to their sexuality or promiscuity 'in order to place opposition leaders on the extreme fringes of Bahraini society and depict their work for civil rights as deviant and foreign to Bahrain'.[90] The prominent activist Maryam Al-Khawaja, for example, was repeatedly called a slut and a traitor throughout 2011.

@yalseyd: 'Shoot this slut! RT @maryamalkhawaja: Just received msg protesters will come from Nuaim, Sanabis and Manama towards #pearl at 3 pm #bahrain'.

AbdullaMNoor: @MARYAMALKHAWAJA so you filthy ignorant slut should shut the fuck up and stay away from Bahrain, thanks to your sugar daddy Iran[91]

@aliahmedxxx مصي عيري و انطمي يا خت الكحبة عبالش ما ندري عن سوالفش في امريكا مص و لحس و متعة ما قول الا كس امش يالقحبة بت القحاب[Translation: suck my dick, you whore. Do what we know you do in America: the sucking, pussy-licking and muta [pleasure marriage]. I've nothing left to say but your mum's cunt you son of a whore.[92]

Global Voices' MENA editor Amira Al Hussaini described such behaviour as having a chilling effect, 'cyberbullying = censorship! Welcome to the new era of freedom in #Bahrain'.[93] Indeed, the prevalence of Bahrain's Twitter trolls prompted several international journalists or activists to write about them.[94] For example, former Al-Jazeera reporter Gregg Carlstrom tweeted in November 2011: 'Bahrain has by far the hardest-working Twitter trolls of any country I've reported on.'[95]

While the Bahrain government were early adopters of Twitter accounts as a means of surveillance, it was never always clear at which point state-led surveillance ended, and pro-government vigilantiism started. In the first half of 2011 in particular, anonymous pro-regime supporters would often use Twitter to inform the Minister of Information (MOI) of people, especially other Twitter users, whom they thought were opposition 'traitors'. This example shows someone reporting the person with the Twitter handle @hussainm89: 'Dear @moi_bahrain can you please arrest this MOFO Hussain Mirza born 1989, he is a traitor.'[96] In another example,

[90] E. Kilbride, 'Too Gay to Represent Bahrain', Cited in, B. Whitaker, 2014, https://al-bab.com/blog/2014/12/homophobia-and-nationalism-too-gay-represent-bahrain
[91] https://twitter.com/AbdullaMNoor/status/440805277885947905
[92] https://twitter.com/aliahmedxxx/status/78587838723145728
[93] Jones, 'Social Media, Surveillance.'
[94] Including Jillian York, (2011) David Goodman (2011) and Brian Dooley (2011). Following the release of the BICI report on 23 November 2011. See Jones, 'Social Media, Surveillance'
[95] Ibid. [96] Ibid.

Twitter user Bahrain First wrote: '@moi_bahrain, please apprehend this moronic traitor he's a wefaqi'.[97] A prominent pro-government Tweeter at the time, Adel Maymoon, encouraged this type of behaviour, stating: 'If u have any names or information about any traitor or terrorist, kindly send it to @moi_bahrain no need to expose his family & children'.[98] One informant reported that her father, an influential former banker, was messaged by a former colleague to ask if he could do as much as he could to get a traitor removed after he was mentioned by the pro-government vigilante @7areghum. Even in 2016, it was still relatively common for Twitter users to direct reports of 'traitorous' political activities to the MOI's Twitter account.

The effect this fear of surveillance had was made clear by several people. One informant stated: 'Be careful, Marc. Don't argue a lot. A lot of people from MoI on Twitter. And if you mention the king justice etc., you might be unable to enter the country. Just be careful plz'.[99] In many instances, especially in 2011, accounts like @7areghum would circulate images of protesters or activists, circle their heads, brand them traitors and ask for personal information such as name, address and telephone number. These images would be supplied by both unknown sources and citizens who often harvested photos of common Facebook friends that they deemed to be traitorous. Such photos could include innocuous images of people simply visiting the Pearl Roundabout during 2011. This cyber-vigilantism was effective in a small, island community like Bahrain, and soon people mentioned by @7areghum would go into hiding.

Accounts like @7areghum demonstrate the potential pitfalls of what Mann calls 'personal sousveillance', that is, the use of technology such as social media to document one's own day-to-day experience.[100] Bahraini activists, sharing their collective joy at reaching the Pearl Roundabout, took images of themselves celebrating. However, such seemingly banal yet defiant and political 'personal sousveillance' can be reappropriated by the regime and its supporters and used as part of its surveillance apparatus.[101] This is nowhere more evident than in Bahrain, where the increasing polarization of society has resulted in citizens using social media as a tool for peer-to-peer to surveillance.

In March 2011, some prominent Tweeters were targeted in a similar way. A photo of 'web terrorists' was circulated on Twitter. It included

[97] https://twitter.com/Bahrain1st/status/50279272459415552

[98] @adelmaymoon, 'If u have you any names or information about any traitor or terrorist, kindly send it to @moi_bahrain no need to expose his family & children', [Tweet by @adelmaymoon], 1 May 2011, https://twitter.com/adelmaymoon/status/64784728217223168

[99] Exchange with Twitter user during March 2011.

[100] S. Mann Sousveillance, 2002, http://wearcam.org/sousveillance.htm

[101] Ibid.

Manaf al-Muhandis, Mahmud Yusif and Muhammad Masqati.[102] After the circulation of the document, these bloggers were subsequently arrested. A year after his release, Manaf al-Muhandis Tweeted, "Today is the anniversary of my detainment. Just because someone posted my picture on Facebook'.[103] Following their release, none of them tweeted anything controversial or political for a considerable time.

ʿAli ʿAbd al-Imam, a prominent blogger, was sentenced to fifteen years in prison for 'spreading false information and trying to subvert the regime'.[104] However, he escaped the island in 2013 after finding a way to get from Bahrain to Britain. Such arrests prompted much fear among other online activists, who were far more reluctant to tweet anything critical of the regime – at least without using a pseudonym. Some informants stated that their family had pressured them not to use social media such as Twitter for fear of arrest. One informant stated: 'I used to Tweet but then when some of my friends got arrested my father sat me down and gave me a looong [sic] talk, guilting me into deleting all my tweets.'

Trolling in Bahrain reached such a pitch that it was addressed in a report commissioned to investigate human rights abuses during the uprising of 2011. The Bahrain Independent Comission of Inquiry report singled out the actions of @7areghum, a Twitter account that 'openly harassed, threatened and defamed certain individuals, and in some cases placed them in immediate danger'.[105] Although the authors of the report noted that @7areghum had broken both Bahraini and international law, there is currently no evidence to indicate that the Bahrain government have asked the US government to subpoena Twitter to release information about the account. This points to an element of complicity or tacit acceptance by the regime, or indeed Twitter, of such actions.[106]

In addition to having a chilling effect on criticism, these trolls were an important source of disinformation. They frequently disseminated information that was controversial, defamatory, sectarian or inaccurate. The phenomenon was especially problematic in 2011. In times of conflict, such disinformation is harmful, as it is also a time when people are feeling

[102] Jones, 'Social Media, Surveillance'.

[103] @Redbelt, 'Today is the anniversary of my detainment Just because someone posted my picture on Facebook. Also because I started #UniteBH', [Tweet by @Redbelt], 29 March 2012, https://twitter.com/Redbelt/status/185324439934738432

[104] Global Voices Advocacy, 'Remembering 'Ali Abdulemam', 7 November 2011, https://advox.globalvoices.org/2011/11/07/remembering-ali-abdulemam/ (accessed 7 October 2015).

[105] *BICI Report*, p. 401.

[106] M. O. Jones, 'Bahrain Activists' Trouble with Trolls', *Index on Censorship Uncut*, 15 May 2012, http://uncut.indexoncensorship.org/2012/05/bahrain-marc-owen-jones-twitter-trolls/

vulnerable, defensive and afraid.[107] While accounts such as @7areghum were never formally identified by activists or NGOs, a similar account named @mnarfezhom was identified as belonging to Salman Al Khalifa, a member of the ruling family.[108] His anti-Shiʿa discourse and critique of the protest movement was not considered problematic by the government, yet he was only questioned by authorities after he slandered influential and Sunni notables.[109] Again, this asymmetry in the application of rule of law reflects a tacit approval by the regime of harassment strategies designed to intimidate opposition members online. What is clear is that such tactics, whether undertaken directly by the government or vigilantes, was facilitated by government inaction in preventing it. As many informants pointed out, it was an important part of the regime's information control strategy.

In addition to the crude use of social media in combating dissent, the Bahrain government are refining more localized forms of censorship. Unlike in countries such as Turkey for example, where the government have been accused of blocking access to certain social media sites on a national scale, the Bahrain government has generally throttled access to the Internet or denied it to specific towns perceived as troublesome. This more targeted form of censorship is useful, as it circumvents criticism by the international community of collective punishment. The tactic was most notable in the case of the denationalization of the prominent Bahraini cleric Isa Qasim. Following the government's revocation of his citizenship, hundreds of protesters camped out in Duraz, where Qasim lived. In addition to creating checkpoints to regulate people's entry and exit from the village, the government ordered the Bahrain telecoms providers to throttle the internet in the Duraz area. Batelco and Zain, two of Bahrain's largest Internet Service Providers, were disabling their 3G and 4G signals between 7 pm and 1 am every day. Also, Batelco was introducing 'astronomical levels of loss and latency into fixed-line internet connections in Duraz'.[110] In other words, they put the internet under curfew. In addition to a form of collective punishment for those in Duraz, the curfew meant that it was extremely difficult for activists or residents

[107] M. O. Jones in J. D. Goodman, '"Twitter Trolls" Haunt Discussions of Bahrain Online', *The Lede* [*New York Times* blog], 11 October 2011, http://thelede.blogs.nytimes.com/2011/10/11/twitter-trolls-haunt-discussions-of-bahrain-online/

[108] Bahrain Watch, *The IP Spy Files: How Bahrain's Government Silences Anonymous Online Dissent*, August 2013, https://bahrainwatch.org/ipspy/ip-spy-files.pdf

[109] S. S. Grewal, 'Probe into Slander on Twitter', *Gulf Daily News*, 7 January 2013, http://archives.gdnonline.com/NewsDetails.aspx?date=04/07/2015&storyid=345115

[110] Bahrain Watch, 'Time for Some Internet Problems in Duraz': Bahraini ISPs impose internet curfew in protest village, 2016, https://bahrainwatch.org/blog/2016/08/03/bahrain-internet-curfew/

Figure 6.1 Cartoon lampooning the internet curfew in Duraz, titled 'Life in Duraz'.

to provide critical real-time updates or media content regarding what became termed 'the siege of Duraz'. While still crude, this localized internet throttling marks a far more nuanced form of repression than a nationwide internet curfew.

Mediated Violence and Its Chilling Effect

While trolling and internet curfews represent a more direct form of censorship, silencing of the opposition can also be achieved by the selective and judicious circulation of information that the government might ordinarily try to hide. For example, several people reported that visual evidence of government atrocities made them more afraid of engaging in dissent (regardless of who circulated the information). The rise of videos and images shared through social media has, in many ways, actually facilitated the process of censorship. As Austin Turk noted, by making the consequences of opposition and resistance so gruesome, many of those exposed become psychologically and/or physically incapable of further criticism and resistance.[111] As such, videos of state

[111] Turk, *Political Criminality*.

violence and brutality may have a repressive effect. If such visual images or videos generate fear of authority, the benefits to the regime are self-explanatory – they may ameliorate dissent. If they further public anger, and increase radicalization that leads to further violence, then the opposition movement will remain fragmented – making it easier for the regime to operate a divide and rule policy. It can be argued that the depiction of state violence in videos or images circulated on social media serves a similar intended function to that of the legal public corporal punishment of yore. Historically, in Bahrain, this took the form of lashes in the market place, frequently administered personally by Charles Belgrave. The location was as important as the punishment itself, and market places were chosen in order to maximize the number of people witnessing the event. The only difference now is that physical location need not constrain the number of those who witness state violence. Videos of violence transcend temporal and spatial boundaries, serving as a permanent reminder of state brutality. Often they go viral, in part because activists know they will attract the attention and condemnation of many in the international press. But it is a double-edged sword, and many will simply become more fearful of dissent for fear of grisly consequences.

While videos of state violence on social media may also provoke anger, they still serve to remind people of the costs of engaging in protest. Indeed, in times of political upheaval, authorities benefit from periodically reminding the public of their vulnerability by showing what happens to those who break the rules. As Turk states: a 'barbarous tactic is the public display of mutilated bodies, or of persons maimed by their ordeals in the hands of police'.[112] By hiding such abuses, the regime is less able to use violence to deter potential troublemakers from engaging in such acts. A truly totalitarian regime like that of Pol Pot would simply eliminate every possible rival, yet authoritarian regimes, less extreme on the scale of tyranny, may target opponents more specifically, and utilize these cases to deter and terrorize the rest of the population. It is a calculation of efficiency rather than morality.

Of course, most of the time the authorities will attempt to limit or prevent people from circulating images or videos of police brutality or state violence. However, periodic reminders of the brutal consequences of engaging in dissent are useful. After all, if people did not believe that the costs of engaging in dissent could result in torture or death, they would be more emboldened in challenging the state. An analysis of comments posted on YouTube videos of political violence in Bahrain

[112] Ibid., p. 155.

indicated that such videos led to polarized responses in which many articulated their political and religious position. Indeed, such videos of political violence could arguably contribute to the increased polarization of fragmentation between Sunni and Shiʿa, or those who 'support' and 'oppose' the current government. This sowing of divisions, though bad for society, assists the regime in their policy of divide and rule. In the 2011 Uprising, supporters of the government circulated videos of protesters throwing Molotov cocktails to defend the actions of the state, while those who wanted reform circulated videos of police brutality to draw attention to their cause. In this sense, it is often people's political position that determines how they interpret or select these videos. In both cases, consumption appears to be a form of validation rather than a challenge to one's own belief system. Nonetheless, the mediated perpetration of violence, regardless of the actor carrying it out, elicits strong responses of fear and indignation.

Scholars of political science and indeed repression will be quick to note that videos of state violence are damaging in the sense that they are a PR disaster. Indeed, using violence incurs significant legitimacy costs. For Bahrain, keen to market itself as a neoliberal space open for global business, videos of police brutality are scarcely likely to attract foreign investors. This sensitivity to reputation was underscored by reminders from the head of public security that circulating videos of the security forces engaged in egregious acts would be considered an act against the nation.[113] Continued use of coercive methods may be useful in the short run, yet coercion 'maximizes alienation', and makes it more difficult for any regime to achieve any legitimacy.[114] This inherent paradox can partially be resolved by distancing the action of state agents from elites who benefit from such violence. That is, state violence depicted on social media was said by the government to be the action of a few bad apples, a small number of policemen over whom the regime had little control. Consequently, there would be some show trials where a few policemen would be convicted, or in the case of Bahrain, convicted but probably let off after a laborious process of repeated trials and appeals. Indeed, court decisions exonerating legal control agents such as police officers are to be

[113] @YusurAlBahrani, 'Chief of Public Security in #Bahrain @Talhassan, claims that who publicize video of @moi_bahrain violations is traitor', 25 December 2012, https://twitter.com/YusurAlBahrani/status/283442087192588288 (accessed 10 October 2015). @Talhassan, '#البحرين يقوم الدجالون والعملاء ببث تلك اللقطات ويبالغون فيها وحسبما يردهم من - تعليمات وبما يحقق لهم ولمن يدفعهم من الدول أهدافهم [Those who broadcast these clips achieve the goals of those other countries that pay them]. https://twitter.com/talhassan/status/283339899518730241, 24 December 2012.

[114] Dallin and Breslauer, 1970, p. 3.

expected in any polity.[115] Of course, the more videos that emerge of state violence and police brutality, the more difficult it is for authorities to convince people that such acts are the work of a few bad apples. Therefore, regulating the number of images or videos of police brutality is perhaps more about controlling the flow of information, and determining when people should be reminded of the state's brutality, rather than any real objection to people witnessing those deeds.

Despite the utility of reminding people of the violent consequences of engaging in dissent, the reliance on short-term methods of coercive force at the expense of political processes that appease the population can be explained by recognizing that such processes would require more wealth and power sharing. As Turk again states, 'alternatives to intimidation may simply be unacceptable because they are perceived to involve intolerable changes in the allocation of resources among competing groups, even to the point of dismantling the existing structures of power and status'.[116] Just as violent repression is seen as a necessary political risk, one that weighs up the benefits of continued protection of resources with those of sharing those resources, the impact of mediated violence poses another conundrum. Do the benefits of intimidating the population through depictions of state violence outweigh the negatives? After all, how does one pacify a population without doing the following: (a) sacrificing significant power and wealth; (b) terrorizing them and (c) convincing them (brainwashing) that the current social order is infallible and true. Indeed, the above is an example that highlights how repressive calculations are not simply about more or less but about when and how often.

The Rise of the Propaganda Machine

The Increasing Need for Propaganda

Shaping the perceptions of citizens about the nature of reality is an important aspect of repression, as it can deter people from supporting social movements via stigmatization, ideology or socialization. While censorship limits the availability and diversity of information available, propaganda attempts to persuade or inform people of the correct viewpoint according to the status quo. Often this involves constructing a specific perception of reality, one in which there are almost always foes and allies.

The most salient strategy of the Bahrain government has been to frame any opposition as being treasonous and violent externally supported fifth columns, operating in Bahrain under orders from a foreign power. Before

[115] Turk, Political Criminality. [116] Ibid., p. 154.

Independence, inside agitation was often attributed to Arab nationalist or Marxist/Leninist leftist movements from Egypt, while after Independence, Iran has often been used as the external 'bogeyman' with a hand in dissent in Bahrain. This tactic is not necessarily new in Bahrain. As early as the 1920s, the British would deliberately frighten Shaykh Hamad with the 'bogeyman of Persian pretensions to get his own house in order'.[117] More recently, this demonization has taken place through the state-controlled media. The media scene in Bahrain has hardly ever been vibrant, and it is only since 2001 that the proliferation of media outlets and the internet has seen a burgeoning of state and non-state discourse attempting to shape public perceptions of opposition movements. Thus stigmatization, demonization and intimidation by way of new media technologies is an increasingly more prevalent tool in the government's repertoire of repression. It is an authoritarian response to media pluralism.

Before the advent of newspapers and satellite TV channels, the government focused less on stigmatizing the opposition and more on countering external propaganda. They also focused their attention on trying to promote the idea that people in Bahrain were better off than in places like Egypt, hotbeds of Arab nationalism. As mentioned earlier, rising Arab nationalism during the 1950s made Britain and the Al Khalifa regime particularly paranoid about the dissemination of Arab nationalist propaganda. On 1 February 1955, the government of Bahrain opened its Public Relations Department. This was done ostensibly to explain the government's policies and achievements but also, as one British official noted, to combat the 'continual incitement against established authority being poured out by the Cairo and Damascus wireless'[118] stations. In 1956, the newspaper *Al Khalij* [The Gulf], edited by the British Colonel Anderson, was set up to spread pro-government propaganda, marking the beginning of the trend of using British officers or former British officers for reputation management on behalf of the Bahrain government.[119] They even co-opted 'Ali Sayyar, the former editor of the more critical *Al Watan,* to write for the paper. Sayyar was once described by the HEC as the 'greatest torch of freedom in Bahrain;' He later resigned from his role in *Al Khalij* due to accusations of collusion with the British.[120]

[117] Viceroy, Foreign and Political Department, to Secretary of State for India, 14 May 1923, p. 761.
[118] C. A. Gault, 27 January 1957, in A. Burdett (ed.), *Records of Bahrain 1820–1960,* vol. 7, Slough, Archive Editions, 1993, p.335.
[119] B. A. B. Burrows, Summary of News, 24 August 1956, FO371/120548, The National Archives.
[120] Note in Margin on, 'Daily in Bahrain by 'Ali Sayyar', 1956, FO371/120548, The National Archives.

The government crackdown of 1956 prompted an almost decade-long hiatus of any remotely critical press, highlighting how challenges to regime authority created long-lasting opportunity closures for opposition. Throughout the 1960s, British paranoia about hostile propaganda led them to keep track of subversive foreign publications. Officials even kept a thematic analysis of propaganda located in Bahrain in 1964, including its likely author and political sympathies. Most of this was seen as Baathist or Arab nationalist, although the British were also suspicious about demands for women's emancipation.[121] This paranoia was somewhat indicative of personalistic attitudes. In 1964, Sir William Luce noted his own as well as Shaykh ʿIsa's fear of the press, stating that Arab nationalist propaganda from the United Arab Republic, Iraq and Cairo was the 'greatest danger to the Ruler'.[122] Shaykh ʿIsa personally believed newspapers would eventually create problems and that the Press Ordinance would be invoked so frequently that there would be no point in even allowing them to start up.[123]

A lack of principled commitment to a free press was evidenced by the same justifications being brought up during dissent in the 1960s. Indeed, the press was merely seen as a temporary instrument designed to mitigate dissent by promoting government reforms. It was, in effect, strategic communication. During the worker and student strikes of 1965, William Luce, like Gault before him in the 1950s, suggested the necessity of a 'lively and strong' broadcasting station 'capable of answering the groundless allegations poured out by Kuwait and other hostile Middle East broadcasting stations'.[124] Despite the recalcitrance of the ruler and the Al Khalifa in allowing a press, the British encouraged them to permit an independent newspaper, *Al-Adwa*, something which Shaykh ʿIsa had reportedly long been against.[125] The first issue was published on 9 September 1965 and was described by the British official J.W.D. Gray as lacking 'spice' on account of the draconian Press Law issued in August 1965.[126] Indeed, such was the government's paranoia about propaganda, that the Press Law was both comprehensive and stifling. Among the requirements were that the editor and owner had to be over 25, and that the papers were not allowed to criticize the ruler or his family or publish

[121] William Luce 1964, FO371/174521, The National Archives. [122] Ibid. [123] Ibid.

[124] W. Luce, Dispatch No. 305, 26 April, 1965 telegram to foreign office, in A. Burdett (ed.) *Records of Bahrain, 1961–1965,* vol. 5, Cambridge Archive Editions, 1997, p. 292.

[125] Arabian Department, 'Minister of State's Visit to the Persian Gulf', 9–16 May 1965, in A. Burdett (ed.) *Records of Bahrain, 1961–1965,* vol. 5, Cambridge Archive Editions, 1997, p. 297.

[126] J. W .D. Gray, Letter to S. J. Nuttall, 14 September 1965, in A. Burdett (ed.) *Records of Bahrain, 1961–1965,* vol. 5, Cambridge Archive Editions, 1997, p. 49.

news that might damage the economy or harm relations with 'friendly nations'[127] All publications brought into the country could be appropriated by the authorities if they contravened any of the articles laid out in the Press Law, and anything that encouraged people to embrace communism was also banned. In short, the press in Bahrain was never intended to be a 'fourth estate', one designed to speak truth to power but a way in which the government could celebrate its own achievements, deploy propaganda and counter news issued by foreign actors. Even in 1974, during Bahrain's brief democratic experiment, the British noted that the government was 'infiltrating the press' and controlled both state radio and state TV.[128]

In addition to celebrating government achievements, propaganda has been used as a tool of intimidation. Government control of the press has allowed them to strategically place information designed to have a salutary impact upon any opposition. In 1979, for example, the British Ambassador Harold Walker believed that the widely publicized expressions of support from Arab governments for the Al Khalifa was enough to convince potentially pro-Khomeini dissidents 'that they were not up against the Bahrain Government alone'.[129] Sometimes the regime exploited the perceived deep-rooted *baḥrānī* fear of the tribal raids from the mainlaind in the 1920s. For example, in 1980 it was thought that a deliberate rumour was spread about Saudi troops being deployed in Bahrain, an act devised to intimidate any *baḥārna* from protesting.[130] As the ruling family and Saudi authorities continued to fear Shiʿa expansionism, the press was used to promote predominantly Sunni Arab unity. In 1982, the British mentioned that there was a 'well-advertised campaign to underline the fact that Bahrain enjoys the support of its Arab neighbours'.[131] During the 1990s Intifada, the Saudis were more demonstrable in their shows of support, staging military exercises predicated around invading a Bahrain overtaken by fundamentalists. It was during the 1990s Intifada that the Saudi Defence Minister Prince Sultan purposefully stated to the BBC: 'We are prepared to stand forcefully by Bahrain if the need arises.'[132] When the Saudi-led Gulf Cooperation Council Peninsula Shield (GCCPS) came over the bridge to help bolster

[127] www.legalaffairs.gov.bh/Media/LegalPDF/K0765.pdf
[128] Tesh, 9 April 1974, The National Archives.
[129] H. B. Walker, 'Bahrain: Annual Review for 1979', 8 January 1980, FCO8/3490, The National Archives.
[130] Passmore, Bahrain Internal, The National Archives.
[131] W. R. Tomkys, Bahrain: Annual Review for 1981,13 February 1982, FCO8/4332, The National Archives.
[132] Cited in Human Rights Watch, *Routine Abuse.*

the Bahraini Security Forces in 2011, it was widely broadcast on state media. Soldiers in heavily armoured vehicles, many displaying the 'V for victory' sign, were broadcast crossing the sea causeway. In addition to a show of force, the presence of Saudi forces potentially evoked the historical 'visceral fear' that many *baḥārna* reportedly have of those on the mainland. This is not necessarily surprising, given the continued oppression of the *baḥārna* living over the water in Saudi's Eastern Province.

Stigmatization and False Balance

In addition to demonizing the opposition through the false or exaggerated creation of links to external powers, the government have also constructed a more simplistic good versus evil binary to stigmatize opposition movements. Here, the government present themselves as a bulwark against violent extremism while seeking to frame the opposition as deviant. A 'frame', according to Goffman (1974), is a means of organizing, classifying and interpreting our life experiences. The frame, or 'schemata of interpretation', enables individuals to label and perceive certain events, protagonists or information, and make sense of them. Crucially framing is about prominence, and involves selection and salience. As Entman stated: 'To frame is to select some aspects of a perceived reality and make them more salient in communicating text, in such a way as to promote a particular problem definition, causal interpretation, moral evaluation, and/or treatment recommendation for the item described.'[133] It has been argued, for example, that media coverage can focus attention on protester violence to the neglect of underlying causes. The media is thus used to polarize, marginalize and disparage groups seen by the status quo as adversarial.[134] Boykoff has argued that the media often frame social movements as violent, freakish, disruptive and ignorant.[135]

The state media, loyalists and numerous Western public relations firms working for the Bahraini government have employed a number of rhetorical devices and narratives that contribute to framing the opposition in a negative light. Here, acts of violence against the state are

[133] Cited in I. Hellsten, J. Dawson and L. Leydesdorff, 'Implicit Media Frames: Automated Analysis of Public Debate on Artificial Sweeteners', *Public Understanding of Science*, vol. 19, no. 5, 2010, pp. 590–608, doi:10.1177/0963662509343136, https://www.leydesdorff.net/implicitframes/

[134] S. Cottle, 'Reporting Demonstrations: The Changing Media Politics of Dissent', *Media, Culture and Society*, vol. 30, no. 6, 2008, p. 856.

[135] Boykoff, *Beyond Bullets*.

exaggerated or focused on, while egregious acts perpetrated against citizens by the state are marginalized. This tactic, as mentioned by Boykoff, is meant to remove support from social movements by painting them in a negative light. There is evidence to suggest that even in its infancy, the Bahraini press has been used as a vehicle to stigmatize opposition. For example, in order to justify its decision to dissolve the National Assembly in 1975 for reasons of national security, the government widely publicized acts of violence perpetrated by those with leftist political associations. One man, ʿAbd al-Rahman Ahmad ʿUthman, a member of the Popular Front for the Liberation of Oman (PFLO), allegedly confessed to throwing a bomb into a police station. His trial was widely published in the now defunct *Gulf Weekly Mirror*. The British explicitly noted that the widespread publicity of the trial was 'to lend support to the government's line that national security was under threat'.[136] Conversely, after the torture and killing of the likely innocent Jamal 'Ali in 1980, the papers carried what British officials described as a 'disingenuous' statement about his death, attributing it to kidney failure.[137] (Thirty years on, the government blamed kidney failure on the death of someone who the BICI also noted died of torture).[138] Here, by minimizing state brutality, the authorities help maintain their position as a moral authority and arbiter of the public good.

The somewhat inexorable rise of international media outlets has prompted a need for tactics that aim to leverage media to the regime's advantage. Given the lack of freedom of the press in Bahrain, publicizing confessions of political prisoners has become a means of attempting to add credibility to what would otherwise be perceived as wholly government-controlled broadcasting. In the 1990s, state newspapers and state TV frequently published images of suspects along with accounts of them having confessed to various political crimes. Amnesty International noted that official investigations into the alleged murder of three policemen by protesters received widespread publicity, while the government killing of civilians received no coverage.[139] The pro-government *Al-Ayam* newspaper was singled out on several occasions by Amnesty International for publishing the names and personal details of those accused in various cases. Amnesty noted that 'articles along similar lines were published regularly in Bahrain's newspapers for several months'.[140] Such trial-by-media undermined the defendants right to be

[136] E. H. Noble, Bahrain Internal, 26 August 1975, FCO8/2415, The National Archives.
[137] C. E. J. Wilton, Bahrain Internal, 14 May 1980, FCO8/3489, The National Archives.
[138] *Gulf Daily News*, 'Ministry denies death rumours', The National Archives.
[139] Amnesty International, *Bahrain: A Human Rights Crisis.* [140] Ibid.

presumed innocent until proven guilty before a court of law, something that is actually guaranteed by Article 20(c) of Bahrain's constitution and Article 14(2) of the ICCPR. Indeed, the publication of such confessions in the press prejudiced any chance the defendants may have had of receiving a fair trial.[141] Similarly, in 1996, Kathy Evans of the *Guardian* reported how the state 'paraded' a 'string of bearded young men with dead staring eyes' on television, all of them confessing to their role in an alleged Iranian-backed plot to overthrow the government.[142] The local papers even dubbed the men 'the faces of evil'.[143]

This trial by media occurred again in 2008[144] and 2010, with the Bahrain Centre for Human Rights (BCHR) and the International Federation of Human Rights (FIDH) accusing the state-controlled media of publishing images of those connected to a terror threat, including lawyers defending the suspects.[145,146] In an alleged plot against the regime in 2010, six out of seven of Bahrain's daily newspapers published the images of the suspects, highlighting a distinct lack of editorial diversity.[147] Amnesty International described the decision as 'nothing less than a form of trial by media in which the accused themselves had no means by which to defend themselves or their reputations'.[148] In another particularly appalling example, Bahrain State Television aired the confession of 'Ali Ibrahim Saqer on 28 April 2011. Saqer was accused of killing two policemen. However, in a macabre twist, Bahrain Television failed to state that Saqer had already been killed in custody on 9 April 2011 as a result of torture.[149] His broadcast confession was, in actuality, posthumous.

141 Ibid.
142 K. Evans, 'Bahrainis Implicate Iran in TV "Coup" Confession', *The Guardian*. Jun 6, 1996, p. 14.
143 XXX
144 R. Khalifa, '(AP) – Bahrain TV Airs Terror Plot Confessions', BCHR, 29 December 2008, www.bahrainrights.org/en/node/2625
145 Bahrain Center for Human Rights, 'ANHRI: Bahrain: Court Holds Mass Hearing for Human Rights Activist', 29 October 2010, www.bahrainrights.org/en/node?page=155&nomobile=true
146 Human Rights Defenders, 'Violent Crackdown Continues to Target Human Rights Defenders', Press Release, 8 September 2010, www.fidh.org/International-Federation-for-Human-Rights/north-africa-middle-east/bahrain/Violent-crackdown-continues-to
147 H. Toumi, 'Bahrain's Prosecution Defends Decision to Publish Suspects' Names and Pictures', Habib Toumi, [web blog], 2 September 2010, www.habibtoumi.com/2010/09/02/bahrains-prosecution-defends-decision-to-publish-suspects-names-and-pictures/
148 Amnesty International, *Crackdown in Bahrain: Human Rights at the Crossroads*, London, p. 16, www.univie.ac.at/bimtor/dateien/bahrain_ai_2011_hr_crossroads.pdf
149 Bahrain Youth Society for Human Rights, 'A Man Died in Custody Confession on Television that He Had Killed Two Policemen', 28 April 2011, www.byshr.org/?p=396

Despite the government's much-lauded announcements of media reforms in the wake of the recommendations made in the *BICI Report*, state media still pursued this form of trial by media. In 2012[150] and 2013, *Al Watan* published the names and photos of terror suspects – a move that is ordinarily illegal, even under Bahraini law.[151] Here again, we see how the social control objectives of repression in Bahrain subvert legal protections when deemed necessary.

Protesters or Violent, Riotous Mobs?

Despite many opposition members branding certain stories as 'fabrications', or *mufabrakat*, instances of alleged protester violence have been highly publicized, leading to the emergence of a violence frame in the stigmatization of the opposition. An attack on a Pakistani muezzin by a group of protesters was highly publicized by the state media who claimed that his tongue had been cut off. Despite this, there were many doubts about the veracity of such claims. These doubts were strengthened by the *BICI Report*, which claimed his tongue was lacerated, and that those found guilty of the attack were tortured into confessing. In a separate instance, pro-government newspapers *Gulf Daily News*[152] and *Al-Ayam* also reported that a Bahraini taxi driver had been killed by 'terrorists',[153] while the more moderate *Al-Wasat*[154] claimed it was a traffic accident.

Although the government could more easily control traditional media, social media posed a challenge to the regime's ability to influence the message. While the government used social media to spread rumours or disinformation, they have used other tactics to try and legitimize particular online news sources. Among the responses by the Information Affairs Authority was the establishment of Social Media Awards along with a grand ceremony.[155] The move was an attempt to confer legitimacy and credibility on certain news sources on Twitter and Facebook. It was even preceded by warnings to avoid spurious social media sources and only

[150] POMED, 'One Year Later'.
[151] @F-albinali, '**@marcowenjones @lawyereemkhalaf** its a concern, NHRI raised it as well. My view is that that's it's a grey area. Something for the defense', 21 February 2013, https://twitter.com/f_albinali/status/304556075405955072
[152] S. S. Grewal, 'Track Down My Father's Killers', *Gulf Daily News*, 15 June 2011, http://archives.gdnonline.com/NewsDetails.aspx?date=04/07/2015&storyid=307919
[153] *Al-Ayam*, 'Terrorists Brutally and Mercilessly Stabbed His Body with Their Knives', 29 March 2011, http://goo.gl/qmhTWC
[154] *Al-Wasat*, 'Funeral of Rashid Mamri in Riffa Cemetry', 23 March 2011, www.alwasatnews.com/3120/news/read/533682/1.html
[155] Bahrain News Agency, 'Shaikh Fawaz Presents Social Media Awards', 8 February 2012, http://bna.bh/portal/en/news/493277

listen to official government ones. Unsurprisingly, one of the winners was the Ministry of the Interior (MoI) and *Al-Watan*, the fiercely pro-government newspaper responsible for various transgressions of local law. In a bizarre move, one of the winners was Lex Birch, an anonymous account that used to Tweet negative information about opposition activists. Lex Birch was awarded 'outstanding resident' by the Information Affairs Authority. He had once claimed that the opposition activist Nabeel Rajab had ordered people to cut off the fingers of British expatriate Peter Morrisey, a story that was never independently verified.[156] Along with Lex Birch, a number of anonymous expat accounts appeared on Twitter to condemn oppositional activity. None of these revealed their true identity, yet the story about Morrisey and the suspicious expat accounts would indicate how keen the government were to make sure that the country's large migrant worker population appeared to support them. This was especially useful for allied Western governments, who could theoretically instrumentalize such narratives to muddy the waters of any discourses that sought to portray their Bahrain ally as a brutal dictatorship. It was never clear if Lex Birch was a real person, yet his fear-mongering anti-opposition narrative was legitimized by the government through this award.

The veracity of government claims of opposition violence has been repeatedly questioned, partly due to their absurdity but also partly due to the fact that some fabrications have been exposed. For example, in the 1990s, the government claimed that parents beat the corpses of their children to make it look like they had been tortured.[157] This myth was repeated in the 2011 Uprising. Here, people who had been at the Pearl Roundabout were accused of making their wounds worse in order to elicit media sympathy. With the advent of social media, attempts to corroborate this misinformation were made. One video was circulated that showed children being made up to look injured, with pro-government supporters claiming it was evidence that the opposition was fabricating wounds. It was later discovered that the video was an unrelated recording from a school in Palestine that showed children putting on makeup for a nativity play. It, had, however, been strategically edited.

Indeed, those who supported the government quickly adopted a discourse of suspicion, where all anti-government stories were perceived as 'fake'. One informant told me that a viral video of Abd al-Redha

[156] @LexBirch, '@NABEELRAJAB well you are, and you proved it by sending out your thugs to amputate #UK citizens fingers #Bahrain. We all know the truth now', 10 February 2012, https://twitter.com/LexBirch/status/167887885960347648

[157] *The Economist*, 'Whitewash', 23 January 1999, issue, 8103, p. 60.

Buhmayd being shot at the Pearl Roundabout was in fact fake and that it had been filmed at a 'famous Iranian studio'. It was, in this case, too difficult for that person to believe that the government would do something so awful. An Australian migrant worker who was an eyewitness to the clearing of the Pearl Roundabout in 2011 highlighted the discrepancy between opposing interpretations of events.

> Suddenly, there was an almost deafening volley of shots fired from the roundabout and without my camcorder, I could see the protesters fleeing away back towards Salmaniya Hospital. I later learnt that several unarmed protesters had been shot by this volley and I was also 'reliably' informed by pro-government students that the injuries they suffered had actually been faked, which was nonsense. (18 February 2011).[158]

In addition to these more overt strategies attempting to associate violence with the opposition, the government have resorted to both subtle and blatant rhetorical devices. Chief among these are constant references to people not as protesters or activists, but as 'vandals', 'terrorists' and 'hooligans' beholden to outside powers. Such terminology is nothing new. An article in the *London Times*, as far back as 1956 reporting on the protests that occurred during the visit of Selwyn Lloyd to Bahrain, was titled 'Hooligans in Control'. Unsurprisingly, it gave no space to comment or demands made by the HEC. While Belgrave was the *Times* correspondent at the time, it was not clear if he wrote that particular piece, although he did use the term 'hooligans' a lot in his diary.

Although there are people in the February 14th Movement known to have used violence, the majority of protesters have remained peaceful. State media, in both English and Arabic, have used a narrative that is designed to conflate fringe violence with the tactics of the entire opposition. The following excerpt from a weekly security report by the Ministry of the Interior highlights this rhetorical sleight of hand: 'The security report brings you a summary of what happened during the week from rioting, vandalism and law-breaking which SOME [original emphasis] still call it a peaceful protest. And through this week's report once again we will show you by footage what has been labelled as peaceful as an act of terrorism'.[159] This rhetoric was regurgitated in the state media or in the writings of loyalist lobbies such as 'Citizen for Bahrain' – a mysterious

[158] T. Mitchell, 'Witness to an Uprising: What I Saw in Bahrain', *The Atlantic*, 14 December 2011, www.theatlantic.com/international/archive/2011/12/witness-to-an- uprising-what-i-saw-in-bahrain/249977/

[159] Bahrain News Agency, 'Bahrain Weekly Security Report 12/07/2012', 12 July 2012, www.bna.bh/portal/en/news/516756#.T_8KWEjw0Z0.twitter

internet-based group set up to denounce the opposition. In an op-ed for the local English-language daily, the *Gulf Daily News* (GDN), Citizens of Bahrain stated the following: 'The opposition claims that its methods are peaceful, but its actions say otherwise. When opposition militants, trained and armed by Iran, are going to such efforts to bring armed conflict to Bahrain's shores'.[160] Again, without providing evidence, this lobby group, itself designed to appear like a grassroots pro-government lobby, buttressed state rhetoric about both oppositional violence and Iranian involvement in Bahrain's affairs.

Discursive Tropes of Violence

Generally speaking, there is a homogeneity to discourses by state or non-state actors attempting to skew the narrative around criminality linked with Bahrain's pro-democracy movement. These techniques follow four broad themes: (1) vilify the victims or the people the victim was associated with (e.g., say they were engaged in nefarious activities or doing something illegal/using weapons); (2) denounce any state responsibility by indicating that the police acted in self-defence; (3) use passive constructions that imply a lack of agency and responsibility when it comes to killing by agents of the state (e.g. instead of saying the victim was killed, say he died. Similarly, suggest a disconnect between the incident and the death of the victim.); (4) legitimise violent police responses by mentioning how they [the police] adhered to protocol and procedure or were just doing their duty. The following excerpt from an MOI statement concerns the death of Husayn al-Jaziri, a fourteen-year-old boy who was killed after being hit directly in the head by a tear gas canister. The numbers from above are used to mark the rhetorical devices used by the MOI in their attempts to abrogate their responsibility and delegitimize opposition claims of police oppression or malpractice.

> The most violent (1) group amassed at around 8 am in the village of Daih where 300 rioters assembled to attack police (1) deployed in the area, with rocks, steel rods and Molotov cocktails (1). Warning shots (4) were fired but failed to disperse the advancing crowd, which continued their attack (1). Officers discharged birdshot to defend themselves (2) and at least one rioter was injured (3) in the process. A short time later, a young man was pronounced dead at (3) Salmaniya Medical Complex.

[160] Citizens for Bahrain, 'Weapons Cache Proves Motives Not Peaceful', in *Gulf Daily News*, 5 January 2014, http://archives.gdnonline.com/NewsDetails.aspx?date=04/07/2015&storyid=368096

In a similar incident in October 2012, when the police shot and killed sixteen-year-old Hussam al-Haddad, the MOI issued the following statement.

The director general of the Muharraq Police dept said that a police patrol was carrying out its duty securing (4) a crowded Al Khalifa Avenue in the middle of Muharraq, when it was subjected to a terrorist attack (1) carried out by a large number of firebombs (Molotovs) (1). This was at 9.30 pm yesterday. The attack endangered the lives of the patrol, civilians, residents and those present, which led to the injury of the patrol, fear among citizens/residents, panic, and damage to public and private property (2). The police dealt with matters in accordance with established legal procedures, (4) appropriate to such cases and defended both themselves and citizens (2 and 4). This resulted in the injury (3) of one of the persons taking part in this terrorist activity (1), who was immediately taken to hospital where he died. To confirm, this was both a terrorist act and attempted murder (1 and 2), intended to take the lives of those policemen on patrol whilst also subjecting citizens and residents to danger. Director general says he had informed the public prosecution of the incident.

The headline about the death of policeman Muhammad Asif read as follows: '*Police Officer Dies in Unprovoked Attack*'. Contrary to the report about the death of Hussain Al Jaziri, which implied Al Jaziri's guilt, and stated that he was participating in the day's 'most violent' protest, the report about Muhammad Asif claims that the attack was unprovoked. The fact the protest was termed 'the most' violent also indicates that the police were under the most duress at this time, further legitimizing their harsh response. Whereas protesters killed by the police are inevitably done so in the name of 'self-defence', police killed at the hands of protesters are done so without provocation. At least this is how it is articulated by official channels. The MOI also chose to frame the deaths of policemen as an act of martyrdom, referring to them as 'duty martyrs'. They do not do this with civilians, suggesting that they are attempting to appropriate the category of 'legitimate victim', adding a sense of religious sanctity and righteous sacrifice to the actions of the security services.

There is a similar asymmetry in announcements of investigations into cases where police or protesters are harmed. In cases where police are harmed, the Ministry of the Interior almost always state that an investigation was launched to find those who were 'responsible'. When protesters die at the hands of the police, an investigation is sometimes launched, although it rarely mentions that the purpose is to find out who is responsible. In the November 2012 follow-up to the *BICI Report*, where the government were meant to be demonstrating their implementation of the recommendations, a detailed list of deaths of protesters during confrontations with the police was included. Interestingly, eighteen instances of police violence that resulted in the death of a civilian were framed as *responses* to dealing with a 'riot'.[161] The term 'riot' implies an orderless, dangerous situation, as opposed to peaceful political expression. Official publications frequently frame and justify the deaths of civilians killed by police as a consequence of dealing with a disorderly and dangerous situation.

While it is perhaps unsurprising that the MOI use these rhetorical devices to demonize protesters and absolve themselves of responsibility, such statements are often the basis of the police's defence argument should they end up in court. This is especially disturbing when the media are prevented from bearing witness to such incidents. Journalists and reporters have often been arrested for covering protests (although they are rarely given an actual reason for their arrest). By removing witnesses from the scenes of such incidents the MOI can exploit an information vacuum, one in which their testimony will lack credible contradiction. This is especially true in a court run by a non-independent judiciary dominated by members of the ruling family, who also run the Ministry of the Interior.

Leveraging External Actors to Demonize Protesters

The state media have also attempted to add legitimacy to their discourse by misrepresenting the words of important international actors. For example, in 2014, the Bahrain News Agency (BNA) put out a news release claiming that Eileen Donahoe, the US ambassador to the UN Human Rights Council, had 'expressed her dismay at violent demonstrations and burning of tires' by Bahrain's opposition.[162] When informed, Donahoe's office denied the story. In another example, the BNA claimed that UN Secretary-General Ban Ki-moon had praised Bahrain's efforts to 'preserve its security and stability hailing the reform process spearheaded by His Majesty King Hamad bin ʿIsa Al Khalifa'.[163] In actual fact, Ban Ki-moon was voicing concern about state violence towards protesters. In yet another case, the chairman of the BICI commission, Cherif Bassiouni, was forced to release a statement saying that his opinions had been deliberately misrepresented by the pro-government

[161] BICI Follow-UpTeam *BICI Follow-Up Report*, November 2012, http://iaa.bh/downloads/bici_nov2012_en.pdf

[162] Bahrain Watch, 'UN Ambassador to UN Human Rights Council', September 2014, https://bahrainwatch.org/media/#!donahoe

[163] Bahrain Watch, 'Secretary General of the United Nations', *Fabrigate*, September 2014, https://bahrainwatch.org/media/#!bankimoon

newspaper *Al-Ayam*.[164] Amnesty International too had to issue a rejoinder after *Akhbar Al-Khaleej* [The Gulf News] claimed that they had issued a statement condemning the opposition for using children as human shields at protests.[165] Other people or international organizations who claim to have been misrepresented or misquoted by Bahrain's government-controlled media include: Member of European Parliament Marietje Schaake, Former US Chairman of the Joint Chiefs of Staff Hugh Shelton, the US TV channel CNN and the president of the International Federation for Human Rights.[166,167] The frequency of the behaviour would imply that it is a deliberate tactic designed to add international and external legitimacy to the state's condemnation of the opposition.

The Iran, Sectarianism and Existential Threat Myth

The importance of creating or exaggerating an existential threat to provoke the real possibility of violence or death is the very essence of securitization. Securing and protecting citizens from a threat gives the state 'legitimacy to undertake extreme measures to protect itself and keep the larger citizenry secure'.[168] The government, via the media, have long exaggerated opposition links to outside groups in order to achieve this securitization, and frame dissent as the influence of ill-intentioned outsiders. Before the emergence of the Islamic Front for the Liberation of Bahrain, the link between Bahrain's leftist movement and external sponsors was deliberately exaggerated by the Bahrain government. This is not mere conjecture but something that was admitted by officials at the time. Even British diplomats noted that 'the extent to which the People's Bloc and PLO [Palestinian Liberation Organization] were taking their orders from outside Bahrain [had] been deliberately exaggerated by the Government'.[169] However, since the Iran–Iraq war and the Iranian

[164] *Fabrigate*, 'Chairman of the Bahrain Independent Commission of Inquiry', Bahrain Watch, https://bahrainwatch.org/media/#!cherif

[165] *Fabrigate*, 'Amnesty International', https://bahrainwatch.org/media/#!amnestyintl

[166] *Fabrigate*, https://bahrainwatch.org/media/

[167] These are but a few. Other known cases include: Souhayr Behlassen, Reuters News Agency; author and broadcaster Joseph Braude; former UK Foreign Office Minister Alistair Burt; British MP Conor Burns; Tunisian Minister of Culture Mehdi Mabrouk; Tunisia's Al Nahda Party; former UK Foreign Secretary William Hague; UN High Commissioner for Human Rights Navi Pillay; the International Federation of Journalists and the UK Under Secretary of State and various UK Lords. See Fabrigate, Bahrain Watch, https://bahrainwatch.org/media/

[168] Fernandez, *Policing Dissent* p. 161.

[169] Tesh, Bahrain's First Parliament, The National Archives.

Revolution of 1979, the bogeyman changed from the communist bloc to Iran. Since that time, the government and the prime minister, in particular, have exploited the media to paint the opposition as a fifth column determined to impose a Shiʿi theocratic state in Bahrain. Consequently, the Bahraini regime has harshly suppressed Shiʿi groups and played the sectarian card to portray the Shiʿa as an Iranian 'fifth column', resulting in dividing Sunna from Shiʿa.[170]

This demonization of the Shiʿa was particularly acute after the alleged coup attempt of 1981, which was widely reported. Criticism of Iran was deliberately made more salient in the press. According to one British official, reports on Iranian subversion in Yemen were given 'pride of place in the local press'.[171] In the 1990s, government officials made numerous statements linking the mass protests and any acts involving violence in Bahrain to hostile foreign powers or entities.[172] In 1995, the Minister of the Interior stated that an extremist religious organization with illegitimate goals and linked with a political entity abroad was behind incidents of sectarian strife and sabotage.[173] Such announcements were undoubtedly made deliberately to detract from the fact that the Intifada was, as one reporter in the *Economist* put it, 'neither exclusively Shiʿa nor hardline Islamist'.[174] On the contrary, the committee tasked with drafting the petition for basic rights and democracy in the 1990s included Sunni religious leaders and even a 'Sunni feminist professor'.[175]

In addition to Iran, the foreign bogeyman has been extended to other Shiʿa or Iranian-backed organizations such as Hezbollah. On '1 May 1995, the State Security Court sentenced Hussain 'Ali al-Tattan to 10 years' imprisonment, Salman ʿAbd Allah al-Nashaba to five years' imprisonment, and eight other defendants to three years' imprisonment',[176] for being members of Hezbollah in Bahrain. Officials also publicized that Shaykh ʿIsa Qassim, based in Qom in the 1990s, guided Hezbollah in Bahrain and that the 250-strong network discovered was only a small part of a labyrinthine network connected to Iran.[177] To bolster this narrative, extensive TV coverage was given to a group of Shiʿi youth who said they were trained in Lebanon and called the

[170] M. Ma'oz, 'The "Shi'i Crescent": Myth and Reality', The Saban Center for Middle East Policy at the Brookings Institution, no. 15, November 2007, www.brookings.edu/~/media/research/files/papers/2007/11/middle-east-maoz/11_middle_east_maoz.pdf
[171] S. P. Collis, 16 January 1982, FCO8/4332, The National Archives.
[172] Amnesty International, *Bahrain: A Human Rights Crisis.* [173] Ibid.
[174] *The Economist*, 'Gazing Backward', 25 March 1995, issue 7907. [175] Ibid.
[176] Ibid.
[177] K. Evans, 'Bahrain Plot "is Led from Qom"', *The Guardian*, 12 June 1996.

'Bahrain Hezbollah'.[178] As others before them, they were most likely tortured into confessing.

In 2013, Erin Kilbride, an American teacher living in Bahrain, was deported for allegedly inciting hatred against the government and ruling family. The Bahrain News Agency published an image of Kilbride's room, replete with a Hezbollah flag hanging on the wall.[179] Sometimes the propaganda was more subtle. In a video alleging to show a police raid on a Bahrain bomb-making lab, a 1,000 Iranian Toman note was placed strategically on the table to make it obvious to the camera.[180] In 2014, Bahrain's foreign minister, Shaykh Khalid bin Ahmad Al Khalifa, said that Hezbollah was behind an explosion that killed a Jordanian police officer working in Bahrain.[181] Given the government's attempts to forge an Iranian link, the veracity of these claims was disputed. Bahrain's government-controlled papers frequently published anti-Iranian cartoons. One example included Bahrain caught in a spider's web, about to be devoured by a spider that had Khomeini's head.[182]

The continuity of anti-Iran tropes throughout the 1980s, 1990s and 2000s reflect a lack of dynamism in power. Indeed, the prime minister was at the forefront of this fear mongering. In a 2012 interview with the German newspaper, *Der Spiegel*, the prime minister said, contrary to the *BICI Report* which had found no Iranian involvement in Bahrain's unrest, that protesters wanted to turn Bahrain into a 'second Iran'.[183]

Strategic Disinformation

A crucial aspect of promoting fear of Iranian involvement in Bahrain's affairs has been through the strategic use of disinformation, often through social media or pro-government op-eds in the daily papers. Here, false news stories have been promoted by hegemonic forces. These

[178] Bahry, 'The Opposition in Bahrain'.

[179] Bahrain News Agency, 'Teacher with Links to Extremists Deported for Social Media Activities and Violation of Labor Laws', 10 August 2013, http://www.bna.bh/portal/en/news/574672

[180] M. O. Jones, 'Bahrain Propaganda Machine is Turned up to Eleven', Marc Owen Jones, [web blog], 13 July 2012, https://marcowenjones.wordpress.com/tag/timoney/

[181] Reuters, 'Policeman Killed in "Terrorist" Attack in Bahrain: Interior Ministry', 8 December 2014, www.reuters.com/article/2014/12/08/us-bahrain-security-policeman-idUSKBN0JM25320141208

[182] 'A Persian Dream'. Artist: Muharraqi. Sourced from @AAK_News Instagram Account, 8 November 2015, www.instagram.com/p/90OGq4JT2u/

[183] *Spiegel* Online, 'Interview with Bahrain's Prime Minister: The Opposition "are Terrorising the Rest of This Country"', 27 April 2012, www.spiegel.de/international/world/interview-bahraini-prime-minister-prince-khalifa-bin-salman-al-khalifa-a-830045.html

stories have typically contained references to Iranian involvement in Bahrain's affairs, or sympathy towards Iran from Bahrain's pro-democracy movement. During 2011, there was a string of false stories claiming that boats from Iran, heading to Bahrain, had been intercepted. An opaque Kuwaiti news portal stated that Qatari authorities had intercepted an Iranian boat smuggling weapons to Bahrain.[184] However, Qatar later denied the story.[185] On 21 March 2011, soon after the Uprising began, King Hamad announced that a foreign plot had been foiled with the aid of Saudi troops. A week later another Kuwaiti news site said that Qatari authorities had intercepted two Iranian ships carrying weapons to Bahrain, a story that Qatar again denied.[186] On 12 November 2011, a few weeks before the release of the *BICI Report*, the government reported that they had discovered another terror cell with links to Iran.[187] This was another case of history repeating itself. In 1975, a similar report was released strategically the day before the government dissolved the National Assembly in August. The press announced that thirty people were arrested from the National Liberation Front and the People's Front. Soon after, the weekly paper *al-Mawaqif* [Points of View] published an article claiming that a ship loaded with arms had been intercepted as it headed towards Bahrain. Many of those arrested also reportedly had anti-government propaganda 'pamphlets ready for distribution'. The only difference between today's 'plotters' and those that came before them is that they are Shiʿa rather than left-wing.[188]

Clearly, there has been a pattern of spurious claims about an impending foreign assault on Bahrain during times of political crisis or on the anniversary of political events. More recently, two days after the second anniversary of the 14th February uprising, the Ministry of the Interior announced that they had arrested eight men who were part of a terror cell with links to Iran, Lebanon and Iraq. Although such occurrences were previously reported in traditional media, the present-day modus operandi has often been for the local press in Bahrain to report content from dubious online Arabic news portals. This news is not

[184] H. Toumi, 'Qatar Denies Seizing Iran Boat Loaded with Weapons', *Gulf News*, 23 January 2013, http://gulfnews.com/news/gulf/qatar/qatar-denies-seizing-iran-boat-loaded-with-weapons-1.1136351

[185] Ibid.

[186] J. Bladd, 'Qatar Denies Seizing Iran Ships Carrying Weapons', *Arabian Business*, 28 March 2011, www.arabianbusiness.com/qatar-denies-seizing-iran-ships-carrying-weapons-390435.html

[187] M. Singh, 'Terror Plot Foiled', *Gulf Daily News*, 13 November 2011, http://archives.gdnonline.com/NewsDetails.aspx?date=04/07/2015&storyid=317594

[188] A. Khalaf, 'A Ship Loaded with Arms and Explosives', *Al-Waqt*, http://bahrainonline.org/showthread.php?t=224765

verified and the provenance of the publisher is often unclear. Nonetheless, the fact the stories originate in ostensibly 'foreign' news sites lends them a veneer of authenticity that would be less plausible had they simply originated in Bahraini media.

As well as these suspicious or 'fake' news stories, government officials have propagated bizarre myths designed to provoke national concern about Iranian expansionism.[189] One such highly improbable story included mentioning that there were tunnels[190] to Iran dug under the Pearl Roundabout. Another unsubstantiated story was that an Iranian drone had been found off the coast of Bahrain.[191,192] In another instance, the Minister of State for Information Sameera Rajab claimed protesters were carrying Bahraini flags with twelve points instead of the usual five. This was an apparent unsubtle allusion to their commitment to Twelver[193] Shiʿi Islam, the dominant strand of Islam in Iran. Sameera Rajab even went on Al Jazeera holding a photo of one of these flags as evidence. Bizarrely, the flag in the photograph she was holding did not have twelve points, although this was not picked up on by the presenter or the guest. The twelve-point flag conspiracy reached such a pitch that the Arabic translation of the *BICI Report* mentioned it, suggesting that high-level and influential forces were inserting anti-Iranian propaganda into a supposedly independent document. Soon after this scandal raised doubts about the integrity of the BICI investigation,[194] the Arabic translation of the report was withdrawn.

Doubling down on the Iranian bogeyman trope, the government announced in 2013 that the February 14th Youth Coalition was backed by Hadi Al Mudarrasi, an exiled Iraqi cleric who had lived in Bahrain, and who had subsequently moved to Iran. Al Mudarrasi had been accused of attempting to stir up unrest in Bahrain during the 1980s.[195]

[189] Lies of Samira bin Rajab [online video],

[190] @busalmani, 'نفق في الدوار يودي على ايران و نفق في عذاري يودي العكر حشى اللي عندكم ارانب مو بشر كله تحت الارض#مسخره #طنبورها #نفق#البحرين [Tunnel under the Roundabout Leads to Iran while Tunnel under Al 0dhari leads to Al-Eker] Bahrain 23 October 2012, https://twitter.com/busalmani/status/260673433485062145

[191] Fajr al-Bahrain, 'competition … enter and put in your information' [web forum], www.fajrbh.com/vb/threads/24682/

[192] *Al-Wasat*, 'Iran Deny Sending Unmanned Aerial Spy Drone Above Bahrain', 23 May 2013, www.alwasatnews.com/3911/news/read/774772/1.html

[193] Twelver Shiʿa Islam is the largest branch of Shiʿa Islam. The name reflects that its adherents believe in twelve divinely ordained leaders, known as the Twelve Imams.

[194] N. Toorani, 'Arabic Report of BICI Withdrawn', *Gulf Daily News*, 30 November 2011, http://archives.gdnonline.com/NewsDetails.aspx?date=04/07/2015&storyid=318698

[195] 'Bahrain: Report on the Carrying Out of Terrorism and the Identity of the February 14 Movement' [online video], 12 June 2013, www.youtube.com/watch?feature=player_embedded&v=D_WBKYBXlY0 Translated from Arabic by the author.

Other sensationalized reports included articles focusing on emotive topics like the exploitation of women and children by the opposition. Faisal Fulad of the government-run Bahrain Human Rights Watch Society stated to the press that 'Iran-backed extremists are using children as human shields'.[196] However, there has been no documented evidence suggesting that this occurred.

Bad News Is Big Business: Western PR Companies

In the modern, globalized era of contentious politics, a protest movement can no longer be repressed solely within the confines of a single state. To market the exogenous Iranian threat myth to the international community, and to stigmatize the pro-democracy movement, Bahrain turned to numerous Washington and London-based PR companies, marking a broadening of the repressive reach of the Bahrain government. While the Bahraini regime and those loyal to the status quo intimidated local dissenters, often through grisly means, bad publicity meant that it became increasingly difficult for Bahrain to demonstrate to its Western allies that it supported human rights. Bahrain's protecting powers have always been sensitive to criticism of the Bahrain regime, and a small industry of reputation management firms have profited from whitewashing human rights abuses in the country. British private companies, taking over the role once held by the British-led PR office in Bahrain, have worked directly to prevent negative coverage of Bahrain. The idea is that protecting the reputation of the Al Khalifa will diminish external support for the protest movement that may risk putting pressure on the status quo.

While Western political and military support has been crucial in bolstering the strength of the Al Khalifa regime and supporting the repressive apparatus, Western PR companies, particular in London and Washington, have played a significant role in burnishing the reputation of the Bahrain regime. The Bahrain government spent $32,504,997 on PR-related activities between 2011 and 2012.[197] The modus operandi of such companies varies. Some have created seemingly independent websites and social media accounts to attempt to influence public opinion, while others have sought to arrange high-level meetings with Bahraini policymakers and

[196] S. S. Grewal, 'Children Used as "Human Shields"' *Gulf Daily News*, 7 June 2013, http://archives.gdnonline.com/NewsDetails.aspx?date=04/07/2015&storyid=354827

[197] Bahrain Watch, *PR Watch: Dragon Association*, 2012, https://bahrainwatch.org/pr/dragon-associates.php

influential Western government officials.[198] Many of these companies have focused on lobbying international newspapers to remove material that could be seen as critical of the regime in Bahrain. For example, Dragon Associates, a London-based company, forced the *Guardian* newspaper to temporarily take down an article written by Bahraini activist Nabeel Rajab and journalist John Lubbock. The article in question detailed how torture had occurred at Bahrain's F1 track, a showpiece location in the government's drive to promote business-friendly Bahrain.[199] The complaint from Dragon Associates was strategically timed ahead of the Bahrain F1, and although the *Guardian* eventually put the piece up again unchanged (albeit with a superfluous addendum), they only did so after tickets for the F1 had already started selling.[200] Thus the intended impact of the piece, which had been to discourage people from going to Bahrain to see the F1, was undermined.

Similarly, the Cable News Network (CNN) decided not to repeat a shocking documentary presented by the journalist Amber Lyon on Bahrain after its first airing caused 'blowback' from the Bahraini government.[201] The Bahraini government also hired British law firm Carter-Ruck to attack the *Independent* for their negative coverage on Bahrain.[202] Bahrain even threatened to sue the *Independent* for allegedly 'orchestrating a defamatory and premeditated media campaign'.[203] As has happened before, Nawaf Mohammad al Mawda, the then acting press and foreign media director for the Information Affairs Authority in Bahrain, claimed that the *Independent* published 'provocative' articles that deliberately targeted Saudi Arabia and Bahrain.[204] Again, we see how criticism in the press of Bahrain and its allies really irks the regime.

Many such PR companies have exploited the Iran-as-a-bogeyman trope. This was done to legitimize the Bahrain government crackdown to the international community in order to diminish global support for Bahrain's opposition, or at least allow Bahrain's Western allies to justify any inactivity on their part. Former British military officials

[198] Bahrain Watch, 'Bahrain Govt Hires 18 Western Companies to Improve Image after Unrest', 23 August 2013https://bahrainwatch.org/blog/2012/08/23/bahrain- government-hires-18-western-companies-to-improve-image-after-unrest/
[199] Interview with Brian Whitaker, February 2012.
[200] Bahrain Watch, *PR Watch: Dragon Association*, 2012.
[201] J. Horne, 'Tn Tn Tn and Torture in Bahrain: 'Puncturing the Spectacle of the "Arab Spring"', in A. Shehabi and M. O. Jones (eds), *Bahrain's Uprising: Resistance and Repression in the Gulf*, London, Zed Books Ltd, 2015, p. 163.
[202] Ibid.
[203] www.journalism.co.uk/news/bahrain-to-sue-independent-over-defamatory-articles/s2/a544720/
[204] Ibid.

and diplomats have been co-opted into writing several op-eds for various publicatons. Notable among them was Harold Walker, who was the British ambassador to Bahrain between 1979 and 1981 during the Iranian Revolution. No doubt his perspective would be perceived as valuable, given that he was in Bahrain during such a decisive period. In a now-removed op-ed published by the Conservative Middle East Council (CMEC),[205] Harold Walker stated that 'the 1979 Islamic revolution' and the impact of Iran [had] been the single most important factor in fragmenting Bahraini society and injecting religion into opposition politics'.[206] However, this strangely contradicts claims he made in the midst of the Iranian crisis. In a diplomatic cable written in 1980, Harold Walker stated: 'Since the Iran/Iraq conflict began, there have, as you know, been virtually no visible signs of support among the Bahraini Shiʿa for Imam Khomeini'.[207] Whether Walker was deliberately following a specific public relations line, was only referring to support for Khomeini or had simply changed his mind is unclear, but he was undoubtedly seen as someone who would toe the Bahrain government's line on Iran. Indeed, Walker appeared to have established a reputation as a reliable scribe for pro Bahrain op eds. In 2012, David Cracknell, the head of London-based PR firm Big Tent Communication, complained to the *Guardian* newspaper about an article written by Dr Kristian Ulrichsen and Dr Ala'a Shehabi that was critical of the Bahrain Government. Cracknell asked the *Guardian* to publish an article that he would provide, written by Harold Walker. Cracknell's request was denied.[208]

The reach of public relations was also evident in investigations designed explicitly to offer transparency about the UK's foreign policy with Bahrain. In a parliamentary report commissioned to evaluate the UK's relationship with Bahrain and Saudi Arabia, the Bahrain government's perspective on the events of 2011 was overrepresented. Of the thirty submissions dealing with Bahrain in Part One of the report, 22 were submitted by organizations or individuals either paid directly by the Bahrain government, or those suspected of doing PR for the government or British officials deemed to hold pro-establishment views on Britain's

[205] I was asked by the CMEC to write a piece on social media in Bahrain. My critical piece was rejected on the basis it did not fit with the Conservative support for the Bahrain government.

[206] H. B. Walker, 'Bahrain after the BICI', *Conservative Middle East Council*, 6 December 2011, http://cmec.org.uk/blog/bahrain-after-the-bici/

[207] Walker, The Shiʿa in Bahrain, 26 October 1980, FCO8/3489, The National Archives.

[208] Bahrain Watch, *PR Watch: Big Tent Communications* 2012, https://bahrainwatch.org/pr/big-tent-communications.php

foreign relations with Bahrain.[209] At least five relatively glowing and separate testimonies were included from members of the same social organization called 'the Bahrain Society'. Interestingly, Bahrain Society's previous chairs include Harold Walker, and Michael Rice, the latter a former PR expert whose company, the Michel Rice Group, was asked to cover the dissolution of Bahrain's parliament in 1975 so that the Bahrain Government could 'present their case abroad'.[210] Indeed, Michael Rice and Co, Ltd, issued press releases for the Bahrain government from 1964 to 1978. As can be expected from a press release, they marginalized dissent and avoided anything critical or controversial, serving instead to emphasize Bahrain's progress and openness. Indeed, the trope of Bahrain's modernity and development has been one pushed by British officials since the 1950s, strategically and as an antidote to perceived subversive ideas.

The role of British elites in spreading this propaganda was drawn out by investigative work, including the monitoring of Bahrain's tendering contracts and the US Foreign Agents Registration Act (FARA). Other British officials, like retired British army officer Graeme Lamb, whose company, G3, was contracted by the IAA in 2011 for £1.5 million, wrote at least six op-eds for newspapers, including the *Guardian* and the *Times* of London. All of these articles attempted to put spin on deflecting criticism from the Bahrain government.[211] The main argument in Lamb's article for the *Guardian* article was, 'Of course, Bahrain could and should do better. However, Iran is a bigger, and a more immediate problem'.[212] The emergence of these narratives addresses how different political interest groups attempt to control, influence and respond to political upheaval within particular countries.[213] It also highlights how the salience of specific narratives is constructed over time and place by a complex network of local and international actors. Indeed, it is the very epitome of a transnational attempt at information control.

[209] M. Jones and J. Horne, FAC Submission Breakdown, Internal Document at Bahrain Watch, 2012, https://docs.google.com/spreadsheets/d/1puCoqyyMvPeJy1fWmVuGqIVOOzGcLsLNuwo94ZFH0UM/edit?usp=sharing

[210] Noble, 26 August 1975, The National Archives.

[211] Bahrain Watch, *PR Watch*, G3, https://bahrainwatch.org/pr/g3.php

[212] G. Lamb, 'Why Narrowly Cast the Push for Democracy as the "Arab Spring"?', *The Guardian*, 22 February 2012, www.theguardian.com/commentisfree/2012/feb/22/democracy-arab-spring

[213] M. M. Howard and M. R. Walters, 'Explaining the Unexpected: Political Science and the Surprises of 1989 and 2011', *Perspectives on Politics*, vol. 12, no. 2, June 2014, p. 401.

Wikipedia Edits

In 2011, it was discovered by the author that someone was editing *Wikipedia* entries in a manner designed to stigmatize the opposition and lionize the Bahraini government. The ubiquitous online encyclopaedia, *Wikipedia*, is a crucial first stop for many people seeking to find information on a multitude of topics. Public relations companies understand this, and, as such, frequently attempt to burnish or control the image of their clients' (and their clients' adversaries) Wikipedia entries. The discovery came shortly before the Bureau of Investigative Journalism revealed that the now-disgraced British public relations company, Bell Pottinger, who had a contract with the Bahraini government, offered a service that involved making Wikipedia edits on behalf of clients. Wikipedia subsequently ran an investigation and suspended a number of accounts they believed were run by Bell Pottinger. Several articles on Bahrain were edited by an account named 'PetersBah', which was investigated by Wikipedia as part of the Bell Pottinger affair. Although Wikipedia could not determine the exact provenance of the account, they deemed that it was 'behaviourally suggestive' of advertising and blocked it.[214] PetersBah exclusively edited Wikipedia entries on Bahraini politics to demonize the opposition and burnish the reputation of the Bahrain government. Table 6.1 is an outline of the nature of these edits, and how they contributed to the lionization or stigmatization of respective actors.

Although the exact identity of PetersBah is unknown, there is evidence to suggest it was an actor close to the government or government sources. By tracking the timestamp of specific changes made to Wikipedia edits, it was clear that PetersBah edited the aforementioned entries of police advisors John Timoney and John Yates before it was first announced in the press that they were coming to Bahrain (which was reported by the *Daily Telegraph*). This would imply that whoever ran the account was a party to the information before it became public. A plausible explanation is that a public relations company working on behalf of the government was briefed ahead of the announcement. The ability of anyone, opposition or otherwise, to make edits to such a ubiquitous platform as Wikipedia suggests that regimes can use companies or people to whitewash human rights abuses, legitimizing international support while also stigmatizing protesters and activists. By attempting to reduce negative press of Bahrain, these companies are

[214] Wikipedia, Wikipedia: Conflict of interest/Noticeboard/Bell Pottinger COI Investigations, https://en.wikipedia.org/wiki/Wikipedia:Conflict_of_interest/Noticeboard/Bell_Pottinger_COI_Investigations

Table 6.1 *Examples of Wikipedia edits*

	Purpose of Edit	Example of Edit
1	To provide positive coverage on initiatives or reforms set up by the Bahrain government	Writing about the BICI commission, PetersBah added content that stressed the panel's independence and value in ending conflict, tropes that painted the government as progressive and willing to address mistakes: 'The panel of investigation is described by human rights group Amnesty International has "an impressive line-up of independent international experts"'[a] and 'US President Barack Obama praised the establishment of the Commission on 2 July 2011 and said that, "by providing an independent assessment of what happened and identifying those responsible, the Royal Commission will play an essential role in advancing reconciliation, justice, and peace in Bahrain'.[b]
2	To provide positive information on persons employed by the Bahrain government	Before the announcement that Bahrain had hired John Yates and John Timoney to help reform the police, PetersBah wished to mitigate potential controversy by showing the policemen in a positive light. He added to John Yates' Wikipedia entry. 'At the time of his resignation, he was Scotland Yard's most trusted detective and has led many of its highest-profile probes for almost a decade. He also won widespread praise for his tenacious 16-month pursuit of senior Labour politicians implicated in the cash-for-honours scandal and was seen by many as a possible future commissioner'.
3	To frame accusation of police violence as a response to protester violence	After the regime controversially shot and killed 16-year-old Ahmed Jaber, PetersBah edited the entry to make it appear as if Jaber provoked the police into action: 'Ahmed Jaber, a 16-year-old Bahraini, was killed during a small riot in which police clashed with youths who were blocking roads and setting bins on fire in Abu Saiba, in western'. PetersBah added: 'According to the Interior Ministry, the boy was killed by a bird-pellet shot fired following an attack on police who also allege that rioters threw [Molotov cocktails] at security forces'.[c]

Table 6.1 (*cont.*)

	Purpose of Edit	Example of Edit
4	To demonise protesters by emphasizing negative stories such as their involvement in torture	PetersBah's contributions mimicked the discourse of the Bahrain government by inverting opposition narratives on torture. In other words, PetersBah wished to emphasize the idea that the opposition was torturing migrant workers. The following edit demonstrates this stigmatization: 'Following the government's attempts to restore law and order to the country following the 2011 Bahraini Uprising, a number of claims of torture emerged. Although predominantly from the opposition alleging government-backed torture, there were also cases of protesters torturing security service members and Asian immigrant workers'.[d]
5	To demonize activists and protesters by suggesting links to Iran	PetersBah made two significant edits to the profile of internationally known Bahraini activist Maryam Al Khawaja. Those edits included information conflating Maryam with Iran. E.g. 'Al Khawaja is closely associated with the Bahrain Freedom Movement led by Saeed Shehabi…who is reported to be funded by Iran'.[e]
6	To frame narrative in a manner that suggests the opposition were undermining progressive initiatives led by the government	'Following the clearance of the Pearl Roundabout the government made an unconditional offer of political dialogue and security forces were withdrawn from the streets. Talks led by the Crown Prince were ruined by opposition radicals, who erected roadblocks manned by armed vigilantes'.

[a] PetersBah, Royal Independent Investigation Commission: Difference between Revisions, Wikipedia, July 2011 https://en.wikipedia.org/w/index.php?title=Royal_Independent_Investigation_Commission&diff=prev&oldid=441362334

[b] PetersBah, Aftermath of the Bahraini Uprising of 2011: Difference between Revisions, Wikipedia, October 2011 https://en.wikipedia.org/w/index.php?title=Aftermath_of_the_Bahraini_uprising_of_2011&diff=prev&oldid=457317643

[c] Ibid.

[d] PetersBah, Torture in Bahrain: Difference between Revisions, Wikipedia, September 2011, https://en.wikipedia.org/w/index.php?title=Torture_in_Bahrain&diff=prev&oldid=451655091

[e] PetersBah, Maryam al-Khawaja: Difference between revisions, September 2011, Wikipedia, https://en.wikipedia.org/w/index.php?title=Maryam_al-Khawaja&diff=prev&oldid=452883882

Table 6.2 *Summary of frames of how the opposition and government were constructed*

Demonizing Opposition	Exonerating the Government
o The opposition protesters are practising dissimulation, or *Taqqiya*. In other words, they may be calling for democracy but are in fact backed by Iran and want to impose a Shi'i theocracy. o The February 14th Youth Movement, in particular, are violent radicals. o The opposition's values are backward and conservative, and they are sectarian. They will harm Bahrain's progressive image. o The opposition is heavily armed.	o Any violence carried out by security forces against protesters is always only in reaction to violence carried out by protesters, labelled as 'terrorists' or 'vandals'. o The country is not ruled by an autocrat but by an enlightened monarchy shepherding its subjects towards democracy. o Torture and police abuse are not systematic but are the result of just a few bad apples rather than orders by any senior officials. o The government has made amends for any mistakes it made last year by commissioning the *BICI Report*.

conforming to the government's desired narrative that Bahrain is a safe space, ripe for investment and the global flow of capital.

Interestingly, the reach of this repression highlights the importance of the growing web of non-state actors invested in laundering the reputations of authoritarian regimes. It is interesting too, that many of these companies known to be doing so are British or American, suggesting a devolution of repressive strategies to non-state, private actors. Table 6.2 highlights a simplified framing analysis of all the documents produced or written by known public relations entities contracted by institutions connected to the Bahrain government. They are broken down into two categories: discourses that demonize/stigmatize the opposition, and those that exonerate or justify heavy-handed government responses.[215]

From Fake News to Fake Journalists and Social Media

Liliane Khalil, the Political Catfish

The rise of social media has increased the opportunities for the government and pro-government forces to stigmatize opposition or spread propaganda. The relative ease of opening a Twitter, Facebook or Youtube account and posting anonymous information means that it has been

[215] For more details on these documents, see https://bahrainwatch.org/pr/

adopted as a widespread tactic of harassment and 'astroturfing'. Here, astroturfing refers to flooding online conversations with propaganda in order to 'turf over' writings and publications seen to be critical of the Bahrain government. In 2011, anytime a blogger or news organization posted an article critical of the Bahraini regime, dozens of accounts would astroturf the comments section, criticizing the author or 'debunking' the criticism of the Bahraini government. In 2011, I and another activist discovered that a public relations company paid for by the Bahrain government had likely created a fake journalist persona called Liliane Khalil.[216,217] Khalil wrote an extensive op-ed published on the site of the author Reza Khalil, an alleged (anonymous) Iranian defector who fled to the United States after working in the Iranian Revolutionary Guard. Khalil's piece noted how the respected Bahraini human rights activist Abdulhadi Al Khawaja and the Bahrain Center for Human Rights were an Iranian-linked clandestine operation. Liliane Khalil claimed to be an Atlanta-based journalist. She had previously written for *BikyaMasr*, a now-defunct Egyptian web news portal that garnered quite a large following in 2010 and 2011. She also wrote for the ironically named *Bahrain Independent*, a news site set up in 2011 to promote Bahraini government propaganda. It was edited by Saqer Al Khalifa, a member of the ruling family who later became the media attaché for the Bahraini Embassy in Washington.[218]

Khalil's rise to prominence was in no small part due to her prolific tweeting about the Arab Spring that earned her a sizeable following. Indeed, before she opened a new Twitter account in May 2011, the number of her Twitter followers was estimated to be over 3,200. Despite this impressive figure, it was difficult to track any trace of Liliane Khalil before about February 2011. As a supposedly renowned journalist, whose jet setting had taken her to Cairo, Israel, Atlanta and New York, it was surprising not to find any significant mentions of her on the web. She also claimed to be on first name terms with disgraced US Representative Anthony Weiner and also claimed to have interviewed several notable figures in the Middle East, including King Hamad, the Bahraini foreign minister, Natan Sharansky, Dr Hanan Ashrawi and Egyptian

[216] This story was broadcast on Al Jazeera and France 24. See M. O. Jones, 'The Hunt for #LilianeKhalil', *Al Jazeera English*, 4 August 2011, www.youtube.com/watch?v=TgCp15kVggI

[217] Despite her singular mention, the investigation into Liliane Khalil was extensive and painstaking. At the time, with the rise of issues like the 'Gay Girl of Damascus', the issue was very revelatory in determining the dangers of social media and what sources to rely on.

[218] The *Bahrain Independent* ceased functioning, 14 July 2011.

diplomat Mohammed AlBaradei. Partly due to her convincing persona, and daringness in using photos of 'herself', she interacted with numerous legitimate commentators and pundits on Twitter without having her identity questioned. Indeed this is perhaps unsurprising, the novelty of social media at the time and dominance of the Internet-as-emancipation paradigm meant that many people let their guard down.

The intrigue and suspicion surrounding Liliane Khalil's veracity first began after her involvement with a group of Tweeters working from the besieged town of Zintan in Libya. The group, using the Twitter handle @operationlibyia, gained many followers after Khalil wrote an obituary for one of their members who had reportedly died. Following the obituary, the group began to ask people to contribute to relief efforts by putting money into their personal PayPal account. However, it was not too long before people began to question the authenticity of @operationlibyia. For example, why was their Arabic so bad? How could they Tweet from a besieged town? After a few days, Liliane Khalil claimed that she had been duped by the group, calling them frauds. Shortly after this statement, Liliane Khalil's Twitter and Tumblr accounts were deleted. As it stands, there remains no discernible trace of the article Liliane Khalil wrote on Tumblr that denounced this group as frauds. The article, which also mentioned two other unknown charities that could be donated to, vanished into thin air.

Liliane's disappearance caused a stir, with many people who knew her online expressing concern for her safety after exposing the scam, others thinking maybe she was part of the scam. This conjecture soon ended when Liliane Khalil re-emerged on Twitter, her new name @Liliane_-Khalil replacing the old but similar @lilianekhalil. Upon her return, Khalil claimed her account had been hacked. The hacking excuse again elicited some suspicion, with people asking questions such as: why would hackers delete all her accounts, including her Tumblr blog and all her articles for *Bahrain Independent*? Did she have copies of her old blogs? If so, why didn't she republish old articles, especially the one about being duped?

Further open source research revealed that her Twitter photo traced back to the LinkedIn profile of a Gisele Cohen, who allegedly worked for a company called Union Healthcare in Atlanta. Other online twitter identities were found to be linked to her profile and biography, including those of a Victoria Nasr, Gisele Mizrahi and Gisele Cohen – among others. Her various claims on Twitter, including alleged interviews with Dr Hanan Ashrawi and Dr Natan Sharansky, were unusual as there was never any evidence of these interviews. She also claimed to have given talks at Oglethorpe University and New York University, although neither of them had heard of her. Despite these claims, Khalil still remained credible in the eyes of many, not least because she was given some form of legitimacy by writing for a Bahrain web blog run by real people who claimed to be setting up a bureau in Atlanta. Also, many of her other claims, such as her working at CNN, or the Turkish News Channel TRT, were simply accepted at face value by many in the online community. The misinformation and fake news at this time were overlooked due to the fact the Arab Spring had heralded a relatively new media landscape, in which issues of authenticity and verification were unfolding rapidly. However, after the' Gay Girl in Damascus' story, whereby a Syrian-American woman called Amina Arraf Tweeting from Damascus was revealed to be Tom MacMaster, an American man studying at Edinburgh University, people grew more wary of fake news and the power of anonymity on social media.[219] As with Amina, well-known commentators had interacted online with Liliane Khalil, some assuming her anonymous identity was simply there to protect her in a dangerous climate. These interactions were not always positive. Her article purporting to expose the Bahrain Centre for Human Rights' links with Iran quoted Dutch academic Katje Niethammer, who responded by posting a video response denouncing Khalil's article as a misrepresentation of her work.

Liliane Khalil was exposed shortly after she claimed she was holding a Gala opening for the *Bahrain Independent*'s Bureau in Atlanta, along with staff from the British Consul. Khalil even posted a photo with women she claimed worked at the consul. When contacted, the consul denied that any such event had existed. The reveal that Khalil was a political catfish and possible fraudster prompted much attention, and was covered by France 24, the *Washington Post,*[220] and Al Jazeera's 'The Stream'. Following the exposé several news organizations invited Liliane Khalil for an interview, but she refused to go on camera, compounding suspicions that the photos she used of the young woman on her social media accounts were not in fact her. Her explanations for her various acts of dishonesty, including posting links to wire content by other journalists, claiming they were her own, were that she was drunk. Later, Khalil stated that she was working for a Bahrain-based PR firm called Task

[219] BBC News, Syria Gay Girl in Damascus blog a Hoax by US Man, 13 June 2011, www.bbc.co.uk/news/world-middle-east-13744980

[220] Elizabeth Flock, 'Liliane Khalil, Another Possible Fake Blogger: Should We Care?', *The Washington Post*, 5 August 2011, www.washingtonpost.com/blogs/blogpost/post/liliane-khalil-another-possible-fake-blogger-should-we-care/2011/08/05/gIQAd2XvwI_blog.html?utm_term=.2acd67c11a90

Consultancy who had, according to documents showing financial contracts between Bahrain entities and foreign companies, been given money by the Bahrain government to conduct public relations. Members of Task Consultancy had claimed on their Twitter accounts to be representing Liliane Khalil after the exposé.

In the rapidly changing media landscape of the Arab Uprisings, the Khalil episode was one of the first real insights into how public relations companies and individuals were generating patently false stories that sought to emphasize the Iran angle. What is more, it marked the beginning of a new trend of people using fake Twitter accounts to masquerade as journalists.

Bot Networks

While Liliane Khalil represented one fake journalist, operated by a real human being, the rise of bot accounts has been prolific. Bots are pieces of code written by humans that perform functions on an automated basis. A common behaviour is for bot accounts to automatically Tweet out messages from Twitter accounts. An investigation I undertook in July 2016 revealed that up to half of the Tweets being produced at any one time on the #Saudi and #Bahrain hashtag were produced by robots. The content of the Tweets reflected Saudi foreign policy and was frequently sectarian. The initial discovery was made after the bots started tweeting about the removal of ʿIsa Qasim's nationality. ʿIsa Qasim was an opposition figurehead, and the removal of his nationality provoked an angry response from both Bahrainis and Saudis alike. As such, social media was used to demonize Qasim. Multiple tweets contained the inflammatory phrase, 'Isa Qasim, the #Shiite #terrorist, telling followers to annihilate #Bahrain's Security Forces'. The conflation of ʿIsa Qasim, an important spiritual leader for Bahrain's Shiʿa with the term 'terrorist', again sought to propagate the idea that Bahrain's opposition was a violent religious fifth column. The volume of the bot Tweets was such that any legitimate discussion on Twitter was drowned out or polluted by fake accounts. In a sample of 10,887 tweets taken in a 12-hour period on 22 June 2016, 51 per cent were from bot accounts. Table 6.3 shows a sample of these Tweets.

The purpose of the bots was not simply to spread propaganda supporting the repressive actions of the Bahrain authorities but to drown out legitimate or critical information. One informant commented that the sheer volume of such bots and fake accounts made Twitter 'politically useless'. While useless might be an overstatement, the presence of propaganda bots has made it much more difficult to determine between

Table 6.3 *A sample of Tweets taken from #Bahrain hashtag on 22 June 2016*

Number of Tweets in Sample	Translation	Original Tweet
2,742	Persians and the Majus (Zoroastrians) hate the Arabs	الفرس والمجوس ......حقد على العرب
946	The Iranian regime is the leader in war and the manufacturing of terrorism and crises #withdrawalofnationalityfrom'IsaQasim #Bahrain #Fitna	النظام الإيراني راس حربة في صناعة الإرهاب و الأزمات https://t.co/ZcOaOUvn1T … #سحب_جنسية_عيسى_قاسم #الفقيه_القائد #Bahrain #البحرين
95	Iran's Mullah's politicize the Hajj (piligrimage) with slogans outside Islam and the Sunna of the Prophet #withdrawalofnationalityfromIsaQasim #Bahrain #Fitna	دولة ملالي #ايران تسيس الحج بشعارات خارجة عن الإسلام و السنة النبوي https://t.co/0HCOKhuJf6 … #البحرين #Bahrain #آية_الله_الشيخ_عيسى_قاسم
1,773	Sowsan Sha'ir*: Bahrain will not listen to the threats of Qasim Suleimani** or others like him. *Sowsan Sha'ir is a pro-status quo Bahraini columnist **QS is an Iranian general who said that the move against 'Isa Qasim would cause a fire in the region.	وسن الشاعر:البحرين لا تعبأ بتهديدات قاسم سليماني ولا غيره https://t.co/zkHjKY0u9O … #سحب_جنسية_عيسى_قاسم #الفقيه_القائد #Bahrain #البحرين

legitimate vox pops and fake accounts.[221] Journalists reporting on Bahrain may then mistakenly confuse bot accounts for the opinions of real people. It has also meant that trending hashtags can be manipulated and gamed in order to promote pro-regime messages.

Grassroots Conspiracies and Sectarian Discourses

Social media has also provided opportunities for ostensibly bottom-up forms of information control through fake news stories and sousveillance. It has created a fertile breeding ground for the spread of various conspiracy theories and alleged evidence of an Iranian-backed plot. Trolls, in particular, have exploited Bahrainis' thirst for information, which naturally increased during the 2011 crisis. However, the lack of credible official information on issues and the government's deliberate

[221] For more on the methodology, see M. O. Jones, 'Automated Sectarianism and Pro-Saudi Propaganda on Twitter', Exposing the Invisible – Tactical Technology Collective, 2016, https://exposingtheinvisible.org/resources/obtainingevidence/automated-sectarianism

obfuscation made the scramble for answers in a febrile environment both desperate and blind.[222] Thousands of sock puppet accounts appeared at key moments in 2011, spreading government propaganda and intimidating opposition figures online.[223] Many of these supposed grassroots conspiracy theories were appropriated by the government to fit their diplomatic strategy. Some verged on the absurd. In one instance, a fake Wikileaks cable that appeared to originate on the loyalist internet message board 'Bahrain Forums' was used by two state newspapers to discredit a critical Sunni parliamentarian. The story accused representative Osama Al-Tammimi of supplying the US Ambassador Thomas Krajeski with private parliamentary documents and asking for US citizenship. The rumour was likely fabricated to discredit a Sunni MP who was sympathetic to the opposition.

Perhaps the most virulent piece of fake news to emerge from social media was the aforementioned Twelve-Point Flag Conspiracy propagated by Sameera Rajab. The twelve-point flag conspiracy started as a video circulated on YouTube, Twitter, Facebook and other messaging services. It quickly received 18,400 views, and was given an air of credibility when a number of online commentators, including a Bahraini PhD student studying at Leeds University in the UK, confirmed without evidence that some loyalist students at the University of Bahrain were being bullied into taking down the official Bahraini flag and told to put one up with twelve points.[224] Another Bahraini, a member of the ruling family, and a former professor of international relations stated on Twitter: 'Do you know what's the story behind the 12 edged flag? Well, all I can say is that majority of Shiʿa in #Bahrain are Twelvism Shiʿa. Research it'.[225] Encouraged by a climate of uncertainty and fear, and legitimized by credible members of the online community and the government, the conspiracy's impact was extensive.

Naturally, the twelve-point flag controversy highlighted the increase of a sectarian discourse that had long been bubbling under the surface. The extent to which those propagating the discourse were government-operated accounts or citizens within and without Bahrain cannot be determined. However, an investigation by members of Bahrain Watch, including Bill Marczak, found evidence suggesting that the Bahraini

[222] Ibid. [223] Jones, 'Social Media, Surveillance.'

[224] @Kalfadhel, 'Many UOB students were bullied to take off the official Bahraini flag (with 5 points) and replace it with the', 12 March 2011, https://twitter.com/KAlFadhel/status/46576218627248128

[225] F. Desmukh, 'Myths and Lies in the Bahrain Infowars' [web blog], 11 April 2011, http://revolutionbahrain2.blogspot.co.uk/2011/04/myths-and-lies-in-bahrain-infowars.html

government was operating social media accounts spouting extremist discourse. This was undoubtedly designed to contribute to sectarian polarization. Bill Marczak noted, 'If the Government did indeed run these accounts, this would raise serious questions about to what extent the Government is inciting its supporters – and the opposition – to violence.'[226]

The Resurrection of Hate Speech

Another pernicious occurrence was the 7areghum Twitter account, which paved the way for the propagation of overt sectarian discourses. Tweets from 7areghum and several other similar accounts set the tone for sectarian hate speech, which had previously been generally present on YouTube videos of political violence in Bahrain. Derogatory anti-Shiʿa terms like *Majūsi, Rawāfiḍ, Ṣafawi, and Walad/abna' al-Mutʿa*[227] were used frequently. Rather than this being a new phenomenon, the language reflected the activation of nascent sectarianism. Before 2010, shortly before the Uprising, anti-Shiʿa rhetoric in some online forums was probably the most salient sectarian theme, representing what can be called 'rich prejudice'. That is, the online demonization of the Shiʿa involved the mobilization of discourses that drew on many aspects of life integral to the construction of identity, including religion, nationality, gender, class, geography and even biology. Indeed, the discourses point to a pervasiveness of prejudice that the government seeks to activate in order to divide the opposition.

Ilsa Schumacher's ethnographic work during the 1980s revealed that the Shiʿa in Bahrain have been perceived by many Sunnis to be illiterate, revolutionary, emotional villagers, farmers or labourers. In the current milieu the discourse suggests that they are perceived to be any of the following: terrorists, uneducated, apostate, traitorous, sexually promiscuous, untrustworthy, violent, deviant, backwards, Iranian, Jewish or Rafadites. Such a rich lexicon of distrust illustrates a belief among some members of the community that the Shiʿa are innately backward. These

[226] B. Marczak, 'Is Bahrain's Government Running Extremist Accounts?', Bahrain Watch blog, 5 August 2013, https://bahrainwatch.org/blog/2013/ 08/05/is-bahrains-government-running-extremist-accounts/

[227] *Majūsi,* meaning Zoroastrian, is a derogatory term often used by Sunnis to describe Shiʿa. *Rawāfiḍ,* meaning rejecter, is often used by Sunnis to mean one who rejects the true Islamic authority and leadership. *Ṣafawi* is another term derogatory term directed Shiʿa. It comes from 'Safavid, the Iranian dynasty that made the state religion of Iran Shiʿa Islam. *Walad/abna' al-mut'a* literally means children of *mut'a. Muta'a* is a type of temporary marriage that some Muslims argue is immoral.

beliefs disregard socio-economic explanations that underpin and motivate political unrest. The endemic nature of this rich prejudice has undoubtedly contributed to a continuation of Shia subjugation, especially because the government is populated with people who hold these beliefs.[228] That the government periodically revive and rejuvenate this prejudice through the media reflects the instrumentalization of sectarianism hate for social control purposes.

Before 2011, such sectarian discourses were already prevalent but were buried mostly online and in the YouTube comments sections. The year 2011 prompted the reintroduction of these ideas in plain sight, in public newspapers and on television. One newspaper, the *Gulf Daily News,* even published a letter that referred to opposition activists as 'termites'. After explaining at length what it is that termites do, the letter concluded: 'The moral is: to get rid of [termites] so that they don't come back. [The only way to do this is] to get rid of the mother (the head) responsible for these destructions. There is no point in capturing and getting rid of baby ants when the mother is still reproducing!'[229] Similarly, Bahrain Television prompted outrage when they used the terms 'cleanse' and 'purify' to describe the police operation of removing protesters from the Pearl Roundabout. They also said that the Pearl Roundabout had been 'desecrated'.[230] Journalist Roy Gutman compared this dehumanizing language with that used immediately before the Rwandan Genocide.[231] By using this type of language, government-approved news agencies were tacitly endorsing the dehumanization and 'othering' of opposition members. Not only was this designed to draw public support away from the social movement but to encourage Bahrainis to believe that critics of the government were legitimate targets for retribution and state repression.

Indeed, despite democratization, state-controlled media is still an avenue for government repression. Reforms to the media post-2011 have done little to change this, presenting an opportunity for circumvention rather than a commitment to free expression. The creation of a media ombudsman in the form of the Higher Media Board (HMB) was nothing

[228] M. O. Jones, 'Here's Looking at YouTube. Neoliberalism, Political Violence, and Racialised CounterSpace in Bahrain', MSc Dissertation, University of Durham, 2010.

[229] www.gulf-daily-news.com/Print.aspx?storyid=305077

[230] Bureau of Human Rights, Democracy and Labor, US Department of State, Bahrain 2011 Human Rights Report, April 2011, www.state.gov/documents/organization/186633.pdf

[231] Roy Gutman, 'While Bahrain Demolishes Mosques, US Stays Silent', *Truthout*, 8 May 2011, www.truth-out.org/news/item/977:while-bahrain-demolishes-mosques-us-stays-silent

more than a reorganization of the censorship apparatus, with control of appointment in the hands of the Al Khalifa. It consists of seven members, 'four of whom will be directly appointed by the King, and one each appointed by the Prime Minister, President of the Shura Council, and the President of the Council of Ministers'.[232] Thus, recommendations from the BICI to create a media body that promoted opposition representation and tempers incitement to violence or hatred through the media have not been implemented.

The fetishization of the Shiʿa and Iranian threat, and the rise of sectarianism through media channels al Naqib argues, is a particular feature of tribal monarchies that became more apparent after the demise of Arab nationalism, to which the Gulf monarchies had all been hostile. Al Naqib adds that this 'tribal consciousness' is becoming more embedded, and facilitated with the rise of new media outputs.[233] Khuri concurs that the regime exploits the polarities inherent in political unions,[234] and this is most easily done along sectarian lines. This factor would certainly explain the emphasis in Bahrain on focusing efforts at stigmatization on the sectarian threat.

The process of dividing society has been further facilitated by the appointment of officials perceived as sectarian. Sameera Rajab was widely viewed as being sympathetic to Saddam Hussein – a figure widely disdained by many Shiʿa everywhere for his sectarian beliefs.[235] Rajab's anti-Shiʿa statements have previously stirred much controversy. However, what Al Naqib calls these 'pathological symptoms'[236] of emerging Sunni tribal exclusivity have long tentacles. The buttressing of such existing sectarian sensibilities with negative media framing has contributed to some of Bahrain's Sunna adopting a government line in which they 'reject the position taken by Sunni liberals that democratization would integrate the Shiʿah'. Instead, conservative Sunna are portraying 'democracy as a vehicle for the Shiʿah to seize power in Bahrain'.[237] As the regime relies more on a policy of divide and conquer, one that creates a small but ideologically extreme core of support, repression will

[232] POMED, 'One Year Later'.
[233] Al Naqeeb, *Society and State in the Gulf and Arab Peninsula*.
[234] Khuri, *Tribe and State in Bahrain*, p. 242.
[235] D. Murphy, 'After Formula One Scrutiny, Bahrain Hires a Fan of Saddam Hussein to Improve Its Image', *The Christian Science Monitor*, 25 April 2012, www.csmonitor.com/World/Security-Watch/Backchannels/2012/0425/After-Formula-One-scrutiny-Bahrain-hires-a-fan-of-Saddam-Hussein-to-improve-its-image
[236] Al Naqeeb, *Society and State in the Gulf and Arab Peninsula*, p. 127.
[237] M. Ma'oz, 'The "Shi'i Crescent": Myth and Reality', The Saban Center for Middle East Policy at the Brookings Institution, no. 15, November 2007, www.brookings.edu/~/media/research/files/papers/2007/11/middle-east- maoz/11_middle_east_maoz.pdf

inevitably become more severe. Strengthened by the support of these Sunni conservatives, 'the regime imposed considerable restrictions and harsh discrimination on Shi'i political representation, employment, education and, for the first time in Bahrain, Shi'i religious worship'.[238] This is all reflected in the state media, which frequently attempts to dehumanize the Shi'a by referring to them in subhuman terms, such as spiders or snakes. To this end, sectarian polarization through the state media is a mutually constructed phenomenon from above and below. The state pushes forward a sectarian narrative, manipulating sensibilities and emotions, while tapping into extant prejudice that leads to hostility and sometimes violence.

Surveillance

The Rise of the Surveillance State

Fuad Khuri noted that the Al Khalifa could once name every family in Bahrain, as well as their history, a feat undoubtedly facilitated by Bahrain's small size. Although this intimate knowledge was vital in understanding what was happening in Bahrain, the ruler also began using tactics of infiltration as early as the 1920s. The ruler reportedly had 'secret agents'[239] in Bahrain's village communities in the 1920s. One British official referred to these as the ruler's 'special proteges among the Baharinah', or 'myrmidons'.[240] However, the 1970s marked a shift in this relationship between the ruling family and Bahraini residents. There arose an increasing distance between not just the Al Khalifa and the *baḥārna* but also between the Al Khalifa and the traditional upper-middle-class merchants, a point noted by Marc Valeri.[241] With the breakdown of this traditional intimacy, came the need for new methods of infiltration. In addition, opposition forces were developing new forms of tactics and complex structures designed to resist traditional attempts at dismantling them.

British tactics of surveillance, honed by various colonial police outfits across their vast Empire, were then brought to bear in Bahrain. They were not always sophisticated, and sometimes ad hoc. When Charles Belgrave

[238] Ibid.
[239] C. K. Daly, 30 September 1923, in P. Tuson, A. Burdett and E. Quick (eds), *Records of Bahrain 1820–1960,* vol. 4, Slough Archive Editions, 1993, p. 136.
[240] S. G. Knox, 'Report on Bahrain Reforms', in P. Tuson and E. Quick (eds), *Records of Bahrain 1820–1960,* vol. 3, Slough, Archive Editions, 1993, p. 779.
[241] M. Valeri, 'State–Business Relations in the Smaller Gulf Monarchies–The Role of Business Actors in the Decision-Making Process,' IDE Discussion Papers 524, Institute of Developing Economies, Japan External Trade Organization (JETRO), 2015.

was commandant of the police in the 1920s, he did, for example, undertake surprise visits of Manama to make sure that his police were working as they should be. However, Belgrave's patrols quickly became something of a quaint parochialism as Bahrain modernized rapidly. The unrest of the 1950s prompted an urgent need to re-evaluate political policing. In 1965, Bahrain recruited Colonel Ian Henderson, who had previously pioneered methods of infiltrating the Mau Mau during his tenure as head of security in Kenya. By capturing, co-opting and turning members of opposition groups, Henderson formed 'pseudo-gangs' or 'counter-gangs' who would then infiltrate opposition networks. While Henderson had grown up in Kenya, and spoke Kikuyu, the language of the Mau Mau, his lack of Arabic, at least initially, would have led him to be more reliant on his Arabic-speaking colleagues. Whether or not this affected his personalist involvement in intelligence gathering is unclear, but it does highlight how Britain's experience of control strategies garnered in other corners of the Empire were deemed useful in a small Gulf state. Moreover, it reflected a standardization of a scalable model of surveillance. Repressive methods, honed by the British, were now perceived as suitable for a rapidly modernising Bahrain.

Henderson's arrival in 1965 coincided with Bahraini labour agitation and the British visceral fear of communism. His surveillance strategy reflected this. The leftist threat in the form of the National Liberation Front, a Leninist-Marxist group with Nasserist leanings set up in Bahrain around 1955, was closely monitored. Later on in the 1970s, the government observed carefully any Bahrainis returning from Soviet or Communist countries. The security services worried that students returning from such countries would establish 'positions of influence in the government',[242] and try to undermine it from within.

To some extent, the tactics of surveillance seemed to work. Special Branch was content to rely on surveillance through the penetration of opposition networks, as opposed to the repeated incarceration and interrogation of suspected political opposition. By the late 1960s, the new methods devised by Henderson and Bahrain Special Branch were relatively effective in controlling leftist opposition. A report published by Special Branch described how surveillance was foundational for controlling the National Liberation Front. The report noted, 'in 1968, [The NLF] was penetrated at all levels by the Bahrain Security Forces, and its organised structure was destroyed'.[243]

[242] Given, Prospects for Bahrain, 29 October 1976, The National Archives.
[243] Bahrain Special Branch, 'The Bahrain National Liberation Front (NLF)', FCO8/3489, The National Archives.

As with students studying in the Soviet Bloc, any former exiles or political dissidents were potential suspects and closely monitored by the security forces. The British Ambassador Robert Tesh wrote in 1973 that those who returned from exile were 'closely watched and occasionally detained by the Security Forces'.[244] But it was not only those going abroad that were viewed with suspicion. The security services remained paranoid about any potential politicians or polemicists. In the run-up to the election for the National Assembly, Special Branch was even 'keeping track' of the activities of 'would-be members'.[245] This reflected the government's paranoia about the democratic turn.

The death of the National Assembly did little to assuage government paranoia. On the contrary, the dissolution of parliament reflected a resurgent securitization, both among the al Khalifa themselves but also British officials. In 1978, three years after the National Assembly was suspended, the British ambassador expressed alarm at Bahraini opposition abroad. He noted that 'the clandestine opposition seems to be inactive within the country, but has continued to work abroad, particularly among students, so that a reservoir of disaffection must be building up'.[246] Edward Given had raised similar concerns the previous year in 1977, once again using the same aquatic metaphor: 'students abroad continue to furnish a reservoir of dissidents'.[247] Despite this fear, Given expressed faith in Henderson's methods, stating that Bahrain's student organizations were "fairly well-penetrated by the security forces'.[248] This successful penetration reflected considerable government investment in monitoring Bahrainis abroad. Indeed, in 1975, the British Ambassador Robert Tesh reported that a million pounds was allocated to 'setting up student officers in foreign universities, presumably to try to control their political activities'.[249]

The trend of monitoring students abroad continued into the 1990s. According to Amnesty International, 'Bahraini students studying abroad, and relatives of political opposition activists or suspects are often subject to arrest and detention on their return to Bahrain.'[250] Amnesty also noted that: 'Many [students] have been subjected to torture or threats in order to force them to cooperate with the authorities, reporting back on the activities and friends of particular individuals. Detainees are left in no doubt

[244] R. M. Tesh, 'Bahrain: Annual review for 1973, FCO8/2181, The National Archives.
[245] Tesh, 'Bahrain Internal', 18 November 1973, The National Archives.
[246] E. F. Given, Annual Review 1978, 10 January 1979, FCO8/3305, The National Archives.
[247] Given, Bahrain Round Up, 20 June 1977, The National Archives. [248] Ibid.
[249] Tesh, Bahrain Internal, 1 March 1975, The National Archives.
[250] Amnesty International, *Bahrain: Violations of Human Rights*, p. 6.

that if they fail to comply, they may be held indefinitely.'[251] In 2011, Bahraini students studying in the UK complained of harassment by the Bahraini authorities. At least nine students in Britain said that their £850 subsistence grants and tuition fees had been axed due to their alleged political activities. One student noted how the Bahraini Ministry of Education informed his father that they had video footage of his son attending a rally in the UK. They asked the father to order the son home.[252]

The reach of this fear of surveillance has also been compounded by Britain's historic support of the Al Khalifa regime. Bahrain activist Jaafar Al Hasabi noted that the threat of surveillance was extended as far as London, especially after two activists were attacked on their way home during the 2011 Uprising.[253] Al Hasabi noted that activists in London did not feel safe anymore, because of spying, and other means. He believed that Britain's relationship with Bahrain meant that anything said there could be relayed back to Bahrain, and that the behind the scenes relationship between Bahrain and the UK was such that activists did not trust British authorities to protect them from surveillance. Al Hasabi attributed specific personal behaviour changes to this surveillance. For example, he would often be careful on the telephone, and only speak to people face-to-face, undermining the supposedly emancipatory potential of technology. The combination of actual surveillance, the threat of surveillance and the visible grisly consequences of engaging in dissent, all combined to create a climate of fear that lessened, for some people, their willingness to engage in contentious activity, whether in the UK or Bahrain.[254]

The Murder of al-Madani: Henderson's Method Challenged

Even after Independence, when Britain began losing its influence in matters of security policy, the role of British officers in maintaining the efficacy of the intelligence apparatus was frequently mentioned as necessary in preserving stability in Bahrain. However, the British were keen to minimize publicity about the extent of British influence in the Bahrain police. Exiled human rights organizations based in the UK, and elsewhere, were increasingly drawing attention to the role played by British

[251] Ibid., p. 9.

[252] R. Booth and J. Sheffer, 'BahrainRegime Accused of Harassing UK-Based Students', *The Guardian*, 15 April 2011, www.theguardian.com/world/2011/apr/15/bahrain-regime-uk-students

[253] J. Al Hasabi, 'Privacy Extra: Jaafar Al Hasabi and Marc Owen Jones Discuss Bahrain and Surveillance' [online video], 19 March 2015, www.youtube.com/watch?v=5ViK48BX24U

[254] Ibid.

officers in abetting human rights violations. Despite this, internal restructuring within the government gave the British some useful political cover. As Robert Tesh noted in 1973, 'the efficient and loyal Special Branch is run by Britons, because no Bahraini could do it. These are now coming under attack (not, as yet, seriously). They have at last been given the protection of a Bahraini Minister of the Interior'.[255]

While the British were very keen to maintain control of the Special Branch and its incumbent surveillance apparatus, they valued the protection of a Bahraini in a superior position. However, they also feared that 'Bahraini control of Special Branch could provoke civil unrest'.[256] The British, for their part, saw an efficient, British-run Special Branch as a bulwark between the local population and the ruling core. Their absence, argued the British, would be disastrous for Bahrain. This rather arrogant perception belied an important tactical shift, itself brought about by differences over surveillance policy. This shift in influence was evident in 1976 following the assassination of the newspaper editor and Shiʿa notable ʿAbd Allah al-Madani.[257] Leftists, who had previously been strictly observed without being interrogated, were now hauled in for often brutal interrogation. With the side-lining of Henderson and Bell and the ascendency of the conservative prime minister, the opposition now bore the brunt of a policy that had perhaps been curtailed by a less coercive form of surveillance.

This shift in tactics also reflected a shift in perceived enemies. While the British had a seeming obsession with leftist subversion, the Al Khalifa and Saudi Arabia were more watchful of Shiʿa or Iranian-backed subversion. Consequently, the Shiʿa were increasingly closely monitored. Roger Tomkys, the British ambassador to Bahrain in 1982, provided an example of this: 'The security forces took some precautionary steps to emphasize their close surveillance of Shiʿi meetings and these appear to have had the desired effect.'[258] The Shiʿi clergy were also closely monitored by the security services,[259] especially during Ashura. Other incentives were also offered. Muezzins were rewarded with a 50 per cent pay rise as 'trouble blew itself out' in 1979,[260] the implication being that they were being rewarded for remaining politically on message or keeping an eye on those among their flock who might be considered subversives.

[255] Tesh, Bahrain: Annual review for 1973, The National Archives.
[256] Wogan, Iran and the Gulf', The National Archives.
[257] Given, Prospects for Bahrain, The National Archives.
[258] Tomkys, Bahrain Internal, 30 October 1982, FCO8/4332, The National Archives.
[259] S. M. J. Lamport, 'Bahrain Security, 8 March 1982, The National Archives.
[260] Walker, Bahrain: Annual Review for 1979, The National Archives.

Although the government valued this extensive surveillance apparatus, it was not always clear how effective it was. Certainly, the increasingly coercive co-optation of 'pseudo-gang' members ran the risk of alienating large swathes of the population. In the short term, however, it was arguably effective. Certain British officials stated that the discovery of the IFLB coup plot in 1981 was due to the efficiency of the surveillance apparatus. On the other hand, a British note scribbled on an internal document mentioned that the then Crown Prince Hamad bin Salman Al Khalifa had told the Jordanian government that the coup had been discovered 'by chance', highlighting an element of confusion as to the true nature of what actually happened.[261] Following the coup attempt, the efficiency of Bahrain's security forces was bolstered by Saudi and UAE money, extending Bahrain's capabilities beyond what would be expected for such a small state.[262] Indeed, regardless of proven efficacy, the antidote to perceived threats has always been increased investment in the surveillance apparatus, by both Bahrain and its close regional allies.

Surveilling the Shiʿa

The regime's distrust of the Shiʿa population has prompted a deepening of the process of administrative surveillance. In 1996, amid the unrest, the government divided the country into four *muhafidhahs* (provinces), each with a governor directly responsible to the Ministry of the Interior. Accordingly, one of the duties of the governor was to maintain public order and security, and each governor could appoint an unlimited number of *mukhtars* responsible to him. As Bahry notes, the 'multitude of local mukhtars gives the government intensified security control over villages as well as urban areas'.[263] In a nod back to the municipality reforms of the 1920s, the purpose of the administrative structure was to exert further control via a deepening of surveillance structures. Specifically, the government made administrative reforms that further increased their power over Shiʿi religious elements.

Similar reforms were made to regulate the Shiʿi clerical establishment more efficiently. While the Ministry of Justice had previously nominated the imams in the Sunni mosques, paid their salaries, promoted or fired them,[264] the Shiʿa had been outside the reach of the government. A new decree in the 1990s would mean that all clerical appointments would be overseen by the Higher Council of Islamic Affairs. The council would screen Shiʿa nominations for clerical positions, as well

[261] Miers, Attempted coup in Bahrain, FCO8/4332, The National Archives.
[262] S. P. Collis, 16 January 1982, FCO8/4332, The National Archives.
[263] Bahry, 'The Opposition in Bahrain'. [264] Ibid.

as decide on expenditure for Shiʿi mosques and matams.[265] The decree also allowed the government to direct scholarships towards students, and thus enable them to control where Bahrainis received their theology education. This administrative sleight of hand could prevent some students from studying in countries perceived as hotbeds of subversion, such as Iran. Indeed, the change of this scholarship policy reflected a commitment to influencing the overall ideological persuasion of existing and future Shiʿi clergy.

The surveillance of the Shiʿi community is perhaps now more persistent than ever before. Paradoxically, the government's distrust of the Shiʿi community has not stopped them using Shiʿa informers. On the contrary, Shiʿa informants are necessary for conducting surveillance of the broader Shiʿa community. This was as true in the 1920s as it is today. During a meeting with a former US ambassador in 2007, prominent Bahrain businessman Faisal Jawad raised the issue of Shiʿa marginalization. Jawad reportedly 'scoffed at the government's distrust of Shiʿa in the security forces, claiming that the police have hired numerous Shiʿa to work undercover in the villages, and these Shiʿa have always worked loyally for the government'.[266,267] Despite this demonstrable but often coerced loyalty, the employment of Shiʿa into sensitive ranks of the military or security apparatus is still seemingly absent. In 2010, the Bahrain Centre for Human Rights told Human Rights Watch that there were 'no Bahraini Shiʿa in the ranks of the Special Security Forces, and that the only Bahraini Shiʿa working for the National Security Agency are a small number of informants and persons holding low-level positions'.[268] However, this loyalty within a discriminatory political system is problematic. Jane Kinninmont noted that the surveillance apparatus is often coerced into place and that Shiʿa 'refusing to act as informants were beaten, slashed with box-cutters, burned with cigarette lighters, or threatened with sexual assault'.[269] Thus while surveillance serves as a conduit for employing Shia into the security apparatus, it is only done so on the basis that those employed work to control their own community.

[265] Ibid. [266] Monroe, 'Prominent Shiʿas Paint Gloomy Picture.

[267] It is worth noting that the Al Khalifa have long relied on co-opted *baḥārna* to assist their domination. In 1923 Daly talks of how *baḥārna* Waziers were appointed to sublet Al Khalifa plots of land and to extort the *baḥārna*. farmers. See 'Administration Reports 1920–1924' [158r] (320/412), in *Qatar Digital Library*.

[268] Human Rights Watch, *Torture Redux*.

[269] J. Kinninmont, Bahrain: Beyond the Impasse, Chatham House, London, 2012, www.chathamhouse.org/sites/files/chathamhouse/public/Research/Middle %20East/pr0612kinninmont.pdf, p. 12.

Government Spying and Technological Shifts

The surveillance apparatus has only become more technologically sophisticated since the recent Uprising. In 2011 foreign expertise was brought in to increase the effectiveness of surveillance. CCTV cameras were installed around the country, but particularly outside Shiʿi villages. This policy reflected the advisory influence of the former British police officer John Yates. Yates did not hide his love for this type of surveillance;. Stating 'CCTV is everywhere [and is] utterly fantastic'.[270] In late 2011, police units dispatched to protests and other incidents often had a cameraman present recording protesters. John Horne noted that such techniques were indicative of UK training: 'This is reminiscent of British Forward Intelligence Teams, used to help police identify and monitor protesters, whose details are then stored on a database.'[271]

New technologies, while providing opportunities for resistance, have also been used by the government in an attempt to undermine protective tactics of anonymity used by many activists. This appropriation of new technology for repressive purposes has been a hallmark of the 2011 Uprising. Despite using anonymous accounts, eleven activists were put in jail in 2012–13 for referring to King Hamad as a 'dictator' (*tāghiyya*) or a 'fallen one' (*saqiṭ*) in Arabic.[272] Their details were obtained by using the internet, and it was often social media that was used as the medium of delivery. These attacks, most likely carried out by Minister of Interior's Cyber Crime Unit (a unit set up ostensibly to tackle online sex crimes) sought to identify the poster's IP addresses, which are assigned every time someone uses the internet via a local provider in Bahrain (e.g. Batelco, Zain, Menatelecom). Because 'Bahraini law requires that every time an IP address is assigned, the internet service provider must record the name of the subscriber of the internet connection, as well as the date and time',[273] IP addresses offer a wealth of information about the target. The telecom authorities must keep this information for at least one year, and the security forces must be able to access this information at any time directly.[274] As a result, simply clicking on malicious links generated from freely available online services sent out by government-operated Twitter and Facebook accounts is enough to reveal the physical home address of anonymous Bahraini activists.

Malicious links were also sent out through 'e-mail, and likely via other services including YouTube, InstaMessage, and mobile messaging

[270] J. Horne, 'Policing Bahrain: the Long Arm of the British', *Open Democracy,* 8 August 2013, www.opendemocracy.net/opensecurity/john-horne-john-lubbock/policing-bahrain-long-arm-of-british

[271] Ibid. [272] Bahrain Watch, 'The IP Spy Files'. [273] Ibid. [274] Ibid.

services including BlackBerry Messenger and WhatsApp'.[275] The government used 'IP spying' on 'journalists, labour unions, human rights groups, activists, licensed opposition groups... whistle-blowers, Sunni groups, vigilantes, and even residents opposed to the seizure of their homes to build a government housing project'.[276] Some targets were even sent malicious links from opposition or activist accounts that had likely been hacked by government agents.[277] This 'social engineering' is genuinely far more effective, as activists are more likely to click on a link they believe is from an ally.

When it comes to technological repression, it is important to reflect on the assemblage of institutions that profit from the production and dissemination of such products. In particular, the growing relevance of European-made surveillance technology was highlighted when it was revealed that the Bahraini Ministry of the Interior was using FinSpy, malware developed by UK-Based Gamma International, to spy on opposition members. FinSpy was able to 'take remote control of a computer, copy its files, activate the microphone, take screenshots, intercept Skype calls, and log every keystroke'.[278] All without the user knowing. Several Bahrainis were targeted with this malware. Those perceived as political dissidents were infected after opening malicious files disguised as banal email attachments. They included Ibrahim Sharif, the Sunni head of the country's liberal Wa'ad party; Muhammad al-Tajir, a prominent human rights lawyer; Hadi al-Musawi, head of Al Wefaq's Human Rights Department and Hasan Mushaymaʿ, an incarcerated opposition leader adopted by Amnesty International as a prisoner of conscience.[279] Several activists were targeted when FinSpy was attached to an email that appeared to come from a real Al Jazeera journalist called Melissa Chan.[280] Saiʿd Shehabi' was among three Bahraini exiles granted asylum in the UK to have their computers targeted with Finspy. Others residing in Belgium and Germany were also targeted.[281] Again, this targeting of the opposition abroad illustrates how Bahrain's repressive apparatus extends far beyond its geographical borders. This delocalization of repression is enabled by the Bahrain government's historic

[275] Ibid. [276] Ibid. [277] Ibid. [278] Jones, 'Social Media, Surveillance', p. 247.

[279] F. Desmukh, 'Bahrain Government Hacked Lawyers and Activists with UK Spyware', *Bahrain Watch*, [web blog], 7 August 2014, https://bahrainwatch.org/blog/2014/08/07/uk-spyware-used-to-hack-bahrain-lawyers-activists/

[280] W. Marczak and M. Marquis-Boire, 'From Bahrain With Love: FinFisher's Spy Kit Exposed?', Citizenlab, 25 July 2012, https://citizenlab.org/2012/07/from-bahrain-with-love-finfishers-spy-kit-exposed/

[281] European Center for Constitutional and Human Rights, 'Gamma/FinFisher: No Investigation into German-British Software Company', 12 December 2014, www.ecchr.de/surveillance

'friendship' with the UK. This is particularly the case when British companies are profiting from selling repressive technology to Bahrain. Other British companies such as Olton, now defunct, also contracted by the Bahraini Government, have advertised their products as being able to use social media to target ringleaders and thus stave off unrest.[282] In an interview, an informant mentioned that part of their mandate was to dig up publicly available information on targets (people) defined by their clients in order to blackmail them.[283]

Other methods of exploiting technology for surveillance in Bahrain have been cruder, yet they demonstrate the security services' commitment to adaptation. The security services exploited vulnerabilities in Zello, a social media application that allowed people to use their phones like walkie-talkies. Fifteen activists were arrested after being tricked into attending a meeting arranged by the police who 'had posted the message through the account of a compromised member'.[284] The police then posted messages via the app saying that they would come and get the activists, 'one by one'.[285] The ability of the authorities to forcefully coerce and compromise activists into accessing and exploiting their social media accounts is well evidenced. Once, in the Q and A session of a presentation on Bahrain at the London School of Economics in 2011, a Bahraini activist claimed that those who were arrested were asked for their Facebook or Twitter login details and threatened when they did not comply. Presumably their accounts were then used for the purposes of social engineering and obtaining details from fellow activists. Indeed, while it is important to note the liberalising or democratising potential of new technologies, the Bahrain authorities have been successful in utilizing them in counter-revolutionary and repressive measures.

Conclusion

The modern information control assemblage in Bahrain has its roots in imperial paranoia about Arab nationalism and communism. The British, who spearheaded the creation of Bahrain's public relations and propaganda apparatus, began doing so in the 1950s. Naturally, Britain's fear of communism and Arab nationalism and the threat it posed to the waning Empire meant that propaganda strategies reflected this. Bahrain's

[282] Jones, 'Social Media and Surveillance.' [283] Interview with former employee, 2014.

[284] W. Marczak, 'Bahrain Watch Issues Urgent Advice for Activists to Stop Using @Zello Due to Security Flaw', *Bahrain Watch*, [web blog], 7 September 2014, https://bahrainwatch.org/blog/2014/09/07/bahrain-watch-issues-urgent-advice-for-activists-to-stop-using-zello-due-to-security-flaw/

[285] Ibid.

Independence, the Iran–Iraq War, the Iranian Revolution and the Al Khalifa's own ethnocentrism created a situation in which the regime became increasingly suspicious of the country's Shiʿi population, as opposed to leftist subversion. As such, informational controls have becoming increasingly sectarian. Both the British and the Al Khalifa were zealous in their application of censorship, yet both differed in their priorities, especially with regard to propaganda.

However, as with other forms of repression, there is evidence of personalistic approaches informing information control strategies. As such, the application of informational controls is rarely consistent. Under the British, Belgrave personally vetted foreign journalists, wrote columns for the London *Times*, and ensured the timely surveillance of his own police force. To an extent, this personalism and autocratic tendency was extended with the recruitment of Ian Henderson, who attempted to recruit his colleagues from Kenya into the Bahrain police. However, this British paternalism gave way to some extent to an equally paternalistic, yet somehow different, form of information control. Following 2001, a clearly discernible group of hardliners took it upon themselves to closely monitor and repress opposition expression. The Al Khalifa ruling elite now exercise an enormous amount of control over media output, whether through unofficial means such as the Khawalid, or appointments on institutions such as the Supreme Media Council. Western tech firms and public relations companies underpin the capability of much of this assemblage, advising, profiting and tacitly encouraging the procurement of their various surveillance or stigmatization services.

The personalistic elements of control that transcend the role of institi-tions mean that elite perceptions of the Shiʿa as an underclass are now being indoctrinated into, and perpetuated by, future generations of Bahrainis. Unsurprisingly, propaganda campaigns, and media framing attempts, have led to an increase in anti-Iranian and anti-Shiʿa rhetoric. However, propaganda is for public consumption, while surveillance is generally not, and therefore surveillance is likely to target any opposition equally, regardless of sect.

The increasing modernization of Bahrain, and its corollary creating of distance between the ruling classes and ordinary Bahrainis, has necessitated a more formalized and complex system of surveillance. Similarly, during moments when Al Khalifa hegemony is threatened, either through democratization measures or social movement pressure, a paranoid reflex seems to kick in, with repressive mechanisms of redundancy implemented to ensure that the new openings are contained. This really gained pace in the 1970s, with the increasing funding of surveillance networks abroad, as well as the growing sophistication of the Special

Branch. In an age where the relevance of controlling digital networks and information systems is becoming integral to state security, and surveillance more and more embedded in technology, the Bahrain government and some who support the government (or oppose the opposition) have sought to use the internet and technologies to extend their digital surveillance network. They have co-opted new technologies to a large extent, weaponizing them in order to deliver a range of payload from spyware to disinformation and propaganda. The value of this advanced surveillance network, especially in a country as small as Bahrain, has long been perceived as crucial. This is especially true should the regime wish to offer any sort of political openings. As Robert Tesh said ahead of the opening of the National Assembly in 1973: 'Crucial to all this will be the Government's will to insist on retaining the means of knowing what is going on and controlling subversion – ie an effective security service with good morals.'[286]

The 2011 Uprising demonstrated that social media in particular can be appropriated by counter-revolutionary forces as a tool of repression. 'Forces' here does not just refer to the state. Indeed, the security services are just one node in a complex network of agents who can use technology to repress dissent. The assemblage of repression includes loyalist vigilantes, public relations companies, the surveillance industrial complex and an environment of permissiveness abetted by Bahrain's strategic relationship with Western allies. Certainly, the ability of both the regime and its supporters to engage in unfettered media and online vigilantism certainly answers the question posed by Marc Lynch: 'Are some groups differentially empowered by the new media?'[287]

[286] Tesh, From Bahrain Embassy, 18 December 1973, The National Archives.

[287] M. Lynch, "New Arab Media Research Opportunities and Agendas" In *Arab Uprisings: New Opportunities for Political Science*, Project on Middle East Political Science (POMEPS Briefings), pp. 5–8.

Conclusion
Between Retrograde Repression and Repression

> Revolution is unlikely to succeed as long as the Kingdom of Saudi remains intact[1]

This book has sought to explore Bahrain's modern history through the lens of repression in order to better understand: (1) what constitutes repression; (2) why certain methods are used at specific times and (3) what role Bahrain's external actors have played in constructing the repressive apparatus and influencing methods of repression. Through answering the first part with an expansive definition of repression, organized according to the master categories of *statecraft, personal integrity violations, legal repression and informational control,* it has been possible to garner insights into particular aspects of repressiveness and the reasons for its use – from the growth of repressive law and the rhizomatic growth of social media surveillance to political strategies designed to provide a façade of safety valves without power-sharing. By doing so, the deficiency of broad causal models has been revealed, indicating that more academic attention needs to be dedicated to how repressiveness is deeply dependent on context, temporality and other factors. These factors include the attitude or ideology of elites, the weakness or strength of the coercive apparatus, the availability of resources (whether technical, monetary or political will), the perception of threat, the nature of the threat, the technologies available and, crucially, the intentions and foreign policy of Bahrain's protectors.

Revisionism, Historic Injustice and Repressive Cycles

The application of the repression template to Bahrain's history has brought to the surface new facts about Bahrain's history. While these have been detailed throughout, there have been some notable historical trends. In particular, the examination of political trials suggests that the

[1] W. R. Tomkys, First Impressions, 4 February 1982, FCO 8/4332, The National Archives.

regime has routinely imprisoned or executed political criminals with little due process or evidence. This is especially true with regard to those accused of killing the newspaper editor ʿAbd Allah al-Madani in 1976, the deportation of the St Helena three and the trial of those accused of attempting to assassinate Shaykh Hamad in 1926. The book has also revised historical accounts of the aforementioned assassination attempt on Shaykh Hamad. It seems in that instance, Charles Belgrave acted as a true eminence grise, throwing members of the Khawalid family under the bus in order to preserve the more useful ʿAbd Allah Al Khalifa, by all means the prime suspect in the case. To the best of my knowledge, this fact has never been revealed in the substantial scholarship on Bahrain during the first part of the twentieth century. Even now, such facts remain remarkably pertinent, as they throw into sharp relief the current tendency to focus on the role of the Khawalid in Bahrain, whose recent rise to power was described by journalist Charles Levinson as partly the result of wounds that 'festered',[2] in the decades following the various trials of the 1920s. Indeed, a close examination of political trials in Bahrain, whether it be that of ʿIsa Qambar in the 1990s or those deported to St Helena in the 1950s, reveal what appear to be systemic attempts to subvert justice, undertaken in order to preserve the interests of the status quo. Such new insights provide interesting examples of those fleeting moments in which the motivations for particular repressive choices can be discerned. They also demonstrate the cyclical tendency of certain aspects of repression in Bahrain's modern history.

In many respects, such facts demand further investigation. Indeed, for colonial or imperial historians, many questions have arisen about the extent of British 'complicity' in the pursuit of Al Khalifa regime maintenance. The idea that the British helped prop up the Al Khalifa regime cannot be in dispute. British officials and citizens were engaged in practices that could have faced legal consequences were it not that Bahrain's nominal independence provided them some autonomy from what could generously be regarded as the burden of imperial overrule. Former colonial officers in the British Empire essentially became what were viewed as mercenaries, and the sovereign state system allowed an informal amnesty for those complicit in abuses in states where they were not citizens but employees. Before Independence, Britain intervened militarily, politically and economically, straying from what they had hoped would be a middle course of pacification and minimal interference in Bahrain. This was

[2] C. Levinson, 'A Palace Rift in Persian Gulf Bedevils Key U.S. Navy Base', *The Wall Street Journal*, 22 February 2013, www.wsj.com/articles/SB10001424127887324595704578239441790926074

particularly evident in the security forces, which were shaped by the British, certainly before Independence, but also afterwards. Indeed, for the British, in the 1920s the police were conceived as a force to restrain Al Khalifa brutality. Following Independence, British diplomats still believed that British officers in the police were crucial in preventing increasing police brutality that could result in civil war.

However, this is not merely an anti-imperial polemic. Indeed, despite the crystallization of Al Khalifa rule through British protection, this study has revealed that the British-led reforms in the 1920s did, for a number of decades, temper the modalities and, in some senses, the extreme brutality of the legacy of conquest of the Al Khalifa regime who had hitherto tyrannised, oppressed and extorted the indigenous *baḥrānī* population. At the same time, the regime that the British had preserved formed the basis of a privileged nucleus that was willing to repress doggedly to uphold a lucrative bargain. Bahrain's Independence, and the subsequent decline of British influence, prompted its subordination to Saudi Arabia which had an enabling effect on more coercive forms of repression. That circumstance, coupled with the Iran–Iraq war and the Iranian Revolution, seemed to result in a culture of revenge whereby the Al Khalifa regime, unrestrained and galvanized by Saudi conservatism, reasserted their previous tribal dominance over the Shiʿa. With the Saudis now conducting the type of regional imperial intervention formerly reserved for the British, the latter has undertaken a more surreptitious, neocolonial form of influence, executed through the sale of weapons, cover-ups, political support and the provision of security expertise.[3] Of course, this begs the question as to whether such support is more harmful in preserving the authoritarian rule. One must be mindful of the 'considerable leverage which accrues to those powers willing to supply advanced military equipment and training to the Gulf states'.[4] Indeed, just as Clive Jones and John Stone broadened the concept of strategic influence to include military sales and the influence of British nationals,[5] the new paradigm of influence must include the growing role of reputational laundering, spyware and other forms of strategic influence.

With regard to foreign actors, this book has highlighted how Bahrain's sovereign insecurity has had an impact on repression. Bahrain's

[3] M. O. Jones, 'Bahrain's Uprising: Resistance and Repression in the Gulf', Open Democracy, www.opendemocracy.net/arab-awakening/marc-owen-jones/bahrain%E2%80%99s-upising-resistance-and-repression

[4] C. Jones, and J. Stone, 'Britain and the Arabian Gulf: New Perspectives on Strategic Influence', *International Relations*, vol. 13, no. 4, pp. 1–24, 1997, doi:10.1177/004711789701300401.

[5] Ibid.

relationship with its suzerains, in particular Britain and Saudi Arabia, has had a significant impact upon determining the repressive methods and choices in Bahrain: from the micro level, such as Saudi Arabia pressuring Bahrain to execute prisoners, to making political gifts contingent on Bahrain abandoning democracy in the 1970s. This is not to overstate the case of a singular variable, yet Saudi has behaved as an *enabler* in forms of repression designed to be more paternal, violent, coercive and draconian. On the other hand, towards the end of the twentieth century the British generally favoured the thriftier alternative of administrative and constitutional reforms. Violence in Bahrain, the British reasoned, would simply focus more anger at British repression in other more 'significant' parts of Empire. Nonetheless, it was British protection of the ruling family in Bahrain that ossified a tribal system, setting the foundations for continued tribal exclusivity and societal discord in Bahrain. Indeed, the various strands, legacies, policies and influences of different agencies make determining particular variables problematic, although there does seem to be some evidence of repressive cultures, i.e. certain methods that are resultant from a confluence of particular ideologies, instruments, experience and attitudes. Despite the relative difficulty of finding comparable locations, comparative studies on places similar to Bahrain would be fruitful in seeing how the evolution of repression changed.

The election of Donald Trump as US president in 2016 has brought into sharp relief the importance of US foreign policy in dictating repressive practice in Bahrain. On Tuesday 23 May 2017, Bahrain's security forces raided the village of Duraz, killing five people and arresting 286.[6] The raid ended an almost-year long siege by the security forces. The Duraz assault was not the result of a sudden change within the Bahrain administration. On the contrary, the raiding of Duraz happened immediately after Donald Trump's visit to Saudi Arabia. The US regime's relationship with Saudi Arabia and their mutual antipathy toward Iran has unshackled the Bahraini regime, allowing it to take an even harder line against dissent without fear of US remonstrations. As such, the first half of 2017 was one of the deadliest in Bahrain's history, and certainly the most deadly since 2011. In January 2017, three young Bahraini men were executed for allegedly killing three policeman – the first time the death penalty had been used in Bahrain since 2010. Shortly afterwards, in February, another three young men were shot at sea after they escaped prison and tried to flee Bahrain by boat. In addition, twenty-two-year-old

[6] The five killed were named as Mohammed Ali al-Sari, Mohammed Kadhem Mohsen, Ahmad Jamil Al-Asfour, Ahmed Hamdan and Mohammad al Ekri.

ʿAbd Allah Al ʿAzjuz reportedly died while running from the police. It is not a coincidence that these killings occurred shortly after the election of Trump. Indeed, Saudi too saw a surge in state-sponsored executions of predominantly Shiʿa political prisoners.

It is not the intention of this book to completely denounce Bahrain's sovereignty. Bahrain, despite its small size, has been able to play off regional tensions between Saudi and Iran for its own benefit, indicating substantial agency. For example, it signed a Memorandum of Understanding with Iran for potential gas sales, mostly to prompt Saudi ire and get Qatar and Saudi Arabia to renege on a decision not to export gas to Bahrain.[7] However, its deference to Saudi has been hard to deny, whether in repression, or even trivial matters, and while the securitization of the Shiʿa threat may suggest that Saudi's influence in Bahrain is reserved predominantly on issues of Gulf Cooperation Council (GCC) security, Bahrain's unwillingness to defy their neighbours is evident in the most banal of matters. For example, the former US ambassador Christopher Henzel noted that Bahrain was unlikely to recognize Kosovo before the Saudis did.[8] Nonetheless, the growth of a GCC alliance seems to reflect an increasing tribal, monarchical and Sunni coalition whose interests transcend the demands of Bahrain's citizens wanting political change, and whose policies will continue to impact on how Bahrain represses internal dissent.

Theoretical Implications

New Insights and Old Generalizations

By examining long term trends in repression, we can see that not only do authoritarian regimes repress differently, but that the same regime represses differently over time due to changing regional politics and internal dynamics. For example, deaths in custody only appear to have occurred after Independence in Bahrain. Such deaths imply a change in certain factors over those years that resulted in the emergence of tactics that are not attributable to the Iranian Revolution. While the reasons for this have been hypothesized in the preceding chapters, it is only through extensive historical analysis that we can ascertain the emergence of such a phenomenon. This is also particularly interesting as it is often the Iranian Revolution or the 1981 coup attempt that are argued to

[7] C. Henzel, 'Bahrain-Iran Gas Deal Still Far Off', 3 February 2009, Wikileaks, https://search.wikileaks.org/plusd/cables/09MANAMA58_a.html

[8] C. Henzel, 'Bahrain Will Follow Saudi's Lead on Kosovo', 19 February 2009, Wikileaks, https://search.wikileaks.org/plusd/cables/09MANAMA97_a.html

have been the critical moments in shifting the regime's threat perception and subsequently increased coercion of the Shiʿa population.[9] However, as this research highlights, such assertions place an erroneous emphasis on the Iranian Revolution, rather than other variables, such as the impact of Independence, the increasing role of Saudi Arabia or the reassertion of the Al Khalifa's legacy of conquest. Thus, this interpretive work has undermined normative assumptions about Bahrain and the region that tend to reflect transatlantic foreign policy objectives that portray Iran as the main agent in creating draconian policy shifts in the Arab Gulf states towards the Shiʿa. In Bahrain's case, what is certainly evident is the extent to which Independence and Saudi ascendency have resulted in deleterious consequences for the country's Shiʿa community. Through the examination of repressive methods, this work has been able to highlight this outcome. Indeed, the tendency to overemphasize the role or the importance of the Islamic Front for the Liberation of Bahrain and the Islamic Revolution in Bahrain's history complements the government's attempts to paint the Shiʿa opposition as a security threat and consequently enact processes, legislation or actions that disproportionally criminalize Shiʿa members of society. Certainly, emphasizing the impact of the Iranian Revolution on Bahrain's internal politics adds credibility and legitimacy to a discourse of national security that runs the danger of positioning discrimination against Bahrain's Shiʿa as being in the interest of maintaining Bahrain's sovereignty.

In addition to revising previous assumptions about events before the 1950s, this is one of the first studies of Bahrain to focus on primary documentation of the immediate post-Independence period. The national archives, coupled with freedom of information requests, have shed interesting light onto a period that has proved to be remarkably insightful into the shifting nature of political decision-making in Bahrain. The period also marked the rise of US hegemony and the activities of leftist organizations such as the Popular Front for the Liberation of the Occupied Arabian Gulf. With these threats and changing dynamics, it was interesting, for example, to compare how the regime treated leftist opposition versus Shiʿa opposition. The aforementioned reassertion of the Al Khalifa legacy of conquest is perhaps the most notable finding of this period. This book has also challenged generalizations regarding repression in the Cold War period, such as the argument that the demise of the Soviet Union made states less autocratic in order to appease the democracy-spreading agenda of the United States. While this may be

[9] L. Louër, 'Sectarianism and Coup-Proofing Strategies in Bahrain', *Journal of Strategic Studies*, vol. 36, no. 2, pp. 245–60, 2013.

true in some contexts, this research – like Christian Davenport's research on repression in authoritarian states – highlights that the death of the Soviet Union did not have a particularly positive effect on Bahrain. In actuality, Bahrain's continued geostrategic importance to the United States meant that its protection of the status quo continued unabated. Indeed, repression has become worse despite the end of the Cold War.

The large timespan combined with a broad conceptualization of repression has also highlighted several other trends, prising open the authoritarian playbook. The growth of legal forms of repression and information control are particularly notable. While it would be tempting to assert, as Foucault does in *Discipline and Punish,* that the growth of these invisible forms of control replaces more coercive and disciplinary measures, it seems that in Bahrain they simply augment them. As we have seen, coercive methods have not abated but increased. This is not to attach a particular value to certain types of repression. If anything, the study has exposed the problems of attempting to rank repression or ascertain levels of severity among its manifested forms. The tendency in the field to focus perhaps on overt physical acts of harm as the more egregious acts of repression is problematic. Surveillance, for example, may not traditionally be seen as a violent form of coercion, yet when it instils anxiety or fear that modifies behaviour, and makes victims less likely to engage in challenges to the status quo, it is fundamentally and physically altering their physiology. Thus, how do we determine where 'physical' coercion begins and ends?

Information control too is a growing tool, and one that has become fundamental to repression since the 1950s in Bahrain. It is also one of the clearer areas where we see innovation. From crude public relations and propaganda to pseudo gangs and now social media, innovation in the field reflects the regime's ability to adapt to new technological challenges. Thus, by expanding the framework for repression, we are inviting people to critically interrogate the very notion of repression and its visibility. Indeed, it is perhaps more insidious to dismiss certain institutions, regulations or actions as benign than to explore the extent to which they regulate our behaviour in a way that deliberately advantages a specific 'elite'.

Perhaps one of the most unexpected yet important contributions in this work is its shedding light on how individual actors within a regime can influence repressive choices. As noted by Jennifer Earl, there is little done on how elite attitudes impact upon the type, frequency and consistency of repression.[10] However, this work has shown, for example, that

[10] J. Earl, 'Political Repression: Iron Fists, Velvet Gloves, and Diffuse Control', *The Annual Review of Sociology,* vol. 37, 2011, p. 263.

under the British Belgrave's influence was pervasive, as was the personal influence of various political agents – from Daly's inexorable documenting of Al Khalifa abuses to a member of the police being in the pocket of the prime minister. In recent times, this research has implicated the prime minister as a key driver of certain repressive strategies. This, in many repects, represents one of the most significant shifts in the past hundred years of repression in Bahrain. This factor ties in with Goldstein's argument that the most critical variable throughout history in determining repressive outcomes is the attitude of policy-making individuals towards dissidents.[11] Indeed, as was noted earlier in this research, 'ideas/beliefs also play a role' in determining response to threats. The prime minister has repeatedly cropped up as a shrewd but malevolent patriarch, keen to preserve both his own interests and those of the Al Khalifa more broadly.

These findings cast some doubt on recent scholarship that has emphasized how the violent repression of 2011 was the result of an 'anti-reform' faction led by the Khawalid and other hardliners.[12] It would perhaps be more accurate to say that any large-scale challenge in Bahrain will be met with violent repression – rather than it being simply the result of a swing to hardliners away from moderates. It's as if hardliners are deferred to in times of crises as opposed to them seizing control as other methods fail. Furthermore, this hardline reaction has been evident since the 1970s. Thus, the importance of old habits is key, as is the significance of ruling family coalitions in controlling dissent. Certainly, the continued role of the ruling family raises questions about the existence of path dependencies, institutional memory or authoritarian learning. In Bahrain, there seems to be notable patterns in responses to unrest, an authoritarian repertoire facilitated by the fact that officials from the same family often hold positions for decades, rather than years. As Justin Gengler noted, 'Khalid bin Ahmad replied that the crown prince would 'bring God only knows what disaster upon the family, and that it is only the older members that "know these people" (i.e., the protesters) and how to deal with them'.[13] In states like Bahrain, where the will of influential members of the ruling family is less tempered by institutional processes, the attitudes of elites will certainly impact upon repression. Crucially, the prime

[11] Goldstein, *Political Repression in Modern America*, p. 558.

[12] See for example, Kinninmont, *Bahrain: Beyond the Impasse,* p. 20; Wehrey, 'The March of Bahrain's Hardliners'; J. Gengler, 'Royal Factionalism, the Khawalid, and the Securitization of "the Shiʿa Problem" in Bahrain', *Journal of Arabian Studies: Arabia, the Gulf, and the Red Sea,* vol. 3, no. 1, pp. 53–79, 2014.

[13] J. Gengler, 'A Different Sort of Coup', 20 March 2011, http://bahrainipolitics.blogspot.de/2011/03/different-sort-of-coup.html

minister, rather than the Khawalid, long seems to have been driving against opposition movements. Writing in 1985, Peter Ivey, the Third Secretary at the British Embassy in Bahrain, noted this historic repressive learning among the ruling family.

> Over the years the Al Khalifa have learned how to deal with rebellions – with a mix of firmness, liberality and favours distributed carefully. By manipulating the various sectors of a society which they of course know intimately with the distribution of government contracts, jobs etc, they have been able to maintain an atmosphere of reconciliation.[14]

The focus of this book has added nuance to numerous generalizations made about the nature of regimes and why they use repression. Depending on how one wishes to quantify repression, this has demonstrated, for example, that political democracy does not necessarily mean a decrease in repression. It is mostly true that personal integrity violations have become worse in Bahrain despite democratization. Could it be, as has been argued, that transitional regimes are the most coercive? Or is it simply that we cannot ascertain what repression would be like in Bahrain had parliaments or other reforms never taken place? Perhaps it could have been worse. Perhaps this is where further comparative studies would yield fruit.

Nonetheless, the combination of perceived increasing political opportunities but limited realities may create a dynamic that encourages collective action yet maintains barriers. What was an opaque ceiling in Bahrain has become a glass one. Alternatively, the influence of personalistic attitudes skews an understanding of threat perception. We have seen, for example, that disagreements between Henderson and the prime minister reflect disagreement over the fear of consequences and fear of appearing weak. The prime minister did, for example, wish to increase repression against the Shiʿa despite Henderson saying it would only make things worse. Rather than assuming, as a norm, that increased dissent is an undesirable outcome, it could be that it is an inevitable part of specific, divide and rule governing strategies.

Notions of whether governments repress according to their strength and weakness have also been challenged. It is perhaps better to examine to what extent regime strength or weakness influences those methods and strategies adopted. For example, the regime's weakness in the 1920s (with threats of the withdrawal of British protection) prompted more conciliatory attitudes from the regime to the population at large. However, rather than extorting and enacting violence against the population,

[14] P. R. Ivey, Bahrain Internal Political, FCO 8/5187, The National Archives.

the ruling family took British advice and accepted a stipend to maintain internal cohesion. Having said this, it is important to bear in mind that any criticism of generalizations in repression studies here are contingent on a definition that may not be applicable to those scholars valuing a more parsimonious conceptualization.

Despite these findings, scholars of repression have long complained of the difficulty of obtaining clear data on how governments calculate the 'onset and escalation of repression'.[15] Bahraini internal documents are not public, and with next to no mechanisms allowing transparency, there is little opportunity to gain a really deep insight into, for example, the workings of the Al Khalifa Royal Court without whistle-blowers coming forward. However, by utilizing multiple sources, especially diaries, government correspondence, leaks and high-level insight, this book has obviated, to some extent, the usual hurdles. Indeed, there is much truth in Tilly's assertion of the utility of focusing on sources as opposed to theories in order to find historical limits to observations.[16]

It would, of course, as a next step, and certainly as a way of balancing out the heavy use of British documents, be invaluable to have access to Saudi documents detailing strategic decision making.To some extent, this was possible; the recent Wikileaks cables of Saudi correspondence did, for example, confirm Saudi's obsession with Iran. However, this offered merely a glimpse into the Kingdom's notoriously secret political machinations. Future studies of repression will still be hampered by these problems, yet continued attention to historical sources and leaked information such as that garnered through Wikileaks, will offer more insights into government strategizing in repression. However, methodological innovation should be considered by those wishing to study repression more expansively.

Moving Away from the State

While much of this research does somehow emphasise the state, this book has also shown that future studies of repression would benefit from being less state-centric. Indeed, 'while living in a world that stresses the interconnection and dissolution of older political units such as states, scholars, activists, politicians, ordinary citizens interested in coercive government activity are consistently attempting to refocus attention back

[15] C. Davenport.

[16] Cited in B. Dill and R. Aminzade, 'Historians and the Study of Protest', in B. Klandermans and C. Roggeband (eds), *Handbook of Social Movements Across Disciplines,* New York, NY, Springer, 2007, p. 305.

onto relevant actors'.[17] In addition to the role of Britain and Saudi Arabia, repression in Bahrain is increasingly the result of a broad global network, whose stakeholders include international companies, foreign governments, and non-state actors. Just as advocacy groups and social movements have turned to the outside world to assist in their struggle, governments too, seek assistance from the outside world to repress dissent. Donatella Della Porta once explored the policing of transnational protest, yet in Bahrain, we can clearly see the development of the transnational repression of local protest, and transnational protest over local repression.[18] It would be interesting to examine these repressive networks in the future, examining where their power nodes lie and what forms they take. Focusing just on states is to miss flagrant examples of privateering or commercial complicity in repressive methods.

This repressive global network also reflects the imperative of transnational corporations in attempting to generate profit from instability, and the increasing role the government of Britain (as a relevant example) has in facilitating that process. From a social justice perspective, better regulation of the arms trade, and more robust treaties and enforcement are required to temper the desire to secure increasingly lucrative arms deals that provide governments such as that of Bahrain with increasing capacity to preserve their position of hegemony. Certainly, in a transnational, globalized environment, focusing on state repression is not necessarily the most appropriate lens. Indeed, it could be argued that such an approach feeds the dominant paradigm about the value of sovereignty that is used by states such as Bahrain to denounce foreign 'interference' that could actually assuage certain types of repression.

In this regard, authoritarianism as a concept is also problematic. While this work departs from quantitative covariate analysis, instead attempting to find the nuance within a state deemed authoritarian, the multiple agencies involved in executing repression has highlighted how the authoritarian framework perhaps focuses too much on the state. By examining methods broadly, we can examine how those authoritarian structures, and their respective networks, as evidenced in Bahrain, stretch beyond the state. Perhaps scholars studying the regime–state nexus may find much of use here. Indeed, the term 'regime' has been used throughout this work, and perhaps better reflects a confluence of actors acting together to attain certain power-maintenance objectives. However, this can make the term, as an analytical unit, somewhat

[17] Davenport, 'State Repression and Political Order'.

[18] D. Della Porta, A. Peterson, H. Reiter, and D. Nelken (eds), *The Policing of Transnational Protest*, Aldershot, Ashgate, pp. 1–13.

slippery, for the case of Bahrain has demonstrated how shifting international politics has significantly altered the nature and make-up of what might constitute 'the regime'.

Furthermore, to place too much emphasis on authoritarian regimes is to shift the responsibility of repression away from key sovereign states within repressive assemblages. This is especially problematic when the states under scrutiny, such as Bahrain, benefit from relationships with states not considered authoritarian – such as the United Kingdom. If, as Bellin argues,[19] authoritarianism robustness is facilitated by foreign support of militaries – then to what extent is examining the subordinate state missing the core problems of authoritarian resilience? From the perspective of rectifying social justice, this aspect needs to be addressed.

Ever-Expanding Webs of Control

As well as the importance of non-state actors and international networks, rhizomatic forms of control, through online or offline vigilantiism have demonstrated the power of society in repressing dissent, especially when mobilized along ideological grounds. This pattern has been particularly evident in the analysis of social media use. As this research has shown, social media can extend the repressive apparatus to citizens. Through trolling, peer-to-peer surveillance, propaganda and other means – those aligned with the hegemonic order can facilitate control strategies that benefit the status quo. Not only does this problematize the utopian potential of social media as a place of democratic emancipation, it also highlights the mixed role of technological determinism and social constructivism in outlining how such technologies are used. This is not to deny the potential liberating aspects of technology, but rather it emphasises the importance of doing future, case-by-case research on the role of social media during unrest in specific countries. The role of specific technologies in repression will certainly be contingent on socio-cultural, economic and political factors.

The relative merits of parsing up repression is that it opens up the path to more interesting theoretical insights into the nature of repression. Rather than seeing repression as a monolithic concept, the proliferation of categories garnered from numerous studies of a similar phenomenon, coupled with inductive research, have created a template that, while tailored to this study, may be useful for other scholars wishing to examine aspects of repression. By using levels of disaggregation, this book has demonstrated that the Bahrain regime has responded 'to different

[19] E. Bellin, 'Reconsidering the Robustness of Authoritarianism in the Middle East'.

challenges with distinct repressive strategies', thus addressing the question posed by Davenport.[20] However, the expansive definition of repression, while giving scope to examine multiple aspects of Bahrain's history, has concurrently made it difficult to go into extreme depth on any one facet of repression. Although depth has been achieved by focusing on Bahrain alone – a long temporal period, coupled with a broad conceptualization of repression, has made generalizations difficult. As Skocpol argues, 'interpretive works can only be judged to be more or less successful at meeting the challenge they set for themselves: finding the most compelling conceptual lenses through which to mediate between meaningful happenings in the past and the concerns of present-day audiences'.[21] Repression is compelling and highly relevant to both Bahrainis and anyone interested in human rights. The benefits, however, should not be undersold, and by uniting disciplines through the concept of repression, this study offers a new approach to the study of national histories.

Given the current regional climate in the Gulf, and the so-called New Middle East Cold War between Riyadh and Tehran, repression in Bahrain is unlikely to diminish. Certainly, Saudi's intervention against what it perceives as Iranian and Shiʿa expansionism in Yemen has exacerbated regional tension, and the rise of ISIS and Mohammed bin Salman, the Saudi crown prince, has both been a catalyst and a symptom of escalating regional tensions. This defensive stance from the likes of Saudi Arabia is only likely to make Bahrain fall more under Saudi control, and acts such as the provocative execution of the Shiʿa cleric Nimr Al Nimr suggest that Saudi Arabia will, in all probability adopt more violent methods of coercion in the near term. Similarly, for students of information control, the increasing evidence that Mohammed bin Salman may have personally ordered the execution of journalist Jamal Khashoggi points to a whole new era of personalism. The future for a more equitable sharing of power in Bahrain is bleak. Bahrain's lack of independence has already, and will continue to impact significantly on repression. American and Saudi military interests in the region equate to transatlantic support for the authoritarian status quo, while Saudi military intervention virtually guarantees that even armed insurrection would have little effect on regime change.

[20] Davenport, 'State Repression and Political Order', p. 18.

[21] T. Skocpol, 'Emerging Agendas and Recurrent Strategies in Historical Sociology', in T. Skocpol (ed.), *Vision and Method in Historical Sociology*, Cambridge, Cambridge University Press, 1985, pp. 356–85.

Bibliography

Abdo, G., 'The New Sectarianism: The Arab Uprisings and the Rebirth of the Shi'a Sunni Divide', *The Saban Center for Middle East Policy at Brookings*, Analysis Papers, no. 29, April 2013, www.brookings.edu/~/media/research/files/papers/2013/04/sunni%20shia%20abdo/sunni%20shia%20abdo

Agamben, G., *Means without End: Notes on Politics*, Minneapolis, MI, University of Minnesota Press, 2000.

Albrecht, H., 'The Myth of Coup-Proofing: Risk and Instances of Military Coups D'état in the Middle East and North Africa, 1950–2013', *Armed Forces & Society*, vol. 41, no. 4, 2015, pp. 659–87. doi:10.1177/0095327X14544518

Al Hasabi, J., 'Privacy Extra: Jaafar Al Hasabi and Marc Owen Jones Discuss Bahrain and Surveillance', [online video], 19 March 2015, www.youtube.com/watch?v=5ViK48BX24U

Al-Hasan, H. T., 'Bahrain's New Labour Scheme: One Step Forward, Two Steps Back?', *Open Democracy*, 5 August 2012, www.opendemocracy.net/hasan-tariq- al-hasan/bahrain%E2%80%99s-new-labour-scheme-one-stepam-forward-two- steps-back

'Ali, A., 'Bahrain's Move to Legalise Repression', *Bahrain Watch*, [Blog], 7 August 2013, https://bahrainwatch.org/blog/2013/08/07/bahrains-move-to-legalise-repression/

Al Naqeeb, K. H., *Society and State in the Gulf and Arab Peninsula*, London, Routledge, 1990.

Al-Rumaihi, E. M. H., 'The Development of Mass Media in the Kingdom of Bahrain', PhD Thesis, University Exeter, 2002.

Al Shehabi, O., Contested Modernity: Divided Rule and the Birth of Sectarianism, Nationalism, and Absolutism in Bahrain, *British Journal of Middle Eastern Studies*, vol. 44, no. 3, 2017, pp. 333–55, doi:10.1080/13530194.2016.1185937

'Divide and Rule in Bahrain and the Elusive Pursuit for a United Front: The Experience of the Constitutive Committee and the 1972 Uprising', *Historical Materialism*, vol. 21, no. 1, 2013, pp. 94–127.

'Political Movements in Bahrain, Past, Present, and Future', *Jadaliyya*, 14 February 2012, www.jadaliyya.com/pages/index/4363/political-movements-in-bahrain_past-present-and-future

Al-Tajir, M. A., *Bahrain 1920–1945, Britain, the Shaikh and the Administration*, London, Croom Helm, 1987.

Anderson, D. M. and Killingray, D. (eds), 'Consent, Coercion and Colonial Control: Policing the Empire 1830–1940', in *Policing the Empire: Government, Authority and Control, 1830–1940*, Manchester, Manchester University Press, 1991.

'An Orderly Retreat? Policing the End of Empire', in *Policing and Decolonisation: Politics, Nationalism, and the Police, 1917–65*, Manchester, Manchester University Press, 1992.

Austin Holmes, A., 'Working on the Revolution in Bahrain: From the Mass Strike to Everyday Forms of Medical Provision', *Social Movement Studies: Journal of Social, Cultural and Political Protest*, 2015, doi:10.1080/14742837.2015.1037265

Bahrain Martyrs, [Instagram Account], 16 February 2014, https://instagram.com/p/ke8XaLxEnT/

Bahry, L., 'The Opposition in Bahrain: A Bellwether for the Gulf', *Middle East Policy*, vol. 5, no. 2, 1997, pp. 42–57.

Balbus, I. D., *The Dialectics of Legal Repression: Black Rebels before the American Criminal Courts*, New York, NY, Russell Sage Foundation, 1973.

Barton, B. F. and Barton, M., 'Modes of Power in Technical and Professional Visuals', *Journal of Business and Technical Communication*, vol. 7, no. 1, 1993, pp. 138–62.

Bassiouni, M. C., Rodley, N., Al-Awadhi, B., Kirsch, P., and Arsanjani, M. H., 'Report of the Bahrain Independent Commission of Inquiry' [BICI Report], 23 November 2011, BICI, Manama, www.bici.org.bh/BICIreportEN.pdf

Beaugrand, C., 'The Return of the Bahraini Exiles, Mapping Middle Eastern and North African Diasporas', BRISMES Annual Conference, July 2008, Leeds, United Kingdom, https://halshs.archives-ouvertes.fr/halshs-00511588/document

Bellin, E., 'Reconsidering the Robustness of Authoritarianism in the Middle East: Lessons from the Arab Spring', *Comparative Politics*, vol. 44, no. 2, 2011, pp. 127–49.

Bhatia, L. and Shehabi, A., 'Shifting Contours of Activisms and Policies for Justice in Bahrain', in A. Shehabi and M. O. Jones (eds), *Bahrain's Uprising: Resistance and Repression in the Gulf*, London, Zed Books Ltd, 2015, pp. 93–134.

Blaug, R., 'New Theories of Discursive Democracy: A User's Guide', *Philosophy and Social Criticism*, vol. 22, no. 1, 1996, pp. 49–80.

Blaydes, L., *State of Repression: Iraq under Saddam Hussein*, Princeton, NJ, Princeton University Press, p. 2.

Bonnell, V. E., 'The Uses of Theory, Concepts and Comparison, in Historical Sociology', *Comparative Studies in Society and History*, vol. 22, no. 2, 1980, pp. 156–73.

Boudrea, V., 'Precarious Regimes and Matchup Problems in the Explanation of Repressive Policy', in C. Davenport, H. Johnston and C. Mueller (eds), *Repression and Mobilization*, Minneapolis, MI, University of Minnesota Press, 2005, pp. 33–57.

Boykoff, J., *Beyond Bullets: The Suppression of Dissent in the United States*, Edinburgh, AK Press, 2007.

'Limiting Dissent: The Mechanisms of State Repression in the USA', *Social Movement Studies: Journal of Social, Cultural and Political Protest*, vol. 6, no. 3, 2007, pp. 281–310.

Braun, A., 'Dissent and the State in Eastern Europe', in C. E. S. Franks (ed.), *Dissent and the State*, Toronto, Oxford University Press, 1989, pp. 111–37.

Braun, V. and Clarke, V., 'Using Thematic Analysis in Psychology', *Qualitative Research in Psychology*, vol. 3, no. 2, 2006, p. 77–101.

Brown, H., 'Domestic State Violence: From the Croquants to the Commune', *The Historical Journal*, vol. 42, no. 3, 1999, pp. 597–622.

Bryman, A., 'Triangulation', *Encyclopedia of Social Science Research Methods*, London, Sage, 2003, http://studysites.sagepub.com/chambliss4e/study/chapter/encyc_pdfs/4.2_Triangulation.pdf

Brynen, R., Korany, B., and Noble, P., *Political Liberalization and Democratization in the Arab World*, vol. 1, Boulder, CO, Lynne Rienner Publishers, 1995.

Cancian, F. M., 'Conflicts between Activist Research and Academic Success: Participatory Research and Alternative Strategies', *The American Sociologist*, vol. 24, no. 1, 1993, pp. 92–106.

Carlstrom, G., 'In the Kingdom of Tear Gas', *MERIP Online*, 13 April 2012, www.merip.org/mero/mero041312?ip_login_no_cache=a560e0ddfd87c30e7b1e14c337e587ee

Cassel, M., 'Even Bahrain's Use of "Miami Model" Policing Will Not Stop the Uprising', *The Guardian*, 3 December 2011, www.theguardian.com/commentisfree/2011/dec/03/bahrain-miami-model-policing

Churchill, W. and Vander Wall, J., *Agents of Repression: The FBI's Secret Wars Against the Black Panther Party and the American Indian Movement*, 2nd ed., Cambridge, MA, South End Press, 2002.

Corradi, J. E. and Fagen, P. W. (eds), *State Terror and Resistance in Latin America*, Berkeley, CA, University of California Press.

Cottle, S., 'Reporting Demonstrations: The Changing Media Politics of Dissent', *Media, Culture and Society*, vol. 30, no. 6, pp. 853–72.

Creswell, J. W., *Qualitative Inquiry and Research Design: Choosing Among Five Approaches*, London: Sage, 2013.

Research Design: Qualitative, Quantitative, and Mixed Methods Approaches, London, Sage, 2003.

Dallin, A. and. Breslauer, G. W., *Political Terror in Communist Systems*, Stanford, CA, Stanford University Press, 1970.

Davenport, C., *Paths to State Repression: Human Rights Violations and Contentious Politics*, New York, NY, Rowman and Littlefield, 2000.

'Repression and Mobilization: Insights from Political Science science and Sociology', in C. Davenport, H. Johnston and C. Mueller (eds), *Repression and Mobilization*, Minneapolis, MI, University of Minnesota Press, 2005, pp. 239–40.

'State Repression and Political Order', *Annual Review of Political Science*, vol. 10, no. 1, 2007, pp. 1–23.

'State Repression and the Tyrannical Peace', *Journal of Peace Research*, vol. 44, no. 4, 2007, pp. 485–504.

How Social Movements Die: Repression and Demobilization of the Republic of New Africa, Cambridge: Cambridge University Press, 2015. [Kindle Edition]

Davenport, C. and Armstrong, D. A., 'Democracy and the Violation of Human Rights: A Statistical Analysis from 1976 to 1996. *American Journal of Political Science*, vol. 48, no. 3, 2004, pp. 538–54.

Davidson, C., *After the Sheikhs: The Coming Collapse of the Gulf Monarchies*, London, Hurst, 2012.

Definitive Report – Report No 230, November 1983, Case No 1043 (Bahrain) – Complaint date: 01-JUN-81 – Closed http://www.ilo.org/dyn/normlex/en/f?p=1000:50002:0::NO:50002:P50002_COMPLAINT_TEXT_ID:2900571

DeMeritt, J. H. R. and Young, J .K., 'A Political Economy of Human Rights: Oil, Natural Gas, and State Incentives to Repress', *Conflict Management and Peace Science*, vol. 30, no. 2, 2013, pp. 99–120, doi:10.1177/0738894212473915

Desmukh, F., 'Bahrain Government Hacked Lawyers and Activists with UK Spyware', Bahrain Watch, [web blog], 7 August 2014, https://bahrainwatch.org/blog/2014/08/07/uk-spyware-used-to-hack-bahrain- lawyers-activists/

Dickinson, E., 'Bahrain's Elections and the Opposition', *Middle East Institute,* 23 December 2014, www.mei.edu/content/article/bahrains-elections-and-opposition

Dill, B. and Aminzade, R., 'Historians and the Study of Protest', in B. Klandermans and C. Roggeband (eds), *Handbook of Social Movements Across Disciplines*, New York, NY, Springer, 2007, pp. 267–312.

Dresch, P. and Piscatori, J. (eds), *Monarchies and Nations: Globalization and Identity in the Arab States of the Gulf*, London, I.B. Tauris, 2005.

Earl, J., 'Tanks, Tear Gas, and Taxes: Towards a Theory of Movement Repression', *Sociological Theory*, vol. 21, no. 1, 2003, pp. 44–68.

'You Can Beat the Rap, But You Can't Beat the Ride: Bringing Arrests Back into Research on Repression', *Research in Social Movements, Conflicts, and Change*, vol. 26, 2005, pp. 101–39.

'Political Repression: Iron Fists, Velvet Gloves, and Diffuse Control', *The Annual Review of Sociology*, vol. 37, 2011, pp. 261–84.

Eisenberger, N. and Leiberman, M. D., 'Why Rejection Hurts: A Common Neural Alarm System for Physical and Social Pain', *Trends in Cognitive Sciences*, vol. 8, no. 7, 2004, pp. 294–300.

Elster, J., *Nuts and Bolts for the Social Sciences*, New York, NY, Cambridge University Press, 1989.

Entman, R. M., 'Framing: Toward Clarification of a Fractured Paradigm', *Journal of Communications*, vol. 43, no. 4, 1993.

Escribà-Folch, A., 'Repression, Political Threats, and Survival Under Autocracy', *International Political Science Review*, vol. 34, no. 5, 2013, pp. 543–60, doi:10.1177/0192512113488259

European Center for Constitutional and Human Rights, 'Gamma/FinFisher: No Investigation into German-British Software Company', 12 December 2014, www.ecchr.de/surveillance

Evans, K., 'Bahrainis Implicate Iran in TV "Coup" Confession', *The Guardian*, 6 June 1996, p. 14.

'Bahrain plot "is led from Qom"', *The Guardian*, 12 June 1996.

Fagen, P. W., 'Repression and State Security', in J. E. Corradi and P. W. Fagen (eds), *State Terror and Resistance in Latin America*, Berkeley, CA, University of California Press, p. 47.

Fairclough, N. and Wodak, R., 'Critical Discourse Analysis', in T. A. Van Dijk (ed.), *Discourse as a Social Interaction*, London, Sage, pp. 258–84.

Fernandez, L. A., *Policing Dissent: Social Control and the Anti Globalization Movement*, New Brunswick, NJ, Rutgers University Press, 2008.

Ferrara, F., 'Why Regimes Create Disorder: Hobbes' Dilemma During a Rangoon Summer', *The Journal of Conflict Resolution*, vol. 47, no. 3, 2003, pp. 302–25.

Foucault, M., *Discipline and Punish: The Birth of the Prison*, trans. A. Sheridan NewYork, NY, Pantheon, 1997, p. 201.

Franklin, R., 'Migrant Labour and the Politics of Development in Bahrain', *Middle East Report 132*, www.merip.org/mer/mer132/migrant-labor-politics-development-bahrain? ip_login_no_cache=a7ae599f50b951b5145fca37 baa546b4#_12_

Franks, C. E. S. (ed.), *Dissent and the State*, Toronto, Oxford University Press, 1989.

Fuccaro, N., *Histories of City and State in the Persian Gulf: Manama since 1800*, Cambridge, Cambridge University Press, 2009.

Gamson, W. A., *The Strategy of Social Protest*, Homewood, IL, Dorsey, 1968.

Gause, F. Gregory, III, 'Beyond Sectarianism: The New Middle East Cold War', Brookings Doha Center Analysis Paper, No. 11, July 2014, /www.brookings .edu/research/beyond-sectarianism-the-new-middle-east-cold-war/

Gengler, J., A Different Sort of Coup, 20 March 2011, http://bahrainipolitics .blogspot.de/2011/03/different-sort-of-coup.html

'Ethnic Conflict and Political Mobilization in Bahrain and the Arabian Gulf,' PhD Thesis, Ann Arbor, MI, University of Michigan, 2011.

'Guilty by Billboard', *Bahrain Politics Blogspot*, [web blog], 10 May 2011.

'The Most Dangerous Men in Bahrain', Religion and Politics in Bahrain, [web blog], 5 June 2011, http://bahrainipolitics.blogspot.co.uk/2011/06/most-dangerous-men-in-bahrain.html

'Bahrain's Sunni Awakening', *Middle East Research and Information Project (MERIP)*, 17 January 2012, www.merip.org/mero/mero011712

'Bahrain's Legal "War on Terror"', Religion and Politics in Bahrain, 17 September 2013, http://bahrainipolitics.blogspot.co.uk/2013/09/bahrains-legal-war-on-terror.html

'Bahrain Drain; Why the King's Sunni Supporters are Moving Abroad', *Foreign Affairs*, 5 September 2014, www.foreignaffairs.com/articles/middle-east/ 2014-09-05/bahrain-drain

Gibbs, J.P. (ed.), *Social Control: Views from the Social Sciences*, London, Sage Publications, 1982.

Gibson, J. L., 'Political Intolerance and Political Repression during the Mccarthy Red Scare', *American Political Science Review*, vol. 82, no. 2, 1988, pp. 511–29.

'The Policy Consequences of Political Intolerance: Political Repression During the Vietnam War Era, The National Archives War Era', *The Journal of Politics*, vol. 51, no. 1, 1989, pp. 13–35.

Goldstein, R. J., *Political Repression in Modern America: From 1870 to 1976*, Urbana, IL, University of Illinois Press, 1978.
Political Repression in 19th Century Europe, Oxford, Routledge, 2010 (first published 1983).
Greenwald, G., 'The US Alongside Saudi Arabia Fights for Freedom and Democracy in the Middle East', *The Guardian*, 12 January 2013, www.theguardian.com/commentisfree/2013/jan/12/us-saudi-arabia-libya-freedom
Gregory, P. R., Shroder, P .J. H. and Sonin, K., 'Dictators, Repression and the Median Citizen: An "Eliminations Model" of Stalin's Terror', Working Paper No. 91, CEFIR/NES Working Paper Series, 2006.
Gresh, A., 'Bahrain: Divide, Repress and Rule', April 2011, http://mondediplo.com/blogs/bahrain-divide-repress-and-rule
Hammersley, M. and Atkinson, P., *Ethnography: Principles in Practice*, London, Routledge, 1995.
Hardt, M. and Negri, A., *Empire*, Cambridge, MA, Harvard University Press, 2000.
Hariri, J. G., 'A Contribution to the Understanding of Middle Eastern and Muslim Exceptionalism', *The Journal of Politics*, vol. 77, no. 2, 2015, pp. 47–90.
Harvey, D., *The New Imperialism*, New York, NY, Oxford University Press, 2003.
Hassan, O., 'Undermining the Transatlantic Democracy Agenda? The Arab Spring and Saudi Arabia's Counteracting Democracy Strategy', *Democratization*, vol. 22, no. 3, pp. 479–95, doi:10.1080/13510347.2014.981161
Hedstrom, P. and Swedberg, R., (eds) 'Social Mechanisms: An Introductory Essay', *Social Mechanisms: An Analytical Approach to Social Theory*, Cambridge, Cambridge University Press, 1998.
Hellsten, I. Dawson, J. and Leydesdorff, L., 'Implicit Media Frames: Automated Analysis of Public Debate on Artificial Sweeteners', *Public Understanding of Science* , vol. 19, no. 5, 2010, pp. 590–608, doi:10.1177/0963662509343136
Hedstrom, P. and Ylikoski, P., 'Causal Mechanisms in the Social Sciences', *The Annual Review of Sociology*, vol. 36, 2010, pp. 49–67.
Hendrix, C. S., 'Measuring State Capacity: Theoretical and Empirical Implications for the Study of Civil Conflict', *Journal of Peace Research*, vol. 47, no. 3, pp. 273–85.
Heydemann, S., 'Upgrading Authoritarianism in the Arab world', Analysis Paper 13, The Saban Center for Middle East Policy at The Brookings Institution, October 2007, www.brookings.edu/~/media/research/files/papers/2007/10/arabworld/10arabworld.pdf
Hill, D. W., 'The Concept of Personal Integrity Rights in Empirical Research,' PhD Thesis, Athens, GA, University of Georgia, 2013.
Hill, D. and Jones, Z. (2014). 'An Empirical Evaluation of Explanations for State Repression', *American Political Science Review*, vol. 108, no. 3, pp. 661–87. doi:10.1017/S0003055414000306
Holes, C., 'Dialect and National Identity: The Cultural Politics of Self-Representation in Bahrain Musalsalat', in P. Dresch and J. Piscatori (eds), *Monarchies and Nations: Globalization and Identity in the Arab States of the Gulf*, London, I.B. Tauris, 2005.

Hoque, Z., Covaleski, M. A. and Gooneratne, T. N. (2013), 'Theoretical Triangulation and Pluralism in Research Methods in Organizational and Accounting Research', *Accounting, Auditing & Accountability Journal*, vol. 26, no. 7, 2013, pp. 1170–98.

Horne, J., 'Policing Bahrain: the Long Arm of the British', *Open Democracy*, 8 August 2013, www.opendemocracy.net/opensecurity/john-horne-john-lubbock/policing-bahrain-long-arm-of-british

'Tn Tn Tn and Torture in Bahrain: Puncturing the Spectacle of the "Arab Spring"', in A. Shehabi and M. O. Jones (eds), *Bahrain's Uprising: Resistance and Repression in the Gulf*, London, Zed Books Ltd, 2015, pp. 151–74.

Howard, M. M. and Walters, M. R., 'Response to Eva Bellin, Ellen Lust, and March Lynch', *Perspectives on Politics*, vol. 12, no. 2, June 2014, pp. 417–19.

'Explaining the Unexpected: Political Science and the Surprises of 1989 and 2011', *Perspectives on Politics*, vol. 12, no. 2, June 2014, pp. 394–408.

Humphreys, S., 'Legalizing Lawlessness: On Giorgio Agamben's State of Exception', *The European Journal of International Law*, vol. 17, no. 3, 2006, pp. 677–87.

Johnson, D. H., 'From Military to Tribal Police: Policing the Upper Nile Province of the Sudan', in D. M. Anderson and D. Killingray (eds), *Policing the Empire: Government, Authority and Control, 1830–1940*, Manchester, Manchester University Press, 1991.

Jones, M. O., 'Here's Looking at YouTube. Neoliberalism, Political Violence, and Racialised CounterSpace in Bahrain', MSc Dissertation, University of Durham, 2010.

Jones, M. O., in J. D. Goodman, '"Twitter Trolls" Haunt Discussions of Bahrain Online', *The Lede* [*New York Times* blog], 11 October 2011, http://thelede.blogs.nytimes.com/2011/10/11/twitter-trolls-haunt-discussions-of-bahrain-online/

Jones, M. O., 'For the Record: Police in Bahrain Throw Molotov Cocktails', *Marc Owen Jones,* [web blog], 18 March 2012, http://marcowenjones.word press.com/2012/03/18/for-the-record-police-in-bahrain-throw-molotov-cocktails/

'Bahrain Activists' Trouble with Trolls', *Index on Censorship Uncut,* 15 May 2012, http://uncut.indexoncensorship.org/2012/05/bahrain-marc-owen-jones-twitter-trolls/

'Social Media, Surveillance and Social Control in the Bahrain Uprising', *Westminister Papers of Communication and Culture*, vol. 9, no. 2, 2013, pp. 71–91.

'Bahrain's History of Political Injustice', *Your Middle East,* 29 April 2013, www.yourmiddleeast.com/opinion/marc-owen-jones-bahrains-history-of-political-injustice_14064

'How the Al Khalifas Took a Quarter of Bahrain's Wealth', *Your Middle East,* 29 April 2013, www.yourmiddleeast.com/opinion/marc-owen-jones-how-the-al-khalifas-took-a-quarter-of-bahrains-wealth_11643

'Bahrain's Uprising: Resistance and Repression in the Gulf', Open Democracy, www.opendemocracy.net/arab-awakening/marc-owen-jones/bahrain%E2%80%99s-upising-resistance-and-repression

'Rotten Apples or Rotten Orchards: Police Deviance, Brutality, and Unaccountability in Bahrain', in A. Shehabi and M. O. Jones, M. (eds),

Bahrain's Uprising: Resistance and Repression in the Gulf, London, Zed Books Ltd, 2015, pp. 207–38.

'Automated Sectarianism and Pro-Saudi Propaganda on Twitter', Exposing the Invisible – Tactical Technology Collective, 2016, https://exposingtheinvisible.org/resources/obtainingevidence/automated-sectarianism

'Saudi Intervention, Sectarianism, and De-democratization in Bahrain's Uprising', in Davies, T., Ryan, H. and Pena, A., (eds), Protest, Social Movements, and Global Democracy Since 2011 (Special Issue), *Research in Social Movements, Conflict and Change*, vol. 39, 2016, pp. 251–79.

Jones, C. and Stone, J., 'Britain and the Arabian Gulf: New Perspectives on Strategic Influence', *International Relations*, vol. 13, no. 4, 1997, pp. 1–24, doi:10.1177/004711789701300401

Jones, T. C., 'Time to Disband the Bahrain-Based U.S. Fifth Fleet', *The Atlantic*, 10 June 2011, www.theatlantic.com/international/archive/2011/06/ time-to-disband-the-bahrain-based-us-fifth-fleet/240243/

Joyce, M., 'The Bahraini Three on St. Helena, 1956–1961', *Middle East Journal*, vol. 4, 2000.

Ruling Shaikhs and Her Majesty's Government 1960–1969, London and Portland OR, Frank Crass, 2003.

Juska, A., and Woolfson, C., 'Policing Political Protest in Lithuania', *Crime, Law and Social Change*, vol. 57, no. 4, 2012, pp. 403–24.

Kafai, N., and Shehabi, A., 'The Struggle for Information: Revelations on Mercenaries, Sectarian Agitation, and Demographic Engineering in Bahrain', *Jadaliyya*, 29 May 2014, www.jadaliyya.com/pages/index/17912/the-struggle-for-information_revelations-on-mercen

Kalmanowiecki, L., 'Origins and Applications of Political Policing in Argentina', *Latin American Perspectives*, vol. 27, no. 2, Violence, Coercion and Rights in the Americas, 2000, pp. 36–56.

Kerr, S., 'Bahrain Pulls Plug on Saudi Media Tycoon's TV Station', *Financial Times*, 20 February 2015.

Khalaf, A., 'Labor Movements in Bahrain', *Middle East Research and Information Projects Report*, no. 132, 1985, pp. 24–29.

'Contentious Politics in Bahrain: From Ethnic to National and Vice Versa, The Fourth Nordic Conference on Middle Eastern Studies: The Middle East in a Globalising World, Oslo, 13–16 August 1998. www.smi.uib.no/pao/khalaf.html

'Opening Remarks, Bahrain: 30 Years of Unconstitutional Rule', Parliamentary Human Rights Group, House of Lords, 25 August 2005, http://jaddwilliam2.blogspot.co.uk/2005/08/royal-dream.html

'The Outcome of a Ten-Year Process of Political Reform in Bahrain', Arab Reform Initiative, 2008, www.arab- reform.net/sites/default/files/ARB.23_Abdulhadi_Khalaf_ENG.pdf

'GCC Rulers and the Politics of Citizenship', *Al-Monitor*, 26 December 2012, www.al-monitor.com/pulse/politics/2012/12/gcc-rulers-use-citizenship

'The Many Afterlives of Lulue', Ibraaz, 28 February 2013, www.ibraaz.org/essays/56

'Foreword', in A. Shehabi and M. O. Jones, M. (eds), *Bahrain's Uprising: Resistance and Repression in the Gulf*, London, Zed Books Ltd, 2015, pp. xiii–xvii.

Khawaja, M., 'Repression and Popular Collective Action: Evidence from the West Bank', *Sociological Forum*, vol. 8, no. 1, 1993, pp. 47–71.

Khuri, F., *Tribe and State in Bahrain: The Transition of Social and Political Authority in an Arab State*, Chicago, IL, University of Chicago Press, 1981.

Kilbride, E., '"Too Gay to Represent Bahrain"': Homophobia and Nationalism in the Wake of a Revolution', *Muftah*, 15 December 2014, http://muftah.org/homophobia-and-nationalism-in-bahrain/#.VjY7hCsl-ao

Killingray, D., 'Guarding the Extending Frontier: Policing the Gold Coast, 1865–1913', in D. M. Anderson and D. Killingray (eds), *Policing the Empire: Government, Authority and Control, 1830–1940*, Manchester University Press, Manchester, 1991.

King, N., 'Using Templates In The Thematic Analysis of Text' in C. Cassell and G. Symon (eds), *Essential Guide to Qualitative Research in Organizational Research*, London, Sage, 2004, pp. 256–70.

'Constructing the Template', [online video], 2008, http://onlineqda.hud.ac.uk/_REQUALLO/FR/Template_Analysis/The_Template.php

'Descriptive and Interpretative Coding', [online video], 2008, http://onlineqda.hud.ac.uk/_REQUALLO/FR/Template_Analysis/Analytic+Descript_coding.php

Kinninmont, J., Bahrain*: Beyond the Impasse*, Chatham House, London, 2012, p. 1, www.chathamhouse.org/sites/files/chathamhouse/public/Research/Middle%20East/pr0612kinninmont.pdf

Kirchheimer, O., *Political Justice*, Princeton, Princeton University Press, 1961.

Klandermans, B. and Roggeband, C. (eds), *Handbook of Social Movements Across Disciplines*, New York, NY, Springer, 2007.

Kleinman, H. M., 'Disappearances in Latin America: a Human Rights Perspective', *N.Y.U. Journal of International Law and Politics*, pp. 1033–1060, 1986–87.

Koopmans, R., 'Repression and the Public Sphere: Discursive Opportunities for Repression against the Extreme Right in Germany in the 1990s', in C. Davenport et al. (eds), *Repression and Mobilization*. Minneapolis, MI, University of Minnesota Press, 2005.

Lambert, L., *The Funambulist Pamphlets Volume 02: Foucault*, Brooklyn, NY, Punctum Books, 2013.

Lansford, T., 'Bahrain', *Political Handbook of the World 2014*, London, Sage, 2014.

Lawson, F. H., 'Repertoires of Contention in Contemporary Bahrain', in Q. Wiktorowicz (ed.) *Islamic Activism: A Social Movement Theory Approach*, Bloomington, IN, Indiana University Press, 2004, pp. 89–111.

Lessware, J., 'State of Emergency Declared in Bahrain', *The National*, 16 March 2011, www.thenational.ae/news/world/middle-east/state-of-emergency-declared-in- bahrain

Lichbach, M., 'How to Organize your Mechanisms: Research Programs, Stylized Facts, and Historical Narratives', in C. Davenport et al. (eds), *Repression and Mobilization. Minneapolis: University of Minnesota Press*, 2005, pp. 239–40.

Lopez, G. A. and Stohl, M., 'State Terrorism: From the Reign of Terror to Ninety-Eighty Four Terrorism', *Chitty's Law Journal*, vol. 32, no. 5, 1984–87, pp. 14–33.

Louër, L., Sectarianism and Coup-Proofing Strategies in Bahrain, *Journal of Strategic Studies*, vol. 36, no. 2, 2013, pp. 245–60.

Lowe, R., 'Bassiouni:New Arab Court for Human Rights is Fake "Potemkin Tribunal"', International Bar Association, 1 October 2014, www.ibanet.org/Article/ Detail.aspx?ArticleUid=c64f9646–15a5–4624-8c07-bae9d9ac42df

Lynch, M., 'New Arab Media Research Opportunities and Agendas' In *Arab Uprisings: New Opportunities for Political Science*, Project on Middle East Political Science (POMEPS Briefings), pp. 57–8.

Mann, S., Nolan, J., and Wellman, B., 'Sousveillance: Inventing and Using Wearable Computing Devices for Data Collection in Surveillance Environments', *Surveillance & Society*, vol. 1, no. 3, 2003, pp. 331–55.

Marcuse, H., 'Repressive Tolerance', in R. P. Wolff, B. Moore, Jr and H. Marcuse, *A Critique of Pure Tolerance*, Boston, MA, Beacon Press, 1965, pp. 95–137.

Marczak, W. and Marquis-Boire, M., 'From Bahrain With Love: FinFisher's Spy Kit Exposed?', Citizenlab, 25 July 2012, https://citizenlab.org/2012/07/from-bahrain-with-love-finfishers-spy-kit-exposed/

Marczak, B., 'Is Bahrain's Government Running Extremist Accounts?', Bahrain Watch, [web blog], 5 August 2013, https://bahrainwatch.org/blog/2013/ 08/05/is-bahrains-government-running-extremist-accounts/

'The "Trivially Fake" Wikileaks Cable that Fooled Bahrain's Press and Parliament', Bahrain Watch, [web blog], 12 September 2013, https://bahrainwatch.org/blog/2013/09/12/the-trivially-fake-wikileaks-cable-that-fooled-bahrains-press-and-parliament/

Marczak, W., 'Bahrain Watch Issues Urgent Advice for Activists to Stop Using @Zello Due to Security Flaw', Bahrain Watch, [web blog], 7 September 2014, https://bahrainwatch.org/blog/2014/09/07/bahrain-watch-issues-urgent-advice-for-activists-to-stop-using-zello-due-to-security-flaw/

Marx, G., 'External Efforts to Damage or Facilitate Social Movements: Some Patterns, Explanations, Outcomes, and Complications', in M. Zald and J. McCarthy (eds), *The Dynamics of Social Movements*, Cambridge, MA, Winthrop Publishers, 1979, pp. 94–125. http://web.mit.edu/gtmarx/www/movement.html

Mc Adam, D., 'Political Process and The Development of Black Insurgency 1930– 1970', in V. Ruggiero and N. Montagna (eds), *Social Movement: A Reader*, London and New York, NY, Routledge, 2008, p. 177–85.

McGarry, J., and O'Leary, B., (eds) 'Introduction: The Macro-Political Regulation of Ethnic Conflict', in *The Politics of Ethnic Conflict Regulation*, Oxford, Routledge, 1993.

Menoret, P., The Saudi Enigma: A History, London, Zed Books, 2005.

Mertens, D. M., 'Philosophy in Mixed Methods Teaching: The Transformative Paradigm as an Illustration', *International Journal of Multiple Research Approaches*, vol. 4, 2010, pp. 9–18.

'Tansformative Mixed Methods Enquiry', *Qualitative Inquiry*, vol. 16, no. 6, 2010, pp. 469–74.

Mills, C. W., *The Power Elite*, New York, NY, Oxford University Press, 1967.

Mitchell, T., 'Witness to an Uprising: What I Saw in Bahrain', *The Atlantic*, 14 December 2011, www.theatlantic.com/international/archive/2011/12/witness-to-an- uprising-what-i-saw-in-bahrain/249977/

Munck, G. L., 'What Is Democracy? A Reconceptualisation of the Quality of Democracy. *Democratisation*, vol. 23, no. 1, pp. 1–26, 2014, doi:10.1080/13510347.2014.918104

Nakhleh, E., *Bahrain: Political Development in a Modernizing Society*, New York, NY, Lexington Books, 2011.

Nakhleh, E., 'Op-Ed: Ian Henderson and Repression in Bahrain: A Forty-Year Legacy', *Inter Press Service*, 18 April 2013, www.ipsnews.net/2013/04/op-ed-ian-henderson-and-repression

The National, 'Emirati Officer Dies in Bahrain Bomb Explosion', 3 March 2014, www.thenational.ae/world/emirati-officer-dies-in-bahrain-bomb-explosion

Nepstad, S. E., *Nonviolent Struggle: Theories, Strategies, and Dynamics*, Oxford, Oxford University Press, 2015.

Nieto, J., 'U.S. Security Policy and United States-Colombia Relations', Latin American Perspectives, vol. 34, no. 1, pp. 112–19.

Nelsen-Pallmeyer, J., *Brave New World Order*, Maryknol, NY, Orbis Books, 1992.

Nonet, P., and Selznick, P., *Law and Society in Transition: Towards Responsive Law*, Abingdon, Routledge, 2009, Ebook.

Okruhlik, G., 'Re-thinking the Politics of Distribution: Lessons from the Arab Uprisings and the Lack Thereof', in *Arab Uprisings: New Opportunities for Political Science*, Project on Middle East Political Science (POMEPS Briefings), pp. 42–3, www.ssrc.org/publications/docs/POMEPS_Conf12_Book_Web.pdf

Oliver, P., 'Repression and Crime Control: Why Social Movement Scholars Should Pay More Attention to Mass Incarceration as a Form of Repression', *Mobilization*, vol. 13, no. 1, 2008, pp. 1–24.

Pallmeyer, J. N., *Brave New World Order*, Maryknoll, NY, Orbis Books, 1992.

Pan, Z. and Kosicki, G. M., 'Framing Analysis: An approach to News Discourse', *Political Communication*, vol. 10, no. 1, 1993, pp. 55–75.

Parolin, G. P., 'Reweaving the Myth of Bahrain's Parliamentary Experience', in M. A. Tetreault, G. O. Okruhlik, and A. Kapiszewski (eds), *Political Change in the Arab Gulf States; Stuck in Transition*, London, Lynne Rienner, 2011, pp. 21–48.

Peerenboom, R., *China's Long March to Rule of Law*, Cambridge, Cambridge University Press, 2002.

PetersBah, Royal Independent Investigation Commission: Difference between Revisions, Wikipedia, July 2011 https://en.wikipedia.org/w/index.php?title=Royal_Independent_Investigation_Commission&diff=prev&oldid=441362334

PetersBah, Maryam al-Khawaja: Difference between revisions, September 2011, Wikipedia, https://en.wikipedia.org/w/index.php?title=Maryam_al-Khawaja&diff=prev&oldid=452883882.

PetersBah, Torture in Bahrain: Difference between revisions, September 2011, Wikipedia, https://en.wikipedia.org/w/index.php?title=Torture_in_Bahrain&diff=prev&oldid=451655091

PetersBah, Aftermath of the Bahraini Uprising of 2011: Difference between Revisions, Wikipedia, October 2011 https://en.wikipedia.org/w/index.php?title=Aftermath_of_the_Bahraini_uprising_of_2011&diff=prev&oldid=457317643

Pino, N. W., and Johnson, L. M., 'Police Deviance and Community Relations in Trinidad and Tobago', *Policing: An International Journal of Police Strategies & Management*, vol. 34, no. 3, 2011, pp. 454–78.

Pion-Berlin, D., 'Theories of Political Repression in Latin America: Conventional Wisdom and an Alternative', *American Political Society Association*, vol. 19, no. 1, 1986, pp. 49–56.

Punch, M., 'Rotten Orchards: "Pestilence", Police Misconduct And System Failure', *Policing and Society*, vol. 13, no. 2, 2003, pp. 171–96.

Rappaport, J., 'Beyond Participant Observation: Collaborative Ethnography as Theoretical Innovation', *Collaborative Anthropologies*, 1, 2008, pp. 1–31.

Reudy, J., 'Review of Arabs in the Jewish State: Israel's Control of a National Minority', *Washington Report on Middle East Affairs*, 6 September, 1982, p. 7, www.wrmea.org/1982-september-6/book-review-arabs-in-the-jewish-state-israel-s-control-of-a-national-minority.html

Ritter, E .H., 'Policy Disputes, 'Political Survival, and the Onset and Severity of State Repression', *Journal of Conflict Resolution*, vol. 58, no. 1, pp. 143–68 doi:10.1177/0022002712468724

Ross, J. I., *The Dynamics of Political Crime*, London, Sage, 2003.

An Introduction to Political Crime, University of Bristol, Policy Press, 2012.

Rowlinson, M., 'Historical Analysis of Company Documents', in C. Cassell and G. Symon (eds), *Essential Guide to Qualitative Research in Organizational Research*, London, Sage, 2004, pp. 301–11.

Roy, S., 'Humanism, Scholarship, and Politics: Writing on the Palestinian Israeli Conflict', *Journal of Palestine Studies*, vol. 36, no. 2, 2007, pp. 54–65.

Ruggiero, V. and Montagna, N. (eds), *Social Movement: A Reader*, London and New York, NY, Routledge, 2008.

Rumaihi, M. G., *Bahrain: Social and Political Change Since the First World War*, London and New York, NY, Bowker, 1976.

Ryan, C., 'New Opportunities for Political Science: IR Theory', in Arab Uprisings: *New Opportunities for Political Science,* Project on Middle East Political Science (POMEPS Briefings), 2012, 55–7.

Scahill, J., 'The Miami model', Democracy Now! on *Information Clearing House*, 24 November, www.informationclearinghouse.info/article5286.htm

Schwedler, J., 'What Should Political Scientists be Doing?', in *Arab Uprisings: New Opportunities for Political Science,* Project on Middle East Political Science (POMEPS Briefings), pp. 5–8.

Sellin, T., *Culture Conflict and Crime*, New York, NY, Social Science Research Council, 1938.

Sharif, E., 'A Trial of Thoughts and Ideas', in A. Shehabi and M. O. Jones, M. (eds), *Bahrain's Uprising: Resistance and Repression in the Gulf*, London, Zed Books Ltd, 2015, pp. 43–68.

Sharlet, R., 'Party and Public Ideals in Conflict: Constitutionalism and Civil Rights in the USSR', *Cornell International Law Journal*, vol. 23, no. 2, 1990, pp. 341–62.

Shehabi, A., 'Bahrain's Sovereign Hypocrisy', The Middle East Channel, *Foreign Policy*, 14 August 2013, http://mideast.foreignpolicy.com/posts/2013/08/14/bahrains_sovereign_hypocrisy?wp_login_redirect=0

Shehabi, A. and Jones, M. O. (eds), *Bahrain's Uprising: Resistance and Repression in the Gulf*, London, Zed Books Ltd, 2015.

Shucair, A., 'Bahrain Begins to Revoke Dissidents' Citizenship', *Al-Monitor,* 4 September 2014, www.al-monitor.com/pulse/politics/2014/09/bahrain-citizens-deprived-revolution

Skocpol, T., 'Emerging Agendas and Recurrent Strategies in Historical Sociology', in T. Skocpol (ed.), *Vision and Method in Historical Sociology*, Cambridge, Cambridge University Press, 1985, pp. 356–85.

Smith, M. A., 'Invisible Crowds in Cyberspace: Mapping the Social Structure of the Usenet', in M. A. Smith and P. Kollock P (eds), *Communities in Cyberspace*, London, Routledge, 1999.

Snow, D. A., and Benford, R. D., 'Collective Identity and Activism: Networks, Choices, and the Life of the Social Movement', in A. D. Morris and C. McClurg (eds), *Frontiers in Social Movement Theory*, New Haven, CT, Yale University Press, 1992.

Strobl, S., 'From Colonial Policing to Community Policing in Bahrain: The Historical Persistence of Sectarianism', *International Journal of Comparative and Applied Criminal Justice*, vol. 35, no. 1, 2011, pp. 19–37.

Stockdill, B. C., 'Multiple Oppressions and Their Influence on Collective Action: The Case of the AIDS Movement'. PhD Dissertation, 1996, Evanston, IL, Northwestern University.

Sullivan, C. M., 'Project MUSE – Political Repression and the Destruction of Dissident Organizations: Evidence from the Archives of the Guatemalan National Police'. *World Politics*, vol. 68, no. 4, October 2016, pp. 645–76.

Sunshine, J., and T. R.Tyler, 'The Role of Procedural Justice and Legitimacy in Shaping Public Support for Policing', *Law and Society Review*, vol. 37, no. 3, 2003, pp. 513–48.

Tatham, D. E., 'Internal Security in Bahrain', 1977, FCO document, www.whatdotheyknow.com/request/164213/response/531538/attach/3/FOI%200544%2013%2

Teo, P., 'Racism in the News: A Critical Discourse Analysis of News Reporting in Two Australian Newspapers', *Discourse & Society*, vol. 11, no. 1, 2000, pp. 7–49.

Tetreault, M. A., Okruhlik, G .O. and Kapiszewski, A. (eds), *Political Change in the Arab Gulf States; Stuck in Transition*, London, Lynne Rienner, 2011.

Tilly, C., *From Mobilization to Revolution*, Ann Arbor, MI, University of Michigan, 1977.

Trew, F. S. E., Bahrain Annual Review 1985, 23 January 1986, FOIA Request from FCO.

Tsou, T., *The Cultural Revolution and Post-Mao Reforms: A Historical Perspective*, Chicago, IL, University of Chicago Press, 1986.

Turk, A., Law as a Weapon in Social Conflict, *Social Problems*, vol. 23, no. 3, 1976, pp. 276–91.

'Organizational Deviance and Political Policing', *Criminology*, vol. 19, no. 2, 1981, pp. 231–50.

Political Criminality: The Defiance and Defence of Authority, Beverley Hills, CA, Sage Publications, 1982.

'Social Control and Social Conflict', in J. P. Gibbs (ed.), *Social Control: Views from the Social Sciences*, London, Sage, 1982.

Walker, H., 'Bahrain after the BICI', *Conservative Middle East Council,* 6 December 2011, http://cmec.org.uk/blog/bahrain-after-the-bici/

Wehrey, F., 'The March of Bahrain's Hardliners', Carnegie Endowment for International Peace, 31 May 2012, http://carnegieendowment.org/2012/05/31/march-of-bahrain-s-hardliners.

Welch, M., *Crimes of Power and States of Impunity: The U.S. Response to Terror,* New Brunswick, NJ, Rutgers University Press.

Whitaker, B., 2014, https://al-bab.com/blog/2014/12/homophobia-and-nationalism-too-gay-represent-bahrain

Wikipedia, Wikipedia: Conflict of interest/Noticeboard/Bell Pottinger COI Investigations, https://en.wikipedia.org/wiki/Wikipedia:Conflict_of_interest/Noticeboard/Bell_Pottinger_COI_Investigations

Wiktorowicz, Q. (ed.), *Islamic Activism: A Social Movement Theory Approach,* Bloomington, IN, Indiana University Press, 2004, p. 92.

'Civil Society as Social Control: State Power in Jordan', *Comparative Politics,* vol. 33, no. 1, 2012, pp. 4–61.

Wilkingson, R., 'Speak Together of Freedom. The Present Struggle for Democracy and Human Rights in Bahrain', *The Parliamentary Human Rights Group,* March 1996, http://bahrain.wikia.com/wiki/Speak_Together_of_Freedom:_The_Present_Struggle_for_Democracy_and_Human_Rights_in_Bahrain,_Robert_Wilkinson,_The_Parliamentary_Human_Rights_Group,_March_1996

Wodak, R., 'What is Critical Discourse Analysis? Interview with Gavin Kendall', *Forum: Qualitative Social Research,* vol. 8, no. 2, art. 29, 2007.

Wolff, R .P., Jr, Moore, B. and Marcuse, H., *A Critique of Pure Tolerance,* Boston, MA, Beacon Press, 1965, www.qualitative-research.net/index.php/fqs/article/view/255/561

Yusif, M., 'Just Bahrain not Welcome at Checkpoints', Mahmood's Den, [web blog], http://mahmood.tv/2011/03/19/just-bahraini-not-welcome-at-checkpoints//

Zald, M. and McCarthy, J. (eds), *The Dynamics of Social Movements,* Cambridge, MA, Winthrop Publishers, 1979, pp. 94–125, http://web.mit.edu/gtmarx/www/movement.html

Reports by NGOs, Commissions, Think Tanks and Committees

Amnesty International, *Annual Report, 1971 1972,* London, Amnesty International Publications.

Annual Report 1972–1973, London, Amnesty International Publications.

Annual Report 1974–1975, London, Amnesty International Publications.

Annual Report 1978, London, Amnesty International Publications.

Annual Report 1982, London, Amnesty International Publications.

Annual Report 1983, London, Amnesty International Publications.

Bahrain: Violations of Human Rights, 1991, London, Amnesty International Publications.

Bahrain: A Human Rights Crisis, 1 September 1995, www.refworld.org/docid/3ae6a9984.html

Bahrain: A Human Rights Crisis, 1996, London, Amnesty International Publications, www.refworld.org/docid/3ae6a9984.html

Report: Bahrain, 1 January 1997, London, Amnesty International Publications, www.refworld.org/cgi- bin/texis/vtx/rwmain?page=publisher&docid=3ae6a9fe0&skip=0&publisher=AMNESTY&coi=BHR&searchin=title&sort=date

Crackdown in Bahrain: Human Rights at the Crossroads, 2011, London, Amnesty International Publications, www.univie.ac.at/bimtor/dateien/bahrain_ai_2011_hr_crossroads.pdf

'Human rights in Bahrain – Media Briefing', 31 April 2012, www.amnesty.ca/news/news-item/amnesty-international-human-rights- briefing-on-bahrain

Bahrain: Reform Shelved, Repression Unleashed, London, Amnesty International Publications, 2012.

201 –15 Report Bahrain, London, Amnesty International Publications, www.amnesty.org/en/countries/middle-east-and-north- africa/bahrain/report-bahrain/

Behind the Rhetoric: Human Rights Abuses Continue in Bahrain Unabated, London, Amnesty International Publications, 2015.

Bahrain: Citizenship of 115 People Revoked in 'Ludicrous' Mass Trial, www.amnesty.org/en/latest/news/2018/05/bahrain-citizenship

Bahrain Central Informatics Organization, Labour Force by Nationality and Sex in Census Years – (1959, 1965, 1971, 1981, 1991, 2001) www.cio.gov.bh/cio_ara/English/Publications/Statistical %20Abstract/ABS2009/CH11/1.pdf

Bahrain Center for Human Rights, 'ANHRI: Bahrain: Court Holds Mass Hearing for Human Rights Activist', 29 October 2010, www.bahrainrights.org/en/node?page=155&nomobile=true

'Individuals Killed by Government's Excessive Use of Force since 2011', 4 April 2011, www.bahrainrights.org/en/node/3864

'Bahrain: Right to Association under Attack as Ministry of Justice Moves to Dissolve Islamic Action Society "Amal"', 20 June 2012, www.bahrainrights.org/en/node/5326

'The Terrorism Law in Bahrain: A Tool to Silence Dissidents', 13 March 2014, www.bahrainrights.org/sites/default/files/Terrorism%20Laws%20in%20Bahrain%20-%20FINAL.pdf

Bahrain Labour Market Indicators, Labour Market Regulatory Authority, Q2, 2015, http://blmi.lmra.bh/2015/06/mi_dashboard.xml

Bahrain Watch, 'Bahrain Govt Hires 18 Western Companies to Improve Image after Unrest', 23 August 2012, https://bahrainwatch.org/blog/2012/08/23/bahrain-government-hires-18-western-companies-to-improve-image-after-unrest/

Access Denied, 2012, https://bahrainwatch.org/access/viewreport.php#findings

PR Watch: Big Tent Communications 2012, https://bahrainwatch.org/pr/big-tent-communications.php

PR Watch, 2012, https://bahrainwatch.org/pr/g3.php

PR Watch: Dragon Association, 2012, https://bahrainwatch.org/pr/dragon-associates.php

'The IP Spy Files: How Bahrain's Government Silences Anonymous Online Dissent', August 2013, https://bahrainwatch.org/ipspy/ip-spy-files.pdf
'UN Ambassador to UN Human Rights Council', September 2014, https://bahrainwatch.org/media/#!donahoe
'Secretary General of the United Nations', *Fabrigate*, September 2014, https://bahrainwatch.org/media/#!bankimoon
'Time for Some Internet Problems in Duraz': Bahraini ISPs Impose Internet Curfew in Protest Village, 2016, https://bahrainwatch.org/blog/2016/08/03/bahrain-internet-curfew/

Bahrain Youth Society for Human Rights, 'A Man Died in Custody Confession on Television that He had Killed Two Policemen', 28 April 2011, www.byshr.org/?p=396
Report: The Recommendations of the Bahraini National Assembly Restrain Human Rights, 8 September 2013, http://byshr.org/wp-content/en-reco.pdf

Bassiouni, M .C., Rodley, N., Al-Awadhi, B., Kirsch, P. and Arsanjani, M. H., 'Report of the Bahrain Independent Commission of Inquiry' [BICI Report], 23 November 2011, BICI, Manama, www.bici.org.bh/BICIreportEN.pdf

Bery, S., 'Nabeel Rajab: Why Did the U.S. State Department Drag Its Feet?', Amnesty International Blog, 21 August 2012, http://blog.amnestyusa.org/middle-east/nabeel-rajab-why-did-the-u-s-state-department-drag-its-feet/

BICI Follow Up Team, *BICI Follow-Up Report*, November 2012, http://iaa.bh/downloads/bici_nov2012_en.pdf

Blaydes, L., State of Repression: Iraq Under Saddam Hussein, Princeton, NJ, Princeton University Press, , p. 2.

Bureau of Human Rights, *Democracy and Labor, US Department of State, Bahrain 2012 Human Rights Report*, April 2012 www.state.gov/j/drl/rls/hrrpt/2012/nea/204355.htm
Democracy and Labor, US Department of State, Bahrain 2013 Human Rights Report, 27 February 2013, www.state.gov/j/drl/rls/hrrpt/2013/nea/220348.htm

Carnegie Endowment for International Peace, 'Arab Political Systems: Baseline Information and Reforms – Bahrain', 2008.

'Denied the right to enter Bahrain', Bahrain Human Rights Organization, Centre for Arab Gulf Studies, January 1996.

Diboll, M., 'Written Evidence from Dr Mike Diboll', Parliamentary Foreign Affairs Committee on the UK's Relationship with Saudi Arabia and Bahrain, 12 November 2012, www.publications.parliament.uk/pa/cm201314/cmselect/cmfaff/88/88vw25.htm

Freedom House, 'Bahrain 2012', https://freedomhouse.org/report/freedom-world/2012/bahrain-0
Freedom on the Net 2012: Bahrain, 2012, www. freedomhouse.org/sites/default/files/Bahrain%202012_0.pdf
Freedom in the World 2015, 2015, https://freedomhouse.org/report/freedom-world/2015/bahrain#.VWius8_BzGc

Global Voices Advocacy, 'Remembering Ali Abdulemam', 7 November 2011, https://advox.globalvoices.org/2011/11/07/remembering-ali-abdulemam/

Human Rights Defenders, 'Violent Crackdown Continues To Target Human Rights Defenders', Press Release, 8 September 2010, www.fidh.org/Inter

national-Federation-for-Human-Rights/north-africa-middle-east/bahrain/Violent-crackdown-continues-to

Human Rights Watch, *Routine Abuse, Routine Denial, Civil Rights and the Political Crisis in Bahrain*, 1997.

Torture Redux: The Revival of Physical Coercion during Interrogations in Bahrain, 2010, www.hrw.org/sites/default/files/reports/ bahrain0210webwcover_0.pdf

'Bahrain: Medics Describe Torture in Detention', 22 October 2011, http://www.hrw.org/news/2011/10/21/bahrain-medics-describe-torture- detention

'Human Rights Watch UPR Submission on Bahrain', 21 November 2011, http://www.hrw.org/news/2011/11/21/human-rights-watch-upr-submission-bahrain

No Justice in Bahrain: Unfair Trials in Civilian and Military Court, 2012, www.hrw.org/sites/default/files/reports/bahrain0212webwcover.pdf

'Bahrain: Vital Reform Commitments Unmet', 28 March 2012, www.hrw.org/news/2012/03/28/bahrain-vital-reform-commitments- unmet

'Bahrain: Promises Unkept, Rights Still Violated', 22 November 2012, www.hrw.org/news/2012/11/22/bahrain-promises-unkept-rights-still-violated

'Interfere, Restrict, Control: Restraints on Freedom of Association in Bahrain', 20 June 2013, www.hrw.org/report/2013/06/20/interfere-restrict-control/restraints-freedom-association-bahrain

Bahrain: Citizenship Rights Stripped Away, August 2014, www.hrw.org/news/2014/08/21/bahrain-citizenship

2016: Bahrain Events of 2015, www.hrw.org/world-report/2016/country-chapters/bahrain

Index on Censorship, 'Bahrain Activist Nabeel Rajab Sentenced to Three Years in Prison', August 2012, www.indexoncensorship.org/2012/08/bahrain-activist-nabeel-rajab-sentenced-to-three-years-in-prison/

International Crisis Group, *Popular Protests in North Africa and the Middle East (III): The Bahrain Revolt*, MENA Report No. 105, 6 April 2011, www.crisisgroup.org/~/media/Files/Middle%20East%20North%20Africa/Iran%20Gulf/Bahrain/105-%20Popular%20Protests%20in%20North%20Africa%20and%20the%20Middle%20East%20-III-The%20Bahrain%20Revolt.pdf

Popular Protest in North Africa and the Middle East (VIII): Bahrain's Rocky Road to Reform, MENA Report, No. 111, 28 July 2011, http://www.crisisgroup.org/~/media/Files/Middle%20East%20North%20Africa/Iran%20Gulf/Bahrain/111-%20Popular%20Protest%20in%20North%20Africa%20and%20the%20Middle%20East%20VII%20-%20%20Bahrains%20Rocky%20Road%20to%20Reform.pdf

International Commission of Jurists, 'Bahrain – Attacks on Justice 2002', 26 August 2002, www.refworld.org/docid/48a57efa0.html

International Commission of Jurists (ICJ), 34th Session of the UN Committee Against Torture, 10 May 2005: Submission by the International Commission of Jurists (ICJ) on the impact of the draft law on counter-terrorism of the Kingdom of Bahrain on its obligations under the United Nations Convention against Torture and Other Cruel, Inhuman or Degrading Treatment or Punishment (UNCAT), 10 May 2005, available at: www.refworld.org/docid/48a57eff2.html

International Trade Union Confederation, 'ITUC Statement on Recent Attacks on Rights of Bahraini Trade Unionists', 11 October 2011, www.ituc-csi.org/IMG/pdf/ITUC_Bahrain_Statement_Final_3_.pdf

Countries at Risk: Violations of Trade Union Rights, 2013.

Jones, J. and Horne, J., 'FAC Submission Breakdown, Internal Document at Bahrain Watch', 2012, https://docs.google.com/spreadsheets/d/1puCoqyyMvPeJy1fWmVuGqIVOOzGcLsLNuwo94ZFH0UM/edit?usp=sharing

Kinninmont, J., *Bahrain: Beyond the Impasse*, Chatham House, London, 2012, www.chathamhouse.org/sites/files/chathamhouse/public/Research/Middle%20East/pr0612kinninmont.pdf

Ma'oz, M., 'The "Shi'i Crescent": Myth and Reality', The Saban Center for Middle East Policy at the Brookings Institution, no. 15, November 2007, www.brookings.edu/~/media/research/files/papers/2007/11/middle-east-maoz/11_middle_east_maoz.pdf

Physicians for Human Rights, *Weaponizing Tear Gas: Bahrain's Unprecedented Use of Toxic Chemical Agents Against Civilians*, August 2012, https://s3.amazonaws.com/PHR_Reports/Bahrain-TearGas-Aug2012-small.pdf

POMED, Project on a Middle East Democracy, 'One Year Later: Assessing Bahrain's Implementations of the BICI Report', November 2012, http://pomed.org/wp-content/uploads/2013/12/One-Year-Later-Assessing-Bahrains-Implementation-of-the-BICI-Report.pdf

Reporters Without Borders, 'Bahrain', http://surveillance

'Media Freedom Still Under Attack in Bahrain', 11 March 2015, http://en.rsf.org/bahrain-media-freedom-still-under-attack-11-03-2015,47675.html

Reudy, J., 'Review of Arabs in the Jewish State: Israel's Control of a National Minority', Washington Report on Middle East Affairs, September 6, 1982, p. 7, www.wrmea.org/1982-september-6/book-review-arabs-in-the-jewish-state-israel-s-control-of-a-national-minority.html

Summary of report submitted by Daniel Walker, Director of the Chicago Study Team, to the National Commission on the Causes and Prevention of Violence, introduction by Max Frankel, E.P. Dutton, New York, 1968, www.fjc.gov/history/home.nsf/page/tu_chicago7_doc_13.html

The National Democratic Institute for International Affairs, 'Bahrain's October 24 and 31, 2002 Legislative Elections', 2002, www.ndi.org/files/2392_bh_electionsreport_engpdf_09252008.pdf

The Political Terror Scale, www.politicalterrorscale.org/countries.php?region=Eurasia&country=Syria&year=2010

Yasin, Y., 'The Cost of Tweeting in Bahrain', *Index on Censorship*, July 2013, www.indexoncensorship.org/2013/07/the-cost-of-tweeting-in-bahrain/

Laws

Law Number 58, Protecting Society from Terrorist Acts, July 2006, www.legalaffairs.gov.bh/AdvancedSearchDetails.aspx? id=2125#.U49LEfldXD1

Part about six months comes from Civil Procedures, www.bahrainrights.org/sites/default/files/Terrorism%20Laws%20in%20Bahrain%20-%20FINAL.pdf

Publication Law of 1965, www.legalaffairs.gov.bh/AdvancedSearchDetails.aspx?id=2184#.Us_OsvRdWwt

Law Number 33 for the Year 2012, amendment to number 221 for the penal code decreed by the law 15 for the year 1976, www.legalaffairs.gov.bh/Media/LegalPDF/K3312.pdf

Law Number 52 of the Year 2012, amendment to some of the penal code stipulated by decree 15 from the year 1976. www.legalaffairs.gov.bh/Media/LegalPDF/K5212.pdf

The National Archives, Qatar Digital Library and other Archives

Wilson, Maj., 'Selections from the Records of the Bombay Government' [107] (149/733), British Library: India Office Records and Private Papers, IOR/R/15/1/732, in *Qatar Digital Library* www.qdl.qa/en/archive/81055/vdc_100022870191.0x000096

'Administration Reports 1920–1924' [84v] (173/412), British Library: India Office Records and Private Papers, IOR/R/15/1/713, in *Qatar Digital Library* www.qdl.qa/en/archive/81055/vdc_100023385510.0x0000ae

'Administration Reports 1920-1924' [119r] (242/412), British Library: India Office Records and Private Papers, IOR/R/15/1/713, in *Qatar Digital Library* www.qdl.qa/en/archive/81055/vdc_100023385511.0x00002b

'Administration Reports 1920–1924' [158r] (320/412), British Library: India Office Records and Private Papers, IOR/R/15/1/713, in *Qatar Digital Library* www.qdl.qa/en/archive/81055/vdc_100023385511.0x000079

'Administration Reports 1920–1924' [158v] (321/412), British Library: India Office Records and Private Papers, IOR/R/15/1/713, in *Qatar Digital Library* www.qdl.qa/en/archive/81055/vdc_100023385511.0x00007a

'Administration Reports 1920–1924' [159r] (322/412), British Library: India Office Records and Private Papers, IOR/R/15/1/713, in *Qatar Digital Library* www.qdl.qa/en/archive/81055/vdc_100023385511.0x00007b

'Administration Reports 1920–1924' [159r] (322/412), British Library: India Office Records and Private Papers, IOR/R/15/1/713, in *Qatar Digital Library* www.qdl.qa/en/archive/81055/vdc_100023385511.0x00007b

'Administration Reports 1920–1924' [195r] (394/412), British Library: India Office Records and Private Papers, IOR/R/15/1/713, in *Qatar Digital Library* www.qdl.qa/en/archive/81055/vdc_100023385511.0x0000c3

'File 6/70 Census of Bahrain population' [45r] (91/228), British Library: India Office Records and Private Papers, IOR/R/15/2/1289, in *Qatar Digital Library* www.qdl.qa/archive/81055/vdc_100035874045.0x00005c

'File 6/70 Census of Bahrain population' [89r] (179/228), British Library: India Office Records and Private Papers, IOR/R/15/2/1289, in *Qatar Digital Library* www.qdl.qa/archive/81055/vdc_100035874045.0x0000b4

'File 9/1 Institution of Reforms & Sunni opposition intrigues' [151r] (318/504), British Library: India Office Records and Private Papers, IOR/R/15/2/127, in *Qatar Digital Library* www.qdl.qa/archive/81055/vdc_100023321443.0x000077

'File 19/165 IV (C 57) Bahrain Reforms' [106r] (242/476), British Library: India Office Records and Private Papers, IOR/R/15/1/340, in *Qatar Digital Library* www.qdl.qa/en/archive/81055/vdc_100023555763.0x00002b

Al Nida Al Arabi, Issue 1, September 1956, FO371/120548, The National Archives.

'Bahraini Police Methods, FCO 8/4332, The National Archives.

Amnesty Report Clipping, FCO8/3893, The National Archives.

Anon, 6 September 1956, FO371/120548, The National Archives.

Anon, 18 July 1960, FO1016/684, The National Archives.

Author unknown, Letter to ITM Lucas, 22 June 1975, FCO8/2415, The National Archives.

Bahrain Special Branch, 'The Bahrain National Liberation Front (NLF)', FCO8/3489, The National Archives.

Bahrain State Radio Transcript, 6 & 7 November 1956, FO371/120548, The National Archives.

'Bahraini Police Methods', FCO 8/4332, The National Archives.

Belgrave, C., 5 January 1929, *Papers of Charles Dalrymple-Belgrave: Transcripts of Diaries, 1926–1957*, Library of the University of Exeter.

British Embassy Bahrain, Letter to Rt Hon Anthony Crossland MP, 29 January 1977, The National Archives, FCO 8/2874, The National Archives.

Burrows, B. A. B., Summary of news, 24 August 1956, FO371/120548, The National Archives.

22 September 1956, FO371/120548, The National Archives.

1 October 1956, FO371/120548, The National Archives.

Bahrain Internal Situation, 6 November 1956, FO371/120548, The National Archives.

12 November 1956, FO371/120548, The National Archives.

15 November 1956, FO371/120548, The National Archives.

Collis, S. P., 16 January 1982, FCO 8/4332, The National Archives.

Bahrain Internal, 20 February 1982, FCO 8/4332, The National Archives.

Bahrain Labour, 12 March 1983, FCO 8/4920, The National Archives.

'The Shiʿa in Bahrain', Bahrain Internal Political, 1984, FCO8/5442, The National Archives.

Confidential, 11 July 1960, FO1016/684, The National Archives.

Copson, Telegram No 165, 16 September 1981, FCO8/3893, The National Archives.

Foggon, G., 28 October 1974, FCO 8/2180, The National Archives.

Foreign Office, Communique to Bahrain, 14 November 1956, FO371/120548, The National Archives

1957, FO371/126918, The National Archives.

Given, E. F., Prospects for Bahrain, 5 July 1976, FCO8/2643, The National Archives.

Prospects for Bahrain, 29 October 1976, FCO8/2643, The National Archives.

Bahrain: Annual Report for 1976, 5 January 1977, FCO 8/2873, The National Archives.

Political Murder in Bahrain, 29 January 1977, FCO8/2874, The National Archives.

Bahrain 1976, 15 March 1977, FCO8/2873, The National Archives.

Bahrain Round-Up, 20 June 1977, FCO 8/2872, The National Archives.

Bahrain: Annual Review for 1977, FCO8/3091, The National Archives.

Gulf Daily News, 'Ministry Denies Death Rumours', April 1980, FCO8/3489, The National Archives.

'Interview with Shaykh Khalifa bin Salman Al Khalifa', 15 Saturday 1982, FCO 8/4332, The National Archives.

Ivey, P. R., Political Expression in Bahrain, 7 July 1985, FCO8/5817, The National Archives.

Bahrain Internal Political, FCO 8/5187, The National Archives

Kinchen, R., Dissolution of the Bahrain National Assembly, 29 August 1975, FCO 8/2415, The National Archives.

Lamport, S. M. J., Bahrain Security, 8 March 1982, FCO 8/4332, The National Archives.

Leading Personality Reports 1977, FCO 8/3090, The National Archives.

Little, W. O. Report by Major Little, in Pamphlet on Bahrain, 1957, FO371/126918, The National Archives.

Luce, W. 1964, FO371/174521, The National Archives.

Lucas, I .T. M., Bahrain 1977, 9 February 1978, FCO 8/3091, The National Archives.

Lyall, W. C., 22 October 1960, FO1016/684, The National Archives.

Miers, C., Attempted Coup in Bahrain, 26 February 1982, FCO 8/4332.

Minutes from Meeting, 1956, FO371/120548, The National Archives.

Moberly, J. C., Bahrain: Use of Torture by the Special Branch, 19 February 1982, FCO 8/4332, The National Archives.

Noble, E. H., Bahrain Internal, 26 August 1975, FCO 8/2415, The National Archives.

Note in Margin on, 'Daily in Bahrain by Ali Sayyar', 1956, FO371/120548, The National Archives.

Office Notice, 29 October 1956, FO371/120548, The National Archives.

Oldfield, K., 15 August 1965, Amnesty International and Political Prisoners, FO371/185355, The National Archives.

30 August 1965, FO371/179790, The National Archives.

Parsons, A. D., Communique to T.F. Brenchley, 18 December 1965, FO371/179788, The National Archives.

Passmore, K. J., Bahrain Internal, 3 December 1980, FCO8/3489, The National Archives.

Passmore, K. J., Letter from Roland Moyle, MP: Bahrain, 16 September 1981, FCO8/3893, The National Archives.

State Security Law, in Internal Political Situation in Bahrain, FCO8/2415, The National Archives.

Sterling, A. J. D., Bahrain: Annual Review, for 1970, FCO8/1638, The National Archives.

Bahrain: Annual Review for 1971, FCO 8/1823, The National Archives.

Staff at UK Embassy Bahrain, Biography of Yusuf bin Ahmad al Shirawi, Leading Personalities, 1976, FCO8/2643, The National Archives.

Tesh, R. M., Bahrain: Annual Review for 1972, 31 December 1972, FCO 8/ 1974, The National Archives.
Bahrain: Annual Review for 1973, FCO8/2181, The National Archives.
Bahrain: Constitutional Development, 12 June 1973, FCO8/1975, The National Archives.
23 July 1973, FCO8/1975, The National Archives.
Bahrain Internal, 18 November 1973, FCO 8/1975, The National Archives.
Bahrain Elections, 11 December 1973, FCO8/1975, The National Archives.
Bahrain: Internal, 17 December 1973, FCO8/1975, The National Archives.
From Bahrain Embassy, 18 December 1973, FCO8/1975, The National Archives.
Bahrain: Internal, 9 April 1974, FCO 8/2180, The National Archives.
Bahrain Internal, 6 May 1974, FCO8/2180, The National Archives.
Bahrain: Internal, 23 June 1974, FCO 8/2180, The National Archives.
Form at a Glance (FAAG), 24 June 1974, FCO8/2180, The National Archives.
Bahrain Internal, 1 July 1974, FCO8/2180, The National Archives.
Bahrain's First Parliament, 8 July 1974, FCO 8/2180, The National Archives.
Bahrain Internal', 8 October 1974, FCO8/2180, The National Archives.
Bahrain National Assembly, 12 November 1974, FCO 8/2180, The National Archives.
Internal Political 1974, 17 December 1974, FCO8/2180, The National Archives.
Annual Review for the Year 1974, FCO8/2414, The National Archives.
Bahrain: Annual Review for 1974, 2 January 1975, FCO 8/2414. The National Archives.
Bahrain Internal, 1 March 1975, FCO8/2415, The National Archives.
Bahrain: Internal, 4 March 1975, FCO8/2415, The National Archives.
Letter to Ivor Lucas, 6 May 1975, FCO 8/2415, The National Archives.
Tomkys, W. R., Meeting Between Minister of State and Bahraini Prime Minister, 18 December 1981, FCO8/3893, The National Archives.
First Impressions, 4 February 1982, FCO 8/4332, The National Archives.
Bahrain: Annual Review for 1981,13 February 1982, FCO 8/4332, The National Archives.
Communique, 16 February 1982, FCO 8/4332, The National Archives.
Trial of Detainees, 15 March 1982, 8/4332, The National Archives.
The December Coup, 21 March 1982, FCO 8/4332, The National Archives.
Internal Political Situation Bahrain 1982, 10 April 1982, FCO 8/4332, The National Archives.
Internal Political Situation Bahrain 1984, FCO8/5442, The National Archives
Tel 75: Internal Security, 27 April 1982, FCO 8/4332.
Communique, 8 May 1982, FCO 8/4332, The National Archives.
Mahdi Tajjir, 16 May 1982, FCO 8/4332, The National Archives.
Communique, 23 May 1982, FCO 8/4332, The National Archives.
Return of Bahraini Deportees from Iran, 5 July 1982, FCO 8/4332, The National Archives.
Bahrain Internal 30 October 1982, FCO 8/4332, The National Archives.
Farewell to Bahrain, 1984, FOIA Request from FCO, The National Archives.
Internal Political Situation 1984, FCO8/5442, The National Archives.

Trew, F. S. E., Bahrain: Annual Review 1984, FOIA Request from the FCO, The National Archives.
Bahrain: Annual Review 1985, 23 January 1986, FOIA Request from the FCO, The National Archives.
Tripp, J. P., Communique to M.S. Weir, 5 April 1965, FO371/179788, The National Archives.
Communique, 16 April 1963, FO1016/684, The National Archives.
18 April 1963, FO1016/684, The National Archives.
The Internal Situation in Bahrain, 1 June 1963, FO371/174521, The National Archives.
The Internal Situation in Bahrain, 1 June 1963, FO371/168670, The National Archives.
Communique to A.D. Parsons, 14 February 1965, FO371/179788, The National Archives.
14 Feb 1965, FO371/179790, The National Archives.
Turnbull, P. E., A review of the structure and organisation of the Bahraini State Police Force, 1965, FO371/179788, The National Archives.
Walker, H. B, Bahrain: Annual Review for 1979, FCO 8/3490. The National Archives.
The Shi'a in Bahrain, 26 October 1980, FCO8/3489, The National Archives.
Bahrain: Annual Review for 1980, 10 February 1981, FCO8/3894, The National Archives.
Bahrain Internal, 18 May 1980, FCO8/3489, The National Archives.
Bahrain Internal, 28 June 1980, FCO8/3489, The National Archives.
The Shi'a in Bahrain, 26 October 1980, FCO8/3489, The National Archives.
Bahrain Internal - Representative Assembly, 19 February 1981, FCO 8/3893, The National Archives.
Weir, M .S., 22 April 1965, FO371/179788, The National Archives.
7 October 1965, FO371/179788, The National Archives.
Wilton, C. E .J., Bahrain Internal, 14 May 1980, FCO8/3489, The National Archives.
Wiltshire, E. P., 30 December 1960, FO1016/691, The National Archives.
Wogan, P. F. M., Bahrain Coup: Trial of Detainees, 16 March 1982, FCO 8/4332, The National Archives.
Letter to Tomkys, W.R., 23 April 1982, FCO8/4332, The National Archives.
Iran and the Gulf, 23 August 1982, FCO8/4332, The National Archives.
Visit to Bahrain by International Red Cross Official, 1965, FO371/179809, The National Archives.

US Embassy Cables

'Advisory Roles of the UK and Certain Others Countries in the Persian Gulf States', US Embassy Manama, 20 February 1975, www.wikileaks.org/plusd/cables/1975MANAMA00217_b.html

Ereli, A., 'A Field Guide to Bahraini Political Parties', US Embassy Manama, 4 September 2008, www.wikileaks.org/plusd/cables/08MANAMA592_a.html,

'Bahrain's Shiʿa Opposition: Managing Sectarian Pressures and Focusing on 2010 Parliamentary Elections', US Embassy Manama, 22 July 2009, www.wikileaks.org/plusd/cables/09MANAMA438_a.html

'Bahrain-Iran Gas Deal Still Far Off', 3 February 2009, Wikileaks, https://search.wikileaks.org/plusd/cables/09MANAMA58_a.html

C. Henzel, 'Bahrain Will Follow Saudi's Lead on Kosovo', 19 February 2009, Wikileaks, https://search.wikileaks.org/plusd/cables/09MANAMA97_a.html

'Scenesetter for Manama Dialogue', December 11–13, US Embassy Manama, 2 December 2009, https://wikileaks.org/plusd/cables/09MANAMA681_a.html

Monroe, W. T., 'Bahrainis Publicly Acknowledge Regional Terrorist Threat', US Embassy Manama, 16 February 2005, https://wikileaks.org/plusd/cables/05MANAMA224_a.html

'Bahraini Political Scene Part II: Royal Family Conservatives Tighten Reins on Politics', US Embassy Manama, 24 May 2006, https://wikileaks.org/plusd/cables/06MANAMA907_a.html

'Government Committees Warn Newspapers about Anti Regime Coverage', 21 June 2006, https://wikileaks.org/plusd/cables/06MANAMA1116_a.html

'Elections Highlights No. 1: Dates Announced, E-Voting Out', US Embassy Manama, 8 October 2006, https://wikileaks.org/plusd/cables/06MANAMA1756_a.html

'Prominent *Shiʿa* Paint Gloomy Picture of Shiʿa Outlook in Bahrain', US Embassy Manama, 9 April 2007, http://webcache.googleusercontent.com/search?q=cache:eZh_8zJoqAoJ:https://wikileaks.org/plusd/cables/07MANAMA328_a.html+&cd=1&hl=en&ct=clnk&gl=uk

'Court Case Against Activists Dropped, But Clashes Flare Up Anyway', US Embassy Manama, 24 May 2007, https://wikileaks.org/plusd/cables/07MANAMA476_a.html

Future of Bahrain: Ambassador's Parting Thoughts, US Embassy Manama, 19 July 2007, https://wikileaks.org/plusd/cables/07MANAMA669_a.html

Stein, R. A., 'Security on Gulf and Bahrain', US Embassy Manama, 30 April 1973, www.wikileaks.org/plusd/cables/1973MANAMA00248_b.html

US Embassy Manama, 'Security on Gulf and Bahrain', 30 April 1973, www.wikileaks.org/plusd/cables/1973MANAMA00248_b.html

US Embassy Bahrain, 'Bahraini Subversive Given Stiff Sentence,' 12 May 1973, www.wikileaks.org/plusd/cables/1973MANAMA00279_b.html

'Bahrain's Foreign Policy', 9 February 1975, Wikileaks, https://search.wikileaks.org/plusd/cables/1975MANAMA00163_b.html

'Bahraini Political Developments: Foreign Minister's Comments', 11 September 1975, Wikileaks, https://search.wikileaks.org/plusd/cables/1975MANAMA01057_b.html

US Embassy Riyadh, 'Bahrain's Arms Requests', 1 March 1978, Wikileaks, https://search.wikileaks.org/plusd/cables/1978JIDDA01545_d.html

US Embassy, 18 July 1978, 'Bahrain's Financial Plight', Wikileaks, https://search.wikileaks.org/plusd/cables/1976MANAMA00964_b.html

Records of Bahrain

'Notes on formation of New Police Force', in P. Tuson and E. Quick (eds), *Records of Bahrain 1820–1960*, vol. 4, Slough, Archive Editions, 1993.

Acheson, J. G., the Deputy Secretary to the Government of India in the Foreign and Political Department, 'British administration in the Bahrain State', 28 May 1929, in P. Tuson and E. Quick (eds), *Records of Bahrain 1820–1960*, vol. 4, Slough, Archive Editions, 1993.

Al-Shabab al-Watani, 1938, in A. Burdett (ed.), *Records of Bahrain 1820–1960*, vol. 5, Slough, Archive Editions, 1993.

Anon, 1965, in A. Burdett (ed.) *Records of Bahrain 1961–1965*, vol. 5, Cambridge Archive Editions, 1997.

Arabian Department, 'Minister of State's Visit to the Persian Gulf', 9– 6 May 1965, in A. Burdett (ed.) *Records of Bahrain, 1961–1965*, vol. 5, Cambridge Archive Editions, 1997.

Barrett, C. C. J., Letter to the Foreign Sec. To the Gov. of India, 28 August 1929, No. 385-S, in P. Tuson and E. Quick (eds), *Records of Bahrain 1820–1960*, vol. 4, Slough, Archive Editions, 1993, p. 570.

Belgrave, C., Letter to Prior, 12 July 1929, in P. Tuson and E. Quick (eds), *Records of Bahrain 1820–1960*, vol. 4, Slough, Archive Editions, 1993.

'The Bahrain Municipality', in P. Tuson, A. Burdett and E. Quick (eds), *Records of Bahrain 1820–1960*, vol. 3, Slough, Archive Editions, 1993.

Brenchley, R. F., Communique to JP Tripp, 26 March 1965, in A. Burdett (ed.) Records *of Bahrain, 1961 –1965*, vol. 5, Cambridge Archive Editions, 1997.

Burrows, B. A. B., 1 July 1954, in A. Burdett (ed.), *Records of Bahrain 1820–1960*, vol. 7, Slough, Archive Editions, 1993.

20 July 1954, in A. Burdett (ed.), *Records of Bahrain 1820–1960*, vol. 7, Slough, Archive Editions, 1993.

5 March 1955, in A. Burdett (ed.), *Records of Bahrain 1820–1960*, vol. 7, Slough, Archive Editions, 1993.

4 March 1956, in A. Burdett (ed.), *Records of Bahrain 1820–1960*. vol. 7, Slough, Archive Editions, 1993.

12 March 1956, in A. Burdett (ed.), *Records of Bahrain 1820–1960*, vol. 7, Slough, Archive Editions, 1993.

Secret to Foreign Office, 15 December 1956, in A. Burdett (ed.), *Records of Bahrain 1820-1960*, vol. 7, Slough, Archive Editions, 1993.

Daly, C. K., 21 November, in P. Tuson and E. Quick (eds), *Records of Bahrain 1820–1960*, vol. 3, Slough, Archive Editions, 1993, p.674.

Tyranny of the Sheikh of Bahrain and his family over Bahrain Subjects, 30 December 1921, in P. Tuson and E. Quick (eds), *Records of Bahrain 1820–1960*, vol. 3, Slough, Archive Editions.

Note on the political situation in Bahrain November 1921, 6 January 1922, in P. Tuson, A. Burdett and E. Quick (eds), *Records of Bahrain 1820–1960*, vol. 3, Slough, Archive Editions, 1993.

From the Agency in Bahrain, 11 April 1922, in P. Tuson and E. Quick (eds), *Records of Bahrain 1820–1960*, vol. 3, Slough, Archive Editions, 1993.

Note on the Political Situation in Bahrain, November 1924, in P. Tuson and E. Quick (eds), *Records of Bahrain 1820–1960* vol. 3, Slough, Archive Editions 1993, p. 669.

25 September 1923, No. 123-C, in P. Tuson, A. Burdett and E. Quick (eds), *Records of Bahrain 1820–1960*, vol. 4, Slough, Archive Editions, 1993.

30 September 1923, in P. Tuson, A. Burdett and E. Quick (eds), *Records of Bahrain 1820–1960*, vol. 4, Archive Editions, Slough, 1993.

'Memorandum', 4 October 1923, in P. Tuson, A. Burdett and E. Quick (eds), *Records of Bahrain 1820–1960*, vol. 4, Slough, Archive Editions, 1993.

Note on the Political Situation in Bahrain, November 1924, in P. Tuson and E. Quick (eds), *Records of Bahrain 1820–1960*, vol. 3, Slough, Archive Editions, 1993.

Draft Letter (Unapproved) from The Secretary to the Government of India to Major P. Z. Cox, 1905–1906, in P. Tuson and E. Quick (eds), *Records of Bahrain 1820–1960*, vol. 3, Slough, Archive Editions, 1993.

Durand, E. L., 'Notes on the islands of Bahrain and antiquities, by Captain E. L. Durand, 1st Assistant Resident, Persian Gulf', 1878–1879, in P. Tuson and E. Quick (eds), *Records of Bahrain 1820–1960*, vol. 2, Slough, Archive Editions, 1993.

Foreign Office, 'Foreign Office to Bahrain', 6 March 1956, in A. Burdett (ed.), *Records of Bahrain 1820–1960*, vol. 7, Slough, Archive Editions, 1993.

Communique to Agency Bahrain, No. 202, 6 March 1956, in A. Burdett (ed.), *Records of Bahrain 1820–1960*, vol. 7, Slough, Archive Editions, 1993.

Communique to Bahrain, Intel 223, 24 December 1956, in A. Burdett (ed.), *Records of Bahrain 1820–1960*, vol. 7, Slough, Archive Editions, 1993.

Fowle, T. C., Communique to Government of India, in P. Tuson and E. Quick (eds), *Records of Bahrain 1820–1960*, vol. 5, Slough, Archive Editions, 1993.

Communique to the Foreign Secretary, in A. Burdett (ed.), *Records of Bahrain 1820–1960*, vol. 5, Slough, Archive Editions, 1993.

Agitation in Bahrain, 12 November 1938, in P. Tuson and E. Quick (eds), *Records of Bahrain 1820–1960*, vol. 5, Slough, Archive Editions, 1993.

17 November 1938, in A. Burdett (ed.), *Records of Bahrain 1820–1960*, vol. 5, Slough, Archive Editions, 1993.

Gaskin, J. C., A reply to First Assistant Resident's request conveyed in his memorandum of the 1st April 1898, 30 April 1898, in P. Tuson and E. Quick (eds), *Records of Bahrain 1820–1960*, vol. 3, Slough, Archive Editions, 1993.

Gault, C. A., 27 January 1957, in A. Burdett (ed.), *Records of Bahrain 1820–1960*, vol. 7, Slough, Archive Editions, 1993.

Gray, J. W. D., Letter to S.J. Nuttall, 14 September 1965, in A. Burdett (ed.) *Records of Bahrain, 1961–1965*, vol. 5, Cambridge Archive Editions, 1997, p. 49.

Haines, Judge, Comments on Disturbances, in A. Burdett (ed.), *Records of Bahrain 1820–1960*, vol. 7, Slough, Archive Editions, 1993.

Higher Executive Committee, 29 March 1955, in A. Burdett (ed.), *Records of Bahrain 1820–1960*, vol. 7, Slough, Archive Editions, 1993.

Horner, Express Message, 1923–1932, in P. Tuson and E. Quick (eds), *Records of Bahrain 1820–1960*, vol. 4, Slough, Archive Editions, 1993.

Knox, Col. S. G., Attack on 'Ali by Dawasir Tribesmen, in P. Tuson and E. Quick (eds), *Records of Bahrain 1820-1960*, vol. 4, Slough, Archive Editions, 1993.

Report on Bahrain Reforms, 1923, in P. Tuson and E. Quick (eds), *Records of Bahrain 1820–1960*, vol. 3, Slough, Archive Editions, 1993.

From Bushire to Secretary of State for Colonies, in P. Tuson, A. Burdett and E. Quick (eds), *Records of Bahrain 1820–1960*, vol. 3, Slough, Archive Editions, 1993.

11 May 1923, in P. Tuson and E. Quick (eds), *Records of Bahrain 1820–1960*, vol. 3, Slough, Archive Editions, 1993.

Speech to Majlis in Bahrain, 26 May 1923, in P. Tuson and E. Quick (eds), *Records of Bahrain 1820–1960*, vol. 4, Slough, Archive Editions, 1993.

Appendix IV to Report on Bahrain Reforms, 26 May 1923, in P. Tuson and E. Quick (eds), *Records of Bahrain 1820–1960*, vol. 3, Slough, Archive Editions, 1993.

Lian, H. C. G., Secret letter from British Residency in Bahrain, 23 July 1959, in A. Burdett (ed.), *Records of Bahrain 1820–1960*, vol. 7, Slough, Archive Editions, 1993.

Loch, G., Communique to the Political Resident, 18 February 1935, in A. Burdett (ed.), *Records of Bahrain 1820–1960*, vol. 5, Slough, Archive Editions, 1993.

Luce, W., Dispatch No. 305, 26 April 1965 telegram to the foreign office, in A. Burdett (ed.) *Records of Bahrain, 1961–1965*, vol. 5, Cambridge Archive Editions, 1997.

Middleton, G., from the British Residency, 18 July 1960, in A. Burdett (ed.), *Records of Bahrain 1820–1960*, vol. 7, Slough, Archive Editions, 1993.

'Notes on formation of New Police Force', in P. Tuson and E. Quick (eds), *Records of Bahrain 1820–1960*, vol. 4, Slough, Archive Editions, 1993, p. 223.

Peace, G .L., and Mawdsley, W. P. R., 31 May 1956, *Report into March Disturbances, 1956*, in A. Burdett (ed.), *Records of Bahrain 1820–1960*, vol. 7, Slough, Archive Editions, 1993, p. 266.

Political Agent, Express Letter, in A. Burdett (ed.), *Records of Bahrain 1820–1960*, Slough, Archive Editions, 1993.

Prideaux, F. B., From the Agency in Bahrain, 24 June 1904, in P. Tuson and E. Quick (eds), *Records of Bahrain 1820–1960*, vol. 3, Slough, Archive Editions, 1993.

Prior, C .G., Communique from Political Agency Bahrain, in P. Tuson and E. Quick (eds), *Records of Bahrain 1820–1960*, vol. 4, Slough, Archive Editions, 1993.

29 June 1929, in P. Tuson, A. Burdett and E. Quick (eds), *Records of Bahrain 1820–1960*, Archive Editions, vol. 4, Slough, 1993.

Letter to the Political Resident, 28 July 1929, in P. Tuson and E. Quick (eds), *Records of Bahrain 1820–1960*, vol. 4, Slough, Archive Editions, 1993.

Public Security Law, in A. Burdett (ed.) *Records of Bahrain, 1961–1965*, vol. 5, Cambridge Archive Editions, 1997.

Report into July Disturbances, in A. Burdett (ed.), *Records of Bahrain 1820–1960*, vol. 7, Slough, Archive Editions, 1993, p. 63.

Riches, D. M. H., 10 April 1956, in A. Burdett (ed.), *Records of Bahrain 1820–1960*, vol. 7, Slough, Archive Editions, 1993.

Minutes, 26 June 1956, in A. Burdett (ed.), *Records of Bahrain 1820–1960*, vol. 7, Slough, Archive Editions, 1993.

11 April 1957, in A. Burdett (ed.), *Records of Bahrain 1820–1960*, vol. 7, Slough, Archive Editions, 1993.

Secretary, Communique to Resident, 12 August 1926, in P. Tuson, A. Burdett and E. Quick (eds), *Records of Bahrain 1820–1960*, vol. 4, Archive Editions, Slough, 1993.

The Agency Bahrain, 11 February 1923, in P. Tuson and E. Quick (eds), *Records of Bahrain 1820–1960*, vol. 3, Slough, Archive Editions, 1993.

Trevor, A. P., 'Bahrain Reforms', in P. Tuson and E. Quick (eds), *Records of Bahrain 1820–1960*, vol. 4, Slough, Archive Editions, 1993.

Tyranny of the Sheikh of Bahrain and his family over Bahrain Subjects, 6 January 1922, in P. Tuson and E. Quick (eds), *Records of Bahrain 1820–1960*, vol. 3, Slough, Archive Editions, 1993.

Letter to Mr Denys de S.Bray, 'Tyranny of Shaikh of Bahrein and his family over Bahrein subjects', 13 January 1922, in P. Tuson and E. Quick (eds), *Records of Bahrain 1820–1960*, vol. 3, Slough, Archive Editions, 1993.

From the British Residency – Bushire, 10 November 1923, in P. Tuson, A. Burdett and E. Quick (eds), *Records of Bahrain 1820–1960*, vol. 4, Slough, Archive Editions, 1993.

Tripp, J. P., Letter to J.A. Shellgrove, in A. Burdett (ed.) *Records of Bahrain, 1961–1965*, vol. 5, Cambridge Archive Editions, 1997.

Communique to M. S. Weir, 26 April 1965, in A. Burdett (ed.) *Records of Bahrain 1961–1965*, vol. 5, Cambridge Archive Editions, 1997.

Viceroy, Foreign and Political Department, to Secretary of State for India, 14 May 1923, in P. Tuson, A. Burdett and E. Quick (eds), *Records of Bahrain 1820–1960*, vol. 3, Slough, Archive Editions, 1993.

Wall, J. W., Communique to B.A.B. Burrows, 5 October 1953, in A. Burdett (ed.), *Records of Bahrain 1820–1960*, vol. 7, Slough, Archive Editions, 1993.

Letter to Political Resident in Gulf, 25 October 1954, in A. Burdett (ed.), *Records of Bahrain 1820–1960*, vol. 7, Slough, Archive Editions, 1993.

Communique to Foreign Office, 4 December 1954, in A. Burdett (ed.), *Records of Bahrain 1820–1960*, vol. 7. Slough, Archive Editions, 1993.

Wiltshire, E. P., Annual Review of Bahrain Affairs for 1960, in A. Burdett (ed.), *Records of Bahrain 1820–1960*, vol. 7, Slough, Archive Editions, 1993.

Weightman, H., to Fowle, 27 October 1938, in A. Burdett (ed.), *Records of Bahrain 1820–1960*, vol. 5, Slough, Archive Editions, 1993.

Annual Reports

Al Khalifah, M. b. S., Annual Report for the Year 1961, *in Bahrain Government Annual Reports 1924–1970*, vol. 6, *Gerrards Cross, Archive Editions*, 1987.

Belgrave, C., Annual Report for the Year 1348 (1929–30)', *in Bahrain Government Annual Reports 1924–1970,* vol. 1. *Gerrards Cross, Archive Editions,* 1986.

Annual Report for the Year 1351 (1932–33), in *Bahrain Government Annual Reports 1924–1970,* vol. 1, Gerrards Cross, Archive Editions, 1986.

Annual Report for the Year 1352 (1933–34), in *Bahrain Government Annual Reports 1924–1970,* vol. 1, Gerrards Cross, Archive Editions, 1986.

Annual Report for the Year 1353 (1934–35), *in Bahrain Government Annual Reports 1924–1970,* vol. 2, *Gerrards Cross, Archive Editions,* 1986.

Annual Report for the Year 1937, *in Bahrain Government Annual Reports 1924–1970,* vol. 2, *Gerrards Cross, Archive Editions,* 1986.

Annual Report for the Year 1357 (1938–39), *in Bahrain Government Annual Reports 1924–1970,* vol. 2, *Gerrards Cross, Archive Editions,* 1986.

Annual Reports for the Year 1955, *in Bahrain Government Annual Reports 1924–1970,* vol. 5, *Gerrards Cross, Archive Editions,* 1986.

Annual Report for the Year 1956, *in Bahrain Government Annual Reports 1924–1970,* vol. 5, *Gerrards Cross, Archive Editions,* 1986.

Bell, J .S., Annual Report for 1970, *in Bahrain Government Annual Reports 1924–1970,* vol. 8, *Gerrards Cross, Archive Editions,* 1987.

Smith, G. W. R., Annual Review for the year 1965, *in Bahrain Government Annual Reports 1924–1970,* vol. 7, *Gerrards Cross, Archive Editions,* 1987.

News Sources

Al A'Ali, M., 'Group Formed to Help Policemen', *Gulf Daily News,* 1 January 2012, www.thefreelibrary.com/Group+formed+to+help+policemen.-a027611748

'20 Years Jailed Backed for Inciting Hatred', *Gulf Daily News,* 30 April 2013, www.gulf-daily-news.com/NewsDetails.aspx?storyid=352350

'Rioters' Parents May Face Jail', *Gulf Daily News,* 4 December 2013, www.gulf-daily-news.com/NewsDetails.aspx?storyid=366155

Al Jazeera, 'Bahrain Strips 72 of Citizenship for "Harming" Kingdom', 31 January 2015, www.aljazeera.com/news/middleeast/2015/01/bahrain-strips-72-citizenship

Associated Press, 'Execution Stirs Protests in Bahrain', 27 March 1996, www.nytimes.com/1996/03/27/world/execution-stirs-protests-in-bahrain.html

Associated Press Archives, Shaikh Mohammed bin Mubarak Al Khalifa, 'Bahrain Crises', [video], www.aparchive.com/metadata/Bahrain-Crises/12dd0996a99586175645c5ab8800cf71?query=bahrain¤t=30&orderBy=Relevance&hits=330&referrer=search&search=%2fsearch%2ffilter%3fquery%3dbahrain%26from%3d21%26orderBy%3dRelevance%26allFilters%3d1990%253ADecade%26ptype%3dIncludedProducts%26_%3d1398696824995&allFilters=1990%3aDecade&productType=IncludedProducts&page=21&b=00cf71

Bahrain News Agency, 'Shaikh Nasser to Launch the Youth Sword and Patronise the Allegiance-Pledge Signing', 12 April 2011, www.bna.bh/portal/en/news/452594?date=2011-04-15

'Shaikh Fawaz Presents Social Media Awards', 8 February 2012, http://bna.bh/portal/en/news/493277

'Northern Police Directorate/ Statement', 24 February 2013, www.bna.bh/portal/en/news/548078

'HM King Hosts Reception Ceremony in London', 12 May 2013, www.bna.bh/portal/en/news/560364

'Teacher with Links to Extremists Deported for Social Media Activities and Violation of Labor Laws', 10 August 2013, www.bna.bh/portal/en/news/574672

Bahrain Mirror, 'Bahrain Mirror Publishes Important Document Regarding Jordanian Police: 499 Policemen are Costing Bahrain 1.8 Million Dollars Per Month', 3 April 2014, http://bmirror14feb2011.no-ip.org/news/14724.html

BBC News, 'US Diplomat Tom Malinowski Expelled from Bahrain', www.bbc.co.uk/news/world-us-canada-28204511

Bladd, J., 'Qatar Denies Seizing Iran Ships Carrying Weapons', *Arabian Business*, 28 March 2011, www.arabianbusiness.com/qatar-denies-seizing-iran-ships-carrying-weapons-390435.html

Booth, R. and Sheffer, J., 'Bahrain Regime Accused of Harassing UK-Based Students', *The Guardian*, 15 April 2011, www.theguardian.com/world/2011/apr/15/bahrain-regime-uk-students

Chulov, M., 'Bahrain Doctors Await the Call that Will Send Them to Prison', *The Guardian*, 30 September 2011, www.theguardian.com/world/2011/sep/30/bahrain-doctors-prison-uprising

Citizens for Bahrain, 'Weapons Cache Proves Motives Not Peaceful', in *Gulf Daily News*, 5 January 2014, http://archives.gdnonline.com/NewsDetails.aspx? date=04/07/2015&storyid=368096

Cockburn, P., 'Bahrain Regime Jails Doctors Who Dared to Treat Protesters', *The Independent*, 30 September 2011, www.independent.co.uk/news/world/middle-east/bahrain-regime-jails-doctors-who-dared-to-treat-protesters-2363331.html

Daily Pakistan, 9 May 2014, https://dailypakistan.com.pk/09-May-2014/100742 , [Urdu].

The Economist, 'Gazing Backward', 25 March 1995, issue 7907.

'Spot the Villain', 3 February 1996, issue, 7951.

'Bahrain's Spreading Flames', 19 July 1997, Issue 8026.

'Sheikhly Fall-Out', 6 December 1998, Issue 8046.

'Whitewash', 23 January 1999, issue, 8103.

'Morning and Questioning, in Bahrain', 13 March 1999, issue 8110.

Evans, K., 'Bahrain plot "is led from Qom"', *The Guardian*, 12 June 1996.

Fattah, H. M., 'Report Cites Bid by Sunnis in Bahrain to Rig Elections', *New York Times*, 2 October 2006, www.nytimes.com/2006/10/02/world/middleeast/02bahrain.html? pagewanted=all&_r=0

Fisk, R., 'Britain at the Heart of Bahrain's Brutality Rule', *The Independent*, 18 February 1996, www.independent.co.uk/news/world/briton-at-the-heart-of-bahrains-brutality-rule-1319571.html

Fuller, T., 'Bahrain's Promised Spending Fails to Quell Dissident', *New York Times*, 6 March 2011, www.nytimes.com/2011/03/07/world/middleeast/07bahrain.html?_r=0

Gambrell, J. Bahrain, Reversing Reform, Restores Arrest Powers to Spies, Associated Press, 2017, https://apnews.com/d1d7dc18390a485cb9461b7b496ef279/Bahrain,-reversing-reform,-restores-arrest-powers-to-spies

Grewal, S. S., 'Track Down My Father's Killers', *Gulf Daily News*, 15 June 2011, http://archives.gdnonline.com/NewsDetails.aspx? date=04/07/2015&storyid=307919

'Probe into Slander on Twitter', *Gulf Daily News*, 7 January 2013, http://archives.gdnonline.com/NewsDetails.aspx? date=04/07/2015&storyid=345115

'ChildrenUsed as "Human Shields "' *Gulf Daily News*, 7 June 2013, http://archives.gdnonline.com/NewsDetails.aspx? date=04/07/2015&storyid=354827

Gulf Daily News, 'No Place for Anarchy", 13 March 2013, http://archives.gdnonline.com/NewsDetails.aspx? date=04/07/2015&storyid=349200

'Societies Seek to Expel Envoy', 12 June 2013, http://archives.gdnonline.com/NewsDetails.aspx?date=04/07/2015&storyid=355162

'Saudi Role Vital', 17 April 2015, www.gulf-daily-news.com/NewsDetails.aspx?storyid=400151

Gulf News, 'New Rule for Bahrain Societies over Contacts', 4 September 2013, http://gulfnews.com/news/gulf/bahrain/new-rule-for-bahrain-societies-over-contacts-1.1227200

Halliday, J., 'Channel 4 Journalists Arrested and Deported from Bahrain', *The Guardian*, 23 April 2012, www.theguardian.com/media/2012/apr/23/channel-4-journalists- arrested-bahrain

Hirst, D., 'Putting the Gulf's Resistance on Trial', *The Guardian*, 15 March 1982.

'Inquiry Into Bahrain Shootings'. *Times* [London, England] 5 Apr. 1956: 6. *The Times Digital Archive*.

'Findings On Riot In Bahrain'. *Times* [London, England] 11 June 1956: 8. The Times Digital Archive.

Hubbard, B., and ElSheikh, M., 'Wikileaks Shows a Saudi Obsession with Iran'. 16 July 2015, www.nytimes.com/2015/07/17/world/middleeast/wikileaks-saudi-arabia-iran.html

Khalaf, A., 'A Ship Loaded with Arms and Explosives', *Al-Waqt*, http://bahrainonline.org/showthread.php?t=224765

Khalifa, R., '(AP) – Bahrain TV Airs Terror Plot Confessions', BCHR, 29 December 2008, www.bahrainrights.org/en/node/2625

Kingdom of Bahrain Ministry of Interior, 'Study to Identify Sites for Approved Rallies', 12 July 2012, www.policemc.gov.bh/en/news_details.aspx? type=1&articleId=13799

Laessing, U., 'Gulf States Launch $20 Billion Fund for Oman and Bahrain', *Reuters*, 10 March 2011, www.reuters.com/article/2011/03/10/us-gulf-fund-idUSTRE7294B120110310

Lamb, G., 'Why Narrowly Cast the Push For Democracy as the "Arab Spring"?', *The Guardian*, 22 February 2012, www.theguardian.com/commentisfree/2012/feb/22/democracy-arab-spring

Law, B., 'New Bahrain Trade Federation Splits Union Movement', *BBC News*, 17 November 2012, www.bbc.co.uk/news/world-middle-east-20324436

'Bahrain Reconciliation Distant among Slow Pace of Reform', *BBC News*, 23 November 2012, www.bbc.co.uk/news/world-middle-east-20449587

Ministry of the Interior Media Center, 'MOI Response to US State Department's 2013 Country Report on Human Rights', 8 May 2014, www.policemc.gov.bh/en/print.aspx?articleId=22819&mode=print

Muhammad, P., 'Foreign Relations: Tit-for-Tat Proposed over Visa Rejections', *The Express Tribune*, 1 April 2014, http://tribune.com.pk/story/689833/foreign-relations-tit-for-tat-proposed-over-visa-rejections/

Murphy, D., 'After Formula One Scrutiny, Bahrain Hires a Fan of Saddam Hussein to Improve its Image', *The Christian Science Monitor,* 25 April 2012, www.csmonitor.com/World/Security-Watch/Backchannels/2012/0425/After-Formula-One-scrutiny-Bahrain-hires-a-fan-of-Saddam-Hussein-to-improve-its-image

Mustin, S., 'Anti-Protest: Bahrain Bans Import of Plastic Guy Fawkes Masks', 25 February 2013, *The Independent*, www.independent.co.uk/news/world/middle-east/anti-protest-bahrain-bans-import-of-plastic-guy-fawkes-masks-8510615.html

New Arab, 'Lebanese Families Given 48 Hours to Leave the UAE', 18 March 2015, https://www.alaraby.co.uk/english/news/2015/3/18/lebanese-families-given- 48-hours-to-leave-the-uae

Now Lebanon 'Mikati Thanks Bahrain for Halting Deportation of Lebanese Nationals', 19 April 2011, https://now.mmedia.me/lb/en/archive/mikati_thanks_bahrain_for_halting_deportation_of_lebanese_nationals

Reuters, 'Bahrain Toughens Penalties for Insulting King', 5 February 2014, www.reuters.com/article/2014/02/05/us-bahrain-law-idUSBREA140KX20140205

'Bahrain Bans Three Clerics from Preaching; Opposition Condemns Move', 8 August 2014, www.reuters.com/article/2014/08/08/us-bahrain-clerics-idUSKBN0G81HQ20140808

'Policeman Killed in "Terrorist" Attack in Bahrain: Interior Ministry', 8 December 2014, www.reuters.com/article/2014/12/08/us-bahrain-security-policeman-idUSKBN0JM25320141208

Singh, M., 'Terror Plot Foiled', *Gulf Daily News*, 13 November 2011, http://archives.gdnonline.com/NewsDetails.aspx?date=04/07/2015&storyid=317594

Toorani, N., 'Arabic Report of BICI Withdrawn', *Gulf Daily News*, 30 November 2011, http://archives.gdnonline.com/NewsDetails.aspx?date=04/07/2015&storyid=318698

Toumi, H., 'Bahrain's Prosecution Defends Decision to Publish Suspects' Names And Pictures', Habib Toumi, [web blog], 2 September 2010, www.habibtoumi.com/2010/09/02/bahrains-prosecution-defends-decision-to-publish-suspects-names-and-pictures/

'Qatar Denies Seizing Iran Boat Loaded with Weapons', *Gulf News*, 23 January 2013, http://gulfnews.com/news/gulf/qatar/qatar-denies-seizing-iran-boat-loaded-with-weapons-1.1136351

Trade Arabia, 'Bahrain to Build $5.59bn Housing Units', 19 September 2012, www.tradearabia.com/news/CONS_222196.html

'Bahrain Bans Public Meetings in Manama', 7 August 2013, www.tradearabia.com/touch/article/LAW/240713

Tran, M., 'Bahrain Accuses Human Rights Leader of Faking Pictures of Beating', T*he Guardian*, 11 April 2011, www.theguardian.com/world/2011/apr/11/bahrain-human-rights-activist-accused

Zahra, N., 'Kalashnikovs Drama in Medics' Trial…', *Gulf Daily News*, 29 November 2011.

'Officer Jailed in Shooting Case', *Gulf Daily News*, 26 June 2012, www.thefreelibrary.com/Officer+jailed+in+shooting+case.- a0294433698

'Sentences Slashed for Officers', *Gulf Daily News*, 28 October 2013, www.gulf-daily-news.com/NewsDetails.aspx?storyid=363780

Arabic [Translated]

Translated from Arabic by the author.

Abode and residency from registration papers for the Tabu department, www.legalaffairs.gov.bh/AdvancedSearchDetails.aspx?id=4406#.Wte_o4jwZyw

Al-Ayam, 'Terrorists Brutally And Mercilessly Stabbed His Body with Their Knives', 29 March 2011, http://goo.gl/qmhTWC

Al Khalifa, K. bin S., 'Prime Minister's Speech to Mubarak bin Huwail', [online video], 7 July 2013, www.youtube.com/watch?gl=GB&client=mv-google&hl=en&feature=plcp&v=YVundvyyNS8&nomobile=1

Al Saud, F., 'Secret and Urgent', Kingdom of Saudi Arabia Ministry of Foreign Affairs, 2011–2012 (1433 Hijra), Wikileaks, https://wikileaks.org/saudi-cables/doc46685.html

Al-Wasat, 'Funeral of Rashid Mamri in Riffa Cemetry', 23 March 2011, www.alwasatnews.com/3120/news/read/533682/1.html

'Iran Denies Sending Unmanned Aerial Spy Drone above Bahrain', 23 May 2013, www.alwasatnews.com/3911/news/read/774772/1.html

Bahrain: Report on the carrying out of terrorism and the identity of the February 14 Movement, [online video], 12 June 2013, www.youtube.com/watch?feature=player_embedded&v=D_WBKYBXlY0

Bahrain News Agency, 'His Majesty Visits the Majlises of al Mahmud and al Musallim in Hidd' June 2011, http://bna.bh/portal/mobile/news/461875

Lies of Samira bin Rajab, [online video], 14 March 2013, www.youtube.com/watch?v=GA4qMgNugys

Political Naturalisation in Bahrain II, [online video], 2011, www.youtube.com/watch?v=QBzFRVY79jA

Tweets, Forums and Blogs

@adelmaymoon, 'If u have you any names or information about any traitor or terrorist, kindly send it to @moi_bahrain no need to expose his family & children', 1 May 2011, https://twitter.com/adelmaymoon/status/64784728217223168

[Translated from Arabic] @busalmani, يقوم الدجالون والعملاء ببث تلك اللقطات ويبالغون فيها وحسبما يردهم من تعليمات وبما يحقق لهم ولمن يدفعهم من الدول أهدافهم 'Tunnel under the Roundabout leads to Iran while tunnel under al 0dhari leads to al-Eker',

Bahrain' 23 October 2012, https://twitter.com/busalmani/status/260673433485062145

@F-albinali, '@marcowenjones @lawyereemkhalaf its a concern, NHRI raised it as well. My view is that that's it's a grey area. Something for the defence', 21 February 2013, https://twitter.com/f_albinali/status/304556075405955072

@Kalfadhel, 'Many UOB students were bullied to take off the official Bahraini flag (with 5 points) and replace it with the', 12 March 2011, https://twitter.com/KAlFadhel/status/46576218627248128

@LexBirch, '@NABEELRAJAB well you are, and you proved it by sending out your thugs to amputate #UK citizens fingers #Bahrain. We all know the truth now', 10 February 2012, https://twitter.com/LexBirch/status/167887885960347648

@Redbelt, 'Today is the anniversary of my detainment. Just because someone posted my picture on Facebook. Also because I started #UniteBH', [Tweet by @Redbelt], 29 March 2012, https://twitter.com/Redbelt/status/185324439934738432

@YusurAlBahrani, 'Chief of Public Security in #Bahrain @Talhassan, claims that who publicise video of @moi_bahrain violations is traitor', 25 December 2012, https://twitter.com/YusurAlBahrani/status/283442087192588288, (accessed 10 October 2015). @Talhassan, يقوم الدجالون والعملاء ببث تلك اللقطات ويبالغون فيها وحسبما يردهم من تعليمات وبما يحقق لهم ولمن يدفعهم من الدول أهدافهم Those who broadcast these clips achieve the goals of those other countries that pay them'. [Translated from Arabic] https://twitter.com/talhassan/status/283339899518730241

Bahrainwatch, 'Bahrain: Please Don't Feed these Trolls', [web blog], June 2012, https://bahrainwatch.wordpress.com/2012/06/08/bahrain-please-dont feed-these-trolls/

Fajr al-Bahrain, 'competition…enter and put in your information', [web forum] www.fajrbh.com/vb/threads/24682/

Documentaries

Bahrain's Policy of Revoking Shiʿa Protesters Citizenship, [Documentary] 2015, www.anabahraini.org/2018/02/18/%E2%80%8Bbahrains-policy-of-revoking-shia-protesters-citizenship-2/-technology/articles/human-rights-organisations-file-oecd-complaints-against-surveillance-firms-gamma-international-and-trovicor.html-in-gulf.html-in-bahrain-a-forty-year-legacy/-arab-spring.html.rsf.org/en/bahrain/-harming-kingdom-150131140438495.html

Index

Books in the Series

1. Parvin Paidar, *Women and the Political Process in Twentieth-Century Iran*
2. Israel Gershoni and James Jankowski, *Redefining the Egyptian Nation, 1930–1945*
3. Annelies Moors, *Women, Property and Islam: Palestinian Experiences, 1920–1945*
4. Paul Kingston, *Britain and the Politics of Modernization in the Middle East, 1945–1958*
5. Daniel Brown, *Rethinking Tradition in Modern Islamic Thought*
6. Nathan J. Brown, *The Rule of Law in the Arab World: Courts in Egypt and the Gulf*
7. Richard Tapper, *Frontier Nomads of Iran: The Political and Social History of the Shahsevan*
8. Khaled Fahmy, *All the Pasha's Men: Mehmed Ali, His Army and the Making of Modern Egypt*
9. Sheila Carapico, *Civil Society in Yemen: The Political Economy of Activism in Arabia*
10. Meir Litvak, *Shi'i Scholars of Nineteenth-Century Iraq: The Ulama of Najaf and Karbala*
11. Jacob Metzer, *The Divided Economy of Mandatory Palestine*
12. Eugene L. Rogan, Frontiers *of the State in the Late Ottoman Empire: Transjordan, 1850–1921*
13. Eliz Sanasarian, *Religious Minorities in Iran*
14. Nadje Al-Ali, *Secularism, Gender and the State in the Middle East: The Egyptian Women's Movement*
15. Eugene L. Rogan and Avi Shlaim, eds., *The War for Palestine: Rewriting the History of 1948*
16. Gershon Shafir and Yoar Peled, *Being Israeli: The Dynamics of Multiple Citizenship*
17. A. J. Racy, *Making Music in the Arab World: The Culture and Artistry of Tarab*
18. Benny Morris, *The Birth of the Palestinian Refugee Crisis Revisited*
19. Yasir Suleiman, *A War of Words: Language and Conflict in the Middle East*
20. Peter Moore, *Doing Business in the Middle East: Politics and Economic Crisis in Jordan and Kuwait*
21. Idith Zertal, *Israel's Holocaust and the Politics of Nationhood*
22. David Romano, *The Kurdish Nationalist Movement: Opportunity, Mobilization and Identity*

23. Laurie A. Brand, *Citizens Abroad: Emigration and the State in the Middle East and North Africa*
24. James McDougall, *History and the Culture of Nationalism in Algeria*
25. Madawi al-Rasheed, *Contesting the Saudi State: Islamic Voices from a New Generation*
26. Arang Keshavarzian, *Bazaar and State in Iran: The Politics of the Tehran Marketplace*
27. Laleh Khalili, *Heroes and Martyrs of Palestine: The Politics of National Commemoration*
28. M. Hakan Yavuz, *Secularism and Muslim Democracy in Turkey*
29. Mehran Kamrava, *Iran's Intellectual Revolution*
30. Nelida Fuccaro, *Histories of City and State in the Persian Gulf: Manama since 1800*
31. Michaelle L. Browers, *Political Ideology in the Arab World: Accommodation and Transformation*
32. Miriam R. Lowi, *Oil Wealth and the Poverty of Politics: Algeria Compared*
33. Thomas Hegghammer, *Jihad in Saudi Arabia: Violence and Pan-Islamism since 1979*
34. Sune Haugbolle, *War and Memory in Lebanon*
35. Ali Rahnema, *Superstition as Ideology in Iranian Politics: From Majlesi to Ahmadinejad*
36. Wm. Roger Louis and Avi Shlaim eds, *The 1967 Arab-Israeli War: Origins and Consequences*
37. Stephen W. Day, *Regionalism and Rebellion in Yemen: A Troubled National Union*
38. Daniel Neep, *Occupying Syria under the French Mandate: Insurgency, Space and State Formation*
39. Iren Ozgur, *Islamic Schools in Modern Turkey: Faith, Politics, and Education*
40. Ali M. Ansari, *The Politics of Nationalism in Modern Iran*
41. Thomas Pierret, *Religion and State in Syria: The Sunni Ulama from Coup to Revolution*
42. Guy Ben-Porat, *Between State and Synagogue: The Secularization of Contemporary Israel*
43. Madawi Al-Rasheed, *A Most Masculine State: Gender, Politics and Religion in Saudi Arabia*
44. Sheila Carapico, *Political Aid and Arab Activism: Democracy Promotion, Justice, and Representation*
45. Pascal Menoret, *Joyriding in Riyadh: Oil, Urbanism, and Road Revolt*
46. Toby Matthiesen, *The Other Saudis: Shiism, Dissent and Sectarianism*
47. Bashir Saade, *Hizbullah and the Politics of Remembrance: Writing the Lebanese Nation*
48. Noam Leshem, *Life After Ruin: The Struggles over Israel's Depopulated Arab Spaces*
49. Zoltan Pall, *Salafism in Lebanon: Local and Transnational Movements*
50. Salwa Ismail, *The Rule of Violence: Subjectivity, Memory and Government in Syria*
51. Zahra Ali, *Women and Gender in Iraq: Between Nation-Building and Fragmentation*

52. Dina Bishara, *Contesting Authoritarianism: Labor Challenges to the State in Egypt*
53. Rory McCarthy, *Inside Tunisia's al-Nahda: Between Politics and Preaching*
54. Ceren Lord, *Religious Politics in Turkey: From the Birth of the Republic to the AKP*
55. Dörthe Engelcke, *Reforming Family Law: Social and Political Change in Jordan and Morocco*
56. Dana Conduit, *The Muslim Brotherhood in Syria*
57. Benjamin Schuetze, *Promoting Democracy, Reinforcing Authoritarianism: US and European Policy in Jordan*
58. Marc Owen Jones, *Political Repression in Bahrain*